A TASK FORCE CALLED
FAITH

A TASK FORCE CALLED FAITH

The Untold Story of the U.S. Army Soldiers Who Fought for Survival at Chosin Reservoir—and Honor Back Home

STEVE VOGEL

Essex, Connecticut

An imprint of The Globe Pequot Publishing Group, Inc.
64 S Main St.
Essex, CT 06426
www.GlobePequot.com

British Library Cataloguing in Publication Information available

Library of Congress Cataloging-in-Publication Data available

ISBN 9781493092895 (cloth) | ISBN 9781493092932 (epub)

∞™ The paper used in this publication meets the minimum requirements of American National Standard for Information Sciences—Permanence of Paper for Printed Library Materials, ANSI/NISO Z39.48-1992.

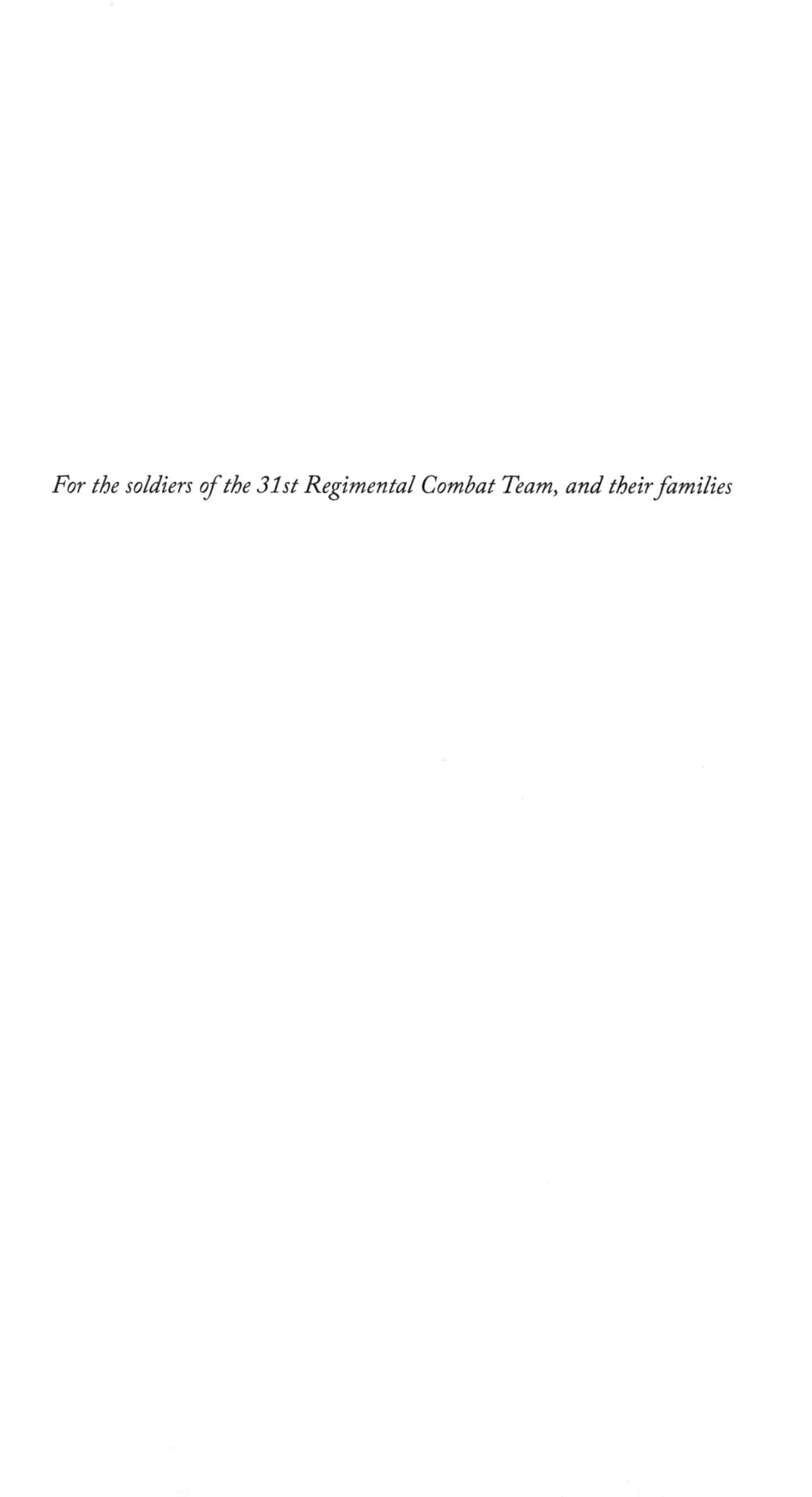

For the soldiers of the 31st Regimental Combat Team, and their families

Contents

Maps

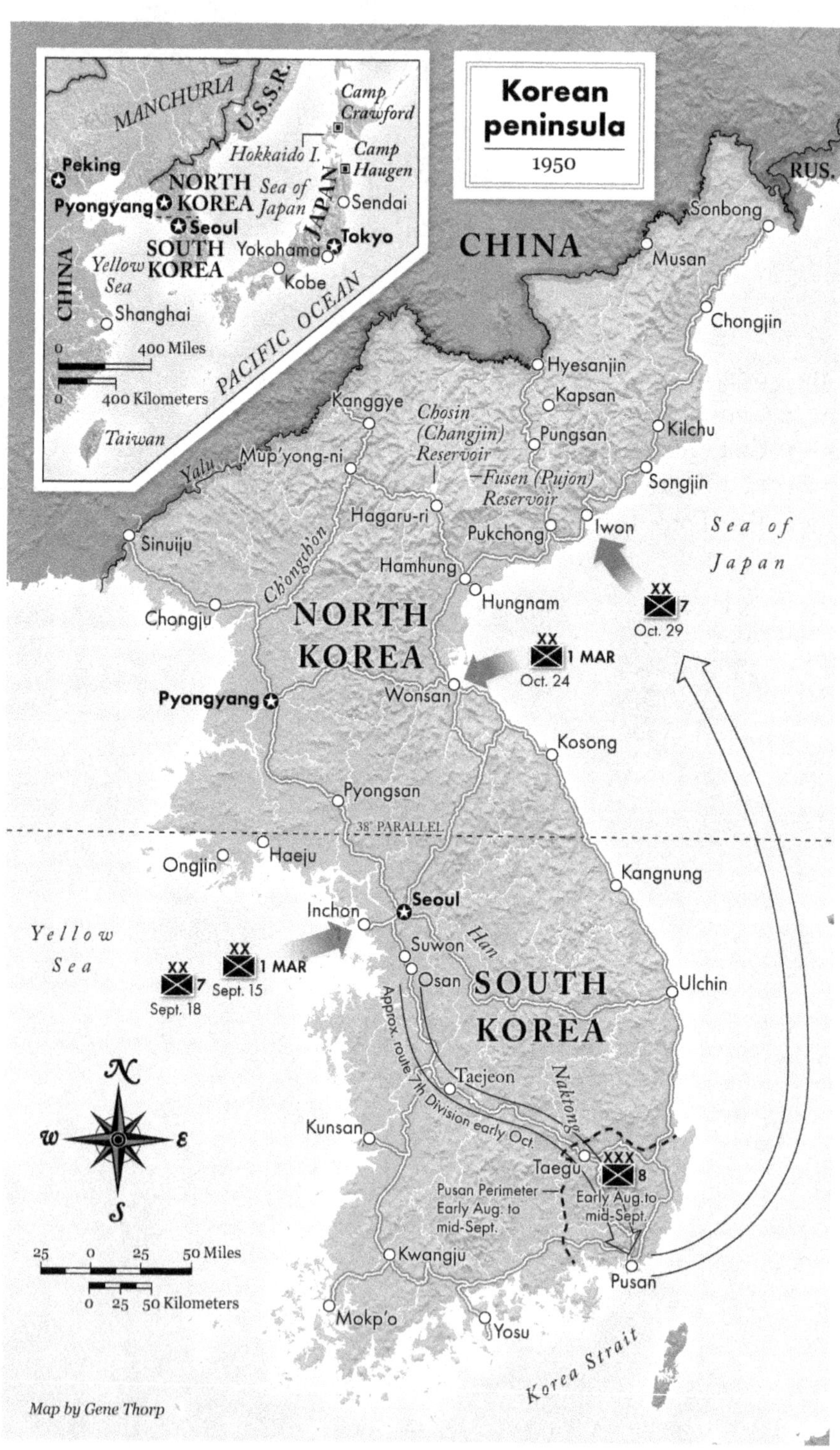

Korean peninsula
1950
MANCHURIA
U.S.S.R.
Camp Crawford
Hokkaido I.
Camp Haugen
Peking
NORTH KOREA
Sea of Japan
JAPAN
Sendai
Pyongyang
Seoul
Tokyo
SOUTH KOREA
Yokohama
CHINA
Yellow Sea
Kobe
Shanghai
PACIFIC OCEAN
0 400 Miles
0 400 Kilometers
Taiwan
CHINA
RUS.
Sonbong
Musan
Chongjin
Hyesanjin
Kapsan
Kanggye
Chosin (Changjin) Reservoir
Pungsan
Kilchu
Yalu
Mup'yong-ni
Fusen (Pujon) Reservoir
Songjin
Hagaru-ri
Pukchong
Iwon
Sea of Japan
Sinuiju
Ch'ongch'on
Hamhung
Hungnam
XX 7
Oct. 29
Chongju
NORTH KOREA
XX 1 MAR
Oct. 24
Pyongyang
Wonsan
Kosong
Pyongsan
38° PARALLEL
Ongjin
Haeju
Kangnung
Seoul
Inchon
Yellow Sea
Han
Suwon
XX 1 MAR
Sept. 15
XX 7
Sept. 18
Osan
SOUTH KOREA
Ulchin
Approx. route 7th Division early Oct.
Taejeon
Naktong
Kunsan
Taegu
XXX 8
Pusan Perimeter Early Aug. to mid-Sept.
Early Aug. to mid-Sept.
Kwangju
Pusan
Mokp'o
Yosu
Korea Strait
N
W
E
S
25 0 25 50 Miles
0 25 50 Kilometers
Map by Gene Thorp

Prologue

Task Force Faith

The men of Task Force Faith came together one last time, for themselves and for their families, but also for the comrades lost on the frozen Chosin Reservoir battlefield more than seventy years earlier.

It was the final reunion of the U.S. Army Chapter of the Chosin Few, a small band of brothers with a bond forged during one of the most brutal and desperate battles in American history. They gathered the last weekend of August 2021 at the Oasis Hotel in Springfield, Missouri—the same place they had returned annually for years, chosen for its location in the middle of the country.

The youngest of them was Max Guernsey, 89, who boarded a Greyhound bus in St. Joseph, Michigan, with a battered brown suitcase and rode twenty-four hours via Chicago and Indianapolis to make it. He still had a metal plate in his head because of the grievous wound he had suffered when shot by a Chinese soldier and left for dead in the snow. Ray Radke, 92, drove more than four thousand miles round-trip from his home in Ferndale, Washington, hard up by the Canadian border. Harry Graham, still limping from the frostbite he suffered in the terrible cold at Chosin, arrived with his son from Mount Joy, Pennsylvania. Grant McMillin, captured and held as a POW for nearly three years, drove with his wife from Elkhorn, Wisconsin. Everyone expected Elmer Schearf to show up from his home in Cape Girardeau, Missouri, but he had been hospitalized two days before the reunion. Just before he died, he asked his family to tell the guys he would see them on the other side.

Al Zentko came from Crawfordsville, Indiana; Monty Piercefield from Belgium, Wisconsin; and Don Tague from Gorin, Missouri. Seven in all made it—a good showing, given how many had died in recent years and how few were still alive. At their age, the old soldiers were taking a risk by gathering in southwest Missouri, then a Covid hotspot amid a surging pandemic. But for the troops who fought in the mountains of North Korea at the Chosin Reservoir in November and December of 1950, risk is a relative term.

The hellish fate of Task Force Faith was one of the cruelest to befall U.S. troops in any war. The 3,100 men from the Army's 7th Division sent into the rugged terrain on the east side of Chosin were ambushed by a Chinese force that would grow to nine times its size. With little food or ammunition, they held on through four days and five nights of bitter close combat, in temperatures that plunged to thirty-five degrees below zero. When it ended, the task force had suffered a terrible mauling, with about 85 percent of its soldiers killed, captured, or wounded.

Everything about the Battle of Chosin Reservoir was extreme: the killing cold, the savageness of the fight, the odds against the outnumbered Americans, the swings of fortune, and, ultimately, the courage and endurance of the troops who fought there.

No Korean War battle carries a larger legacy than Chosin. In the seventy-five years since it was fought, no battle has come close to claiming as many U.S. Army soldiers and Marines as those lost at Chosin and during concurrent fighting during the Chinese offensive against the U.S. 8th Army in northwest North Korea. Almost as many American service members died during the Chosin campaign as did in twenty years in Afghanistan. Chosin was the moment the Cold War turned into a savage and exceedingly dangerous conflict. The Chinese offensive turned the outcome of the war, changing what seemed to be a sure American victory that would have unified Korea into an uneasy standoff that continues to this day, looming ever larger with a nuclear-armed North Korea.

The soldiers of Task Force Faith paid a heavy price for the catastrophic miscalculation made by General Douglas MacArthur, who waved off signs of a major Chinese intervention as his forces drove toward the Yalu River in November 1950. MacArthur sent the powerful X Corps, under the command of Army Major General Edward M. "Ned" Almond and including the 1st Marine Division and the Army's 7th Infantry Division, to lead the attack through eastern North Korea. Almond, an ambitious and aggressive commander, ordered his troops into the mountains around the Chosin Reservoir as part of a general offensive expected to end the war, with talk of getting the boys home by

Christmas. The Marines, led by Major General O. P. Smith, moved 15,000 men to the west and south of the reservoir. The 7th Division, assigned at the last minute to send troops to the east side of the reservoir, hastily cobbled together a much smaller force of 3,100 soldiers, designated the 31st Regimental Combat Team (RCT), or Task Force Faith, as it would become known. The 31st RCT was rushed, poorly equipped and with little time to prepare, to the east side of Chosin. The lead battalion, under the command of Lieutenant Colonel Don Carlos Faith, moved up a winding mountain pass leading to the reservoir and followed the road to a point halfway up the east shore. The charismatic Faith, a World War II veteran who jumped into Normandy on D-Day, was from a distinguished military family and considered one of the Army's most promising young officers, though he had no experience leading men in combat prior to Korea.

While X Corps moved to Chosin, the Chinese 9th Army Group was on the move as well: 150,000 soldiers slipped largely undetected into the mountains around the reservoir with orders from Chinese leader Mao Zedong to "annihilate" the unsuspecting U.S. force. On the night of November 27, the trap was sprung. Seven Chinese divisions launched a massive attack against the Marine and Army forces on both sides of the reservoir.

For the Marines, the resulting Battle of Chosin Reservoir has become legend, justifiably one of the proudest episodes in Marine Corps history. Despite being surrounded by a larger force, the 1st Marine Division fought its way out of the Frozen Chosin, inflicting tremendous damage on the enemy and carrying out its wounded and many of its dead.

For the U.S. Army, it was a different story. Facing proportionately even greater odds than the Marines, the Army task force punished two Chinese divisions, leaving them unable to attack the Marines. But the 31st RCT paid a terrible price in casualties, and its attempted breakout ended in disaster. Task Force Faith suffered nearly 1,000 dead or missing and 1,500 wounded. Those who were able to escape made their way out alone or in groups, many of them staggering on foot across the frozen reservoir for miles before reaching U.S. lines at Hagaru-ri, near the reservoir's southern tip. After the wounded were evacuated by air, only 385 soldiers were able to join the 1st Marine Division for the fighting retreat out of the mountains.

Overshadowed by the Marines' successful escape from Chosin, the fate of Task Force Faith was quickly forgotten, and to the extent it was remembered, the Army officers and soldiers were said to have disgraced themselves. A U.S. Navy chaplain who was with the Marines at Chosin accused the Army task force of cowardice, claiming that its officers and soldiers had thrown down their weapons and run, and that many had feigned injuries to get evacuated. The accusations ran in newspapers across the United States. A magazine article contrasted "the shame" of the Army at Chosin with the "glory" of the Marines. The entire 1st Marine Division was awarded the high honor of the Presidential Unit Citation for its actions at Chosin, but the 31st RCT was removed from the paperwork by Gen. Smith, the Marine commander, who said that only units that had made a "direct contribution" to the breakout should be honored.

For decades, the survivors of Task Force Faith have fought to clear their names of unfounded charges of cowardice, correct a flawed historical narrative, and reclaim the honor they won at the frozen reservoir.

On the third morning of the Army Chosin Few reunion—the last full day the men would be together—the old vets put on their best clothes and gathered in an Oasis conference room for a memorial service remembering those lost at Chosin and in the years since. A table in the front of the room held the chapter's wooden memorial, a cross adorned with the Star of Koto-ri, the symbol of the Chosin Few. It represented the star that troops saw through the clouds at the end of a snowstorm, promising clearing weather to escape the treacherous mountains. A plaque at the memorial's base read, "In Memory Of The Fallen—Army Chosin Few."

David Hillis, a retired Army chaplain leading the service, told the men the story they had lived: The terrifying night attacks. The subzero temperatures and howling winds. The weapons freezing up, and men dying of cold in their foxholes. The exhaustion. The wounded soldiers slaughtered in the trucks. "There are those of you that not only brought back your physical wounds—and you took a while to heal from those—you brought back as well your inward wounds," the chaplain said. "The memories that you could not escape. The nightmares. For many, the frostbite, the amputations, the months in the hospital, and then wondering, 'Lord, why me?' And then, having to fight for your honor was unbelievable. For I believe that you won that honor on those five days."

One by one, the last men of Task Force Faith rose from their seats and approached the memorial. Small American flags lay on the table for each of them to pick up and place in peg holes in the base of the memorial. Don Tague,

95, went first, maneuvering his walker to the table and placing his flag. "Amen," was all he said. Monty Piercefield, 94, wearing a blue Army beret, placed his flag and raised his shaking right arm in salute. Ray Radke, with his buzz-cut white hair and still looking like the tough Army sergeant he was in Korea, took two steps back after placing his flag and gave the memorial a smart salute.

Harry Graham, Max Guernsey, Grant McMillin, and Al Zentko placed their flags. Elias Wood, another veteran expected at the reunion, was not there. "He so wanted to make it, but his heart gave out six weeks ago," said his wife, Betty. She and her daughter, Tammy, drove up on his behalf from their home in Gardner, Louisiana. They approached the memorial, clutching a framed photograph of Elias, and placed the flag for him.

Chaplain Hillis led the group in a final prayer. "What an appropriate name—Task Force Faith—because you had faith not only in your commander, you had faith in each other," he said. "Faith in those who stood beside you against all odds. No matter how brave you are, you're going to be afraid. Courage is really about faith. And that's what this was about, Task Force Faith."

Before their last dinner together and the final sad farewells the next morning, there was the business of formally disbanding the U.S. Army Chapter of the Chosin Few. The men sat around a table with Charmaine Francois-Griffith, the chapter secretary. "We've come to an end," she said. Her father, Jerry Francois, a radio operator who had been bayoneted by Chinese troops at Chosin and survived nearly three years of captivity, had helped found the Army chapter. He and other Army veterans had attended a reunion of the National Chosin Few organization, founded in 1983 and dominated by Marines, but they felt ignored and occasionally insulted. In 1986 Francois, Max Guernsey, and fourteen others formed the Army chapter. Soon dozens—and then hundreds—of Task Force Faith veterans joined them. For many of them, reuniting with comrades for the first time since Chosin was cathartic. No one would ever be able to understand or heal their memories except for the men who stood there with them at the reservoir.

Before Jerry Francois died in 2012, he made Charmaine promise that she would keep the chapter running and look after the guys. She had done that, but time had culled the ranks, and now their numbers were down to about two dozen members, most of them too frail to travel to reunions anymore. The past several years had been particularly rough. The 2020 reunion was canceled because of the pandemic, and just in the past few months, the chapter president, Ernie Wotring, and one of the directors, Elliott Sortillo, had both died.

It had fallen to the seven men left around the table to bring it to an end. There were just too few of them left to continue, they all agreed.

One pressing issue was finding a home for the Army Chosin Few memorial. It was precious to them, a gift from a Korean American doctor whose family had escaped from North Korea aboard a ship filled with refugees when MacArthur's forces were evacuated from North Korea after the battle. Charmaine reported that the chapter had contacted several museums to see if they would take the memorial, but there had been no takers yet.

There was silence around the table. It felt like another slap at Task Force Faith. Nobody wanted to see the memorial end up in a museum storage container, never to be seen again. The veterans agreed that Charmaine should bring the memorial back to her home in Colorado for safekeeping until they found the right place for it. "One way or the other, the memorial is safe and secure and in the hands of people who understand it and respect it until we find a home," she told the men.

Charmaine updated them with the latest on the more than 400 31st RCT soldiers whose remains were still missing. In 2018 North Korea turned over fifty-five boxes of human remains to the United States, most of them recovered from the east side of Chosin, and some identifications had been made. "These are your guys," Charmaine said. "Your men." It was personal to all of them. While they might not be alive to see it, it was comforting to know that more Task Force Faith soldiers would finally be coming home to their families.

As the meeting came to an end, one matter felt unfinished. Despite the Army chapter's best efforts to correct the record, Task Force Faith remains largely forgotten to history, and the sacrifices made by its soldiers little appreciated.

"It's all Marines," Charmaine said. "And it's all about the glory of the Marines and how brave they were at Chosin. And that the Army cut and ran, that you guys had no leadership, that you laid your weapons down. That's the story—that's the way the history was written."

The truth about the 31st RCT would come out, she insisted. "I want you to know that will not stop here," Charmaine told the men. "That your story is going to go on. And it will go on through my family, through your children who've been here, and through the other people who are here with you today. Your story will be told. And it will be told, and it will be told."

Part I

The Road to Chosin

Chapter 1

AN END TO THE PEACE

Tokyo, Sunday, June 25, 1950

Army Lieutenant Alexander Haig arrived just after dawn at the Dai Ichi Building in downtown Tokyo, headquarters to General Douglas MacArthur, supreme commander of the Allied forces in occupied Japan. Haig had just returned from his honeymoon and was not eager to spend Sunday in the office, but there was no getting around his turn as duty officer. Any hopes for a quiet morning were dashed when he answered the telephone and found himself speaking to John Muccio, the U.S. ambassador to South Korea.

Over a line crackling with static, Muccio reported stunning news. A large North Korean Army force, supported by tanks and aircraft, had swept across the South Korean border at 4:00 that morning and was racing toward Seoul, the capital. It was a full-scale invasion, meeting little resistance from surprised and unprepared South Korean troops. There had been many border violations over the past year along the tense Cold War frontier, but none of them had amounted to much. Haig wondered if this was another minor incursion. As if reading his mind, Muccio added sharply, "Lieutenant, this is not a false alarm."

Haig steeled himself to call his boss, Major General Edward "Ned" Almond, MacArthur's chief of staff. The high-strung and imperious Almond—Ned the Dread, as he was often called—was a feared figure at the headquarters. "Ned Almond could precipitate a crisis on a desert island with nobody else around," one officer said.

Though Almond had attended his wedding in Tokyo a month earlier, Haig was intimidated by the chief of staff. "Almond was far too powerful a personality to be contained by any novel or movie; he had to be experienced in real life to be believed," Haig later wrote. The general possessed a volcanic temper as well as "frosty blue eyes in which there was a perpetual glint of skepticism," Haig recalled.

Almond was in the office himself, catching up on paperwork after a busy week. Several telegrams from Korea reporting border incidents had already arrived that morning, and Almond's first thought was that it was another border raid. But when Haig called, he demanded specifics. "Muccio called this operation an invasion, quote unquote?" Almond asked. When Haig confirmed this, Almond hung up on his aide and immediately called MacArthur.

In his darkened bedroom at his home at the American Embassy, MacArthur had already been awoken by a telephone call with the news. "I had an uncanny feeling of a nightmare," he later wrote. It reminded him of the shock he had felt nine years earlier in Manila as commander of the U.S. forces in the Philippines, when he learned of the Japanese attack on Pearl Harbor. "It couldn't be, I told myself," MacArthur wrote in his memoir. "Not again! I must be asleep and dreaming."

But hearing "the crisp, cool voice of my fine chief of staff, General Ned Almond" on the telephone shook him from his reverie, MacArthur recalled.

"Any orders, General?" Almond asked.

Whatever orders came, the soldiers of the Army's 7th Infantry Division had an uneasy feeling that they would be involved. Five years after the end of World War II, the soldiers and families of the 7th Division were living the happy, cushy life of a peacetime occupation army in Japan. The demands of duty were light, family life was carefree, and war was a distant memory. The division's soldiers were "products of the snack bar, comic book, Geisha house culture" of postwar occupation troops in Japan, one officer said disapprovingly.

News of the North Korean invasion reached the division's 31st Regiment at the Sunday morning chapel service at Camp Crawford, the regimental headquarters near Sapporo, on the northern island of Hokkaido. A Japanese Lutheran clergyman who directed the choir for the Protestant service had heard a report on Japanese radio and informed Major Marty Hoehn, the regiment's Catholic chaplain. Word quickly spread through the chapel and across the camp. They heard nothing official for several hours, and then Hoehn and other officers gathered around 2:00 p.m. for an emergency staff meeting. Armed Forces Radio, broadcasting to GIs across Japan, interrupted the *Amos 'n' Andy* show with a news flash reporting the invasion. Rumors were already floating that some divisions in Japan would be put on alert.

At Camp Haugen, on the island of Honshu, home to the division's 32nd Regiment troops from the 865th Antiaircraft Artillery Battalion were called in from pass Sunday and put on alert because of fears that the Soviets might launch an air attack. "It looks really bad," Cpl. Donald Hamilton, a medic with the regiment's 1st Battalion, wrote to his parents in Indiana. "As of yet they haven't put us on alert, but I look for them before long."

Sgt. Sam Muncy was lounging on his bunk at Camp Crawford when he saw his platoon sergeant rushing from one squad leader to another. He figured something was up. Muncy wasn't worried though—his overseas tour was up, and he had orders to return to the United States the following day. "I had already turned in all my stuff," he recalled. "I didn't even have a rifle—just two sheets and a pillow. The next morning I was supposed to get on a ship at Yokohama and go home."

But Muncy got nervous watching the grave expressions on faces around the barracks. He rushed to headquarters, where a group of officers and noncommissioned officers (NCOs) were huddled around a map of Korea. "The North Koreans went across the parallel this morning," an officer said.

"I'm on orders to go home," Muncy reminded him. The officer fixed a steady gaze on Muncy. "Your orders have been canceled," he said.

President Harry Truman, home for the weekend in Independence, Missouri, was no less shocked when Secretary of State Dean Acheson telephoned with the news Saturday evening, reaching him shortly after 10:00 p.m. Missouri time. Flying back to Washington Sunday afternoon, Truman worked himself up into a dander, thinking of the parallels to Fascist aggression in the 1930s, such as the German Anschluss of Austria, the Italian invasion of Ethiopia, and the Japanese seizure of Manchuria. "If this was allowed to go unchallenged it would mean a third world war, just as similar incidents had brought on the second world war," Truman later wrote.

It was quite a change. Earlier that year, at a press conference, Acheson had not even mentioned South Korea when discussing the U.S. strategic defensive perimeter in the Far East. Korea had long been on the back burner for the United States despite its strategic position as a gateway between the historically imperial powers of Japan, Russia, and China. The nation had suffered under Japanese occupation from 1905 until the final days of World War II, when Soviet forces entered the war against Japan in August 1945 and moved into northern Korea. The Pentagon hastily proposed dividing the Korean peninsula roughly in half at the 38th parallel, creating an American occupation zone in the south and a Soviet zone in the north. Nobody bothered to consult the Koreans. The Soviets accepted, and in 1948, the division hardened into the creation of North and South Korea. In the North, Kim Il Sung, a communist and one-time guerilla commander, was installed in power by the Soviets. In South Korea, the United States supported the nationalist leader Syngman Rhee, overlooking his corrupt and authoritarian tendencies because he was staunchly pro-American and anticommunist.

Back in Washington on Sunday evening, Truman met with senior cabinet and military leaders. The assumption in Washington was that the invasion had to have been orchestrated by Soviet leader Josef Stalin and might be just the first step in Soviet aggression around the globe—perhaps toward Berlin, Japan, or Iran. Truman said there was "complete, almost unspoken acceptance on the part of everyone that whatever had to be done to meet this aggression had to be done." Instructions were sent that evening to MacArthur, authorizing him to send ammunition and equipment to South Korea to help defend Seoul. But Monday evening, Truman received word from the general that the capital was on the verge of capture, South Korean forces were collapsing, and American nationals were being evacuated from the country. After Truman huddled with his advisers, further instructions were sent to MacArthur that night, authorizing him to use his air and naval forces south of the 38th parallel to clear North Korean troops from South Korea. It would be done under the auspices of the United Nations (UN), with the security council on Tuesday approving a U.S. resolution requesting member states to send whatever assistance was necessary to repel the invasion.

Shocked as he had been by the invasion, MacArthur was even more surprised by Truman's speedy decision to intervene in Korea. Truman, now in his fifth year as president, was no longer the untested Missouri politician thrust onto the world stage after the death of Franklin D. Roosevelt. He had a bantam rooster's cockiness about his judgment and leadership. Though no fan of the president, MacArthur later admitted to a grudging respect for "the little bastard." Truman, he added, "reacted instinctively, like the gutter fighter he is—and you've got to admire him."

MacArthur seemed unworried that his command was not remotely prepared to take on such a mission. The United States had withdrawn its occupation forces from South Korea in 1949. Contingency plans for a North Korean invasion did not even envision the possibility of U.S. military intervention.

Accompanied by Almond, MacArthur flew to South Korea on June 29 aboard his C-54 plane, *Bataan*, to inspect the front. Just four days into the war, Seoul had already been captured, forcing the party to land at the Suwon airfield, twenty miles south of the capital. A Russian-made Yak fighter-bomber had just attacked the runway and moved threateningly toward *Bataan*, but it was chased off by American P-51 Mustangs.

MacArthur, sporting his trademark crushed cap, sunglasses, and large corncob pipe, was unperturbed by the chaos and appeared buoyant when he stepped off the plane. In a nearby schoolhouse, the party received a briefing from members of an American military survey party who had been sent to assess the situation. The news was not good. South Korean defenses were crumbling in the face of the North Korean invasion force, which included six infantry divisions that were well supported by modern Soviet-made T-34 tanks, heavy artillery, and Yak warplanes. North Korean troops, many with experience fighting alongside Mao Zedong's Red Army in the Chinese Civil War, were proving well disciplined and well trained.

As soon as the briefing ended, MacArthur slapped his knee. "Let's go up to the front and have a look," he suggested. A battered Dodge sedan carried MacArthur and Almond, trailed by several jeeps. The convoy struggled north up the road against a flood of refugees and truckloads of South Korean troops fleeing to the rear, having apparently put up scant resistance. "I haven't seen a wounded man yet," MacArthur complained to Almond. "Nobody is fighting."

The visit lasted eight hours—long enough to convince MacArthur that U.S. ground forces needed to be committed immediately. Back in Tokyo, MacArthur sent a message to Washington saying he wanted to rush a regimental combat team (RCT) to South Korea, followed by two full Army divisions. Though it was the middle of the night in Washington, Gen. J. Lawton Collins, the Army chief of staff, quickly approved the RCT. But when Collins said approval of the divisions might take a few hours, he was steamrolled by MacArthur, who demanded the matter be brought to the president immediately. By 5:00 a.m. June 30 in Washington, with remarkably little consideration, Truman had agreed to commit U.S. troops to a ground war on the Asian mainland.

The forces MacArthur commanded in Japan as the supreme commander for the Allied Powers were part of a diminished U.S. military—one that was a far cry from the massive global force that had helped win World War II. The number of Americans in uniform had shrunk from 12 million in 1945 to 1.5 million by 1948. Truman, fixated on cutting costs after the war, had worked with Congress to slash the defense budget. The state of U.S. armed forces in 1950 made the decision to rush to war all the more remarkable.

The 7th Infantry Division was one of four divisions making up the U.S. 8th Army, which occupied Japan. All four were badly understrength, at half their designated size, a deficiency mirrored in Army units around the world. Infantry regiments had only two battalions instead of three. Infantry battalions had three companies instead of four. The 8th Army had "just the merest skeleton of a military command," Almond said. Equipment was of deteriorating World War II vintage. Radios did not work. Machine guns were inoperable. Ammunition left in storage since the end of the war was corroding. With limited funding and units spread all over Japan, the 8th Army was unable to train above the battalion level.

The 24th Division was the least combat-ready of the four divisions in Japan, but as it was based on the southernmost Japanese home island of Kyushu, it was the closest to South Korea and would be sent first. The 25th Division, the next closest, would go second, followed, if needed, by the 1st Cavalry Division. The 7th Division, based the farthest north, would remain in Japan for now, serving as the home guard. Emptying Japan of all U.S. troops was seen as "exceedingly risky," Haig recalled. The 31st Regiment would stay on Hokkaido due to the concern that Soviets might try to seize the island, as Stalin had considered during World War II. The 7th Division soldiers were uneasy, uncertain whether they would remain in Japan for the duration of the war or be sent to Korea. "I look for this to start something big, but I hope not," Cpl. Hamilton wrote to his parents. "There is news that comes on the radio at 11:00 at night and almost everyone in the barracks does not go to bed until they hear the news."

On July 1, the vanguard of troops from the 24th began flying into the airfield at Pusan, a key port city on South Korea's southeast coast. Crowds of South Koreans cheered and waved flags as the force of 440 American soldiers—named Task Force Smith, after its commander, Lt. Col. Brad Smith—moved north on the highway from Pusan. "It made us feel like we'd already won," Smith recalled.

On July 5, Task Force Smith dug in along the highway north of Osan, awaiting the approach of North Korean forces. "The rumor was as soon as they saw American troops, they'd turn around and go back," recalled Lt. Carl Bernard. A column of thirty-three North Korean tanks rolled down the highway, and Bernard's bazooka teams began firing from positions thirty yards away. When the tanks kept coming, the lieutenant figured his nervous men were not shooting straight. He grabbed a bazooka and fired, but to his shock, the rocket bounced off a tank. The American 2.36-inch rockets could not penetrate the heavy armor of the T-34 tanks.

Smith and Bernard could see more tanks approaching, followed by a line of infantry stretching back for miles. Task Force Smith was quickly overrun, suffering 185 casualties. "We had a pretty good idea right then that we had something that was going to cause us a hell of a lot of woe," Smith said. "We weren't ready to fight, there's no question about it."

In six years in Japan, MacArthur had never once visited any of his occupation divisions. He acknowledged privately that his troops were unprepared to fight a war on short notice, but characteristically, he took no responsibility.

The legendary American general, 70 years old when North Korea invaded, remained a conquering hero of World War II to much of the American public, often seen as virtually infallible, certainly by himself but also by many at his Tokyo headquarters and in Washington. As a commander, he was capable of bold strokes of strategic genius but also of a blindness born of hubris.

MacArthur was the Army's senior officer, "senior to everyone but God," as one officer put it. Some of the more sacrilegious staff at the Dai Ichi went even further, adopting "There is no god but MacArthur" as their motto. It was said tongue in cheek perhaps, but MacArthur often was treated more like a deity than an Army officer by subordinates and supposed superiors alike.

MacArthur had been a general since World War I, when he commanded a division in France. He had become the youngest superintendent at West Point in 1919, then the youngest Army chief of staff in 1930, at age 50. While overseeing the creation of the Philippine Army, he had retired from the U.S. Army in 1937. But in the summer of 1941, with the Philippines under threat from the Japanese empire, President Franklin Roosevelt called MacArthur back to duty as commander of U.S. Army Forces in the Far East, headquartered in Manila. MacArthur's performance in World War II began with baffling failure but ended in triumph. After learning of the Japanese attack on Pearl Harbor on December 7, 1941, MacArthur's command did not disperse its aircraft at Clark Field, making them easy targets for Japanese planes when they attacked nine hours later. MacArthur was soon forced to move his headquarters to the island fortress of Corregidor in Manila Bay, and in February 1942, FDR ordered him to evacuate to Australia. His forces on the Bataan Peninsula and Corregidor surrendered within months. As the commander of the Southwest Pacific Area, MacArthur, together with Admiral Chester Nimitz, orchestrated an island-hopping strategy that enabled Allied forces to bypass Japanese strongholds while pressing deeper into enemy territory. On October 20, 1944, after Allied forces including the 7th Division made an assault landing on the Philippine island of Leyte, MacArthur waded through the surf and proclaimed, "I have returned," fulfilling a vow he had made when he had escaped two years earlier.

It was MacArthur who accepted the surrender of the Japanese aboard the USS *Missouri* in August 1945. After the war MacArthur remained in Japan, refusing invitations from Truman to come home for consultations and public honors. Instead, he focused on his new role as supreme commander for the Allied powers (SCAP) in Japan, helping shape the country into a modern democracy.

The general rarely left Tokyo, living with his wife Jean and 12-year-old-son Arthur on the U.S. embassy grounds in a palatial house with a grand entrance hall, seven bedrooms, a banquet room, and salons. Jean, a gracious and petite Tennessean who was 20 years his junior and in private called her husband Sir Boss, dedicated herself to running a smooth and tranquil household for the general, overseeing a staff of Japanese and Filipino workers.

The residence was about a mile from the Dai Ichi, meaning number one in Japanese, a one-time insurance company building that had survived the firebombing of Tokyo. MacArthur's daily arrival at the general headquarters, or GHQ, would draw large crowds of Japanese onlookers, with white-gloved

Army military police (MPs) on hand to keep order—"like the changing of the guard at Buckingham Palace," one officer recalled.

GHQ in Tokyo was an insular world, far removed from the Pentagon and White House, enabling MacArthur to work with the independence he wanted from Washington. He treated the Truman administration like a "suspicious foreign government," the U.S. State Department's George Kennan later observed. A coterie of senior staff officers who had been with MacArthur since before or during the war were known as the Bataan Gang and were largely regarded as sycophants by those on the outside. Their numbers had dwindled by 1950 but still included Maj. Gen. Courtney Whitney, his chief confidant, and Maj. Gen. Charles A. Willoughby, chief of intelligence.

Only one outsider had penetrated MacArthur's inner circle: Ned Almond. Though Almond had never served with MacArthur—or even met him—before arriving in Tokyo in 1946, he had worked his way into his favor—so much so that another nickname behind his back was Ned, the Anointed.

Almond was a Virginian born in 1892 in the Shenandoah Valley. The grandson of a Confederate officer, he was raised with a reverence for the Confederacy and had a mean streak of racism that only worsened with age. He attended Virginia Military Institute, where he where he learned to venerate Thomas "Stonewall" Jackson, who had been an instructor at the school until the start of the Civil War. When Almond graduated in 1915, the yearbook sent him off with the words "Sic'em Ned," meant to tease his potential as a lady-killer but also serving as an apt summary of his approach to life and war.

Almond was commissioned as an Army lieutenant just as the United States entered World War I, sailing to France in 1918 with the 4th Division as a company commander in a machine gun battalion. He was wounded during the fighting in the Marne Valley in August, later received the Silver Star for his actions, and after recovering in a hospital, returned to command the battalion through the Meuse-Argonne offensive. Almond had already picked up a reputation for aggressiveness. "He wouldn't step two paces to the rear for the devil himself," a contemporary said. After the war, Almond served as an instructor at the Army's Infantry School at Fort Benning at a time when George C. Marshall was the assistant commandant of the school. The future Army chief of staff was impressed with Almond, and thereafter, he was labeled a Marshall Man, marked for success.

In the months after Pearl Harbor, Marshall was looking for White Southern officers of "especially high professional qualities" to stand up and lead Black units in the still-segregated U.S. Army. Marshall's theory was that as a Southerner, Almond would understand "Negro capabilities," so he was chosen to command the Black 92nd Division. The division's training was marked by tensions between White officers and Black soldiers, and Almond was faulted by an inspector general for giving little consideration to "racial understanding." Arriving in Italy in 1944, the division's regiments were committed to combat piecemeal, and after initial success pursuing retreating Germans north of Rome, they collapsed in the face of stiff resistance along the Gothic Line in the Apennines. "The infantry literally dissolved each night abandoning equipment and even clothing in some cases," a disappointed Marshall wrote to General Dwight Eisenhower, the Allied supreme commander. All the 92nd regiments but one were pulled back and replaced by other units.

Almond disgracefully blamed the race of his soldiers. "The white man . . . is willing to die for patriotic reasons," he said. "The Negro is not." Black soldiers saw it differently, including one who called the division "a slave unit for white masters." Black newspapers in the United States defended the troops of the 92nd and called for Almond's removal. The *Chicago Defender* complained that the Black soldiers were fighting not only Nazis but also "Dixie race haters."

After a reorganization, the 92nd performed better during the final offensive in northern Italy in spring 1945. But as the offensive progressed in March, Almond received devastating news. His only son, Capt. Edward M. Almond Jr., West Point class of 1943, had been killed by a German sniper in France as his unit approached the Rhine River. It was a bitter loss for the elder Almond, particularly since he had written to his son's commander, saying he should be given a combat assignment, not a safer staff position. Compounding the general's grief, he received notification at the same time that Maj. Thomas Galloway, a P-38 fighter pilot who was married to Almond's daughter and who had been missing since being shot down over Normandy in July, had been declared killed in action. Almond insisted on staying on duty with the 92nd despite the dual blows.

Reflecting the Army's prevailing prejudice at the time, the War Department absolved Almond of blame for the 92nd travails. But the war ended without his earning any of the glory won by many of his peers, officers such as Omar Bradley, Joe Collins, George Patton, and Matthew Ridgway. Almond was disappointed to be left behind. According to Haig, many Army officers of the time believed that Almond would have ended the war with four stars if he had been given command of one of the "regular divisions," as Haig put it. Certainly, Almond thought so.

With his career prospects looking bleak, Almond was assigned to the Pacific. But his luck picked up when he arrived in Tokyo in 1946. MacArthur's chief of staff, Maj. Gen. Paul Mueller, was an old friend, and he picked Almond for a position as MacArthur's personnel chief.

MacArthur, skeptical of outsiders, particularly those who had served in the European theater, was impressed with Almond's ability and work ethic. Despite his faults, Almond was a brilliant dynamo—"a phenomenally gifted soldier," in Haig's view. In 1948 Eisenhower would rate Almond as one of the half dozen ablest officers in the Army. Within a few months, Almond was chosen to fill a vacancy as deputy chief of staff, bringing him into closer contact with MacArthur. When Mueller rotated back to the United States in January 1949, MacArthur approved Almond as his new chief of staff.

It was a particularly powerful position at the Tokyo GHQ because MacArthur did not wish to interact with his underlings and required everyone to go through the chief of staff on any matter. Almond took full advantage, jealously guarding access and thereby making himself even more powerful. Only Whitney and Willoughby could see MacArthur without his blessing.

MacArthur liked to play the man in the white hat at GHQ and let his chief of staff be the hatchet man. It was a role that came naturally to Almond, who had no problem denying requests, scolding subordinates in front of others, and making incessant demands. Arrogantly confident in his own opinions, Almond would often override staff recommendations and substitute his own decisions. Most of his staff considered him "a slave driver," recalled Maj. Joe Gurfein. "I don't think he ever worried about being liked," Gurfein added. "He worked 18 hours a day and expected everyone else to do the same."

Some grumbled that Almond's rise with MacArthur was due to an "instinctive knack for ingratiation,"but Omar Bradley, who was then chairman of the Joint Chiefs of Staff, was among those who thought otherwise. "Almond was not the usual yes-man or sycophant that seemed to gravitate to MacArthur's staffs," Bradley later wrote, adding that Almond had "extraordinary ability."

Almond may not have been a sycophant, but he was something potentially even more dangerous—a true believer. MacArthur had a powerful aura, and Almond was captivated by it. He "had an almost mystical belief in General MacArthur's genius," said Lt. Col. Bill McCaffrey, who served with Almond in World War II and joined his staff in Tokyo. Almond "absolutely hero worshipped [MacArthur] without stint, without reservation, without any critical judgment at all," he added.

MacArthur, for his part, "admired [Almond] almost without reservation and regarded him as his right arm," Haig recalled. MacArthur prized loyalty from subordinates above all else, and Almond delivered that in spades—he was "loyal to an extreme" in the view of Brig. Gen. Edwin "Pinky" Wright, the operations chief at GHQ. In return, MacArthur protected Almond from retribution: He was untouchable.

After the demise of Task Force Smith, the rest of the 24th Division landed in Pusan by July 6, the same day Lt. Gen. Walton "Johnnie" Walker, commander of the 8th Army, arrived to take over operations in Korea. The 24th was fighting delaying actions, desperately trying to buy time for more U.S. forces to arrive from Japan. The 25th Division, next in line, began boarding ships in Japan July 8.

MacArthur had decided the best way to relieve pressure on Walker's troops and reverse the North Korean gains was a bold amphibious assault far in the enemy rear. He already had a landing site in mind: Inchon, an industrial port west of Seoul. On July 15, MacArthur directed Almond to prepare requisitions for the troops and equipment needed for the amphibious landing. To keep it secret, Almond adopted the name X Force and set up its headquarters in a small airplane hangar at the GHQ motor pool in Tokyo. MacArthur instructed Almond to put together the X Force staff from inside GHQ and "not from outside sources" to make sure MacArthur kept control.

Initially, the invasion force was to include the 1st Cavalry Division, headquartered northeast of Tokyo, but the situation along the American defensive perimeter was getting so precarious that the division was instead being rushed to reinforce Walker's troops.

That would leave the 7th Division as the last one remaining in Japan, and MacArthur had been assured he could use it for his amphibious assault. MacArthur leapt at a suggestion from Lt. Gen. Lem Shepherd, the newly appointed commander of Fleet Marine Force, Pacific, that he request the 1st Marine Division, based at Camp Pendleton, California, be brought up to full strength and sent to Japan to join his X force. The Joint Chiefs were reluctant, but MacArthur browbeat them until they agreed on July 25. Now MacArthur would have the force he needed for Inchon.

MacArthur left the 7th Division commander, Maj. Gen. David Barr, in the dark about his plans to use the division at Inchon. By late July Barr's division was spread all over Japan, occupying camps left by the divisions fighting in Korea. Barr was at the division headquarters at Sendai on July 26 when he received a call from GHQ telling him to report to Tokyo. He was needed immediately, so MacArthur sent *Bataan* to pick him up.

At the Dai Ichi, Barr received orders that left his head spinning. "My instructions from GHQ were to assemble the division, receive replacements, retrain it and be ready for an amphibious landing in thirty days," he recalled. "That seemed like a considerable task.... As a matter of fact, it seemed so great that I didn't even question it."

The 7th Division was now even more understrength than it had been at the start of the war. Over the past month, it had been stripped of some of its most experienced junior officers and NCOs to fill in the three divisions already sent to Korea, all understrength themselves. The 7th Division was now at less than half strength, short 9,117 men, including 290 officers. It had suffered "decimation," Almond acknowledged. The shortages were proportionally even greater in some key combat areas, as many of the division's most battle-tested World War II veterans had been hastily transferred to the other divisions. It had been stripped of communications and artillery specialists badly needed by the 24th and 25th Divisions. Now the 7th badly needed its own.

Originally activated in 1917, the 7th Division had seen action in France in World War I and in the Aleutians, the Philippines, and Okinawa in World War II. It had more experience in Korea than any other American unit, having received the surrender of Japanese troops in southern Korea at the end of the war and then patrolling the 38th parallel as an occupation force for more than three years. After the establishment of the North and South Korean states, the Soviets and Americans pulled out their occupation troops. In 1949 the 7th Division was the last to leave. Some groused that if Washington had left American troops in South Korea, the division would not now be heading into war. "A classic example of the striped pants boys getting our chestnuts in the fire," recalled Lt. Col. Bill Paddock, the division's operations officer.

One of the division's three infantry regiments, the 31st Regiment, had a history that was both colorful and tragic. It was famous in the Far East, sent to Vladivostok in 1918 after the Russian Revolution to secure the Trans-Siberian Railroad, enabling czarist Russian army units to escape from Bolshevik troops. The regiment had served between the wars in China and was stationed in the Philippines when World War II broke out. The 31st Regiment troops defended against invading Japanese at Corregidor and the Bataan Peninsula before being ordered to surrender. Its soldiers had suffered terrible casualties through the Bataan Death March and imprisonment in Japanese camps. Some of the old-timers with the 31st had served with MacArthur in the Philippines and weren't terribly fond of him for escaping to Australia while they were left for the Japanese.

Reflecting their heritage, the soldiers of the 31st called themselves the Polar Bears, and their regimental crest was a Siberian bear. It was fitting that the Polar Bears were based near Sapporo in Hokkaido and were accustomed to heavy winter snow in the surrounding mountains and forests. Some trained as ski troopers and learned winter survival skills.

The regiment's other nickname was America's Foreign Legion, reflecting that from its formation in 1916 in Manila, the 31st had never served on continental U.S. soil. It still felt like a foreign legion. That was part of its appeal for Cpl. Ray Radke, who had spent his early years growing up poor on a dairy farm in northern Illinois. He had already done one stint in the Army, enlisting at 17 and serving in Panama, but his company commander discouraged him from reenlisting. "I was carousing, drinking a lot, enjoying life," Radke recalled. "He was probably right." Back in the United States, Radke bummed around the southwest, riding the rails, until he got to El Paso, Texas, where police picked him up twice for trying to hitchhike out of town. Fed up, Radke made his way to the Army recruiting office in El Paso and spoke to the recruiter. "I told him I wanted to get as far away from the United States as I could," Radke recalled. They looked at the map of the world on the office wall, and the recruiter pointed to Japan. "He said, 'Well, the 7th Division is up here in northern Japan. The 31st Regiment is the farthest north, on the island of Hokkaido. I could assign you to 7th Infantry, and you could probably talk your way to the 31st.' So that's exactly what happened."

Radke was very pleased with what he found. Camp Crawford was a comfortable setup, with platoon-sized brick barracks and plenty of showers and latrines. Outside the gates of the camp were a host of diversions for GIs. "Them were the days," Radke recalled. "Sitting around in the whore houses, drinking beer, playing with the girls." He wasn't the only one; Chaplain Hoehn fretted about the high venereal disease rate at Camp Crawford.

Others found more wholesome entertainment. Cpl. Ray Vallowe and his best friend, Cpl. Eldon Ervin, were radio operators with the 57th Field Artillery (FA) Battalion, which was based at Camp Crawford in support of the 31st Regiment. On early summer days, after rolling up their telephone wires, the two would pull their communication trucks between the many cherry trees around Sapporo and eat their fill.

Many of the regiment's officers were married with children. Jerry McCabe, a self-described "wet-nosed lieutenant" from Baltimore assigned to the 31st Heavy Mortar Company, was a newlywed, living with his wife, Peg, in Sapporo. Maj. Harvey Storms, the executive officer of the 3rd Battalion, 31st Regiment, lived in a house outside Sapporo with his wife, Helen, and their three young boys. He was from a family of ranchers in La Feria, a town in the southeast tip of Texas near the Mexican border. After graduating from Texas A&M in 1939 with a degree in agriculture, he married Helen, who was from a nearby family of farmers. After the United States entered World War II, Storms enlisted in the Army, taking part in the invasions of North Africa, Sicily, and Italy. Friendly and good-natured, Storms befriended villagers outside Genoa who would fondly remember him for years. Storms came home after the war and taught agriculture, but missing the Army, he reenlisted in 1948 and was sent to Japan.

Helen had been relieved when it looked like the 7th Division would remain in Japan, particularly since she had recently learned she was pregnant with a fourth child. But that was not to be. "Daddy came home one day, and he and Mama sat down at the dining hall table," recalled Sam Storms—at 9, the eldest of the boys. Harvey told her he would be leaving in several weeks for a camp near Mt. Fuji, where the 7th Division would assemble and train before going to Korea. "I remember her crying and sobbing," said Sam.

Now that it was clear the Polar Bears were going to Korea, some officers whispered their concerns about the regimental commander, Col. Richard P.

Ovenshine, a gray-haired and stately gentleman. He had briefly commanded a regiment at the end of the Okinawa campaign but had little combat experience, and at age 50, many thought he was too old and inexperienced to go to war. "It was the opinion of the majority of us that he had had no combat experience AND THAT HE SHOULD HAVE BEEN REPLACED," Hoehn later wrote in a letter. "He was mild mannered, fatherly, one might say," he added disapprovingly. Hoehn, a one-time parish priest in Brooklyn, had the bona fides to make such judgments, having served as a chaplain in North Africa, Sicily, and across northwest Europe with Patton's 3rd Army.

Not surprisingly for a regiment that had been through Bataan, the 31st had a reputation as a hard-luck unit. Some considered it a bit of a dumping ground for problem soldiers, and by virtue of its isolated location, it was often last in line for replacements and equipment. But that isolation and reputation bred an us-against-the-world pride among many of the men and officers.

Training in Hokkaido was constrained, with no live fire and no exercises conducted above the battalion level. Nonetheless, smaller units were constantly in the field; Ovenshine intensified training when the war broke out, and by the time they were alerted, the 31st Regiment had reached a high state of readiness.

Most considered the 7th Division's best regiment to be the 32nd Regiment, stationed at Camp Haugen, a former Imperial Japanese military airfield on the northeast coast of Honshu, the largest Japanese island. "The 32nd was a class outfit—head and shoulders above the others," said Charles Davis, Barr's aide-de-camp.

The 32nd Regiment had been on occupation duty in Korea until early 1949, when it withdrew to Japan and took over the camp from a regiment of the 11th Airborne Division, which was being recalled to the United States. The 32nd had been reconstituted with an unusual mix of cavalry, infantry, and airborne troops, including paratroopers with the 11th Airborne who wanted to stay in Japan. A cavalry squadron from the 12th Cavalry Regiment near Yokohama was added to the mix, including the squadron commander, Lt. Colonel Don Carlos Faith, who was given command of the 1st Battalion, 32nd Regiment.

Col. Allan Maclean, a robust West Pointer, was the first commander of the reconstituted 32nd Regiment, and he spent a year molding it into a cohesive unit from the airborne, infantry, and cavalry elements. Within a few months, the 32nd Regiment had the highest combat effectiveness rating given by 8th Army headquarters. The 32nd Regiment had three of the ablest battalion commanders among all the units being sent to Korea, and of the three, in the judgment of military historian Clay Blair, the standout was Faith.

Faith launched an extensive training program as soon as he took command, keeping the battalion in the field much of the time for over a year, sometimes for two or three days at a time and sometimes for two or three weeks. "We trained hard, and we trained day and night," recalled Bob Jones, one of Faith's staff officers. "We trained on the ground up in the mountains. It was not that we anticipated anything, but that was just his nature. . . . And it paid off."

In spring 1950 Maclean was reassigned to 8th Army headquarters. The new regimental commander, Colonel Charles Beauchamp, considered Faith's 1st Battalion as his best-trained and best-led battalion "due entirely to the initiative, energy, and esprit instilled in it by Don."

Faith was big, handsome, and gregarious, with brown eyes and dark brown hair sometimes worn in a crew cut. He was close to six feet tall with no fat, as he constantly ran around Camp Haugen to stay fit. He was married to the former Barbara Ann Wilbur of Louisiana, and they had a 4-year-old daughter, Barbara Ann, known as Bobbie.

Faith was from a family that had a tradition of military service since their arrival in Pennsylvania prior to the American Revolution. A Faith fought with Mad Anthony Wayne at Paoli during the Revolutionary War and another with William Henry Harrison at the Battle of Tippecanoe during the War of 1812. Faith's great-grandfather served under Ulysses Grant at Vicksburg during the Civil War. His father, Don Carlos Faith Sr., was an Army brigadier general during World War II who was chosen by George Marshall to organize and train what became known as the Women's Army Corps (WAC).

Given his name and dark complexion, many assumed Don Carlos Jr. was of Spanish descent, but his heritage was Scotch-Irish—his grandparents apparently just liked the name. Paddy, as he was known to family and friends, was born in Indiana and grew up on Army posts in the United States and overseas, including three years in Tientsin, China. He wanted to attend West Point but failed a physical due to two missing molars—considered a "dental deficiency." He went to Georgetown University School of Foreign Service instead and considered a career with the State Department. But in the summer of 1941, believing U.S. entry into the war to be inevitable, Faith joined the Army. He graduated in February 1942 from the U.S. Army Officer Candidate School at Fort Benning, Georgia, among the top ten in his class of two hundred.

Brig. Gen. Matthew Ridgway—just arrived at Benning as assistant division commander for the 82nd Infantry Division, which he was helping transform into an airborne division—had the pick of the crop for an aide-de-camp. Ridgway chose Faith, describing him as "an awfully likable youngster" with a "winning smile . . . superior physique, great athletic ability and an alert mind and positive qualities of leadership."

Ridgway was on his way to becoming one of the ablest Army commanders in World War II, taking command of the 82nd Airborne and eventually the XVIII Airborne Corps, and Faith was along for the ride. He accompanied Ridgway through North Africa, Sicily, and Italy. By the time of the D-Day invasion, Faith was a major and serving as Ridgway's headquarters commandant, jumping with him into Normandy hedgerow country. Through the fighting at Arnhem, into the Ardennes, and across the Rhine to the Elbe River, Faith became a confidant and friend to the hard-charging Ridgway, not the easiest man to cozy up with. "Don and I so often enjoyed a glass of cognac when combat tension had relaxed," Ridgway later wrote to Barbara Faith. Don Faith, by then a 27-year-old lieutenant colonel, was en route with Ridgway to MacArthur's headquarters in Manila when word came of Japan's surrender.

Faith's ticket with Ridgway had given him a unique view of the war from the highest levels, including interactions with Eisenhower and other senior commanders. He had a great champion in Ridgway. "I could have asked for no more devoted assistant, or finer Aide, associate and companion—conspicuous for high-principled integrity, selfless devotion to duty, fearlessness in combat, modesty, compassionate consideration for others, cheerfulness and sense of humor," Ridgway later wrote. But what Faith had not done at any time during the war was command troops in combat.

After the war, Faith had served with the Army's advisory mission in Nanking, China, assisting Chiang Kai-shek's National Revolutionary Army in its struggle against Chinese communists. Faith forged a close relationship with the director, Dave Barr. The victory of the Chinese communists in October 1949 forced the mission out of China, and both Barr and Faith ended up in Japan. Given command of the 7th Division, Barr likely was involved in the selection of Faith as the 1/32 commander. The general would visit the 32nd frequently and always stopped by to see Faith. "Theirs was a close and somewhat a father and son relationship," Bob Jones recalled.

Faith was well aware that he lacked combat command experience. "I think he regretted the fact that he was working for Ridgway as headquarters commandant aide because he never really got down with the troops in World War II," said Jones. Faith was hardly alone. None of the three 32nd Regiment rifle battalion commanders had combat command in World War II. The same was true at higher ranks and in other divisions. Of the first eighteen Army regimental commanders sent to Korea, fifteen had none. The Army policy at the time was to give officers who had served well in vital staff roles in World War II a chance to command troops. It had not been much of a problem in peacetime, but now they were going to war.

Faith worked to remedy his shortcomings in experience, but it was difficult, given the training restrictions in population-dense Japan. He "realized exactly that he was very short on experience with using the artillery support battalion," Jones recalled, so he arranged on his own to spend a week with the 48th Field Artillery Battalion at Camp Zama south of Tokyo, a long journey from Camp Haugen. "That was the type of person he was," Jones said.

When the war broke out, Faith had been due to rotate soon back to the United States, but he immediately went to Barr and told him he wanted to go to Korea. He had been run off the mainland once, Faith told colleagues, and he wasn't going to be run off again.

By early August Walker's forces had fallen back to a defensive line that became known as the Pusan Perimeter, a toehold behind the Naktong River in the far southeast corner of South Korea that included the vital ports of Pusan and Pohang.

In Tokyo the X Force planners at GHQ were deep into planning for Operation Chromite, MacArthur's amphibious landing at Inchon, with the 1st Marine Division landing first and the 7th Division as the follow-on force. Since the X Force included two divisions, Almond recommended to MacArthur it be designated a corps. MacArthur agreed and asked what name the corps would take. Corps in the U.S. Army are traditionally designated with Roman numerals, so Almond proposed turning the *X* in X Force into the Roman numeral 10, hence X Corps.

An important question remained: Who would command this force? Given Inchon was an amphibious operation and the primary invasion force was the 1st Marine Division, most expected a Marine general would be chosen. MacArthur's operations chief, Pinky Wright, recommended Shepherd, the Marine Pacific commander. On the morning of August 10, Almond posed the question to MacArthur, who replied he would have an answer later that day. Almond returned to MacArthur's office in the afternoon. "You will be the landing force commander," the general told Almond.

Almond professed to be shocked. "This was a complete surprise to me and I told him so," he later wrote. Almond also pointed out that he was already chief of staff and would be unable to do both jobs.

MacArthur waved off the concern. "We will all be back here in a month," he told Almond.

Almond wasn't the only one surprised. The Joint Chiefs were astonished, seeing it as a high-handed MacArthur ploy to block the Pentagon from choosing a Navy or Marine commander with experience from World War II amphibious landings in the Pacific. Collins, the Army chief of staff, had long disliked Almond and was incensed by the choice.

No one had more reason to be unhappy than Johnnie Walker. The 8th Army commander had been a tough, aggressive armored corps commander serving under Patton during World War II. He was short and squat and low on charisma, but while Walker didn't look much like a general, he was "a fighting little son of a bitch," Patton said approvingly.

But he was not a MacArthur man, nor was he equipped temperamentally for the internecine struggles of GHQ. Almond and Walker had been friendly as young officers, but that changed after Walker arrived in Japan. Almond limited Walker's access to MacArthur and regularly snubbed the 8th Army commander. Walker was on the outside looking in. But to make it worse, MacArthur intended to keep X Corps as a separate command from the 8th Army, meaning Almond would report directly to MacArthur, bypassing Walker altogether. With Almond wearing the dual hats of X Corps commander and MacArthur's chief of staff, Walker would have to go through his lower-ranking rival as the 8th Army and X Corps competed for limited supplies, equipment, and men. Many disputes were settled by scribbling the initials GASS on a memo—"General Almond Said So."

For MacArthur, what mattered most was having a loyalist in position who would never question his directives, no matter how risky and how much heartburn they created in Washington. "I think more than anything else, MacArthur wanted to pull the strings from Tokyo," said Ridgway, then deputy chief of staff for operations for the Joint Chiefs. "He wanted that corps under his direct command."

Almond had quickly dismissed his own reservations and embraced command of X Corps, which would give him the chance to grab the laurels that had eluded him in World War II. As McCaffrey later noted, "General Almond desired one thing above all else in life. Military Glory."

Beijing, August 4, 1950

Mao Zedong's alarm was growing. The Chinese leader had met in Beijing with Kim Il Sung in May and agreed to support the planned North Korean invasion, though he had not been enthusiastic. Mao raised the possibility that the United States would intervene and asked Kim if he wanted China to position troops in Manchuria, along the border with North Korea, as a precaution. Kim had brushed off the offer—"arrogantly," in Mao's view—insisting that North Korea would capture all of Korea too quickly for the United States to intervene. Kim was wrong, and now, the North Korean invasion was bogging down along the Naktong. On August 4, Mao called his politburo together to discuss the worrying developments.

It had been less than a year since Mao had proclaimed the new People's Republic of China after the Red Army's decisive defeat of Chiang's Nationalist forces in October 1949, ending decades of fighting. Chiang and the remnants of his defeated army had retreated to the island of Taiwan—then often called Formosa—one hundred miles offshore of mainland China.

The war in Korea had disrupted Mao's plans to invade Taiwan, finish off Chiang, and unify all of China. The elite 9th Army Group, under the command of General Song Shilun, had been south of Shanghai, preparing for a major crossing operation. Two days after the North Korean invasion, Truman sent the U.S. 7th Fleet into the Taiwan Strait, which ran between the mainland and the island. The presence of the U.S. warships in the Taiwan Strait had forced Beijing to postpone the invasion.

The speed of the U.S. intervention in South Korea, together with the deployment of the 7th Fleet, had surprised and angered the new Chinese government. Chinese Premier Zhou Enlai, Mao's trusted deputy, called it tantamount to a declaration of war. Mao considered the UN forces now building up in South Korea to be a direct threat to the fledgling Chinese Communist nation. Failing to respond would send a signal to the world—and, just as importantly, the Chinese people—that the new Chinese government was weak, a paper tiger, little different than the nationalists. If the Americans won this war, they would pose an even greater danger to China.

Mao argued that any UN movement to the north toward the Yalu River border called for Chinese intervention in the war. Massing manpower on the Yalu as a defensive deterrent would not be enough, Mao believed; Chinese troops should prepare to advance into North Korea and set a defensive line one hundred miles south of the river, he told Zhou. Mao's mind, at least, was made up. On August 5, he sent a telegram to his military command: "Get ready for fighting in early September."

In early August, the 7th Division began assembling at the base of Mount Fuji, the iconic cone-shaped volcano sixty miles southwest of Tokyo. On August 5, the 7th Division headquarters at Sendai moved to Gotemba, at the eastern base of the mountain, home to the Camp Fuji training ground—land where Samurai warriors had once trained. The 32nd Regiment arrived in mid-August, setting up over a hill from the headquarters. The 31st Polar Bears followed soon afterward.

Some families opted to stay in Japan, hoping their soldiers would return soon. "It was supposed to be a real short war at that point," recalled Col. Herbert Powell, commander of the division's 17th Regiment. Many others were returning to the United States. The McCabes decided Peg should return to Maryland, as she was pregnant and expecting their first child. Barbara Faith likewise left with her daughter, Bobbie, to move in with her parents at their home in Alexandria, Louisiana.

Harvey and Helen Storms and their three young boys left Sapporo on a train on August 20 and traveled all night, crossing the strait between Hokkaido and Honshu aboard a train ferry, and then continued to Tokyo. It was a long, hot journey, and it was just starting. Once they reached Tokyo, Harvey would continue with the troops on the train to Camp Fuji, while Helen and the children would travel on to the Tokyo airport and fly home to Texas.

Harvey and Helen had agonized over whether she and the boys should stay in Hokkaido or go back to La Feria, where they had a home on a ten-acre tract. Harvey's parents, who owned fields of cotton and grains, lived next door. Helen was worried that if she went home, she and the boys would be separated from Harvey longer and that they would be stuck halfway around the globe when the war ended and the troops returned to Japan. But Harvey persuaded Helen that his mind would be more at ease knowing she was home with family to help with the boys and her pregnancy.

The Tokyo train station was jammed, filled with GIs on their way to war, families on their way home, and the regular flood of Japanese travelers. Two Army lieutenants told Storms that the troop cars at the rear of the train would be detached from the rest of the train, staying in Tokyo until that evening. That would give him the chance to spend the day with Helen and the boys before they took another train to the airport that evening. But when Storms went back to move his bags into the troop cars, the conductor insisted the entire train, including the troop cars, would be leaving momentarily.

Harvey rushed back to the platform and into the station to find his family and say a hurried goodbye. Ernie, the youngest, was puckering up to cry. Sam, the eldest, stayed with the family's luggage while Helen and the two younger boys went back to the train to see Harvey off. "They walked down the ramp with Daddy, but probably after about twenty yards he turned and looked back at me, and had kind of a forlorn look," Sam remembered. Sam didn't think to wave goodbye.

Chapter 2

WE SHALL LAND AT INCHON

Mt. Fuji, Monday, August 21, 1950

The race to rebuild the decimated 7th Division was on, and the scene at the Mount Fuji staging area was beyond chaotic. "It is a three ringed circus," the division's operations officer, Lt. Col. Bill Paddock, wrote in his journal.

Trains carrying 7th Division units from across Japan were arriving three times a day. Tents sprung up, covering the black lava on the shoulder of the snow-capped mountain. Replacement troops from the United States were pouring in, many of them barely out of boot camp. "It is a helluva mess," wrote Paddock, a tough-minded officer who had served as an airborne artillery battalion commander in World War II. "To top it all off we have to reequip and try to train."

Beyond that, thousands of bewildered South Korean citizens had been rounded up from the streets of Pusan and shipped to Japan in a desperate attempt to fill out the 7th Division. "There never was a division in history in the Pickle we are in," Paddock wrote August 22. "With thousands of untrained replacements thrown on us and then to have all these Koreans tossed in for good measure, oh brother!"

MacArthur ordered "every effort" be made to equip the 7th Division to be at full war strength and ready for combat by September 15, the day set for the Inchon landing. All soldiers meant to replace 8th Army casualties in Korea were diverted to Fuji.

Across the United States, soldiers' lives were being upended. Lieutenant Lloyd Mielenz, who just finished at West Point as a member of the class of

1950, was one of many newly minted second lieutenants who suddenly had their graduation leave cut short. Mielenz was home in New Jersey when orders came sending him immediately to Fuji, where he joined A Battery, 57th Field Artillery. Private Huey French, a 15-year-old, had been visiting home in Childress, Texas, in July when his leave was likewise cut short. He had grown up idolizing his older brothers, who had all served in World War II, and when an Army recruiter came to town in March 1950, Huey convinced his mother to sign enlistment papers saying he was 17. It was plausible—he was a big, strapping boy at six feet, two inches tall. "Our mother knew that if she did not consent that he would find a way to get in," Huey's twin sister, Joan, recalled. "She never dreamed that there would be a war, or that they would send him overseas." Trained as a Browning Automatic Rifle (BAR) man, Private French arrived at Fuji and was assigned to C Company, 32nd Infantry. They dubbed him The Kid.

PFC Grant McMillin had just finished several specialized artillery courses at Fort Sill, Oklahoma, when the war broke out, and he volunteered for Korea. "Oh, you're not going to Korea, we have too much money invested in you," his 1st sergeant told him. "You're going to train guys to go there." McMillin went home to Lake Geneva, Wisconsin, over the Fourth of July weekend and bought a car, a 1947 Plymouth convertible, red with white seats. "It was mint," he recalled. McMillin was back at Fort Sill when his 1st sergeant shook him out of a deep sleep. "How would you like to sell your car?" the 1st sergeant asked.

McMillen said he didn't want to sell his car. "Where you're going, you need a tank, you don't need a car," the 1st sergeant said. "You're headed for Korea." McMillin sold his car and soon found himself at Fuji, assigned to the 57th Field Artillery.

Some of the new arrivals were seasoned veterans. John Edward Gray, from a poor farming family in North Carolina, had enlisted in the Marine Corps at age 17. He had been an antiaircraft gunner on the USS *Maryland* in World War II, serving at Peleliu and Leyte and surviving a kamikaze attack. After the war he had gone to Davidson College on the GI Bill and earned a commission as an Army officer. Gray was preparing for a three-year assignment to the Far East Command, where he'd be accompanied by his wife and young son, but his orders changed, and he alone was rushed to Japan. At Fuji he was assigned to M Company, the heavy weapons company for the 3rd Battalion, 31st Regiment. The company commander, Capt. Earle Jordan, rejoiced when he learned of Gray's combat experience and infantry training. Gray assured him he was a skilled mortarman. "You sure as hell better be," Jordan said.

Two highly experienced majors were assigned to Don Faith's 1st Battalion, 32nd Infantry, and arrived the same day. Wesley Curtis, 32, a scholarly and soft-spoken West Point graduate from Arkansas's Ozark Mountains, had served in the Pacific as a platoon and company commander with the 27th Infantry Regiment "Wolfhounds," while Crosby Miller, a Virginian and 1940 Virginia Military Institute graduate, had commanded tank companies under Patton's army across Europe. Because of their rank, they would be expected to take over as the battalion executive officer and operations officer from Bob Jones and Ed Scullion, who were both captains. Curtis and Miller reported together to Faith. "He greeted us in a frank and friendly manner—and promptly told us in a frank and friendly manner that he didn't want us!!" Curtis recalled. Faith explained that he had a bond with Jones and Scullion, both of them combat-experienced World War II veterans. They had trained together, they knew and understood each other, and he wanted them with him in Korea. Miller thought that was "perfectly understandable," though Curtis was a bit miffed.

Gen. Barr told Faith he needed to take Curtis and Miller—it would have been foolish to turn away two combat-experienced officers of their caliber. Faith accepted them without further protest; Jones and Scullion would accompany the battalion as company commanders. Despite the awkward start, Curtis found himself deeply impressed with the battalion commander. "Lt. Col. Don Faith was a remarkable young man," Curtis would recall decades later. "He was open, frank, friendly, candid, forceful—and had a high degree of charisma and leadership," Curtis added. "I liked and respected him—he was popular with troops—and his potential value to the Army was unlimited."

But Curtis was concerned by Faith's lack of combat leadership experience and that he had not attended the Command and General Staff School or the advanced course at the Infantry School. Faith was instead given credit for the courses because of his World War II experience, another common Army practice at the time. Faith had "proven leadership," Curtis said, but the Army "placed him in his position without providing him required training in the fundamentals of his profession."

In all, some 390 officers and 5,400 enlisted men were sent to build up the 7th Division. These included cadres of highly experienced soldiers from the

Infantry School at Fort Benning and the Artillery School at Fort Sill who were sent to restore units that had been shuttered as part of the budget cuts. But the stream of GIs pouring into Fuji was not going to be nearly enough to bring the division up to full strength.

In August, faced with this grave shortage, MacArthur requested that the South Korean government provide thousands of citizens who could help fill the gaps. Rhee's government acted with its usual efficient brutality. The National Police cordoned off several blocks in Pusan and closed in, grabbing any male who looked even marginally able to serve in the military. The hapless men were given no opportunity to go home to pack possessions or even to contact their families to tell them what had happened. They were put on ships and sailed straight to Japan.

The Koreans, eventually given the Army acronym KATUSAs (Korean Augmentees to U.S. Army) but also called ROKs (from Republic of Korea), began arriving at Yokohama on August 18. Some were schoolboys still clutching their schoolbags; others were older men well past their prime. One man had been nabbed on the street while out getting medicine for his sick wife; he arrived in Japan still holding her medicine. A few were in business suits, many others were just in shirts and shorts, and some were in shorts only. The majority had only sandals or cloth shoes. "They were stunned, confused and exhausted," recalled Barr, the division commander.

Lt. John Gray was sent with trucks to Yokohama to pick up a contingent of ROKs for the 31st Regiment. Gray watched in dismay as the Koreans walked down the gangplank in single file to the dock, where they were greeted by an Army delousing team spraying them with clouds of DDT to kill lice. Gray and his men counted out about 400 Koreans, loaded them on trucks, and drove them sixty miles to Fuji.

Once there, they were issued fatigues and dog tags with their names. Army doctors gave them physicals and shots, while dentists pulled parasitic worms out of their throats. "They are a sad lot, recruited from the streets and sometimes forcibly, young and often sick and stupid; and we have to make soldiers of them in about two weeks—what a helluva job," Paddock wrote in his journal.

Each ROK was paired with his own GI in a buddy system—sharing a pup tent and eating and training together. "To practically every soldier went a Korean," Barr said. "We stressed the idea that we wanted every soldier to feel that his Korean was the best treated [and] the best trained. . . . They were given the same clothing, the same equipment and the same treatment as the American soldier. General MacArthur specifically directed this."

Like many MacArthur innovations, it worked better in theory than in practice. Very few of the Koreans spoke any English, and even fewer GIs spoke any Korean, so most communication was via sign language. The culture shock for Americans and Koreans alike was enormous, starting with the strange Western foods the Koreans encountered in the mess tents. "We had to post a U.S. soldier at the chow line; otherwise the ROK would cover their roast beef, potatoes, gravy and vegetables with a half inch of sugar; diarrhea would be rampant," recalled Major Lester Olson, the 31st Regiment operations officer. Others put Tabasco sauce on their cornflakes.

The biggest problem was differing views regarding sanitation. "The KATUSAs would relieve themselves, diarrhea and all, around the pup tents, sometimes at night right at the tent entrances," Gray recalled. "This caused some KATUSAs to be hit in the head with entrenching tools."

It fell to the squad leaders and platoon sergeants to sort out misunderstandings. This cut into their already short time to train the soldiers and create cohesive units out of many new arrivals. "The ROK soldier became part of our problem, not a part of the solution," recalled Captain Erwin Bigger, one of Faith's company commanders.

Gradually, the situation improved. Koreans who spoke a bit of English were assigned to each platoon to act as an interpreter. Storms, overseeing the training of the Koreans assigned to the 31st Regiment, spent two days teaching the ROKs how to sight and aim the rifles and then brought them to the firing range. "They surprised us all with the accuracy of their shooting—and most of them claim they have never fired a gun before!" Storms wrote Helen.

The Americans and Koreans tended to get along better when a GI treated his buddy as an equal. Roy Oxenrider, a 17-year-old from Muir, Pennsylvania, assigned to a recoilless rifle squad in A Company, 32nd Infantry, was paired up with a young Korean named Joung He Su. "He was my shadow," recalled Oxenrider. "Joung was a good soldier, alert, serious and very courageous and I liked him as a person."

By the end of August, the 7th Division had received 8,000 Koreans—a full one-third of its strength—without major disaster. Even Paddock was somewhat relieved. The ROKs, despite "the mange, worms, [and] language barrier seem miraculously to be doing OK," he recorded in his journal.

MacArthur pushed ahead with plans for a landing at Inchon despite the numerous dangers it presented. In many respects, it would have been hard to find a less suitable location for an amphibious landing. There were no beaches, only mud flats and stone walls. The currents in the channel were notoriously dangerous. The range between high and low tide was thirty feet, one of the greatest on earth. At low tide, a landing force would have to cross a thousand yards of mud flats. The only day in the next six weeks when the tide would be high enough for landing craft to reach the seawalls and piers was September 15. The invasion force would have only a few hours to land before the water would recede, leaving enormous potential for catastrophe.

Almond was MacArthur's chief Inchon acolyte, fending off doubters. When Rear Adm. James Doyle, the Navy's lead planner for the operation, said that MacArthur needed to receive a detailed briefing about the dangers of Inchon, Almond was dismissive. "The General is not interested in the details," he told the admiral.

"He *must* be made aware of the details," Doyle insisted, forcing Almond to eventually back down.

Maj. Gen. Oliver Prince Smith, the commander of the 1st Marine Division, which would be making the landing, shared Doyle's concerns. Soft-spoken and professorial, with white hair and brilliant blue eyes, the tall and gaunt Smith looked less like a Marine general and more like "a small-town druggist, a man whom older ladies would call nice looking if only he would put on a little weight," as author Martin Russ put it.

Smith arrived in Tokyo on August 23, after a long journey from Camp Pendleton, California, and reported as instructed at the Dai Ichi at 5:30 p.m. Almond kept Smith waiting ninety minutes before meeting with him. Smith had extensive amphibious experience in World War II, including at Peleliu and Okinawa, but when he tried "to point out a few of the facts of life" about the difficulties Inchon posed, Almond waved him off. There would be no organized enemy resistance, and any difficulties would be "purely mechanical," Almond said flatly.

"My first impression of General Almond was distinctly unfavorable, and, unfortunately, that impression was not materially improved by later association," Smith recalled. "He had no amphibious experience, yet he was very positive in his judgments regarding such operations, and pronounced these judgments in a supercilious manner."

Smith was also irritated that Almond insisted on calling him "son," even though they were roughly the same age and Smith was senior by date of rank. Almond called almost everyone "son," including other generals—he meant it in a "fatherly" way, according to Haig—but Smith had a prickly pride and was the sort to take offense.

The tensions were exacerbated by service rivalries. The Marines were unhappy that X Corps command had been given to an Army general with no amphibious experience, and Smith resented being under an Army general in the first place. He had worked with the Army at Okinawa and found it exasperating. But at the heart of the matter were two strong-willed and diametrically different personalities. "Smith and Almond were just like two dogs at each other's throats," said Col. Jack Chiles, Almond's operations chief.

On August 23, a delegation from the Joint Chiefs of Staff, including Collins, the Army chief of staff, and Adm. Forrest Sherman, the chief of naval operations, arrived at the Dai Ichi to convey the Pentagon's deep reservations about the Inchon landing. Just before the meeting, Almond went into MacArthur's office. "General, they're coming in to argue you out of Inchon. Don't let them do it."

There wasn't much chance of that. After patiently listening to presentations from Collins and Sherman outlining the problems with Inchon, MacArthur took his turn. He launched into a spellbinding forty-five-minute soliloquy invoking a great military gamble of the past, when British Gen. James Wolfe scaled the Heights of Abraham at Quebec Ciy to surprise the French in 1759. The very impracticality of Inchon would similarly guarantee the element of surprise, MacArthur declared. "I realize that Inchon is a 5000 to 1 gamble, but I am used to taking such odds," he concluded. "We shall land at Inchon and I shall crush them."

There was a stunned silence in the room. After several more feeble attempts to change the plan in the days that followed, the chiefs wired their surrender to MacArthur. It would be Inchon.

Beijing, August 23

The same day as MacArthur's tour de force, Mao received a briefing from Zhou Enlai's military secretary, Lei Yingfu, who had been analyzing intelligence about what course of action the Americans might take. Lei predicted that MacArthur was likely preparing for an amphibious landing deep behind North Korean Army lines, and moreover, considering MacArthur's aggressive personality, he thought Inchon was the target. Its very unlikeliness would appeal to MacArthur, Lei suggested. Impressed by the analysis, Mao directed Zhou to inform Kim Il Sung.

Mao then questioned Lei further about MacArthur's personality. Lei said the American commander was "famous for his arrogance and stubbornness."

"Fine! Fine!" Mao replied. "The more arrogant and more stubborn he is the better."

On August 26, the 7th Division headquarters received the operational plans and learned for the first time of the amphibious landing at Inchon. MacArthur had assigned the 7th Division the code name Bayonet for the invasion, a name it would wear proudly. The rank and file were kept in the dark, but with the training taking on increased urgency, the troops "felt something big was going to happen," Gray recalled. They figured they would soon be sent to South Korea, but many assumed they would be shipped to Pusan to bolster the perimeter.

It wasn't clear they were ready. Lt. Jim Mortrude, a seasoned 28-year-old combat veteran from Seattle who had served as an infantry squad leader in North Africa and Europe during the war, arrived at Fuji in the final days of frantic preparations and was assigned to command a C Company platoon in Faith's 1st Battalion. Mortrude was dismayed at the men's discipline, training, and combat skills. During a night exercise, Mortrude inspected the platoon perimeter at 2:00 a.m. and found every man asleep. The lieutenant ordered all the soldiers out of their foxholes and had them conducting walking patrols in the middle of the night. He was interrupted by a voice demanding, "What the hell [is] going on?"

It was Faith. In the chaos, Mortrude hadn't even met him yet. "I rather testily explained that since my people had no respect for tactical security, I was starting their retraining in guard duty from scratch," Mortrude recalled.

Faith nodded approvingly. "Good," he said. "I sure hope it works."

Almond inspected the 7th Division on August 31 and was overall pleased with its progress, but after watching the performance of the 3rd Battalion, 31st Infantry, in a training exercise, he told Barr the "situation in this battalion was not particularly good."

Almond considered the 1st Marine Division the best troops he had. The division was 25,433 strong—all Marines except 110 Korean interpreters. Almond noted that a large percentage of its troops were drawn from active Marine reserve units, many of them with World War II combat experience. "The Army should have done the same but did not!" he recorded in his diary.

The Marines, for their part, made little effort to hide their contempt for the 7th Division. "Its quality was in no way comparable to that of the 1st Marine Division," Smith said. The Marines' respect for the 7th Division, Haig recalled, "was ostentatiously low."

Haig conceded that the 7th Division was "a ragtag outfit," noting that one-third its strength consisted of "South Koreans, many of whom, only a few weeks before, had been terrified, ill-clothed, half-nourished civilians." On the other hand, he added, many soldiers and officers in the 7th Division "were the very best that the Army had to offer."

After what the Army had done to it, it was a miracle that the 7th Division had come as far as it had. But with the date for Inchon looming, the time for preparing was running out. "This was a division that was faced with the bloody job of learning its trade and building esprit while fighting and dying," said Haig.

Lt. Col. Bill McCaffrey, the X Corps deputy chief of staff, was blunter in his assessment. "Basically I was shocked by the 7th Division," he later said. "It was a disaster going somewhere to happen."

Yokohama

In the first days of September, the 7th Division prepared to move 18,000 men the sixty miles from Fuji to the port of Yokohama. "Plans were made and changed, made and changed many, many times before we finally had one that would meet with the approval of all concerned above—and then those plans were changed several times," said Harvey Storms. In the midst of everything, Typhoon Jane, one of the worst storms to hit Japan in years, landed on the country's southeast coast on September 3, with 110-mile-per-hour winds. At Fuji, soldiers rushed to lower the tents to the ground and then took cover under them, but there was no protection from the "drenching fusillade" of rain coming in sideways. The storm "just about blew us away," recalled Gray.

Finally, the division moved out by train to Yokohama, and on September 6, the first troops began loading troop ships. Cranes lowered jeeps and trucks into the cargo holds. Long lines of infantrymen from the 3rd Battalion, 31st

Regiment, loaded with gear, moved slowly down the docks toward their ship, the USS *General George M. Randall*, most paired up with their ROK buddies. Inside their packs were two days of rations, a mess kit, underwear, a change of socks, and personal gear. An American missionary had positioned himself near the gangplank and offered pocket-sized Gideon copies of the New Testament. PFC Ed Reeves took one with a quiet thank-you and slipped it into his shirt pocket.

Aboard the *Randall*, there were twice as many troops on board as there were bunks, and other ships were similarly packed. Despite the crowded conditions—or perhaps because of them—many of the units managed to smuggle aboard their Japanese houseboys to help with kitchen work in Korea. They snuck on dressed as GIs and mixed in with the ROKs, and were kept off the ship manifests. Among them was Kenzo "Benny" Takatsu, who came aboard with Cpl. Robert Tait with Headquarters Battery, 57th Field Artillery.

After four days the ships were finally all loaded on Sunday, September 10. The division was set to sail early the next morning. Storms tried to call Helen from Yokohama but was denied permission; X Corps had barred all such communication out of fear that the plans for the invasion would slip out.

For any superstitious GIs, heaven and earth provided ominous signs. Shortly after 3:00 a.m. Sunday, a 6.6 magnitude earthquake centered just across Tokyo Bay from Yokohama jolted soldiers awake. The *Randall*, 622 feet long and twenty thousand tons fully laden, suddenly "gave a big shudder and was shoved away from the dock," Storms wrote Helen. The quake caused no serious damage to the invasion force; far more worrisome was the approach of a new storm, Typhoon Kezia, with 125 mph winds, even stronger than those of Jane. It was on a course forecast to put it over the Korea Strait over the next several days, directly into the path of the invasion force.

Given the narrow window for landing at Inchon, there was little choice but to set sail as planned on September 11. Two tugs pushed the *Randall* away from the dock and turned her around, and the transport joined an invasion flotilla of some 260 ships, including those carrying the 1st Marine Division, which had set off from the port of Kobe.

As they sailed along the coast of Japan on September 12, the seas were getting quite rough from Kezia's approach. Reaching the southern tip of Kyushu early the next day, the troops found the conditions had grown even worse. The ships pitched about in forty-foot seas, their propeller screws coming out of the water. "My God, you'd think they were going to tip over, the sea was rolling so bad," recalled Beauchamp, the 32nd Regiment commander. Ammunition crates and vehicles on the decks broke loose, and soldiers scrambled to lash them back down. Two of the five jeeps that made up Almond's mobile command post were blown overboard.

Half the GIs figured they were about to die, and the other half were so seasick they hoped they would. Buckets for vomit were distributed throughout the troop compartments, but virtually every man detailed to empty them ended up sick himself. "A troop compartment with several hundred seasick soldiers jammed together and unable to go on deck is several degrees worse than Dante's description of the innermost rings of Hell," said Lt. James Dill, a 31st Regiment artillery officer. "I was ready to storm the beach single handed just to get on solid land."

Adm. Doyle, aboard the flagship *Mount McKinley* carrying MacArthur, Almond, and Smith, considered it one of the worst storms he'd ever experienced at sea. Fortunately for MacArthur and the invasion force, Kezia veered northeast on September 13, sparing the armada the worst of its winds and a potential catastrophe before they reached Inchon.

The 7th Division battalion commanders had been briefed on Inchon prior to departure, and some of their key officers were read into the plan after the ships set sail. But most of the junior officers and enlisted men remained oblivious as to their destination. Lt. Gray and his men were still convinced they were on their way to Pusan. But once they reached the Yellow Sea and continued sailing north up the coast of South Korea, escorted now by Navy cruisers and destroyers, it became clear they were headed elsewhere. Commanders brought their units together and briefed the men that they would soon be landing at Inchon. "Not that anyone cared much," recalled Monty Piercefield, the operations sergeant for Faith's battalion. Still suffering from seasickness, the soldiers had lost much of their curiosity about their destination.

Inchon, September 15

The North Koreans had belatedly recognized that Inchon was the probable target of the invasion force based on the heavy air and sea bombardment of defenses guarding the port in recent days, but it was too late to build up much defense. Kim had refused to heed the Chinese warnings in August that the Americans were preparing for an amphibious landing and that Inchon was the most likely spot.

At 6:30 a.m. on September 15, the 5th Marine Regiment began landing on Wolmi-do, the island protecting the mouth of the harbor, meeting minimal resistance and securing the entire island by noon. A second assault with the afternoon tide onto the mainland met mostly similar success, and by the end of the day, 13,000 Marines were ashore with light casualties. MacArthur had already sent a message to Vice Adm. Arthur Struble, commander of the U.S. 7th Fleet: "The Navy and the Marines have never shone more brightly than this morning."

Almond was anxious to get the 7th Division into the fight, and he insisted that Doyle pause the unloading of supplies for the Marines to instead get the Army troops ashore. The 32nd Regiment was first, landing unopposed on the morning of September 18 with the mission of securing the Marines' right flank, freeing them to cross the Han River for the attack on Seoul. The regiment moved eight miles inland, digging in that evening in hills south of Inchon. Shots were heard around eleven that night, and it soon grew into a fusillade of fire all around the area, almost as if the 2nd Battalion were being overrun. It turned out some green troops, jumpy on their first night at war, had been firing at each other.

The 32nd took over the Marine positions during the day on September 19. Col. Lewis "Chesty" Puller, the legendarily hard-nosed officer who commanded the 1st Marine Regiment, was infuriated that the 32nd Regiment was late, but the real problem was the lack of good coordination between the Army and Marine division headquarters. It would not be the last episode.

Moving forward on September 20, the 32nd was driving east in a flanking movement toward the Seoul-Suwon highway, the key artery needed to link up with the 8th Army, fighting to break out from the Pusan Perimeter. Faith's 1st Battalion was in a heavy firefight, and movement through the mine-strewn farming land was painfully slow. When A Company on the left flank bogged down on a hill, Faith grew impatient with its progress and personally led an attack capturing the high ground. "I found out then what kind of battalion commander I had," recalled Major Ed Stamford, a Marine forward air controller assigned to Faith's battalion. "Luckily, we didn't run into any opposition. . . . Otherwise we would have probably lost the command group right there."

Capt. Bob Jones, commanding C Company on the right flank, was moving on foot to capture an enemy-held hill that commanded the approach to Suwon. Jones was short in stature—his nickname was Scochie, a phonetic pronunciation of the Japanese word for small. But he was one of the most universally respected officers in the battalion—"a top-notch combat trooper," said Crosby Miller. Raised by an Army doctor in Arizona after being orphaned at age 10, Jones had served with the 502nd Parachute Infantry Regiment through much of World War II, jumping into Operation Market Garden as a company commander. Having seen hard combat before, he had not been eager to leave his wife and 12-year-old daughter in Japan.

Jones had led his first and second platoons almost to the hill's summit and was turning around to deploy his third platoon when he felt like he'd been kicked in the chest by a mule. He dropped to his knees, hit by long-range machine gun fire. "I thought I was mortally wounded and waited for the pain to subside a little and waited to succumb entirely," he recalled. Miller, standing nearby, helped Jones rip open his fatigue jacket. A .30 caliber machine gun bullet had pierced his flesh but was sticking out of his chest. It had hit a steel button on the jacket's left breast pocket and burrowed through a fifty-page notebook as well as a twenty-page company roster before stopping on a rib. Miller plucked the bullet out and handed it to Jones. "Must have been meant for some other Bob Jones," Miller remarked. Jones rejoined his company, and they captured the hill.

By the end of the day, the 32nd Regiment had taken Copper Mine Hill, the last high ground before the highway, suffering 7 dead and 36 wounded, as well as three tanks destroyed by landmines. Beauchamp escaped death when his jeep struck a mine that killed his driver and wounded his radioman, Sgt. Arthur Mercier. Nonetheless, Smith complained that day to Almond that the 32nd Regiment was being timid in its advance, trying to outflank the North Koreans rather than root them out.

The 31st Regiment Polar Bears had landed on September 19, one day after the 32nd Regiment, and moved southeast, securing the Suwon Airfield on September 22. Its mission was to link up with units from Walker's 8th Army once they broke out from the Pusan Perimeter.

The 3rd Battalion had suffered few casualties, and as each day passed, the men were growing confident and cheerful, Storms wrote Helen. "We Americans are still prone to underestimate the other side and I am trying not to do that, but it is hard."

Two big fights lay ahead: the battle for Seoul and the battle between Smith and Almond. MacArthur wanted Seoul captured by September 25, the three-month anniversary of the North Korean invasion. Considering himself omniscient on matters involving the Far East, MacArthur believed the "oriental mind" put great stock in such calendar events. More concretely, reinstalling Rhee's government so quickly could be strategically decisive, keeping the Chinese out of the war.

But resistance stiffened as the Marines approached Seoul, where the North Korean defenders had been reinforced by a division and numbered 20,000. Almond pressed Smith for more progress, but the 5th Marine Regiment, attacking from the west, had been bogged down for days in a brutal fight. On the evening of September 23, Almond suggested that Smith maneuver his 1st Regiment to attack Seoul from the southeast, creating a pincer movement that could dislodge the North Korean army from the capital. Smith declined, unwilling to split his forces; he wanted the 1st Regiment to join the 5th Regiment in attacking from the west.

Almond was infuriated, believing Smith's course was plodding and unimaginative, taking needlessly high casualties for little territory gained. If Smith had been an Army general, Almond might have relieved him, but firing a Marine commander would undoubtedly create a firestorm at the Pentagon. Instead, he gave Smith an ultimatum: Either make significant progress within twenty-four hours, or Almond would bring in the 7th Division's 32nd Regiment to attack Seoul from the southeast. "General Smith liked this not at all, which concerned me very little inasmuch as I was trying to serve General MacArthur's preference of capturing Seoul as soon as possible," Almond later said.

The next day, the Marines had not advanced far. Almond summoned Smith to a commanders' meeting that afternoon and icily informed him that the 32nd Regiment would make an assault across the Han River at 6:00 a.m. the next morning to attack Seoul from the southeast. Moreover, Almond directed that Smith provide the Marines' amphibious tractors, or AMTRACs, to carry the Army soldiers across the nearly two hundred-yard-wide river.

"Those AMTRACs are Marine property," Smith protested.

"They are the property of the United States government and I propose to use them," Almond replied.

Almond had a second goal—he wanted to make sure the Army shared the glory for capturing Seoul. "Dave Barr is doing a fine job with the 7th and tomorrow he gets his chance at a big operation (just as the Marines did several days ago)," he wrote his wife, Margaret, that night. "It will even things up a bit."

As usual, Almond was brimming with confidence. "I hope to send [MacArthur] a telegram tomorrow night 'Seoul is ours, just three months after Korea was invaded,'" he told Margaret. "We are doing wonderfully and it is such a pleasure to command where you are never in doubt."

Han River, Dawn, September 25

A heavy ground fog shrouded the 32nd Regiment as it assembled along the Han at the village of Sinsa, across from Seoul's southeast quarter. The regiment's mission was to capture several high points across the Han, including the highest point in Seoul, South Mountain, which rose from the river and ran into the city. Before first light, Almond arrived at an observation post overlooking the crossing point, dragging along Adm. Struble to show off the event.

The 2nd Battalion loaded into the Marine AMTRACs, crossed the river unscathed at 6:30 a.m., and began moving up South Mountain against light resistance. It was soon followed by Faith's 1st Battalion, which, after landing, headed east along the river toward its objective, Hill 120. Jim Mortrude's C Company platoon was in the lead, but the lieutenant was having trouble finding the company objective on the Japanese hachured map. Faith simplified it for him. "Pick the highest ground you can find and grab it," he told Mortrude.

Almond soon decided he wanted a closer look and rode an AMTRAC across the Han, landing right on the heels of Faith's battalion. He quickly collared Faith, apparently unhappy with his progress. It was not normal for a corps commander to issue direct orders to a battalion commander, but Almond was not a normal corps commander—he would regularly "interfere outrageously in minor tactical matters," recalled McCaffrey, the X Corps deputy chief of staff.

After speaking with Faith, Almond marched up the high ground just secured by the 1st Battalion, quizzing soldiers who were busy taking positions on the hill. Almond then continued to the regiment's forward command post, where he interrogated Lt. Col. Charles Mount, the 2nd Battalion commander. The X Corps commander hit the roof when he learned that both battalions had stopped pending coordination with the other, a delay he blamed on poor communication between Faith and Mount. Almond gave Mount "quite a dressing down for his inactivity," Smith said.

With Almond's prodding—or perhaps in spite of it—the 32nd Regiment had secured South Mountain and the surrounding high ground by midafternoon. That evening, some North Koreans began withdrawing from the city, while others stayed to fight delaying actions. Almond took great satisfaction from his maneuvering, believing it to be key to the capture of Seoul. Smith was derisive of the Army performance, insisting in his journal that the Army's contribution was "negligible."

As he had been determined to do, Almond declared victory that evening, September 25, announcing to reporters just before midnight that the capital had been liberated on the three-month anniversary of the invasion. That much of the city remained under North Korean control and heavy fighting would continue for several days apparently mattered not to him.

The next morning, the 32nd Regiment worked to clear the area around South Mountain and the hills to the east of remaining North Korean forces. In the 1st Battalion zone, Jones's Charlie Company moved down from the hills and into the town on city streets, initially encountering no resistance. Mortrude's platoon, again at the point, was approaching the city racetrack when it suddenly came under devastatingly accurate fire. Six GIs were killed and many more wounded. With his platoon pinned down, Mortrude raced through heavy enemy fire to reach three nearby Army tanks and directed their machine guns toward enemy positions. After getting his platoon to cover, Mortrude ran back to the ambush site twice under a deluge of fire to pull wounded men back to safety, brave actions for which he would be awarded the Distinguished Service Cross.

Lt. Col. McCaffrey observed the 1st Battalion in action that afternoon and thought Faith had done a poor job. As an officer who had led men through combat in World War II, McCaffrey resented Faith's rise to command. "I thought he was spoiled," McCaffrey later said. "He was an army brat. He'd been a sort of a front runner, now he was commanding an infantry battalion and I had the feeling he should get his face dirty like the rest of us had."

McCaffrey reported to Almond that Faith had failed to properly communicate and coordinate supporting fire for his rifle companies. Almond spoke to Barr about it that evening and was "greatly concerned" about it, according to Barr. But the division commander retained his confidence in Faith.

Among the C Company soldiers wounded in the fight for Seoul was 15-year-old Huey French, The Kid. When his mother back in Texas received a letter from him mentioning his wound, she was so upset that she contacted the Red

Cross and disclosed his real age. She was assured Huey would be pulled out of Korea and likely be home by Christmas.

Donald Hamilton, the C Company medic from Indiana, was kept busy patching up the wounded. "There is really some bloody messes around here," he wrote to his parents at his home in rural Greene County, Indiana. Right before the war had started, Hamilton had told them he was looking forward to getting out of the Army and getting back to Indiana, maybe using his training as a medic to find a job as a safety worker with a construction company. Even helping out on the family farm was sounding good. "I don't like to put up hay, but I believe I like it better than dodging lead," he wrote.

Those plans were on hold. "I am about half afraid to make plans for the future because everyone who had it planned what he was going to do when he got out either got killed or bad hit," Hamilton wrote home after the battle for Seoul. "I had a good friend who never talked about anything but his future and now he is rolled up in a blanket in the army graveyard on a hill just outside of Inchon. He never had a good time like other boys because he saved his money, and what good did it do him? He was cut almost in half by a 30 cal. machine gun."

As MacArthur predicted, Inchon had proven decisive. With their rear threatened, North Korean defenses started to crumble in the face of the 8th Army's counteroffensive, and by September 23, they were in full retreat. The 8th Army followed them north in hot pursuit.

"The war is going very well," Storms wrote Helen on September 25. "If other forces aren't thrown in from the north and China then this 'police action' will be finished!"

On the night of September 27, the Polar Bears were positioned several miles north of Osan, in a blocking position to protect Seoul from retreating North Korean units. They were already in a fight with several North Korean tanks when they opened fire on more tanks advancing from the south. But those were U.S. tanks—an armored task force from the 1st Cavalry Division, arriving sooner than expected.

The confusion was quickly sorted out. "A roar of cheers went up to celebrate the historic link-up of X Corps and 8th Army forces," Lieutenant Gray recalled. The war, it seemed, "was virtually over."

Chapter 3

AN UNKIND AND INEXORABLE FATE

Seoul, September 29, 1950

Ned Almond had big plans for an elaborate ceremony restoring South Korea's government in Seoul, including military honor guards and a triumphant parade into the city with the 1st Marine Division band. ("We had left our band instruments in Kobe," O. P. Smith dryly noted in his log.) When Almond proposed that X Corps battalion commanders report to his headquarters to plan the ceremony despite continued fighting in the city, Smith protested that there was still a war going on. Almond sent Tokyo his suggested program, but it was too much even for MacArthur, who told the X Corps commander that he would take care of the ceremony.

Landing at Kimpo Airfield at 10:00 a.m. on September 29, MacArthur strode past Walker, the 8th Army commander, to greet Almond, who was wearing a starched field jacket open at the neck to show a snappy black silken ascot. "Ned, my boy," MacArthur said affectionately. A motorcade drove the official party into war-ravaged Seoul to the bomb-damaged National Assembly Hall, even as Beauchamp's 32nd Infantry and the Marines were fighting in the northern suburbs. As MacArthur spoke, the concussion from distant artillery shelling shook loose shards of glass from the skylights, which showered onto the floor. "Like most people around me, I hastily put on my helmet," recalled Haig. MacArthur paid no mind to the ruckus, declaring Seoul liberated and then leading the audience in the Lord's Prayer.

Inchon had succeeded precisely as MacArthur had predicted, leaving those who had doubted him without a leg to stand upon. It had reinforced his own sense of infallibility. Wariness in Washington about expanding the war largely evaporated. Truman, with new confidence in MacArthur and with the backing of Secretary of State Acheson and other advisers, favored expanding the war to destroy the North Korean Army, depose Kim Il Sung, and unify Korea. On September 27, the Joint Chiefs gave MacArthur the green light to cross the 38th parallel into North Korea. The one caveat was that the chiefs wanted only South Korean troops to be used in the areas closest to the Chinese border; there was no sense in provoking China by having American GIs on the Yalu River. "We want you to feel unhampered tactically and strategically to proceed north of 38th parallel," Secretary of Defense George Marshall wrote MacArthur.

On September 28, MacArthur sent the Joint Chiefs his plan for invading North Korea. With his love of the bold stroke, MacArthur wanted to make another amphibious landing—this time, on the opposite coast of the Korean peninsula. While Walker's 8th Army moved north overland from Seoul toward Pyongyang, Almond's X Corps would board ships and land at Wonsan, a port on North Korea's east coast about one hundred miles above the 38th parallel. From there, X Corps would strike back west, creating a second avenue of attack toward the North Korean capital.

While convoluted, there was some rationale for the plan. Although on opposite coasts, Wonsan and Pyongyang were situated roughly parallel at the relatively narrow waist of the Korean peninsula, about 125 miles apart. The cities were connected by a road and rail line, offering the best path through the rugged Taebaek Range, which ran north to south and divided the peninsula. An X Corps attack from the east offered a backdoor to Pyongyang around prepared defenses that might confront the 8th Army attack from the south.

But MacArthur's grand plan carried with it enormous problems and logistical complications. Instead of rushing east from Seoul to exploit Inchon and cut off the rapidly retreating and demoralized North Korean forces, X Corps would be loaded onto ships, raising the risk that the North Korean forces would escape. Smith's 1st Marine Division would load back onto the ships at Inchon and sail around Korea to Wonsan. But because Inchon would be so congested, the 7th Division would have to move by road and rail to Pusan on the southeast coast, boarding ships there for the landing at Wonsan. Instead of supplies coming into Inchon, men and supplies would be sent out.

Moreover, X Corps would be kept as a separate command under Almond rather than folded into the 8th Army, as almost everyone, including Walker, had expected. The 8th Army's lack of control over X Corps had already led to several missed opportunities for cutting off escaping North Korean forces. Walker tried in vain to persuade MacArthur to include X Corps in his command for the drive north—or failing that, at least to have X Corps move overland to Wonsan rather than tying up port facilities. But MacArthur refused. Keeping Almond and X Corps separate maintained MacArthur's independence from Washington. Almond, having tasted corps command, was eager to keep it.

Barr and his staff wanted to pursue the retreating North Koreans, believing it made no sense to send the 7th Division in the opposite direction. But Almond brushed off all doubters who had the temerity to question MacArthur's second amphibious landing. "That's what you said about Inchon," he told them.

Even MacArthur's nominal superiors, the Joint Chiefs of Staff, were cowed. "The success of Inchon was so great, and the subsequent prestige of General MacArthur was so overpowering, that the Chiefs hesitated thereafter to question later plans and decisions of the general, which should have been challenged," Collins, the Army chief of staff, acknowledged in his memoir.

MacArthur was left unchecked. "From then on," said Collins, "he seemed to march like a Greek hero of old to an unkind and inexorable fate."

Beijing, Early October 1950

Shortly after midnight October 3, K. M. Panikkar, the Indian ambassador to China, was roused from bed and asked to come immediately to Zhou Enlai's official residence. Panikkar served as something of an intermediary between the United States and China, and the Chinese premier had a simple message he wanted passed on to Washington: If the Americans crossed the 38th parallel, China would be forced to intervene. The warning reached Washington but was largely dismissed. Despite concern that intervention was possible, some considered the message a Chinese bluff and Panikkar too much of a leftist to be fully trusted.

Mao had convened the politburo's standing committee on October 2 to consider entering the war. South Korean forces had crossed the border the day before, further convincing Mao that China must intervene. But most members had deep reservations, believing the country was too exhausted economically and militarily to take on the United States. Seeking more support, Mao called for a meeting of the full politburo and sent an airplane to pick up Peng Dehuai, the commander of the Northwest Military Region. Peng, Mao's longtime ally from the days of the Long March, was a rugged fighter, a peasant soldier with a bulldog face who had become one of the People's Liberation Army's (PLA's) most experienced generals. While loyal to Mao, he was one of the few leaders willing to challenge him. In turn, Mao trusted and respected Peng.

As the meeting continued on October 5, Peng spoke in favor of intervention, arguing that if American troops reached the Yalu River, they would be positioned to invade China. It would be better to fight the Americans in Korea than in China. Peng's words swayed the balance, and the politburo agreed that day to send troops to Korea. China would intervene.

That same day, the 7th Division began moving south to Pusan as ordered, taking a circuitous, 280-mile route down dusty roads away from the direction of battle. The Polar Bears led the way, hitting the road before 4:00 a.m., followed a few hours later by the 32nd Regiment.

The 7th Division was given priority over the 8th Army forces pursuing North Korean troops, including the 2nd Infantry Division, newly arrived from Fort Lewis, Washington. The 7th Division was moving south at the same time the 2nd Division was racing north on the same narrow and decrepit roads, creating numerous logjams. MacArthur, Almond, and the rest of the high command ignored the simple solution of reassigning the 2nd Division to X Corps and the 7th Division to Walker's command, which would have negated the need for two divisions to race across the country to swap positions.

Accidents were the inevitable result. A truck carrying troops from the 31st Regiment's K Company rolled and landed upside down, with all the men under it. One soldier was killed and at least a dozen injured, many with broken legs. "We know not why we were sent to Pusan—nor why there was such a rush doing it," Storms wrote to Helen after arriving on October 7. "Just in the 3rd Bn, 2 trucks were wrecked with two men killed and 25 injured—needless—a screwy war!"

The chaotic rush was for naught. The Navy discovered that Wonsan Harbor had been sown with several thousand mines, a vast number that overwhelmed its minesweeping capabilities. The target date to begin landing at Wonsan—October 20—looked increasingly doubtful. Shipping out the Marines from Inchon tied up that port for ten days, reducing the flow of supplies for the 8th Army to a trickle and slowing its advance. The worst fears were realized as substantial numbers of North Korean troops were able to slip north. "Our move to Pusan against the flow of the Eighth Army was absolutely asinine and allowing the N Korean Army to escape was inexcusable," said Paddock, the 7th Division operations officer.

As they sat in Pusan, the men of the 7th Division grew restless. "We still don't know where or whether we will be used further in this conflict," Storms wrote Helen on October 11. "I imagine we will be."

Adding to the uncertainty, Almond abruptly relieved Ovenshine as commander of the 31st Regiment on October 5, just as the movement south began. He was replaced by Col. Allan Maclean, who had commanded the 32nd Regiment prior to the war and was recommended by Barr. Almond had been dissatisfied with Ovenshine's handling of the regiment around Suwon, even though the regiment had won a "stirring victory" in the view of Korean War historian Clay Blair. The problem may have been more fundamental. "I suspect that General Almond considered me too old . . . and not sufficiently aggressive," Ovenshine later said. "I considered General Almond to be impulsive."

Beijing

Mao notified Kim Il Sung on October 7 that the politburo had approved China's intervention in Korea. As window dressing, the troops sent into Korea would be called volunteers and their uniforms stripped of Chinese insignia, a charade that Mao hoped would allow China to claim it had not entered the war. The following day, Mao named Peng Dehuai as commander of the newly created Chinese People's Volunteer Force (CPVF), which involved little more than a change of name for existing PLA units.

On October 9, the 9th Army Group, under the command of General Song Shilun, was ordered to prepare for movement to Manchuria along the Yalu River border with North Korea. Song, an expert at guerilla warfare who had commanded a regiment at age 24 during the Long March, was regarded as a clever, if quick-tempered, tactician. The 9th Army Group, which had captured Shanghai during the Chinese Civil War and was considered one of the PLA's elite forces, had been in training for the now-postponed invasion of Taiwan. The army group, still positioned on the southeast coast around Shanghai, had been strengthened considerably for the Taiwan operation—each corps had four divisions instead of three, each division had four regiments instead of three, and each regiment had four battalions instead of three—and numbered close to 150,000 soldiers. Now this powerful force would be going to Korea.

On October 14, Mao telegrammed orders for Song's 9th Army Group to leave Shanghai and the surrounding area within two weeks and then await his order to move to Manchuria.

Wake Island, October 15, 1950

Douglas MacArthur did not salute when President Harry Truman came down the ramp of the presidential aircraft *Independence* at Wake Island, a tiny coral atoll in the Western Pacific. Truman later noted tartly in his memoir that MacArthur's "shirt was unbuttoned, and he was wearing a cap that had evidently seen a good deal of use." Nonetheless, they greeted each other cordially and were each surprised at their instant rapport. "I liked him from the start," MacArthur later said. Truman described their conversation as very friendly—"much more so than [he] had expected."

Truman had asked several weeks earlier to have a face-to-face meeting with the general to discuss the war. With midterm elections looming in November, some suspected politics were at play and believed Truman wanted to borrow some of MacArthur's luster. MacArthur had grumbled about making the trip, though compared to Truman's long flight from Washington, the general's journey from Tokyo had been far shorter, an accommodation made so as to not remove him for too long from his headquarters.

Meeting in a communications building at the airfield, Truman and MacArthur sat with senior officials along for the trip, including Joint Chiefs of Staff Chairman Bradley; Adm. Arthur Radford, commander of the Pacific Fleet; and White House Special Advisor Averell Harriman.

MacArthur briefly reviewed the military situation in Korea. There was little enemy resistance remaining in South Korea, and he expected formal resistance in the north to end by Thanksgiving. "It is my hope to be able to withdraw the Eighth Army to Japan by Christmas," MacArthur said.

When Truman asked about the possibility of Chinese intervention, MacArthur replied that there was "very little" chance. "Had they interfered in the first or second months it would have been decisive," he said. "We are no longer fearful of their intervention."

MacArthur was not alone in this opinion. A CIA assessment issued October 12 reported "no convincing indications of an actual Chinese Communist intention to resort to full-scale intervention in Korea." Moreover, neither Truman nor any of his advisers disagreed with MacArthur. There were no follow-up questions about Chinese intervention or even a further discussion of the topic.

There was a bit more disjointed and perfunctory talk, mostly about postwar arrangements. The meeting wrapped up after ninety minutes, and a communique was prepared in which Truman declared there had been a "very complete unanimity of view."

Lunch had been planned but was scrapped when MacArthur asked to skip it, pleading that he needed to get back to Tokyo. Following cordial goodbyes, Truman and his entourage took off five hours after landing on Wake to return to the United States, while MacArthur returned shortly afterward to Japan. There had been no substantive review of the dangers of the UN movement to the Yalu River. In the view of MacArthur biographer Clayton James, Wake Island had been a missed opportunity "to change a tragic course in history."

Pusan, October 16

The soldiers of the 7th Division began boarding ships on October 15 but remained in the dark about their destination. "We never hear much news over here," Donald Hamilton wrote to his parents. "I guess they just don't want us to get our hopes built up. I still believe I will be back to Japan or the states before Christmas." Rumors were flying about their destination. Some were sure they were heading back to Japan. Harry Graham and his comrades from B Company, 32nd Infantry, boarded their ship thinking they were heading to Germany to bolster defenses against a feared Soviet invasion. "Hell, we were ready to go home at that point," recalled Grant McMillin, with the 57th Field Artillery.

Actually, they were going nowhere, at least for the time being. Much to Almond's frustration, the demining of Wonsan Harbor was painstakingly slow. The 7th Division would have to sit on ships indefinitely in Pusan Harbor.

Barr, the 7th Division commander, was fuming. "This delay was frustrating to the extreme—especially so since I had been hurried so in getting loaded when there was so much that should have been done in way of vehicular maintenance and equipping of troops," he said. All his vehicles were left with summer-weight oil in their crankcases, even though they were moving north into rapidly approaching freezing weather.

As they waited, the men of the 31st Regiment were introduced to their new commanding officer, Colonel Allan Maclean, who blew into Pusan like a typhoon. "Mac" Maclean was a big, burly, ruddy-faced Scotsman, looking every inch an infantryman. He was a member of the West Point class of 1930, playing tackle on some of the great Army football teams of the era. Maclean had also boxed as a heavyweight at the academy, retaining a pugnacious nature and whirlwind energy. "Just be careful when he decides to move, because if you were in the way, you got pushed out of the way," recalled Beauchamp, a classmate at West Point. "Friendship was seldom a passing thing with him, because the intense nature of his personality forbade such," he added.

Maclean made a quick impression on the Polar Bears. He was big on training and made use of the downtime aboard the ships, putting the men through vigorous physical exercises and having them climb ropes and ladders, trying to harden them for the coming winter. He roamed ship corridors, booming out greetings, but stopped dead in his tracks when he found something he didn't like. The colonel "completely blew his cork when he saw some food on the windshield of a jeep that was on the deck," recalled Cpl. Jerry Francois, a communications specialist. "I thought for a while he was going to shoot him a 2nd lieutenant. He had the fear of God in all of us. You can classify him as a Patton of the infantry."

Maclean had a history with the 31st Regiment, having served with the Polar Bears in the Philippines in the mid-1930s. He had been a staff officer in World War II, coordinating battlefield assignments for units arriving in Europe after the Normandy invasion. Maclean was no stranger to the 7th Division, having commanded the 32nd Regiment for a year before turning command over to Beauchamp in spring 1950. He was on the 8th Army operations staff when the war broke out and served as Walker's roving representative on battlefields across Korea.

Most of Maclean's staff liked and respected him, seeing the officer as a more competent, aggressive, and mission-oriented commander than Ovenshine. Even McCaffrey, not one to toss around compliments lightly, admired Maclean. "I was tremendously impressed with him," McCaffrey later said. "He was confident, aggressive and I thought sensible."

But like so many other Army regimental commanders in Korea, Maclean had never commanded a unit in combat.

Pyongyang, October 20

On October 19, South Korean troops entered Pyongyang, followed a day later by the U.S. 1st Cavalry Division. Johnnie Walker and his 8th Army had shown up Almond, capturing the North Korean capital while X Corps troops were still sitting on boats. For a commander who had been consistently shortchanged by Almond and MacArthur, it was sweet vindication. MacArthur flew into Pyongyang on October 20 for a quick celebratory visit. "The war is very definitely coming to an end," he later told reporters.

But it was a bit awkward. The main reason for landing X Corps in northeast Korea—to provide a second avenue of attack on the capital—was now entirely moot. So was the secondary goal of securing Wonsan as a port, as the ROK I Corps, racing up the northeast coast, had captured the city days earlier. But scrapping X Corp's landing altogether would have meant admitting MacArthur's plan was ill-conceived from the start. MacArthur would have to come up with a new plan, and he already had one in mind.

On October 24, MacArthur issued new orders to Almond: Instead of attacking west after landing, X Corps would attack north to the Yalu River. MacArthur also told his field commanders that he was lifting Pentagon restrictions that barred U.S. forces from entering a buffer zone along the Chinese border and allowed only South Korean troops to go all the way to the Yalu. His commanders were now authorized to "use any and all ground forces" to secure all of North Korea. Though this contradicted the instructions the Joint Chiefs had given him, MacArthur did not bother consulting Washington. When the Joint Chiefs learned of MacArthur's order, they quickly cabled their objections. MacArthur replied sharply that his action was a "matter of military necessity," claiming South Korean forces could not take all of North Korea on their own. Though MacArthur had clearly overstepped his authority, the Joint Chiefs rolled over once again, unwilling to challenge him.

The stage was set for U.S. forces to advance to the Yalu River, a decision journalist and historian David Halberstam considered the greatest American military miscalculation of the twentieth century.

Wonsan, October 24

Ned Almond was beside himself. Not only had X Corps missed the capture of Pyongyang, it remained trapped aboard ships for another week, unable to launch its new mission to the Yalu. Almond clashed with the Navy admirals, pressing them to speed up the demining operation. But they insisted on completing the work safely. Two minesweepers had already been sunk by mines, with 92 casualties.

For six days, in what was dubbed Operation Yo-Yo, ships crowded with Marines sailed up and down off the coast of Wonsan, waiting for the green light to land. The 7th Division was still aboard ships in Pusan Harbor, waiting for the Marines to land. On October 24, Almond decided he would go ashore by helicopter to establish X Corps headquarters in Wonsan. Haig was sent ahead in a small Navy boat carrying Almond's gear. A stiff, cold wind from Siberia was blowing, and the boat bobbed up and down in big swells before capsizing just offshore. Haig, pitched into water over his head, struggled unsuccessfully to keep the general's bedroll above the surface, but he made it ashore. Hours later, suffering from a fever and cough, Haig was called to see Almond in the new X Corps Command Post (CP). "Damn it, Haig," the general exploded, "you got my bedroll wet! Can't you do anything right?"

Almond was on the cover of *Time* magazine that week. The accompanying profile, headlined "Sic 'Em, Ned," was a largely sympathetic profile of the "whip-cracking" general. "To some he seems an insufferable martinet," *Time* said. "Those who know him best say his professional manner, at times as tough as armor plate, is only the protective covering for a courtly, convivial, even sentimental off-duty personality." That was news to many on the X Corps staff. For his part, Almond complained the article was "a little severe" but was pleased with the attention. At least it evened the score with O. P. Smith, who had appeared on *Time's* cover after Inchon a month earlier.

The main body of the 1st Marine Division began landing on October 26 at Wonsan. Entertainer Bob Hope, traveling with a United Service Organizations (USO) troupe, was already performing ashore when the Marines arrived. "They were kind of humiliated about that," recalled McCaffrey.

Both the 1st Marine Division and the 7th Division had now been out of combat for three weeks, and the latter remained stuck in Pusan. X Corps' new mission was to advance to the Manchurian border as fast as possible, with the 1st Marine Division on the west flank, the 7th Division in the center, and the ROK I Corps on the east.

Almond had decided it would be useless to land the 7th Division at Wonsan since it would then need to immediately move north through territory already captured by South Korean forces. Searching for a new landing spot further north, Almond had scoured the mountainous coast in *Blue Goose*, a small artillery spotter plane that frequently carried him around Korea. About one hundred miles northeast of Wonsan, Almond had his pilot circle low and found what he was looking for—Iwon, a pocket of level ground with beaches and unmined waters, not far from a road corridor leading to the Yalu River. The Navy was not happy about upending the landing plans at this late hour, but Almond was insistent. The 7th Division would land at Iwon.

Aboard the USNS *Antalok*, Pusan

Halloween was approaching, and the Polar Bears were still sitting aboard ships. There had been a brief flurry of excitement on October 23, when the ships received orders to pull out. "All ships in convoy had anchors pulled up and were just ready to get up steam—then anchors were dropped and here we sit," Harvey Storms wrote Helen.

Storms, aboard the USNS *Sgt. Sylvester Antalok* transport ship with the rest of the 3rd Battalion, played endless chess matches against other officers. He went regularly to church services, though he complained to Helen about the 3rd Battalion chaplain, Captain James Conner, "a cussing, hard-drinking Episcopalian. I just can't understand how he drinks more whiskey straight and seems to relish it than any person I have ever seen. Don't pass that on." The chaplains organized variety shows every night on the ships, featuring corny comedy sketches and music from soldiers who had managed to bring instruments on board. One evening the men on *Antolak* watched *Scott of the Antarctic*, a British film about Robert Falcon Scott's doomed 1912 expedition to reach the South Pole. "No excitement, just wind and snow, and, I guess, some good acting, only we couldn't understand their language," Storms wrote.

Admittedly, life on ship was cushy, at least compared to the usual infantryman's lot. "Darling, our food on ship is wonderful," he told Helen. "Always have at least two choices of main dish, ice cream two or three times a week—wonderful cooks. This navy is the life." By October 29, though, the *Antolak* was "getting low on water and supplies—so they are going to have to move us somewhere, soon," he wrote.

"This outfit I am in has been just like one of those 'good' Texas Tornadoes—blowing and twisting and ready to tear anything up that gets in its way out on the wide open, barren plains, and finding nothing to tear up or down, blows itself out," Storms wrote to family friends in Texas. "We've been the luckiest of any outfit in the battle zone—have had little enemy fire at all. Not that I am griping, understand. Honestly, though, I've never been too worried about getting back to Helen and those boys."

Chapter 4

INTO NORTH KOREA

Iwon, North Korea, October 29

The 7th Division began landing in North Korea shortly before noon on October 29, meeting no opposition. Landing craft carrying the 17th Infantry Regiment disgorged thousands of GIs and hundreds of vehicles onto the sandy beach. The operation continued into the night, with the beach lit up by the headlights of jeeps and trucks. Sherman tanks towed trucks filled with cargo and equipment across the soft sand to the nearby coastal highway.

Gen. Dave Barr was on the beach to greet the troops, having come ashore by small boat from the USS *Eldorado*, the flagship for the amphibious task force carrying the division. Even as unloading continued, the 17th Regiment began moving north up the highway, toward the Yalu River only 120 miles away—but over forbidding mountainous terrain. The 31st and 32nd Regiments would be landing in the following days.

"We are going to the Manchurian border, destroying any enemy we find in our path," Barr told correspondents. The words, though certainly appropriate for an amphibious landing, sounded a bit bellicose coming from Barr, a gentle, rumpled, and portly soul who would have been more at home teaching on a college campus than leading a division into combat. Bill McCaffrey, the X Corps deputy chief of staff, viewed him as "a nice old guy" who had no business commanding in war. Within some circles of the 7th Division, there was "a general lack of confidence in his ability, openly discussed by both troops and officers," Lt. Jim Mortrude recalled.

Barr, from Nanafalia, Alabama, was an armor officer who had served as chief of staff for the Sixth Army Group in France during World War II. But he had not led men in combat since World War I, when he was awarded the Silver Star with the 18th Infantry in France. In the late 1940s, as chief of the 1,000-man Army mission advising Chiang Kai Shek, Barr had seen firsthand the corruption and ineptness of his Nationalist army. In secret testimony to a congressional committee six months before Mao took power, he correctly warned that the Chiang's government was doomed. Barr then became chief of staff for the 8th Army in Tokyo but disliked working for Johnnie Walker and asked to be reassigned. Based on Barr's seniority, MacArthur had assigned him to fill a vacancy commanding the 7th Division. Barr was content in that position until the war broke out, then offered to relinquish command when the division was sent to Korea, partly for family reasons and partly because he doubted his ability to command in combat. Since Barr had already asked for one reassignment, Almond refused to take the matter to MacArthur.

Barr and Almond had been on friendly terms as fellow junior officers from the South during the interwar years. But their relationship was much more fraught now, particularly since Barr was reporting to Almond. Barr disliked the corps commander's dictatorial ways, while Almond was frustrated by Barr's indecisiveness. "[Barr] was an inept, vacillating commander who exasperated Gen. Almond continuously," recalled Col. Chiles, the X Corps operations officer. "In my opinion only their long personal friendship kept him from being relieved."

Paddock, the 7th Division operations officer, was among those who thought Barr was underestimated. "He was courtly, kind, friendly, very intelligent, capable and I think aware of his shortcomings," Paddock said. "He was not the loud-gung-ho type but this is not to be held against him." Barr commanded with loose reins, but he demanded results.

Some thought Almond should have relieved Barr. Paddock had a different assessment: "He was a helluva better division commander than Almond was a corps commander."

The same day the 7th Division began landing, Mao Zedong telegraphed Peng Dehuai with recommendations that the 9th Army Group prepare to counter X Corps, which included two South Korean divisions from the ROK I Corps. "Song Shilun's army group must be surely used and deployed on the eastern front where the U.S. 7th Division and ROK Capital and 3rd Divisions are very likely to make northward attacks," Mao wrote.

Warnings were flashing of a major Chinese intervention. On October 28, the 26th ROK Regiment, part of Almond's X Corps command, was moving north from the North Korean city of Hamhung when it collided with an enemy force at Sudong. In heavy fighting the next day, the South Koreans captured 16 prisoners whose uniforms bore no insignia, but they were obviously Chinese. They had been captured in the heart of X Corps territory, roughly midway between the Marine landing at Wonsan and the Army landing at Iwon. Sudong was on the road leading to the Changjin Reservoir, or, as it was known on the Japanese maps the Americans were using, Chosin.

This was not the first UN encounter with Chinese forces. On October 26, as the ROK 6th Division moved in the 8th Army zone toward the Yalu in northwest North Korea, it ran into a Chinese division at Onjong-ri, suffering heavy casualties. On that day, as historian Allan Millett noted, "the Korean War changed, but only the Chinese knew it."

MacArthur's headquarters downplayed the significance of the first encounter, reporting to Washington that the enemy troops may have been volunteers and that "there was no positive evidence that Chinese Communist units, as such, had entered Korea." But the report acknowledged it was a possibility.

Almond, at least, was concerned. On the afternoon of October 30, the X Corps commander flew to the ROK I Corps headquarters in Hamhung and had a look at the 16 Chinese prisoners captured the previous day. They were the first Chinese prisoners captured in his zone, and he wanted to interrogate them personally rather than wait for intelligence reports from his staff.

Almond ran them through close-order drills, checking if they could keep formation. "They looked like a mob," recalled Lt. Col. Frank Mildren, the X Corp deputy chief. Still, Almond noted they were well equipped for winter in their boxy padded-quilt uniforms.

Working with an interpreter, Almond questioned each of the prisoners individually, out of earshot of the others. "What is your mission?" Almond asked.

"Our mission is to drive south of the Yalu River," one answered.

"How far?" Almond asked.

"To Pusan." The captives added that their political commissars had told them "they would drive the Americans into the sea."

This was "rather unsettling news," recalled McCaffrey. That night, Almond radioed a message addressed personally to MacArthur reporting that the prisoners were not volunteers and that he believed they were regulars from Chinese units that had crossed the Yalu, and that "probably others would follow." MacArthur forwarded Almond's message to the Joint Chiefs.

Charles Willoughby, MacArthur's chief of intelligence, scoffed when he saw the report. The imperious Willoughby, born in Germany and still with the heavy accent to prove it, had been MacArthur's intelligence chief since 1939. It was said Willoughby acted so Prussian that all he was missing was a spiked helmet. Most intelligence officers in the Far East command were afraid to challenge Willoughby, as he had MacArthur's ear.

One of the few opinions O. P. Smith and Almond shared was skepticism about the validity of Willoughby's intelligence. "Willoughby made up his mind as to what he wanted to have happen and shaped his intelligence reports accordingly," Smith later said. Almond privately doubted his competency, but MacArthur trusted Willoughby, so Almond had learned to tolerate him.

For a month Willoughby had reported the Chinese had 44 divisions in Manchuria, including 29 positioned along the Yalu. But by the end of October, Willoughby was convinced China had missed the window for intervening in the war. He aggressively challenged any intelligence suggesting otherwise.

Willoughby told Almond he didn't believe he had Chinese prisoners, so Almond invited him to come see for himself. Willoughby flew to Korea and conceded the prisoners were Chinese, but he insisted they were likely volunteers or stragglers.

Regardless of Willoughby's verdict, a powerful warning was delivered on the night of November 1 in the 8th Army zone in northwest North Korea. Following the 6th ROK's fight with the Chinese force a few nights earlier, Walker had decided to bolster his forces for his movement north, ordering the 1st Cavalry Division to leave Pyongyang and attack to the Yalu. As darkness fell on the evening of November 1, the 8th Cavalry Regiment, positioned ahead of the rest of the division near the town of Unsan, suddenly found itself under a massed infantry assault by enemy troops firing burp guns and throwing grenades. Two Chinese divisions were attacking the 8th Cavalry and the nearby 15th ROK Regiment, overwhelming the far-outnumbered Americans and South Koreans. By the following morning, more than 800 men of the 8th Cavalry were casualties.

That same day, the 7th Marine Regiment relieved the 26th ROK Regiment and continued cautiously north on the road to Sudong, where the South Koreans had encountered the Chinese a few days earlier. That night, the 7th Regiment was attacked by a large Chinese force that managed to infiltrate between the two lead Marine battalions. In a pitched battle the next day, the Marines inflicted punishing damage on the Chinese force, identified as a Chinese Communist Forces (CCF) division, the 124th.

Whatever Tokyo thought, it was plain to the commanders on the ground they were fighting Chinese regulars.

Iwon, November 4

The 31st Regiment Polar Bears climbed down rope ladders from the troopships onto infantry landing craft with heavy packs on their backs. Nobody was shooting at them, so the most precarious moment came when L Company's Elmer Schearf fell while descending, thankfully not killing himself.

As the landing craft packed with GIs started for the beach, the captain of the troop transport USNS *David C. Shanks* stood on the bridge, waving his cap at the soldiers and sounding several blasts from the ship's horn. "Good luck, 31st!" he called. "God be with you."

The mountains in the near distance looked higher and the weather was colder than anything they had experienced in South Korea, but Iwon's wide, soft sand beach was the most immediate problem. "We had a hell of a time getting into Iwon because we were landing on a sandbar and our trucks were getting stuck and everything was haywire," recalled PFC Grant McMillin.

But the regiment finished landing that day and moved north by foot, in jeeps, and in trucks on dirt roads, passing curious North Korean civilians who stood at the side, gazing at the GIs. The 31st mission was to secure supply lines and guard the left flank of the 17th Regiment, which was now seventy-five miles north, on its way to the Yalu River.

Beauchamp's 32nd Regiment began landing later on November 4, the last of the 7th Division regiments to come ashore. The 32nd had seen the most action in the division after Inchon and was now in reserve. That night, a group of 32nd officers and troops gathered around a campfire on the beach. It looked like the war was about to be over and that the 32nd might not get back in the fight. It was ironic, as its more veteran officers believed that the regiment had finally hit its stride. Curtis, who had been so concerned about the regiment at

Fuji, now considered the 32nd battle-tested and efficient. Capt. Erwin Bigger, a seasoned World War II paratrooper, believed the 1st Battalion had proven itself in the fight for Seoul. "We were no greenhorn outfit," recalled Bigger. "We had pride and esprit." But now they could do little except speculate on which division would be stuck with occupation duty and when everyone else would go home.

Major Spencer Edwards, the regiment's highly regarded intelligence officer, was inside the operations tent, studying the latest intelligence summary from X Corps and plotting the enemy locations on his map, Curtis recalled. After a while, Edwards joined the others on the beach and stared into the fire before speaking. "I predict that the United States Army is headed for the worst disaster in its history," Edwards said.

People around the fire smiled awkwardly. Edwards continued, citing intelligence doctrine he had taught as an instructor at Fort Riley, Kansas: "A commander must base his estimate on the enemy's capabilities—not what he believes the enemy's intentions to be."

Curtis finished the story: "The group smiled again—those school teachers and their manuals—they just don't apply in this crazy war in Korea."

The Chinese attack on the 8th Army reversal had, in fact, alarmed MacArthur. On November 5, without bothering to inform the Joint Chiefs, he ordered the Far East Air Force under Gen. George Stratemeyer to bomb the Korean end of all the Yalu River bridges. Stratemeyer, nervous about carrying out an order that clearly violated the instructions to stay clear of the Manchurian border, alerted the Pentagon. The Joint Chiefs, with Truman's concurrence, quickly countermanded MacArthur's order, worried about inciting China.

MacArthur erupted at the news, firing back a message apocalyptic even by his standards. "Men and materiel in large force are pouring across all bridges over the Yalu from Manchuria," he wrote. "This movement not only jeopardizes but threatens the ultimate destruction of the forces under my command."

MacArthur said he would comply with the Joint Chief of Staff's instructions, but he made it clear he would not be responsible for the disaster that ensued. "Every hour that this is postponed will be paid for dearly in American and other United Nations blood," he wrote. MacArthur's language completely contradicted a reassuring cable he had sent the Joint Chiefs on November 4, saying that "many fundamental logistic" hurdles made a large Chinese intervention unlikely.

A stunned Bradley telephoned Truman and relayed MacArthur's message, and the president reluctantly acquiesced to the bombing. Secretary of Defense Marshall tried to calm MacArthur with a note November 7, pledging that the administration was "intensely desirous" of supporting his command but adding a point that seemed to have escaped the general: "We are faced with an extremely grave international problem that could so easily lead to a world disaster."

On November 8, around seventy B-29s and hundreds of fighter-bombers were launched on raids attacking Yalu bridges, causing only limited damage to the spans.

Reflecting MacArthur's concern, Almond was uncharacteristically cautious for a few days. He had been pressing O. P. Smith to move the 7th Marine Regiment toward the Yalu River along the road going further into the mountains toward the Chosin Reservoir. Smith's other two infantry regiments were on defensive missions assigned by X Corps, and Smith did not want to push one regiment into the mountains alone. When Almond visited the 1st Marine Division headquarters on November 7, Smith was pleasantly surprised to find the X Corps commander suddenly receptive to his warnings against dispersing the forces. "General Almond had apparently been somewhat sobered," Smith noted.

Almond acknowledged as much. "The mountain and winter situation in which we now find ourselves does not admit of anymore 'blitzkriegs,'" he wrote on November 6 to a friend at the Pentagon. "We are confronted with both an enemy and a terrain which will require the most methodical and difficult efforts to overcome."

Fusen Reservoir, November 8

There were hints of winter in the air by the time the 31st Polar Bears made it up to the Kaema Plateau late on the night of November 6, after the long road march from Iwon. The Kaema was a vast, heavily forested highland known as the roof of Korea, filled with mountains and valleys exposed to Siberian winds blowing from Manchuria. The regiment set up headquarters in the crossroads village of Untaek, on the road leading to the Fusen Reservoir.

In the days that followed, the regiment spread out in the mountains, spanning all possible avenues of approach into the 17th Regiment's west flank. They sent out patrols to the surrounding mountains and villages and flushed out small pockets of enemy soldiers. On November 8, Lt. Col. Bill Reilly's 3rd Battalion advanced toward Fusen, on the western edge of the regiment's assigned zone. Maj. Storms was up front with the advance guard, Capt. Auburn Marr's Item Company, as it moved along the east slope of Paek-san, a 7,700-foot mountain.

A battalion-sized force of 450 Chinese soldiers waiting in ambush on the forested slope let the lead platoon, commanded by Lt. Donald Halverson, move into the trap and then opened up with machine gun, mortar, and rifle fire. Halverson was killed in the barrage. Storms quickly rallied nearby troops, and they moved forward to support Marr's company in their attack on the mountainside.

Reilly, who was three hundred yards to the rear, brought up more troops. Lt. Gray and his mortar platoon hastily unloaded an 81 mm mortar and ammunition from their truck and assembled it while under Chinese fire, soon firing barrages that raked the enemy entrenchments. The Chinese battalion was forced to withdraw, leaving 64 dead scattered across the mountainside.

The fight was the first between the 7th Division and Chinese Communists, and Halverson was the first officer of the 31st killed in North Korea. After recovering from its initial surprise, Reilly's battalion had done well, and the mood the next day at the regimental headquarters was celebratory. "Ole W. J. Reilly has been itching for a fight and one of his outfits did some tangling late yesterday afternoon, and according to the colonel [Maclean] they did very well," Capt. George Rasula, the regiment's assistant operations officer, wrote to his wife, Lucy.

Storms had performed bravely and would soon receive the Silver Star for his actions. But in the letter he wrote to Helen and the boys the next day, he told them nothing about the fight, only confessing to being exhausted. "I am so tired in body and mind," he wrote. "There are so many things I'd love to tell you about, but feel that I might endanger lives somewhere if I try to tell you what is happening. I'll tell you all about us one of these sweet days when I get home."

Several enemy soldiers had been captured by the 3rd Battalion. When questioned, they said were from the 376th Regiment of the 126th Division—a different Chinese Communist Forces division than the one the Marines fought at Sudong. "This seemed to us positive confirmation of serious Chinese participation in the war," Gray recalled.

However, Maclean's report on the encounter at Fusen was met with much skepticism at GHQ in Tokyo, which had decided that the CCF were not present in any significant numbers in the 7th Division zone. When Beauchamp visited Maclean at his CP on November 9, the 31st commander told him about the encounter. "I'm convinced they were Chinese," Maclean said.

"I had the impression that he was having difficulty convincing people they were CCF," recalled Beauchamp.

Then, as quickly as they had appeared, the Chinese disappeared. At dawn November 7, the Marines below Chosin found the Chinese forces to their front had simply vanished. The Polar Bears' fight with the Chinese on November 8 was the last encounter anywhere in the X Corps zone for days. The Chinese were also gone from the 8th Army front out west, along the Chongchon River.

But on the same day, an entirely new and far more powerful force—Song Shilun's 9th Army Group—150,000 of the best Chinese troops—began moving into North Korea. It included three armies of 50,000 men: the 20th, 26th, and 27th Armies, each with four divisions. Song had the 20th Army cross first. The 27th Army followed, crossing at Linjiang. The 26th Army would wait further back as the reserve.

Their destination was the Chosin Reservoir.

The high-altitude man-made lake, surrounded by foreboding mountains, lay along one of the few roads leading through the North Korean highlands to the Manchurian border. With Mao's agreement, it had been selected by Song and Peng Dehuai as the ideal spot to lay a trap for X Corps.

Peng's plan was to draw the force north into the mountains, cut off the sole road leading in, and then destroy the American forces. "The key is to lure the enemy to move inland deeper and more dispersed, for us to destroy them one by one," Mao telegrammed Peng November 5.

The withdrawal of the 124th and 126th divisions was meant to encourage X Corps to advance north while covering the secret march of the 9th Army Group toward the Chosin Reservoir. The movement would have to be entirely undercover, only at night, and without radio transmissions or even the bugles and whistles smaller units traditionally used to communicate. The armies were taking different routes to Chosin, and they faced journeys of 120 to 200 miles. The routes would take them first across the rugged Rangrim Mountains, a heavily forested range with peaks ranging from three thousand to six thousand feet, and then through the Kaema Plateau.

Mao, concerned by X Corps' movement north, had insisted that Song accelerate the 9th Army Group's move to Chosin by weeks, drastically shortening the preparation time. There had been no time for weapons inspection, drills, and, critically, training on how to protect themselves against aerial attacks. Perhaps worst of all, Mao's rush also meant that the 9th Army Group was crossing the border into the mountains of North Korea without nearly enough winter clothing. Two-thirds of its troops had no winter coats, and none had winter gloves. When trains carrying the Korea-bound troops stopped at the Shenyang train station in northeast China, a senior regional commander was stunned to see the soldiers wearing light canvas shoes and quilted cotton uniforms designed for the mild winter weather of subtropical southeast China. He hurried back to his headquarters and asked everyone to donate their winter clothing. He made it back to the train station with 641 winter coats—a drop in the bucket.

The Joint Chiefs, nervous about the Chinese attacks in the X Corps and 8th Army zones, sent MacArthur a feeble message on November 9, suggesting that his objective of destroying the North Korean Armed Forces "may have to be reexamined." U.S. intelligence had increased its estimate of Chinese forces in Manchuria from twelve to twenty divisions, which seemed like quite a bit if China had indeed planned only limited operations in Korea. Even Willoughby allowed that there was some risk, reporting on November 10 that there was a considerable enemy buildup in the Chosin-Fusen area and warning that the Chinese might now be capable of "launching offensive operations."

MacArthur brushed away the Joint Chiefs' suggestion. The disappearance of the Chinese from his front had restored his vim. Their attacks, MacArthur decided, had only been a limited effort to save face and preserve a "nominal foothold" in Korea for the North Korean forces. He concluded that the Chinese had had enough of American air attacks and artillery bombardment. Though MacArthur recognized that China still had the capability for a major intervention, he was convinced that if the Chinese dared cross the Yalu in force, they would be decimated by air power.

In his reply to the Joint Chiefs on November 9, MacArthur said that failing to push all the way to the Manchurian border would be the "greatest defeat of the free world in modern times," likening it to the appeasement of Hitler at Munich. He said he was going ahead with the 8th Army offensive, which was tentatively set for November 15 and would scour North Korea clean of all communist forces. Washington again bowed to his wishes.

"We sat around like paralyzed rabbits while MacArthur carried out this nightmare," Secretary of State Acheson later wrote.

As went MacArthur, so too did Almond. The X Corp commander did not stay "sobered" for long about the dangers of plunging forward. By November 11, Almond was anxious to get back on the attack and ordered the 7th Division to resume its move north to the Yalu. Powell's 17th Regiment would remain in the lead, continuing up the road that led to Kapsan, a key town twenty miles from the Yalu; Maclean's 31st Regiment would move up, protecting Powell's flank, while Beauchamp's 32nd Regiment would take Maclean's position southeast of Fusen Reservoir. On November 13, Almond ordered Smith to have the 7th Marine Regiment seize ground around Hagaru, a village at the southern tip of Chosin Reservoir.

Almond's goal was to reach the Yalu as quickly as possible—not just to defeat the enemy but to beat the 8th Army to the river. "General Almond was always trying to be farther north than Eighth Army," recalled McCaffrey. "In any given day, he wanted X Corps' front line north of wherever Eighth Army was. It was a childish competition." Almond made it clear to Barr that the 7th Division was to win the race.

Almond's insistence on pushing the 7th Division north meant it was separating further from the 1st Marine Division, which was still slowly approaching Chosin. The distance between the two divisions was even greater than it looked on a map, as a steep mountain range between them meant the route connecting them was a long, circuitous route south via Hamhung.

The dangers of the move north grew dramatically with the early arrival of winter on the Kaema Plateau. On the night of November 10–11, temperatures plunged, falling from thirty-two degrees Fahrenheit to eight below zero in a matter of hours, accompanied by 20 to 30 mph winds. At the 31st Polar Bear's headquarters at Untaek, Chaplain Hoehn's thermometer recorded fourteen below zero Fahrenheit. That was balmy compared to some spots in the X Corps zone that reached thirty below.

The Marines were relatively well equipped with winter gear; the Army, less so. The gear—both in quality and quantity—varied unit by unit and, sometimes, soldier by soldier in the 7th Division. Ironically—and sadly—the Polar Bears had nothing like the high-quality winter clothing and equipment used in their maneuvers training as ski troops in the mountains around Sapporo. Instead of the warm mountain sleeping bags they'd used in Japan, many soldiers had blanket-type sleeping bags. Their field jackets were made of cotton and their combat boots unlined. Many soldiers had cotton caps with no earflaps; the 7th Division surgeon reported to Almond that proper headgear and scarves "are badly needed."

Like many soldiers, Storms donned virtually every piece of clothing in his pack. From the inside out, Storms wore a T-shirt, a long-sleeved wool undershirt, a wool sweater, a fatigue jacket, a pile-line jacket, and a waterproof parka on his upper body. Below, he wore cotton drawers, long johns, two sets of fatigue pants, three pairs of wool socks, and shoepacs. He wrapped a towel around his face and ears and under his helmet, leaving only his eyes showing. "Boy, I look like a gangster," he wrote Helen.

The situation was only marginally better in Beauchamp's 32nd Regiment. Sgt. Charlie Gebhardt had grown up on Chicago's West Side and thought he knew tough winter weather, but the cold in North Korea was in a different league. The troops in Faith's 1st Battalion generally had field jackets, long underwear, pile liners, and parka shells, but they were short on gloves. A truck showed up and dumped cold weather gear on a tarp for the troops to sift through; Roy Oxenrider was able to get mittens but no gloves, and as was the case for many soldiers, there was no liner for his parka shell, leaving it as little more than a windbreaker. The battalion's vehicles lacked chains and tarp covers, and tents were scarce.

Almond cabled Tokyo, reporting the 7th Division had an "urgent need" for 250 squad tents and five hundred oil-burning stoves. "Soldiers are freezing for lack of shelter," he warned. Some equipment would be sent, but most of it, not in time.

By November 15, Beauchamp's 32nd Regiment had joined the rest of the division on the wintry plateau, taking a blocking position at Sinhung, a village twenty miles north of Hamhung at a junction of several roads and stream valleys. The regiment protected the X Corps communication lines, patrolling the area on foot. It was a pleasant, quiet spot with a picturesque coating of snow. It seemed as if the war had passed them by. "It was kind of nice in a way, sort of a pretty valley, and we called it Happy Valley," said Gebhardt.

Despite the cold, morale was good. "Everyone expected the war to end in a few days," Maj. Curtis recalled. On the battalion's first day there, soon after dark, a call came into Faith's headquarters from one of the companies, which reported that they had shot an intruder and to please send a truck to bring the intruder to the battalion CP. "Faith looked puzzled and stated he didn't know what was happening but he was going to find out," recalled Stamford. "He soon returned and announced that he was sending the cooks with a truck to bring in the intruder."

The soldiers had shot an ox that wandered into their lines. The next day, the troops enjoyed the first fresh beef they had eaten in quite a while. "Tough, but tasty," said Stamford.

The 7th Marine Regiment reached the burned-out and largely deserted village of Hagaru-ri on November 14. It had taken the Marines four days to move the eleven miles from Koto-ri. That was no accident. Smith was trying to buy time to build up supplies and concentrate his division, delaying right up to the point of insubordination. "All of us at division HQ used every trick in the bag to slow our advance," recalled Col. Alpha Bowser, the 1st Marine Division's chief of operations.

Visiting the Marine headquarters on November 15, Almond pressed Smith to speed up. Almond wanted to split the division, sending the 7th Marine regiment to continue fourteen miles up the west side of Chosin to the village of Yudam-ni while the 5th Marine Regiment went up the east side of the reservoir. Meanwhile, the 1st Marine Regiment was still fifty miles south, providing security on the sole road leading to Chosin. Smith argued that the advance should be delayed until the 1st Marines were relieved of their security mission and could join the rest of the division at Chosin. But there was no debate as far as Almond was concerned. MacArthur had ordered the advance to continue, and he would comply.

After the meeting, a frustrated Smith wrote a long letter to Marine Commandant Clifton Cates. Smith did not like the idea of stringing his division along a single two hundred-mile-long mountain road all the way to the Chinese border. "I have little confidence in the tactical judgment of the Corps or in the realism of their planning," Smith wrote. "There is a continual splitting up of units and assignments of missions to small units which puts them out on a limb."

Part of the problem was that the Army and Marines had wildly different operational philosophies. Army doctrine called for a division to move cross-country at full speed while relying on higher headquarters to protect its rear and send up logistical support. Marines would seize a bridgehead, set up a defensive perimeter, and build up supplies before advancing. Smith's deliberate pace with the 1st Marine Division left Almond and his headquarters gnashing their teeth. "Its slow movement frustrated us Army people who expected a Patton-like dash," recalled Maj. Joe Gurfein, a planning officer at X Corps headquarters. "The Marines are great fighters, but the word offense means different things to Army and Marines."

MacArthur and Almond wanted to get to the border before winter set in, but as far as Smith was concerned, that race was over, and they had lost. "I believe a winter campaign in the mountains of North Korea is too much to ask of the American soldier or marine," he told Cates.

The single road to Chosin, which twisted tortuously up to the plateau, would be vulnerable to both the weather and enemy attack. Smith wanted an operations base where supplies could be stocked and an airstrip for C-47 transport planes that could carry in supplies and carry out casualties. Smith and Maj. Gen. Field Harris, commander of the 1st Marine Air Wing, scouted out locations for the construction on November 16 and picked a site on the south side of the village.

Though there would be later claims that Almond thought the airstrip was unnecessary, it was standard procedure in X Corps for a division to build an adjacent landing strip within twenty-four hours of establishing a command post, and he wanted Smith to build it quickly. "Desire you expedite completion C-47 landing field your forward area north of Hagaru-ri," Almond cabled Smith on November 17. "Report location of site. Daily report desired on progress and estimated time of completion." The real point of contention was who should build it: Smith thought X Corps should at least help because the Marine engineer battalion was already tied up fixing the road and bridges, but Almond insisted it was the division's responsibility.

Almond was not thinking in terms of evacuations and supplies. The main reason he wanted airstrips built was so he could fly in to visit his subordinate commands whenever he pleased and find out what was going on. That was particularly so with the Marines; getting information from Smith and his staff was like pulling teeth, and he believed his visits would spur the Marines into action. "The Marines were hardly ever glad to see him," recalled Haig.

Almond had eleven liaison planes at X Corps at his disposal. "The only Almond assistant with a soft job is his jeep driver," an Associated Press reporter wrote. "The general won't drive two miles if he can fly." But the small planes lacked deicing and navigation equipment, and with the worsening weather, it was becoming more difficult to reach the high-altitude X Corps bases. After nearly being stranded at the 17th Regiment headquarters when its airstrip was socked in by clouds, Almond lobbied Tokyo for a C-47, which could fly in such conditions.

Almond made industrious use of his time in the air, studying bridges and hills to see how they might affect his advance and watching his truck convoys to make sure they were moving with discipline. The commanders of any units he found lagging would face his wrath. Yet despite the aerial overview, Almond somehow missed the big picture of what was happening on the ground. "Moving by air from one unit to another in a few minutes, he failed to recognize that the dispersion of his troops was much greater on the ground than it appeared to him when flying between units," noted Michael Lynch, Almond's biographer.

Almond's aggressive push north was raising some alarms among MacArthur's staff at GHQ. Pinky Wright, chief of operations, was worried about X Corps' wide dispersion. Its units were spread over distances of close to one hundred miles, both from north to south and from east to west, and they were hardly in a position to support each other, much less the 8th Army. At least as worrisome was the enormous gap opening up between the 8th Army and X Corps—thirty-five to fifty miles by air and even greater by road.

MacArthur was unconcerned with the gap, believing the terrain was too rugged for the enemy to take advantage. Nonetheless, with MacArthur's approval, on November 10, Wright alerted Almond in a letter that X Corps needed to do everything possible to support the 8th Army, including possibly reorienting his attack to the west to protect Walker's right flank. Almond did his best to ignore the letter and continued his drive to the Yalu. After five days, he sent Wright a reply insisting that the best way for X Corps to help the 8th Army was to continue attacking north while being ready to move west if needed. By word and deed, Almond made it clear he did not wish to subordinate his advance to the 8th Army.

But MacArthur sided with Wright, and on November 16, he ordered Almond to make a plan for reorienting his attack to the west from Chosin. This alternate plan, aimed at cutting a key enemy supply route and attacking the rear of any Chinese forces facing the 8th Army, would be executed only at MacArthur's order. As an apparent sop to Almond, MacArthur allowed X Corps to continue its drive north to the Yalu, but he specified using "minimum forces only."

Accordingly, the X Corps staff went to work on a plan that would have the 1st Marine Division attack west from Chosin. But the 7th Division would continue its drive toward the Yalu along the Pungsan-Kapsan axis, an attack that would pull the division farther away from Chosin—and away from supporting the 8th Army.

Almond's plan did call for sending a regimental combat team from the 7th Division to the east side of Chosin to protect the Marines' eastern flank. This would allow Smith to concentrate the 1st Marine Division on the reservoir's west side, as the Marine commander had persistently requested. But Almond did nothing to prepare the 7th Division for this, apparently viewing the attack west as a contingency plan that would not need to be executed. Instead of having one of the Army regiments prepare for movement to Chosin—and despite MacArthur's admonition to use "minimum force only" in the drive to the Yalu—Almond wanted the 31st and 32nd regiments to join the race for glory to the Manchurian border.

Through his stubborn determination, Smith had succeeded in keeping his 1st Marine Division relatively concentrated. Dave Barr had no such luck with his 7th Division. "Our biggest problem was logistics as we were spread from hell-to-breakfast over harsh terrain with a poor road net," recalled Paddock.

The division's three rifle regiments were scattered so far apart in mountainous terrain that they couldn't reach each other by radio. By road they were so distant from each other—and from headquarters—that flying by small airplane was the most practical way to travel between them. Even within the regiments, the rifle battalions "were way out of supporting distances from each other," Paddock said.

Almond had far more control over Barr than he did over Smith. "We being Army had to explicitly obey Almond and put up with his interfering with our chain of command whereas Gen Smith of the Marines didn't and wouldn't," Paddock said.

As ordered by Almond, the 7th Division continued its drive to the Chinese border. Powell's 17th Regiment captured Kapsan on November 19, putting the Yalu in striking distance. The following day, Almond ordered Barr to move Beauchamp's 32nd Regiment from the Fusen area toward the Yalu River, leaving much of the 7th Division far from Chosin.

Almond was feeling increasingly confident. Writing his wife, Margaret, in Tokyo, on November 18, he conceded that "the enemy is a bother" but said X Corps was doing well despite the weather and terrain. "We have good clothing and food and there is no real reason for us to complain."

Certainly, Almond had no reason to complain. His personal command vehicle was equipped with electricity, a refrigerator, hot running water, and a flush toilet. His headquarters mess was stocked with linen, Japanese china, silverware, and silver napkin rings. Aides rotated flying to Tokyo on the daily airlift and bringing back fresh fruit, vegetables, and meat.

Almond had at his disposal "3 good cooks, 3 waiters and a white table cloth and I have it run as we run a table at home," he reported to Margaret. He also had two "very faithful" Puerto Rican orderlies. "One runs my van and the other a little shack where we have a big hot bath." Almond also requisitioned a villa in Hungnam to use as his private residence. Ordered to redecorate, Haig hired Korean artisans to build a "magnificent" sunken bathtub of mosaic tiles, and he placed beautiful hand-painted vases he'd found in the Hamhung marketplace in the reception rooms. When President Rhee and his wife visited Almond, he gave them a tour and proudly pointed out the vases, crediting Haig with finding them. "Mrs. Rhee, a brusque and outspoken woman who was an Austrian by birth, fixed the general with a disdainful stare," Haig related. "'Then your aide should know for future reference,' she said, 'that in Korea vases of this kind are used as chamber pots.'"

La Feria, Texas, Sunday, November 19

Helen Storms was tired Sunday evening. The baby was kicking, she was caring for the three boys, and she was worried about her husband. But she picked up her pen. "I really have very little news to write—but can't let myself retire until I have whispered an 'I love you' by ink," she wrote to Harvey.

"Precious sweetheart, every week seems to get long and longer without you," she continued. "Nearly Thanksgiving and you are still fighting." The two younger boys, Billy and Ernie, were asking when Daddy was getting home. "They are getting anxious as am I."

The news that day was full of reports of the 17th Regiment's rapid advance toward the Chinese border. "Seems that the 17th is in Kapsan and Col. Powell says his men captured it without loss of a single life. Sounds unbelievable but I hope it's true," Helen wrote.

"Now that means 7th Division is 21 miles from Yalu River. I'm afraid if they go too fast they might be encircled—but guess they have thought of that long before I did."

3rd Battalion, 31st Infantry Headquarters, November 20

Harvey Storms sat at a table in a schoolhouse serving as the 3/31 headquarters, which was lit up and warm, thanks to a generator the battalion had managed to procure. "A soprano is warbling away on one of the men's radios," he wrote Helen. "Really, it is very 'homey' but not for me, because I'd much rather be sitting at home with you in my lap telling you all this than just writing it!"

After nearly two weeks of being spread out in the mountains, protecting the 17th Regiment's flank, the Polar Bears had been pulled back from the front and were consolidating. In his letter, Storms explained to Helen why she had heard so little about the 31st Regiment in the news. "We, the 31st, have been so widely spaced out that if the enemy knew just how far, they could have walked right through us and wiped us out," he wrote.

Yalu River, November 21

George Patton had peed in the Rhine when the 3rd Army reached the river in 1945, and Ned Almond was determined to do the same in the Yalu. On November 20, the 17th Regiment advanced on foot from Kapsan over icy mountainous roads in the bitter cold weather against slight North Korean Army resistance, then stopped for the night on a ridge overlooking the river.

Almond flew into Kapsan that evening, and the next day, he and Barr accompanied the lead troops into the river town of Hyesanjin, which was deserted and already almost entirely destroyed by bombing. The Yalu here, near its source in the mountains, was no mighty waterway, stretching about fifty to seventy-five yards wide and largely frozen except for a narrow channel that was still flowing. The GIs could see Chinese sentries across the river. "No one fired at us, and we fired at no one," Barr recalled. "The Chinese looked at us from across the river, and we looked at them."

In a celebratory mood, various senior officers and aides joined Almond by the river and "performed the hallowed ritual of urinating in the Yalu," recalled Bill Paddock, one of the participants.

Back at X Corps Headquarters, a cable arrived from Tokyo: "Heartiest congratulations, Ned, and tell Dave Barr the 7th Div hit the jackpot. MacArthur." It was, seemingly, a high point for MacArthur, Almond, the 7th Division, and the United States in Korea.

9th Army Group Headquarters, Northeast North Korea, November 21

The first of the three armies of the 9th Army Group had arrived at its target as well. The 27th Army, 50,000 strong, closed in the Chosin area by the night of November 20. It had been an arduous journey. For seven nights, the men had marched in the dark through the mountains, covering their tracks in the snow as they moved. They rested during the day in the forests, concealed from air surveillance. Anyone out in the open during the day would freeze in place whenever a plane was overhead. No fires were allowed for fear they would be spotted by U.S. aircraft.

With temperatures in the Kaema highland plunging to twenty or thirty degrees below zero, the rushed entry into Korea with scant winter gear had proven calamitous. Soldiers stationed along the border were astonished at the lack of winter clothing carried by 9th Army Group troops as they crossed into Korea.

The subzero weather had been tortuous for the soldiers, who were largely from southeast China and accustomed to subtropical weather. "We lacked gloves, caps and even winter shoes," recalled Captain Wang Xuedong, a company commander with the 58th Division of the 20th Army. His division alone lost 700 men to severe frostbite during the march. In some units, soldiers took turns sleeping but never for more than an hour; otherwise, they could freeze to death. Most squads had only one or two cotton-padded quilts, which were placed on the ground to be shared by ten or more soldiers. The troops huddled together and hugged each other's feet to keep them from freezing.

Horses pulled smaller artillery guns, but in some spots, they refused to continue along treacherous icy cliff trails. "It was just too slippery and dangerous," recalled Wang. "The men came up with the idea of laying down their comforters on the cliffs to cover the snow and ice. The idea worked, and they led their horses safely through the pass."

A Chinese division traveled far more lightly than an American division, carrying roughly five pounds of supplies per man per day, barely a tenth of what a U.S. division carried. With very few trucks and the bridges and roads damaged, most heavy artillery pieces had to be left at the border. Soldiers had to carry all the ammunition, including mortar and artillery shells.

Without fires, the troops could not cook rice, so they carried concentrated cakes of wheat, soybean, and corn flour, which they packed into a sock. The rations were so inadequate—in quantity, vitamins, and calories—that many soldiers suffered malnutrition. "We had to take with us whatever we needed, or whatever we could carry on our shoulders," said Wang. "When our regiment ran out of food, we had to trade our blankets, towels and even medicines with local Koreans for their rice, corn and vegetables."

After hundreds of hungry soldiers in the 26th Army tried to desert, Song executed a battalion commander in an attempt to restore discipline. The hunger, hardship, and death the soldiers suffered on the move to Chosin were "even worse" than the Long March, Song later said.

To the west, the 13th Army Group had likewise crossed the Yalu undetected, and eighteen Chinese divisions were in place to spring a trap on Walker's unsuspecting 8th Army. In all, China had infiltrated nearly 400,000 troops through some of the most inhospitable terrain on earth and the harshest weather imaginable, almost entirely undetected by the world's most technologically advanced superpower. It was, by any measure, a remarkable achievement.

On November 20, Peng sent orders to Song Shilun for the 9th Army Group to attack X Corps on the night of November 25, the same day Chinese forces to the west were scheduled to launch their attack on the 8th Army. Peng did not want to wait, fearing that once the attack in the west started, X Corps would withdraw from Chosin and escape the trap.

But Song replied on November 21 that his forces would not be ready by then. The 27th Army still needed several days to get in position around the Chosin Reservoir. The 20th Army was farther back in the Kaema highlands and would need to rush for days to reach Chosin. The 26th Army was even more distant. The 9th Army Group would not be ready, and Peng had no choice but to delay the attack at Chosin until November 27.

Almond issued instructions that he wanted "maximum photo and news coverage" of all the Thanksgiving dinners being served across northeast Korea to X Corps troops. Turkeys had been distributed to every unit, and there was nothing like Thanksgiving dinner coverage to assure the families back home that their boys were being treated well.

There was no press, however, at Almond's own Thanksgiving dinner at X Corps headquarters, possibly because of its extravagance. It was a fancy affair, with a cocktail bar, place cards, and even dinner candles that Almond had flown in from Tokyo via courier. O. P. Smith had been looking forward to a simple turkey meal with his staff at the 1st Marine Division mess, but he along with Barr were obliged to attend the dinner at X Corps headquarters with a clutch of senior officers.

Smith congratulated Barr for reaching the Yalu, and the 7th Division commander told him the entire operation had been conducted "on a shoestring, never at any time having on hand more than one day's supplies." Given the nearly impassable roads, this had been risky, Smith noted in his journal. Had an enemy attack succeeded in cutting off the road behind them, the 17th Regiment might have been decimated. "However," Smith added, "his reaching the border did make a fine communique."

At the 31st Regiment headquarters near Untaek, Ray Radke and his pals from the headquarters company enjoyed simpler fare, celebrating Thanksgiving in a barn strewn with straw that they called The Pigpen. Figuring to be returning to Japan soon, they made plans for reestablishing the NCO club back at Camp Crawford on Hokkaido. "One of the medics had medical alcohol, we spiced it up with grapefruit juice and had a roaring time," Radke recalled. "Hell of a hangover, though."

Thanksgiving came a day early to Happy Valley. It looked like 1/32 might be moving out in the next day or two, so Lt. Col. Faith ordered the Thanksgiving meal served on Wednesday.

In keeping with Almond's orders, the 32nd Regiment was being sent north to back up the 17th Regiment on the Yalu and to extend the American position on the river further west. The 2nd and 3rd battalions had already departed Happy Valley, and the 1st Battalion would be leaving any day.

Faith was eager to get back in the action and swore to Capt. Stamford that he would cross the Yalu one way or another. "He looked forward to the time when he would sneak across the river and say he had put his foot in Manchuria," Stamford recalled. "He mentioned to me at one time that he was looking for another fight and he thought the battalion was ready for it, the way the men were acting."

Before eating their Thanksgiving meal, the troops worked off excess energy with some intercompany football games—rough enough that several soldiers were left with minor injuries and bruises. "The battalion was ready for a fight," Stamford recalled.

"We had everything, soup to nuts, we even had turkey and cranberries," said Private Harry Jacobs of B Company. The meal was "all served hot but then froze in your mess kit before you could eat it," added Sgt. Clarence White, also in B Company. "But, all in all, we were in good spirits." At his own expense, Faith also supplied each company mess with locally procured beef, so the men ate well.

The 1st Battalion was a close-knit group by then, and Faith was much admired and liked by its men. "The battalion commander had, I should say, faith in his troops and his troops had faith in him," Stamford said.

It was, especially in retrospect, an idyllic day. "I have never sat down to a Thanksgiving dinner after that without thinking about our dinner," Roy Oxenrider recalled years later.

Oxenrider and his Korean counterpart, Joung He Su, had road duty, checking civilians coming from the north to make sure they were not smuggling ammunition. "We had to wait to be relieved before we could go eat," he recalled. That only made the food taste that much better. "What we did not know then, but for most of us, this would be our last real meal for over a week, and of course, for so many, many of our friends, it was their last Thanksgiving."

Chapter 5

TO CHOSIN

North Korea, Friday, November 24, 1950

A tremendous barrage of artillery on the 8th Army's front signaled the start of MacArthur's great offensive to end the war. The United Nations divisions rolled forward from the Chongchon River, accompanied by optimistic predictions of reaching the Yalu in a matter of days. MacArthur flew to the 8th Army headquarters for the jump-off, touring the front and meeting with commanders. Reporters traveling with MacArthur reported him saying he hoped to have the GIs "home for Christmas."

Back on the plane for the flight back to Japan, MacArthur unexpectedly directed his pilot, Tom Story, to fly north to the Yalu and follow the river all along the Manchurian border so he could personally reconnoiter what was happening behind enemy lines. Story tried to talk the general out of it—the plane was unarmed and could be hit by antiaircraft fire or attacked by fighters—but MacArthur insisted. Nervous aides and correspondents donned parachutes, but MacArthur refused one, instead gazing peacefully out the window and puffing on his pipe. "All that spread before our eyes was an endless expanse of utterly barren countryside, jagged hills, yawning crevices, and the black waters of the Yalu locked in the silent death grip of snow and ice," MacArthur later wrote. There was no sign of the enemy.

At the 17th Infantry headquarters in Hyesanjin, Colonel Herbert Powell received a call on his field telephone from the commander of his antiaircraft battery, who was reporting that an unknown four-engine aircraft had been spotted but was too high to shoot down. "Well, if he comes down within range, open fire," Powell replied. The plane stayed high, waggling its wings in salute to the regiment, and the flight continued undisturbed back to Japan. MacArthur had avoided one disaster that day.

Back in Tokyo, MacArthur issued a communique boasting that the UN campaign against North Korean forces was "approaching its decisive effort." The general explained that X Corps in the east and the 8th Army in the west represented the two arms of a pincer coming together to envelop the enemy. "If successful this should for all practical purposes end the war, restore peace and unity to Korea [and] enable the prompt withdrawal of United Nations military forces," MacArthur announced. Apart from revealing his plan for X Corps to shift its attack to the west, the communique also made it clear to Peng Dehuai that the huge Chinese infiltration around MacArthur's forces was still undetected.

The shift to the west was also a surprise for the X Corps division commanders. MacArthur had ordered Almond to execute Operation Plan 8, the contingency plan that would redirect X Corps' attack from north, toward the Yalu, to instead attack west, in support of the 8th Army.

Almond had done nothing to prepare X Corps to redirect its attack, and both Dave Barr and O. P. Smith were caught by surprise. Much of the X Corps staff had huge reservations about the attack west and had hoped Tokyo would not go through with it. "It was an insane plan," General Clark Ruffner, Almond's chief of staff, later wrote in a letter. "You couldn't take a picnic lunch in peace time and go over the terrain in Nov. & Dec." Almond's staff officers were worried that X Corps was so scattered across the landscape that it was in danger of being cut to pieces. "We were all trying to get General Almond to exercise some caution in attacking over the mountains," recalled Bill McCaffrey, the X Corps deputy chief of staff. "But General Almond was not about to protest an order from General MacArthur. After all, everyone had said Inchon wouldn't work."

The 1st Marine Division would attack west from Yudam-ni in support of the 8th Army. That meant the 7th Division needed to send a regimental-sized task force to replace the 5th Marine Regiment on the east side of Chosin Reservoir, a modification Almond had offered in order to meet Smith's wise insistence that he would need the 5th Marines to join the 7th Marine Regiment in the attack west. Almond suggested that Smith begin his attack while the Army task force moved toward Chosin, but Smith declined to do so until the 5th Marines were relieved. Almond, anxious to launch the attack, ordered

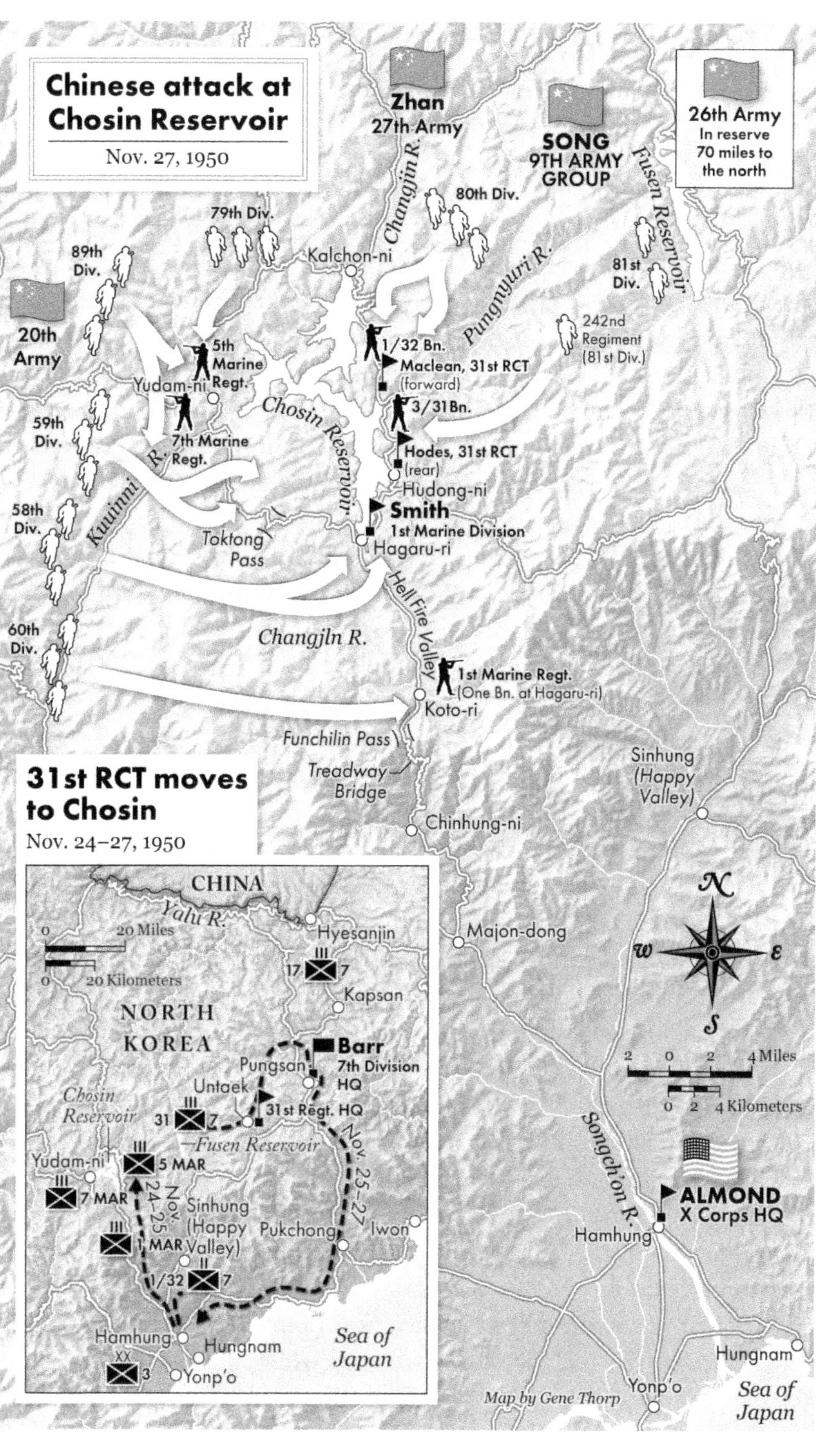

Chinese attack at Chosin Reservoir
Nov. 27, 1950
Zhan
27th Army
SONG
9TH ARMY GROUP
26th Army
In reserve
70 miles to the north
Changjin R.
Fusen Reservoir
80th Div.
79th Div.
89th Div.
20th Army
Kalchon-ni
Pungnyuri R.
81st Div.
242nd Regiment (81st Div.)
1/32 Bn.
Maclean, 31st RCT (forward)
5th Marine Regt.
Yudam-ni
Chosin Reservoir
3/31Bn.
59th Div.
7th Marine Regt.
Hodes, 31st RCT (rear)
Hudong-ni
Kuuinni R.
58th Div.
Smith
1st Marine Division
Toktong Pass
Hagaru-ri
Hell Fire Valley
60th Div.
Changjln R.
1st Marine Regt.
(One Bn. at Hagaru-ri)
Koto-ri
Funchilin Pass
Treadway Bridge
Sinhung (Happy Valley)
Chinhung-ni
Majon-dong
N
W
E
S
2 0 2 4 Miles
0 2 4 Kilometers
Songch'on R.
ALMOND
X Corps HQ
Hamhung
Hungnam
Yonp'o
Sea of Japan
Map by Gene Thorp
31st RCT moves to Chosin
Nov. 24–27, 1950
CHINA
Yalu R.
0 20 Miles
0 20 Kilometers
Hyesanjin
17 7
Kapsan
NORTH KOREA
Barr
7th Division HQ
Pungsan
Untaek
31st Regt. HQ
Chosin Reservoir
31 7
Fusen Reservoir
Nov. 25–27
Yudam-ni
5 MAR
7 MAR
Nov. 24–25
Sinhung (Happy Valley)
Pukchong
Iwon
1 MAR
1/32
7
Hamhung
Hungnam
Sea of Japan
3
Yonp'o

Barr to relieve the 5th Marines on the east side of Chosin with at least one battalion by noon the next day, November 25.

Barr was shocked when he conferred with Almond at X Corps headquarters on Friday morning. Much of the 7th Division was on or near the Yalu River, as Almond had previously ordered. The Chosin Reservoir was 250 miles away by road. "I made a feeble protest that I couldn't possibly command another force that far away nor supply it either," Barr recalled. "General Almond assured me that Corps would take care of that."

Almond knew that Faith's 1st Battalion had just been released from the Corps reserve, and he asked Barr where it was located. "I told him it was moving that day to go up and join the 32nd Infantry on the border," Barr recalled. "He ordered it stopped immediately, to be turned around and started toward the Chosin Reservoir."

Smith was pleased that the Marines would be relieved of responsibility for the east side of Chosin. "I finally talked Gen. Almond into letting us off the hook on that," Smith later said.

Now the 7th Division was on the hook.

Happy Valley, Friday, November 24

Before dawn, Faith's 1st Battalion was moving for the 160-mile road march to the 7th Division's rear CP at Pukchong, the first leg of their journey to join the 17th Regiment on the Yalu River. Faith went ahead by himself to get instructions from Col. Beauchamp, the regimental commander, leaving Maj. Crosby Miller, his executive officer, to move the battalion. Because of the lousy radio communications in the mountains, Faith had been out of communication with headquarters for three days.

Miller had been a tank company commander and staff officer at Normandy and the Ardennes and was one of the most combat-experienced officers in the battalion. He was one of many armor officers assigned to the 7th Division in the desperate rush to fill infantry vacancies. Faith had ribbed Miller about that when he joined the battalion at Fuji. "Don told me to continue to wear my Armor insignia until I proved that I was an Infantryman," Miller recalled. "After our action in taking Seoul, he personally pinned crossed rifles on me."

Around 9:00 a.m., the battalion column reached the outskirts of Hamhung, where it was stopped by a liaison officer from Corps headquarters. Miller was told to have the battalion turned around while he reported to the Corps headquarters for further instructions. The liaison officer had missed Faith, who had already passed Hamhung and was on his way to Pukchong.

While Miller went to the headquarters, Maj. Curtis reassembled the battalion in a nearby school yard. The soldiers took advantage of the break to wolf down C-rations. A broadcast from Tokyo announcing the 8th Army's offensive came over Capt. Ed Stamford's radio. "The word was that American divisions in Korea would be back in Japan by Christmas," Curtis recalled. Cheers erupted as the news quickly spread among the troops.

At X Corps headquarters, Miller met with Almond and Barr, who told him to immediately move the 1st Battalion to Chosin and to push up along the east side of the reservoir, where it would be attached to the 1st Marine Division for now. The generals instructed him to get up the road as far as possible that day. Because of the rush, the battalion was being sent without tanks, artillery, or antiaircraft vehicles. Those would come later, along with the rest of the task force.

Once Miller rejoined the battalion at the school yard, Curtis was sent ahead with guides to pick an assembly area for the night. At noon the 1st Battalion headed north on the road to Chosin.

With one infantry battalion on its way, Barr scrambled to assemble the rest of the regimental combat team, or RCT, to be sent to Chosin. An RCT was, in essence, a souped-up infantry regiment—three infantry battalions, plus artillery, engineering, and other supporting units that would allow the RCT to operate without division support.

In his usual rush, Almond wanted X Corps' attack to kick off from Chosin on the morning of November 27, even though MacArthur had given him discretion to attack when ready. Almond ordered Barr to have the entire RCT positioned east of the reservoir by noon, November 27.

Because Almond had insisted on racing to the Yalu, the 7th Division was hardly in a position to make this deadline. "It was scattered all over the place," recalled Paddock, the division operations officer.

Barr had wanted to concentrate his regiments before sending any force to Chosin, but Almond's demands made that impossible. "Corps insisted we get there as fast as we could, piecemeal or not," Paddock said. Barr could not assign the mission to one regiment, which would have been far preferable and in keeping with Army doctrine. The remaining two 32nd Regiment infantry battalions had reached Samsu, approaching the Manchurian border, and were too far away to join Faith's 1st Battalion at Chosin. The 17th Regiment remained at the Yalu and, likewise, was too distant. That left Maclean's 31st Regiment, whose units were scattered between the Fusen Reservoir and Pungsan, a long trip to Chosin but closer than the rest of the division.

At the 7th Division CP, Barr had a hurried conference with Maclean. The colonel was put in command of an ad hoc unit, including Faith's battalion from the 32nd Regiment and two infantry battalions from the 31st Regiment: Lt. Col. Bill Reilly's 3rd Battalion and Lt. Col. Richard Reidy's 2nd Battalion. Two batteries from the 57th Field Artillery Battalion would be sent, along with a third from the 31st Field Artillery Battalion. The 31st Tank Company, a 7th Division antiaircraft battery, and other supporting units were also attached. It was designated the 31st Regimental Combat Team, or more informally, Task Force Maclean.

Many of the units had never trained or fought together before. "It was a collection of strangers who happened to be closest and were grabbed out of the air by X Corps," Curtis later said.

Task Force Maclean was being sent to the Chosin Reservoir "poorly supplied, poorly organized, weak and under equipped," Paddock said.

La Feria, Texas, 1:00 p.m., Friday, November 24

When Helen Storms heard the reports that MacArthur had said the troops could be home by Christmas, she immediately went to the grocery store. "News is sounding so good, I'm going to bake a fruit cake for Christmas—as you may be home," she wrote to Harvey on Friday afternoon. She bought several pounds of paper shell pecans—Harvey's favorite snack—and put them away to save for him.

"I shouldn't let my hopes get the best of me—but oh, I just go wild thinking about you and that some miracle could take place and you could be here a month from now," she wrote. "Oh! What a dream! I'll really be satisfied if you get here before the baby comes."

Chinhung-ni, 6:00 a.m., Saturday, November 25

After eighteen hours on the road, Don Faith caught up with his battalion at midnight. He had driven all the way to Pukchong only to learn that his battalion had been turned around and was on its way to Chosin. He found them at Chinhung-ni, where Marine traffic control had stopped them for the night, at the foot of the long winding pass leading up to the plateau. The troops slept restlessly on rocky, snow-covered ground in the bitter cold. All night there was traffic heading north, carrying supplies for the Marines.

The Marine traffic control officer gave them permission to move out at first light. Just a few hours after arriving, Faith was back on the road, departing with Curtis for Chosin at 6:00 a.m. Miller followed a half hour later, leading the battalion. The road began to climb almost immediately, heading up toward the Funchilin Pass. What had been a two-lane road became a twisting one-lane trail—snow-covered, rough, with almost no vegetation.

The road twisted tortuously up, climbing 2,700 feet over eight miles along a path cut through rock. The road was bordered on one side by steep mountain slopes and, on the other, by a long, precipitous fall. "It was nothing but an oxcart road, really, and you started climbing pretty steeply," said Sgt. Charlie Gebhardt.

Even wearing all their warmest clothing, including their pile jackets, two pairs of socks, and wool scarves tied around their heads underneath their helmets, the men riding in the back of the trucks were freezing. Every time the trucks came to a stop, Lt. Mortrude insisted his platoon soldiers get out and stomp their feet to restore circulation, worried they would get frostbite.

They reached the most frightening stretch of the pass, with a cliff on one side and a terrifying chasm on the other. A concrete bridge crossed over four enormous steel pipes that carried water from the Chosin Reservoir to power stations in the valley below. It was an obvious choke point—if the bridge were blown, there would be no way back out.

Reaching the plateau, they felt even colder. Two miles in, they drove through the village of Koto-ri, held by a Marine battalion safeguarding the road. From there, the road continued on relatively flat ground, following the Changjin River valley another eleven miles to Hagaru-ri, near the southern tip of the Chosin Reservoir.

Hagaru—a shortened version of the village's name often used by the Americans—was now a bustling Marine base with a tent city. Though the village had been badly damaged by bombing, there were still some scattered concrete buildings and homes standing. South of town, the 1st Marine Engineer Battalion was hard at work building the airstrip, scraping the frozen ground with bulldozers.

The reservoir lay at an elevation of 3,870 feet in the midst of mountains, with high forested ridges along both the east and west sides rising 6,000 to 7,000 feet above sea level. Even though they were freezing, the men gawked at "the largest mountains most of us had ever seen," recalled Sgt. Clarence White of B Company—certainly bigger than any he had seen back home in South Carolina.

The Japanese had created the reservoir when they dammed the Changjin River in the late 1920s to create a hydroelectric plant. The flooding of the river valley and adjoining stream valleys created a vast, Y-shaped lake that stretched forty miles from south to north, with many appendages and coves. It was both beautiful and foreboding.

The road split in Hagaru, and Faith's party continued to the right and up the east side of the reservoir. The dirt road, mostly covered with snow, was hardly wide enough for two vehicles. Miller studied the rugged terrain carefully as they continued up the east side. The land rose sharply from the reservoir and was cut deeply by valleys carrying streams to the lake. The road twisted up, down, and around these hills and valleys, going around the wider inlets of frozen marshland but crossing several small streams on narrow wooden or concrete bridges.

A narrow-gauge railroad, built by the Japanese to support mining and lumber operations, ran up the east shore, sometimes running alongside the road and, elsewhere, veering off to more level ground along the edge of the reservoir and crossing streams on unfloored wooden trestles. Near the tiny village of Sasu-ri, there was a large sawmill, which a Marine engineering company had managed to get working.

They were heading for the 5th Marine command post when they ran into the regimental commander, Lt. Col. Raymond Murray, driving south. Murray, a veteran of Guadalcanal, Tarawa, and Saipan, was tall and rangy, with high cheekbones that gave him the appearance of a hawk. "His looks alone stamped him as a leader," Smith later said. Murray said he had been expecting Faith, but he then expressed amazement that a single Army battalion was supposed to relieve a Marine regiment more than four times its size. He assigned Faith to a nearby piece of high ground commanding the road, designated on the maps as Hill 1221 based on its height in meters. Murray said he had "no definite plans" yet for when the 5th Marines would pull out but asked Faith to report to his command post for a general orientation once his battalion had arrived.

The Marines and Army did not operate on the same radio frequency—a major headache—so communication would have to be in person or by messenger.

It was 3:00 p.m. before all the trucks of the slow-moving convoy arrived at Hill 1221. The battalion took position on the high ground above a hairpin curve, setting up a defensive position alongside the Marine units already there. As C Company took over some well-prepared positions on the ridgeline, Mortrude was briefed by a young Marine squad sergeant, who told him a Chinese reconnaissance patrol had attacked the previous night and tried unsuccessfully to drag a wounded Marine from his position. Faith sent patrols out to the east and northeast, but they found no sign of a Chinese force.

The 1st Battalion now had 715 GIs and about 300 ROKs, down from the 500 Koreans they had been assigned at Fuji. Some had been wounded or killed in action; others had deserted or been encouraged to leave. They had "been both culled and integrated by combat and the 'buddy system,'" said Mortrude. Some of the troops had become quite attached to their Korean buddies, and relations were "relatively cordial." Mortrude had picked the best trained ROK, Chung Yung Te, to be the Korean platoon sergeant. Despite all the language difficulties and cultural differences, Mortrude was glad to have the ROKs. After his platoon had been ambushed in Seoul, he had even recruited two Christian mission students who picked up weapons from fallen GIs and fought alongside the Americans. Mortrude persuaded Jones to let the two students join his platoon, and they accompanied the troops to Chosin.

Charlie Company was now under the command of Capt. Dale Seever, a 27-year-old Kansan who had taken over when Bob Jones was promoted to major and became the battalion adjutant. In Mortrude, Jones had one of the finest platoon leaders in the battalion, one in whom all the officers had great confidence. "He was a very fine young officer—the tower of strength type—highly respected by all," said Curtis.

Mortrude was pleased with the growing combat skills his platoon was showing. "Our fire discipline had greatly improved," he said. "Our soldiers held their fire on order, even at night." They had also become skilled at using suppressive fire while advancing to overrun enemy positions. But one continuing concern for Mortrude was night security. Too many times, he still found soldiers who were supposed to be on watch asleep in their foxholes, especially between 2:00 a.m. and 4:00 a.m. Mortrude had made it a point to always walk the defensive line during that time. He was satisfied when one of his sergeants told him that the "troops were more concerned with me than the enemy catching them asleep."

As soon as the 1st Battalion arrived, Faith; Curtis; Maj. Wayne Powell, the battalion's intelligence officer; and Capt. Erwin Bigger, the heavy weapons company commander, drove to Murray's command post. Murray and his staff briefed them on what patrols had found and what they knew about the area. "Little was known of the enemy situation or plan for future operations," Curtis recalled. A Marine patrol that morning had encountered several small groups of Chinese soldiers but found no sign of a large-scale enemy presence. One of Murray's battalion commanders, Lt. Col. Robert Taplett, had made a reconnaissance by helicopter over the area that day and seen no sign of significant Chinese activity. Murray told Faith that he would be going to a meeting at the 1st Marine Division headquarters the next morning and would get more information for the Army officers. Faith's group continued another four miles up the road to the northernmost Marine position, held by Taplett's 3rd Battalion. They made a reconnaissance of the area and then returned to the 1st Battalion headquarters before dark.

It was a quiet night on Hill 1221. As usual, Mortrude scheduled himself for the 2:00 a.m. "witching hour" shift. He checked the platoon area and was infuriated to find only one man awake. Mortrude awakened the platoon sergeant and ordered him to organize walking patrols for the rest of the night. "If we couldn't manage security from the foxholes, then we would do it the hard, uncomfortable way, above ground," Mortrude recalled. "I was insistent one way or another that we have effective night security."

8th Army Front, Saturday Evening, November 25

The 8th Army offensive had made good progress over two days, advancing north from its positions along the Chongchon River, fifty miles north of Pyongyang. But at 8:00 p.m. on Saturday evening, Peng unleashed the 13th Army Group offensive along the 8th Army front, catching the UN force by surprise. Receiving reports at his headquarters, General Walker found it difficult to gauge the extent of the Chinese attacks.

Two infantry battalions from Maclean's 31st Regiment scrambled all day, but by nightfall on November 25, both were still a long way from Chosin. Maj. Hugh Robbins led the regimental quartering party, which had moved south all day across snow-covered trails before stopping for the night at the 7th Division rear command post at Pukchong. Maclean—Colonel Mac, as the men called him—met the quartering party at the CP and briefed them on their mission.

Maclean and several staff officers left early the next morning for the day-long journey to Chosin, followed soon by Robbins and the quartering party. But moving entire infantry battalions was a much more cumbersome affair. Some troops rode in open rail cars from Pukchong to Hamhung, a particularly freezing way to travel. From there, they were loaded onto trucks, which were scarcely warmer, particularly once they started the climb to Chosin.

Intelligence was all over the place. As of November 26, the 1st Marine Division intelligence section reported the Chinese force around Chosin had no offensive capability and was capable of conducting "no more than a delaying action against our advance." In Tokyo Willoughby estimated there could be between nine to twelve Chinese divisions in North Korea, but he suggested November 25 that they were withdrawing. When Ruffner, Almond's chief of staff, expressed concern about intelligence maps showing multiple Chinese divisions in the X Corps zone, Willougby assured him the units "were symbolic with token strength." MacArthur remained convinced the Chinese would not intervene on a major scale. "If he did not want to believe something, he wouldn't," Matt Ridgway later said. Almond likewise thought there were no more than one or two Chinese divisions in X Corps' area.

But there were some troubling episodes and bits of intelligence around Chosin. Around 1:30 a.m. on November 26, a group of civilians from the village of Sinhung-ni, east of Chosin, came to a 5th Marines outpost and reported that a dozen Chinese soldiers had killed some villagers. The next morning a patrol went to the village and verified the killings, but they found no Chinese. Air observers that day reported to Marine headquarters that there were "numerous signs of enemy activity all through the area immediately north and east of CHOSIN Reservoir."

It was becoming apparent to O. P. Smith that the Chinese soldiers around Chosin came from different divisions than the ones encountered earlier in the month, but it was difficult to get a complete picture. "The Chinese in front of us are like the will o' the wisp," he wrote to his wife, Esther. "They appear in small groups and retire as soon as we fire on them."

Maj. Powell, Faith's intelligence officer, working with Korean interpreters, questioned families and other small groups of civilians coming from the north. "They said the Chinese intended to take back the reservoir in the near future," Capt. Stamford recalled. It was hard to believe, given the lack of large-scale enemy activity, he added. "Everyone more or less pooh poohed the idea," said Stamford. "They couldn't take it from us."

On November 26, on the reservoir's west side at Yudam-ni, the Marines captured three soldiers from the CCF 60th Division, who described in remarkable detail the 20th Army's plans for drawing in UN forces at Chosin, waiting for two regiments to pass north of the Chinese force and then cutting off and destroying them. But the Marines were skeptical that privates would have such detailed information, and they suspected the soldiers may have been planted by the enemy to deliver misinformation. The information was sent to X Corps but apparently not passed on to Task Force Maclean.

Hill 1221, Sunday, November 26

The weather was clear and cold Sunday morning. The men of Faith's 1st Battalion spent the morning caring for equipment, building shelters, and replenishing their rations and fuel from the 5th Marine Regiment supply depot.

At 11:30 a.m., Brig. Gen. Henry Hodes, 51, the assistant 7th Division commander, arrived by jeep at the hut on Hill 1221 serving as Faith's command post. Barr had sent Hodes to serve as his eyes and ears and to assist the task force. The West Point graduate was a seasoned combat commander who had led the 112th Infantry Regiment through France before being wounded.

Barr thought highly of Hodes, though his subordinate did not return the respect. Hodes privately called Barr an "old woman" who should not be commanding an Army division, according to Maj. Ray Lynch, an operations officer who accompanied Hodes to Chosin. Hodes "did the generaling" in the 7th Division, Barr's aide, Charles Davis, later said. Hammering Hank, as he was known, was a notably gruff and taciturn officer. "General Hodes was not given to a show of emotion," recalled Lynch. "He would grumble every now and then, but said little."

Hodes told Faith that the 3rd Battalion, 31st Infantry; the 57th Field Artillery Battalion; and the 31st Regiment's Heavy Mortar Company were on their way to Chosin. Maclean and his staff would be arriving soon, followed by the regiment's Intelligence and Reconnaissance (I&R) Platoon and detachments of medical and communications personnel. The 31st Tank Company was also en route, but its arrival time was unknown because of the road conditions and the weather. Once Maclean arrived, he would take command of the composite task force and Faith's battalion would be released from Marine control.

Hodes had little other information, telling Faith the overall situation in the X Corps area was "vague" and that the 7th Division's mission was uncertain pending clarification of what was going on with the 8th Army's fight to the west. Faith suggested to Hodes that if the Marines were able to provide a tank platoon and artillery support, his battalion would be ready to attack to the north before the rest of the task force arrived. Hodes wisely rejected the plan.

Shortly afterward, the general left for Hagaru in his jeep while Faith, accompanied by Curtis, Powell, and his company and platoon leaders, headed north to make a detailed reconnaissance of the forward Marine battalion area. Faith clearly had not given up on moving to the location, believing "it would be a good defensible position plus a good place to jump off from," recalled Gebhardt, a battalion intelligence specialist who went on the reconnaissance. They returned to their command post before dark. It was another cold night, with temperatures dropping to twenty-five below zero in the area.

At X Corps headquarters in Hungnam, Almond received word that the 8th Army had been attacked by a large Chinese force and that the right flank manned by the ROK II Corps was in danger. Almond sent the information to Smith at the 1st Marine Division. But once again, the news was not passed on to Task Force Maclean.

Hill 1221, Sunday Evening, November 26

At 6:00 p.m., a messenger sent by Murray arrived by jeep at Faith's command post with word that the 5th Marines would be pulling out early the next morning to join the 7th Marine Regiment at Yudam-ni. Faith's battalion, which was directed to remain in place to protect the Marines' right flank, would be the only force on the east side of Chosin until the rest of the Army task force arrived. Since Faith was still under the 1st Marine Division's control, he called Murray to ask if he had any additional instructions for the battalion. Murray replied that he did not but suggested Faith go no farther north without orders from the 7th Division.

Maclean arrived with several staff officers around 7:00 p.m., after a long journey from Pukchong. It was a reunion of sorts, as Maclean had commanded the 32nd Regiment when it was reconstituted in Japan in 1949. There was "much mutual respect and admiration" between the colonel and the officers who had been with him, Bob Jones recalled. Maclean had been particularly fond of Faith, with whom he had worked closely in building the 32nd into a cohesive unit. "There was a warm and affectionate relationship between Maclean and Faith, and after a year of such close relationship they knew each other's minds and thought much alike," Bob Jones observed. "So there was no 'breaking in' period required when these two met again in the Chosin Reservoir." Curtis, who was not one of the old gang from Japan and had never met Maclean before, was not comforted by the similarities between the two, observing that Maclean and Faith "complimented each other in brashness."

Maclean reported that the 3rd Battalion and 57th Field Artillery were expected to arrive by the end of the following day. In keeping with Almond's instructions, Maclean said he planned to attack north as soon as the rest of the task force closed in the area. Given that the Marines would be abandoning their forward positions in the morning, Faith recommended to Maclean that his battalion move forward the next day to the site, which he described as "an excellent position." Maclean approved the plan. He was eager to have the task force in position to launch the attack. The battalion staff immediately began to coordinate the move with the 5th Marine Regiment.

It was a fateful decision. Curtis considered the move reckless. Hill 1221 was the key strategic point on the east side of the reservoir, with a commanding view of the road. The hairpin curve on its east side was a perfect site for a roadblock. It was the best defensive ground in the area, and it seemed risky to Curtis to leave it before most of the task force had arrived, including the tanks, the artillery, and the antiaircraft weapons. "Maclean should have assembled his command on the high ground at the hairpin curve before moving any further north," Curtis later said. It was not hindsight, he added. "I could not even attract Faith's attention with suggestions of caution."

Maclean established his command post in a schoolhouse in the tiny village of Hudong-ni, about one mile south of Hill 1221. More of the task force leadership arrived during the evening, including the quartering party led by Hugh Robbins. At 8:30 p.m., Lt. Col. Ray Embree, commander of the 57th Field Artillery, arrived and reported to Maclean that the remainder of the task force, including Embree's artillery battalion and the two additional infantry battalions, was on the move and expected to arrive before dark the next day.

But that was not entirely correct. Unknown to Maclean and the other officers at Chosin, one of the infantry battalions—Reidy's 2nd Battalion—had not even begun the journey. Maclean had been told by X Corps staff that morning that the 2nd Battalion would follow the 3rd Battalion closely. But the 2nd Battalion was scattered southeast of Pungsan on antiguerilla operations and still needed to be assembled. It did not even receive its orders to Chosin until the next day, November 27.

Monday Morning, November 27

The 5th Marines began moving out from the forward perimeter at first light. The snow was worn off the road by the heavy traffic, and before long, trucks were kicking up clouds of dust.

Taplett's 3rd Battalion was not waiting for the Army to take over the northernmost positions before pulling out. It was "a very sorry 'relief in place,'" Curtis later said. "They were gone by the time we got there!" The 5th Marines had no time for pleasantries—they were to pass through the 7th Marines as soon as they arrived at Yudam-ni and immediately go on the attack.

Maclean was equally eager to get moving. Joined by Faith and Robbins, he made a reconnaissance of the northernmost positions vacated by the Marines. They spotted the bodies of two Chinese soldiers who had been shot in front of a Marine outpost two nights earlier, but they saw "nothing in particular to arouse any suspicion" of a large Chinese force in the area, Robbins recalled.

Maclean gave the go-ahead for Faith to move up the 1st Battalion. "[Maclean] was not anxious but merely eager to get into our zone so a rapid move to the north could begin with least possible delay," Robbins recalled. Maclean made it clear that the task force would not attack until all the battalions had arrived, including Reidy's 2nd Battalion.

Maclean may have been feeling pressure from Almond to advance rapidly. According to Embree, the X Corps commander spoke to Maclean sometime on November 27, likely when Almond came through Hagaru on his way to view the Marine attack from Yudam-ni. "The key to what happened to the 31st

Regimental Combat team is the briefing and verbal instructions that General Almond gave to Col Maclean," Embree recalled years later. But exactly what Almond told Maclean is a mystery. "Tho Col Maclean and I enjoyed a very close personal and working relationship, he told me he could not reveal the contents of the discussion with General Almond," Embree said.

Faith's 1st Battalion began moving north to the forward perimeter at 1:00 p.m., with trucks shuttling back and forth, carrying troops and equipment. Because the battalion was short on trucks, a platoon of six Army two-and-a-half-ton trucks from the 515th Truck Transportation Company had been assigned to accompany the battalion on the attack north. Like many Army transportation units at that time, the soldiers in the 515th were all Black, except for the platoon commander. Ironically, given that one-third of the 7th Division was now made up of South Koreans, the division had no Black soldiers. Truman's 1948 order desegregating the Army was being slowly implemented, and the 7th Division had not yet been integrated. But everyone that truck driver Sgt. Joe Ager encountered seemed glad to have the additional hands and equipment. "They deployed us like we were part of them," Ager recalled. "We were all in a tight situation, unfamiliar territory, so we were nice to one another."

The Marines left well-situated defensive fortifications positioned on both sides of the road that was spread over two miles on a horseshoe-shaped range of hills. But it was more ground than Faith's battalion could cover—the Marine battalions at Chosin had about 30 percent greater strength than the Army battalions.

Captain Ed Scullion's Able Company was placed on the forward slope of high ground to the left side of the road, while Seever's Charlie Company took the forward slope of high ground on the right side of the road. They held commanding positions over the road, but there was a gap between the two companies where it passed through on a saddle. Baker Company, under Captain Wallace Turner, carried the perimeter south from C Company's right flank. Many of the Marine foxholes were left empty because the Army battalion lacked manpower and weaponry, leaving some gaps in the line, with one particular weak point existing on the boundary between C and B companies. Faith's CP was located in a house in a ravine behind the C Company line. Capt. Bigger's D Company (heavy weapons) was across the road, on the west side, with its 81 mm mortars covering the open rear of the horseshoe along with the headquarters company. Overall, Faith and his commanders were satisfied. "The battalion was thinly spread, but the position had excellent control of the ground and the key road to the north," said Miller.

9th Army Group Headquarters, November 27

Song Shilun was optimistic. All the 9th Army Group forces had reached their designated positions, and it was clear the Americans had no inkling of the scale of the Chinese infiltration around Chosin. The four divisions of the 27th Army were positioned north and east of the reservoir and had completed attack preparations. The 20th Army's four divisions were west and south of Yudam-ni. The 26th Army was positioned as a reserve farther north. Song had issued orders to attack on all fronts around the reservoir that night.

Song had made good use of surprise, mobile operations, and night attack during the Chinese Civil War to destroy Nationalist units, and he intended to do the same with the Americans at Chosin. The tried and true Red Army practice was to surround the enemy and cut off their route of supply and retreat. One force would make a frontal assault while another went around a flank to cut the exit from behind.

But there were surprises in store for Song as well. The Chinese were expecting to meet one Marine regiment at Yudam-ni, not two. The Chinese believed the 5th Marine Regiment was either at Hagaru or divided between Hagaru and the east side of the Chosin Reservoir. Chinese intelligence had not yet picked up the fact that an Army task force had relieved the 5th Marines, freeing them to join the 7th Marines. Song had allotted enough force that he felt sure could destroy a single regiment at Yudam-ni. The 79th Division would attack from the north, the 59th Division would cut off the road to the south, and portions of the 89th Division would block the Marine attack to the west. Likewise, Song was confident he had allocated enough force to destroy the Marine base at Hagaru. The 58th Division would attack from the southwest, while the 60th Division cut the road leading south to Koto-ri.

The 80th Division, reinforced by one regiment from the 81st Division, was to annihilate any forces on the east side of the reservoir, and if successful, join the attack on Hagaru. The main force of the 81st Division was to move down the western side of the Fusen Reservoir, with the goal of cutting off contact across the mountains between the 1st Marine Division and the 7th Division. The Chinese believed the U.S. Army 31st Regiment was still in the vicinity of the Fusen Reservoir. If the attacks around Chosin succeeded, they would destroy the 31st Regiment at Fusen. The last-minute movement of Task Force Maclean would throw a kink in those plans.

"American troops are nothing extraordinary," Song told his commanders. "They depend on two things: airplanes and artilleries. But we have two better things: attack and defense. We will defeat them as long as we are perfect at our things."

The Marine attack west launched from Yudam-ni that morning did not make it far before running into roadblocks and stiff Chinese resistance. But there was no inkling yet at the 1st Marine Division headquarters about how precarious the situation was.

More ominous was an urgent message sent by Gen. Johnnie Walker to the Dai Ichi in Tokyo around noon, which reported that 8th Army troops to the west were retreating in the face of a full-scale offensive by 200,000 Chinese. The right flank held by the ROK II Corps had collapsed, endangering the entire 8th Army. Almond received word of this in the evening but did not alter his plans.

Given the Chinese actions, Barr called Almond and told him he was going to withdraw his forces back from the Yalu River, but the X Corps commander insisted he stay and rout out any remaining North Korean forces. "You're going to stay up there until you get it cleaned out, and you had better turn to and do it," Almond snapped.

More elements of Task Force Maclean began arriving at Chosin during the afternoon. Trucks carrying Reilly's 3rd Battalion, 31st Infantry, came up the eastern side of the road in the afternoon as the Marine convoys continued pulling out.

There was some friendly bantering back and forth as truckloads of Marines jolted past the arriving Army troops. "We were calling them doggies, and they were calling us jarheads," recalled PFC Warren Wiedhahn, a mortarman with the Marine 2nd Battalion. The Marines joked that they were going home because "the Army occupation troops had arrived," said Lt Gray. It was easy to spot the Marines, with the camouflage cover on their helmets and their canvas leggings, and their uniforms were a much lighter shade than the dark green worn by the Army.

Cpl. Jerry Francois managed to climb into the back of a Marine five-ton truck and swipe twenty-nine cases of rations. "I was observed by Col. Reilly, who informed us that we were stealing government property," Francois recalled. "I told him we weren't stealing government property, we were just stealing from the Marine Corps." They kept the food.

Reilly was well liked and respected by his troops and fellow officers alike. "I don't know of a man in the 3rd Battalion that wouldn't follow Col. Reilly any place he went," Francois later said. Reilly, a Vermonter and 1939 West Point graduate, had been captured by the Germans during fighting in the Ardennes in December 1944. He escaped from a POW camp several months later and reached Allied lines. Reilly was a bit aloof but considerate of his men, as well as a cool head in tight situations. "He had nerves of steel," said Francois.

The Polar Bears had been on the road virtually nonstop for two days and were arriving frozen, hungry, and exhausted. The Marine convoys had been given priority, so it had been a long, cold trip, driving at a snail's pace, with stops for short cat naps and to eat cold C rations. Much of the drive up to the plateau had been at night. Capt. George Rasula, riding shotgun in a jeep, spent his time nervously making sure his driver did not fall asleep on the treacherous road.

Maclean had the 3rd Battalion set up on the south side of a large inlet where the Pungnyuri River flowed into the reservoir, about four miles south of Faith's battalion. It was on low ground, bordered on the north by the frozen inlet and on three sides by high ground and ridges, including a hill that dominated the site, marked Hill 1456. The narrow-gauge railroad ran along the reservoir shore until reaching the inlet. There it followed the undulating southern bank of the inlet, mostly along an embankment that offered some protection from an attack over the ice. At other times, the line ran through cuts in the terrain that allowed the tracks to stay on level ground. While it was virtually impossible to find any site at Chosin that did not have some high terrain around it, the Pungnyuri inlet was a particularly bad location. "It's a nice area, but it's not too defensible," Faith remarked.

Maclean likely picked the site because it was closer to Faith's battalion than Hill 1221, and its relative flatness could make it a good staging area for the attack north planned for the morning. He was expecting that the 3rd Battalion would only be there for the night. Maclean was still hoping the 2nd

Battalion would arrive that evening, and he was perhaps planning to place it at the abandoned positions on Hill 1221.

Lead elements of the 57th Field Artillery reached Hagaru by midday, but the battalion was held up for hours there, waiting for the departing 5th Marines to clear the road junction leading to Hudong-ni. The artillery arrived in the inlet through the afternoon, with A Battery in the lead and B Battery making it late in the day. The battalion was not at full strength, with only two of its three firing batteries. A separate battery of 155 mm howitzers that was supposed to be sent was scrubbed because of traffic delays on the road.

After reconnoitering the area, Maclean and Embree, the 57th commander, placed the two firing batteries in the inlet near the 3rd Battalion. Each battery had six 105 mm howitzers, which could fire far enough to also support Faith's battalion four miles to the north. The 31st Heavy Mortar Company, equipped with 4.2-inch mortars, set up midway between the two infantry battalions, positioned to provide fire support in both directions.

Key additional firepower arrived late afternoon in the form of one platoon from D Battery, 15th Antiaircraft Artillery Automatic Weapons Battalion, under the command of Capt. James McClymont. While the task force faced little aerial threat, the self-propelled antiaircraft weapons could do much damage to enemy ground forces. The platoon had four M19 tracked vehicles, known as Twin 40s, each mounted with two 40 mm Bofors antiaircraft guns. It also included four M16 half-tracks, known as Quad-50s, each carrying four 50-caliber machine guns that enabled it to fire 1,800 rounds a minute. The platoon set up in a small cove near the 57th Field Artillery headquarters, about a mile south of the inlet where the 3rd Battalion and 57th Field Artillery firing batteries were located.

Hudong-ni, Monday Afternoon, November 27

Back at the regimental CP, Maclean grew concerned about several reports of Chinese troops to the north and east of his task force. The Marines had passed along intelligence reports from civilians about several hundred Chinese soldiers in the village of Pungnyuri, which lay upriver from the inlet where the 3rd Battalion was positioned. Moreover, a patrol dispatched by Faith the previous evening reported seeing 200 enemy soldiers in a valley to the northeast of Hill 1221. Maclean also had the reports Maj. Powell had gathered from refugees about Chinese troops in the hills who planned to recapture the reservoir.

When the 31st Regiment Intelligence and Reconnaissance Platoon arrived at the regimental command post at Hudong-ni in the afternoon, Maclean directed the platoon leader, Lt. Richard B. Coke Jr., to take his unit on the trail up the Pungnyuri valley to locate any enemy presence. Beyond the village of Pungnyuri, the trail led in the direction of the Fusen Reservoir, an area Maclean remained concerned about following the 3rd Battalion's fight with a Chinese battalion three weeks earlier. Gen. Hodes, also at the CP, wanted Coke to determine whether the trail might provide an alternate route to Fusen, which, by air, was only 25 miles from Chosin but, by the circuitous land route via Hamhung, was 140 miles.

Coke, a paratrooper from San Antonio, Texas, was "the sharpest soldier I'd ever met," said a sergeant who served under him. The I&R Platoon, which included 42 GIs, had 4 seasoned NCOs who had been with the unit since the days when the 31st Regiment had patrolled the 38th parallel in Korea as part of the post–World War II occupation force. They also had 10 of the best ROK soldiers in the battalion, along with Cpl. Roy Shiraga, a Japanese-American from Spokane, Washington, who had been assigned to the I&R platoon to help communicate with some of the ROKs who spoke Japanese.

The platoon, equipped with two 60 mm light mortars and six jeeps mounted with 50-caliber machine guns, took off up the trail. It was soon out of radio contact with the regiment. That was not considered unusual, given the rough terrain and poor radio equipment.

Convoys carrying Reilly's 3rd Battalion and Embree's 57th Field Artillery rolled in all afternoon. Darkness was falling by the time many of the units arrived at the Pungnyuri inlet. The late arrival meant much of the setup had to be done in the dark, including preparing defensive lines, setting up switchboards for the artillery, and erecting tents.

Reilly and his staff were told by the departing Marines that their patrols had identified a battalion-sized enemy force five miles north on the reservoir's east shore—but that the force was moving north on a delaying action and not a serious threat. Reilly hurried to set up a perimeter and position his automatic weapons. He sent out local reconnaissance patrols and established outposts.

Organization of the defense was complicated by the fact that it was done in the dark, without a chance to reconnoiter the ground, Reilly later said.

Capt. William Etchemendy's L Company, assigned the northern perimeter, crossed a concrete bridge over the inlet, and took position on a ridge rising north from the river. Etchemendy, 39, a hardened combat veteran from Nevada, had been a platoon leader in Normandy, the Ardennes, and Hurtgen Forest and had been wounded twice in battle. Given the concerns about the possible Chinese presence up the Pungnyuri, Etchemendy established an outpost on high ground overlooking the valley, manned by SFC Willard "Bill" Donovan's weapons platoon, including a mortar section and recoilless rifle.

Capt. Auburn Marr's Item Company and Capt. Robert Kitz's King Company were positioned on the south side of the river, facing northeast on a ridge that rose rapidly south from the valley until it joined Hill 1456. K Company was tied into L Company on low ground near the bridge, while I Company continued the perimeter up the ridge. But the 3rd Battalion lacked the manpower to continue the perimeter line all the way to the summit of Hill 1456, leaving I Company's right flank exposed to unoccupied higher ground.

To guard against approaches from that high ground, Capt. Jordan's M Company (heavy weapons) set up blocking positions facing southeast and south. The men in Lt. Gray's mortar platoon grumbled at all the work involved—digging emplacement for the mortars in the frozen ground, setting up the mortars and aiming stakes, registering fire on critical approaches, and digging foxholes. It seemed like a lot of work for nothing, as they would be abandoning the position in the morning. But Gray and his platoon sergeant insisted it be done.

In midafternoon, Capt. Robert Drake's 31st Regiment Tank Company arrived at Hudong-ni after a long trip with twenty Sherman tanks crawling up the mountain road. Drake, a West Point graduate and combat veteran who had seen action in Europe, wanted instructions on where to position his tanks. Maclean was not at the headquarters, so Drake left the tanks at Hudong-ni to refuel and continued north by jeep to look for the task force commander. He could not locate Maclean but found Faith at his CP. The battalion commander directed him to keep the tanks at Hudong-ni for now, as it was getting late. "Faith told me to move my company north on the following morning as he did not think it was safe to move at night," Drake recalled.

When Drake asked about the enemy situation, Faith said they had only "vague" information about Chinese in the area. "He said the Marine units which his battalion had replaced had reported very little activity," Drake said. Faith was confident his position was solid.

Drake drove back to rejoin his tanks at Hudong-ni. Along the way, Drake's Korean interpreter reported that his radio had intercepted a weak signal. They were speaking Chinese.

At the 1st Battalion's forward position, troops spent the day digging in and registering fire from the artillery batteries and mortar company. The infantry companies set up outposts and trip flares in front of their lines to provide early warning of enemy action.

Roy Oxenrider and Joung He Su were determined to improve their position on the A Company line—no easy task. "Our foxhole was only about 18 inches deep, so we pushed the snow back and started digging," Oxenrider recalled. "The ground was frozen hard as a rock for about two feet." They kept at it for hours until finally satisfied, settling into their foxhole to await the evening.

Late in the afternoon, Faith met with his company commanders to review plans for the attack. The 1st Battalion was to move out at dawn and seize the road junction at Kalchon-ni at the north end of the reservoir. Reilly's 3rd Battalion would then pass through the 1st Battalion lines and move north, while the 1st Battalion would send patrols to the north and be ready to assist.

Faith placed Capt. Stamford's five-man Tactical Air Control Party (TACP) with Scullion's Able Company so it could run air support from Marine Corps fighters and bombers for the attack the next morning. Stamford had been a dive bomber pilot in the South Pacific during World War II. The stocky, barrel-chested Marine was much admired by the battalion's officers as a cool and tough operator. He had bonded with Faith, who gained a fast appreciation of the firepower Stamford could quickly and accurately bring to bear on behalf of the battalion.

Shortly before dark, in the battalion operations tent, Sgt. Piercefield received a report from an aerial reconnaissance plane that a battalion or more of enemy troops had been spotted on the road heading south toward the 1st Battalion position. Faith sent a small long-distance reconnaissance patrol to head up the road to Kalchon-ni to look for any Chinese troops.

By early evening, the 2nd Battalion had still not arrived. Maclean was growing concerned, and he was rethinking plans for the morning attack. After conferring with Hodes over dinner, the colonel scrubbed his plan to stay the night at the regimental headquarters. Instead, he departed Hudong-ni to visit the battalions and stay the night at a forward regimental command post Major Robbins had set up about a mile south of Faith's battalion. Likely, he wanted to speak to the battalion commanders in person rather than rely on radio communication, which was spotty at best.

When Maclean arrived at the 3rd Battalion headquarters in the inlet at 7:30 p.m., Reilly reported they would be ready in the morning to pass through Faith's battalion and attack north. But Maclean decided against moving forward without the 2nd Battalion in position to follow. He told Reilly that the 3rd Battalion's attack was being delayed twenty-four hours and was only to be launched upon his order.

Maclean had not heard anything back yet from the I&R Platoon, which was another worry. Possibly this was because of the poor radio communication, or possibly it was something else. Maclean directed Reilly to send a strong patrol up the Pungnyuri trail in the morning, accompanied by some of Drake's tanks.

Maclean continued north in his jeep to Faith's 1st Battalion at the forward perimeter. The colonel still planned to have the 1st Battalion move forward to the northern end of the Chosin Reservoir. Seizing the road junction at Kalchon-ni in the morning would set the stage the following day for the rest of the task force to pass through Faith's battalion and attack north toward the Manchurian border.

After receiving a copy of the attack order at 8:30 p.m., Faith summoned his company commanders to his CP, with instructions to bring along their mail orderlies. Bob Jones had just arrived at the forward perimeter, having hitched a ride in a two-and-a-half-ton truck carrying two weeks' worth of mail, including some early Christmas presents and cookies. He was greeted like Santa Claus. Jones had been at the Yalu River with an advance party when the battalion was rerouted to Chosin, and it had taken him three days to catch up.

After Faith issued the attack order, everyone took a few minutes to relax around the CP stove and open letters and packages from home. Then, accompanied by their orderlies heavily laden with mail, the commanders headed back into the cold, bringing the attack order to their respective companies. The patrol that had been sent north to Kalchon-ni had not yet returned.

A bitter, ceaseless wind from the north was blowing off the ice. The Chosin Reservoir was largely frozen solid, with ice easily thick enough to support troops and even jeeps. Temperatures sank rapidly with the darkness, on their way to twenty below zero. The Kaema Plateau was the coldest place in Korea, cut off by mountains from warmer sea air but open to the north, exposed to the Siberian winds blowing from Manchuria. It was just their luck—the GIs, the ROKs, the Chinese soldiers—that the winter of 1950 was the coldest in the highland in a half century.

A bright gibbous moon rose around 6:00 p.m., but before long, it clouded over. "It was beginning to snow, slowly at first, and then it got serious and got colder, so cold that you could not stay warm in a mountain sleeping bag, which was the warmest piece of equipment we owned," recalled Sgt. Clarence White of B Company. The older NCOs told the soldiers to change their socks periodically and keep the extra pair inside their shirt to keep them from freezing. "It was too cold to remove anything, too cold to do anything," White said.

"There was some hopeful discussion of a hot meal . . . but nothing materialized," recalled Lt. Mortrude. It was C-rations again for dinner. Along the C Company line, Mortrude directed each of his squads to build a warming fire in empty foxholes where the men could rotate in to warm up. But he soon got calls from company and battalion headquarters ordering him to extinguish the fires—they were nervous the glow could be spotted by the enemy.

Across the reservoir at Yudam-ni, each Marine company had warming tents with diesel stoves, where Marines could rotate through to warm up and dry their clothing and maybe get a cup of hot coffee or soup. "We didn't have any of that," said Jones. Supply trucks carrying that equipment for the Army task force had not yet arrived, another casualty of the rush.

All Mortrude could do was periodically walk the platoon line to make sure the men were alert and not letting their feet freeze in their foxholes. "In some cases we would order seemingly benumbed troops out of their holes to move around with us to restore circulation," Mortrude recalled.

On the A Company line on the left flank, alert orders had been issued to the platoons, requiring one man in each foxhole to be awake. "We settled in for the night, tired, cold, hungry," recalled Sgt. Willis Via.

The 1st Battalion, having arrived at Chosin two days ahead of most of the task force, was in decidedly better readiness than the units still settling in at the inlet. "By nightfall the battalion was as ready as it ever would be for any attack," said Miller.

Pungnyuri Inlet, Monday Evening, November 27

Four miles south, the 3rd Battalion defensive perimeter at the Pungnyuri inlet did not look very strong to Lt. Gray, dominated as it was by the high ground around it. "I felt uneasy about our vulnerability in what was a forbidding, frozen mountain wilderness," Gray recalled.

It was dark by the time Cpl. Francois helped lay telephone wire across the river to the L Company outpost manned by Sgt. Donovan's platoon, two hundred yards up the trail leading to the village of Pungnyuri. Everyone was working on adrenaline. "Two days of no sleep, most of us," Francois said.

It was a particularly vulnerable moment, with units still arriving and not yet in high readiness. Almond's rush to Chosin had enabled Smith to consolidate his two forward Marine regiments at Yudam-ni, but it had come at considerable cost to Task Force Maclean.

Smith acknowledged as much. "These units had been moved north in great haste and piecemeal," he wrote in his journal. "In their hurried movement they had brought little tentage and few stoves with them. Moreover, many of the men were not properly outfitted with cold weather clothing and equipment." One of the Army battalion commanders asked at Hagaru if the Marines had parkas his men could use, but there were no extras to spare for "these poor devils," Smith said.

Task Force Maclean had roughly 3,100 soldiers, including about 2,500 GIs and 600 ROKs, with units spread over ten miles at seven different locations along the road, strung along from the forward perimeter occupied by Faith's 1st Battalion, 32nd Infantry, to the 31st Regiment headquarters at Hudong-ni—all largely in positions where they would be unable to support each other. "One more day in the reservoir area would have seen us in much better posture defensively," said Capt. Bob Drake, the 31st Tank Company commander. "The day we never got."

Francois's team finished laying wire to the outpost around 8:00 p.m. and hurried back inside the inlet perimeter. Francois had never seen the 3rd Battalion this quiet. "Everybody was really tense," he said. "Like there was something wrong that was going on, but they couldn't pinpoint it."

Part II

The Battle of Chosin Reservoir

Chapter 6

THE FIRST NIGHT

Monday–Tuesday, November 27–28

With darkness approaching, Lieutenant Richard Coke halted the Intelligence and Reconnaissance Platoon for the night several miles up the Pungnyuri trail at a cluster of huts marked on the map as the village of Kanunmul. It was a good defensible site at the base of a steep hill overlooking the trail and the narrow-gauge railroad running parallel to it.

Coke had already left his 3rd Squad with a dozen men under SFC Sam Muncy about two miles beyond the 3rd Battalion position at the inlet. They were to serve as quick-reaction reinforcements in case the other two squads ran into trouble, or as a fallback position if the platoon needed to make a hasty retreat. Muncy's squad could also relay emergency requests for fire support to the 31st Heavy Mortar Company, assuming the radios worked.

At Kanunmul, 1st Sgt. Paul Embry, a veteran platoon sergeant, worked with SFC John Q. Adams, the 1st Squad leader, and SFC Richard Cooper, the 2nd Squad leader, to pick sites fifty yards apart for the two squads. The men established a half-dozen machine gun positions commanding both the trail and a cut through which the narrow-gauge railroad track passed.

The troops broke several entrenching tools digging foxholes in the frozen ground and were exhausted by the time they finished. After everything was set up, those not on watch crawled into sleeping bags. Cooper and one of his soldiers, Cpl. Jim Arie, set up their bags inside a hut near one of the 2nd Squad's machine gun positions and fell into a deep sleep.

At about 6:00 p.m., well past dark, a lone American jeep pulled into the platoon perimeter. It was carrying mail that had arrived by truck earlier in the evening. Since it was the first mail from home in weeks, someone at the regimental headquarters at Hudong-ni must have decided it would be a morale booster to send a jeep to deliver the platoon's mail. The driver had no problem finding the platoon, following the only trail leading up the Pungnyuri.

The driver emerged from the jeep and was immediately cut down by a spray of gunfire from outside the perimeter. The night exploded with the sounds of gunfire, bugles, and yelling. "We got up and started shooting," recalled Arie. "I didn't see anybody, I shot at flashes."

Trip flares lit up the night. Adams could see a column of Chinese troops moving through the railroad cut, five abreast. The platoon's machine guns opened up and took a heavy toll on the Chinese. But more troops kept coming through, fanning out around the perimeter. Cpl. Donald Trudeau was firing his Browning automatic (BAR) rifle so fiercely that the barrel was glowing red. Then his position was overrun. Trudeau's firing stopped.

Adams dashed to the platoon command post but found that Coke and Embry had already headed out to reconnoiter the situation. Back outside, he saw them about fifty yards south of the perimeter, moving back toward the platoon, but they were cut off by advancing Chinese troops. Embry was killed by enemy fire while Coke was shot and taken prisoner. Rushing back to the CP with his radio operator, Adams tried to call Muncy's squad. Moments later the door was flung open. A grenade was thrown in and exploded, killing the radio operator, destroying the equipment, and burying Adams in debris.

After recovering his senses, Adams made his way back out. Most of the platoon's positions had been overrun. Those men able to escape fell back into a makeshift perimeter around the CP. Cooper and Adams pulled a 60 mm mortar from a jeep. They tried firing rounds directly at enemy concentrations and then elevated the mortar to nearly its maximum angle, hoping to create a protective ring of fire around the remaining platoon troops. It worked momentarily, but then the Chinese pressed in and overran the CP area. Adams was struck in the forehead by a rifle butt but managed to bayonet his attacker. In the chaos that followed, Adams, Cooper, Arie, and several others were able to escape up the hill behind the CP. From above, Adams watched Chinese troops herding together surviving GIs and ROKs, shooting several who were too wounded to walk.

The I&R Platoon never stood a chance. It had been hit by the entire CCF 239th Regiment. The force—several thousand strong, by Adams' estimate—soon continued down the trail toward the Pungnyuri inlet, where the 3rd

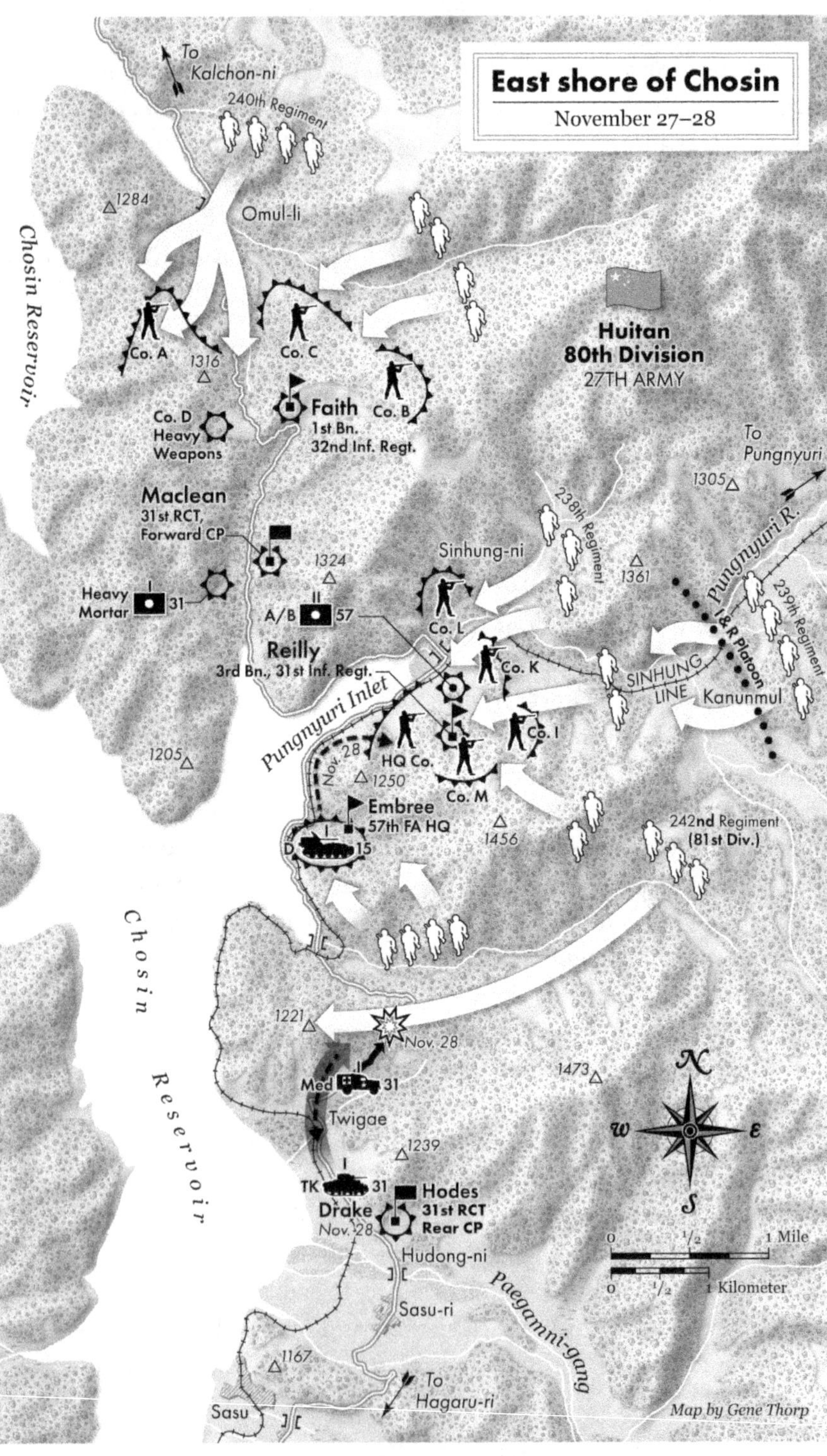

East shore of Chosin
November 27–28
To Kalchon-ni
240th Regiment
1284
Omul-li
Chosin Reservoir
Co. A
Co. C
Co. B
1316
Faith
1st Bn.
32nd Inf. Regt.
Co. D Heavy Weapons
Huitan
80th Division
27TH ARMY
To Pungnyuri
1305
Pungnyuri R.
238th Regiment
Maclean
31st RCT, Forward CP
1324
Sinhung-ni
1361
239th Regiment
Heavy Mortar
31
A/B
57
Co. L
I & R Platoon
Reilly
3rd Bn., 31st Inf. Regt.
Co. K
SINHUNG LINE
Kanunmul
Pungnyuri Inlet
Co. I
1205
Nov. 28
HQ Co.
1250
Co. M
Embree
57th FA HQ
D
15
1456
242nd Regiment
(81st Div.)
Chosin Reservoir
1221
Nov. 28
Med
31
Twigae
1473
1239
TK
31
Hodes
31st RCT
Rear CP
Drake
Nov. 28
Hudong-ni
Sasu-ri
Paegamni-gang
1167
To Hagaru-ri
Sasu
0
1/2
1 Mile
0
1/2
1 Kilometer
Map by Gene Thorp

Battalion, 31st Regiment, and the 57th Field Artillery remained unaware of its approach.

At its position atop a hill several miles back, Muncy's squad had received no radio calls from the platoon. Yet there were ominous signs. "We heard gunfire," recalled Cpl. Roy Shiraga. "Lots of it."

Hudong-ni, Monday Night, November 27

A 31st Medical Company convoy rolled into Hudong-ni in the late evening, including about a half-dozen ambulances and jeeps carrying medical equipment, along with the regimental surgeon, Maj. Harvey Galloway, and other doctors and medics. It had been a long and arduous journey, with several vehicles breaking down on the treacherous road up the pass. Inside the 31st Regiment command post, Capt. Henry Wamble, the medical company executive officer, learned that Col. Maclean had gone forward for the night. Gen. Hodes was asleep on a cot in the operations center. So Wamble spoke with Capt. Drake, the tank company commander, who passed along Faith's recommendation against traveling on the road at night. Drake suggested that the medical convoy remain in the Hudong-ni perimeter until morning. But Wamble believed his instructions obliged him to push forward to join the rest of the medical company already at the inlet. After a short pause, the medical convoy continued up the dark road.

Not long after the convoy disappeared into the night, the radio sets inside the CP burst to life with a series of rapid transmissions. The voices of excited radio operators were drowned out by the sounds of automatic weapons firing.

Forward Perimeter, 11:00 p.m., Monday Night, November 27

In their hillslope foxhole on the A Company line, Roy Oxenrider and Joung He Su had nothing to eat but some crackers and compressed cocoa powder from their C-rations. Even worse, they had to consume the cocoa dry, as the water in their canteens was frozen. Down below, the cooks at the company headquarters were preparing to serve the troops a hot breakfast in the morning. But dawn was long hours away. Though it scarcely seemed possible, the temperature was continuing to drop, approaching thirty below zero. Other than an occasional tree popping in the extreme cold, it had been quiet on the A Company perimeter. The wind was blowing hard and steady, swirling snow all around. Oxenrider took a break, sitting down in his foxhole and pulling his poncho over his head. He lit one of his remaining cigarette butts while Joung stayed on watch. "I had only got a couple of puffs when Joung started jabbering excitedly, kicking me," Oxenrider recalled. He hurriedly stubbed out the butt and pulled off the poncho. Joung was firing his rifle. Oxenrider joined in, shooting at some Chinese soldiers they saw scampering back down the hill.

It quieted down at their front. But they could hear occasional firing elsewhere along the A Company line. Lt. Cecil Smith, the A Company executive officer, recognized that the Chinese were probing the American defenses. These probes could serve many purposes: draw fire to learn where the perimeter lay; find the exact location of foxholes and heavy weapons; determine enemy strength; find strong points, weak points, or gaps in the line; create diversions; or simply encourage the GIs to waste ammunition. Often it was best not to take the bait. Smith ran along the perimeter, yelling, "Don't fire!" But the Chinese had likely learned what they wanted by then.

The firing could be heard down at Faith's CP. Everyone's first thought was that the ROKs were spooked. "Are those Koreans firing at each other again?" Faith asked.

But they grew concerned when the shooting was followed by some grenade explosions. Trip flares went off in front of A and C companies. Checks revealed that Chinese patrols were hitting all along the battalion perimeter.

On the C Company line, Mortrude received a call from his squad on the left flank that they had spotted people crawling toward them. He directed his men to hold their fire while he rushed to the scene. From the hillside, he could see the figures lying in the snowy brush fifty yards below. Mortrude launched two fragmentation grenades at them from his carbine, which succeeded in rousting the Chinese back down the hill without giving away his platoon's individual positions. Again, there was quiet.

27th Army Headquarters, Monday Night, November 27

The wait to attack was agonizing for the soldiers of the 27th Army. Gen. Zhan Da'nan, the 27th Army assistant commander who was in charge of the Chinese forces on the east side of the reservoir, intended to encircle and destroy all the American units in his zone. He had assigned the mission to the 80th Division, which included the 238th, 239th, and 240th regiments and was bolstered by the 242nd Regiment from the 81st Division. In all, Zhan had more than 14,300 troops for the attack, outnumbering the Army task force by nearly five to one.

Of the three armies in the 9th Army Group, the 27th was considered the most combat effective, with a distinguished record in the Chinese civil war. And of the dozen divisions Peng had arrayed around Chosin, the 79th and 80th Divisions were considered the best. The 80th Division was under the command of Rao Huitan, a highly experienced fighter who had joined the Red Army in 1930 and had commanded troops at almost every level.

Nonetheless, the plans quickly went awry. The 238th Regiment was supposed to lead the attack down the Pungnyuri to the inlet, but two of its battalions, using old World War II Japanese maps, had gone to the wrong locations, four miles from where they were supposed to stage. The attack had to be delayed for hours while the two battalions were repositioned.

"Why don't we start our attack?" Zhang Guijin, a political commissar with the 239th Regiment, asked the regimental commander. "We're freezing to death out here." It was not hyperbole. For hours, the 238th Regiment's security company soldiers had been lying in the snow motionless, positioned for attack. When the attack order finally came, Song Xiesheng, an assistant captain with the 238th Regiment, sent messengers to alert the security company. The messengers returned and reported all the soldiers in the company had frozen to death. Song was stunned. "Are you sure?" he asked. But there was no mistake. They had checked every soldier and found only frozen corpses.

The 240th Regiment was to attack south on the reservoir road to the northern position occupied by Faith's 1st Battalion, 32nd Infantry. The 242nd Regiment was to approach the reservoir from the east, with the mission of cutting the road between the inlet and Hudong-ni. The 242nd had already occupied the abandoned Hill 1221 positions and ambushed the 31st Medical Company convoy. The 238th and 239th regiments had come down the Pungnyuri trail. The 239th, in the lead, had wiped out the two forward squads of Lt. Coke's 31st I&R Platoon but had bypassed Muncy's 3rd squad, either not spotting them or not wanting to waste time eliminating such a small force.

By now, Chinese commanders recognized from interrogating prisoners that they were facing soldiers from the U.S. Army 7th Division—and not Marines. A 239th patrol had captured several 31st Regiment soldiers from an outpost along the inlet perimeter and learned that the Army task force commanders had no idea such a large Chinese force was positioned outside their lines, preparing to attack.

The attack orders were being relayed to all units. The Chinese only used radios and telephones at their higher headquarters. Below the battalion level, orders were relayed with simpler methods: messengers running between units, green and red flares, and, most distinctively, bugles, shepherd horns, and whistles.

The system made careful coordination difficult, if not impossible, and it may have been primitive. But in this terrain, it often performed better than the bad radios and vulnerable telephone lines the U.S. Army was using.

Forward Perimeter

Around 12:30 a.m. on the A Company line, Roy Oxenrider and Joung He Su began hearing a strange cacophony of sounds—"whistles, bugles, horns, screaming and bells," Oxenrider recalled. In minutes the soldiers began taking mortar and small-arms fire. Then they could see columns of Chinese troops advancing up the hill. These were no probes. "The Chinese hit full force," Oxenrider said. "It did not take us long to figure out what was happening. It was the signal for the Chinese to attack."

At the A Company headquarters back along the road, Captain Ed Scullion burst out of his command post to investigate the firing. "Don't shoot, don't shoot," he yelled. Possibly, he believed that the ROKs were shooting each other or that the Chinese were probing his lines again. The captain had only walked a few yards when a Chinese soldier with a burp gun shot Scullion in the face and killed him.

A sizable number of Chinese soldiers had stealthily infiltrated the A Company perimeter—perhaps taking advantage of a lack of alertness and making their way through the wide gaps between foxholes or going around the company's right flank via the road.

Captain Stamford, bedded down in a bunker near the CP he shared with several other Marines from the TACP, was awoken by the shots and Scullion's yelling. A poncho the Marines had placed on one end of the bunker to keep out snow was pulled aside, and Stamford could see a fur-rimmed face illuminated in the moonlight. Stamford fired his .45, but the Chinese soldier had already dropped a grenade in the bunker. It exploded atop Stamford's sleeping bag, wounding one Marine but leaving Stamford unscathed. An A Company machine gunner cleared the Chinese off the bunker. After emerging and learning that Scullion was dead, Stamford, now the senior officer on the scene, took command of A Company and began organizing the men to clear the Chinese infiltrators out of the company's CP area.

Soldiers on the A Company perimeter could hear the shooting and yelling to their rear. But they had no time to find out what was happening. Mortar fire was raining on Cpl. Donald McAlister's outpost on A Company's far left flank, followed by a rush of Chinese troops. "We had our hands full trying to hold our position, as the enemy was all over us," McAlister said.

Across the road, on A Company's right flank, C Company was also under attack. "We were hit heavy and hard, on all sides," said SFC John McGuire. "The attacks were unremitting." A 75 mm recoilless rifle crew managed to get off one shot before being overrun and the weapon dragged away by the enemy.

1st Battalion CP

Reports started coming into Faith's headquarters via phone, radio, and runners, describing attacks along each company position. Calls for artillery and mortar fire were received from both A and C companies. In the communications room, the SCR-300 radio burst to life with a call from one of the companies: "Jesus H. Christ! Somebody help! They're all over the fucking place." The transmission was cut off. "I kicked somebody to tell the colonel," recalled Cpl. James Smith, Faith's radio operator.

Faith instructed Lt. Hugh May, the motor officer, to bolster security around the battalion headquarters, and then he called Captain Erwin Bigger, the heavy weapons commander, to the CP. Bigger and Faith had been friends since their World War II days in the 82nd Airborne. Despite his boyish looks, Bigger was one of the most respected and combat-tested officers in the battalion, and Faith relied heavily on his expertise.

A garbled message had come in from A Company reporting that Scullion might be dead, but then radio and telephone contact went out. "Something may have happened to Ed Scullion," Faith told Bigger. Faith turned to Capt. Robert Haynes, the assistant operations officer. "You had better go up there and see what has happened," he told him.

The color drained from Haynes's face. He was a reservist with no infantry background. Bigger volunteered to accompany him—his weapons company's machine gun and recoilless rifle sections were positioned with A Company, so he knew the layout of its perimeter.

Bigger and Haynes climbed the winding road toward the A Company position, five hundred yards forward, and as they came close, they were challenged by a prone figure in a parka lying in the road. "We thought he was a ROK and replied with the countersign," said Bigger. Then Bigger noticed the soldier was aiming his rifle at them. "Bob, that guy is going to shoot—hit the ditch!" he called. They dove as the Chinese soldier fired, but Bigger heard Haynes grunt, hit by a round in the stomach. Bigger was trying to check Haynes's condition when he saw three more Chinese soldiers rushing at him, throwing grenades. Bigger beat a hasty retreat to the battalion CP, shaken at having to leave a wounded comrade behind.

The A Company mess sergeant, SFC Jeremiah Casey, overhearing that Haynes remained wounded on the road above, pulled together a party of headquarters soldiers to try to rescue the captain. But as they approached, Chinese troops on the road drove them off, and Casey was killed during the valiant attempt.

Inside the CP, Faith and Maclean were still trying to piece together what was happening. The area was overrun with Chinese, Bigger told Faith. "One minute we were planning an attack," Bigger recalled. "The next, we were fighting for our lives in a situation where we knew little of what had hit us." Maclean had heard enough to call off Faith's dawn attack.

No artillery fire was coming from the 57th Field Artillery at the inlet despite the increasingly urgent requests from the line companies. The mortarmen did their best to fill the void. Bigger worked mightily, shifting D Company's 81 mm mortar positions around to cover every request for fire from B and C companies. But A Company was left without fire support, as its radios were out and the Chinese had cut the telephone wires connecting it to Bigger's mortars. The two wire teams sent to restore the connection were lost, apparently intercepted by infiltrators.

Lt. Jerry McCabe, a fire direction officer with the 31st Heavy Mortar Company located two miles south, was unable to reach either of his forward observers with the 1st Battalion via radio and feared they had been wounded or killed. So McCabe—described by one of his men as "a crazy Irishman"—strapped a heavy radio set on his back and went forward himself, crawling on his belly first through a Chinese position and then into the 1st Battalion perimeter without being shot. McCabe called back accurate fire direction for his 4.2-inch mortars the rest of the night.

The mortar fire helped, but the silence from the howitzers was frustrating for the desperate infantry units on the perimeter. "We could not understand why we could not obtain supporting artillery fires," Bigger said. Part of the problem was that the Chinese had also cut telephone wires that ran to the artillery at the inlet. After much effort, radio communication with the inlet was established around 1:00 a.m., and Faith learned of a much more serious problem: Both the 57th Field Artillery and the 3rd Battalion, 31st Infantry, were under heavy attack at the inlet. They were fighting for their lives and in no position to support Faith's battalion.

Hudong-ni, Early Tuesday Morning, November 27

Capt. Clifton Hancock, the 31st Medical Company's motor officer, passed through Hudong-ni around midnight, hurrying to catch up with the medical convoy. The company mess truck had broken down on the road leading to the reservoir, and Hancock had stayed back with his jeep to help repair it.

On the south slope of Hill 1221, where the road rose toward a hairpin curve, Hancock found the tail end of the convoy—several medical vehicles riddled with bullet holes. The convoy had made it about two miles up the road from Hudong-ni when their path was blocked by Chinese soldiers who had put logs across the road, then sprayed the blocked vehicles with fire.

The jeep carrying Maj. Galloway, the regimental surgeon, had been near the front when it was riddled with machine gun fire. Galloway was hit once in the right leg, twice in the right arm, and once in the head. "Fortunately, I did not lose consciousness and knew just what nerves had been hit and what area of my brain had been hit," Galloway recalled. His driver, Cpl. Donald Jeter, was hit in the arm but was able to put the jeep in low gear and power over the log blocking its path, breaking free from the ambush and flooring it north toward the inlet.

Most others in the convoy were not so lucky. Hancock found about a half-dozen survivors, including the company 1st sergeant, Master Sgt. Clarence Lee, who described the ambush and its aftermath. "The enemy had been systematically walking down each side of the convoy shooting any individual they found alive," Hancock recalled. A few survived by playing dead.

The attack had paused upon Hancock's arrival. But as he spoke to Lee, Chinese soldiers on the slope resumed firing. Hancock's party gathered the survivors and hurried back to Hudong-ni. Their arrival with news of the ambush hit the CP like a lightning bolt. Hodes, awoken by the commotion, ordered a message be sent to the 3rd Battalion, 31st Infantry, at the inlet, directing it to dispatch a platoon to the scene of the ambush to look for any more survivors and retrieve the vehicles.

But even as the message was sent out, alarming reports arrived from the forward battalions. "By this time the radio in the CP was red hot, everyone was reporting enemy action," recalled Lt. J. Howard Burton, an officer in the tank company. Because of the poor signal, the reports were frustratingly garbled, breaking off mid-sentence. "Bits of unclear information came to us over a multitude of radios," said Maj. Lynch, Hodes's operations aide. "Usually the source was uncertain other than we got the picture that the units up forward were eyeball to eyeball with the Chinese."

The radios the task force had been issued were underpowered WWII surplus models that had been hastily rebuilt in Japan after the North Korean invasion, and they were often defective. The handheld SCR-536 walkie-talkies were no match for the terrain and cold, even within companies. The backpack-mounted SCR-300s had better range, but their batteries quickly weakened in the cold. In this mountainous, freezing setting, the radios were failing badly—with fatal consequences.

A frustrated Hodes was unable to reach Maclean, the task force commander, or any of the battalion commanders—Faith, Reilly, or Embree. Lynch tried radioing the 7th Division CP, about sixty miles northeast, using the most powerful radio the task force had, an SCR-193, hoping to reach Lt. Col. Paddock, the division operations officer. To his great surprise, Gen. Barr answered the call.

Hodes was summoned to the radio, which was inside a three-quarter-ton truck parked near the schoolhouse. The radio signal was weak, and Hodes had to yell to be heard. "Maclean is trouble," he shouted. The situation was very fluid and tenuous, Hodes told Barr. The task force would need plenty of air support at daylight. Hodes also reported that Reidy's 2nd Battalion, 31st Infantry, had still not arrived and that he could not understand the delay. Before the generals could finish the conversation, the radio signal was lost and could not be reestablished.

Hodes decided to have Drake's 31st Tank company attack north at daylight to try to break through to the forward battalions. Tank commanders were sent to their tanks to await further orders. Hodes was also concerned that Hudong-ni might itself be attacked. Soldiers on watch reported seeing

Chinese troops on high ground just to the north. Maj. Carl Witte, overseeing security at the CP, ordered some tanks placed in defensive positions around the perimeter.

The weather was worsening with the arrival of a 20 mph Siberian wind. Lynch had served in some of the bloodiest and most star-crossed operations of the Italian campaign during World War II, including Salerno, San Pietro, and Rapido, and he had a sense of foreboding about what was unfolding at the Chosin Reservoir.

Inlet Perimeter, Early Morning Hours, Tuesday, November 28

The night had begun relatively quietly at the inlet. Near the K Company CP, cooks were preparing chow for the morning. The company's soldiers were without sleeping bags because the truck carrying them hadn't arrived yet. As the cold night wore on, Capt. Robert Kitz, the company commander, gave permission for warming fires to be built in the rear area.

The 3rd Battalion headquarters put out an alert around 10:00 p.m., after receiving a report that Chinese had attacked an artillery unit to the rear. Kitz called in his platoon and section leaders and told them to extinguish all fires and double their guards. "We were on 100 percent alert, which means nobody sleeps," said SFC Ed Farley, who was in charge of the company's 60 mm mortar section.

Sometime after midnight, the men could hear off-key bugle signals sounding from ridges across the way, then whistles. It was undeniably eerie to hear on the dark and cold night. "It sounded like they were playing taps," recalled Sgt. Bill Rowland of I Company.

At their 3rd platoon location, PFC Ed Reeves and Ho-Yah Bak had been scanning the front for movement and not seeing anything. That changed in an instant. They suddenly saw Chinese soldiers in winter white uniforms approaching. Multiple enemy squads were charging up the ridge in their direction and firing. All up and down the line, GIs were calling for medics.

The Chinese assault was pouring down the Pungnyuri trail, and it built quickly in volume. The 239th Regiment launched strong attacks along the ridge line where L, K, and I companies manned the perimeter north to south, the brunt of the assault coming against K Company, which was in the center. Squads of Chinese soldiers attacked K Company's 3rd Platoon positions, drawing fire that provided cover for other squads to move through the forty- to fifty-foot gaps between foxholes.

The 3rd Platoon leader, Lt. Jack Brooks, a 24-year-old Georgian, was infuriated when Chinese soldiers bayoneted several of his wounded soldiers in their foxholes. After running out of ammunition, Brooks swung his rifle at the enemy like a club. He drove them out and chased them down the ridge but was not seen again, apparently killed in action.

The main assault overran one K Company platoon and soon forced the entire company to withdraw in disarray. Reeves and Ho fell back, mixed in with enemy soldiers as they ran downhill toward the inlet interior, expecting at any minute to be hit by GI slugs from the front or Chinese fire from the rear. As they approached the M Company position, Reeves was relieved to hear a call from an American officer: "Hold your fire, GIs are coming in." A machine gun temporarily stopped firing, and Reeves and Ho joined a group defending the M Company headquarters. "Get those rifles working," an officer told them. "The whole Chinese army's trying to come through here."

The collapse of K Company, which held the center of the defensive line, exposed both the right flank of L Company and the left flank of I Company. Etchemendy's L Company, on the northernmost portion of the battalion perimeter, was hit hard especially on its exposed right flank but held its position. The I Company commander, Auburn Marr—at 41, one of the oldest officers in the battalion and known as Pop—sent messengers to each of his platoons, telling them to hold at all costs. But the Chinese overran at least one platoon and broke through the I Company line. "We thought the whole bugle blowing whistle tooting Chinese Army was upon us," recalled one of Marr's messengers, 19-year-old PFC Lewis Shannon.

By 1:30 a.m., the K Company CP was overrun. "They were on us before anyone knew it," said SFC William Mahon, a K Company supply sergeant. The cooks busily preparing breakfast with their ROK helpers suddenly found their mess tents overrun, and the company kitchen was soon in flames. Some of the cooks and ROKs fled further to the rear in panic. Others grabbed their rifles and took up positions behind nearby trucks to fire at the onrushing attackers.

Hundreds of Chinese soldiers were streaming into the inlet perimeter, overrunning the eastern half of the bivouac area and catching the 3rd Battalion headquarters and support units by surprise. Some of those units had arrived after dark and had not dug in adequately. "We was all sitting there just like ducks," recalled Cpl. Francois. Many GIs sleeping in the open or in pup tents were caught unaware and bayoneted in their sleeping bags. Following Zhang's instructions, troops from the 239th Regiment soldiers fired into tents, killing GIs before they could get out.

It was total chaos. Attackers were intermixed with defenders, and uniforms were hard to distinguish in the darkness. Some GIs and ROKs were shooting at anything that moved. "I feel sure many men were killed by friendly fire," said Staff Sgt. Harry Scott, a radio repairman with the Headquarters Company.

The soldiers of the 9th Army Group were good night fighters, with excellent camouflage discipline, and able to close in under fire. The divisions at Chosin had no heavy artillery, just a few 75 mm field guns each, along with plentiful mortars and rocket launchers. Song Shilun's tactics emphasized getting his troops close to neutralize the heavy American firepower.

The Chinese attacks at Chosin were not human wave attacks, as sometimes depicted. Each assault was more like a battering ram, made in a column along a narrow front, throwing platoons or squad-sized units at a chosen point one after another until the troops broke through or died trying. The attacks often continued despite terrible losses, as Chinese company and platoon commanders had little leeway to alter plans, particularly given the limited communication with higher headquarters.

Attacking troops would approach enemy lines at a walk or trot, looking for a weak point. Falling snow worked in their favor, obscuring visibility, enabling them to get close. And the rugged terrain and snow masked sounds, so an American unit on one side of a ridge might not hear a unit on the opposite side being attacked.

If the Chinese broke through enemy lines, they did not focus on wiping out defenders along the perimeter. Instead, most troops rushed into secondary and rear areas, making little or no attempt to stop and reorganize. The goal was to create as much damage and chaos as possible, trying to destroy the Army unit integrity.

The leading CCF troops often carried only grenades to use against foxholes, bunkers, and command posts, which required getting close. Sometimes, they were able to infiltrate close enough to get in range, but it often meant running uphill into enemy fire and taking heavy casualties. The second and third squads of Chinese attackers generally carried rifles and machine guns to provide covering fire for the grenadiers. Some of the attackers carried no guns but instead picked up weapons from fallen comrades, of which there was no shortage.

Troops from the CCF 2nd Battalion, 239th Regiment, followed the communication wires that led to command posts located in three houses along the roadside. Captain Li Changyan divided his 4th Company into teams to assault each house. One team attacked the hut in the center, which housed the Air Force tactical air party assigned to the 3rd Battalion. They killed the forward air controller, Air Force Lt. Olin Johnson, and damaged the radio equipment—a serious blow that left the battalion unable to coordinate air support. A second team headed toward the southernmost hut several hundred yards down the road, housing Earle Jordan's M Company headquarters.

A third assault team attacked the 3rd Battalion headquarters in the largest and northernmost house. They sprayed it with machine gun fire and tossed grenades inside, killing or wounding several officers and enlisted men. Bill Reilly, the battalion commander, was shot in the leg. As the Chinese team tried to break into the house, Reilly sat facing a window with his .45, shooting enemy soldiers one at a time as they tried to climb in. "Seems like they just wouldn't stop coming—standing on their comrades' bodies to get in," Reilly later told his wife, Celeste.

Lt. James Anderson, the battalion's assistant operations officer, gravely wounded by a grenade, was frustrated because he could not get his pistol out of his holster. "Bill went over to help him and saw why," Celeste Reilly said. "His right arm was missing." Anderson did not realize it. Reilly took the lieutenant's pistol out and placed it in Anderson's left hand. The lieutenant seemed satisfied and stayed in position, holding the gun until he died.

Capt. Changyan's assault moved on, following the communication wires toward the field artillery positions.

Reilly gave himself a syrette of morphine. Around 3:00 a.m., a Chinese concussion grenade came flying through the window and exploded, knocking him unconscious.

More Chinese troops who had broken through the inlet perimeter came pouring through, joining the assault on M Company. Lt. John Gray's 81 mm mortars, positioned just to the northeast of the M Company CP, were targeted. "Suddenly I found many strange-looking Chinese soldiers in white, quilted uniforms and fur caps bearing down on my mortar positions," Gray recalled. The mortarmen fired their rifles at the enemy, but that did little to stop the onslaught. The carbines they had been issued did not have much stopping power in the first place; moreover, the oil in their guns had frozen, and the bolts would jam after one shot. In any event, the numbers of Chinese were overwhelming. Gray's mortarmen were hit by a hailstorm of long-handled concussion grenades, and they were soon struggling in hand-to-hand combat with the determined Chinese attackers.

Seeing the mortar positions were overrun, Capt. Jordan shouted for Gray's platoon to fall back to join the defenses around the mud-wall and thatched roof hut serving as M Company's CP. At the new position, Gray tossed his carbine in favor of an M-1 Garand, lost by a dead or wounded GI. Not only did the Garand deliver a more powerful shot, but its longer length made it more useful for defensive parries and butt strokes. "It was the most desperate hand-to-hand fighting imaginable," said Gray.

The M Company inner perimeter around the CP became a bastion of defense. Streams of wounded men came into the perimeter. Any ammunition they had was taken by GIs manning the defenses, who were running low. Inside the CP the wounded were given rudimentary care by other wounded. The soldiers outside held the tight ring around the M Company CP against heavy fire and repeated assaults. But elsewhere in the inlet, the Chinese continued to sweep through.

A Battery, Inlet Perimeter

The 105 mm howitzers of A Battery, 57th Field Artillery, were positioned about five hundred yards southwest of the overrun K Company line. Around 2:45 a.m., Lt. Keith Sickafoose, the forward observer attached to K Company, came sprinting into the A Battery CP to report that infantry was retreating to their position. Capt. Harold Hodge, the Battery commander, went to each gun section and perimeter defense position, telling the men to fight as long as they possibly could.

Lt. Lloyd Mielenz, the battery security platoon leader, rushed to one of his machine gun positions and could vaguely see dark figures in the snow. "I didn't know whether they were our infantry or the enemy," Mielenz recalled. He hesitated to open fire, fearing he would be killing GIs.

Infantrymen came pouring into A Battery's positions with the Chinese on their heels. Within minutes, the log hut housing the battery CP was hit with several bursts of machine gun fire. Hodge and his executive officer, Lt. Thomas Patton, hurried outside and found chaos. Retreating GIs and ROKs as well as attacking Chinese were rushing through the area, yelling in English, Korean, and Chinese. It was nearly impossible to tell who was who in the dark.

A grenade landed next to two cans of gasoline near the CP, exploding and set the hut ablaze, providing some visibility. PFC Bob Hammond, an 18-year-old cannoneer, was on an embankment overlooking the CP and could see two quilted figures standing at the edge of the burning building, warming their hands. "Are those Chinese?" he asked the soldier next to him.

"Yeah," the soldier answered. "I think so."

"How come nobody's shooting them?" Hammond asked.

"I don't know," the soldier answered. Whether it was human empathy for fellow freezing soldiers or just confusion, the two Chinese soldiers were left alone.

A more pressing concern was the group of Chinese soldiers who were climbing onto an M16 Quad 50. Mielenz feared if they captured the half-track vehicle, they could turn it on GIs in the perimeter, so he sent Hammond to get a bazooka. The private quickly returned with Staff Sgt. Robert Stansfield, who fired a rocket at the half-track, scattering the enemy.

The antiaircraft guns, with their fearsome destructive power, were a prime target of the Chinese assault. "There were hundreds of screaming Chinese, all coming straight at me, it seemed," said Staff Sgt. Robert Ayala, the gunner on an M19 positioned near A Battery. "I just lowered my Twin 40s and blasted the hell out of them."

Nonetheless, the Chinese assault continued their sweep toward the A Battery howitzers. Hammond, who had taken a position with a half-dozen other soldiers around one of the guns, saw a company of enemy soldiers one hundred yards away, all racing toward them. There was "no time left to do anything with the howitzer," he recalled. Hammond got a couple of shots off from his rifle before he turned to take off, but he stumbled to the ground. He saw spurts of snow jumping off the ground as bullets hit a few feet from him. Hammond got back up and sprinted toward B Battery, some three hundred yards to the south.

B Battery, Inlet Perimeter

Cpl. Anthony Mora and Cpl. Richard Vendinghouse, sitting in a foxhole on the B Battery perimeter, were puzzled when they heard what sounded like an air horn coming from the direction of A Battery. "Sounded like a Greyhound bus . . . and we knew it couldn't be, because the roads were too small for something like that," Mora recalled.

Several B Battery officers, sleeping in a small stable, awoke to the same noise. "We listened and soon decided that the truck horns were bugles," said 1st Lt. Ted Magill, a forward observer. "Shortly thereafter, the building in which we were bedded down was riddled by machine gun fire." They rushed out to help man the perimeter.

Most of those inside the A Battery perimeter, including some infantrymen from all three rifle companies, prepared to retreat to B Battery around 3:30 a.m. Sgt. Stanford Corner, an A Battery medic, risked his life numerous times by running into small arms and mortar fire to collect wounded soldiers, then carrying them on his back to a hut where he set up an impromptu aid station. When the decision to retreat was made, Corner loaded the wounded into a truck, covered them with blankets, and drove them to B Battery. The retreat was another disorganized affair, but B Battery officers established order and put the arriving men into defensive positions. B Battery had a good defensive perimeter, which grew stronger with the new arrivals, and the position held firm against heavy assaults by the Chinese for the next forty-five minutes. Along with the M Company perimeter to the south, B Battery became a rallying point for the GIs and ROKs.

Forward Perimeter

Four miles to the north, the situation faced by the 1st Battalion was grim, though not nearly as dire as at the inlet. In the A Company headquarters area, soldiers under Capt. Stamford's command went on the offensive against the Chinese infiltrators who had killed Scullion and overrun the area. Lt. Carlo Ortenzi, the company's mortar officer, led a counterattack that recaptured lost ground, inflicted heavy casualties on the Chinese, and blocked them from advancing on Faith's headquarters. Before long the interior had been largely cleared of the enemy.

But fierce fighting continued along the A Company perimeter. The Chinese captured a gun pit on the line and began firing a machine gun at surrounding American positions. In the foxhole to the immediate right, Sgt. Willis Via thought he was taking friendly fire but realized the occupants of the neighboring pit were Chinese when they tossed two concussion grenades at his squad. "We fired in the direction of the muzzle flash and took it out," he recalled.

Around 2:00 a.m., a new threat came rumbling down the road dividing A Company from C Company. The 240th Regiment had been bolstered with a North Korean tank and an armored self-propelled gun, which the Chinese commanders hoped to use to exploit the gap between the companies. But the pass carrying the road between the companies was guarded by a D Company recoilless rifle squad on the east side of the road. The rifle, which fired a 75 mm high-explosive projectile, was manned by James Godfrey, who had been busted from sergeant to private first class for misconduct. But Bigger, the D Company commander, considered it lucky that Godrey had been assigned to his weapons company. "He could do more with the 75 mm RR than anyone I have ever seen," said Bigger.

As the armored vehicles approached the gap, Godfrey took each out with well-placed shots. As soon as he fired, a force of 100 Chinese soldiers who had crawled unnoticed to within forty yards of the squad charged, trying to overrun the position. Godfrey swung his weapon around and cut down the attackers. He also eliminated an enemy mortar position and helped repel five successive attacks on the C Company line. Able Company restored its lines, and the battalion held the eastern perimeter, thanks in no small measure to Godfrey.

Along the battalion's right flank, the fighting was equally desperate. By 3:00 a.m., a Chinese company had captured a knoll on the boundary of B and C companies, giving them a critical piece of high ground between the two units. When an assault threatened to break through the B Company line around 4:30 a.m., Captain Wallace Turner sent every available man in the company headquarters, including the cooks, to help hold the line. "They said leave everything behind, just bring your guns and ammunition, we need you bad up here,'" recalled Private Harry Jacobs, who dutifully left behind his pack with medical supplies, food, and letters from home. The reinforcements turned the tide, though Jacobs never saw his pack again.

Dr. Lee Yong Kak, a South Korean doctor who had been assigned to the 1st Battalion as an assistant surgeon, was deep in slumber when a medic woke him up and said he was urgently needed at the aid station. There he found the battalion surgeon, Captain Vincent Navarre, working alongside the medics, dressing the wounds of injured GIs and ROKs.

Wounded men were being carried in gray-faced, half-frozen, and groaning with pain, their uniforms smeared with mud, snow, and blood. Many of the casualties were from the brutal hand-to-hand combat on the A Company line. So many wounded were arriving that the overflow had to be put in the adjoining CP, which was the only other spot with heat and light. Soon that was filled too, so some were placed in a cold mess tent. Capt. Lawrence Brunnert, the battalion's Roman Catholic chaplain, was soon taking the place of the doctors at the sides of the soldiers, ministering to the dying.

57th Field Artillery HQ, Western Base of Hill 1456

Dawn was approaching, but the Chinese were not done launching attacks for the night.

About a mile south of the inlet, Ray Embree's 57th Field Artillery headquarters, accompanied by a platoon from Capt. McClymont's D Battery, 15th AAA, had spent a quiet night bivouacked alongside a cove. They were shielded from the inlet by a ridge running between the positions and had heard nothing of the life-and-death battle underway for hours just to their north. Any radio calls made from the inlet, including those from Embree's two firing batteries, were not received.

PFC Grant McMillin was trying to get some sleep as the morning slowly lightened when he heard his first sergeant yelling, "Everybody out, they're going to hit us!" McMillin jumped up. "You could see the columns of troops coming out the mountains behind us," he recalled.

The troops coming up the road from the south were from the CCF 242nd Regiment, which had occupied Hill 1221 and ambushed the medical company convoy. A second large Chinese force, likely one of the 238th Regiment battalions that had gotten lost during the night, had crossed a shoulder of Hill 1456 and was approaching from the southeast. The two Chinese columns were apparently on their way to attack the American troops at the inlet from a new direction, and they were not expecting to encounter an additional force along the way, particularly one armed with lethal antiaircraft weapons.

Heavy mortar fire dropped around Embree's headquarters, grievously wounding Cpl. Eldon Ervin. Cpl. Ray Vallowe, his close friend from their days picking cherries outside Sapporo, was quickly at Ervin's side but was helpless to do anything. "My best buddy was dying from mortar shrapnel to the throat, choking on his own blood," Vallowe recalled. "He could not be saved." Another good friend, PFC Charles Smith, had been hit in the shoulder. His wound did not look terribly serious, but in the deep freeze, Smith went into shock and died soon after Ervin.

At the nearby 15th AAA headquarters, McClymont heard the mortar fire and learned that his 1st Platoon was under attack. He rushed from his CP and climbed onto a nearby M19, commanded by SFC Robert Denham. McClymont raised his field glasses to his eyes. In the faint light, he glimpsed movement on the side of a hill by the road leading to Hagaru. Focusing the glasses further, he could make out a column of soldiers two hundred yards down the road, heading to his position. An illumination shell burst overhead, and then McClymont could see them clearly, in their dark quilted uniforms and fur caps with ear flaps. He had no doubt they were Chinese. McClymont ordered Denham to open fire. "The twin 40s crumped simultaneously, and the tracers leaped out," he later wrote. "Immediately, the high explosive shells burst in the column of men, and I ordered fire at full automatic. In only seconds, there was no movement from the column."

Then McClymont felt someone tugging on his ankle. It was a cook, saying he was wanted on the field telephone. McClymont jumped off the vehicle and picked up the phone in the CP tent. "Those are friendly troops out there, cease fire!" Lt. Colonel Robert Tolly, the 57th FA operations officer, urgently told him.

"My heart sank," McClymont recalled. "I had just erased a whole column of men." He ran back to the M19 and ordered Denham to stop firing.

It was not true—the troops were Chinese. The 57th headquarters mistakenly thought the column coming up the road was the long-awaited 2nd Battalion, 31st Infantry. But McClymont had no time to sort out the confusion. The second Chinese force had come across a shoulder of Hill 1456 and was attacking their position from the southeast. The enemy were pouring machine gun and sniper fire into the D Battery area, and McClymont could see the 1st Platoon CP was burning.

McClymont organized some of his men to try recapture the CP, but as they ran up the road, they were ambushed by Chinese soldiers who had commandeered a sandbagged bunker. McClymont and his men fired bazooka rockets at the bunker and hit it with grenades, but they weren't able to wipe out the occupants until they ran up to the sandbags and poured rifle fire over the top.

Approaching the CP, they came under a hailstorm of small-arms fire from a nearby hillside. McClymont rolled for cover underneath a trailer loaded with .50-caliber ammunition. He was firing back at the Chinese until one of his men yelled a warning: "Captain, get the hell out of there, that trailer is on fire!" McClymont scrambled to safety moments before the ammo began to pop off. Just then, one of his M19s opened fire on the hillside, catching the Chinese troops in the open. Once more the Twin 40s, each gun firing 120 high explosive rounds per minute, proved devastating against infantry.

Once the shooting stopped, McClymont entered the CP and found Warrant Officer Roscoe Calcote sprawled facedown on the floor, dead. Four enlisted men had also been killed and several others wounded. Calcote had thrown back numerous grenades tossed into the CP until one exploded in his hand, a survivor told McClymont. Though severely wounded, Calcote continued shooting his pistol at the enemy until he was hit by a burst of automatic fire.

At the nearby 57th FA headquarters, Embree, the battalion commander, had been seriously wounded in the upper legs by small-arms fire, and Maj. Max Morris, Embree's executive officer, lay dead on the ground outside. One M19 had been knocked out of action by the Chinese.

But McClymont's antiaircraft weapons had effectively eliminated both attacking Chinese columns, preventing them from continuing north to attack the inlet and opening an additional front that might have finished off the beleaguered American units.

Inlet, Early Morning, November 28

The arrival of dawn gave the infantry and artillery troops rallying inside the B Battery perimeter the opportunity to retake positions lost during the night. At daybreak Lt. Henry Traywick, the 3rd Battalion motor officer, led a counterattack to recapture the 3rd Battalion CP. Word was that Reilly had been killed in the assault, and Traywick's men liberally blasted the area with machine-gun and small-arms fire to clear it of Chinese. Traywick went into the CP expecting to find Reilly's body, but instead, he discovered the battalion commander alive but unconscious. He had been stripped of his weapons and left for dead by the Chinese. Captain Melville Adams, the battalion supply officer, had a serious chest wound. Lt. Anderson and several enlisted men were dead.

Just to the north, infantry and artillery troops led by a trio of captains—Marr, the I Company commander; Kitz, the K Company commander; and Hodge, the A Battery commander—launched an assault on foot to retake the captured A Battery howitzers. The attacking Americans were hit by Chinese mortar fire, and Lt. Mielenz was flipped into the air when a shell exploded next to him. Mielenz's men used his belt as a makeshift tourniquet to stop the bleeding from his shredded left leg and carried him to an aid station.

But the attack soon scattered the Chinese defenders. The fighting around the howitzers had been heavy all night. "There were enemy dead all around the guns and a few laying across the trail legs of the guns," said PFC Shannon of I Company.

To the surprise and relief of the artillerymen, they found that the Chinese had failed to destroy any of the captured howitzers, reflecting poor coordination and communication between the enemy forces during the chaotic night. There was another surprise. "We then discovered that approximately 30 men from Battery A had remained in their foxholes and had continued fighting even though they were completely overrun," Patton said. Emerging from the bunkers, the artillerymen promptly put their 105s to use against the retreating Chinese.

Casualties had been high; about a third of the battery troops had been killed or wounded or were missing, including 15 ROKs and 1 GI marched off by the Chinese. But A Battery had been reconstituted. Patton credited Hodge's leadership for getting the men through the night, "his coolness under heavy fire being almost unbelievable."

Hodge, a 28-year-old Iowan, had been with the 101st Airborne Division when it was surrounded at Bastogne by the German Army during the Battle of the Bulge six years earlier. But he had never experienced anything like the fight that first night at the Chosin Reservoir. "The Battle of Bastogne," he told Patton, "was a picnic compared to this."

Chapter 7

THE FIRST DAY

Tuesday, November 28

With the morning light, Zhan Da'nan, the CCF 27th Army assistant commander, ordered his units to withdraw. At the inlet, bugles sounded, the signal for the Chinese troops to pull out and retreat into the hills. From the high ground overlooking the inlet, Wang Kefu, operations chief for the 239th Regiment, looked around the surrounding ground and saw hundreds of his men in their mustard-colored uniforms lying motionless, not retreating. All were dead. Wang began to weep.

Despite taking the Army units by complete surprise, overrunning their lines, and cutting off their escape route, Zhan was stunned by the number of casualties he had taken. The 80th Division had been devastated, losing some 3,200 men, or nearly 30 percent of its troops. The 238th Regiment alone had lost 58 percent of its combat troops. The 240th Regiment, which had been attacking the northern perimeter, had only expected to encounter one company. Instead, they had found Faith's 1st Battalion and suffered heavy losses, with one company losing three-quarters of its troops. The 81st Division's 242nd Regiment, which had run into the lethal American antiaircraft weapons in its attack from the south, lost seven of ten attacking companies.

Zhan's command had been hampered during the night by confusion and poor communication. Telephone wires connecting the 80th Division headquarters to its regiments had been cut by U.S. shelling soon after its attacks began, leaving the division commander, Rao Huitan, unable to communicate with the attacking forces. There had been no coordination between the 238th and 239th Regiments when they broke into the inlet perimeter—one of the reasons the American artillery pieces had been left unscathed.

"We were told that the enemy force was a paper tiger," Song Xiesheng, an assistant captain with the 238th Regiment, told scholar Xiaobing Li in 2008. "Therefore, we organized massive attacks. Hundreds and hundreds of soldiers charged the enemy without artillery coverage and firepower protection. Then we found out the enemy was not a paper tiger, but a real tiger with strong firepower and combat effectiveness."

It was clear that the U.S. force on the east side of the reservoir was significantly stronger than Chinese commanders had expected. The Americans had recovered from their surprise and were successfully counterattacking, showing they remained potent. Though he had an entire division reinforced by an additional infantry regiment, Zhan feared it was not enough to destroy the American force.

The Chinese offensive in North Korea had achieved total surprise against the most powerful and technologically advanced military in the world. Song Shilun's 9th Army Group had struck X Corps with seven divisions and 70,000 soldiers, attacking the U.S. forces at seven locations. Song had effectively surrounded the 8,200 Marines at Yudam-ni; the 3,100 GIs and ROKs east of the reservoir; and the 3,000 Marines and 600 Army soldiers at Hagaru. The CCF 79th Division had launched a major assault on the two Marine regiments at Yudam-ni. One regiment from the 89th Division blocked the road leading west from Yudam-ni, while the 59th Division maneuvered to cut off the Marine regiments' escape route south to Hagaru. The 60th Division had cut the road leading south from Hagaru to Koto-ri, cutting off the route south for all the U.S. units at Chosin.

The Chinese attack at Yudam-ni took the 1st Marine Division by "distinct surprise," according to a Marine report, and the two regiments suffered more than 500 casualties, with one company overrun. To the east the Army task force had suffered some 420 dead, missing, or wounded during the night.

But the Chinese success had come at a terrible price to Song's men. His calculations had been thrown off by the last-minute arrival of the Army task force east of the reservoir, which left the Chinese unexpectedly facing two Marine regiments at Yudam-ni. Instead of concentrating enough force at Yudam-ni to wipe out the Marines, he had dispersed his forces to attack on both sides of the reservoir, watering down his huge manpower advantage. The Chinese attacks had done great damage. But they had failed to destroy any of the American units.

Song had underestimated the firepower of the U.S. Army and Marine units. The 9th Army Group had lost an astonishing 10,000 men in the first night of fighting on both sides of the reservoir. The 80th Division, fighting Task Force Maclean on the east side of the reservoir, had suffered the most, with the highest casualty rate of all seven Chinese divisions attacking the first night at Chosin.

Forward Perimeter, Tuesday Morning, November 28

With the Chinese withdrawal and the arrival of daylight, Capt. Haynes was finally recovered from the road where he had lain since being shot on the way to A Company. He was brought into the 1st Battalion CP area, still alive but suffering from his stomach wound and long hours of exposure. Capt. Navarre, the battalion surgeon, took one look at him and shook his head. Haynes was given last rites and died soon afterward.

Soon after dawn, four Marine Corsairs arrived overhead, a welcome sight to PFC Roy Oxenrider, who was still in his foxhole with Joung He Su on the A Company line. Capt. Stamford directed the planes to attack the area behind a ridge three hundred yards beyond the line, where Chinese troops had retreated and been firing mortar shells at the 1st Battalion. The Corsairs dropped napalm to force the enemy troops into the open, and then strafed them with 20 mm cannon fire. That took care of the mortar fire.

Faith had the battalion working to recapture ground lost during the night. The Chinese had not withdrawn from the knoll overlooking the boundary between C and B companies. The two companies launched an attack but without artillery support, made no progress. The situation worsened when the Chinese penetrated C Company's right flank. But Faith had resourcefully organized all available headquarters and service troops into an effective infantry company to protect the rear. Led by a pair of dauntless liuetenants, Hugh May and Henry Moore, they rushed up the draw and drove the Chinese back to the crest of the hill. But there the enemy remained.

The Chinese were also hitting B Company hard, threatening to break into the battalion rear. Maj. Curtis picked his reliable operations NCO, Sgt. Monty Piercefield, to take some of the service troops and secure a hill behind the battalion headquarters. Piercefield led a dozen cooks wading through knee-deep snow up the hill. Once they reached the ridgeline, they moved east toward the sounds of firing. Piercefield's heart jumped when he spotted several Chinese soldiers aiming a captured .30-caliber machine gun in their direction. "But they couldn't get it to work, so they took off," Piercefield said. "So we got the machine gun back, but we couldn't get it to work either." The hill, though, remained secure, and the rear of the battalion protected.

At first light Colonel Maclean departed Faith's headquarters by jeep to check in with his 31st Regiment's forward command post, under the command of his adjutant, Hugh Robbins. Though they were located only one mile behind Faith's battalion in an exposed and poorly protected area, the little command group had not been detected by the Chinese. Robbins and his men had spent an uneasy night listening to heavy fire to their front and rear. "The enemy 'who wasn't there' in earlier reports was very much there and giving our units the fight of their lives," Robbins recalled.

After arriving at the CP, Maclean described the Chinese attack on the 1st Battalion at the forward perimeter, telling Robbins that "things were pretty much under control up there and that all units of the battalion were holding OK." Maclean had been impressed with Faith's cool command during the chaotic night.

The situation at the inlet sounded much more tenuous. The CP had learned that the 3rd Battalion headquarters had come under heavy attack and that one of the 57th Field Artillery batteries had been overrun. Maclean received reports in quick succession that both battalion commanders at the inlet—Reilly and Embree—had been wounded in the fighting. "The picture of these two battalions was grim indeed," Robbins said.

Inlet Perimeter, Tuesday Morning, November 28

PFC James "Doc" Blohm, a medic with the 31st Regiment, was shocked when he arrived at the inlet in the morning. He had spent the night near the 57th Field Artillery headquarters a mile south, treating wounded from the fighting there. But nothing prepared him for the carnage revealed by the morning light at the inlet. "The perimeter was a scene lifted from the pages of Dante's Inferno," Blohm said. Hundreds of dead bodies—American, Korean, and especially Chinese—lay everywhere, many frozen in grotesque poses. Soldiers had been bayoneted in their sleeping bags. The GI and ROK bodies in their green uniforms were far outnumbered by the Chinese corpses in their quilted uniforms, either white or mustard yellow, depending on their regiment. Two lieutenants with B Battery, Ted Magill and Keith Sickafoose, toured the entire inlet perimeter after daylight and counted about 2,500 Chinese bodies. "I never saw so many dead people before," Reilly later wrote to his parents. "Far more than the Battle of the Bulge."

Burned-out vehicles, some still smoking, were scattered about, along with weapons and equipment. A headquarters company mess truck had been ransacked, and a Chinese soldier had run off with a frozen turkey from Thanksgiving that the mess sergeant had saved to make soup, but he'd only made it about ten yards before dropping it on the ground, where it lay, still frozen.

Officers and sergeants moved about in the numbing cold, "trying to create order out of chaos," Blohm said. Ammunition was taken from the dead and given to the living. Company first sergeants were making head counts and checking rosters, trying to figure out who was dead, wounded, or missing. A squad leader from the headquarters company was found dead outside the company CP, apparently shot by his men, who had mistaken him for an enemy soldier when he came around the corner in the dark. "Two men from his squad lost control of themselves because they were sure they had killed him," said Capt. Herbert Bryant, the company commander. The first sergeant tried to console the men, telling them it could have been anyone who shot him.

Litter parties carried the wounded to already overcrowded aid stations. Some had to be left outside, covered with blankets and sleeping bags. The medical convoy ambush had been a serious blow to medical support for the task force. Dozens of medical company personnel had been killed, captured, or wounded. The jeep that carried Maj. Galloway, the regimental surgeon, from the ambush had made it to the inlet. But with his serious head wound, Galloway was simply one more patient to be treated by Capt. Sterling Morgan, the overworked 3rd Battalion surgeon. As casualties were treated, Chinese mortar shells lofted from the hills landed in the inlet, wounding more men and drawing counterfire from the 57th Field Artillery howitzers.

"The battalion was stunned, not only by its casualties but by the loss of leadership," recalled Lt. John Gray. Maj. Clifton Couch, the executive officer, had made it through the night unscathed but, in the morning, was hit in the chest by a sniper round. He was brought gravely wounded and unconscious into the battalion CP.

Reilly remained in command of his battalion and had reoccupied the CP, where he was able to sit up and meet with his company commanders and platoon leaders. "He did not seem much different from his usual self," said Earle Jordan, the M Company commander.

Reilly briefed the leaders on what he knew. "First he told us that we were cut off from the 1st Marine Division," said SFC Farley. The rest of the Army task force was also "under heavy attack." Reilly wanted the perimeter shrunk and tightened up.

Harvey Storms, now the senior officer below Reilly, oversaw the realignment, directing Bill Etchemendy's L Company to pull back from across the Pungnyuri River. This meant crossing the inlet bridge exposed to potential enemy fire. "Amazingly, the Chinese didn't bother us at all and I figure they were recuperating and reorganizing from the tremendous casualties which we had inflicted during the night," Etchemendy said. Storms had the company set up along the inlet shore past the bridge, tying into what remained of K Company.

But SFC Bill Donovan's L Company weapons platoon remained positioned with a rifle squad and mortars in its outpost across the river on the high ground up the valley. They had been bypassed by the Chinese during the night. At first light, a bullet struck right above Donovan's head into the door of the hut he was using as a CP. Donovan could see the Chinese rushing up a gully toward their position. "We'll shoot it out until we're ordered back," he told his men.

The close quarters fight was vicious. Firing a 60 mm mortar on an enemy one hundred yards away would be cutting it close, and the Chinese were only twenty-five yards away. Donovan had the mortars firing almost straight up in order to drop on the enemy and keep them from overrunning the position. When word finally came from Etchemendy to pull out, they retreated across the bridge and set up their mortars inside the new perimeter.

Further south, Sergeant Jim DeLong's K Company machine gun squad was similarly alone in a ridgetop outpost, unnoticed during the night by the attacking Chinese. When daylight came, DeLong looked down the reverse slope of the ridge, where he saw a company-sized Chinese unit busily digging in right below their position. DeLong quietly told everyone in his squad—7 GIs and 5 ROKs—to get out a grenade and throw them on his signal. Then they would open up with their machine gun. "I passed the word to open fire," DeLong said. "They didn't know we were there."

They quickly learned. The Chinese took casualties but recovered from their surprise and furiously attacked the squad. DeLong's machine gunner was killed by a shot to the head and several ROKs were also fatally hit. As the squad retreated down the hill toward the inlet, the assistant gunner was shot in the stomach and fell on top of DeLong, who carried the wounded man over his shoulder. GIs in the inlet spotted the men coming and fired over their heads, trying to keep the pursuing Chinese at bay. The squad made it in and bolstered the K Company perimeter.

Hudong-ni, Tuesday Morning

At the 31st Regiment headquarters, Gen. Hodes was eager to launch the 31st Tank Company. After conferring with Capt. Drake, Hodes issued orders to attack north to the site of the medical convoy ambush. Drake, 27, a West Point graduate and tank commander with the 20th Armored Division in Germany in World War II, was confident, expecting little more than a road-clearing operation for his M4 Sherman tanks. It was a formidable force of sixteen tanks, armed with 76 mm cannons, grouped in three platoons of five tanks apiece, plus Drake's command tank. A fourth platoon stayed back to protect the Hudong-ni perimeter.

Hodes rode with Drake in the latter's jeep behind the tanks, but he left command of the attack with the captain. Master Sgt. James Thompson, a medic who had survived the ambush, volunteered to ride with them to identify where the Chinese had attacked the convoy. They soon approached the turn where the road rose along the south side of Hill 1221. Thompson asked that they stop so he could point out suspected Chinese positions on the mountain slope. Hodes, Drake, and Thompson, joined by Drake's driver, stood on the road, looking over the terrain. As they studied Drake's map, a sniper's bullet struck Thompson in the head, spraying blood over the map and killing the sergeant instantly. "General Hodes looked at me and said, 'Lad, we better hit the ditch,'" recalled the driver, 17-year-old Beryl Williams.

While they took cover, Drake ran to his command tank. The captain directed one tank platoon to continue up the road while a second platoon went off the road to attack up the south face of the hill. He kept his third platoon behind his command tank as a reserve.

The Chinese 3rd Battalion, 242nd Regiment, was waiting for the tanks, with one company positioned on Hill 1221, to the west of the road, and a second company positioned on lower ground on the east side. During the ambush of the medical convoy the night before, the Chinese had captured several U.S. Army 3.5-inch bazooka rocket launchers, which were quite effective against tanks.

When the tanks on the road were within twenty yards, an antitank team hiding in the low ground sprang out and swarmed over the tanks "like bees," Drake said. The two lead tanks were both hit by rockets and knocked out, one remaining on the road and blocking it, the other sliding off to the side.

Drake sent his third platoon onto flat marshland to the east, trying to provide flank support for the tanks on the road, but the heavy Shermans quickly bogged down in the softer ground and were attacked by Chinese troops, who scrambled up their sides. The "little fellows" strained mightily to open heavy engine compartment doors to drop in grenades, Drake said, but most were swept away by machine gun fire from other tanks. Two tanks remained stuck, spinning their turrets to keep the Chinese at bay. The tanks attacking up the slope of Hill 1221, meanwhile, were having trouble negotiating the icy hillside. One rolled over on a steep incline and was disabled. Two others threw tracks, leaving them unable to move.

By now, Drake said, "I realized we had more of a fight than I expected." He needed infantry troops to clear out the Chinese troops dug in on the hill. One of the hard-learned lessons from the fighting in Italy in World War II was that tanks operating in mountains needed infantry to clear the high ground. There were no infantry troops at Hudong-ni, but Drake radioed the CP, requesting they send any soldiers available to help the tanks.

Maj. Witte, the security commander at Hudong-ni, cobbled together a composite platoon of mechanics, cooks, bakers, and engineers who were rushed forward to join the battle. They would need to fight their way up the slope of Hill 1221 against dug-in Chinese troops and try to root out enemy positions commanding the hairpin curve, a task that would have been daunting even for seasoned infantry. Air support would have helped, but they had no forward air controller or radio to direct air strikes. The makeshift infantry bravely attacked up the hill, making several attempts to get around the Chinese right flank, but were "badly shot up," said Drake.

Capt. Hancock, the 31st Medical Company motor officer, and Master Sgt. Clarence Lee, the company 1st sergeant, had brought up an ambulance to treat the wounded. They struggled to keep up with the steady flow of casualties brought to their makeshift aid station. Hancock and Lee had limited medical supplies, as much of the company's supplies had been lost in the ambush. They used underwear to dress wounds and rationed their morphine, using one syrette to last for two or three wounded men. The ambulance made several trips, carrying wounded back to Hudong-ni. Despite the ambulance markings on the doors, they took heavy small-arms fire that killed at least one wounded man. Then Lee was killed by a shot to the head.

Maj. Marty Hoehn, the 3rd Battalion chaplain, had driven up in a jeep to offer his services and launched his own rescue effort. At 46, Hoehn had seen heavy combat in World War II and possessed a combative streak mixed with a crusader's zeal. Despite admonitions against it from the chief chaplain in Tokyo, he carried a .45 pistol with him everywhere he went in Korea. Had Hoehn lived in an earlier time, Bill McCaffrey later said, "he would have been a Knight Templar and a great threat to the Saracens."

Seeing the predicament of the men, Hoehn rushed repeatedly into heavy fire to get to the side of wounded men, ministering to them, treating their wounds, and pulling some to safety. The chaplain, irate that the Chinese were shooting stranded tankers, joined an attack up the hill. Hoehn "grabbed a submachine gun and began shooting—each time asking God's forgiveness," Drake said.

"He was right there in the middle of a banzai charge, helping wounded," said PFC Donald Cook. "He seemed to be everywhere at the same time."

Despite such heroics, by midday, it had become obvious to Hodes and Drake that the tank attack had failed. If it hadn't been before, it was now clear that the Chinese possession of Hill 1221, with its command of the only road, posed a serious threat to the task force. Drake told Hodes that with better infantry and air support, the tanks could make another attempt to break through. While Drake worked to extricate the tanks, Hodes returned to Hudong-ni in the captain's jeep with the hope of arranging better support for a second attack.

X Corps Headquarters, Tuesday Morning

Ned Almond was not particularly concerned about the attacks around the Chosin Reservoir the previous night, even though his headquarters had received an urgent telephone report at 9:50 a.m. from Maj. Lynch at Hudong-ni, reporting alarming details about the attack on the Army battalions east of the reservoir: Artillery positions had been overrun. There was no telephone communication with the forward units, only unreliable radio transmissions. A medical company convoy had been ambushed. The tank company had launched an attack. The task force needed medical assistance, improved communication, and small-arms ammunition. The 2nd Battalion still had not arrived and was badly needed.

Shortly before 11:00 a.m., Almond, accompanied by Lt. Haig, departed Hamhung in a small L-17 liaison plane to fly to Chosin, intending to "visit the units I thought most needed an inspection," the general later said. They landed in Hagaru at 11:30 a.m. and were taken by jeep to the 1st Marine Division CP to meet with O. P. Smith. The Marine commander had arrived by helicopter in Hagaru shortly before, having moved the division headquarters that morning from Hungnam.

Almond and Smith discussed the Chinese attacks. By the X Corps commander's account, they agreed the overall situation had not changed sufficiently and not enough was known about the Chinese intent to make any changes to the mission. But Alpha Bowser, Smith's operations chief, recalled the Marine general was less than enthusiastic at Almond's insistence to proceed with the attack. "That man must be crazy," Smith muttered afterward.

Almond wanted to visit Faith's 1st Battalion on the east side of the reservoir and took off in a Marine helicopter just before 1:00 p.m. Landing near Faith's CP, Almond popped out of the bubble-nosed helicopter, looking fresh and clean in his new parka and starched cold-weather pants. Haig followed, carrying the general's briefcase. Faith sent a jeep to pick up Almond. Maclean drove up at the same time from his nearby forward headquarters to join the conference at Faith's headquarters.

Standing outside the battalion CP, Almond immediately made it clear to Maclean and Faith that he expected the Army task force to attack north to the Yalu as planned. Maclean, likely feeling pressure from Almond, agreed that the attack could be resumed once the task force was joined by Drake's tanks and the still-missing 2nd Battalion. "He was cheerful and confident and determined," Almond later said. Faith, though, seemed tense and dubious about the whole proposition. Based on intelligence picked up from Chinese prisoners, Faith told Almond they were being attacked by elements of two Chinese divisions.

"That's impossible, Colonel, there aren't two Chinese communist divisions in the whole of North Korea," Almond declared. He told Faith not to worry about the Chinese; they were just stragglers retreating north and represented no serious threat to the Army task force.

The men around the CP who had lived through the previous night were stunned. "The officers present were amazed at Gen. Almond's remarks about the CCF stragglers," said Lt. May. "That was a beauty," agreed Capt. Bill McNally, the 31st Regiment communications officer.

That Almond would make such a claim was astonishing. He was well aware by now of the collapse of the 8th Army to the west. He had met with Smith and knew about the heavy fighting at Yudam-ni and the threat of encirclement. The Army perimeters had been penetrated the previous night, and the ground commanders were now telling him they had been hit by elements of two divisions. Quite a few frozen American bodies were stacked near the CP, and many dead Chinese were scattered about, lying in mute testimony to the ferocity of the fighting the previous night.

Yet Almond clearly did not grasp how precarious the situation was—nor did he seem interested in learning. The general insisted that the enemy forces the task force had battled during the night were simply remnants from the Chinese divisions that the Marines had demolished at Sudong and that Reilly's 3rd Battalion had scattered weeks ago at Fusen Reservoir.

Faith wore a look of disbelief as Almond spoke. "He wasn't going to be insolent or anything, he wasn't that kind of a man," recalled Sgt. Charlie Gebhardt. "But I could tell."

Almond did not use his brief time on the ground to ask about the previous night's attack or find out what equipment and supplies his commanders on the ground needed. Instead, the general announced he had three Silver Star medals to hand out: one for Faith and the other two for soldiers selected by the battalion commander. Faith tried to decline the honor, but Almond insisted. He told Faith to pick two more recipients and to gather troops to watch the presentation. Almond loved giving out medals on the spot in the field in Korea, emulating a habit of MacArthur's; others suggested he saw Napoleon as his role model. Almond believed this sort of dashing, immediate recognition inspired the troops.

To Faith and the men watching, it was ludicrous; they needed ammunition, not medals. Faith looked around and spotted Lt. Everett Smalley, a C Company platoon leader who had been wounded trying to recapture the knoll. He called Smalley over, then stopped Sgt. George Stanley, a headquarters company mess sergeant. "Stanley, come here and stand at attention next to Lieutenant Smalley," Faith told him. He called nearby soldiers over to assemble around the group.

Smalley, though not undeserving of recognition, was embarrassed; he had been hoping the helicopter was carrying medical supplies and was bewildered to be getting a medal instead. The randomness of the recognition cheapened the meaning of the decoration. Almond pinned the medals to the parkas of the three men and shook their hands. Haig dutifully scribbled down the names of the medal recipients in his notebook.

Then Almond addressed the assembled troops and assured them all was well. "The enemy who is delaying you for the moment is nothing more than remnants of Chinese divisions fleeing north," the general declared. "We're still attacking and we're going all the way to the Yalu. Don't let a bunch of Chinese laundrymen stop you."

Whether it was his racist contempt for the Chinese or his arrogant refusal to accept facts that contradicted his preconceived opinion, Almond was fatally underestimating the threat posed by the enemy. Maclean, having witnessed the attack at the forward perimeter and having received reports on the precarious situation at the inlet, should have been more forceful in making sure Almond understood the realities on the ground.

Pulling Faith aside, Almond spread a large map on the hood of a jeep. The general pointed to the high knoll occupied by the Chinese. "You are in a dangerous, low ground area and should improve your present front line defensive position to include that high ground," he told the battalion commander. Faith, of course, was well aware of that. His men had been trying all morning to recapture the ground. But he bit his tongue and simply said he would try. Almond then took off by jeep, back to his waiting helicopter, "bidding all farewell and good luck," the general recalled.

As soon as Almond departed, Faith ripped the Silver Star off his parka. He tossed it into the snow. "What a damned travesty," Faith said.

Wes Curtis went up to Faith and asked him what guidance Almond had provided.

"You heard him," Faith muttered. "Remnants fleeing north."

HUDONG, TUESDAY AFTERNOON

Hammering Hank Hodes, returning to the 31st Regiment CP from the tank attack, exploded when he learned that Almond had just departed the forward perimeter after meeting with Maclean and Faith.

"Well, what in the hell did he tell Maclean to do?" Hodes demanded of Lt. Col. Berry Anderson, the regimental operations officer.

Anderson replied that as far he could find out, Almond had handed out some medals, given a pep talk, and flown off. Maj. Lynch had never seen Hodes so angry. This had been the opportunity to organize a breakout. The task force was bloodied but remained powerful. Every hour that passed would leave it running lower on ammunition and supplies and suffering more casualties. Almond could have ordered Faith's battalion to immediately move south and consolidate with the rest of the task force. He could have tried to coordinate an attack on Hill 1221 by the infantry battalions from the north and the tanks from the south. Almond had done none of that. "Why the Corps CG did not issue instructions which would have prevented or at least minimized the developing tragedy before the situation became hopeless was appalling to General Hodes," Lynch recalled.

Maclean and Faith knew nothing about the 31st Tank Company's fight to reach them, which was still underway. The Sherman tanks had reliable radios, but they would only communicate with other tanks; by some inexplicable Army logic, they did not net with the infantry radios. And even though they were only five miles from Hagaru, the command post had no radio communication with the 1st Marine Division headquarters because their radios were on different networks.

Almond told the Army commanders nothing about the tank attack, even though his X Corps headquarters was informed about it before he had left Hamhung. Almond hadn't bothered to liaison with Hodes, the senior Army commander at the reservoir, or anyone at the regimental headquarters. Almond did nothing to arrange for resupply or address communication problems. Almond would later claim that Faith and Maclean "knew as little about the Chinese forces" east of the reservoir as he did. That was not true; he chose not to listen.

Hodes's view darkened further when word arrived at Hudong-ni that the missing 2nd Battalion, 31st Infantry, was still nowhere near Chosin. The general smoldered for a bit in front of the CP stove, restlessly stabbing at a can of C Rations. Then he got up and declared he himself would take a jeep to Hagaru with the hope of arranging help for the cutoff battalions. Hodes shrugged off Anderson's warning that the Chinese may have cut off the road to Hagaru by now. But the general agreed to ride in a tank rather than a jeep when it was pointed out that he would be able to use the tank's radio to communicate with the CP via the tanks remaining at Hudong-ni.

After arriving safely at Hagaru, Hodes spoke briefly with Gen. Smith. According to Lynch, Hodes hoped to arrange for a Marine helicopter to fly him to the Army task force, where he could instruct Maclean to have Reilly's 3rd Battalion attack Hill 1221 from the north at the same time that Drake's tanks attack the hill from the south. Such a coordinated attack, particularly with airstrikes and follow-on support from Faith's 1st Battalion, would have a good chance of succeeding.

"Why did this not happen?" Lynch later said. "There was no chopper available to Hodes."

The Army had no helicopters at Chosin and was reliant on those belonging to the Marine Observation Squadron 6 (VMO-6). The four-seat Sikorsky helicopters and their Marine pilots were performing yeoman service and made forty flights at Chosin that day, including twenty-three evacuations of wounded Marines from Yudam-ni, as well as sixteen transportation flights. Other than those ferrying Almond to Faith's CP and back, none were for the Army. As a one-star, Hodes did not have the same pull as Almond. But given the desperate straits the 31st RCT faced, the Marines should have flown Hodes to the Army task force that day.

To make matters worse, by late afternoon, radio communication was lost between Hudong-ni and Task Force Maclean at both the forward perimeter and the inlet. "After that, information dwindled progressively to zero," Lynch said. Hodes was unable to reach Maclean or any of the battalion commanders—not by helicopter, telephone, or radio—and his hope of coordinating an attack evaporated.

Maclean's decision the previous night to leave the regimental headquarters at Hudong-ni and move to his forward CP, near Faith's battalion, could be seen now as a mistake, as it left him unable to communicate with Hodes and separated him from his intelligence and operations staff. But if he had stayed at Hudong-ni, he would have been no better able than Hodes to communicate with the forward battalions. Neither was a good option.

The real problem was the disastrous lack of communication between the cutoff battalions and any higher headquarters—with the regimental command post at Hudong-ni, 1st Marine Division headquarters at Hagaru, 7th Division headquarters at Pukchong, or X Corps headquarters at Hamhung. By Army practice, responsibility for reestablishing broken communications lay with higher headquarters. Almond could have taken some steps to fly in better equipment—a Marine radio to communicate with Hagaru or a tank radio to communicate with Hudong-ni—yet he did nothing in that regard. Nor did Barr, Hodes, Smith, or anyone else. Apart from Almond's visit, said Wes Curtis, "our battalion was out of communication with the outside world." The communication breakdown, X Corps historian Shelby Stanton noted, "bordered on command criminal negligence."

Almond had squandered the best opportunity to save the Army task force. During his visit, he had failed to get an assessment of the situation, and he had refused to listen to Faith. "I wanted to find out his needs and to show him that we appreciated his problems at the moment," Almond later said. He failed miserably on both counts.

Almond's insistence that Task Force Maclean attack north rather than consolidate and move south to Hagaru "is a matter which he must take up with his Maker," Lynch later said.

Hill 1221

After extricating his tanks from the marshland east of the road, Bob Drake was ready to retreat to Hudong-ni. The attack had been a disaster. Dozens of men had been killed or injured. Four tanks had been lost. Litter teams gathered all the remaining wounded soldiers they could from the hillside to the ambulance, but as they left for Hudong-ni, Capt. Hancock worried there had been others they had not reached. The ambulance, by then, was so shot up that a tank had to tow it the final stretch into the perimeter.

Chaplain Hoehn, who would be awarded the Silver Star for his heroism, brought up the rear, following a tank that had run out of ammunition. He stewed over the failure. "It disgusted me to see the enemy . . . squirm around in some open patches on the hills but no one could shoot as all were riding away rapidly as possible," Hoehn later wrote.

Back at Hudong-ni, two tanks under Lt. Richard Henson were sent out to scout for a route to the northeast around the Chinese roadblock. That mission ended with no route found and Henson dead, killed by a Chinese soldier who feigned surrender and then shot the lieutenant with a machine gun. The Chinese remained in control of Hill 1221. The three cut-off battalions at the inlet were more isolated than ever.

Inlet Perimeter, Tuesday Afternoon

All afternoon soldiers at the inlet worked to improve their defensive positions before nightfall. The soldiers of M Company battled the frozen ground to dig deeper holes and build higher parapets at the insistence of Earle Jordan, their robust and indomitable company commander. "We had no reason not to expect another attempt to eliminate us sometime during the hours of darkness," said Jordan, a big Yankee from Maine. Jordan had experienced heavy fighting in Italy during World War II while in the same regiment as Maj. Lynch, who considered him "a vital soldier," one of the most outstanding he'd ever seen. Jordan's men had held their ground during the night's fighting, but the cost had been high. Lt. Gray's mortar platoon alone had suffered 12 men killed, 2 missing, and 25 wounded. Jordan had been wounded by a grenade and had frostbite in both feet, but his contagious optimism built back confidence shaken by the night's attack.

Spirits rose further during the afternoon at the sight of the battery of M19 Twin 40s and M16 Quad 50s from the 15th AAA rolling up the road, coming from their position a mile south, to reinforce the battered and undermanned inlet defenses. Capt. McClymont placed them so they protected the artillery batteries and covered all avenues of approach to the perimeter with interlocking fire. As part of the inlet consolidation, B Battery moved up and took a position next to A Battery, with A Battery on the east side, guns facing north, and B Battery to the west, with guns facing south.

Reilly ordered an afternoon counteroffensive to try to regain some of the ground lost during the night fight. He was hoping for air support, but the loss of the Air Force tactical air party the previous night made it hard to coordinate. SFC Farley's K Company platoon put out orange panels to help the planes identify targets, but a snowstorm blew in, covering up the panels. A flight of planes came in for a strike and had to abort when they could not spot the panels. Reilly's men met little resistance and were able to regain some ground, but the Chinese remained in control of all the high ground to their front.

Reilly passed word for soldiers to pick up the Chinese weapons and ammunition and use them to help defend the perimeter. The GIs were puzzled to find many of the attackers were carrying American Thompson submachine guns. "There were Tommy guns with the pistol handle fore and aft, like in the gangster movies," recalled McClymont. Ironically, many of the weapons used by the Chinese at Chosin were American made, including mortars, light and heavy machine guns, and Tommy guns. They had originally been supplied by the United States to Chiang Kai-shek's Nationalist forces and had then been captured by Mao's army. The Chinese also had Japanese weapons surrendered at the end of World War II. Some of their most ubiquitous weapons were reliable Soviet-made 7.62 mm submachine guns, nicknamed "burp" guns by the GIs for the sound they made when fired.

McClymont, handy with guns and an expert marksman from his boyhood days of hunting and wandering the woods near Mount Rainier in Washington state, tried a couple of Tommy guns and picked out one for himself, also helping himself to a canvas apron worn by some Chinese soldiers to carry clips for the submachine guns. Like many of the Americans, McClymont had noticed the Chinese didn't have as many problems with guns jamming as did the GIs. "I quickly discovered why the tommy gun fired and fired and fired," he recalled. "The Chinese weren't using much oil in that below zero weather!"

Late in the afternoon, Air Force C-47 aircraft appeared over the inlet and dropped pallets bearing sixteen tons of supplies for the regiment. Yellow and red parachutes opened up as they fell, their color startling against the bleak background. But strong winds caught the parachutes, carrying the bulk of the supplies south to the Chinese. One crate that a GI patrol managed to retrieve was found to contain toilet paper but no ammunition. "It became another big joke," said Francois.

Capt. Conner, the whiskey-loving 3rd Battalion chaplain, made the rounds, bolstering morale with his Bible and flask. He had been everywhere during the night, helping bring wounded into the aid station and constantly exposing himself to danger to check on men around the perimeter. "Men pouring fire into the Chinese attacks were encouraged by his touch on their shoulder and his calm voice asking, 'How are you doing, son?'" recalled Reeves. "Then, after offering a sip of whisky to give the GI strength against overwhelming fatigue, he moved on." But then Conner himself was seriously wounded, hit by shrapnel or small-arms fire in the buttocks, and the men to whom the chaplain had been ministering took him to the battalion aid station.

What comfort the chaplain had provided could not disguise the increasingly grim situation. All day, the soldiers could see columns of Chinese troops on distant snow-covered ridges to the east, far out of range, moving south, some on horseback.

Late that day, Reilly summoned his company commanders and platoon leaders for another conference. "We . . . were told that we were to hold our ground, as the rest of the [task force] were going to try and join us if at all possible," Farley recalled. Reilly reported that multiple Chinese divisions had attacked all around the Chosin Reservoir and that every American outfit had been cut off.

"We went back to our platoon and told them just what was going on and the morale of the men was still very good," Farley said. "As night was coming on and it was getting awful cold the men knew there was no chance to get any sleep as there would be 100 percent alert all night."

Forward Perimeter, Tuesday Afternoon

The 1st Battalion fight to retake the high knoll captured by the Chinese continued through the afternoon, led by Dale Seever, the C Company commander. Jim Mortrude's ever-reliable platoon was moved to the company's right flank to help with the counterattack. "For the sake of time and weight, we reluctantly abandoned our bedrolls with the assurance of the executive officer that the bags would be brought right up to us at night," Mortrude recalled.

The platoon attacked east up the ridgeline leading to the knoll, at first with no resistance but then encountering a series of lower enemy-occupied knolls. Around 3:00 p.m., Marine Corsairs called in by Capt. Stamford appeared overhead. Every time Stamford called Mortrude to report a plane was on station and ready to strike, the lieutenant heaved a white phosphorus grenade as far out in front as he could, and the white smoke would mark the spot for the pilot to hit. Mortrude and his men marveled at the skill of the Marine pilots, who flew so close and low that the soldiers could look down from their knoll into the cockpit of the aircraft and wave to the pilot.

Maclean tried to get more air support via the SCR-300 radio in his command jeep, which was able to contact aircraft overhead. Maclean's radioman, Sgt. Arthur "Frenchy" Mercier, reached some Air Force P-51 Mustangs on their way to another mission. Maclean took the radio and requested they put gunfire on the slope of the Chinese-held hill. "Sorry, sir," a pilot answered, "but we have our orders."

MacLean was not satisfied with that. "If I have to come up there, I'll shove my boot up your ass!" he shouted. "Now zero your guns on that . . . slope and don't leave until every round is spent." The Mustang pilots complied.

With the air support, C Company advanced, but they were stopped short of the highest knoll by heavy enemy fire that the aircraft could not suppress. The Chinese were well dug in on the reverse slope, and they had brought up several heavy machine guns. Every time the GIs closed in on the knoll, Chinese troops pulled back to allow the machine guns to rake the crest.

Master Sgt. Leo Russavage, the battalion sergeant major, pulled out his pistol and led a charge up the hill. He was felled by burst of machine gun fire. The loss of Russavage, a World War II veteran and one of the finest soldiers in the battalion, was a blow to Faith and his men. "His death stunned and saddened all of us," Bigger said.

Soon after, with darkness approaching, Faith stopped the attack and ordered his forces to consolidate. Mortrude's platoon was ordered to fall back to the previous knoll and dig in for the night to protect the company's right flank. Their promised sleeping gear did not materialize. "We never saw the bags again and suffered considerably," Mortrude said.

Just before sundown, Able Company soldiers spotted several hundred enemy troops coming down the road accompanied by a Russian T-34 tank and several self-propelled guns. Stamford was able to direct flights of Corsairs and Royal Australian Air Force F-51 Mustangs to strike the column "with devastating result," he recalled.

With the Chinese controlling the roads, Maclean had ordered his forward CP to move "with all haste" into the forward perimeter. Apart from Maclean, Robbins, and the radio crew, most of the 35 men were thrown into the company lines. "We could not very well operate as a regimental CP at that time in a normal manner when every man was needed to man a weapon for defense," said Robbins.

Maclean and a small cadre of his regimental staff joined Faith and his staff in the small mud farmhouse serving as the joint headquarters. "The occasional crack of small arms fire going overhead from the Chinese and the answering sputter of our own machine guns and deep chug of our mortars could be heard as we stood by and made plans for the coming night," recalled Robbins. Capt. Raymond Vaudreaux, the 1st Battalion supply officer, reported a critical shortage of every type of ammunition.

At the battalion aid station, dressing material was getting short. Nevertheless, Dr. Lee Yong Kak treated several wounded Chinese who were brought in. They looked very young to be soldiers, Lee thought. "How many battalions attacked us?" Lee asked one of them in Chinese. It was a much larger force than a couple of battalions, the soldier replied—it was three regiments.

Lee was shocked. "Brother, we are gonna have another big fight tonight," he told himself.

All available men, including clerks, cooks, and drivers, were put on the perimeter. Joe Ager and the other Black truck drivers from 515th Truck Transportation Company were paired off with soldiers from Faith's 1st Battalion. It wasn't official, but the 7th Division now had Black soldiers. "I guess this was the first integrated unit," said Ager.

All day small groups of survivors from the 31st Regiment Intelligence and Reconnaissance Platoon had been cautiously working their way around hills and valleys, trying to make their way back to American lines while avoiding Chinese patrols. Concealed in scrub vegetation on a hilltop perch, SFC John Adams, the 1st Squad leader, had watched Chinese rearguard troops comb through the area where the I&R Platoon had been overrun the previous evening. Adams moved carefully to the backside of the hill, where he spotted about a half-dozen men huddled in a clearing. Working his way closer, Adams saw they were other survivors from the platoon, including the 2nd Squad leader, SFC Dick Cooper, as well as Cpl. Jim Arie and Cpl. Ananias Janvrin. "Most everyone was wounded or frostbitten or both, and nobody had any ammunition except me," Arie recalled. Janvrin soon died from his wounds. "In our condition, all we could do was to evade capture and work our way back to the reservoir," Arie said. Deep behind enemy lines, the 1st and 2nd squad survivors had a long way to go.

SFC Sam Muncy's 3rd Squad, which had been bypassed by the Chinese during their attack down the Pungnyuri the previous night, was closer to the reservoir but still in grave danger. The squad had been working its way back to American lines during the day when they were spotted by a platoon-sized Chinese patrol, which opened fire, killing several squad members. In escaping the attack, the survivors split up, with Muncy and several others moving toward the inlet while Cpl. Roy Shiraga and two others took a more northerly route. "In falling back we played cat and mouse with that patrol all day," Shiraga said. "We moused, they catted." Just before nightfall, Shiraga's group reached the 1st Battalion perimeter and were straight away added to the defenses. Muncy's group made it to the inlet perimeter, where they were welcomed into the beleaguered K Company line.

Hagaru-ri, Tuesday Afternoon

As the afternoon progressed, it was becoming increasingly clear to Gen. Smith that the X Corps units at Chosin "were up against a massive force." The Marines at Yudam-ni had identified three CCF divisions—the 59th, 79th, and 89th. Maclean's Army task force east of the reservoir had identified the 80th Division, as well as elements of a second division—the 81st. Another two divisions—the 58th and 60th—had been identified around Hagaru. Smith was also alarmed by the weak defenses he had found at Hagaru after his arrival that morning. Though about 3,000 Marines and 600 Army soldiers were at the base, the only infantry was a Marine battalion that was short one rifle company—not much, given the size of the perimeter. Apart from two Marine artillery batteries, the rest of the troops were from an assortment of service, support, supply, headquarters, and engineer units.

"Hagaru-ri had to be held at all costs," Smith later said. At the junction of the roads leading up the east and west sides of the reservoir, it also lay atop the only road leading back to the sea. Marine engineers were working furiously to complete the airstrip, which had become obviously critical to survival. The base held stockpiles of rations, fuel, and supplies crucial for the surrounded American force. Had the Chinese attacked Hagaru as part of their surprise offensive the previous night, they may well have overrun the base. Several weeks later, Smith would flippantly attribute that failure to Chinese intelligence "of a low order—and I don't mean their military intelligence." In fact, Song Shilun wanted to attack the base. Had the reinforced 80th Division succeeded in destroying the U.S. forces east of Chosin, its orders were to continue on to attack Hagaru in conjunction with an attack from the west by the 58th Division. Instead, the 80th Division had suffered such high casualties in its fight with the Army task force that continuing its attack to Hagaru was impossible.

Though he had not received permission from X Corps, Smith gave orders at 5:00 p.m., canceling the Marine attack from Yudam-ni, considering it "rash" to carry on with Almond's plan. "Under the circumstances I considered it unwise to continue offensive operations," he wrote. "We were now engaged in a fight for our lives and it was necessary to assume the defensive at all points until the situation clarified."

Maclean and Faith had no such leeway. Their hands had been tied earlier that day by Almond's emphatic direction to continue their attack north.

At 6:30 p.m., Hodes sent an urgent radio message to Gen. Barr at the 7th Division headquarters, asking him to do anything possible to speed the 2nd Battalion's arrival at Chosin. But the 2nd Battalion had only arrived at Hamhung that evening.

Upon his return from Chosin to X Corps headquarters in Hamhung late Tuesday afternoon, Almond was given a top-secret message from GHQ. MacArthur wanted him to fly immediately to Tokyo for a conference. Gen. Walker, the 8th Army commander, was also being summoned, so there could be no missing the magnitude of the meeting. Almond hurried to the nearby Yonpo Airfield accompanied by McCaffrey and several other aides, then boarded a C-54 Skymaster and took off at 5:00 p.m. Almond's departure was so abrupt and secret that his own X Corps headquarters reported him missing, forcing patrols to be sent out from Hagaru to search for the Corps commander until the mistake was realized.

At the Dai Ichi in Tokyo, MacArthur had recognized what Almond had not. The shaken commander in chief sent a long radio message late Tuesday afternoon to the Joint Chiefs at the Pentagon, acknowledging that the UN forces under his command in North Korea faced a grave crisis. "The Chinese military forces are committed in North Korea in great and ever increasing strength," he wrote. "No pretext of minor support under the guise of volunteerism or other subterfuge now has the slightest validity. We face an entirely new war."

The message arrived at the Pentagon just before dawn, Washington time, Tuesday, and quickly made its way up the chain of command. At 6:15 a.m., Omar Bradley, the Joint Chiefs of Staff chairman, called Truman and reported that the Chinese had "come in with both feet."

Truman was stunned by MacArthur's grim assessment. Three days earlier, the general had kicked off his offensive with grand pronouncements of quickly bringing the war to a close. Now his military forces faced disaster. It was the "worst situation we have had yet," the president said at his morning staff meeting. At an emergency meeting of the National Security Council, Secretary of State Acheson warned the country might be on the verge of World War III.

MacArthur followed up his message to the Joint Chiefs by issuing a nearly identical public communique reporting that 200,000 Chinese troops had been committed against the UN forces. "This has shattered the high hope we entertained that the intervention of the Chinese was only of a token nature on a volunteer and individual basis," he declared. As usual, MacArthur took no blame, implying it lay with Washington: "This command has done everything possible within its capabilities but is now faced with conditions beyond its control and strength."

Beijing, Tuesday, November 28

Mao Zedong was delighted with the reports he was receiving on the success of the Chinese offensive, both against the 8th Army on the western front and X Corps at the Chosin Reservoir. "This is the best opportunity to massively destroy the enemy and fundamentally solve the Korean issue," he wrote in a telegram on Tuesday to Peng Dehuai at the Chinese People's Volunteer Force headquarters in North Korea.

"It is absolutely feasible to annihilate" the 1st Marine Division and the Army's 7th Division at Chosin, Mao added.

La Feria, Texas, Tuesday Evening, November 28

Billy had a fever and Ernie had a cold, so Helen Storms had put the two younger boys to bed by the time she began her letter to Harvey. As she typed, Sammy was at her feet on the floor with a copy of the Army and Navy Hymnal, singing every song he knew.

The news that day was filled with distressing reports about the Chinese intervention. "Poor MacArthur has his hands tied," she wrote. "It looks like suicide for our men unless the UN does go all out in a third world war. No one wants that."

Helen had given up her brief hope that Harvey would be home for Christmas, so she had mailed him the pecans she had bought for him and also sent two boxes of cookies she had baked—one, dream bars; the other, pecan crescents. In truth, she was coming to terms with the likelihood he would not even be back before she was due to give birth in February. "I don't mind having this baby without you so awfully much, but it is the uncertainty of your whereabouts and safety that keeps me so heavy hearted," Helen wrote.

She added, "I do have faith and confidence, but oh, the agony I suffer sometimes when I let it slip."

Chapter 8

THE SECOND NIGHT

Tuesday–Wednesday, November 28–29

Forward Perimeter, 8:00 p.m., Tuesday

Another attack was coming—the only question was when. Most of the GIs figured the Chinese would strike as soon as the sun went down and the threat of the Corsairs was gone. Yet early evening at the forward perimeter had been strangely quiet. Inside the hut serving as the 1st Battalion, 32nd Regiment, headquarters staff officers were huddled around a small gasoline stove, making small talk and occasionally nodding off from their exhaustion. Faith and Maclean had retired to a side room in the hope of dozing before the attacks started.

But Faith was unable to sleep. Around 8:00 p.m., he came into the communications room and called up each of his company commanders, checking if there was any enemy activity. All quiet, he was told. But a few minutes later, Faith learned that communication with the 57th Field Artillery batteries at the inlet had gone out. "That was a blow which was greeted by silence from the colonel as he realized now that he would be without the help from a usually strong defensive weapon," said Maj. Robbins. On top of that, several of the battalion's heavy mortars had cracked in the extreme cold, so even less supporting fire would be available.

There had been no further contact with higher headquarters since Almond's absurd insistence during his afternoon visit that the task force attack north. That was clearly impossible, but they had been given no alternatives. "I was aware of Col Faith's feelings about the situation that we were in," said Capt. Bigger. "We were receiving no guidance, instructions, orders or whatever about what our actions were to be." The loss of so many men—Capt. Scullion and Master Sgt. Russavage among them—had left Faith in a subdued mood.

The harsh weather deepened their gloom. The temperature was twenty-four below and sinking fast. By later calculations factoring in windchill, it felt as cold at times as seventy-five to one hundred degrees below zero. The troops at Chosin were fighting in cold without parallel in U.S. military history, with the possible exception of the Army Expeditionary Force sent in 1918 to Archangel, Russia, where they battled Bolsheviks near the Arctic Circle. Even the notorious cold during the battles of Trenton and Princeton, the winter at Valley Forge in the Revolutionary War, and in the Ardennes during the Battle of the Bulge was less severe.

The men who suffered the most were the ones up on the hillsides, most exposed to the cold, with their rations and water still frozen. "Eating or drinking was nigh on impossible," said SFC Willis Via, A Company.

On the Able Company line, Roy Oxenrider had cut a hole in his mitten for his trigger finger, but then his bare finger froze to the metal trigger. He had to pull the skin off his finger to free it from his rifle. After that, he put his mitten on backward and used its thumb for his trigger finger. It wasn't ideal, but at least his rifle worked. Up on the line, that meant a lot. "So many weapons would not operate or fire properly because of the cold," he said. "I protected my weapon above all else."

Inlet Perimeter, Tuesday Evening

Four miles to the south, along the inlet perimeter line manned by the men of the 3rd Battalion, 31st Infantry, the wait for the Chinese attack did not last long. Sgt. DeLong's K Company squad, recovered from their morning scramble from their outpost to the friendly lines, had spent the day digging into their position and bracing for the night. "We knew that we were surrounded," said DeLong. "We knew that we were going to have a battle. It was just a question of how long and how many of them were going to come at us." K Company was down to about 60 men, one-third of its strength, so it looked to be a long night.

DeLong's friend, Sgt. Ernest Fontaine, was in the next foxhole, armed with an M-1 rifle. At 32, Fontaine was older than most GIs in the company. He had no wife or girlfriend, and he'd been orphaned as a child and raised by a grandfather in Rhode Island. Admittedly, Fontaine was not the best peacetime soldier. "In Japan he would get paid, go to town, and drink until he didn't have any more money," said DeLong. "Then he would come back and soldier for about 26 days. He would get paid and go AWOL again until he went broke. Then he would come back and soldier again. As long as he didn't have any money, he was a good soldier."

But Fontaine had combat experience few could match, having served with the legendary Merrill's Marauders in Burma during World War II. DeLong and the other soldiers looked up to Fontaine, listening to his lessons on how to survive as a combat soldier. "He was the best wartime man we had in K Company," said DeLong. "He knew what to do."

That made Fontaine's quiet pessimism as they waited for what the night would bring all the more concerning. "Jim, we're not going to stop these people," he told DeLong. "I know how they fight, they'll just keep coming at us until they overrun us."

The 80th CCF Division barely waited for the sun to go down before attacking the inlet at several spots around the perimeter. The 239th Regiment launched company-sized attacks of several hundred men from the south and east on the K and I company lines, firing mortars and assaulting with automatic weapons and grenades. "They hit us every place you could think of," said Capt. Kitz, the K Company commander. "It was here and there and all over the perimeter."

DeLong's hand was soon raw from hitting the machine gun lever to keep it firing. The position held by DeLong and Fontaine held, but the Chinese broke through elsewhere on the thinly stretched K Company line, capturing a machine gun position and cutting the company's communications with the rear.

Kitz got word of the penetration and, lacking communication with the rear, ran back to try to arrange fire support for the company. That angered some K Company soldiers, who believed he should have stayed at his command post and sent a runner instead. "To me and some of [the] men he turned chicken and left us," said SFC Farley.

Lt. John Gray's mortar platoon had set up some positions facing south and east to support K and I companies in the hopes of preventing a disastrous breakthrough, like the previous night. Gray's observer with I Company radioed that the entire east ridge was under heavy attack and that K Company, to his left, desperately needed fire support. But Gray's heart sank when he found his radio and telephone communication with K Company was out. The only choice was to fire blindly on pre-plotted points on the Chinese avenues of approach, but lacking timing and coordination, the mortars were of little help.

Gray didn't realize how serious the penetration was until he heard a warning on the battalion net radio that the Chinese were inside the perimeter. Looking to the southeast, he saw numerous shadowy figures moving quickly across the snowy landscape toward his position. Gray ordered his men to rush into their forward defensive blocking positions and begin firing. Enemy mortar barrages fell all around them, and one shell exploded near Gray, severely wounding his thigh. Gray was able to reach his M-1 rifle and fire it at several approaching Chinese soldiers, but then he was hit with a burst of fire from a Tommy gun, which destroyed his rifle, wounded his right hand, and knocked him into the rubble of a destroyed wall behind him.

All around him, the soldiers of M Company struggled in hand-to-hand combat with enemy infiltrators. Lying in the rubble, Gray desperately worked with his uninjured left hand to pull his .45 pistol from his right hip holster, getting it out just in time to empty the clip at point-blank range at three enemy troops advancing at him, one with a bayonet. Mortar shrapnel had nicked an artery in Gray's thigh, and he was bleeding profusely. The platoon medic placed a tight compress bandage on the wound, gave him a shot of morphine, and helped him to the battalion aid station.

It was scarcely any safer in the surgeon's tent, where bullets snapped through the canvas and shot holes through everything, including the containers meant to hold alcohol and disinfectant. Capt. Morgan, the battalion surgeon, had himself been hit but still was "working frantically with stacks of wounded," Gray said. After a bit, Gray decided his wounds paled in comparison to some of the others, so he grabbed an M-1 rifle belonging to another casualty and hobbled back to his platoon's defensive position, where he found M Company had managed to clear the remaining Chinese from the company's area.

As with the previous night, the 80th Division attack was severely hampered by poor communication, with units inside the perimeter fighting separate, uncoordinated fights in different directions. Some of the Chinese soldiers were most interested in finding food. "They appeared to stop at K Company's kitchen and have a party," said Capt. Bryant, the Headquarters Company commander.

From there, infiltrators headed for the 3rd Battalion CP, the site of so much carnage the night before. Lt. Col. Reilly was inside, along with Maj.

Storms; Capt. Bob McClay, the adjutant; and Lt. Jule "Rocky" Rybolt, the communications officer.

As the Chinese approached, an M16 Quad 50, positioned about one hundred yards behind the CP, began firing wildly. "Their first two bursts went right through our CP," said McClay. One round tore away half of Rybolt's cheek and neck. Another hit Reilly in the right leg. "We got word to the gunners who corrected their aim and thereafter took a terrible toll of Chinese," said McClay.

But the toll on Rybolt was terrible too. Born with a club foot that had been surgically repaired, Rybolt had made five combat landings as a glider pilot during World War II and been awarded the Air Medal. An injury to the foot kept him from sailing with the battalion to Inchon. "He could've missed the war but refused," Celeste Reilly later said. Instead, he caught up to his unit in South Korea by wearing a tightly laced boot to keep the swelling down. Rybolt was taken to the battalion aid station, clinging to life. Reilly had suffered another serious wound but remained in command of the battalion.

A Chinese attack coming up the road and leading to the inlet from the southwest that evening was particularly alarming, as it meant the enemy controlled the road back to Hudong-ni. "It was sobering to realize we were cut off and surrounded," said Lt. Gray.

The incursions ended with all of the Chinese soldiers inside the perimeter killed. But more attacks were underway, and the night was still young.

Tokyo, Tuesday Night

The plane carrying Ned Almond touched down at 9:30 p.m. at Haneda Air Force Base in Tokyo, where a colonel from the Far East Command waited with instructions for the X Corps commander to proceed immediately to MacArthur's home at the U.S. Embassy compound. A meeting at the Dai Ichi at that hour would have attracted unwanted attention. Almond, still in battle dress uniform, arrived to find MacArthur and Walker waiting, along with top commanders and staff, including Willougby, the intelligence chief; Vice Adm. Turner Joy, commander of Naval Forces Far East; and Gen. Stratemeyer, the Far East Air Force commander. The atmosphere was grim.

MacArthur asked first about Walker's situation with the 8th Army in the west, which, at that point, was seen as being in a more precarious position than X Corps. Walker's force was still in full retreat, trying to cover its right flank exposed by the collapse of the ROK II Corps. But Walker was cautiously optimistic that the 8th Army could settle down to form a defensive line in front of Pyongyang.

When MacArthur asked about X Corp's situation, Almond was gung ho, no less irrationally optimistic than he had been earlier that day during his visit to Task Force Maclean. He said he expected that both the 1st Marine Division and the 31st RCT could continue to attack west and north from the Chosin Reservoir, thereby relieving pressure on the 8th Army. Despite his visits to the Marines and Army at Chosin that day, Almond did not yet comprehend the unfolding disaster. "Neither one of us [Almond and Walker] knew the strength of the Chinese," Almond later said. "We each stated so much. . . . [W]e all thought that . . . it was possible for the Marine Division to push forward to the northwest and thereby protect Walker's right flank."

But even from Tokyo, MacArthur seemed to have a better understanding of the gravity of the situation than Almond. The conference continued until 1:30 a.m. MacArthur did not make any decisions and would give orders in the morning. But Almond could sense a change coming. He instructed his aides to alert his headquarters in Hungnam to a possible change in X Corps' mission.

Forward Perimeter, Midnight

The evening had remained quiet for Oxenrider, Joung, and the rest of the Able Company soldiers on the 1st Battalion left flank. SFC Via and Sgt. Sylvia watched snow start to fall, sprinkling some small pine trees to their front. It would have looked idyllic if it wasn't so cold. Then, like a Macbethian Birnam Wood, the pine trees seemed to move. "The trees fell over and a wave of Chinese ran at us, spraying us with burp gun fire," Via recalled. Sylvia was hit in the right thigh. Via's face, spattered with frozen dirt, was bleeding.

Similar probing attacks were taking place all along the 1st Battalion perimeter. After a Chinese artillery barrage was cut short by a lack of ammunition, the 240th Regiment launched its attack, sending its battalions to assault both the left and right sides of the perimeter. By 1:00 a.m., the tempo and force of the attacks accelerated. Bugles, whistles, and horns were sounding, and attacks were coming all along the 1st Battalion line.

At the headquarters, Col. Maclean joined Faith and the others in the small radio room, listening to the increasingly alarming reports coming in by phone and radio. "All companies were getting savage attacks from the Chinese who were attacking with rushes of men regardless of losses which our troops were dealing out," said Robbins. Faith, on edge, ordered Robbins, McNally, and several other staff officers lingering in the radio room to go outside and join the defenses around the CP.

Charlie Company was being hit hard, and the left flank of Baker Company was wavering. The battalion's heavy mortars were firing in support of the line companies, but one round fell short and landed about fifty yards east of the CP, shaking the building and knocking out a machine gun.

Then Lt. Anthony Mazzulla, a B Company platoon leader, reported that the Chinese had broken through the company's left flank and were heading down a draw leading directly to the battalion CP. Faith ordered all remaining headquarters personnel to rush up the draw and stop the attack. B Company managed to quickly close the gap in the line, and the attack was smothered before it went far.

From the din surrounding the CP, it sounded to Robbins as if every weapon in the battalion was being fired. "The mortars were throwing out their rounds as fast as they could be loaded; machine guns kept up their incessant bursts," he recalled. "Shadowy figures kept coming and going about the entrance of the CP as wounded were helped or carried bodily into the relative safety of the area. . . . A ghostly light pervaded the whole scene as a light snow began to fall and through this curtain a faint moon tried vainly to shine. Flashes of fire from bursting shells and flares intermittently lighted the area and added to the weird lighting effect."

With the intensity of enemy mortar and small-arms fire picking up and the task force ammunition supplies dwindling, the battalion's position looked increasingly precarious. Maclean turned to Faith and told him to consider whether the 1st Battalion should fall back to join the rest of the task force at the inlet. He was leaving the decision to Faith as battalion commander, but Maclean "strongly advised him to do so," said Maj. Curtis.

Faith did not take much persuasion. The battalion already had about 100 wounded who would need to be carried out. "Faith's big concern was to get them to a position where they could be evacuated," Bob Jones said. Given the acute ammunition shortage, Faith believed it would be better to pull out and fight back to join the rest of the task force before running out of ammunition. Then came word that Able Company's left flank had been pushed back, with one platoon cut off and considerable casualties, including the platoon leader.

The Chinese penetration threatened Bigger's mortar positions and also left the battalion CP vulnerable to being overrun.

That decided the issue. Around 2:00 a.m., with Maclean's concurrence, Faith ordered the battalion to prepare to withdraw. McNally, the regimental communications officer, was called into the CP to receive the orders and relay them to the company commanders. Orders went out to units via telephone, radio, and messenger. The 3rd Battalion CP at the inlet was reached by radio and alerted to the pending move.

Faith delivered the word personally to Dr. Navarre at the battalion aid station. "We are moving out," he told the surgeon. Orders were given to empty all the kitchen trucks, including all the cooking equipment and rations, so they could be loaded with wounded.

The withdrawal was to be conducted under cover of a complete blackout. That meant no fires to destroy abandoned equipment. Faith and Maclean planned to move out at 4:00 a.m., which they calculated would provide enough time to complete the four-mile move in darkness and arrive at the inlet around sunrise. That would allow the battalion to cross into the perimeter in daylight, reducing the danger of friendly fire.

Inlet Perimeter, Midnight

Sgt. Grantford Brown, the commander of an M19 positioned on the northern side of the inlet perimeter, told his gunner, Sgt. Robert Ayala, not to leave his station under any circumstances during the battle. That left Ayala, who only had a summer uniform, with few options to stay warm as the night wore on. "All I could do was shake my arms and legs to keep from freezing," he said. The 20-year-old Ayala, one of thirteen children from a Dallas, Texas, family, was entirely unused to such cold.

Ayala's best friend, Cpl. John Strack, the gunner on an M16, had come by earlier to check on him. "Think we'll ever get out of this?" Strack asked.

"John, some of us will, some of us won't," Ayala answered.

Unlike the southwest sector of the perimeter, the northern sector had been relatively quiet so far. That changed around midnight, when Capt. McClymont heard horns blowing outside the perimeter. "Then there came a withering stream of small arms fire, and mortar shells began to land through the area," he said. It was obvious to all that the AAA weapons were a key target. The

Chinese had plotted their positions during the day, and intense and accurate mortar fire began raining down around the guns.

Brown, a courageous and capable NCO, was exceptionally skilled at directing the fire of the Twin 40s. But more than that, Lt. Ted Magill noted, "the most impressive thing about him was his calmness and good humor under the most trying of circumstances."

This was just such a moment. Brown saw a rush of Chinese soldiers coming toward the perimeter. At his command, Ayala began firing the Twin 40s, the flash of its bursting high-explosive shells lighting up the night. "It looked like daylight with all of the firing going on," said Ayala.

A second rush of Chinese troops approached the perimeter and was again met with a torrent of fire from Brown's M19. In the chaotic din of the fight, nobody noticed that a Chinese soldier had broken through the perimeter and was clambering up the side of the M19. "I was up on the turret directing fire when he climbed up alongside of me," Brown later told McClymont. "I saw he was carrying something and he looked Chinese to me, so I hit him with my fist."

Brown felt as if he'd broken his wrist, but the infiltrator fell over the side. Just as he hit the ground, he was shot and killed by Sgt. Kim, the squad ROK, who was positioned underneath the M19. Up on the turret, Brown found what the Chinese soldier had been carrying—a six-inch-wide bamboo tube packed with explosives, with two fuses leading out. "Had that fellow been able to find his matches, or had Sergeant Brown been less alert, that M19 would have been blown sky high and the perimeter would have been breached," said McClymont.

Ayala felt lucky to have survived. But when he learned his friend Strack had died in the fighting at his M16, Ayala felt guilty about his grim prediction earlier in the day. "I shouldn't have said that. That night, he got killed. Yeah, that was my best buddy."

The 57th Field Artillery guns were likewise a prime Chinese target and came under heavy attack. The B Battery gun crews were firing the howitzers all night, leaving them exposed to Chinese mortar shells, and they took extremely heavy casualties. The executive officer, Lt. Clyde Morrison, as well as Lt. Robert Styslinger—both from western Pennsylvania—were killed, along with four chiefs of section and numerous cannoneers. One of the section chiefs, SFC Donald Nitz, was decapitated by a mortar.

One officer entirely unscathed was the B Battery commander, Capt. Ted Goss: He stayed in the hut serving as the command post throughout the battle, never exposing himself. "He was just sitting there and other times he was laying on the ground," said Lt. William Eichorn, commander of the battery security platoon. "I did not see him performing any duties."

The battery's junior officers and NCOs took it upon themselves to fill the gap. When Goss crawled in his sleeping bag that night, Lt. Magill, a 24-year old Floridian who started the night as a forward observer, took command of the battery.

B Battery was also lucky to have Sgt. Edgar Copelan as chief of the firing battery. Copelan, an easygoing Georgian who had served in World War II, was "thoroughly proficient in the use of the 105s," said Magill. Copelan had the crews lower the gun tubes as far down as possible to the ground, with fuses set to a minimum arming range, firing so that the shells ricocheted off the frozen ground for maximum fragmentation against the advancing Chinese infantry.

For many GIs, surviving the night came down to having leaders the likes of Brown and Copelan at their side. "These two men performed magnificently and provided great inspiration for their soldiers," said Magill.

The K Company line also did its part in defending the B Battery howitzers against Chinese infiltrators carrying explosives, who tried to rush through gaps in the perimeter. DeLong's machine gun squad and Fontaine, armed with his rifle, were taking a fearful toll on the Chinese. "They kept trying to do that and we kept repulsing them," said DeLong.

The Chinese assault culminated in a company-sized rush with about 100 enemy, and much of it seemed focused on Fontaine's foxhole. "I knew that they were coming in on him so I turned my machine gun as far as I could," DeLong said. "I couldn't get it any further, though. I tried to keep them off of him, but I couldn't stop them. They just came so fast and so hard." Finally, the attack subsided. DeLong hollered over to Fontaine's hole. "You alright?" he asked.

Fontaine did not answer. DeLong got out of his hole and went over to check on him. "He was shot right between the eyes," DeLong said. "And he had 21 Chinese lined up in front of his hole."

By now DeLong had seen many men in K Company die. But losing Fontaine hit him especially hard. "I cried like a baby," he said.

Forward Perimeter

Bullets were flying over the 1st Battalion aid station as soldiers helped medics carry stretchers of wounded from tents onto trucks and ambulances in preparation for the withdrawal. Snow was falling hard, and footing had become treacherous.

The kitchen trucks did not have enough room for all the wounded, so other trucks were ordered to be emptied—among them, the regimental CP truck, to Maj. Robbins' dismay. Sgt. Radke, assigned the job of emptying the truck, dumped the field desks and other contents onto the side of the road. The truck was also carrying two eight-foot-long wooden crates bearing the regimental colors, which Maclean always insisted be brought along to be displayed outside his tent. Radke felt a pang of regret as he tossed the crates holding the flags to the side of the road. "I thought, 'Dammit, we should do something about those colors,' but it didn't rank real high with me," he said. There were other pressing needs at the moment—namely, loading the now-empty truck with seriously wounded soldiers.

The preparations for the withdrawal were rushed and chaotic. It didn't help that many key junior officers and NCOs had been killed or wounded, leaving gaps in leadership. Two hours after the decision to withdraw, some units fighting on the perimeter still had not received word of the plans to withdraw.

Lt. May's men had a Chinese prisoner with badly frozen hands and feet. "I gave him some rations and cigarettes and left him making his way northward," May said. "His feet were so badly frozen he could only hobble along."

Faith had directed Maj. Miller to organize a rear guard for the move using A Company to protect the convoy. Miller made his way over to the company's position by following the din from the ongoing Chinese attack on the left flank. At the CP, Lt. Cecil Smith, commanding the company following Scullion's death, reported that a counterattack to reach the cutoff 1st Platoon had failed but he was about to launch a second attempt. Miller briefed Smith on the withdrawal plans and gave Smith approval to continue with the second counterattack. But Miller told him that when the order to withdraw came, the company would have to pull out—whether or not they had rescued the platoon.

Drivers began trying to start trucks and jeeps—no easy feat, given frozen engines and dead batteries. With his driver in a foxhole guarding the perimeter,

Robbins had to hand crank his lifeless jeep himself. His arm nearly gave out before the engine finally turned over.

Some vehicles refused to start and would have to be left behind. Faith instructed May, the motor officer, "to cripple the vehicles but not to destroy them." Maclean and Faith were still under orders from Almond to attack north; undoubtedly, they were skeptical this would ever happen, but preserving the option of recovering the vehicles might assuage the X Corps commander. May and his men removed coils and coil wires, which would prevent the Chinese from starting the vehicles but could later be reinstalled. Faith also directed that fuel be drained from all abandoned vehicles. "We had to drain tanks, and make sure [those] we took, both tanks were filled with gas," said Sgt. Ager, with the 515th Transportation Company.

Ager watched Faith oversee the withdrawal preparations and felt encouraged by his assured sense of command. "I thought that if we were going to get out of this mess, he was going to be the man to take us out," said Ager.

Trucks, ambulances, and jeeps lined up on the road facing south, with columns of infantry lined up on either side. Faith's plan called for B and C companies to protect the flank of the convoy while A Company protected the rear.

At 4:30 a.m., the withdrawal began with C Company in front, moving on high ground paralleling the road on its east side. Capt. Seever, the company commander, had a leg wound, so he chose Lt. Mortrude to lead the way with his platoon. Mortrude and his men pulled out from their ridgeline position and moved back on steep ground overlooking the road. "This we did without enemy resistance, but with much slipping and sliding down the hillside," recalled Mortrude. The rest of the company followed in hasty confusion. Two lieutenants argued over the order of withdrawal, and some soldiers did not wait their turn to pull off the hill. But there were no serious mishaps and little response from the Chinese. On the road below, the convoy crawled slowly forward in the dark.

B Company held its position on the high ground until C Company had cleared, then pulled out without incident, staying also on the east side of the road on still higher ground than C Company. Their departure was so quiet that Harry Graham didn't even notice they were gone. Graham had been positioned by himself with a radio in an outpost forward of the B Company line, with instructions to call back with any enemy movement. In the rush to get ready, the company neglected to send word to Graham that they were leaving. After a while, the silence was deafening. "I didn't see any more of our guys back there," he recalled. "I said, 'I wonder what's going on, where they at?' So I crawled back and got back, wasn't nobody around." Graham figured they had headed south. His radio was too heavy to lug around, so he put a bullet through it to keep the Chinese from using it, and then took off in the darkness, looking for his company.

A Company, still battling the Chinese on the battalion's left flank, faced the most difficult extraction. Lt. Smith's second attempt to reach his cutoff platoon had failed, and with the withdrawal already underway, Maj. Miller made the difficult decision that there was not time for a third try. "I ordered Lieutenant Smith to move out, knowing that the protection of the battalion rear was more important than relieving the cut off platoon," Miller said. Before they could pull out, the Chinese launched another attack. "They paid dearly as most of them were clearly silhouetted against the snow," Miller said. The heavy casualties inflicted gave A Company time to withdraw from the hill and take position guarding the rear of the truck convoy.

"The Chinese followed closely," Miller added, "blowing weird calls continuously on their bugles," apparently signaling the American withdrawal to other units.

Roy Oxenrider was part of the contingent guarding the rear, which took heavy fire from Chinese troops following them down the mountainside. The GIs kept them at bay with small-arms fire and occasional bursts with light machine guns.

But before long, the Chinese stopped firing and broke off the pursuit, having discovered the Americans' abandoned supplies. Many of the Chinese troops at Chosin had had little or nothing to eat for days, so finding any food, even strange American C rations, was heavenly. It bought time for the battered 1st Battalion to successfully withdraw with only light interference.

When Zhan Da'nan received word that the American force at the forward perimeter was withdrawing south on the road, he issued orders for the 239th Regiment to stop the column before it could join with the Army force at the inlet. Zhang Guijin's 2nd Battalion hurriedly set up a roadblock.

About halfway to the inlet, Faith's column reached the 31st Heavy Mortar Company, which had been positioned by itself for two long nights between the two American perimeters. Captain George Cody, the company commander,

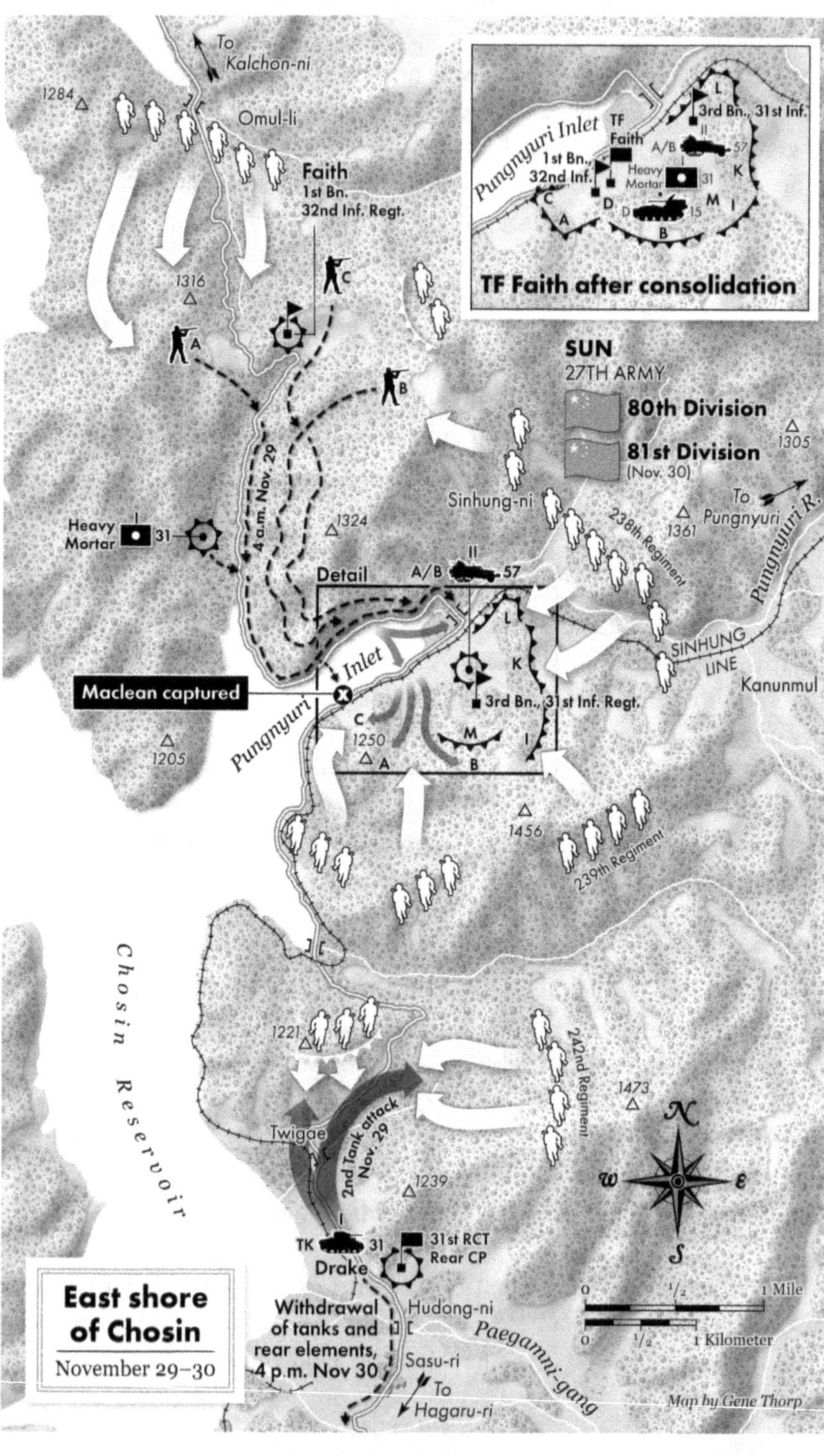

To Kalchon-ni
1284
Omul-li
Faith
1st Bn.
32nd Inf. Regt.
1316
C
A
B
4 a.m. Nov. 29
Heavy Mortar
31
1324
Detail
A/B
II
57
L
K
I
M
C
B
A
1250
Inlet
Pungnyuri
Maclean captured
3rd Bn., 31st Inf. Regt.
1205
1456
239th Regiment
SUN
27TH ARMY
80th Division
81st Division
(Nov. 30)
1305
Sinhung-ni
238th Regiment
1361
To Pungnyuri
Pungnyuri R.
SINHUNG LINE
Kanunmul
Pungnyuri Inlet
TF Faith
1st Bn., 32nd Inf.
3rd Bn., 31st Inf.
Heavy Mortar
D
15
TF Faith after consolidation
Chosin Reservoir
1221
242nd Regiment
1473
Twigae
2nd Tank attack Nov. 29
1239
TK
31
Drake
31st RCT Rear CP
Withdrawal of tanks and rear elements, 4 p.m. Nov 30
Hudong-ni
Paegamni-gang
Sasu-ri
To Hagaru-ri
0
1/2
1 Mile
1 Kilometer
East shore of Chosin
November 29–30
Map by Gene Thorp

had the force "drawn up in a circle 'Wagon Train style,' and had been left unmolested by the Chinese," Bob Jones said. Faith paused the withdrawal to incorporate the company into the column.

While the column was stopped, Maclean and Faith, accompanied by Jones, Bigger, and Stamford, continued forward with a small number of troops to reconnoiter their approach to the inlet. Dawn was breaking as the command group reached the mouth of the inlet, where the road made a sharp turn to the east, following the north bank of the Pungnyuri River.

Looking across the ice of the inlet in the early morning light, Maclean, Faith, and the rest of the command party could see the 3rd Battalion and 57th Field Artillery in a fierce fight with the enemy. "Chinese were pouring down the surrounding hill toward the perimeter of the units," Bigger said. "The quad 50 machine guns and the dual 40 mm anti-aircraft weapons . . . were taking a heavy toll of the Chinese columns. It was like being a spectator at a large screen movie for a moment." Mortars flashed in the hills to the southwest as the Chinese poured fire into the inlet. Smoke from the fighting hung over the perimeter "like a deadly pall," obscuring the view, but from what the officers could see, it was a scene of utter devastation.

The command party continued down the road. The inlet was about five hundred yards across at the mouth of the river; it stayed close to that width for about a mile before narrowing near a bridge and causeway that carried the road over the Pungnyuri and some frozen marshland. Before long, they could see that the Chinese had built a log roadblock on the southern end of the bridge, which appeared to be covered by enemy fire.

Faith quickly formulated a plan for a two-pronged attack on the roadblock. He would have Charlie Company, which he could hear moving along the hillside above the road, go up to the crest of the hill and then follow the ridgeline down to a point where they could attack the roadblock from above. Faith would lead B Company on an attack from the road. He had practically no radio communication with his units during the move, owing to dead batteries and the hilly terrain, and the snow on the hillsides made it virtually impossible for messengers to quickly run between the units. So Faith resorted to using his booming voice.

As the men of C Company stumbled and slipped their way along the hillside, exhausted and freezing cold, Faith hailed Mortrude. "He shouted for me to lead the column over this high ground and attack the enemy roadblock down in the valley below, while he hit it frontally," Mortrude said. Two C Company platoons began a long, slow climb up toward the snow-covered ridge.

Faith, Maclean, and the rest of the command party continued down the road toward the roadblock, reconnoitering for a place where the troops might cross the frozen inlet. About halfway between the mouth of the inlet and the bridge, they came under small-arms fire from across the ice.

The attacking Chinese troops had infiltrated the southern bank of the inlet, moving through rough ground lined with brush, tall grass, and small, scrub-covered islands that provided cover. Maclean was unable to see the Chinese troops along the bank and believed the fire was coming from his own 31st Infantry troops.

Leaving Maclean behind, Faith continued down the road with a small group to get a closer look at the bridge. From his vantage point, Faith recognized that the fire was coming from Chinese troops on the south shore of the inlet.

Further back, Maclean, Bigger, and Jones looked across the inlet and spotted a column of troops coming up the road from the south, approaching the American perimeter. Maclean was convinced it was his long overdue 2nd Battalion. "Those are my boys," he shouted.

"Col. Maclean was at first overjoyed for he felt that that was the remainder of his regimental combat team he had been expecting," said Bigger. But Bigger and others weren't so sure. Between the smoke, fog, and dim early morning light, the visibility was poor. Moreover, the Chinese soldiers wore fur caps that resembled those worn by some GIs. "At a distance it was hard to distinguish one from the other," Bigger said.

Maclean grew alarmed when saw that his 3rd Battalion troops inside the inlet were firing at the approaching column. "My God, those are my troops and they are going to kill each other," he exclaimed. Maclean made a quick decision to go across the ice to halt what he thought was friendly fire between two of his battalions. "He felt it was his moral duty to try and stop the firing," said Jones. "It was a very brave thing to do." Maclean, he added, "likely felt that they would recognize him as their commander, as he was a tall and familiar figure to all his troops."

Before taking off, Maclean hurriedly rattled off an oral five-point operational order. "Here, take this order and give to Faith," Maclean told Bigger. Faith was to be told that the relief column was in sight, that Maclean would establish his regimental CP in one of the houses visible across the inlet within the perimeter, and that Faith was to meet up with the colonel there. Once the 1st Battalion had entered the perimeter and tied in with the 3rd Battalion, Faith was to work to secure the high ground around the inlet.

With that, Maclean started walking down from the road toward the ice, instructing his radioman, Sgt. "Frenchy" Mercier, to follow. Mercier, studying the approaching column with his binoculars, thought they were Chinese. "Sir, they don't look like ours," he told the colonel. Maclean impatiently waved off the warning. "Frenchy, come here," he ordered. Mercier complied, and the two men walked toward the ice before Maclean reconsidered. "Frenchy, go back up," the colonel said. "We're going to need that radio later."

Maclean continued alone onto the ice. Everyone watching was uneasy. "We yelled at him to make sure, but he kept going," Bigger said.

From different vantage points along the north shore, Faith, Jones, Bigger, Curtis, and others watched Maclean cross. The colonel began running across the ice and waving his arms, trying to get the attention of his 3rd Battalion troops in the inlet. Maclean was well out onto the ice when the officers saw him fall as if he had been shot, but he got up. He pressed on, falling and arising, as many as four times in all. "Each time he got up and proceeded onward," said Jones. Some witnesses said they saw Maclean's body jerk each time before falling, as if hit by a bullet.

Despite the heavy fighting in and around the inlet, some troops inside the perimeter noticed the strange sight of Maclean coming across the ice, including Lt. Magill and Sgt. Copelan of B Battery. "He was a large man and we had a clear line of sight," said Magill.

Witnesses on both sides of the ice saw Maclean being grabbed by soldiers as he reached the south shore of the inlet, then disappearing behind brush and small folds of land. "He was hit several times and staggered, fell and finally was led off the ice by what appeared to be Chinese soldiers," said Magill. "Some friendly troops on the south side of the bridge were trying to assist Col. MacLean but were unable to reach him in time."

It had been a courageous but foolhardy act by Maclean. Across the inlet Bigger watched with dismay as the task force commander "was seized and hustled away behind a hill. That was the last we saw of Col. Maclean—a man who exuded confidence, leadership and high morale."

Chapter 9

THE SECOND DAY

Wednesday, November 29

Shocked as he was by MacLean's disappearance, Faith immediately moved forward with his attack on the Chinese roadblock. He rounded up some B Company troops, including a party of soldiers with 1st Sgt. Richard Luna. The men came tumbling down the steep and slippery hillside, hitting the road so hard that some men were injured or broke their weapons. Rather than continuing on the road for a frontal attack, Faith led the soldiers down to the inlet ice to assault the bridge from the flank.

They attacked across the ice toward the roadblock, firing as they moved at Chinese troops along the inlet south bank. Lt. Henry Moore, commander of Faith's Ammunition and Pioneer Platoon, joined the assault with a half-dozen men, knocking out enemy positions on both sides of the bridge.

Across the ice, the 3rd Battalion headquarters had received a radio message shortly before dawn that the 1st Battalion was arriving, and they hurriedly instructed troops guarding the northern perimeter not to shoot at the soldiers crossing the ice. "This message was passed along as loudly as we could yell," said Capt. Bryant, the 3rd Battalion headquarters and headquarters company commander. In the roar and confusion of the ongoing battle, not everyone got the message, but there was no serious friendly fire.

For many men inside the perimeter, the sight of the 1st Battalion GIs streaming across the ice was a pleasant surprise. They "suddenly came barreling down the shore road to our north, knifing their way through confused Chinese soldiers everywhere," said Lt. John Gray, the 3rd Battalion mortar platoon leader. "We were extremely glad to see them, but I am not so sure that they saw much refuge in our perimeter because of the picture of carnage that it presented."

Faith joined B Company troops in removing the logs blocking the bridge. They came under Chinese fire, forcing them to take cover behind abutments supporting the bridge, but they soon drove the enemy off and opened up the road. After their arduous climb to the ridgeline overlooking the bridge, two C Company platoons arrived at their attack position just in time to see Faith's group breaking the enemy roadblock below.

Faith instructed Dale Seever to send some of his C Company troops across the ice to look for Maclean. The troops attacked the area along the bank where Maclean had disappeared, killing some Chinese, but they found no sign of the colonel. "There were considerable dead CCF soldiers in that area and some escaped," said Maj. Jones. "We looked at all of them trying to locate Col. Maclean but without success."

The convoy carrying the wounded remained halted about a mile behind the bridge, with everyone there uncertain about the reasons for the long delay. Maj. Robbins, with the convoy, remained in the dark about Maclean's disappearance and the fight at the roadblock. "We waited for what seemed hours and were getting more concerned by the minute as we knew the Chinese behind us would not fool around all day . . . and would soon be hot-footing down the road toward us." Indeed, a squad of Chinese came trotting up the road around a bend and suddenly came upon the rear of the convoy and "perhaps were as surprised as we were," said Robbins. "In a moment firing was going on all over the place and seemingly in all directions." The Chinese were quickly run off, and calm was restored.

Robbins went forward in his jeep to find out what the delay was. He had a bad feeling when he came upon Maclean's empty jeep and the colonel's radioman, Sgt. Frenchy Mercier, and bodyguard, Sgt. Sastines Salazar—both usually glued to Maclean's side—looking worried. They excitedly told Robbins about the colonel's disappearance.

Shortly afterward, Faith came striding up the road with word that his men had cleared the roadblock and were holding the bridge. He gave Robbins instructions to start up the vehicles and send them down the road. With the bridge and causeway still under enemy fire from the surrounding hills, each vehicle would need to dash across an exposed stretch of road and then over the bridge to make it into the perimeter.

When the trucks reached the mouth of the inlet, Jones sent the trucks down the road to Faith and Maj. Miller, who directed them across the bridge one at a time. The trucks took heavy small-arms fire from the river valley northeast of the bridge. Marine Corsairs, making their first appearance of the morning, put suppressive fire on the Chinese positions at Capt. Stamford's direction. Each truck driver was "floor-boarding the accelerator of his vehicle as we one by one ran the gauntlet," said Robbins. Some vehicles were hit, but no serious casualties were reported as the convoy regrouped inside the perimeter.

Just about every vehicle had made it over by the time Sgt. Charles Garrigus, the assistant motor sergeant for the battalion, drove his truck over the bridge and into the perimeter. Then Garrigus spotted two ammunition trucks still on the other side, apparently abandoned by skittish drivers. Garrigus was not going to stand for that. He was a farm boy from rural Indiana who loved tinkering with motors and driving heavy equipment, and he had found a happy home in the Army. On his own volition, he sprinted three hundred yards across the ice, jumped into the cab of the first truck, and drove it over the bridge and into the perimeter. Then he dashed back across the ice to fetch the second truck. By now, Garrigus's actions were drawing fire from Chinese positions. The second truck was riddled with fire as he raced across the bridge. Garrigus pressed forward, reaching the perimeter safely with a precious load of ammunition just as the engine died. Every truck made it across safely—in no small measure, thanks to Garrigus. But one jeep hauling medical supplies simply vanished.

Most of the GIs crossed the ice about two hundred yards southwest of the bridge to get to the inlet, further from the Chinese guns in the hills, but not out of range. They moved in groups of six to eight to avoid giving the enemy big targets to hit.

It was about five hundred yards across the ice at that spot, but to PFC Tom Marker, with the 31st Heavy Mortar Company, it felt a lot farther. "The Chinese fired at us all the way, and it was the longest mile I ever ran," he said. Corsairs swooped over the heads of the GIs, firing their .50-caliber machine guns at Chinese positions and showering empty bullet casings to the ice. "The casings hit us in the head—like God-sent rain," said Marker.

With the American force consolidated and U.S. planes in the air, Zhan Da'nan, assistant commander of the 27th Army, stopped the attack, his forces once again reeling from the heavy casualties they had suffered. The 80th Division was crippled. It had suffered more than 6,150 casualties, about 60 percent of its combat strength. None of his four attacking regiments had more than half of their men remaining. The 238th Regiment, which had numbered more than 3,600 men two days earlier, now had only 300 soldiers still capable of fighting, and they had to be reorganized into six infantry companies of about 50 men apiece. Three infantry companies and one machine gun company were all that could be mustered from the 239th Regiment. Those not wounded were suffering from frostbite, hunger, and exhaustion.

Zhan personally interrogated several American prisoners and learned that the 80th Division was facing troops from both the 31st and 32nd Infantry Regiments. Chinese intelligence estimated that they were faced with the entire 31st Infantry Regiment augmented by one battalion from the 32nd Regiment and one artillery battalion. That was effectively twice as much infantry—four battalions instead of two—as was actually the case, but apparently, the ferocity of the American fight convinced the Chinese they were facing a larger force.

Zhan nonetheless believed the CCF remained in a stronger position and that the U.S. Army task force was vulnerable. The Americans had clearly been seriously hurt by the Chinese attacks. They remained surrounded, and as their ammunition and supplies dwindled, their advantage of superior firepower would diminish. The tanks at Hudong-ni had been unable to break through so far, and their air support could not help the Americans at night.

Zhan called 9th Army headquarters, asking for reinforcements. The 80th Division had been too weakened by casualties to succeed, Zhan reported, but with reinforcements, he was confident the Army task force could be annihilated.

Once all the wounded were safely into the inlet, Faith crossed the ice on foot with Bigger. "We skirted across the ice as unobtrusively as possible," said Bigger. They made their way into the perimeter through one of the railroad cuts in the uneven ground along the shoreline. For all they had endured at the forward perimeter over the last two nights, Faith's men were shocked by what they found at the inlet.

"There were hundreds of dead Chinese everywhere, inside the perimeter and out, strung out along the perimeter in contorted shapes and heaps," said Sgt. Via of A Company. He and others could not understand how the 3rd Battalion had held their positions against so many attackers. Looking at all the casualties, Roy Oxenrider said, "I thought to myself that we had not improved our chances."

Some GIs lay dead on the ground, still holding carbines in their frozen grips. "How the Chinese were finally pushed back out as dawn came and how those soldiers of the 3rd kept firing until the Chinese retired to the protection of the surrounding hills will be a tribute to that unit forever," said Hugh Robbins.

Dr. Lee Yong Kak walked around the perimeter. "I couldn't walk five steps without stumbling over enemy dead," he said. It was unsettling to see such graphic evidence of the horrendous level of casualties the enemy was willing to accept and yet keep attacking. Many of the foxholes held dead ROKs who had stayed in their holes when they were overrun, making them easy targets for enemy grenades.

The raised railbed, which ran alongside the edge of the reservoir and inlet along the western and northwestern side of the perimeter, was covered with hundreds of bodies, mostly Chinese. "Here and there I could spot GIs and ROKs intermingled with the pile of CCF," said Lee. "They had fought till the last and prevented CCF from overrunning us."

Maj. Robbins made his way to the 3rd Battalion headquarters. "Dead and wounded GIs laid in and around the Korean mud house that served as a CP," he said. Robbins counted 20 dead Chinese in their quilted uniforms and canvas shoes just within a few yards of the CP, their bodies strewn about in the snow and inside nearby foxholes.

In the nearby 3rd Battalion aid station, Robbins found Capt. Henry Wamble, the 31st Medical Company executive officer, who had been wounded when his convoy was ambushed the first night. Wamble, a longtime close friend of Robbins from their time serving together in Japan, had been shot through the lungs and could barely talk above a whisper. "I was shocked to see Henry in such a state," Robbins said. "He was pessimistic about our chances of getting out and showed me his forty-five pistol which he dragged out from under the blanket which covered him. He told me then that he would shoot himself rather than let the Chinese capture him."

At the CP, Lt. Col. Reilly was sitting up on a stretcher with his myriad of wounds evident, including the bullet hole in his leg and grenade fragments on his arms and shoulder. "He was in good spirits and chatted with me about the situation in general," said Robbins.

Faith came in and immediately conferred with Reilly, and he was briefed on the 3rd Battalion's situation by remaining staff officers, including Maj. Storms, now the battalion's second in command. Faith learned that the Chinese had the perimeter surrounded, except along the reservoir shore.

After seeing the serious wounds of Reilly and Lt. Colonel Embree, and with Maclean still missing, Faith assumed command of the 31st RCT—or Task Force Faith, as it would become known. He placed Maj. Miller in command of the 1st Battalion. "Faith, Miller and I spent the rest of the morning trying to figure out what was left of the 3rd Battalion's rifle companies," Curtis said. Faith made plans to consolidate the two infantry battalions and the field artillery in a tight defensive circle.

Faith set up the regimental CP in a railroad cut near another cut where Miller set up the 1st Battalion CP. Tarps were stretched across the railroad cuts to provide roofs, and canvas was hung along both sides to cut down the wind. The setup kept Faith in close proximity to his core group of trusted commanders, including Jones, Bigger, Curtis, and Miller.

Faith had acted quickly to assert command, but Bigger could tell Maclean's disappearance weighed heavily on him. "This caused Col. Faith much distress," said Bigger. "The two men were much attached to each other."

Faith had not given up on finding Maclean, sending out more patrols to search for him. But they all came back empty-handed.

Hudong-ni, Wednesday Morning

At 8:00 a.m., Capt. Drake kicked off a second tank attack, trying to break through the Chinese roadblock on Hill 1221. After losing four tanks the day before, he was down to twelve tanks for the attack, but it was still a formidable force. This time, infantry accompanied the tanks from the start, but once again, it was a small, makeshift force, including a composite platoon of cooks, clerks, and ROKs from the regimental headquarters company; a platoon of engineers from the 13th Engineer Battalion; and an antitank mine platoon—about 30 men in all, including three officers.

The Chinese remained dug in around the roadblock, with the 3rd Battalion, 242nd Regiment, still holding the high ground on both sides of the hairpin turn in the road. But now, it had been reinforced by the regiment's 2nd

Battalion, and burned-out ambulances from the medical convoy ambush had been positioned with the knocked-out tank to further block the road.

Drake approached cautiously, keeping his tanks back and firing on Chinese positions from a distance, inflicting heavy casualties on the enemy but doing little to reduce the roadblock. Marine Corsairs requested by Hodes showed up overhead. But with no ground controller to guide them, their fire was largely ineffective and inaccurate, hitting Chinese positions on the hill but also the attacking American infantry. After four hours of fighting with substantial infantry casualties but no progress in reaching the roadblock, Drake ordered a withdrawal, feeling gloomy about the prospects of breaking through.

Ironically, there was a potential route for bypassing the roadblock, but Drake did not know about it. The narrow-gauge railroad running along the eastern side of the Chosin Reservoir, which generally ran parallel to the road, broke off just south of Hill 1221, running on the west side of the hill along the reservoir shore, while the road went around the east side through the hairpin curve. "I was totally unaware of the existence of the railroad bed," Drake later said. "Otherwise, I might have tried to use it as a route to bypass the hairpin turn." The route may not have worked, as the railbed was narrow and the Chinese on Hill 1221 may have been able to knock out a tank and block the route for other tanks. But it was another missed chance.

Inlet Perimeter, Wednesday Afternoon

As the day wore on, various soldiers who had been left behind during the 1st Battalion withdrawal from the northern perimeter caught up with the task force. The A Company platoon that had been cut off by the Chinese the previous night and left behind managed to break away and arrive safely in the inlet. Harry Graham, forgotten at his outpost when B Company pulled out, caught up and made it across the inlet, bullets chipping the ice around him as he ran.

Sgt. Clarence White of B Company had become separated from his unit when he slipped on the hillside at dawn and fell twenty-five feet, hitting the road so hard that he broke his carbine. Trying to catch up, he'd come under machine gun fire, so he dove off the road. He crawled on his belly through the snow and then onto the ice of the inlet, getting snow caked all over his uniform. "By now I guess I looked like a snowman," he recalled. When he stood up to wave his arms, trying to get the attention of the troops in the inlet, he drew fire from some GIs, who apparently mistook him for Chinese in his white-coated uniform. He dropped back to the ice. "Every time I moved, I drew fire," he said. "I started moving very slowly on the ice now, like a snake but I was a lot slower." White finally succeeded in getting a GI's attention, and they stopped firing at him.

He made it to the south shore. "As I crawled up the bank of the inlet, there stood LTC Faith," said White. "He was uncanny about being everywhere, or at least it seemed so. We had a great respect for him. He was a natural born leader."

The consolidation of the three battalions inside the inlet cheered up many of the troops, as did the very visible sight of Faith in command. "I felt better when I saw Colonel Faith in the middle of the perimeter," said PFC James Ransone of Baker Company. "Here was a lieutenant colonel in the middle of everything."

"You couldn't beat the morale," recalled Cpl. Francois. "For some stupid reason, I think these guys thought they were winning, and so did I."

Sardonic comments were made about MacArthur's hope to have the troops home by Christmas. He didn't say which Christmas, the joke went.

The Chinese had three main avenues of attack into the inlet: from the northeast down the Pungnyuri trail, from the high ground to the southeast, and along the road and railbed approaching from the southwest.

Faith reorganized the defenses, strengthening and slightly expanding the existing perimeter. The 3rd Battalion's three rifle companies—from north to south, Etchemendy's L Company, Kitz's K Company, and Marr's I Company—remained in place, protecting the eastern perimeter, supported by Jordan's M Company (heavy weapons). The newly arrived 1st Battalion's rifle companies took over the defenses along the north, west, and south flanks of the perimeter, previously guarded by the 3rd Battalion's headquarters and heavy weapons companies. Turner's B Company was placed along the southern perimeter, tying into I Company's right flank; it moved up to more elevated ground but was still below the higher positions on Hill 1456 held by the Chinese. Smith's A Company guarded the southwest corner of the perimeter, where the road from the south came along the reservoir shore and turned into the inlet. Seever's C Company spread out along the long inlet shore, protecting the northern side of the perimeter and sharing the responsibility for guarding the road approach from the southwest with A Company. Charlie Company's defensive line continued to the inlet bridge, where it tied in with L Company. Cody's Heavy Mortar Company was placed in the center of the inlet, joining the 57th Field Artillery and D Battery, 15th AAA in being ready to fire in all directions to defend the perimeter. Bigger's D Company (heavy weapons) was positioned behind A and B Companies, providing support along the southern and southwestern perimeter. Faith kept a platoon of Bigger's company available as a task force reserve.

The perimeter was considerably stronger now, but that didn't change the fact the Chinese held the high ground to the south and east. "Faith decided to defend a relatively small perimeter on low ground rather than to attempt to seize high ground and defend an over-extended perimeter," said Curtis. Faith also tried to improve the position on the southern perimeter by getting A and B Companies up on the ridgeline. They met stiff resistance "and had to settle by dark for a very unsatisfactory position on low ground—with the Chinese on high ground looking down on us," said Curtis.

Mortrude's C Company platoon was given a key position to defend on the western edge of the perimeter, blocking the road and railroad bed approach from the southwest. The area was covered with the bodies of Chinese soldiers who had been mowed down during the night by the AAA guns. Mortrude directed his men to search the corpses for grenades, and they collected many potato mashers for later use. He also had the platoon gather all the bodies into one spot so they would not be confused for infiltrators when the Chinese attacked in the dark.

Able Company dug in at its new position on the southwest side of the perimeter, getting ready for the night. "Everyone was exhausted and hungry," said Sergeant Via. "We tried to thaw a gallon can of corned beef hash on a gas squad stove. The can and meat inside were burnt while the center was still frozen." Some of the men tried to grab a little sleep, but the results were equally unsatisfying. They were under constant sniper fire from the hill to their left front.

All around the perimeter, soldiers worked to dig deeper foxholes, looking for that extra inch that might save their lives. Others tried to find M-1 rifles to replace their carbines, which continued to prove almost useless in the unceasing cold. Private Harry Jacobs of B Company could tolerate his carbine no further after it had refused to shoot during the last night's fight. "I try to fire the thing and it's frozen," he complained. "I've got it down in the foxhole, kicking at it, it wouldn't work." Once his unit was set up in the inlet, he took the carbine to the company kitchen. "Here, son of a bitch thing froze on me last night, can you give me a rifle?" Jacobs asked. A cook obliged, giving him an M-1. "Old reliable," Jacobs called it.

With ammunition and supplies dangerously low, Faith assigned Maj. Robbins to take charge of task force supplies. Robbins set up a central collection point so the dwindling supplies could be meted out equally to units around the perimeter. The 57th Field Artillery, the antiaircraft battery, and the mortar units had all expended an enormous amount of ammunition and would need to use what remained more judiciously.

The number of ROKs with the task force had dropped. Many had been killed or captured, but a substantial number had deserted. Dragooned off the streets, lacking real training, and fearful of the Chinese, some of the ROKs took advantage of the chaos to disappear. "When they started to desert, if I'd been in their shoes, I might have done the same thing," said Sgt. Charlie Gebhardt. "I can't blame them." PFC Ed Reeves's foxhole mate, Ho-Yah Bak, disappeared during the fighting, and Reeves was not sure if he had been killed, been captured, or had run off.

Bigger was among those not sorry to see the ROKs leave, complaining that they wasted ammunition and refused orders. "They fired wildly at anything and everything," he said. "They probably shot as many Americans as Chinese. This added to the discipline and control problems enormously. Many took off their uniforms and melted into the countryside."

But many ROKs stayed and continued fighting alongside the GIs.

Capt. Navarre set up the 1st Battalion medical tent in a railroad cut near the CP, with a tarp stretched over the cut to keep additional casualties under cover. The disappearance of the jeep hauling supplies was a blow, as it had been carrying two of the aid station's three medical chests, leaving the doctors desperately short on surgical equipment. Medics used ponchos and jackets to make improvised litters for carrying newly wounded soldiers to the aid station. A makeshift stove had been set up to provide a little warmth. Sgt. Leon Pugowski, a headquarters company cook, had managed to save two stoves during the move and had set them up to heat soup and coffee for the wounded.

Faith came by in the afternoon to check on the wounded and talk to the doctors. "Dr. Lee, you look very tired," the colonel said.

"No, sir, I'm as fresh as you are," Lee replied, drawing a laugh from Faith.

McClymont's men had captured two Chinese who had been trying to blow up D Battery's AAA weapons during the previous night's fight. Questioned by an ROK who spoke Chinese, the captives said their commanders had placed a bounty on the AAA guns. "The Chinese soldier who knocked one of those vehicles out was promised a great prize," said McClymont. He warned his crews to be ready again that night.

It was understandable why the Chinese were desperate to take out the weapons. Through the day, the AAA guns continued hitting targets of opportunity with great lethality. Sgt. Radke had just finished digging in near the inlet shore, about fifty yards from a Quad 50, when a Chinese platoon across the ice came into view, marching along the road in a column of three or four. "That quad 50 opened up on them, and they were all gone, just like that," Radke said.

Around 3:30 p.m., two Air Force C-119 Flying Boxcars appeared over the inlet. Captain Stamford had earlier radioed Corsair pilots to have them relay the task force's urgent requests for ammunition, rations, and supplies. After a pair of trial runs, the cargo planes began dropping crates of supplies that were attached by harnesses to parachutes. But the incessant wind blowing from the north and northwest carried many of the parachutes out of the perimeter, dropping the crates into the waiting hands of the Chinese to the south. Others fell into the no-man's-land between the two forces. Some GIs were shot trying to retrieve the wayward drops.

One parachute failed to open. The attached crate dropped like a stone, heading toward the spot where Radke was standing before crashing in the midst of a nearby group of ROK soldiers, hitting one of them. "I was yelling, 'Watch out! Watch out!' and he had just looked up," Radke said. The edge of the crate sliced open the ROK's head, killing him instantly. It was the young South Korean who had been nabbed by police on the streets of Pusan in August, when he was out picking up medicine for his wife. "The wife probably never did figure out what happened to her husband," said Radke.

To make matters worse, that crate and others were filled with 76 mm shells for the tanks, which were at Hudong-ni. The tank ammunition was useless at the inlet. Conversely, the drop included none of the desperately needed 40 mm ammunition for the M19s. "Although I personally asked [a pilot] to do everything in his power to get us 40 mm ammunition, none was ever received. NONE!" McClymont later wrote. Only forty rounds of the 105 mm shells needed for the howitzers were received, and the amount of mortar shells was not much better.

The medical supplies were likewise sadly deficient. "We never got enough bandages, morphine or ammunition in sufficiently varied types," said Stamford. They did receive castor oil and other nonessential supplies.

Hudong-ni

Captain Drake saw the parachutes dropping four miles to the north, and then shortly afterward, aircraft appeared over the Hudong perimeter and made a generous drop of ammunition. "We were elated!" Drake recalled. Then soldiers retrieved the crates and found they all held 40 mm ammunition meant for the M19s at the inlet. There were no 76 mm shells for the tanks. There was not even any .30- or .50-caliber ammunition for their machine guns, which were down to their last few belts. "It turned out to be a tragic mistake," said Drake.

9th Army Group Headquarters, Wednesday Afternoon

At his headquarters eleven miles north of Chosin, Song Shilun held a council with his senior commanders. The 9th Army Group had suffered tens of thousands of casualties over the course of two nights and had little to show for it. The fight with the 8,000 Marines at Yudam-ni had ground to a bloody standoff. On the east side of the reservoir, the 80th Division had been decimated in its fight with the 31st RCT, and Song had received Zhan Da'nan's report that he would be unable to destroy the Army unit without reinforcements. Ninth Army intelligence now estimated they were facing more than 10,000 American troops around Chosin, more than twice what they had anticipated.

Prisoner interrogations had revealed something of interest to the Chinese commanders. According to an official Chinese Army history of the war, "only after the first two attacks had 27th [Army] found out they were facing one of [the] American army's elite forces: the 31st Regiment of the 7th Division." It was known as the Polar Bear Regiment "because it fought so brilliantly in Siberia" at the end of World War I, the history added.

But now the Polar Bears were vulnerable, and destroying a regiment with a vaunted history in the Far East would be a coup. Song sought recommendations from his commanders on how the 9th Army Group could still meet Mao's directive to destroy the American units at Chosin. Peng Deqing, the 27th Army commander, recommended that they destroy the 31st Regiment first, as the Army unit was completely cut off on the east side of the reservoir. The 20th Army commander, Zhang Yixiang, concurred, saying the 31st "had become the weakest link of the X Corps" and could be more easily wiped out than the Marines.

Song agreed and decided to shift the main focus of his attack away from the Marines at Yudam-ni and make the Army task force his priority. He would mass force to destroy the smaller, weaker Army force and gain a desperately needed victory. Annihilating a regiment might at least partly assuage Mao's and Peng's demands for the destruction of the American forces.

The main force of the 81st Division would move from its position west of Fusen Reservoir and join the 80th Division in surrounding and destroying the Army task force. The 27th Army's 94th Division, which had been held in reserve, would be ready to enter the battle at any moment. The 58th Division at Hagaru and the 79th Division at Yudam-ni would conduct suppression attacks to prevent the Marines from coming to the rescue of the Army task force.

At 2:00 p.m., Song cabled Peng Dehuai at his Chinese People's Volunteer Force headquarters in northwest North Korea, reporting that the 9th Army Group was changing their operations in order to concentrate its main effort to the east side of the Chosin Reservoir, with the goal of annihilating the U.S. Army task force. Song also reported that he was ordering the 26th Army, which had been held north as the 9th Army Group reserve, to march "day and night" to Chosin to bolster his weakened force. Once the Army task force was destroyed, the 9th Army Group would turn its attention back to destroying the Marines at Yudam-ni and Hagaru.

"We will concentrate our forces to wipe them out one by one," Song wrote.

Majon-dong, Wednesday Afternoon

In the tiny crossroads village of Majon-dong, the 2nd Battalion, 31st Infantry, had been waiting hours for trucks that X Corps had promised would carry them forward. Instead of moving out in the battalion's own trucks from Hamhung that morning as originally planned, an X Corps colonel had issued orders for the troops to ride by train to Majon-dong, twenty-two miles from Hamhung, barely one-third of the way to Hagaru. There X Corp trucks were supposed to be waiting to carry them forward. Lt. Col. Richard Reidy and his 2nd Battalion command group drove to Majon-dong by jeep and linked up with their troops, who all arrived by train by 10:15 that morning. There they sat. "No trucks were available," reads the battalion command report. The promised X Corps trucks had already come through Majon-dong and been sent forward, carrying supplies north. Even more infuriatingly, the 2nd Battalion's own trucks arrived that morning, but they had already been assigned by some X Corps functionary to haul ammunition, and the orders were not changed.

After waiting fruitlessly all day, the 2nd Battalion formed a defensive perimeter and prepared to spend the night in Majon-dong. It was asinine and incompetent work by the X Corps staff, an astonishing failure, given the urgent need the 31st RCT had for the reinforcements. The pleas of Maclean, Hodes, Barr, and others to rush the battalion to Chosin had been no match for military bureaucracy.

Inlet, Wednesday Afternoon

Late in the day, several Marine helicopters landed in the inlet, close to the reservoir shore. Hodes had managed to get them dispatched from Hagaru to evacuate a few of the casualties, including the two wounded battalion commanders, Reilly and Embree.

Reilly's condition had worsened. His leg wound had become infected, and he was in a morphine-induced daze at the aid station that day, barely able to speak. Still, according to his radioman, Cpl. Francois, he protested strenuously, not wanting to leave his men. Embree likewise "was arguing about it," said PFC McMillin, with the 57th Field Artillery headquarters. "He was pretty good [about] sticking with us." The two battalion commanders were told their evacuations had been ordered by higher headquarters. Reilly and Embree were flown out, a sight that did little to boost morale. Faith placed Maj. Storms in command of the 3rd Battalion and Lt. Col. Tolly in command of the 57th Field Artillery.

The helicopters made at least one return trip before darkness fell, evacuating several other seriously wounded patients, including Maj. Galloway, the regimental surgeon with the head wound. In all, about 8 to 12 wounded were flown out, according to Capt. Morgan, the 3rd Battalion surgeon.

There was hope Lt. Rybolt, the 3rd Battalion communications officer wounded by the friendly .50-caliber fire, could be saved. "We took Lt. Rybolt down to the lake as he was going to be the next one out," Capt. Bryant said. "The chopper did not return, and, after dark, we brought him back to the aid station. He came close to getting out."

It's puzzling why Hodes did not use the opportunity to fly into the inlet. The small Marine Sikorsky helicopters only had a single bench behind the pilot's seat for passengers, and litter patients had to be stretched across the passenger compartment, with their feet dangling out the helicopter window. Possibly, Hodes did not want to take up space that would have prevented a wounded man from being evacuated.

But it was a lost chance to gain critical communication and coordination. Faith needed to know that the 2nd Battalion was not, in fact, close to arriving. That misconception had already cost Maclean and the task force dearly. With Drake's tanks unable to break through after two attacks and the 2nd Battalion increasingly unlikely to reach the inlet at all, there was an urgent need to alert the 31st RCT that they would need to break out on their own.

Some task force officers thought a senior officer would be flown in to replace Maclean, as was to be expected when a regimental commander was lost in action. Hodes was the obvious choice, being the 7th Division's senior officer in Hagaru. He could have flown in with staff and communications, taking over command of the task force while allowing Faith time to plan a breakout, or vice versa. "Although senior officers could get in by helicopter, not one came to take over," Bigger later noted.

It may have been that no one at Hagaru knew yet of Maclean's disappearance. While Hodes may have learned about it when the helicopters returned to Hagaru with the wounded battalion commanders, there is no evidence that he did. Reilly and Embree were apparently quickly put on small planes out of Hagaru and then moved on to an Army hospital in Osaka, Japan. Reilly was in no condition to be debriefed. "He had no memory of leaving Korea—just of waking up in the hospital," Celeste Reilly, his wife, later said. But the continued lack of knowledge and understanding about the situation facing the task force only underscores the critical need to have established better communication.

There were many steps that could have been taken to help the 31st RCT. A liaison officer from higher headquarters could have flown in to make sure the task force was receiving ammunition, gasoline, medical supplies, batteries, rations, and other urgently needed supplies. An Air Force ground controller could have been flown in to join the 3rd Battalion, replacing Lt. Johnson, killed in the initial attack. Officers could have been flown in to replace Reilly and Embree. Combat-experienced officers and NCOs from other Army units could have been sent in to replace at least some of the many key platoon and squad leaders who had been lost.

None of that was done. The last orders Faith had received was Almond's demand the previous day that they attack north. The task force officers were frustrated by the lack of specific instructions they were receiving—or even what higher headquarters they should look to for guidance. It felt as if they had been deserted, Bigger said.

HUNGNAM, WEDNESDAY, 5:00 P.M.

Darkness was falling when the cub plane carrying a chagrined Ned Almond approached the X Corps headquarters at Hungnam. It was just a five-minute hop from Yonpo Airfield, where an Air Force C-54 carrying him back from Tokyo had landed at 5:00 p.m. The X Corps runway—which was actually a city street—had to be lit up with gasoline pots to guide the small plane to a safe landing.

Almond hurried into the headquarters, as there was much to do. Just before Almond's departure from Tokyo at noon, MacArthur had directed him to pull X Corps back from the Chosin Reservoir and the Yalu River and concentrate his forces in an enclave around Hamhung and Hungnam on the coast. Walker's 8th Army was to fall back and form a defensive line along the Chongchon River. Almond acknowledged three decades later that MacArthur's decision was "the right one in view of the conditions that obtained all along the front which was over-extended on our part. We had been caught in a mess by an unknown enemy strength. . . . [T]he superior strength of the enemy and the nature of the terrain were too much for us."

That realization was coming very late for Task Force Faith.

Inside the X Corps war room, Almond huddled with his senior staff, including Gen. Ruffner, his chief of staff, and directed them to prepare a new order to stop the attack and withdraw X Corps to the Hamhung area.

The X Corps situation had only grown graver in the twenty-four hours since Almond had flown to Tokyo. An X Corps intelligence report that evening estimated there were 40,000 CCF troops in the Chosin area, with another 12,000 nearby and more troops streaming into the gap between X Corps and the 8th Army. The two Marine regiments at Yudam-ni remained cut off and surrounded, and the Chinese had launched a heavy attack against Fox Company, the only unit holding the critical Toktong Pass leading back to Hagaru. The situation with the Army task force east of Chosin was obviously dire, though Almond and his staff still did not comprehend how bad it was.

The Marine base at Hagaru had come under heavy attack by the CCF 58th Division Tuesday night. The initial attack came from the southwest and temporarily broke through the Marines' defensive lines. Some infiltrators reached the airstrip—still under construction and barely a third complete—but were driven off by Marine engineers who jumped off their bulldozers and picked up rifles. A second attack was launched against East Hill, which loomed over the eastern side of the perimeter and was held by a mixed force of Marines and Army engineers. The defenders were quickly knocked off the top, but they counterattacked and established a line just below the crest, holding on through a night of bitter, bloody fighting. It was clearer than ever that Hagaru had to be held, but it was not clear that it would.

Koto-ri, held by the bulk of Chesty Puller's 1st Marine Regiment and an assortment of other units, including a battalion of British Royal Marines, was under siege by the Chinese, who controlled the road leading to Hagaru. But O. P. Smith, desperate for reinforcements to hold Hagaru, ordered Puller to send some of his force at Koto-ri to try to break through and reach Hagaru, eleven miles to the north.

Accordingly, a column of reinforcements under Col. Douglas Drysdale, commanding officer of the British 41st Commando Battalion, departed Koto-ri Wednesday morning. The column included more than 900 troops, including 250 Royal Marines, one company of Marine infantry from Puller's regiment, a Marine tank company, and a company of GIs—B Company from the 1st Battalion, 31st Infantry Regiment. About halfway to Hagaru, the column, given the name Task Force Drysdale, was ambushed by the CCF and cut to pieces. Only about 300 men made it to Hagaru. The rest were killed, captured, or made it back to Koto-ri.

It will never be known what might have happened had Reidy's 2nd Battalion, 31st Regiment, reached Koto-ri in time to join Task Force Drysdale on the attack north. The addition of the Army battalion would have doubled the size of the force and provided considerable additional firepower. Perhaps it would have only increased the numbers of casualties, given how the terrain would have kept the column strung out along the road. But it's also possible that a considerably larger portion of Task Force Drysdale would have broken through to reach Hagaru. Hodes was "most disappointed" to learn that the 2nd Battalion was not part of the reinforcement column that reached Hagaru, said Lynch, the general's operations aide. If even some of the 2nd Battalion had then continued on to Hudong, it would have provided the large infantry force Drake needed for his tanks to break through the Chinese roadblock at Hill 1221.

Instead, the Chinese remained firmly in control of all the roads around Chosin, and Task Force Faith was more isolated than ever.

By 9:00 p.m., the new orders had been prepared. Almond approved Operational Order 8, which stopped the X Corp attack and directed that preparations begin to withdraw forces to the Hamhung/Hungnam perimeter. Almond also issued Operations Instruction No. 19, ordering all Army units at Chosin, including the 31st RCT, to be put under the operational control of Gen. Smith and the 1st Marine Division as of 8:00 a.m. the next morning. The reason, Almond later said, was "so that General Smith might coordinate the battle shaping up in his immediate area." Placing the 31st RCT under the control of the 1st Marine Division would have made sense from the start, given how far removed the task force was from 7th Division headquarters. Quite possibly, Almond had balked at placing the task force under Smith's command because of his frustration with the Marine commander's caution. "Turning command over to Smith on the 29th when the situation had turned desperate only confirmed what [Almond] should have done in the first place," Maj. Roe, a 7th Marine Regiment intelligence officer at Chosin, later observed.

Bizarrely, Almond's order also directed Smith to immediately deploy one of the Marine regiments at Yudam-ni back to Hagaru and then proceed up the east side of the reservoir to link up with the 31st RCT. That evening Smith received a telephone call from X Corps headquarters. "The whole scheme of maneuver was changed, that the Army battalions on the east side of the Chosin Reservoir, who were now cut off from us, were attached to me and I was to extricate them, and that I was to withdraw the 5th and 7th Marines and consolidate around Hagaru-ri," he wrote.

Almond's instructions showed that even though he had acquiesced on stopping his attack, he remained divorced from reality. The Marine regiments at Yudam-ni were fighting for their lives and in no position to rescue the 31st RCT.

La Feria, Texas, Wednesday Night

The news from Korea had continued to be unremittingly grim, with 200,000 Chinese troops reported to be attacking MacArthur's forces. As of yet, the Chosin Reservoir was little more than a dot on newspaper maps of North Korea, with no full understanding among Americans of just how grave the situation faced by their troops was. But Helen Storms had heard and read enough to be deeply worried.

"Dearest Sweetheart," she wrote Wednesday evening. "These days of decision certainly are critical. Oh, how heavy my heart has been all day—just thinking about what I am afraid that the U.S. will do. Sometimes I think that the men in Washington don't care and don't know anything. . . . It sounds as if you might be cut off from all supply lines if something is not done in the next few days. You may already be cut off for all I know."

The boys had been put to bed but were being rambunctious. "They don't want to go to sleep until I get all the lights out and am in bed myself," she wrote. "So, guess I must say goodnight. . . . Soon be time for the newscast too—I listen to them all. I probably shouldn't, but can't stay away from the radio."

"To say that we love you is putting our feeling very mildly—but we mean it with every implication that the imagination can conceive."

Chapter 10

THE THIRD NIGHT

Wednesday–Thursday, November 29–November 30

The calm that prevailed around the inlet once night fell on Wednesday was puzzling, but not in any way relaxing. "From dark until midnight the area was ominously quiet," said Wes Curtis.

Eerie bugle calls drifted in from the north from time to time. Distant artillery fire could be heard from across the reservoir, where the Marines remained surrounded at Yudam-ni. The Chinese made some small-scale probing attacks around the perimeter, keeping the troops on edge.

Every now and then, when the rifle companies suspected enemy movement toward their front, the mortarmen would fire off a star shell—an illumination round that would light up the ground below as it slowly descended, attached to a parachute. Jim McClymont, the D Battery commander, was looking toward the frozen inlet when a star shell went off and lit up a group of men on the ice. Everyone was momentarily startled until they realized it was another group of GIs, who had been cut off during the withdrawal and were coming into the perimeter with great relief. "How they hollered, laughed, and were glad to see us," said McClymont.

After that, things quieted down again. The temperature was plunging, reaching thirty degrees below zero but feeling even colder with the northwest winds out of Manchuria blowing at 15 or 20 mph.

Late that night, Don Faith walked along the perimeter line, checking foxholes to see how the men were coping with the cold. A machine gunner was found frozen to death, sitting in his position at the gun. Anyone who dozed off for more than thirty or forty-five minutes risked dying, and some did.

Almost everyone had some degree of frostbite. Some men were becoming lethargic, unable to focus in the punishing cold. Faces were swollen and bleeding from the stinging wind. "To say that we were unprepared for arctic-type temperatures is a vast understatement," said Lt. John Gray.

Taking care of bodily functions was "both painful and hazardous." It wasn't worth the risk to get out of a foxhole, so GIs used their helmets and tossed the waste as far as they could.

On the Able Company line, Sgt. Via's hands were growing numb. He had taken off his gloves that morning to squeeze off some rounds from his rifle during a firefight on the way into the inlet and, in his haste, left them on the ground, a mistake he sorely regretted now.

At C Company's position on A Company's right flank, Lt. Mortrude was happily wearing a Chinese greatcoat he had salvaged from "an unusually large enemy KIA." Wearing it inside of his parka gave him a bit of a bloated look, but he didn't care.

In the surrounding hills, the bloodied CCF 80th Division was in no condition to launch a major attack that night. The reinforcements Zhan Da'an had requested had not yet arrived.

His troops were suffering as much as the GIs from the cold, if not more. Soldiers slept in the open, hugging together, trying to get a little warmth. They wrapped themselves in anything they could find to protect against what a Chinese Army history called "the killing cold in the night."

The frigid temperatures were wreaking havoc on their weapons. More than half the mortars they fired did not explode, a failure the Chinese blamed on the cold. "Thousands of rifles were broken apart like a frozen ice stick during the night," the history reported.

"In spite of all the unimaginable difficulties, commanders of 9th Army [were] determined to make another all out effort to wipe out the besieged American troops," reads the history. Even in the 80th Division's depleted condition, the commanders gave orders for limited attacks that night to try to further weaken the 31st RCT. The dreaded antiaircraft weapons were the prime targets.

Around midnight, the moon vanished behind clouds, and snow started to fall. "Seemed as if the stars themselves had even stopped twinkling," McClymont said.

The captain was sitting in his foxhole CP with his captured Tommy gun by his side, as well as several grenades stacked on the edge of the hole within easy reach. McClymont was just starting to drift off when he was jolted alert by sudden firing from a foxhole near the edge of the inlet. "I grabbed my glasses and could faintly see running figures out on the ice, running towards us," he said. A star shell revealed a large force of Chinese attacking across the ice. Almost instantly, one of McClymont's M16s opened up with all four of its .50-caliber machine guns. With each gun firing 450 rounds a minute and every fifth round a tracer, GIs watched as the Quad 50 "spectacularly repelled" the Chinese attack virtually single-handedly.

But there were more probing attacks all around the perimeter. The once-quiet night was filled with explosions and fire. "Our artillery began to wham away and the cough of our mortars started up," said Maj. Robbins. "Next the machine guns on our perimeter took up the clatter."

The Chinese had plotted the positions of the artillery guns and antiaircraft weapons during the day and now hit them with heavy mortar fire. Determined, squad-sized assaults followed, with troops carrying Bangalore torpedoes, trying to reach the guns and their crews. When the .50-caliber machine guns on one of his M16 half-tracks suddenly fell silent, McClymont ran over to investigate. The gunner was dead, shot through the head as he sat in the turret. His feet had become tangled inside the turret, and the other crew members were unable to lift him out. McClymont crouched on the floor of the half-track and felt around the armored front of the turret. "I could get my hand up inside the turret and I turned his feet while the rest hauled him up and out," said McClymont. "We laid him down by his half-track and another gunner slid up and into that turret." The Quad 50 rejoined the fight.

The Chinese launched a concerted effort to reach Sgt. Harold Haugland's M19. Haugland exposed himself to intense fire to direct the fire of his Twin 40s at vulnerable points where attacking troops threatened to break through the perimeter. The 40 mm fire beat back the attack. But Haugland was severely wounded in the foot and had to be carried to the aid station.

While he was being treated, the enemy launched another attack. Haugland, a strapping 22-year-old raised on a ranch in Montana, wrapped his wounded foot in cloth and found an empty cardboard ration box to use as a shoe. He limped his way back to his M19, resumed command, and again directed fire at the attackers. Calamity threatened when an enemy mortar set an ammunition trailer ablaze next to his M19. Though 40 mm shells on the trailer were exploding, Haugland coolly walked in front of the vehicle and guided the driver to a safe location, where they resumed firing and again fought off the attack.

Nearby, Sgt. Grantford Brown's normal five-man crew was down to three because the assistant gunner and the driver had gone to replace casualties on other M19s. That left only Brown; Sgt. Ayala, his gunner; and Cpl. Celestino Chavez Jr., their loader. Chavez, a bespectacled 19-year-old from Gallup, New Mexico, seeking to emulate his three half brothers who had served in World War II, had enlisted in the Army over the protests of his mother. Shortly before 3:00 a.m., the Chinese assaulted their position. Chavez was seriously wounded during the attack, but he refused to leave his position, as there was no one available to replace him. Chavez "kept on loading my guns," Ayala said, and Ayala kept on firing.

After the attack was broken by their fire, Chavez, weakened by loss of blood, collapsed unconscious and fell off the M19 to the ground. Ayala helped carry Chavez to the little hut the medics were using as an aid station. "All they could do was put him into a sleeping bag with no medicine," Ayala said.

The heaviest attack of the night was on the southwest corner, where the road and railbed entered the perimeter. A large Chinese force in white uniforms descended from the hill to the south and hit Able Company with several assaults, one after another. They overran a roadblock defended by a recoilless rifle, dragging some of the crew away into the night. Baker Company, on the A Company left flank, was hit in similar fashion. "We heard what was now familiar sounds, the bugles, the whistles, then wave after wave of Chinese," said Clarence White. "There were so many so close together you couldn't miss, and we killed many that night."

Some enemy troops penetrated the lines, but they accomplished little. "They too were seeking warmth and food," said White. "We would kill most of them during the early morning as they went through our areas." On the north side of the road, C Company held the line.

The attacks had been less intense than on the previous two nights, but the task force had suffered another 100 men dead, wounded, or missing. "The ever-increasing number of casualties was becoming a critical problem," said

Lt. Magill, the de facto commander of Baker Battery. "The men were very concerned about being hit because they knew there was a good chance that they would freeze to death if they were immobilized. The remaining medical personnel were close to exhaustion and there were few medical supplies."

Though it came at a great cost in lives, the Chinese had succeeded in whittling down the American firepower advantage. Magill's battery had lost one of its six howitzers. Haugland's M19 was badly damaged in the fight and could no longer move, though it could still fire. The loss of the ammunition trailer loaded with the dwindling supply of 40 mm shells was a serious blow.

When Ayala went to check on Chavez at the aid station that morning, he learned that the corporal who had refused to leave his post had frozen to death in his sleeping bag. "I guess he had lost too much blood," said Ayala.

Chapter 11

THE THIRD DAY

Thursday, November 30

Dawn once again brought a reprieve. The Chinese pulled back to higher ground, dragging some of their dead with them, but leaving most scattered around the perimeter, soon to be covered by blowing snow. "When it got light, they just sort of faded away—like somebody said timeout," said Sgt. Radke.

Corsairs came overhead, encouraging further Chinese retreat. The GIs took advantage of the lack of enemy fire to build some fires to thaw out. "We were all so cold, that we could hardly move, couldn't hardly pull the trigger anymore," said Lt. Mortrude, whose men had endured another night without sleeping bags.

The soldiers also used the lull to gather the bodies of GIs and ROKs in a location close to the inlet shore, not far from the bridge, where they were somewhat out of sight but never out of mind. "The dead at the disposal site were stacked three and four high, like cordwood," said medic Doc Blohm. The men tried to bury a few bodies, but given the numbers of dead and how frozen the ground was, it was futile.

PFC Bob Hammond took off his boots to massage his numb feet, but his left foot was so swollen that he couldn't get the boot back on. Two of his A Battery squad mates took Hammond to the wall of GI dead, looking for a bigger boot that might fit, but the corpses were so frozen that they were unable to pull any boots off. Finally, they tied a cardboard C-ration box around Hammond's foot, and he made do with that.

Around the inlet, sergeants did a check on the ammunition levels in their squads and platoons and found almost everybody was low. At 10:00 a.m., another airdrop brought supplies, but not much ammunition. The 105 mm shells for the howitzers were running low. "The amount tapered off until we were getting hardly any at all," said Lt. Patton. Once again, there were no 40 mm shells for the M19s.

Majon-Dong, Thursday Morning

After waiting almost a full day for transportation, the 2nd Battalion, 31st Regiment, had been given back its trucks by X Corps and was finally able to resume its journey north at 6:45 a.m. But the Corps operations chief, Lt. Col. Jack Chiles, threw confusion into the mission by giving the battalion a second task, directing it "to keep the road open to the south to Hamhung."

Near the top of the Funchilin Pass, the column came under Chinese machine gun fire that destroyed two of the lead jeeps. Troops moved out from the trucks and returned fire, supported by .50-caliber truck-mounted machine guns. Two Army trucks were destroyed in the fierce fight, but the battalion forced the enemy back and took control of the pass.

Lt. Col. Reidy, the 2nd Battalion commander, realized the Chinese would again close the critical pass as soon as the battalion moved forward. Reidy was unsure of which order to follow: continue his attack north, to reach Koto-ri, or keep the road south open. "He chose the latter course since it was the later order and felt he could not do both," Major Joe Gurfein, a planning officer at X Corps headquarters, later said. The 2nd Battalion's painfully slow movement to Chosin was largely X Corps' fault, but what Bill McCaffrey termed Reidy's "lack of aggressiveness" certainly was not helping.

Reidy was not able to reach X Corps by radio, so he sent a liaison officer back to headquarters to recommend that either another unit be sent to hold Funchilin Pass or that the 2nd Battalion remain in place. Either way, the battalion was in no position to help Task Force Faith.

Hamhung, Thursday Morning

The bleak situation facing the 31st RCT was written all over Dave Barr's face when he arrived at X Corps headquarters. "General Barr was in a near state of catatonic shock at the way events were running," said. McCaffrey. "It was a very depressing situation."

Hodes had telephoned Barr that morning from Hagaru with grim new information on the condition of the 31st, probably obtained from Lt. Col.

Embree or others among the handful of wounded who were evacuated from the inlet late Wednesday. Hodes had learned that Maclean was missing and that Faith was in command. Hodes had given up on getting the tanks to the inlet, and it was clear that the 2nd Battalion would not arrive in time. The entire 31st RCT could be lost.

"I have no doubt that [Barr] was personally devastated by what was happening to the officers and men of his division," McCaffrey said. The general now faced a crisis "for which he was neither trained nor I think naturally qualified."

Hagaru, Thursday Morning

As of 8:20 a.m., Task Force Faith was under the overall command of O. P. Smith. It was not a responsibility the Marine general wanted. He had his hands full as it was with the 5th and 7th Marine regiments cut off at Yudam-ni and with Hagaru gravely threatened.

Hodes, now out of the chain of command, went to the Marine headquarters at 8:30 a.m. to meet with Smith, reporting that neither the Army tanks at Hudong-ni nor the 2nd Battalion reinforcements could help the 31st RCT. "General Hodes reported to me that the cut off battalions had about 400 casualties and that it was impossible for them to fight their way out," Smith said. "The inference was that they should be extricated by a larger force."

Smith seemed to think the Army troops were shirkers. "They are about 5 miles north of us and I do not see why they cannot do something," he wrote in his log. "They want to be rescued."

Faith and the 31st RCT had had no contact with Hagaru or with Hodes or Barr in at least twenty-four hours, and they could not have made any request to be rescued. Hodes was likely relaying a request from Barr or Almond. "General Hodes was quite embarrassed about asking us for help in extricating the Army troops," Smith's operations chief, Bowser, said. "He recognized that what he was asking was impossible. Any Marine force from Hagaru strong enough to blast its way through to the GIs would have left our perimeter dangerously vulnerable."

Smith told Hodes he had no infantry to spare. "I directed General Hodes to draw up in my name a dispatch to the task Force directing it to make every effort to improve its situation by working toward us, but to do nothing which would jeopardize the safety of the wounded," Smith wrote in his journal. Faith was to be told that no infantry support could be provided but also that unlimited air support was available.

Smith described his dispatch as "carefully worded," and it was that. It was so carefully worded as to be meaningless. How was Faith to move 400 wounded soldiers toward Hagaru without putting them in jeopardy? Getting ammunition to the task force and establishing direct communication was what would "improve its situation."

"Smith's words 'improve your position' and 'do nothing to jeopardize the safety of the wounded' came from a commander who had no knowledge of the situation that existed at the Inlet, nor did he take action to find out and contribute something," Capt. George Rasula, the 31st Regiment's assistant operations officer, later said.

Bad as the situation was facing Task Force Faith, it was about to get worse. Hodes asked Smith for permission to withdraw the Army troops, including Drake's 31st Tank Company, from Hudong-ni to Hagaru. "This request was granted," Smith noted in his log.

It was astonishing that Hodes made the request—and no less astonishing that Smith approved it. The tanks were positioned to play a critical role in any breakout by the 31st RCT, but now the generals intended to pull the armor out before any attempt could be made. Almost certainly, Hodes had made the request after consulting with Barr. The two apparently had decided that if the Marines were unable to rescue the Army task force, it was doomed, and the best thing to do was cut their losses. "My conclusion at the time was that . . . they decided it was hopeless to try and do something for the 31st," McCaffrey later said.

Hodes "thought that the 31st Rear at Hudong-ni was vulnerable," Drake later said, and he feared the tanks could be lost if the Chinese cut off the road back to Hagaru. Hodes also believed that the 31st Regiment tanks "could significantly assist in the Hagaru defense," Drake said. "What was more important—to hold Hagaru-ri or to hold Hudong-ni?"

As for Smith, he was not likely to turn down an opportunity to add a company of Sherman tanks to his beleaguered Hagaru defenses.

X Corps Headquarters, Hamhung

At 8:00 a.m., Ned Almond assembled his X Corps staff to review MacArthur's orders to discontinue the attack and concentrate his forces around Hamhung. The news from up north was unrelentingly bad, with the Chinese reported to control the main supply route south of Koto-ri.

Almond's alarm grew when he met with Barr at 9:20 a.m. to discuss the 31st RCT situation, which may be when he learned of Maclean's disappearance. "His loss is a great shock to me," Almond wrote in a letter soon afterward.

Almond and Barr considered sending Hodes to replace Maclean. "I urged such a course, and at the meeting of General Almond [and] General Barr I am certain it was discussed," McCaffrey later said. "General Barr had great confidence in Faith. He did not want to risk Hodes. Some remark he made to General Almond, I remember clearly, about not throwing good men away."

Almond decided to fly to Hagaru that afternoon to discuss the situation with Smith at the 1st Marine Division headquarters. During his meeting with Barr, Almond called the Marine commander, apparently to inform him that both he and Barr would be visiting. Immediately after his meeting with Almond, Barr departed Hamhung, flying in a small plane to Hagaru. There he would take one of Smith's helicopters to the inlet and meet with Don Faith.

Hudong-ni, 11:00 a.m.

With 18 remaining Sherman tanks, the 31st Regiment rear headquarters at Hudong-ni was a strong midway point between the Task Force Faith position at the inlet, four miles to the north, and at Hagaru, five miles to the south. The garrison was manned by 325 troops, including 176 from Drake's 31st Tank Company, 105 from the 57th Field Artillery Headquarters Battery, and 44 from the 31st Regiment's Headquarters and Headquarters Company. The supply dump held about 260 tons of equipment and supplies, including the large amount of the airdropped 40 mm ammunition desperately needed for the M19s at the inlet. Two of Drake's tanks were armed with 105 mm howitzers that would have been formidable weapons to keep the road north of Hudong-ni clear of enemy troops and made it more difficult for the Chinese to put up roadblocks.

With Hodes in Hagaru and Maclean missing, the regimental operations officer, Lt. Col. Berry Anderson, 41, was now the senior officer at the rear headquarters. Anderson had joined the regiment at Fuji and was promoted after another officer was wounded in the fighting around Suwon. In his short time at the regiment, Anderson's know-it-all manner had managed to rub many of his fellow officers the wrong way, even the usually affable Maj. Storms. Anderson was good at quoting field manuals, but not much of a leader. "He sure has a lot to learn about handling men," Capt. Rasula complained in a letter to his wife.

Anderson was known as a heavy drinker, and at one point, Maclean had considered replacing him. Ironically, Maclean had left his personal belongings at Hudong-ni, including a supply of whiskey, which Anderson "decided to use, but not to share," Chaplain Hoehn complained. Drake considered Anderson "highly nervous and confused in tight situations" and had seen very little of him since arriving at Hudong-ni, as Anderson rarely strayed from the schoolhouse. "He was not one to risk exposure to enemy fire," Drake said.

The schoolhouse was now taking sniper fire, and the garrison had suffered casualties during sporadic firefights as the Chinese put pressure on the perimeter. But the Hudong-ni position was likely not in immediate danger of being overrun. "It was obvious that the Chinese had no intention of attacking a perimeter defended by so many tanks," said Rasula.

At 11:00 a.m., Anderson received orders to move to Hagaru. They are recorded in the 7th Division records as coming from the 1st Marine Division, as both Hodes and Barr no longer had the authority to issue orders to any of the Army elements at Chosin. According to Maj. Lynch, Hodes relayed the orders to Anderson via the tank radio in Hagaru that he used to communicate with Hudong-ni. Smith intended to use the tanks to bolster the defenses at Hagaru, as Drake was told he would be given a piece of the Marine perimeter.

No one at Hudong-ni objected to the order. "On the ground at the time, there were many reasons to make our move logical," Drake said. The tank ammunition was exhausted, though more could have been dropped. There were worries that the Chinese would cut the road leading back to Hagaru. There were wounded men at the garrison who needed medical help.

What Drake and the others at Hudong-ni did not know due to the lack of communications was how much worse the situation was at the inlet—that the task force had more than 400 casualties; that Maclean and many officers were dead, wounded, or missing; and that the task force would soon have to fight its way out of the inlet. "I personally knew nothing about the situation north of Hudong-ni except that there was a fight," said Drake. "Had I known more, I might have influenced the decision."

Inlet Perimeter, Thursday Late Morning

Lt. Mortrude had been instructed that morning to have his men establish a landing zone near the reservoir shoreline in case any helicopters came to evacuate casualties. When a Marine helicopter flying over the frozen reservoir veered toward the inlet, he went to meet it.

Mortrude, expecting an evacuation flight, was surprised when the portly form of Gen. Barr popped out. The 7th Division commander wore a grim look on his face. "He discouraged my enthusiastic welcome with a brusque response and stalked off to locate Colonel Faith," Mortrude said.

Several officers escorted Barr to the regimental CP, where they found Faith, who'd had no advance word of the general's visit. For two officers with a close, almost father-son relationship, it was likely a painful conversation. At least two regimental officers, including Maj. Robbins and Capt. McNally, the communication officer, were present for the meeting. Faith described Maclean's disappearance, telling Barr that the colonel "fell four times and when he got up the fourth time the Chinese grabbed him and took him away." Faith told Barr he now had 500 wounded men, "which were his great concern," Barr recalled.

Faith put on a brave face. "Lt. Colonel Faith felt that he would be able to fight his way out," Barr related several months later. "However, the situation was much more serious than he realized. We were completely cut off from furnishing any reinforcements."

Barr "told us there was no chance of any reinforcements, in fact, he had tears in his eyes," McNally said. "He was a good ole fellow. And [he said] that he wasn't going to tell us that he was sending reinforcements, because he couldn't, he didn't have any to send, and if we got out, we'd have to fight our way out."

Barr described the futile attempts by Hodes and the 31st Regiment tanks to reach the inlet. "His information was that a tank-led task force had been trying for two days to reach our surrounded garrison and had been severely mauled and turned back in the attempt to break through to us," Robbins said. "Then did we realize the full gravity of our situation."

Barr also told Faith that the long-awaited 2nd Battalion would never reach the inlet. "There was no possibility of getting the Seventh Division reinforcements in to help the surrounded force," Barr said.

Barr's visit was likely the first word Faith had that he was now under the command of the 1st Marine Division. It is not known if Barr was aware by then that orders had been given to withdraw the tanks from Hudong-ni or what, if anything, he told Faith about plans to remove the tanks. Presumably, Barr relayed word that X Corps was planning to withdraw from the reservoir. But Barr gave Faith no instructions, as the task force was no longer under his command. Nor is it known if Barr delivered the dispatch Smith had asked Hodes to prepare. But the gist of the message was clear: Apart from air support, Task Force Faith was on its own.

"Colonel Faith decided that he would prepare to fight our way out of the trap, but wanted to get better supplied with ammunition before making the effort," Robbins said. Barr "promised to do all he could to get us better supplied by air," Robbins added.

It was a short meeting, no more than half an hour. Word of Barr's visit had sparked hope among some GIs that the task force's predicament was finally getting some high-level attention. "We jumped to conclusions that help was on the way," said Lt. Gray.

But anyone close enough to see Barr's demeanor as he departed was disabused of that notion. "After his meeting with Col. Faith, he returned to his helicopter and immediately left the inlet," said Lt. Magill, the acting B Battery commander. "He did not spend any time trying to encourage the troops."

In retrospect, Magill added, "Barr must have decided that the battle was about over for the perimeter defenders and that there was little chance of any of them surviving the engagement."

Hagaru, Early Afternoon Thursday

After landing back at Hagaru, Barr conferred with Smith. The Marine general considered Barr "a pretty good egg," noting that "our relations were always cordial." Possibly, this was because Barr never seemed to challenge Smith about anything. "Upon his return, General Barr agreed with me that Task Force Faith, with air support, could improve its situation," Smith wrote.

Smith's summary of Barr's meeting at Faith's headquarters, whether it was based on anything the Army general told him or on his own interpretation, would have struck those present at the inlet as bizarre. Barr "gave them a pep talk," according to Smith.

Barr did take one concrete action at his meeting with Smith, but it was in no way helpful to the 31st RCT. He told Smith that since Hodes was no longer in the chain of command for the Army task force, he would be withdrawn from Hagaru "to relieve all concerned of embarrassment," according to Bowser. It was odd, given all the pressing needs of the task force, that avoiding ruffled feelings for Smith and Hodes was seen as a priority and that removing the senior Army officer from the scene was somehow considered a good idea.

Shortly after 2:00 p.m., the L-17 carrying Ned Almond landed at the Hagaru airstrip. Almond went straight into two pyramidical tents by the airstrip for the conference with Smith, Barr, and Hodes. The bravado of the commander who, two days earlier, had demanded that Faith not be deterred by "a bunch of Chinese laundrymen" was gone, replaced by a commander who recognized that X Corps was in danger of destruction. Almond had dropped talk of consolidating and holding the position at Hagaru and now wanted Smith to fall back toward Hamhung as quickly as possible. The Corps commander "wants all speed backwards," Smith wrote in his log.

Almond remained full of bluster, though. Flying over the Funchilin Pass on his way up, he had been outraged to see the 2nd Battalion, 31st Regiment, was stopped with infantry still in the truck, and the X Corp commander demanded to know who was responsible for the battalion's movement. "I pointed out to him that by Corps order all movements up to Koto-ri were to be coordinated by the Corps," Smith said. Almond then demanded Barr relieve Reidy, the battalion commander. Barr protested, saying that "he was not aware of the situation which confronted the battalion commander."

Indeed, it was Almond's staff who had botched getting trucks to carry the battalion, as well as his chief of operations who had told Reidy to secure the road, further delaying the battalion's movement. On the spot, Almond telephoned Ruffner, his chief of staff, at Hamhung and ordered him to get word to Reidy to move immediately to Koto-ri.

The discussion turned to the 31st RCT's predicament. Almond, possibly taking his cue from Smith, seemed to think part of the problem was that Faith was not taking aggressive action. "General Almond told General Barr that if the acting commander did not attack he should be relieved," Smith said.

It was an unfounded, almost ludicrous concern. Whatever his faults as a commander, lack of aggression was not one of them. Faith had received no orders from anyone in the forty-eight hours since Almond had told him to attack north. With Maclean's concurrence, Faith had acted to consolidate his battalion with the rest of the task force at the inlet. With no relief force able to reach the inlet, Faith had just told Barr he believed the 31st RCT could fight its way out but needed ammunition for the breakout. As he had done in the past, Barr defended Faith, saying he had great confidence in him. "Barr got hostile and insisted there was no reason for relief," Smith wrote.

Rather than relieving Faith, who was doing an admirable job under the circumstances, Almond should have sent Hodes to replace the missing Maclean. The assistant division commander carried a rank that presumably would have received better support and supply of ammunition and gasoline than Faith was being given. As an experienced regimental commander in World War II, Hodes could have taken command of the breakout effort or at least provided guidance to Faith in the planning. Almond also should have ordered X Corps to send experienced officers to replace the company and platoon leaders lost in the fighting. Almond's inaction on this score amounts to perhaps one of his "worst command failures" with X Corps, in the judgment of historian Roy Appleman.

Neither Smith, Barr, nor Hodes mentioned to Almond that Smith had approved the Army generals' request to withdraw the 31st Regiment Tank Company from Hudong-ni. Given the relevance of the tanks to the survival of the 31st RCT, one can speculate that they feared Almond's reaction. But it was also a startling oversight on Almond's part that he did not ask about the tanks and how they might be used to support the breakout. "The tanks should have been used, of course, in conjunction with Faith's withdrawal," Almond said decades later.

Before reboarding his plane at 3:30 to fly back to X Corps headquarters, Almond ordered Smith and Barr to "submit a plan for the withdrawal" of the 31st RCT from the inlet. He directed Barr to bring the plan back to Hungnam and report to him by 6:00 p.m.

Once Almond departed, Smith decided all that was pointless. Again, he found Barr very accommodating. "We talked it over after Almond left, and I said, 'We can't do anything about going up there for those people until the 5th and 7th Marines fight their way in to us; then maybe we can do something about it,'" Smith said. "And Barr agreed with me. So we didn't have to do anything about that."

It was true Smith had no available Marine force he could send to extricate the 31st RCT. But there were many other things he and Barr could have done, none of which they did.

First and foremost, they could have tried to establish communication with the 31st RCT, which remained an enormous void. Though Smith now had command and control of the 31st RCT, the 1st Marine Division did nothing to establish communication with the subordinate unit.

The VHF radio used by Stamford, the Marine air controller assigned to Faith, could not reach Hagaru. It could, however, send messages to be relayed by pilots overhead, extending the effective range for miles. It was also capable of tuning any high frequency used by the U.S. forces. "Had we been given a frequency by a pilot or had Gen Barr brought one with him, or someone air dropped one, we could have been in business," Stamford later said. "The 1st Mar Div Air Section knew what kind of equipment I had."

Smith and Barr could have made sure the 31st RCT received the ammunition it needed, which Barr had promised to do. Getting 40 mm shells for the M19s would have been a nice start. Nor did the commanders do anything about replacing any of the key company, platoon, and squad leaders who had been lost and whose leadership would be missing in a breakout. They did nothing to improve the task force's terrible lack of medical supplies.

Smith and Barr did nothing to arrange artillery support for the 31st RCT. A battery of 105 mm howitzers from the 11th Marine Regiment at Hagaru was firing missions in support of the isolated Marine Fox Company holding Toktong Pass. No thought was given to having the same guns fire to support Task Force Faith's breakout, even though Hill 1221, the key position held by the Chinese, was in range of the howitzers.

Instead of stripping the Army tanks from Hudong-ni, Smith could have countermanded his order. His headquarters could have directed the Army tanks to attack the roadblock at Hill 1221 at the same time Faith attempted his breakout. Smith had his hands full with trying to get the Marine regiments out of Yudam-ni, but this makes the decision to remove Hodes from the scene all the more inexplicable. Even with the lack of radio communication, Barr, Hodes, or another officer could have been flown back to the inlet with a plan for a coordinated attack.

While Smith promised unlimited air support for the 31st RCT, nothing was done to address a critical shortcoming that severely limited the value of the air support. Faith only had one air controller for the entire task force, compared to at least one controller for each Marine battalion. The Air Force controller attached to the 3rd Battalion who had been killed the first night had not been replaced—neither had his destroyed equipment. If the Marines had no available controllers to fill the gap, the Air Force almost certainly did.

Despite the task force's heavy casualties, no Marine helicopters were made available to the 31st RCT that day. When Stamford radioed a request on

Thursday for the Marine helicopters to evacuate some of the most seriously wounded Army troops, the request was denied. "We learned that other units in similar trouble had priority over us and we could not have their services that day," said Maj. Robbins. All eighteen evacuation flights that day served the 1st Marine Division.

"The helicopter never came back, although we had plenty who could have used the lift service," said Capt. McClymont.

27th Army Headquarters, Thursday Afternoon

In the mountains north of Chosin, the 27th Army prepared to carry out Song Shilun's plan to annihilate the 31st RCT.

The 81st Division was moving southwest from its positions near the Fusen Reservoir to join the battered 80th Division. The two divisions had established a combined headquarters at Sinhung-ni to better coordinate the attacking regiments. The joint headquarters was under the command of Sun Ruifu, the commander and political commissar of the 81st Division and an experienced divisional leader in the Chinese Civil War. Overseeing the operation was Tao Young, the deputy commander of the 9th Army Group, who joined Zhan Da'nan, the assistant commander of the 27th Army, at the combined headquarters.

Zhan would have the fresh 241st Regiment from the 81st Division lead the assault on the inlet. The regiment, which was expected to arrive in the evening from Fusen, would attack from the west and southwest. The division's 242nd Regiment was sent south to set up more roadblocks between the inlet and Hagaru to block the withdrawal south and stop reinforcements from coming to its aid. The 80th Division's 238th Regiment would come down the Pungnyuri trail and attack the inlet, while the 239th Regiment would join the attack from the southwest. "This time the offensive force was much stronger," said Capt. Wang, the company commander with the 58th Division, which was attacking Hagaru.

On paper the two divisions had a strength of more than 20,000 troops. However, given the enormous casualties the 80th Division had suffered in its fight with the 31st RCT, the available attacking force was substantially less, probably about 14,000. But the Army task force was likewise much weaker than when it had started, with hundreds dead or missing and 500 wounded; the number of combat-capable troops available at the time could not have been much more than 2,000. The 31st RCT was outnumbered by about 7 to 1. Pulling the tanks and men out of Hudong-ni would worsen the odds considerably.

X Corps intelligence reported that pressure was slackening that day on the Marines at Yudam-ni and suggested that the Chinese may have disengaged to move south for an attack on Hamhung. The movement of the 81st Division from Fusen was likewise interpreted as a possible second line of attack on Hamhung. But the real target was the 31st RCT, on the east side of the Chosin Reservoir.

Inlet Perimeter, Late Afternoon

Don Faith had been shaken by Barr's visit and the news he had delivered. "Col Faith was not his usual self after this," Lt. Hugh May said. "He would at times seem to lose his concentration, something I had never seen him do before."

May's rank belied his experience and his role as one of the most capable Army officers at Chosin. The 34-year-old Floridian had served as an enlisted man with the 757th Tank Battalion in North Africa and Italy during World War II, earning a battlefield commission in the drive north from Rome. May had served under Faith since the latter took command of the 1st Battalion and considered him one of the finest officers he'd ever known. But May had noticed a change in the normally self-assured commander that began after his meeting with Almond and seemed to grow more evident.

"Faith seemed to have lost confidence in himself at times during the last couple of days," May said. "I know he had lost confidence in the higher command, and I could quote him on that."

May knew Faith as an officer who could study a map intently and "then turn and issue a complete attack order of battle quoting coordinates, hill numbers etc., and never once look back at the map. . . . His coverage was so exact that company commanders and others seldom had any questions."

But now, May said, "Faith surely was not in any condition to do this. . . . He was at times as though in a trance, but only momentarily."

The role of exhaustion cannot be overestimated. Since departing Hamhung at 6:00 a.m. on November 24 to drive to Pukchong, only to be turned around to catch up with his battalion at midnight on the way to the Chosin, Faith had very little opportunity for rest. Like most of his soldiers, Faith had been operating with little or no sleep since the Chinese attack three nights earlier. Back at Hagaru, Smith was careful about getting rest, he assured his wife,

Esther. "Loss of sleep is not an aid to clear thinking," he wrote her. With every night as a fight for survival, Faith had no such luxury. The unrelenting cold compounded the problem, leaving men with slowing cognitive functions—almost punch drunk at times. These conditions make the failure to bring in fresh officers to replace Maclean and other leadership casualties all the more egregious.

Perhaps Faith's most glaring lapse was not improving the task force's communication with higher command. Given the failure by all his levels of higher command to take any steps at establishing communication with him, Faith should have taken the initiative to do it himself. Stamford's radio, which provided an opportunity for contact with the outside world, was used only sparingly (apart from air control) and then apparently just for resupply requests. Faith and Stamford never discussed setting up a system to relay messages via the aircraft overhead.

Communication within the task force was lacking as well. "Very little information was flowing from Faith's CP," May said. "There was very little of the who, what, why, when and where forthcoming."

Curtis was the most critical, feeling he was not taken into confidence by Faith. "He never revealed the details of his conversation with General Barr," Curtis later said. But other officers had been present at the meeting or knew what had been said, including Robbins, McNally, and Miller.

"I never felt any lack of communication," Miller said. "Faith told us everything we needed to know."

Faith likely recognized that the task force's chances of survival were slim, and perhaps that was a message he did not want to give to his command. "I think Faith knew it before most of us," said May.

As evening approached, the GIs braced for the inevitable Chinese attacks. Marine Corsairs overhead "kept the enemy busy so we could prepare for another night of hell," Mortrude said.

"We left our foxholes and drew dead Chinese bodies up close as ramparts," said Sgt. Via of Able Company. "It also prevented live Chinese pretending death and later surprising us."

The Chinese did not even wait for darkness to launch a series of attacks on the southwest corner of the perimeter, where the road and railway entered the boundary between A and C companies. The assaults were stopped, with heavy casualties inflicted on the Chinese. But the ferocity of the attack did not bode well for the night.

Late in the afternoon, Faith huddled with Curtis to plan counterattacks against any penetrations of the perimeter, creating reaction forces with troops from the headquarters units and the 1st Battalion heavy weapons company.

Some rifle companies had suffered 50 percent casualties, not including their walking wounded, and support troops were being pressed into service to fill in gaps in the line. Soldiers with frozen hands and feet were sent back from the aid stations to their units. "We were very short of manpower and we couldn't let those with frostbite take off from their post," said Dr. Lee Yong Kak. The 1st Battalion Aid station was using undershirts, handkerchiefs, towels and torn strips of parachutes for bandages and had run out of fuel and water. "We ate snow," said Lee. "Coffee was available only for wounded."

Every officer in Captain Jordan's Weapons Company had suffered wounds of one kind or another, some multiple. Lt. Gray, with his shattered right hand and arm swollen and his gaping thigh wound infected and oozing blood, hobbled around, trying to make himself useful until Jordan spotted him and ordered him to stay in a company dugout.

Airdrops brought in at least one .50-caliber machine gun and some much-needed .50-caliber ammunition and 4.2-inch mortar shells, but once again, there were no 40 mm shells for the Twin 40s. As darkness fell, some of the final airdrops, with bullets for the rifles and carbines, went awry when snow began to fall and Stamford lost radio contact with the planes. Parachutes carried the ammunition into Chinese lines.

Word had spread that the task force would soon need to break out from the inlet. "We heard that there was to be no relief for us, that we would have to fight our way out to join the Marines in Hagaru-ri," said Capt. McClymont, the D Battery commander.

"Remarkably the troops remained in pretty good spirits, everything considered," said Lt. Magill of B Battery. "What they lacked in unit training and experience, they more than made up for in courage and determination."

Said Major Curtis, "As darkness settled the word was passed: 'Hold out one more night and we've got it made.'" Some believed it; some did not.

Hudong-ni, 4:00 p.m.

By late afternoon, hurried preparations were underway to withdraw the tanks and rest of the rear headquarters elements from Hudong-ni. Troops blew up the stacks of 40 mm ammunition meant for the M19s at the inlet and burned the rations dump. Chinese snipers on the ridge overlooking the perimeter fired some rounds that hit the schoolhouse, heightening the sense of urgency.

At 4:00 p.m., the withdrawal began with some tanks at the point and others serving as the rear guard, while troops on foot were guarding both flanks. Just as the final trucks and tanks of the convoy moved out, a half-dozen GIs appeared in the Hudong-ni perimeter. It was a band of survivors from the destroyed 31st Intelligence and Reconnaissance Platoon, including SFC John Adams, SFC Dick Cooper, and Cpl. Jim Arie. Moving south in a valley east of the reservoir, the group had managed to evade capture for three days. "How we were able to do that is beyond me, as we saw many Chinese, but we did," Arie said. They showed up just in time to hop on the last departing trucks. "Five minutes later would have been too late," he added.

The Chinese wasted no time in taking over the abandoned site. "At the time we pulled south the CCF were coming down the ridge," Rasula said. Chaplain Hoehn had no illusions about what the withdrawal meant. "By our departure the enemy was given free rein to establish themselves along the road from that forward point to the edges of Hagaru," he said.

Two tanks that had been disabled in the fighting with the Chinese were towed by other tanks for about a mile until they came to a steep switchback that could not be navigated. Concerned about holding up the convoy and nervous about the small-arms fire they were taking, Anderson ordered the two tanks destroyed.

Drake was in a hurry to get to Hagaru and position his remaining tanks in the Marine perimeter while there was still light. "I rode back in my jeep and was jubilant to be leaving our shaky positions at Hudong-ni," he said. Drake had a miniature bottle of bourbon in his belongings and decided the moment was right to open it and share with his driver. "We entered the Hagaru perimeter in a gay mood ready to resume the fight!" Drake recalled.

Hodes, who had not yet received the order pulling him out of Hagaru, was awaiting the tanks' arrival with Major Lynch at the eastern edge of the perimeter. He had been worried that with darkness rapidly falling, the Hudong-ni convoy would come under Marine fire, but they entered around 5:00 p.m. without incident.

Drake's tanks were immediately resupplied with ammunition and positioned along the base of East Hill in a tight formation, fifty to one hundred yards apart, covering about one thousand yards of the line and greatly strengthening the Marine perimeter. Most of the able-bodied soldiers from the Hudong-ni contingent were also thrown into the East Hill defenses.

Even though it was now clear that the 31st RCT would have to fight its way out, the only friendly force between the inlet and the Marine base at Hagaru had been withdrawn. With the tanks gone, Task Force Faith had been effectively abandoned.

Hungnam, Early Evening

Ned Almond, seemingly alone among the senior commanders, had not given up on getting help to the 31st RCT. "Almond was at first frustrated and then increasingly enraged by the failure to break through and rescue these men," recalled Al Haig. Back at X Corps headquarters, he sent a flurry of messages to Tokyo proposing different solutions, none of them feasible.

First, he sent a message to MacArthur reporting the 31st RCT was isolated with 400 wounded soldiers, but he added an optimistic spin. They "must wait for a slow helicopter evacuation, then these 2 [battalions] can drive through [enemy] road blocks," Almond reported. Considering not a single wounded soldier had been evacuated from the inlet in the past twenty-four hours, it would be quite slow indeed.

A bit later, Almond seized on word from his staff that portions of the Chosin Reservoir had not frozen over. "Possibility exists of evacuation via seaplane provided boating to plane can be arranged," Almond cabled to Tokyo. "Urgently request all assistance exploring above including manning seaplanes, drop of rubber rafts and sea air rescue boats." Planes went up to scout the thickness of the ice, but the idea went nowhere.

Next Almond learned only three of the Marine helicopters at Chosin were still operational. At least one had been hit by enemy fire and needed to be repaired; another would soon be shot down and the pilot killed. "Urgently request all possible assistance in obtaining more helicopters," he wrote Tokyo. "Minimum 8 requested." But it was impossible to get more helicopters to Chosin in time to help Task Force Faith.

At 9:30 p.m., Almond had Haig send a final message, which was marked priority:

Grapefruit scheduled for my plane did not arrive. Request you dispatch by first courier two cases and bill Quartermaster.
Signed Almond.

Washington, Thursday Afternoon

The plight of MacArthur's forces in North Korea was front-page news across America, with huge headlines reporting that the 8th Army was in full retreat, and that the 1st Marine Division and elements of the Army's 7th Division were surrounded by the Chinese at Chosin Reservoir. Anxious parents flooded Marine Corps and Army headquarters with long-distance phone calls, trying to find out if their sons were alive. Rumors of who was dead or missing circulated among 7th Division spouses in Japan and the United States.

The Joint Chiefs, alarmed at the potential loss of the 1st Marine Division, cabled MacArthur, asking for his plans: "[What is] the positioning of X Corps the units of which appear to us to be exposed?" MacArthur's rather blasé reply on Thursday suggested that Almond had the situation well under control and that the chiefs should not believe what their own eyes saw on the maps. "The Corps commander has been enjoined against any possibility of piecemeal isolation and trapping of his forces," MacArthur wrote. "While geographically his elements seem to be well extended, the actual conditions of terrain make it extremely difficult for an enemy to take any material advantage thereof. Signed MacArthur."

The 1st Marine Division and the 31st RCT were, of course, already isolated and trapped, at least for the moment, and the Chinese seemed to have taken quite good advantage of the terrain. MacArthur clearly understood the danger X Corps faced—he had pulled in the reins on Almond's attack, and he was spending every night anxiously pacing the floor at his home at the embassy residence. But he apparently did not want to give the Joint Chiefs the satisfaction of admitting it. Omar Bradley, the Joint Chiefs of Staff chairman, was predictably infuriated by MacArthur's response, later calling it "utterly absurd and insulting," and the exchange further strained tensions with the Pentagon.

Responding to questions at a press conference on Thursday in Washington, President Truman implied that using an atomic bomb to stop the Chinese in Korea was under active consideration and that MacArthur could use the weapon if he chose. Within minutes, wire service bulletins went out reporting that Truman was considering nuclear war, creating an uproar in capitals around the globe, from London to Paris and New Delhi to Riyadh. The White House issued a clarification later that day saying that only the president could authorize the use of the bomb, and no such authorization had been given. But the country—and the world—remained on edge.

La Feria, Texas, Thursday Evening

Helen Storms's unborn child was kicking so much that she couldn't hold the typewriter on her lap as she preferred, so she hunched over the coffee table to type her letter to Harvey. "Precious Angel," she began. "Again, I have lived in darkness. The news says the enemy have you trapped."

It was Thanksgiving Day in La Feria, even though most of the nation had celebrated the holiday a week earlier. Parts of the country had never gone along with a congressional resolution signed by President Franklin Roosevelt in 1941 that established Thanksgiving as the fourth Thursday in November, instead preferring the traditional last Thursday in November, which, in 1950, was November 30.

Schools in the area had closed today rather than a week earlier, and family friends had invited Helen and the boys to spend the day with them. "I was saved many hours of agony by getting this invitation," she wrote Harvey. "I know that if I had spent this day alone I would have cried and prayed my eyes out."

Helen had little news to pass along. "It seems so trivial," she wrote. "I just can't talk about anything while you are in such peril. Please forgive me." She would be going to bed soon. A tube had burned out on her bedside radio, so she was going to lug the living room radio upstairs to listen to the news when she woke up at night, as she did every night.

"I am praying that you will come through, and I do have so much faith in your prayers," Helen wrote in closing. "How terrible it would be to have to live without you. . . . What a wonderful husband and father you have grown into. . . . Our lives from now on will be so sealed together that no power on earth can take that unity from me."

Chapter 12

THE FOURTH NIGHT

Thursday–Friday, November 30–December 1

Once darkness arrived, the temperature fell precipitously, on its way to nearly thirty below zero. The GIs could hear the usual bugle calls and whistles in the hills, and signal flares lit the night. It was the start of sixteen hours of darkness. In his B Company foxhole shared with another soldier, Private Harry Jacobs figured it was his last night on earth. He was only 19.

"It was so cold in that foxhole, . . . we had our legs together, trying to keep one another warm, and I start crying because my ribs started to hurt," Jacobs said. "And he said, 'Go ahead, cry if it'll make you feel better, but you know what Harry? Tonight it's going to snow.' I said, 'Gee, if it snows it'll get colder.' He says, 'No, if it snows the temperature is going to go up."

A heavy snow soon began to fall, and it did seem to get a bit warmer, and Jacobs felt a bit better.

Along the C Company line, Jim Mortrude's platoon sergeant, SFC Charlie Campbell, and his Korean counterpart, Chung Yung Te, worked to heat some C-ration coffee on a small squad burner that Chung always carried. The stove did not work very well because of the altitude and the cold, and the coffee was only lukewarm when distributed to the soldiers. "The troops appreciated it more, I think, for the effort than for sustenance," Mortrude said. It was typical of the two sergeants, both outstanding soldiers, to make such efforts.

Mortrude made his usual rounds along the platoon line, making sure that everyone was alert and no one was freezing to death. His helmet was covered with a white pillowcase, purloined from the ship that had carried them to Iwon. He figured it offered some camouflage in the snow, while the salvaged

Chinese greatcoat he wore hanging below his parka provided a bit of extra warmth. "I was confronted by an hysterical truck driver who was frenzied by [my] bizarre appearance," Mortrude recalled. "After he refused to be reassured by my voice, I was rescued by one of our automatic riflemen who threatened to 'cut him in half' if he didn't 'leave the lieutenant alone.'"

Don Faith made the rounds as well, putting on a good face for the men. The doubts and exhaustion that Lt. May could see at the CP were gone when Faith stopped to check on the wounded at the 1st Battalion aid station, where the sight of the task force commander bolstered spirits. "Col. Faith looked more confident than ever before . . . and so were we," said Lee Yong Kak.

Sinhung-ni, Combined 80th and 81st Division Headquarters, Thursday Evening

Soon after dark, Zhan Da'nan, assembled with the senior commanders of the 80th and 81st Divisions, gave orders for what he expected would be the final attack on the Army task force. With the arrival of the 81st Division, he had four regiments ready to assault from four directions.

Given his huge numerical advantage—his forces now outnumbered the American task force by about 9 to 1—Zhan was confident his troops could annihilate the Army RCT. "The enemy was compressed into a small, narrow area," said a Chinese Army history. "There was no hope of rescue."

Inlet, Thursday Night

The attack began with a fifteen-minute barrage of light artillery and mortar shells. The muffled booms of the guns, followed by the whistling of projectiles, sent Hugh Robbins and other officers rushing for cover in foxholes near the regimental CP. Shells began bursting around the perimeter. "Incoming steel splinters went swishing and singing through the air all about our emplacements," Robbins said. Calls for medics rang out from several directions.

The heavy fire lifted. Then Chinese assault teams that had crawled closer during the barrage opened fire with burp guns and rifles. "The air over my head was alive with the buzz and crack of the incoming bullets," said Robbins. "We could hear the yells of our own troops mingled with those of the Chinese as the outer defenses clashed."

The initial assaults were turned back by steady defenses along the rifle company lines. The troops were fighting better now than on the first night; by the fourth night, none of them were green. "We survived because of what we had learned the first night; hold our ground and keep shooting," said Capt. Bryant, the 3rd Battalion headquarters company commander. "I think everyone knew after that first night there was no place to go."

Even as the attacks grew in intensity as midnight approached, with mounting American casualties, the Chinese were at first unable to break through anywhere on the perimeter. Despite Zhan's unified command post, coordination and control of the attacking regiments did not seem much better than on previous nights.

It may have helped that Erwin Bigger, Faith's ever-resourceful heavy weapons Company commander, came up with the idea of firing a different colored flare every time the enemy fired a flare and blowing a whistle whenever the enemy blew a whistle. "In any event, the enemy attack, though determined, did not appear to be too well coordinated or concentrated," said Wes Curtis.

But after midnight, the attacks reached an unprecedented ferocity. "The enemy appeared determined to over-run the perimeter at all costs," Curtis said. The Chinese launched a headlong assault toward the roadblock on the perimeter's southwest corner manned by A Company, but they were repulsed with heavy casualties.

With desperate hand-to-hand fighting at points along the eastern perimeter defended by the 3rd Battalion, Faith launched his reserve several times to restore temporary breakthroughs. "Occasionally a Chinese soldier would infiltrate inside the perimeter and run about like a madman spraying with his burp-gun until he was killed," said Curtis.

Baker Battery, supporting B Company along the southern perimeter, lowered its howitzers as far as they would go and fired directly into the Chinese attackers. Lt. Keith Sickafoose, who had a field telephone line to the infantry units, directed fire to stop the penetrations, but more calls kept coming. "Oh, shit!" Sickafoose called. "They've broken through again." The battery continued firing, keeping the Chinese assaults at bay, but the supply of high explosive shells was running perilously low.

PFC Grant McMillin of the 57th FA Headquarters was assigned to a 7-man reaction squad. "If the Chinese broke through any place in the perimeter, we were to plug the hole and push them out and hold until we got help," he said. McMillin was running with his squad to a penetration on the high ground along the southern perimeter when he felt a blow to his foot and tumbled into the snow. A bullet had struck near his right ankle.

McMillin managed to crawl and limp his way back to the battalion aid station, which was overflowing with wounded. "If you're going to get help, you'll have to help yourself because I've got everybody out working on wounded," the aid station first sergeant told him. McMillin took his boot off and found the bullet had entered through the arch of his foot and gone out near his ankle, leaving an exit wound the size of a silver dollar. It was so cold that the blood had frozen and the wound was no longer bleeding. McMillin opened his medical pouch, poured some sulfa powder on the wound, and bandaged it. He could not get his boot back on, so he took an extra pair of socks that he carried under his shirt and put them on his wounded foot. He found he could move around pretty well with three socks. McMillin went off to rejoin his unit. "I didn't consider myself wounded," he said.

Around 3:00 a.m., the Chinese broke through the northeast corner of the perimeter where the 1st and 3rd battalions' lines met near the inlet bridge, taking control of a knob of high ground and proving difficult to dislodge.

The intensity of the attacks was only building as the night wore on. "Between 0400 and 0600 every man in the perimeter was in a defensive position operating a weapon," said Curtis. "The question was whether the perimeter could hold out until dawn."

The enemy mortar fire was not only more plentiful but also more accurate than on previous nights. All three battalion aid stations took hits. At the 1st Battalion aid station, a shell landed near Capt. Navarre, the battalion surgeon. "The force lifted me a few inches, tipped me over, chewed the outside of my right pants leg in a moth-eaten pattern, and wafted the helmet from my head," he recalled. But he continued treating wounded. Two shells hit near the 3rd Battalion aid station, injuring several medics and freshly wounding some of the casualties. A shell slammed into the corner of the hut housing the 57th Field Artillery aid station, killing a medic.

Capt. Cody's 31st Heavy Mortar Company had exhausted virtually all of its 4.2-inch mortar shells, so most of its men were fighting as riflemen. Their position was hit by a heavy barrage of mortar fire, killing 6 of the 8 men in a squad. Lt. Jerry McCabe was directing fire when a Chinese mortar exploded near him, wounding him in the arm and leg and leaving him unconscious in the snow, unnoticed in the dark.

The mortar company troops included Joey and Johnny Snock, 21-year-old twins from Apollo, Pennsylvania, who had joined the Army together and remained inseparable. Any time Johnny got in trouble, it was Joey who would get him out of it. This time, Joey was seriously injured, so Johnny went to get a medic. But when Johnny got back, his brother was gone—dragged off as a prisoner by the Chinese.

Pitched battles continued all around the perimeter. The 3rd Battalion rifle companies faced strong assaults along the east and southeast perimeters at the same time that the 1st Battalion was coming under an extremely heavy attack from the southwest, along the road into the perimeter.

Lt. May assembled a team of cooks and drivers armed with several machine guns to help bolster the defenses at the road on the boundary of Able and Charlie Companies. The Chinese were taking enormous casualties, and the GIs and ROKs, much fewer, yet "these suicide attacks" kept coming, May said.

SFC John "Mac" McGuire of C Company had survived several Japanese night "Banzai" attacks while serving with the 108th Infantry Regiment in the Pacific during World War II, but this was of a different order. "None of those attacks compared in scope to the ordeal encountered at Chosin Reservoir," he said. "The below zero weather, incessant attacks and sheer ferocity of onslaught combined for a far more deadly effect. It seemed at times as if they had more bodies than we had ammo."

For a while it looked like the Chinese assault would break through, and officers prepared for a last-ditch stand against a massive penetration. "We were in danger of being overrun," said Capt. Stamford. But the soldiers of A and C companies held firm.

Once again, the Quad 50s and the Twin 40s from D Battery, 15th AAA, were the targets of multiple assaults as the Chinese desperately tried to knock the deadly weapons out of the battle. Along the southwest perimeter, two M19 Twin 40s and two Quad 50s inflicted terrible casualties on the Chinese attackers. "They paid," said Charlie Gebhardt. "You'd see mounds around them. They tried very hard to get them."

Though the Chinese were unable to destroy the AAA guns, the attacks succeeded in consuming much of the remaining ammunition for the weapons. Even as the intensity of the attacks picked up, McClymont was forced to ration ammunition, ordering his gunners to fire only two of the four machine guns on the Quad 50s and only one barrel of the Twin 40mm guns. It was "a draconian decision" given the ferocity of the attacks, said PFC Hodaviah Hensley, one of the M16 crew members. But McClymont had little choice.

Inlet, Predawn Friday

As dawn approached, Jim Mortrude was standing by his command post behind the C Company line with his platoon sergeants, Campbell and Chung, and Cpl. Alfonso Camoesas, the platoon medic, when they were all blown off their feet by a mortar shell.

Campbell and Chung were both wounded. Mortrude and Camoesas, who were unhurt, brought the two platoon sergeants into a more sheltered portion of the CP. Chung was only slightly wounded, with shrapnel in the legs and back. Camoesas checked out Campbell and didn't find any serious wounds. "No, I'm all torn up," Campbell said. "I think I'm a goner." He asked Mortrude to get his wallet out so he could take a last look at his family pictures. Mortrude assured Campbell he would be fine, gave him the photos, and then was called to the CP telephone. A few minutes later, Camoesas came over to Mortrude and told him Campbell had just died. "I was completely shocked, because I didn't think we'd lose him," Mortrude said. He wished he had stayed with Campbell.

The Chinese still held the knob that they had captured during the night near the inlet bridge. Faith ordered a counterattack, and the call went to Bigger's D Company to send a reaction force. First Lt. Robert Wilson, the company reconnaissance officer, took the assignment and assembled about two dozen soldiers. "Come on, all you fighting men!" he called. "We've got a counterattack to make." They were short on ammunition and had a total of only three grenades, but they took off. Wilson led the way, carrying a captured Tommy gun.

They reached the base of the Chinese-held knob and were heading up when Wilson was knocked down by a bullet in the arm. He resumed the attack but was hit a second time. "That one bit," Wilson said, before getting up again and moving forward. A bullet to his forehead put him down for good. SFC

Fred Sugua took over, but he was killed several minutes later as well. The men continued the fight up the knob. Though they were unable to dislodge the Chinese, they had contained the enemy penetration.

At the combined command post, Tao Yang, the assistant commander of the 9th Army Group, ordered his forces not to withdraw at daylight, as had happened the previous three nights, but to remain in place and continue the attack until the Army task force was annihilated.

Tao's orders notwithstanding, most of the ground assaults subsided when it became light, likely due to sheer exhaustion and the enormous casualties the Chinese had suffered during the long night. After close combat all night, only one man in the 3rd Company, 240th Regiment, was still alive in the morning. Even units not fighting had suffered terribly. Every soldier in the 5th Company, 240th Regiment, manning a roadblock all night in case the Americans attempted to breakout, was reported to have frozen to death, save a liaison officer and a straggler.

But plenty of Chinese remained in low ground around the inlet, three hundred to four hundred yards away, firing machine guns and mortars into the perimeter and laying down grazing fire that hit GIs when they moved from their foxholes.

At daylight a group of Chinese infantrymen infiltrated the Baker Battery gun position, lobbing hand grenades until they were shot down by the artillerymen. Then a lone figure came running at Lt. Magill as he stood by a 105. "Some of the cannoneers were yelling at me to shoot him, but he was wearing a GI field jacket and I thought he was American," said Magill. "He jumped on me, wrapped his legs around my waist and started hitting me on the helmet with a 'potato masher' hand grenade. Fortunately the grenade didn't go off and I killed him with a carbine bayonet that was tucked into my boot. The cannoneers thought it was pretty funny."

The mortar fire remained unrelenting. On the A Company line, Sgt. Via was in a foxhole with Cpl. Sammie Hubbell, a light weapons infantryman from Okmulgee County, within the Muscogee Nation Reservation in Oklahoma. Hubbell was telling Via about a letter he had written to his family for Christmas. "We both heard the whistle of incoming mail, both crouched in the hole, back to back," said Via. When the shell hit, the sergeant heard a pop, like a burst paper bag.

"I'm not going to make it," he heard Hubbell say.

"I looked at Hubbell, his eyes rolled in his head," Via said. "He died. He had taken shrapnel in the heart. His last thoughts were of his family and Christmas."

The 1st Battalion aid station's squad tent in the railroad cut was filled with about 50 casualties, and another 35 wounded were outside. Many of the aid men who had been bravely bringing casualties in from the perimeter had themselves been killed or wounded. Lee was working on patients inside when he heard a loud metallic sound nearby. "All of us hit the ground," he said. "An enemy shell had exploded right outside of the station. We hurried to find those casualties sitting there. Many of them died instantly." The doctors and medics treated the fresh wounds as best as possible, but there were virtually no supplies left.

In the gray morning light, Lee walked over to several nearby foxholes that had held through the long night of fighting. Each was occupied by a GI and an ROK: a GI machine gunner with an ROK ammunition man in one, a GI mortarman and an ROK assistant in another.

Said Lee, "Now they were so closely attached together they almost looked like brothers."

Don Carlos Faith, the 1st Battalion commander. "He was open, frank, friendly, candid, forceful—and had a high degree of charisma and leadership," Wes Curtis said. "His potential value to the Army was unlimited." SOURCE: DPAA

Allan Maclean, the 31st Regiment commander. "Just be careful when he decides to move, because if you were in the way, you got pushed out of the way," another officer said. SOURCE: DPAA

Harvey Storms would take command of the 3rd Battalion. "We Americans are still prone to underestimate the other side and I am trying not to do that, but it is hard," he wrote to his wife, Helen. SOURCE: DPAA

The 3rd Battalion commander, Lt. Col. Bill Reilly, center, with Maj. Berry Anderson, left, and Maj. Lester Olson, right, at the Mount Fuji staging area in Japan, where the 7th Division rushed to prepare for war. SOURCE: RASULA, GRP

Maclean and Faith in Japan. "There was a warm and affectionate relationship between Maclean and Faith," Bob Jones observed. "They knew each other's minds and thought much alike." SOURCE: USAHEC

Maj. Wes Curtis, right, with Capt. Bob Haynes at Fuji. Despite his admiration for Faith, Curtis worried about his lack of combat command experience. SOURCE: USAHEC

Marine Maj. Gen. O. P. Smith, Army Maj. Gen. Ned Almond, and Navy Rear Adm. James Doyle aboard the USS *Mount McKinley*. "Smith and Almond were just like two dogs at each other's throats." SOURCE: OPSC

Gen. Douglas MacArthur, center, and Almond, right, watch the shelling of Inchon. MacArthur was "senior to everyone but God." Almond had an "almost mystical belief" in his genius. SOURCE: NARA

Brig. Gen. Henry Hodes. Hammering Hank, as the assistant 7th Division commander was known, "did the generaling" in the division. SOURCE: NARA

Bob Jones was one of the most universally respected officers in the 1st Battalion—"a top-notch combat trooper." SOURCE: KWE

John Edward Gray, one of many young officers who were rushed to Japan to help fill out the 7th Division. SOURCE: COURTESY OF THE GRAY FAMILY

Monty Piercefield was sent from the United States and assigned as an operations sergeant in Faith's battalion. SOURCE: KWE

Lt. Jim Mortrude, a seasoned 28-year-old combat veteran, turned his green C Company platoon into one of the best in Faith's battalion. SOURCE: USAHEC

Ray Radke reenlisted in the Army to get as far from the United States as possible. He got his wish and was assigned to the 31st Regiment Polar Bears on the northern Japanese island of Hokkaido. SOURCE: COURTESY OF RAY RADKE

The 7th Division had not been integrated with Black soldiers, but Joe Ager and the other truck drivers from the 515th Truck Transportation Company effectively integrated the defenses at Chosin. SOURCE: COURTESY OF THE AGER FAMILY

Lt. Anthony Mazzulla was a platoon leader with B Company, 32nd Regiment. SOURCE: DPAA

Troops from the 31st Regiment Polar Bears land at Iwon on November 4, 1950. "Good luck, 31st!" called the captain of a troop transport. "God be with you." SOURCE: GRP

Almond, left, speaks to Maclean, right, as Maj. Gen. Dave Barr looks on at the 31st Regiment headquarters in Untaek on November 12. The X Corps commander was eager to resume the attack to the Yalu. SOURCE: NARA

An aerial view looking north across the frozen Pungnyuri inlet on the east shore of Chosin Reservoir, where Almond rushed an ad hoc task force under Maclean's command with little planning or preparation. SOURCE: USAHEC

Medics carry off a wounded soldier from the outpost manned by SFC Bill Donovan's L Company weapons platoon in front of the inlet perimeter on the morning of November 28. SOURCE: DONOVAN, GRP

A Chinese soldier wounded by a grenade thrown by Donovan. Questioned by the South Korean soldier squatting next to him, the prisoner talked freely about Chinese troop strength. SOURCE: DONOVAN, GRP

A Battery and its 105 mm howitzers were recaptured on the morning of November 28, after being overrun during the night by the Chinese. The ground inside the inlet perimeter is strewn with the bodies of dead Chinese, GIs, and ROKs. SOURCE: USAHEC

The inlet perimeter "was a scene lifted from the pages of Dante's Inferno," Doc Blohm said. Officers and sergeants moved about in the numbing cold, "trying to create order out of chaos." SOURCE: USAHEC

Five soldiers in a dug-in position overlooking the frozen inlet to the southwest, with task force trucks visible in the background. SOURCE: GRP

A soldier moves through debris after the first night's battle in the inlet perimeter. Smoke hangs in the air, likely from the firing of the howitzer in the background. The view is looking to the southeast. SOURCE: USAHEC

An airdrop lands in a small gully in the inlet perimeter as soldiers from K Company prepare to move out and retrieve the supplies. Many airdrops landed in Chinese-held ground. SOURCE: DONOVAN, GRP

Several Marine helicopters landed near the inlet shore on on November 29 to pick up wounded, including battalion commanders Reilly and Embree. SOURCE: DONOVAN, GRP

A downhill view shows the inlet, causeway, and bridge, with dead in the foreground and soldiers and vehicles in the background. SOURCE: GRP

An M19 crew fires at groups of Chinese across the Pungnyuri inlet on the mountainside. The Twin 40s, which took a heavy toll on the Chinese, were the targets of repeated attacks. SOURCE: DONOVAN, GRP

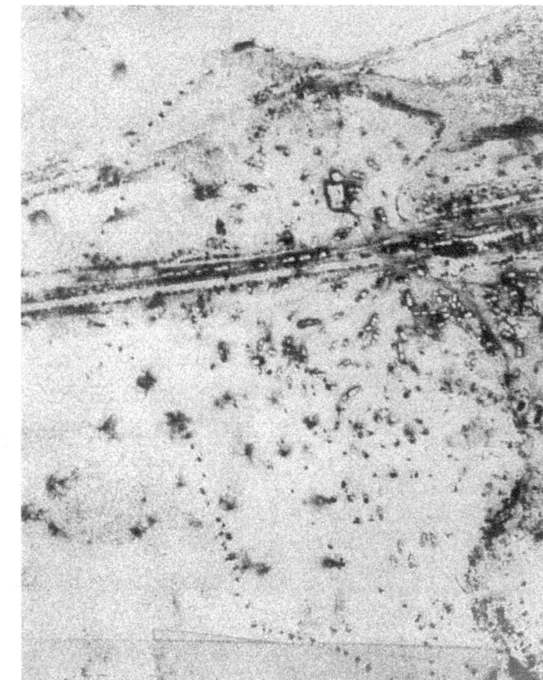

Aerial view of the inlet perimeter, taken from a U.S. reconnaissance aircraft before the breakout. Trucks are lined up on the road. The trace of foxholes marking the perimeter's southwest sector is visible. SOURCE: GRP

Caught in a heavy cross fire early in the breakout, 1st Battalion soldiers take cover along the reservoir bank, while others run up to form a skirmish line and return fire. Hill 1250 lies ahead, and beyond that, Hill 1221. SOURCE: DONOVAN, USAHEC

Soldiers from M Company, part of the rear guard, move along the railroad bed under heavy fire from the hill to the rear. A dead soldier lies in the foreground. Trucks are on the road below the bank on the left and are not visible. SOURCE: DONOVAN, USAHEC

Task Force survivors move south on the reservoir ice toward Hagaru late in the afternoon on December 1. SOURCE: USAHEC

Capt. George Rasula, left, and Lt. Hodges Escue, right, standing near the southern end of the reservoir, helped process 31st RCT survivors as they arrived at Hagaru. SOURCE: GRP

Barr, left, with Capt. Bob Drake. At Hodes's request and likely with Barr's concurrence, O. P. Smith ordered Drake's tanks to withdraw from Hudong-ni before the breakout. SOURCE: USAHEC

Soldiers from the provisional 31st moving south from Hagaru on December 6. SOURCE: U.S. DEPARTMENT OF DEFENSE

Troops from the provisional 31st arrive in the Koto-ri perimeter on December 7, after fighting from Hagaru. "Some seemed to be in shock even though they continued to walk," a soldier said. SOURCE: GRP

The bodies of U.S. Marines, Army soldiers, Royal Marines, and ROKs were buried on December 8 in a mass grave at Koto-ri "in a kind of final fraternity," Maggie Higgins wrote. SOURCE: OPSC

Bobbie Faith, left, and her mother, Barbara, at the dedication for a school named after her father at Fort Benning, Georgia, in 1952. SOURCE: COURTESY OF BOBBIE BROYLES

The old soldiers of the 31st RCT stood at attention when the Presidential Unit Citation was awarded to the unit in 2000, nearly fifty years after the battle. SOURCE: GRP

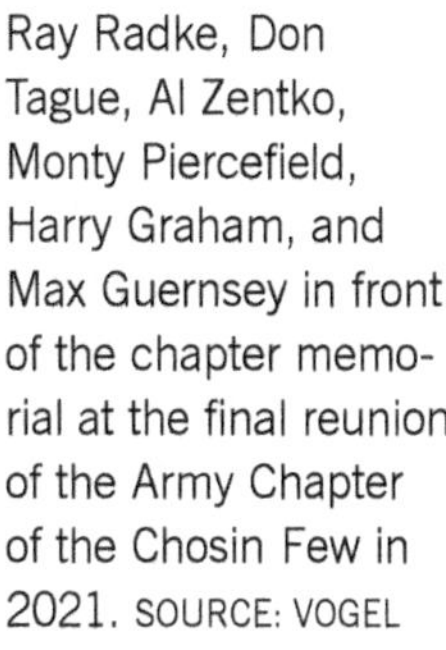

Ray Radke, Don Tague, Al Zentko, Monty Piercefield, Harry Graham, and Max Guernsey in front of the chapter memorial at the final reunion of the Army Chapter of the Chosin Few in 2021. SOURCE: VOGEL

The funeral of Don Faith at Arlington National Cemetery in April 2013. "Now the soldier is coming home," John Gray said. SOURCE: U.S. ARMY

As North Korean Army officers watch, Jennie Jin, right, works with another DPAA official to secure one of fifty-five boxes of remains turned over by the North Korean regime in Wonsan in July 2018. SOURCE: U.S. ARMY

Sam Storms, center, and his brothers Ernie, left, and Robert, right, visit their father's grave at Arlington National Cemetery in July 2022. SOURCE: VOGEL

Part III

The Breakout

Chapter 13

BREAKOUT MORNING

Friday, December 1

By dawn the soldiers of Task Force Faith had been in a brutal fight for survival for eighty hours in subzero weather. "It was said we were in hell when it froze over and we believed that to be a true description," said PFC Roy Oxenrider. "None of us thought we would leave this place alive but we never stopped fighting."

Almost everyone had been wounded in one way or another, if not by a bullet or shrapnel, then with frozen feet or hands. Their dirty and unshaven faces were pocked with ugly patches of frostbitten skin. Many were gaunt from hunger after days with scant rations. "Among our still-fighting survivors, many appeared to be walking dead," recalled Lt. John Gray.

Most had had little or no sleep for days, apart from catnaps. Some of the men "were like zombies," joking about being killed, said Cpl. Jerry Francois. Death was so ubiquitous they had become almost numb to it.

Wounded men who had frozen during the night now lay in the gray light in grotesque stiffness. They were carried to the growing collection points for the dead. Dozens of Chinese killed during the night also lay scattered through the inlet.

It was clear the task force could not survive another night like the last one. Don Faith had still not received orders to withdraw, but he saw little choice but to attempt a breakout. With scores more men wounded during the night, the number of casualties needing evacuation had reached 600. Their fate weighed heavily on the task force commander. "Lt Col Faith's greatest desire was to get the wounded out to a place where they could be taken care of," said Bob Jones.

Surrounded by a much larger force and almost out of ammunition, Faith knew the 31st RCT would need strong air support to have any chance of succeeding. He instructed Capt. Stamford, the Marine forward air controller, to try contacting any planes overhead. "At daylight Col Faith made preparations to fight south to Hagaru-ri and had me send a message requesting aircraft and to notify [General Barr] of his contemplated action," Stamford wrote in a subsequent report.

The weather was like a gray curtain coming down on their hopes. The Chosin Reservoir and surrounding mountains were socked in with low clouds, and snow flurries flew through the air. Unless the weather cleared, there was no chance of getting any air support or aerial resupply.

Stamford tried for a while to contact fighters overhead and finally succeeded, relaying Faith's request. Around 9:00 a.m., despite continued awful weather, a single low-flying Marine fighter bomber flying off the USS *Leyte* managed to break through the clouds and appeared over the inlet. He reported good news to Stamford—the weather report received on the carrier that morning was for the clouds to break up around noon and the day to turn mostly sunny. "The pilot stated that he would guide more tactical aircraft into the area shortly after noon if the weather improved any as was forecast," Curtis said.

Faith huddled with Miller and Curtis and made his final decision. The task force would "try to break out of the perimeter and reach Hagaru-ri in a single dash rather than risk another night in the perimeter," Curtis said.

The planning was rushed. "We knew we had to take advantage of daylight and a break in the weather," said Curtis. During the all-night battle for survival, Faith and his staff had little chance to plan the breakout despite the likelihood that one would have to be attempted. This again pointed to the void left by the failure of Almond and Barr to replace Maclean and other key lost officers.

Undoubtedly, they would face fierce Chinese resistance along the way to Hagaru. If the task force launched the breakout at noon, that would leave them little more than four hours of light to reach the Marine perimeter. The pilot had reported that "there were no friendly forces on the road between the perimeter and Hagaru-ri," said Curtis. While it is not known whether Barr had told Faith the tanks were being pulled out of Hudong-ni, the pilot's report would have been a clear indication the American armor was no longer there.

Despite the by-now-well-known Chinese capabilities for night fighting, Faith and his staff did not plan for any intermediate objective where the task force could reform and hunker down for the night if reaching Hagaru proved impossible. There were not many locations along the winding, mountainous route that would serve to set up a defensive perimeter. Hill 1221 would have been one possibility, though the Chinese now held the strategic position in strength. There was one site that would have been ideal: Hudong-ni—if the tanks had still been there. Faith would have had a ready-made perimeter waiting, and the tanks could have launched a coordinated assault to help the task force break through Hill 1221.

Perhaps Faith, knowing the tanks were gone, decided that he had no choice but an all-or-nothing fight to reach Hagaru.

At 10:00 a.m., Faith called a meeting at his CP to issue orders to his unit commanders, including Maj. Miller, Maj. Storms, and Lt. Col. Tolly, now commanding the 1st Battalion, 3rd Battalion, and 57th Field Artillery, respectively. Key officers including Jones, Curtis, and May were also present. "Colonel Faith stated he was taking it on himself to order a withdrawal and that all communications with higher headquarters were out," said Miller. "Further, no assistance by the Marines was possible."

Said Jones, "Faith made it very clear that he had no orders from anyone, and that his decision to break out of the perimeter to the south to regain the Marine lines was solely his own."

The commanders reviewed the ammunition situation, which was abysmal. Small-arms ammunition was dangerously low across every unit. All ammunition was to be picked up from the dead and wounded and given to those able to fight.

Tolly reported the artillery battalion only had a few rounds of 105 mm ammunition left. Capt. Cody, commander of the 31st Heavy Mortar Company, said the 4.2-inch mortars were nearly depleted. Only two of the M19 Twin 40s were still operating, and in any event, Capt. McClymont reported, virtually all the 40 mm ammunition was spent. The howitzers and heavy mortars were useless without ammunition, and towing them out would slow the convoy. Faith instructed the artillery and mortar commanders to fire their last shells just prior to the breakout and then destroy the weapons.

The priority was getting the casualties out, Faith said. "He emphasized that no wounded men would be abandoned," Curtis said.

The two-and-a-half-ton trucks would be used to carry the wounded out. Each one was to be unloaded and all the supplies and equipment they were carrying, destroyed, to make room for the casualties. Many of the trucks could not be started in the cold or were so riddled with bullet holes in the tires and radiators that they could no longer run. Any truck that could not operate was to be destroyed.

In order to keep the convoy as compact as possible, Faith directed that the smaller, quarter-ton trucks and their trailers also be destroyed, as well as all jeeps, except those carrying radios or mounted with machine guns.

The tactical formation was designed to protect the truck column carrying the wounded. Faith chose the 1st Battalion to lead the way out, with Capt. Seever's Charlie Company making the initial breakout. They would attack the enemy positions outside the southwest of the perimeter and clear the road for the convoy to follow. "The plan was to march down each side of the truck column as fast as possible and fight any resistance hit," said Jones.

The artillerymen of the 57th Field Artillery and the mortarmen of the 31st Heavy Mortar Company would serve as riflemen in the middle of the column, guarding the flanks of the convoy. The 3rd Battalion would serve as the rear guard.

The initial attack would be accompanied by airstrikes from Corsairs, coordinated by Stamford, and there was to be continuous air support as the column fought its way down the road. Faith instructed the Marine captain to request at least ten aircraft overhead at all times to cover the withdrawal.

At Miller's request, Faith assigned one of the remaining M19 Twin 40s to lead the column; even without ammunition, the fully tracked, tank-like vehicle could help knock down physical roadblocks.

When the meeting ended, the unit commanders dispersed to hurriedly prepare for the breakout while Faith delivered instructions to the regimental staff. "Col Faith came by our hole and in a few quick sentences told me that the time had come to get out of there," Robbins said. "He told me that we must get the word out to get the trucks warmed up and the wounded loaded onto those trucks."

Robbins and other regimental officers began rounding up the drivers and getting troops organized for the breakout. As Robbins walked toward the 57th

CP, a mortar explosion knocked him sideways to the ground. He was hit in the arm, and his leg was gashed. Capt. McNally, overseeing the destruction of his jeep, took shrapnel in his left leg and hip. The shell had taken two regimental officers out of the fight. Neither one could walk, and both soon found themselves being loaded onto trucks with other wounded.

At about the same time, Capt. Bigger was standing near the 1st Battalion CP with Lt. May, Lt. Jim Campbell, and several other officers when a mortar round slammed into the center of the circle. "I recall feeling as though I had been hit with a log and falling like a sack of rocks," said Campbell, a machine gun platoon leader with Bigger's company. He was badly wounded, with shrapnel in his leg. Bigger was seriously injured as well, with fragments hitting his leg, back, and arm and knocking his right eye out of its socket.

May, who was unhurt, helped drag the injured to safety. At the battalion aid station, Capt. Navarre, the surgeon, managed to get Bigger's eye back in its socket and put a patch over it. Jones, unhurt by the blast, had some whiskey on hand and gave Bigger a shot. "I can almost remember its warmth and stimulation to this day—and I am not a particularly drinking man," Bigger recalled decades later. "But I will always love Bob for that drink!"

At the 1st Battalion CP, Miller issued orders to his company commanders. Charlie Company, with Lt. Mortrude's platoon at the point, would lead the way and destroy or contain any resistance while the convoy passed through. Charlie Company would then fall back, and Baker Company would take the lead, then D Company. If the resistance was too strong for one company to overcome, the next company in line would be committed. Able Company, under Lt. Smith, would guard the left flank of the convoy.

Storms called together his company commanders and staff at the 3rd Battalion CP. "He said we were going to withdraw to Hagaru and soon as the weather permitted," said Capt. Bryant, the headquarters company commander. Storms instructed his officers to unload all the battalion's two-and-a-half-ton trucks and load them with wounded. Most of the other vehicles were to be destroyed. Storms directed Bryant to follow the convoy and assist the rear guard. Bryant asked what to do with two Chinese prisoners locked in a stall. Storms said to unlock the lock but leave it in the hasp.

At the 57th Field Artillery, the orders to destroy the howitzers hit the cannoneers hard. "I never thought I would see the day when I would have to destroy guns," said SFC Carroll Price, chief of an A Battery detail. All sights were smashed. Major Curtis came upon a battery section sergeant who was firing his last rounds at a large group of Chinese on the mountainside to the northeast, making them scatter. Curtis asked him if he knew how to destroy the block of his howitzer when it was time to pull out. "I'm not leaving this piece," the sergeant answered emphatically. "If they (the Chinese) get it, they're going to have to take me with it."

Said Curtis, "For all I know he may have stayed with his piece."

With Chinese troops crawling closer to the perimeter, the 3rd Platoon, 32nd Heavy Mortar Company, fired its last half-dozen 4.2-inch mortar shells at maximum elevation so they landed about two hundred feet in front of their position. Then they threw termite grenades into the tubes. "After that we fought as riflemen," said PFC Charles Bennett.

Faith, waving a .45 in his right hand, strode up to Magill, the acting Baker Battery commander. Faith looked "off the wall" with stress, the lieutenant recalled. "Everyone was at the end of their rope," he said. Faith appointed Magill a provisional infantry company commander and hurriedly directed him to organize any available artillery troops to help guard the forward left side of the column.

Everyone in Cpl. Anthony Mora's Baker Battery machine gun squad was dead or wounded, so Lt. Eichorn, the battery security platoon commander, brought Mora 13 bakers, cooks, and supply troops from the headquarters company. "Morrie, this is your squad now," the lieutenant said. They were assigned to clear ground on the right side of the column. Eichorn addressed the men before leaving them with Mora: "If anybody can get you out of here alive, Morrie can get you out."

The troop preparations for withdrawal left the perimeter less defended and more vulnerable. Concerned that a Chinese attack might break through before the planes arrived, Faith went to the 1st Battalion aid station and asked all walking wounded who could to go back on the line to bolster the defenses. "If we can hold out forty minutes more we'll get air support," he implored, standing at the tent entrance. Not many responded, so Faith tried a more direct appeal. "Come on, you lazy bastards, and give us a hand," he said.

That drew more of a response. Lt. Campbell, unable to walk with his leg injury, found a carbine with one round in it and crawled twenty yards to a firing position in a ditch. "That was as far as I could go," Campbell said. Someone found him later and carried him back to the aid station.

Hagaru, Friday morning

At 11:00 a.m., the 1st Marine Division headquarters issued orders directing the 31st RCT to "move south to Hagaru-ri at the earliest." While no troops could be sent, "maximum air support" would be available.

The orders changed nothing, as Faith had already taken the matter into his own hands. Moreover, there was no way to immediately transmit the orders to the 31st RCT, as neither Smith nor Faith had taken any steps to establish communication. Flying the orders in via helicopter was not an option, given the weather. The message was periodically broadcast over open radio channels but was not received for some time.

Hagaru had been under a fierce onslaught overnight, but by dawn, the base remained in Marine hands. The heaviest fighting had been on East Hill, where successive Chinese assaults knocked back the Marine and Army defenders. Many of the attacks came down East Hill, directly toward the position taken by the tanks of the 31st Tank Company. Silhouetted by a burning gasoline dump and a house afire on the ridge, the Chinese attackers took tremendous casualties. "They literally charged down the mountain slopes in hordes with bugles blowing," said Captain Drake. "We fought all night." Several hundred Chinese lay dead on the ground in front of the tanks in the morning.

Gen. Hodes, who still had not yet received his orders to depart Hagaru, watched the tanks fend off the Chinese from Drake's position. "These tanks were instrumental in stopping a major Chinese effort," said Ray Lynch, who observed the action with the general. The Army tanks "performed excellently" in defending East Hill, said Col.Bowser, Smith's chief of operations.

In the morning, Gen. Barr dispatched a small liaison plane to Hagaru to bring Hodes back to the 7th Division headquarters. "I've been ordered out," Hodes told Lynch. Almost certainly, he was not happy about it. The major drove the general to the Hagaru airstrip, still under construction, where Hodes boarded the plane and flew off.

Possibly, Barr believed withdrawing Hodes was necessary to get Smith to assume his command duties over the 31st RCT. Smith "did not try to exercise any control over 7th Div. troops until after Hodes left," Bill McCaffrey, the X Corps deputy chief of staff, later told historian Roy Appleman.

Barr and Hodes would thus be in Hungnam when the 31st RCT breakout began. "There were 2600 men dying up there, and I haven't forgotten that one either," McCaffrey said. "Those two G.D. general officers should have been up there."

Unlike the Army task force at the inlet, the two Marine regiments at Yudam-ni had no enemy contact the night of November 30 to December 1. "The enemy counteroffensive appeared to have slacked in its intensity to a considerable degree," Smith noted. The Marine headquarters did not recognize that the main Chinese effort was now being directed at the 31st RCT on the east side of the reservoir.

At 8:00 a.m. on Friday, the 8,000 men of the 5th and 7th Marines began their withdrawal from Yudam-ni, bringing their 500 wounded troops. Some 85 dead Marines were given a field burial and left behind. The 1st Battalion, 7th Marines, under the command of Lt. Col. Ray Davis, had been given the mission of relieving Fox Company at Toktong Pass, and it was to head east overland through the hills in a daring flanking maneuver to reach the company.

At Hagaru, Marine Lt. Col. Thomas Ridge, in charge of the perimeter defenses, "was pretty low and almost incoherent" when he came to see Smith Friday morning, according to the general. Ridge told Smith he did not see how he could hold the airstrip and ridge from another attack. "All I could tell him was that both these points had to be held" until the two Marine regiments at Yudam-ni reached Hagaru, Smith said.

"Had Hagaru-ri fallen, these two [Marine regiments] would have faced a bleak prospect," Smith later wrote.

Inlet, Late Friday Morning

As the breakout preparations accelerated, the rain of Chinese mortar fire grew more intense and more accurate. It was obvious what the Americans intended to do. "They had the high ground and we could not conceal our actions," said Bryant.

More and more GIs and ROKs were wounded or killed by enemy fire. "As men became indifferent to the instinct of self-preservation they started exposing themselves unnecessarily," Wes Curtis said.

Curtis and Dale Seever were sitting on the edge of a foxhole, discussing the withdrawal, when a mortar shell landed ten feet away, but it injured neither man. The nearby explosion was barely worth comment. Seever looked at Curtis and shrugged. "Major, I feel like I'm a thousand years old," he said.

All around the perimeter, soldiers scrambled to get ready for the withdrawal. They unloaded trucks to make room for the wounded. Gas was drained from disabled vehicles and transferred to those that would run. Soldiers ransacked trucks, jeeps, and trailers before they were destroyed, looking for bullets or fabric of any kind that could be used as bandages or clothing.

Hugh Robbins, lying face down on the bed of a truck with other wounded men, could see the preparations through the slats. Artillery gunners dropped phosphorus grenades down the muzzles of their howitzers. Drivers stabbed the tires of their jeeps with bayonets and set the vehicles ablaze. Supplies, records, and documents were soaked in gas and ignited.

At Able Company, ammunition details went around to the squads, checking and dividing up the remaining bullets and grenades. Oxenrider was given seven rounds for his carbine and five rounds for his .45. There were no rounds left for the 57 mm recoilless rifle that served as his squad's weapon. Oxenrider had to use two of his .45 rounds almost immediately as the Chinese made a probing attack close to his location.

Aid men rushed to carry wounded men from the battalion aid stations and load them onto the waiting trucks. Parachute silks had been spread on the truck beds to provide a little warmth and cushion, and the wounded men were given spare blankets and sleeping bags.

There were too many serious casualties to fit on the truck beds, so the soldiers had to improvise, making additional levels in the trucks to lay down more wounded. Stretchers and planks were laid crosswise above the truck bed, with the ends resting on side benches, creating a second level on which to lay the wounded. Those able to walk sat on the benches, and lesser wounded men were placed at the tailgate, armed with rifles.

Most of the trucks were carrying at least two dozen wounded. Only one truck was available for the roughly 50 wounded men in Jordan's M Company. He and his men pulled lumber from the house serving as the company CP to build an ambulance with litters stacked three high.

The dead would have to be left behind. That was bad enough for the GIs, but what made it worse was the need to search the frozen corpses for any ammunition and even to strip some of the clothing from the bodies to give to wounded men.

Capt. Conner, the 3rd Battalion chaplain wounded several days earlier, had recovered enough that he was able to hold a short funeral service for some of the dead, who lay in rows along the road. Then the chaplain was loaded onto one of the trucks with other wounded.

Trucks were lining up on the road inside the perimeter by 11:00 a.m.—around thirty trucks in all, plus some jeeps. Everything now depended on the arrival of the planes.

Only two M19s were still operational. Grantford Brown's M19, with Cpl. Ayala as the gunner, was chosen to lead the convoy and took position at the front, with a total of sixteen rounds of 40 mm ammunition left. The other M19 was to be the final vehicle in the column, protecting the rear, but the cold had weakened its batteries, and it would not start. Brown's M19 drove back, successfully jump-started the second vehicle, and returned to the head of the convoy.

Four M16s, armed with the Quad 50s, remained, but two of them refused all efforts to start and had to be abandoned. "We booby trapped them the best we could," said McClymont. The other two M16s took position in the column, though neither had much .50-caliber ammunition left.

Soldiers searched the perimeter for any remaining wounded. Somebody found Lt. McCabe of the 31st Heavy Mortar Company still lying in the snow where he had been wounded during the previous night's fighting, and he was put on a truck.

PFC Bob Hammond of A Battery, limping around on frozen feet, was with his squad, which had been assigned to flank security. But SFC Billy Allen, his section chief, directed him to get into one of the trucks. "Your feet are so bad that I don't think you can keep up with us," said Allen, a 29-year old Kansan and World War II veteran. Hammond protested, insisting he could keep pace.

"It's an order," Allen said, boosting Hammond up over the tailgate. "See you when we link up with the Marines."

The soldiers anxiously awaited the order to move. The ceiling had lifted a bit, but they were still under total cloud coverage, with the crests of the surrounding hills not visible. Precious daylight hours were slipping away.

As they waited, some soldiers grabbed a rare opportunity to eat whatever they could scrounge up. Sgt. Joe Ager with the 515th Truck Transportation

Company used his bayonet to dig out the contents from a frozen can of fruit cocktail and dumped it into his field jacket pocket, taking out the chunk to nibble on once in a while. Bryant split a can of frozen franks and beans with his first sergeant. "It was like eating buckshot," the captain recalled.

Lt. Magill sat in his foxhole, sharing half of a frozen peach with his sergeant, wondering if it was his last meal. Two B Battery sergeants had been killed that morning by a mortar round that had also peppered Magill's legs with shrapnel. The skies remained overcast, and it looked like the Chinese were gearing up for a major attack. "I felt that we were about at the end of the road," Magill said.

Bigger—still in a daze from the mortar strike and, possibly, the shot of whiskey—was lying on his back, looking at the gray sky. "I remember falling snowflakes as if in slow motion and then a patch of blue sky through a break in the overcast, then a lone Corsair finding its way down through that break," he said.

The skies were clearing. Several more Corsairs dove through the hole in the clouds. Soldiers erupted in cheers. "We're not through here," Faith told Frenchy Mercier, who was now serving as his radioman. "We're going home."

Faith gave orders to move out. "Men, out of your holes, let's go!" All around the perimeter, platoon leaders and squad sergeants picked up the cry. At the Able Company position, Roy Oxenrider heard a yell: "Able, on the road." He jumped out of his foxhole.

Mortrude led his platoon out of their positions to the head of the column for the breakout. He had injured his knee during the night while launching a rifle carbine flare from a kneeling position on the ice and was having trouble walking, so Maj. Miller directed him to command the platoon from the M19 at the head of the column.

Before Mortrude climbed up onto the M19, Faith gave the lieutenant simple instructions: "Break through and keep going."

Chapter 14

BREAKOUT AFTERNOON

Friday, December 1

The attack began on Don Faith's order. Sgt. Grantford Brown's M19 led the way, lurching down the road with Lt. Mortrude in the turret and his platoon trotting along on each side. The rest of C Company followed behind, passing through the task force roadblock held by Able Company and moving forward to clear the Chinese-controlled road. Baker Company was behind Able, ready to join in clearing the high ground east of the road.

"We had started a beautiful assault, with much enthusiasm," said Capt. Bigger, who had procured two mortar-aiming stakes to use as canes and taken a seat in a jeep. "Our spirits had been raised by the appearance of the Corsairs. We were ready to get out of this situation."

Shortly after noon, pilots reported to Hagaru that the task force was on the move. Lt. Col. Berry Anderson, the senior Army officer at the 31st RCT rear headquarters, received a report relayed by an Army observation plane: "They were coming out. They were coming down the road and they were going to try to bring all their wounded out with them by trucks."

Faith rode directly behind C Company in his distinctive command jeep, loaded with radios and a side-mounted .30 caliber machine gun. Faith had slept as little as anyone but somehow looked crisp for the breakout, with his pressed brown wool officers uniform shirt, a sheepskin vest under a clean parka, and a shiny helmet. "He looked outstanding and stuck out from the rest of us," said PFC James Ransone of Able Company.

The confidence of some officers and soldiers was boosted by their expectation that the Army tanks would still be on the route and able to help. "We knew there was a company of tanks behind us," said Sgt. Monty Piercefield, who was up front with the command group.

A short way outside the perimeter, the Chinese had made a roadblock with logs across the road, covered by automatic weapons and small-arms fire. The 241st Regiment, manning the roadblock, was ready to meet the attack head-on. Ed Stamford, positioned close to Faith, had Corsairs fly several dummy runs just beyond the perimeter, keeping the Chinese momentarily frozen in their foxholes. But the column had not gone far when a furious burst of automatic weapons fire sent Mortrude ducking behind the shield of the open turret.

Men on both sides of the column fell from the withering fire as others dropped to the ground, seeking cover. Faith jumped out of his jeep and ran forward to the lead elements, getting the men back on their feet and resuming the assault. He instructed Stamford to place an air strike on the Chinese position.

Mortrude watched hopefully as a Corsair flying fast and low approached from the rear and dropped a canister of napalm. The jellied gasoline, first used in the Pacific during World War II, was a relatively new weapon, but the Chinese had already learned to fear its terrible capacity to burn men alive. To Mortrude, it seemed the canister tumbling through the air had been released too soon, and he and Cpl. Ayala, the gunner, crouched behind the turret. Napalm splashed off the side of the M19 and onto the left side of the road.

Mortrude felt the heat as a sheet of flame flashed overhead. One of the M19 crew members came off the vehicle, aflame and screaming. Magill and other soldiers threw him to the ground and smothered the flames, but the man was mortally burned. "If I had not ducked below my turret I would have been killed too," said Ayala.

The wall of flame and heat sprayed out and enveloped about 15 soldiers, most from C Company, some of them dying immediately, while others were horribly burned. Navarre, the 1st Battalion surgeon, saw a soldier "black as soot and whirling about with a blue flame issuing from his head like a Bunsen burner."

Maj. Robbins, lying in the back of a truck, watched through the slats. "I could see the terrible sight of men ablaze from head to foot, staggering back or rolling on the ground screaming for someone to help them," said Robbins. He recognized one of the burning figures as Master Sgt. Dave Smith, his assistant sergeant major and "one of the finest men I have ever known." Smith ran until he dropped. "I was powerless to do a thing for him," said Robbins. "I had to turn my head."

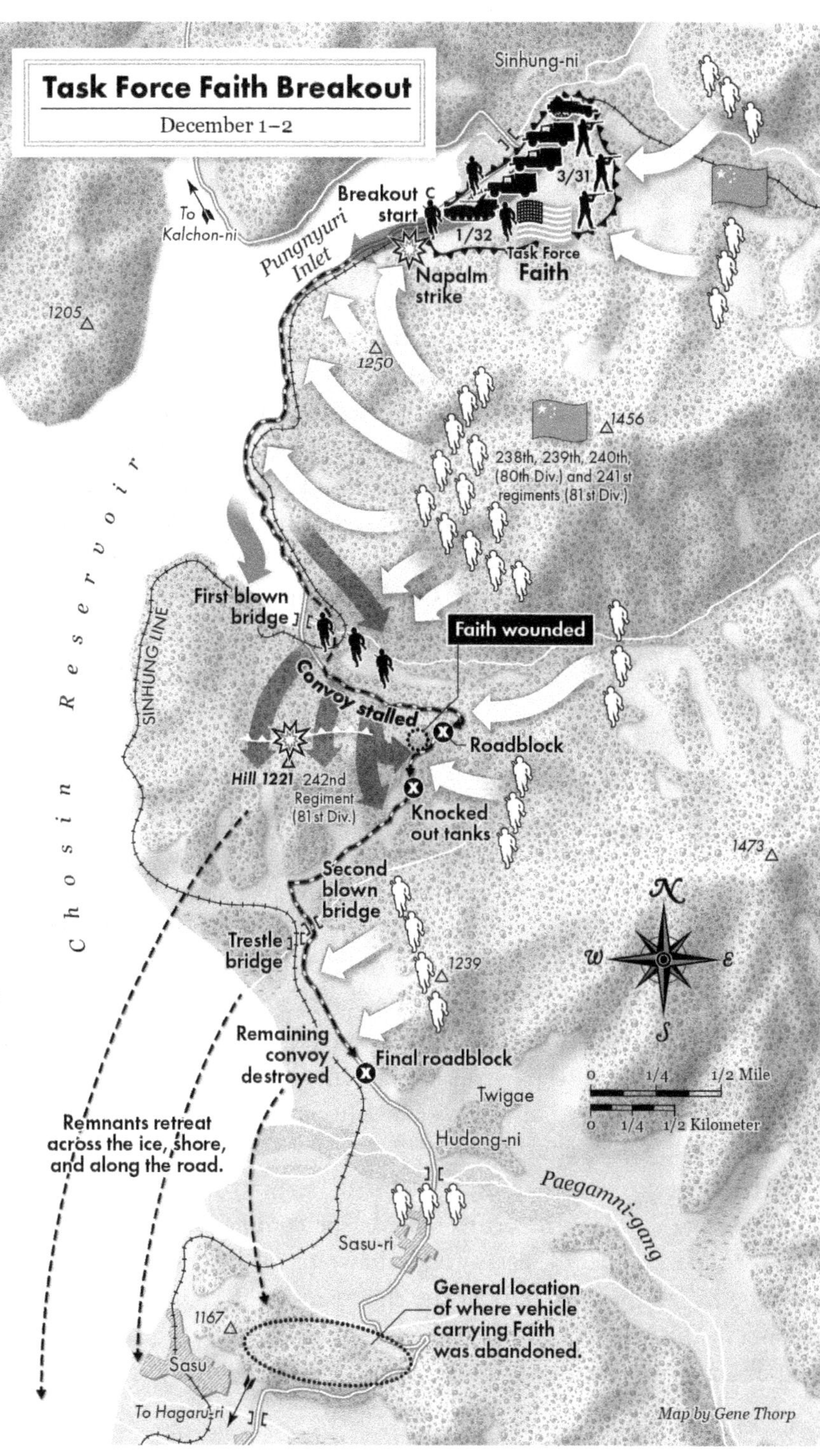

Task Force Faith Breakout
December 1–2
Sinhung-ni
To Kalchon-ni
Breakout start
3/31
1/32
Task Force Faith
Pungnyuri Inlet
Napalm strike
1205
1250
1456
238th, 239th, 240th, (80th Div.) and 241st regiments (81st Div.)
Chosin Reservoir
SINHUNG LINE
First blown bridge
Faith wounded
Convoy stalled
Roadblock
Hill 1221
242nd Regiment (81st Div.)
Knocked out tanks
1473
Second blown bridge
Trestle bridge
1239
Remaining convoy destroyed
Final roadblock
Twigae
0 1/4 1/2 Mile
0 1/4 1/2 Kilometer
Hudong-ni
Remnants retreat across the ice, shore, and along the road.
Paegamni-gang
Sasu-ri
General location of where vehicle carrying Faith was abandoned.
1167
Sasu
To Hagaru-ri
Map by Gene Thorp

Lt. George Foster, one of Mortrude's fellow C Company platoon leaders, stood dazed, his face and clothing scorched. Foster "walked up to another officer, asked him for a cigarette, received, and walked away, never to be seen again," according to Major Jones.

Lt. Henry Moore, the commander of the 1st Battalion's Ammunition and Pioneer Platoon, was terribly burned. "His hair gone, eye glasses gone, and most of his clothes burnt off from the waist up," recalled Hugh May. "He was parched to a dark brown, & in places black and open burns. The only way I could tell it was him was when he spoke to me." Moore could still walk and lead; he refused to get in a truck and continued on foot with his men.

Sgt. John Nagy's face was burned when he turned and saw the blast coming at him. PFC Grant McMillin rushed over and cut Nagy's hood off with his bayonet. "His face within seconds had frozen, because it was all blistered," McMillin said. A ROK soldier who dove in the roadside ditch caught the full force of the backwash from the napalm ignition. Getting to his feet, the soldier "took three faltering steps toward me and collapsed and died on the road," Stamford said.

PFC Roy Oxenrider had jumped for a nearby foxhole when he saw the napalm canister dropping and had not quite made it all the way in when the burst scorched his clothing. Looking over, he saw a dozen men completely on fire and several others partly burned. Oxenrider was unhurt, but he was unable to find his foxhole buddy, Joung He Su, and concluded he was one of the victims. "Had he been alive, he would have found me," Oxenrider wrote decades later. "He had been my shadow, faithful and courageous, a good soldier. I have never forgotten him, or the screams of those comrades who burned alive."

GIs ran up to help the victims, but it did little good. "We took off our helmets and picked up snow and threw it on the burning victims, and it became steam instantly," said Sgt. Joe Ager. "The screams and all, I heard them for years."

In the minutes after the napalm strike, the attack faltered. The men were shocked, demoralized, and disorganized. "It took a lot of wind out of the sails of the guys," said Charlie Gebhardt.

Faith's response at that critical moment "showed him as a true leader," Stamford wrote in a later report to the Marine commandant. "He moved out among the men and met the enemy with drawn pistol. By this demonstration of courage he rallied the men and put the enemy to flight, thus averting disaster."

Some of the GIs and ROKs had turned around, showing signs of retreat. Faith put a stop to that with his .45. "He pointed it generally at the retreating men but did not fire, and shouted at them to turn around and face the enemy," Stamford said. "They did so."

Said Bigger, "Col. Faith was the force behind getting the attack and breakout moving again. He was all over the place, exhorting, ordering, threatening—he moved the unit with the force of his personality."

Deadly as the napalm had been to Task Force Faith, it caused even greater casualties among the Chinese troops. The Corsair had been flying at more than 350 mph when it dropped the canister, and the major portion of the napalm splashed on enemy positions. "I saw many on the higher ground to our front come out of their holes as flaming torches and die immediately," said Stamford.

C Company charged ahead, and a pitched battle was quickly underway. As they moved forward, Seever, the company commander, asked Stamford for rocket fire on a culvert running beneath the road from which the Chinese were throwing grenades. Stamford instructed a Marine F7F Tigercat fighter pilot who was rolling into a strafing run to bring his fire closer to the American positions until the plane's tracer fire hit the ditch, just twenty yards in front of the lead American elements.

"That's the spot, give me a rocket," Stamford radioed. The pilot obliged, and a rocket slammed into the culvert, taking out the Chinese inside. The explosion was so close to the American position that the pilot feared he had killed Stamford or some GIs. They were unscathed, and the task force broke through the position and continued down the road.

Inlet

The 3rd Battalion, which had remained inside the perimeter defending the rear when the attack started, began to pull out of the inlet as the convoy moved forward. In the chaos, not everyone got the word.

Jordan, the M Company commander, was surprised to see the 3rd Battalion headquarters move out. "I received no instructions or mission whatsoever," Jordan later said. "As a matter of fact we would have been left in position if we had not observed the people between us and the lake pulling out." Jordan ordered his men to follow.

John Gray, lying in a dugout and feverish from his infected leg wound, could hear frenzied preparations going on all around him. Several of his men dragged him from the dugout, along with his helmet and rifle, and Jordan ordered him placed in the cab of one of the trucks. "It was like catching an unannounced train pulling out of a station—grab hold or be left behind," said Gray.

The rear guard movement from the inlet began with a disastrous development. The crew of the M19 assigned to bring up the rear had run its engines after getting jump-started, but the sergeant, worried they would run out of gas, ordered the driver to shut them off. "This fool, he let it die down," Cpl. Ayala, whose M19 had provided the jump start, later complained. Now that it was time to go, the M19 refused to start again, with no jump available. To make it worse, it had been given some of the limited 40 mm ammunition, which, like the vehicle, had to be abandoned.

Without the Twin 40 firepower, the 3rd Battalion was having trouble breaking contact with the Chinese forces coming down the hills around the inlet. "As soon as we got out of our positions they just started moving right in," said Kitz, the King Company commander.

One of the remaining M16 half-tracks was directed to pull out of the line and rush back to help the 3rd Battalion break free. The driver, PFC Hodaviah "Hode" Hensley, barreled down the road to the west end of the hill, where the crew blasted the slope with heavy fire from its Quad 50 machine guns. In return, the crew drew a barrage of Chinese mortar, machine gun, and small-arms fire. "We backed, twisted and turned, using every evasion tactic we could think of," said Hensley. "The CCF fire was murderous, especially their mortar fire."

Several 3rd Battalion machine gun crews also stayed behind to keep the Chinese at bay. "Our orders were to hold the enemy to give the trucks time to get away," said Staff Sgt. Harry Scott, the assistant machine gunner for a cobbled-together crew from the headquarters company. They fired until the Chinese had closed to within 150 feet. "We picked up the machine gun and ran like deer to the road and set up again," Scott said.

A company-sized group of Chinese soldiers chased the convoy, trying to overrun the last three trucks, and they killed some of the rear guard troops with sprays of automatic fire. But the defenders bought time for all the trucks to get out. Maj. Storms, leading an attack on the left flank as the battalion exited the perimeter, was wounded but able to keep fighting and continue command of the 3rd Battalion.

Hensley's M16 half-track fired at the Chinese until it ran out of ammunition. The crew broke contact and raced back on the road, exiting the perimeter and finding the task force already out of sight. They passed through the horrific scene of the napalm strike. "Bodies, both GI and Chinese, were all over the place," said Hensley. Soon after, they ran out of fuel and ditched the half-track. Moving on foot, they sought a place to hide from the Chinese troops quickly closing in from behind.

With the task force cleared from the inlet and broken through the 241st Regiment's roadblock, Zhan Da'nan had sent three more regiments—the 238th, 239th, and 240th—in pursuit. A battalion from the 242nd Regiment was positioned on the heights of Hill 1221, ready to fire on the Americans as they approached, and a second battalion was on the way to reinforce the hill.

The column surged forward, C Company still in the lead, taking small-arms and automatic weapons fire from the high ground on the left, the marshes on the right, and the road in front. At a turn in the road, the Chinese had built a log barricade blocking the road, but the M19 "busted it open, and . . . kept going," said Ayala. The infantry and trucks followed.

Maj. Miller, commanding the 1st Battalion, ordered Baker Company to move up on the left flank to help clear out enemy positions. The company was taking fire from a heavy machine gun until a BAR man sprayed the position and silenced the gun.

Sgt. Clarence White of B Company and his friend Cpl. Ralph Boughman, a company cook, rounded a curve at the base of Hill 1456 and were crossing an open field when they came under machine gun fire. They took cover behind a haystack but were quickly surrounded by Chinese soldiers and taken prisoner. The captors took their mittens and then talked amongst themselves. "I think some wanted to just shoot us; the others did not," said White.

Just then a Corsair flew overhead, firing its machine gun. The Chinese went for cover, and White and Boughman began sprinting to catch up with the convoy, about fifty yards away. They had not made it far when a machine gun firing from the hill cut them both down. White's wound was slight, but Boughman was in bad shape. White crawled back to Boughman, who was lying on his back. "I'll never forget the look of innocence on his face," White said.

"Don't leave me," Boughman told White.

"Ralph, I won't," White promised his friend. Boughman closed his eyes and died.

The firing had stopped. White tried to drag Boughman with him but, in his weakened condition, only made it ten feet. He continued to the convoy and found another friend with B Company, Willis Van Merter, and asked for his help. "We were going back to get Ralph's body," White said. An officer stopped them. They needed to move forward.

Roy Oxenrider's Able Company squad moved along the edge of the reservoir, using the bank for cover and trying to get behind a machine gun firing on the convoy. As they crossed a frozen cove, the machine gun swung in their direction. Oxenrider was shot through both thighs and knocked to the ice.

"Come on, Roy, get up. We got work to do," his squad leader, Sgt. Harold Verseman, called. The rest of the squad was moving forward. Oxenrider tried to get up but felt paralyzed.

"I've been hit," Oxenrider yelled back.

Verseman turned around and came back through a hail of bullets chipping the ice around them. He grabbed Oxenrider by the arm and pulled him to the bank, out of the line of fire. After calling for medics, he turned to Oxenrider. "Roy, I'm sorry, but I have to go," he said, and he took off to catch the squad. The medics bandaged Oxenrider's legs, carried him to a truck, and lifted him over the tailgate. It was the last truck in the column.

Drivers in particular were being targeted by the Chinese, and Oxenrider's truck lost four in quick succession. "Any man who slipped into the seat of one of those trucks was committing suicide," he said. "All knew it, but it stopped none. The trucks never lacked drivers. As one was hit, he would be dragged out, another took his place. . . . Each of those guys was a hero."

Sgt. Via, who had continued forward with the Able Company attack, was shot in the left ankle and was lying in a ditch by the road, up to his elbows in snow, when he heard someone call his name. It was Private Humphrey Wilson, who had given him fits back at the barracks in Japan, as he was always late for formation, out of uniform, or needing a shave. "This was one time I was glad to see him late," said Via. Wilson gave Via his mitten shells to keep the sergeant's hands from freezing. Via joined other wounded soldiers lying by the roadside, hoping the trucks would arrive soon to pick them up.

Cpl. Anthony Mora's makeshift squad of B Battery cooks, bakers, and clerks, moving on the right flank of the convoy, was ambushed by Chinese soldiers hiding in snow-covered holes. Several men were killed and others wounded, and Mora was shot by a bullet that hit him in the thigh, then wedged against his spinal cord. "I shook all over and I thought I was dying," Mora said. "But after a while I thought, 'Hey, I'm not dying, I'm going to survive.'"

Mora's rifle had frozen up, and he needed one that worked. He crawled over to get one from nearby dead soldiers, but the first several weapons he tried would not fire either. A Chinese soldier found Mora lying in the snow and started beating him with a rifle butt, breaking his nose and knocking out his front teeth. Mora reached for the last remaining rifle. "I pointed it at him and he wasn't worried about it," Mora said. "And I pulled the trigger and it went off. And I killed him."

Mora crawled toward the convoy, continuing even after being shot again, this time in his foot. Lt. Eichorn, his platoon commander, spotted him and ran over, throwing the corporal over his shoulder and carrying him up to one of the trucks.

Rear Guard

The 3rd Battalion, bringing up the rear, moved along the reservoir shoreline, exposed to heavy Chinese fire from the hills on their left flank. "We had a tremendous number of casualties at that point," said Bill Etchemendy, the L Company commander.

Men began drifting to the right off the road. Kitz did a poor job of keeping K Company on its rear guard mission, with some of his troops going out on the reservoir ice because of the heavy fire. The ice broke in several places, and men fell into the water. "Some got in and some didn't," Kitz said. "I got in the water and was lucky to get out." After making it back to shore, the company continued down the road behind the trucks.

"We were staying back to the rear trying to fight a rear-guard action, and we were getting massacred," said Cpl. Jerry Francois.

Lt. Lester Rulik, an L Company platoon leader, was hit in the legs by enemy machine gun while he and SFC Bill Donovan led the unit across a frozen cove. Donovan and his soldiers tried to drag him across the ice without success, so they left him to get a stretcher. When they returned, they saw Chinese soldiers shooting and bayoneting all the wounded soldiers on the ice. A Chinese soldier shot Rulik, killing him instantly. An enraged Donovan shot and killed the soldier. Then the men continued forward.

1st Battalion

Up front, the troops were moving fast, maybe too fast. As the 1st Battalion moved forward past the log barricade, both Maj. Miller and Maj. Curtis sensed some loss of control. Troops were under heavy fire from the hills to their left, and they were drifting to the right side of the road, where its embankment provided some shelter. Elements of B and C companies had become mixed after the napalm attack. "At the initial success of the breakout, a sort of hysterical enthusiasm seized the troops," said Curtis. "They flooded down the road like a great mob and tactical control broke down almost immediately."

A brief pause to reorganize would be helpful, Miller thought, but communication even within each battalion was an enormous problem. There was little radio contact within the column because of the terrain, dead batteries, and faulty equipment, leaving runners or personal contact as almost the only way to communicate. Both of his radio operators were missing, so Miller sent runners forward to Baker and Charlie Companies, trying to get them to slow down, but the messages did not seem to get through.

As the column surged forward, there was no way for the rear to communicate with the front. Faith, Miller, Storms, and other commanders were enormously handicapped, with little ability to communicate, coordinate, and have the units mutually support each other.

The truck carrying Hugh Robbins moved forward in jerks and halts. Looking through the slats of the truck, Robbins saw dead Chinese and American soldiers lying on the sides of the road and in ditches, "their blood forming pools from which steam rose into the freezing air."

In the face of that horror, Robbins was struck by the spirit of the men. "GIs were sacrificing everything in the fight to bring the wounded to safety," he said. "Soldiers passing our truck called out encouragement to us and grinning as they went forward to blast more Chinese or fall themselves. The enemy was giving way now and our guys sensed it, following them more closely and with greater courage."

Mortrude and his men were in the front. The lieutenant had abandoned riding in the M19 after the napalm calamity, feeling safer on the ground, and limped along the best he could. Following the road along the shore of a cove that led to the northern base of Hill 1221, they arrived around 2:00 p.m. at the most serious obstacle yet. A short concrete bridge, running about twenty feet across a stream feeding the reservoir, had been blown in the middle, which collapsed much of it into the gully.

It was unanticipated, even though it was not particularly surprising that the Chinese would have blown the bridge—an obvious way to slow the retreating column. None of the aircraft had reported a bridge was blown. Faith and his staff had not requested any aerial reconnaissance, nor had any been offered by the 1st Marine Division headquarters. There was only one road out, and the trucks would have to cross the stream regardless of advance knowledge. But knowing the bridge was out might have spurred Faith and his staff to have a contingency plan in the event that the task force could not reach Hagaru before nightfall.

Miller, arriving at the head of the column behind the M19, surveyed the situation. The trucks would have to go upstream a short distance; down a steep embankment; across the narrow ice-covered stream and a wide, semifrozen marsh; and back up an embankment to rejoin the road. The M19 had no trouble crossing, but it was a different matter for the trucks.

The motor column turned off the road and onto the stream bed, bumping over frozen mounds of grass and dirt. The truck carrying Robbins was one of the first to try. "For about 100 yards we bounced and crashed up and down over those hummocks with the wounded screaming in anguish as they were jostled and slammed into one another on the truck bed," said Robbins. With a final jarring crash, the truck's front wheels broke through the stream's ice surface and became firmly stuck, going nowhere. Despite the cold, Robbins began to sweat as enemy fire zipped around the truck.

A few trucks made it across. Sgt. Charles Garrigus, the motor transport NCO who had already bravely driven trucks into the inlet during the consolidation two days earlier, once again rose to the challenge, skillfully driving his truck through the marsh and then returning on foot several times more under fire to bring other trucks across.

But most trucks could not make it, getting stuck in the stream or mired in the marsh. The convoy behind was jamming up, exposing the trucks to fire. Miller directed Brown's M19 to turn around and use cables to tow out each truck unable to make it across. It would be a long, painstaking process. Lt. May directed the crossing operation like a traffic cop, ignoring the heavy fire around him.

Work parties braved Chinese fire and frigid water again and again to hook up the trucks. Brown's crew winched them across, one by one, all the while hearing soul-shaking screams from those inside. "They were just crying and hollering out, but we had to do it," said Ayala.

Faith surveyed the scene at the blown bridge and found "the situation there was under control and the crossing of vehicles was slowly progressing," May recalled. The task force commander continued forward to scout the road ahead.

What he learned was deflating. A large enemy force occupied Hill 1221, giving the Chinese command of the road. Moreover, they had set up a substantial roadblock where the road curved sharply around the hill.

The roadblock was a formidable obstacle at the key pressure point on the road to Hagaru. Built with logs and defended by at least two heavy machine guns, it was located at the southern end of the hairpin turn in the saddle that carried the road between the eastern base of Hill 1221 and another hill rising to the east. Two 242nd Regiment battalions, its troops wearing the mustard yellow uniforms of the 81st Division, were strongly situated on and around Hill 1221, using the positions the 5th Marines had prepared.

As trucks gradually crossed the stream and took position on the steep road, awaiting the rest of the convoy, Chinese troops fired ferociously into the convoy from above. "The continual smack of slugs slapping the truck was unnerving to me as I expected any minute to be hit by the next one," said Robbins. Casualties "set up a mournful racket" as they suffered new wounds, Robbins said. Sitting in another truck, Lt. Smalley, the wounded C Company platoon leader randomly picked to receive the Silver Star from Almond, was killed by a rifle shot through the head.

Soldiers on the road and along the flanks were also being hit, as were medics trying to render aid. The newly wounded were picked up and squeezed as best as possible into the already full trucks, sometimes atop other men. "Wounded men in pain were crammed like sardines," said PFC Charles Bennett.

The roadblock clearly had to be destroyed to stop the slaughter of soldiers on the road and wounded in the trucks, and Faith wasted no time trying. He gathered available troops and led an assault up the steep road toward the hairpin curve. Approaching the roadblock, the attack was met by a torrent of fire. Taking many casualties, the 1st Battalion troops fell back. "The retirement looked like a rout," said Stamford, watching from down the road.

Another threat could be seen developing to the north. The delay at the blown bridge had given Chinese troops bypassed at the inlet time to catch up and set new positions on high ground across a valley parallel to the road running along Hill 1221. Large numbers of Chinese could be seen starting to move down the high ground toward the column. While the assault on the roadblock was underway, 3rd Battalion troops moved up the valley below the road to protect the convoy from those troops. But by moving against that threat, the 3rd Battalion left the rear of the column exposed.

The Polar Bears' attack did not fare well, as they came under heavy fire from the enemy across the valley as well as from at least 300 Chinese positioned to their northeast. The Chinese manning the roadblock at the hairpin curve also directed machine gun fire at the 3rd Battalion troops, forcing them to break off the attack.

The Polar Bears were then ordered—apparently by Faith—to move toward the road to help clear the Chinese off Hill 1221. But this exposed the left flank of the truck column to long-range fire from the Chinese forces across the valley. An air strike called by Stamford kept the Chinese at bay for the time being, but the rear and left flank of the convoy remained dangerously exposed. The reinforcements brought by Zhan had given the Chinese an overwhelming numbers advantage, and it was proving difficult for the task force to protect the convoy.

As the crossing continued at the stream, Crosby Miller went up the road on foot to see if the Chinese had been cleared from the high ground covering the road. He got his answer when he spotted a heavy machine gun trained on him from just above the road. Miller dove for the ditch but was hit by three bullets in the upper left leg and another bullet that clipped off the last three fingers of his left hand, taking his wedding ring with it. Miller was able to cover his left hand with his right-hand glove, which was quickly soaked with blood and soon froze, stopping the bleeding. "Nothing could be done about the leg, so I lay in the ditch taking stock of a very sorry situation," he recalled.

Miller sent a lieutenant to tell Faith he had been hit and to reiterate the desperate need to clear Hill 1221. "The ditch and road around me were dotted with dead and wounded with casualties increasing every minute," Miller said. "I tried to get men around the trucks to move directly up the hill and clear it, but each man who tried it became a casualty."

Curtis was standing near a jeep-mounted radio artillery observer's radio when it received a message being broadcast in the clear around 3:00 p.m.: "To

Colonel Faith: Secure your own exit to Hagaru-ri. Unable to assist you. Smith." Said Curtis, "This was the first instruction that Colonel Faith had received from higher headquarters in 48 hours and in effect directed him to do what he had decided to do three hours previously."

Soon afterward, Curtis was shot in the leg by a rifle. Maj. Jones—still unscathed as others dropped all around him—applied a pressure bandage to stop the bleeding and found a tree limb that Curtis could use as a crutch. Though he could only walk with difficulty, Curtis began looking for an alternate route for the trucks to get around the hill. At the base of 1221, the railroad split off from the road, running around the western base of the hill along the shore of the reservoir. Curtis decided to follow the railroad line, joined by Capt. Conner, the wounded 3rd Battalion chaplain, who had left his truck to help. Along with several enlisted men, they limped along the railroad bed for several hundred yards until they came under enemy mortar fire. It was a narrow bed atop an embankment, and with the route covered by the Chinese, it was clear to Curtis that it would not work as an escape route for the trucks. They returned, and Curtis slowly made his way up the hill toward the roadblock.

Some men had reached their limit. A significant number of rear guard troops followed the railroad bed around the western side of Hill 1221, essentially abandoning the convoy. Capt. Bryant, the 31st headquarters company commander, tried to get men to stop and take up defensive positions. "They would not reply and some would almost walk into me with blank stares on their faces," he said.

So many company commanders, platoon leaders, and squad leaders, exposed as they were leading attacks, rallying soldiers, and keeping the truck column moving, had become casualties, taking a heavy toll on leadership when it was most needed.

"All people have their breaking point, I don't care how good they are," said Jones. "Some breaking points are higher than others."

Not every truck made it across the stream, with several lost to enemy fire before they could reach the site and the wounded men in the back killed or captured. As Oxenrider's truck approached the bridge site, the driver was once again shot—the fifth killed or wounded since he had been onboard. The truck crashed into a shallow ditch on the right side of the road, leaving the rear exposed to direct enemy fire.

Oxenrider, near the tailgate, desperately tried to get out of the truck and finally found the strength to topple over the back, hitting his rib cage on the trailer hitch on his way down. He rolled into the ditch and began crawling into the brush, accompanied by two other wounded soldiers who had also managed to get out of the truck. Before long, they heard screams, grenades, and shooting. "We knew no one else would get off that truck alive," said Oxenrider. "That scene haunts me to this day. Some of those men were stuck fast, frozen in their own blood."

The last two trucks to make it to the stream were both hit while crossing, one knocked out by small-arms fire, while the driver of the second truck was killed. May and his work party managed to get the wounded out from both trucks and reload them into other vehicles, all while under heavy fire.

The crossing had taken at least two hours, eating up critical time needed to reach Hagaru-ri before dark. The chances looked bleak, with another seven miles to travel and a major roadblock ahead. There was no air cover after dark, but with no plan in place to halt for the night, there was little choice but to try to make it.

They would have to do it without the invaluable help of the antiaircraft weapons. The last remaining M16 half-track made it across the stream after inflicting heavy damage on Chinese positions with its remaining .50-caliber ammunition. But the M16 was knocked out of action by Chinese fire from above on Hill 1221, and a number of wounded men being carried on top of the half-track were killed.

Brown's M19, which had done such yeoman service leading the column, was on its last gasps after the stream crossing, firing its final rounds of 40 mm shells at Chinese machine gun positions to the left. "Knocked three of them out, and that was it," said Ayala. "That was the end of my ammunition. And not only that, we ran out of gas." Brown got the M19 off the road so it wouldn't block the convoy. Faith instructed the crew to form an infantry assault team to attack a machine gun position on Hill 1221.

Finally, as daylight was beginning to wane, the trucks started moving again.

Harvey Storms waited at the blown bridge until the crossing operation was finished. He and Capt. Bryant then walked up the road to catch up with the convoy, which was slowly moving up the hill. "There were trucks with steam spewing from broken radiators, wounded and dead drivers being pulled out of truck cabs and other men taking their place, trucks pushing others to help them up the hill," said Bryant. "It was a horrible sight."

Across the valley to the left, Storms and Bryant could see Chinese troops coming down the distant hills and beginning to cross the valley to attack the convoy. Corsairs directed by Stamford flew overhead, strafing the ground below the rising road to keep the Chinese back. The planes dropped napalm on Chinese positions, temporarily putting a stop to their fire.

Storms saw that the Chinese guns firing on the stalled convoy from Hill 1221 had to be taken out. He directed his men to save their ammunition for an assault, telling PFC Donald Mayville from his headquarters company to break off a fruitless firefight with some distant Chinese soldiers. "Don, quit shooting, we're going to need those bullets," the major said.

Storms and Capt. Bob McClay, the battalion adjutant, gathered some nearby 3rd Battalion troops. "Let's take the hill," Storms told the men. They launched their attack, making good progress at first. "I was about five yards to Storms' right and halfway up the ridge when the Chinese really opened up from above us," said McClay.

Storms was hit multiple times but kept leading the men up the hill. "He must have had 10 or 12 bullet holes through his field jacket," recalled Sgt. Bill Rowland. Storms finally collapsed, with wounds to his right arm and chest. He instructed nearby men to continue up the hill and attack the roadblock from above. Then he began sliding down the icy hill. "I watched him roll clear to the bottom," said McClay. The men kept attacking, driving the Chinese from the position, and they continued along the ridge toward the roadblock.

On the road below, the gravely wounded Storms was put in a truck, but he soon got out. "Although wounded, Storms continued to be one of the prime movers in keeping the convoy going," Bill Etchemendy said. "He was constantly in the thick of the action, rallying troops, fighting Chinese and generally keeping the convoy moving."

Faith strode up and down the road, ignoring enemy fire, gripping his .45, and working to get groups to clear the hill enough to permit an attack on the roadblock. "Most of the officers . . . had become casualties and the troops were clustered around the vehicles drawing fire toward the wounded," said Stamford. "Col Faith succeeded in getting them away and headed up the hill."

He stopped periodically at his jeep to fire its side-mounted machine gun at Chinese positions. "He really exerted authority, and he laced it with profanity," said Sgt. Ager. "Somebody said Colonel Faith could curse by music and not miss a note. He kept the .45 out all the time. Whenever he was talking, he was waving it around, so we knew he was in charge."

Faith became infuriated when he spotted two apparently uninjured ROK soldiers tying themselves to the undercarriage of a truck, hoping to ride to safety. One of the men kept saying in Japanese that he was hurt. Faith leaned under the truck and pointed his .45 at the men, ordering them to come out and rejoin the fight. "They refused," said Bigger. "He shot both of them."

It was a shocking and terrible moment, but it was barely noticed in the midst of the surrounding horror.

Bigger volunteered to go forward and help get the column moving. "There were so many wounded far worse than I that I gave up my place in the jeep and began walking," he said.

Limping his way with his canes to the front of the convoy, Bigger found the trucks stopped and "exposed to a murderous fire" from the Chinese on the steep hillside that began abruptly at the roadside. Several attempts to attack up the hill had proven costly. Exhausted soldiers were taking cover between the trucks and the embankment. "The men were reluctant to get going when they looked about and saw men on all sides of them being shot down from the fire from the Chinese above them," said Robbins, who watched from the truck.

Bigger began flailing at the men with his canes. "If you are going to die, do it while in the attack," he shouted. "Let's get moving and secure this hill."

Bigger's efforts snowballed. Other officers began rallying the troops, more and more men joined in, and soon, several teams were assaulting the hill, including one led by Bigger. "He had only a 45 pistol on his hip, a stick under each arm, and one eye almost out," said Sgt. Clarence White, who joined the attack. "He had been hit many times but was leading the attack with two sticks for crutches."

Lt. Mortrude, who had been wounded by a sniper's bullet that grazed his forehead, staggered forward and arrived shortly before the attack was being launched. He heard rallying cries from around the hillside: "Come on, GI!" Mortrude had lost his rifle when he was wounded, so he grabbed an M1 rifle and a bandolier of ammunition from a wounded ROK and followed the assault. Already, the hill was dotted with the bodies of GIs who had fallen in the attack.

Sgt. Via, lying wounded in the ditch, watched as an officer drove up in a jeep and jumped out. His upper body was burnt and his uniform, blackened and shredded. It was Lt. Henry Moore, still unvanquished from the napalm attack. "Men, listen to me," he called. "If we don't get to the top of that mountain, we are all going to die here." Moore headed up the hill, and the men followed him. "I turned and started crawling up the mountain as fast as I could," Via said.

Other assaults on Hill 1221 were underway from different points around the same time. Lt. John Gray, riding in the cab of his truck in a groggy reverie from fatigue and the pain of crossing the stream, had been jolted to reality by the sounds of the convoy being laced with machine gun and rifle fire. Soldiers guarding the trucks shouted warnings to take cover. Gray lost his balance as he exited the cab, slamming onto the frozen roadside and feeling excruciating pain in his wounded thigh.

Gray crept forward in the ditch running on the right side of the road, hoping to locate someone who could give him instructions, but all he saw was a dead officer slumped in the cab of a truck. He met several NCOs in the ditch, who agreed to assault the hill. Some men refused to join, too far in shock to respond to an officer and NCOs they did not know. But many agreed, and Gray and the sergeants organized 30 men into three 10-man squads.

They started up the hill in a skirmish line, their feet crunching in the snow. Fearing they were making too much noise, Gray signaled for a slower pace. It was a steep climb, several hundred yards to the top, and Gray kept slipping on the snow, one step back for every two forward. But the Corsairs flying overhead were keeping the Chinese in their holes, and the assault was not met with enemy fire. As they approached the top, Gray was startled to see dark shadows converging on them from the right. To his surprise and joy, it was another party of GIs, led by his company commander, Earle Jordan, who had launched his own assault of about two dozen men up the nose of 1221.

The combined force, under Jordan's command, continued toward the Chinese position at the top. Lt. Robert Schmitt, Jordan's machine gun platoon leader, led the charge, one arm holding a rifle and the other in a sling from a wound suffered two days earlier. They were less than one hundred yards away before the Chinese spotted them and opened fire with machine guns and automatic weapons. Snow splashed heavily into the air from the enemy fire, and some GIs fell, including Schmitt, hit by a machine gun bullet. He was mortally wounded but urged the men to continue forward. The GIs hit the Chinese position with BAR fire and hand grenades and carried the attack into the emplacements, killing some of the remaining enemy in hand-to-hand fighting and chasing off the others.

"We took it and arrived at the top with 10 men and no ammunition," said Jordan. It came at a heavy cost, with nearly one-third of the men killed or seriously wounded.

Down on the road, Faith, his .45 drawn, was directing more men up the hill to join the attacks.

Private Harry Jacobs of Baker Company followed a group of a half-dozen soldiers up the hill and ran into heavy fire. "First I see two guys in front drop, and then two other guys drop, and then the guy in front of me, when he fell down, I could see a bullet hole and blood squirting about 12 inches high, like a fountain," he said. Jacobs could not see where the shots were coming from until a Chinese soldier suddenly popped out from a foxhole on the ridgeline right in front of him. Jacobs fired instinctively and dropped the man, and when a second enemy soldier rose from the hole, he shot him as well. Jacobs had scarcely absorbed this when he felt a whack in his back. He had been shot, and he fell and rolled into the hole with the two dead Chinese soldiers.

"For the life of me, I could not look at them guys," he said.

The Bigger attack carried the GIs to the top of the hill and into the middle of the Chinese positions. "The Chinese started running down the ridgeline toward the east and about a dozen of us were firing and chasing them," said White. "Even though we took great losses, I know theirs were many more."

The Chinese broke under the assault and ran down the ridge and across the saddle. "Those that did not run were quickly killed in their foxholes," said Mortrude. At least one Chinese soldier was choked to death by an enraged American. Mortrude recognized the location as the very spot on Hill 1221 his platoon had occupied when they first arrived at Chosin.

Lt. Patton, the B Battery executive officer, had started the breakout with 15 Headquarters Battery soldiers assigned to help cover the left flank. Only 4 were left by the time they reached the blown bridge, where an infantry captain ordered him to move forward through the valley below the road and then attack the roadblock. Patton assembled a new group of 15 men, most from the artillery battalion, and moved forward, taking several casualties when they were strafed by a Corsair. They made it to a ditch near the roadblock before they were pinned down by enemy fire. Patton took about 10 men up Hill 1221 to try to get around the roadblock, reaching the top after knocking out a machine gun nest with a hand grenade. They went back down the hill and rejoined the road at a position behind the roadblock. The group attempted to attack the roadblock from the rear but quickly retreated in the face of heavy fire.

Patton took stock of their situation. "Only four of us had ammunition left," he said. They decided to head south in hopes of reaching friendly lines. As they moved down the road, stragglers on the south side of Hill 1221 ran down to join them. The group soon ballooned to dozens of men, including some GIs led by Lt. Cecil Smith, the acting A Company commander, who'd come down the hill after running out of ammunition. The group was taking fire from the high ground around them, so they moved out onto the frozen reservoir, fighting off Chinese soldiers who were trying to cut them off.

Capt. John MacDonald and Capt. Lou Droste, flying an Air Force C-47 cargo plane that had just dropped off supplies along the North Korean coast for retreating ROK forces, were on their way back to their airfield in Seoul when a radio call diverted them to Hagaru-ri. Their plane was needed to evacuate casualties from the surrounded base. Though the Hagaru-ri airstrip was only 40 percent complete, an Air Force C-47 had successfully touched down on a test flight earlier that afternoon to the cheers of troops. Half an hour later, it took off, carrying out 24 casualties. The airstrip was now officially open.

Droste turned the plane inland, and within a few minutes, they had left behind the brown terrain along the coast and were flying into snow-covered mountains. MacDonald, handling the navigation, soon located the Hagaru-ri airstrip, which didn't look much bigger than a postage stamp.

Three C-47s were already on the ground, leaving room for no more, so the airstrip controller requested they circle for forty-five minutes before landing. They headed north over the Chosin Reservoir. To MacDonald, the terrain appeared so bleak and frozen that survival seemed almost impossible, irrespective of the brutal battle underway. The lake looked like "a many-armed white octopus that had dropped, frozen into stillness amid the trees and rocks," he recalled. But as they circled back to Hagaru, the pilots noticed two groups of dots on the ice, moving south.

On the ice below, Lt. Patton saw the C-47 overhead. His group was being trailed by a contingent of CCF soldiers, and Patton was unsure what direction led to safety. He and several other soldiers began stamping a message in the snow with their feet.

Up above, MacDonald saw that the men were making trails in the snow. "It looks like they're writing something, Lou," he said. "Let's go around again." They dropped to two hundred feet above the ice and slowed the plane to 110 mph. There, clearly stamped into the snow, were the words "WHICH WAY."

MacDonald tore a piece of paper out of the plane's logbook and hastily scribbled a note. He drained the water from his canteen, rolled up the note, and slipped it inside. Droste brought the plane on another run, this time fifty feet above the ice, while MacDonald went back to the cargo compartment and helped the crew chief pull out the jump door. When the plane was directly overhead, they dropped the canteen. MacDonald caught a glimpse of pale faces below turned up as it fell.

Patton fetched the canteen from the snow and read the note: "Keep to the center of the reservoir—UN Troops holding Hagaru-ri—Have requested air cover—Good luck fellows."

Hagaru, Late Friday Afternoon

Around 4:00 p.m., the 1st Marine Motor Transport Battalion command post on the northeast corner of the Hagaru perimeter was notified that pilots had spotted friendly troops on the ice, moving toward Hagaru. Shortly before dark, the unit commander, Lt. Col. Olin Beall, was called to the perimeter, where his men pointed out objects moving on the ice. Beall sent out a squad of Marines to investigate, learned they were soldiers from the 31st RCT, and set up checkpoints to guide in the men. "They were a disorganized mob, many hysterical with fright and only a few of them were armed," Beall reported.

It was Patton's group, which now numbered about 100 GIs and ROKs. The soldiers, about three-quarters of them wounded by Patton's estimate, were inside the perimeter by about 6:00 p.m. "Among them were able bodied stepping out with seeming vigor, others who were wounded and were coming along at a crawl or in whatever way they could," said Col. Bowser, Smith's chief of operations.

"I requested aid for the column which was back on the road and was told they didn't have sufficient forces to go out to help and still hold the perimeter," Patton said.

By late afternoon, the column's survival was becoming increasingly precarious. Trucks in the front had been knocked out by Chinese fire, thus blocking the road and stopping the convoy again. More precious time ticked away. "We had been stalled too long now and it was growing darker by the minute," said Robbins. "The Reds were on the hillside shooting us like ducks on a pond."

Etchemendy, the L Company commander, was wounded in the leg and put in a truck. "As trucks were knocked out, people would unload the wounded and place them in other vehicles while under fire," Etchemendy said. "This must have happened to me half a dozen times or more, and I marveled at the courage and strength of those keeping the convoy moving, one of whom was Major Storms."

Enemy mortar fire was creeping toward the truck column, including much-feared white phosphorus shells, which could burn men up in seconds. "As those mortars continued to come closer and closer I made up my mind right then and there to get the hell off that truck," said Robbins. He pulled himself up from between other wounded and dropped to the ground behind the truck, carrying a carbine with a full clip of ammunition.

Assaults were underway all around him. "Many of our guys charged up the hills trying to drive off the Chinese and get the fire off the wounded," said Robbins. He and Lt. Charles Curtis, the M Company recoilless rifle platoon leader, rallied about 20 men and launched their own assault. As he limped his way up the hill, Robbins could not see the Chinese positions above, but he felt their fire hitting all around the makeshift squad. Robbin's carbine jammed after he fired it twice, so he threw it down and took one from a dead GI. They made it to the top as darkness was falling.

PFC Lewis Shannon, the Item Company messenger, was one of those soldiers that others in the company were always glad to see. Already that afternoon, he had repeatedly dashed out into the road under heavy fire, dragging, carrying, and goading as many men as he could to safety.

PFC Floyd Scalph, Shannon's friend, found him near the roadblock and complained that his hands were frozen because he had no gloves. To prove the point, Scalph struck Shannon's helmet three times with one of his bare hands.

"It sounded exactly the same sound as metal striking metal," Shannon recalled. Shannon unbuttoned Scalph's uniform so he could place his hands close to his body for warmth and told him to keep moving his fingers.

"Are we going to get out of here?" Scalph asked.

"Stay with me," Shannon replied. "We will get out of here even if it kills us."

Sgt. Ben Dryden, the first sergeant for the 31st Heavy Mortar Company, ambled back along the column, ignoring incoming gunfire. The hard-bitten, 40-year-old NCO, known as Pappy to his men, paused to unsling his carbine and fire at enemy troops who were getting too close. At each truck, Dryden stopped to speak to the wounded, delivering a chilling message. "Column ain't going to move," he told the men in Ed Reeves's truck. "A roadblock's ahead and nothing to break it with. Ammo's gone. Most trucks won't run or the drivers are dead. Anybody who can move out better do it now." Dryden continued toward the head of the column, calmly helping soldiers where he could. Reeves tried to crawl out from his sleeping bag but passed out.

Capt. James Conner and Cpl. Tom Marker joined one of the groups fighting their way to the top, with the Episcopalian chaplain stopping to minister to wounded men on the hill. From the ridge, GIs could see the Chinese troops had reached the rear of the convoy and were running down the line of vehicles, throwing white phosphorus grenades into some of the trucks. Conner saw they had reached trucks carrying his wounded men from the 3rd Battalion. The chaplain told several soldiers he was going back to stay with the trucks and to try to stop the Chinese from killing the men. Marker watched incredulously as the chaplain turned back and "ran as a man possessed right through the Chinese lines to be with his burning men." Conner fell once, possibly shot, but got back to his feet and reached the trucks. He soon disappeared from sight.

Cpl. Donald Hamilton, the medic from C Company, had teamed up with Junior Price, a soldier also from Greene County, Indiana. They had reached the ridge when Hamilton heard a soldier below yelling for a medic. Hamilton paused momentarily and then began to head back down.

"Don't do it," Price called after him.

"I've got to," Hamilton replied. He scrambled down the hill and was gone.

PFC Doc Blohm, 31st Regiment, was in a truck, caring for wounded, when several vehicles in the rear of the column were overrun. "Chinese climbed into the trucks loaded with wounded, then shot and bayoneted helpless men," he said. "Some trucks were drenched with gasoline, the men burned alive. . . . It was murder, pure and simple."

When Chinese soldiers came to his truck, Blohm shot the first one who climbed in and, in turn, was hit with fire that broke his arm and the stock of his rifle. "It so angered me that I used my good arm to hit the next Chinese with what was left of my rifle," he said. Blohm dove over the other side of the truck and hid in nearby marsh grass.

The scene around the trucks was horrible. "Men were carrying wounded men, dragging wounded men, others crying in pain, calling for help. There was little help to be had," Blohm said. "Most were as bad off as the next. It was something to forget, but I can't." As darkness fell, Blohm took off running. He saw bullets striking all around him, but he kept going.

Two trucks carrying about 50 seriously wounded men from the 57th Field Artillery had fallen behind after crossing the blown bridge. Approaching the hairpin curve, Cpl. McMillin and other wounded men heard fighting ahead. The two trucks pulled over, and the drivers disappeared; it was unclear if they had gone to join the fight or had lost their nerve and abandoned the convoy. It was nearly dark, and the trucks were taking heavy fire from the side of the hill. McMillin got out to return fire from the ground while other wounded fired from the trucks.

With the trucks surrounded, McMillin's 1st sergeant decided to surrender in the hopes of saving the wounded, and he walked onto the road, holding up his white handkerchief. McMillin immediately dove under one of the trucks with his rifle. "I didn't want to be surrendered," he recalled. "And I crawled under and tried to get out the other side, but all that was out there was Chinese bayonets." McMillin left his rifle behind and came out.

He and 9 other soldiers who could walk were marched down the road toward the inlet. As they moved away, McMillin could hear firing coming from the direction of the trucks. "I don't know if they were shooting the wounded or not," he said. "But I figure, one way to look at it, I guess, is if they don't shoot them, they're going to freeze to death. So probably shooting was the best way to go."

It looked like it would be McMillin's turn next. He and the other prisoners had gone a short distance when they were made to kneel in a ditch. "Four or five Chinese soldiers walked up on the bank behind us with Thompson submachine guns, and we shook hands and said goodbye, because we knew we were going to get shot," said McMillin.

By dusk the air cover was thinning. Planes already overhead stayed as long as they could, but no new ones arrived. Stamford—known to the pilots by his call sign, Boyhood One-Four—had done a remarkable job all day directing strikes, even with the handicap of being the only controller for a column spread out over a mile. But as daylight waned, Stamford was having "extreme difficulty" running missions to support troops assaulting Hill 1221.

"The pilots of the aircraft were cluttering up the air with their own transmissions," Stamford complained. His transmitter was weak compared to those in the aircraft, so any pilot pushing his mike button down to talk was blocking Stamford. He was having trouble getting a word in edgewise. "A flight leader was talking to his flight about the targets he saw and wanted to hit," he said. "I was unable to run the planes that were trying to work with me."

Sam Folsom, a Corsair pilot, was horrified by what he saw happening to the convoy. "I was so close that I could look into the backs of the trucks as I flew over, and see the feet sticking out, stacked in there like cordwood," he said. Folsom fired all his ammunition and rockets at Chinese coming down the hilltop in the snow but felt it was a drop in the bucket, given the number of the enemy. He was so desperate that he briefly considered trying to cut them down with his propeller. Folsom felt helpless. "It was the most heartbreaking and frustrating few moments of my life," he said.

Two other Corsair pilots, Ed Montagne and Tom Mulvihill, dropped some rifle ammunition in canisters on the road near the trucks for the troops. "We could see the troops huddled around the vehicles and up the side of the hill, their black forms against the snow," said Montagne. GIs were clubbing Chinese off of the trucks with their rifles.

The pilots were shaken by what they saw. "We hung around until after dark, strafing and trying our best to keep the Chinese from them," said Mulvihill. "But it was all over, there was no doubt about it."

Tokyo

At MacArthur's headquarters at the Dai Ichi that evening, an air report arrived, summing up the situation east of Chosin in a few curt words: The 31st RCT was "in desperate straits."

Atop Hill 1221, Dusk

A ray of hope remained at the top of Hill 1221. At a great cost in lives, the soldiers of Task Force Faith had succeeded in clearing the Chinese off the hill.

Down below on the road, word spread that friendly troops had been spotted at the top. Wounded men were unloaded from the disabled trucks and crammed into others, and the disabled trucks pushed off the side of the road to clear the way. Around 5:00 p.m., as darkness fell, the column once again inched forward toward the roadblock.

Atop Hill 1221, Bigger organized a defense to hold the positions. Soon they could mount an attack on the rear of the roadblock below. Between the Bigger and Jordan groups, as well as other smaller bands that had made it to the top, they had a decent-sized force.

It was a moment of exhilaration. "This unplanned, unorganized, soldier-led assault will always be the highlight of my infantry career—a triumph of the individual initiative, determination, bravery and sacrifice of the American soldier," Jim Mortrude later said.

But the moment did not last long. In the dying light, Corsairs roared over the hill and strafed the men with machine gun fire and rockets, mistaking them for Chinese.

Bigger stood up, trying to wave the Corsairs off, but was nearly shot. Mortrude, who had already almost been hit by napalm and machine gun fire from Corsairs that day, now found himself on the receiving end of air-to-ground rocket fire. He and his makeshift squad jumped for cover in the captured positions and escaped injury.

Sgt. Via, following Lt. Moore, had just reached the top when the air strike hit. He dove for a hole, as shell casings clanged off his helmet. "I reached up and felt my head, not expecting to have one left," he said.

Lt. Magill of Baker Battery led a group that suffered many casualties during its fight up the hill. "As soon as we entered the Chinese trenches, an air strike came in and plastered us," Magill said. "We were worked over with rockets [and] machine gun fire. . . . The air strike finished off most of the remaining soldiers."

The friendly fire was a "disaster," said Harry Scott. "After a lot of hand-to-hand fighting we took the hill only to be shot up by our own planes."

The victims included several of the bravest officers who had kept the men moving. The greatly admired Lt. Moore, so grievously burned by napalm at the start of the breakout, was killed by the strike. Capt. Seever, the C Company commander, limping badly from his leg wound suffered four days earlier and using a stick as a cane, also died. "Only two weeks before he had learned that his wife had given birth to his first son," recalled Wes Curtis.

Most disastrously, the air strike snuffed out much of the momentum from the men's remarkable achievement in capturing Hill 1221. "At this point we lost control of those who had responded so valorously moments before," Bigger said. "Men began to stream down the west side of Hill 1221 toward the reservoir."

Bigger could only hobble after them.

Chapter 15

BREAKOUT NIGHT

Friday–Saturday, December 1–2

Don Faith was not giving up. Hill 1221 had been cleared. But the Chinese still held their strong roadblock at the hairpin curve. Conferring with Maj. Bob Jones at the head of the column, Faith devised a plan for taking out the Chinese position. Faith and Jones would separately sweep through the hillsides on both sides of the roadblock, gather as many men as possible, and then link up on the road to attack the position from behind.

Faith and Jones each made their way around the roadblock, gathering dozens of exhausted, freezing, and leaderless men—many, if not most of them, wounded. In the darkness, what little unit integrity remained had vanished, with so many officers and NCOs dead or wounded.

Faith gathered about 100 men and Jones around 200. "I met him very shortly and we formed up our men on each side of the road," said Jones. Faith got soldiers to their feet and lined them up. "There was no organization left," said Jones. "It was a question of just sheer leadership to go out and pick those people up and say, 'Okay. We're going for this.' And Faith led them. He had to."

Some soldiers refused, too far gone to respond. But many others joined in. "Those soldiers whom we were able to gather together and to whom we could explain our plan were also scared, shocked, injured and cold, but they still retained discipline, and the realization that an effort had to be made to reduce the road block so the convoy of wounded could proceed toward the Marine lines," said Jones.

Jones and his men were to attack from the east, or the right side of the road, while Faith attacked with his men from the west, or the left side of the road. Faith's route would take his team through the rougher, steeper terrain along the slope of Hill 1221. The Jones team moved quickly through the brush, firing small arms and throwing grenades in the general direction of the roadblock. "We knew the fire was down there and we silenced it," said Jones. Most of the Chinese manning the roadblock were either killed or chased off. Realizing they were being flanked, the Chinese escaped with at least one of their heavy machine guns and rushed to the ridge east of the road and Hill 1221.

Once his team had cleared the roadblock, Jones tried to find Faith in the dark, but the task force commander's group was farther back and not in view, its progress slowed by the rough terrain. Jones continued with some of the men past the roadblock and around the hairpin curve toward the column, five hundred yards down the road, where he hoped to get the trucks moving again.

The friendly fire air strikes on Hill 1221 had not chased off all the American forces atop the ridge. Some groups had escaped unscathed, including Capt. Jordan's small group. Unaware of the attack by Faith and Jones, Jordan launched his group down the hill, intending to also hit the roadblock from the rear.

Jordan only had about 10 men left, with Lt. Gray among them, and they had no ammunition. His plan was to bluff their way down the hill, crashing through the brush, trying to sound like a much bigger force than they were. "We assaulted the roadblock by yelling, shouting and making as much noise as possible," said Jordan. Not knowing that the Jones attack had already silenced the roadblock, Jordan and Gray were surprised to meet little Chinese resistance. Reaching the roadblock, Jordan and his men began removing logs to dismantle the barrier. "It was about this point that we heard a voice demand who was making all the noise," Jordan recalled.

It was Col. Faith. He was about fifty to seventy-five yards off the road, up the slope of the hill, moving with his soldiers through brush and small birch trees. The snow on the ground made it possible to make out their movement in the night. Jordan approached and could see Faith had a blanket over his shoulders. After a brief conversation, Faith continued forward with his group, evidently to make sure the hillside was clear of Chinese. Jordan returned to his men and continued dismantling the roadblock.

A few minutes later, Jordan heard a nearby explosion that sounded like a grenade, then voices speaking loudly. Capt. Stamford, who was following Faith from a distance, heard a short burst of light automatic fire interrupted by a loud report and then silence. "The quiet became eerie," said Stamford.

Jordan went over to investigate. A soldier told him that Faith had been hit and he wasn't sure if he was dead or alive. A Chinese soldier hiding in a hole in the brush had thrown a fragmentary grenade, which exploded close to Faith and badly wounded him. Lt. Fields Shelton, with the 31st Heavy Mortar Company, had been near Faith and was slightly wounded by the same grenade. Shelton tried to help Faith down to the road, but they could not make it. He wrapped Faith in a blanket and went to the truck column for help.

Aid men dispatched with a stretcher soon found Faith and carried him back to the column, a sight terribly disheartening to the men. "His being brought back to the convoy wounded had quite an effect on the survivors there," said Lt. Jim Campbell.

"My God," a soldier exclaimed.

"I saw it was Colonel Faith, and my heart sank," said Cpl. Ager.

The stretcher was initially placed atop the hood of Faith's jeep, but to keep him warm, he was soon moved into the cab of a two-and-a-half-ton truck being driven by PFC Russell Barney, with the 1st Battalion headquarters company. Sgt. Anthony Biebel, C Company, who helped place Faith in the truck, saw that he had at least three wounds from grenade fragments, "two in the side very near the heart and one in the stomach." It was clear his condition was grave.

With Faith being tended to, Jordan and his men, joined by other troops, worked to dismantle the roadblock. It was urgent to move quickly, before the Chinese could recapture the position. "When they recovered from their surprise, we knew the enemy would soon get wise to the size of our small force and the tenuous hold we had on the road, and then they would be back in strength," said Gray.

Gray volunteered to go back to the convoy and help get it moving. He stayed off the road to avoid Chinese fire but slipped on the slope of Hill 1221, sliding like a toboggan down toward the trucks and ripping open his thigh wound. "I wondered what else could go wrong," he said.

Gray cut an odd figure, with a makeshift tourniquet made from a tree branch on his leg and the holster for his .45 turned around so he could pull the pistol out with his uninjured left hand. But with so many officers dead, wounded, or missing, he filled a vacuum in leadership for the task force. "He really took over," said Ager, who was among the men who joined Gray's efforts. "He seemed to know how to give orders and get people to follow his direction."

Maj. Jones was already working with Lt. May, the motor officer, to assemble soldiers and get the trucks moving. More trucks had been disabled by enemy fire, and almost all had flat tires. Others refused to start, as they had dead batteries or were out of gas. "Many of the trucks seemed to sit like silent, eerie phantoms on the dark road," recalled Gray.

Jones instructed May to unload the wounded from one of the disabled trucks and then push it over the side of the mountain to get it out of the way. They had to do the same with a second truck, then a third. Capt. Lawrence Brunnert, the Roman Catholic 1st Battalion chaplain and a veteran of World War II, helped May oversee moving the wounded to other already-full trucks.

Cries of wounded men rang through the cold night air as exhausted work parties moved them to other trucks. "We stacked them four deep, crisscrossing them so as not to smother those on the bottom," said PFC John Williams of I Company. "We ran out of space so we stacked more wounded on the hood of the truck." Other wounded were placed atop fenders. Soldiers who had died in the trucks, of which there were many, were taken off and placed by the road to make room for more wounded.

At the rear of the convoy, Stamford worked with soldiers to unload two more disabled trucks. Injured men helped push the trucks off the road, straining so hard they tore open their wounds and bled again. Stamford crammed more wounded on the remaining trucks. Capt. Navarre, the 1st Battalion surgeon, was hit in his knee and lying in the ditch when Stamford picked him up by the seat of his pants and the back of his coat and tossed him in a truck. "There's always room for one more," the Marine captain said.

In the darkness and chaos, focused on getting the column started, Jones had not yet learned that Faith was wounded. "I didn't know then that he had become a casualty and had been put into a truck," said Jones. "I could not locate him and thus took charge of all the [troops] I could physically contact and control." When the front of the column was ready to move, Jones instructed May to assemble a fire team of 20 to 30 riflemen to move up along the road, through the hairpin curve, and make sure it was still open for the convoy. May formed two teams and placed them on both sides of the road, instructing them to hit the ground in case of ambush and then fire upon the flash of the enemy weapons. They had gone little more than one hundred yards when they came under fire from the high ground on the hill across the saddle from 1221. But the Chinese only got a short burst off from a machine gun before May's men knocked it out with rifle fire.

The front of the column began to move, though other trucks further back were still being packed with wounded. Overloaded trucks strained to make it up the steep grade, exposed to long-range fire from Chinese across the valley. Walking wounded clung to the sides of the trucks. Casualties were stacked so high on the hood of the truck PFC Williams was defending that the driver could not see, so Williams sat on the left front bumper and called out directions. Some trucks still refused to move, their engines dead or their drivers incapacitated. It was becoming obvious that it was impossible to carry all the wounded. There were many casualties still scattered along the road and others lying wounded on Hill 1221.

Jones reconsidered what to do. "By this time so many wounded were without transportation that even though the column was started many hundreds would be left where they lay," Jones later reported. He decided that the "only solution" was to leave guards with the stranded wounded men and take as many able-bodied and walking wounded as possible to try to break through to Hagaru-ri to get a rescue force sent. Brunnert, the chaplain, was among those who volunteered to stay with the wounded men along the road.

The trucks that were still operable continued around the hairpin curve. At least ten trucks had been lost by now, some overrun by the Chinese and others abandoned after the wounded had been unloaded. But some twenty to twenty-five trucks and jeeps made it around to the south side of Hill 1221—no victory, certainly, yet a testament to the resilience of many Task Force Faith soldiers despite all they had been through.

They had not gone far when the convoy came upon a new obstacle—the knocked-out Sherman tanks and the ruins of the ambushed 31st Medical Company vehicles, left behind from the vicious fighting days earlier at Hill 1221. The Chinese had added some debris to further block the road and were firing on the position from the east. The ghostly wreckage was a foreboding sign for the men in the convoy, evidence of the scale of the Chinese attack.

It was here that Jones and the main body left the truck column. About 75 to 100 soldiers would stay with the convoy to protect the trucks. Jones instructed them to try to remove the roadblock and get the convoy moving again.

Jones believed getting a rescue force offered the best chance for survival for the wounded. But it was an agonizing choice to leave the convoy, he later said. "That's sort of like deserting the wounded who needed you," Jones said. "But you knew you had to get to the enemy, and so you had to leave them and go in a roundabout way to try to get to the enemy to try and solve the problem. That's a pretty difficult decision to make."

Jones was taking about 200 men with him. Before departing, he ordered a check of ammunition. "We found only a few rounds per man, in some cases none," said May. They redistributed the bullets so that each man had four or five rounds. Jones sent Sergeant Monty Piercefield to take several soldiers and head south on the road ahead of the main body. "You're going to be my point," Jones said.

The Jones group was joined by the small band led by Maj. Robbins, who had come limping down Hill 1221. "We formed two long lines of soldiers on each side of the road and moved out quietly down the road to the south," Robbins said. Soon they were out of sight from the trucks.

Other groups of soldiers were already moving toward Hagaru. After dismantling the roadblock, Capt. Jordan and a small group of men, all of them walking wounded, moved south down the road to make sure it was open for the column. Approaching Hudong-ni, they spotted another enemy roadblock. With no ammunition to attack, Jordan sent a messenger back to the column to warn of the danger and then skirted the enemy position by moving off the road to the west. A bit further south, they came under enemy fire near the logging village of Sasu-ri, but they escaped unharmed and continued south.

After being rousted off Hill 1221 by the friendly fire, Lt. Mortrude's group consolidated at the bottom with the group led by Capt. Bigger, who was still walking with the help of his mortar-aiming stakes. As they moved across the ice, Chinese troops tried several times to intercept them. "We would drive them back by running at them with desperate shouting and shooting," said Mortrude. Eventually, they discovered a surreal scene. "We came across one wounded American soldier and one wounded and one dead Chinese, literally frozen to the ice of a watering hole," Mortrude recalled. "The American said the Chinese had shot him after initially indicating friendship as they hosted him to a drink from 'their' watering hole. He had retaliated by shooting both of them."

Unlike Jordan, Bigger, and Mortrude, some officers were doing little to help the convoy. Capt. Kitz, the K Company commander, had led a group up Hill 1221 but decided the Chinese roadblock was too large to attack. "The only thing left to do was to take off across country, which we did," Kitz said. The group headed across the reservoir ice and, by the time they reached Hagaru-ri, had swollen to 210 men, a number of them wounded.

Many GIs were moving on their own. Private Harry Jacobs, lying in the foxhole where he had been shot atop Hill 1221, felt blood running down his back and recovered his senses. "I said, 'Well, boy, this is a hell of a place to die. What do I do? I'm getting the hell out of here. Where do I go?'"

Jacobs moved warily, keeping an eye out for the Chinese soldier who had shot him, and made his way down the south slope of the hill. He rolled his way over the railroad berm running west of the road and made it to the reservoir. He began running on the ice but felt it cracking beneath his feet. Jacobs laid down, took off his helmet, filled it with water, and took a long drink, his first in days. Then he worked his way to more solid ice further offshore and kept going until he reached the shoreline at Hagaru. A Marine barked at him to halt. He was in a minefield, but he had made it.

X Corps HQ, Hamhung, 9:00 p.m.

At X Corps Headquarters, Hank Hodes received a grim telephone call at 9:15 p.m. from Maj. Lynch in Hagaru. Lynch reported that two groups of troops from the 31st RCT had reached Marine lines. Most of them were wounded, and virtually all were suffering from frostbite. One ROK walked in with one foot frozen and the other a stump. Many other wounds were just as bad. They were getting medical care, food, and shelter from the Marines. Lynch reported that a "lookout is being maintained for the remainder of the 31st RCT including motor column."

At Hodes's direction, Lynch delivered a message to General Smith's headquarters: "Gen. Hodes requested that you consider sending out an Armored-Inf Force at Daylight 2 Dec to intercept this motor Clm of the 31st Inf," the handwritten note stated.

"Use our TKs," the note added—a reference to the Army's 31st Tank Company tanks that Smith and Hodes had agreed to withdraw from Hudong-ni.

The Trestle Bridge

The troops remaining with the convoy cleared debris to create a bypass in short order, allowing the trucks to get around the tanks and destroyed vehicles. Before long, the front section of the convoy began inching past the wreckage.

At the bottom of the south slope, about a mile past the roadblock, the abbreviated convoy encountered a new obstacle: a demolished bridge over a stream. Lt. Gray and Lt. Henry Traywick, the 3rd Battalion motor officer, surveyed the scene. The stream looked too deep to ford, and it seemed likely the surface ice would crack under the weight of the trucks. This time, there was no tracked M19 to pull the trucks over. But reconnoitering further, they discovered the Chinese had left untouched a timber trestle bridge that carried the narrow-gauge railroad tracks over the stream. The trucks would have to go off the road and across a rice paddy and then up the embankment to the railroad tracks to reach the trestle bridge. The Chinese had either overlooked it or figured the bridge was too narrow to carry the trucks.

Traywick thought it might just be wide enough. They brought a two-and-a-half-ton truck down to test. It was as close as could be. From end to end, the cross ties could just carry the tire-to-tire width of the trucks. Moreover, there was no decking over the cross ties. Going very slowly in first gear, the test truck was able to bump its way across. It would be precarious, and it would have to be done painfully slowly.

Bob Jones and his group had opted not to cross the trestle bridge for fear of walking into an ambush. Following the railroad line seemed risky. "We are sitting ducks in this cut if they catch us in it," Jones told May. They decided to make a run for the darkness of the lowland along the frozen stream valley. As they crossed the ice, the men came under fire from the Chinese on the high ground but escaped injury.

They rejoined the road and continued south until they came under heavy fire from automatic weapons at a Chinese roadblock above Hudong-ni. "The column disintegrated to a certain extent, but the majority of them ran for the ice and skirted around the roadblock," recalled Jones.

Monty Piercefield and his group had already moved well down the road entirely unscathed, perhaps undetected or perhaps left alone to preserve the position of the Chinese forces waiting for the convoy. "After a bit, I turned around, it was a bright night, and hell, there was no troops behind us,"

Piercefield said. "I thought we were leading the battalion out. There was no one back there." Piercefield and his men hurriedly backtracked until catching up with a column of soldiers heading out to the ice of the Chosin Reservoir.

Capt. Stamford arrived at the trestle, leading a group of trucks from the rear of the convoy. After scouting the crossing and conferring with GIs at the scene, the captain went into a small hootch near the road to smoke a cigarette.

Several soldiers were doing the same. Stamford lit a cigarette, and the flare of the match illuminated the silver oak leaves on the collar of one of the men. It was Lt. Col. Tolly, who had assumed command of the 57th Field Artillery after Embree was evacuated. Tolly had shown little leadership up to this point, and he showed none now. "I became annoyed when none of the officers present, and particularly the lieutenant colonel, made a move to take command, even if he was an artillery officer," said Stamford.

Stamford went back outside and found the truck carrying Faith. "He could barely talk, and seemed to be in extreme pain and on the verge of losing consciousness," Stamford recalled. He asked Faith if he wanted the convoy to continue to Hagaru tonight.

Faith responded weakly but clearly: "Yes."

It was another endless and painful ordeal for the trucks to cross the trestle, but at least they were not under fire. "Wounded men inside the trucks screamed as the trucks bounced over the rough rice paddies and trestle," recalled Wes Curtis. Crosby Miller, lying on the hood of Stamford's jeep, felt fortunate to have a ride, but crossing the trestle bridge was agonizing. "Jolting over the exposed ties, coupled with wounds and cold, left me, by this time, in pretty bad shape," he said.

Sgt. Radke helped guide the trucks across. It was impossibly close, the ties not even wide enough to hold the entire tire. PFC John Williams, still sitting on the bumper of his truck, guided the driver over the trestle. "From my perch I could see the front left tire," he said. "Inch by inch, we crept across and back on the road."

Traveling on foot with the convoy, Lee Yong Kak, the assistant 1st Battalion surgeon, reached the trestle, where a soldier told him he had seen the wounded Capt. Navarre in one of the vehicles waiting to cross. Lee rushed over, opened the rear door, and found Navarre sitting amidst many wounded GIs. Despite his serious leg injury, the battalion surgeon assured Lee he was all right. "Such a gallant, sincere and hard-working man, who treats casualties ceaselessly," Lee remembered. "Now he was a wounded man himself. I wept in the dark. He was still making a big smile. He was probably trying to encourage me."

Navarre and the other wounded were thirsty, so Lee went down to the stream, broke through the ice, and brought back a canteen cup of water. It wasn't enough, so he took a GI's helmet down to the nearby reservoir, filled it with fresh snow for the men to share, and said goodbye to Navarre.

The trucks that had made it across the trestle bridge lined back up on the road, awaiting the rest. As Curtis limped along the road, a soldier stopped him and told him Faith was seated in the cab of the truck he was passing. For some reason Curtis never knew, Faith had always called him Butch. "Colonel, this is Butch," Curtis said. "How are you doing?"

Faith replied in a firm voice: "Let's get moving."

Curtis worked his way up the column. At one of the trucks, he spoke with Master Sgt. Ivan Long, intelligence sergeant for the 31st Regiment, who had been shot in the chest and arm during the fighting at the hairpin curve and briefly captured by the Chinese before escaping. Long knew the terrain well, and he told Curtis that the reservoir shore was a short distance to the west and then Hagaru not far to the south. Long suggested someone cut across the ice and tell Hodes to "bring those tanks up at daylight."

Curtis asked him why he didn't do it. "If I start walking again, I'll start bleeding again and I will never make it," Long replied.

Curtis decided he himself should try to make it to Hagaru. "No one else in the vicinity was able to walk," he said. He left the column, carrying his .45 pistol with two rounds. Curtis made it to the ice and headed south.

By around midnight, the majority of the remaining trucks had made it over the trestle bridge. As the crossing continued, the lead vehicles in the convoy began moving slowly down the road. Harvey Storms, who had continued on foot despite his serious wounds, finally agreed to get back on a truck after crossing the trestle. "He was bleeding badly and was terribly weakened so he was finally lifted to the lead truck on which I was riding," said Etchemendy. "He must have been hit several times and I remember that he was holding one bloody hand up and it looked like it had been partially shot off."

Approaching Hudong-ni, the lead elements of the convoy came to a halt when they began taking fire from high ground about two hundred yards off the road. The nose of the hill lit up with muzzle flashes. Word filtered back through the column that another roadblock lay ahead.

As one of the last trucks tried to cross the trestle bridge, its right front wheel dropped over the edge of a cross tie, leaving the truck and the wounded on board perilously hanging. Gray and Traywick worked with some soldiers to get the front end of the truck jacked up and the wheel angled back onto the tie. While the work progressed, a warning arrived from troops up the road that the lead trucks approaching Hudong-ni were taking fire from a roadblock and that enemy had been spotted moving on the hill just east of the road.

Leaving a work party to finish getting the trucks across, Gray and Traywick moved toward the sound of a heavy firefight. Gray scanned the snow-covered high ground to the left, hoping the report of enemy on the hill was a false alarm. At first, he saw nothing, but his heart sank as he spotted large groups of shadowy enemy troops moving down the hill in relays, one after another, and forming up on flat ground just east of the convoy. "I was shocked to realize how many there were," Gray said. "Their numbers appeared to be a battalion-sized force, and I knew then that this was the moment of truth, because the enemy had far more men than we had remaining ammunition rounds."

The bitter irony was that Hudong-ni was where many of the junior officers and soldiers had expected to find 31st RCT tanks and support troops. "We had hoped to link up with our regimental troops," said Gray. "With their help, we could have finally extricated all 31st RCT forces back to Hagaru-ri."

"The thing was, they weren't there," said Charlie Gebhardt. "We had expected to run into them. We could help each other to get into Hagaru."

"I thought there would be some [American troops] there, but there was nothing, nothing," said Ray Radke. "There were a lot of Chinese."

The moon was burning with unreal intensity, the brightest many GIs could ever remember seeing. The temperature, thirty below zero, remained shocking.

The column had been stopped for at least half an hour, not approaching the Chinese roadblock. The wait felt interminable to Miller, still on the jeep hood. He checked the half-dozen soldiers near him and found that only two had weapons with ammunition. Around midnight the silence was broken by two mortar rounds hitting about one hundred yards off the road. Then another two rounds hit closer in. It was probably just a matter of time before the trucks would be hit, Miller figured.

The driver of the lead truck, the heroic Sgt. Garrigus, came to Miller and asked permission to make a run for it. He had gone forward on foot one hundred yards and not seen or heard any movement. "It was a choice of the unknown against the known danger," said Miller. "I told him to move out."

Led by Garrigus, the column of trucks took off, making it unscathed about two hundred yards. But as the lead truck rounded a bend in the road near the base of a hill just north of Hudong-ni, the column was hit by a fusillade of rifle and machine gun from the hill. Garrigus was killed and his truck partly tipped over into the ditch, blocking the road. The barrage also killed the drivers of the next two trucks. "The column was stopped cold and being punished unmercifully by a hail of lead," said Miller.

Chinese troops at the roadblock fired antitank rockets into the trucks. Storms, riding in the lead truck, was killed. Etchemendy fell out of the truck and began crawling away.

Miller rolled off the hood of the jeep into the ditch, away from the hill. The two Marines in the jeep, Cpl. Myron Smith and PFC Billy Johnson, had been killed. What remained of Task Force Faith was disintegrating. "It was here . . . that the efforts of many men and officers to fight off overwhelming numbers of the enemy to get their wounded to safety finally collapsed," Miller later wrote. "It is true that some broke earlier under the pressure but many fought well up to this point. There was no doubt in my mind when the column was hit this last time that the battalion was no more and it had become a case of every man for himself."

Miller found himself next to a wounded soldier in the ditch, who began crawling away across open ground toward the shelter of the railroad berm. Silhouetted on the snow, he was shot and killed.

Miller realized that the Chinese would soon rush the convoy and that his best chance was to get clear of the trucks. His hands would freeze crawling through the snow without gloves, so he dragged himself out to the soldier who had just been shot. "I made sure he was dead, but before I could get his gloves, a burst of machine gun bullets hit all around my head," Miller said. He was not hit and pulled himself back to cover.

Miller then crawled down the ditch to the lead truck, where he found Lt. Mazzulla, a Baker Company platoon leader, sitting in the back. Mazzulla, 26, a one-time altar boy born in the Bronx and raised in Rhode Island, was a highly regarded junior officer who had graduated from Providence College and served in World War II. Mazzulla was frozen to the seat by his blood-soaked uniform, and he asked Miller to help free him. No one else alive was around. Miller could not climb into the truck because of his wounded leg and hand, but he was able to reach up and give Mazzulla his pocket knife. Mazzulla tried to free himself but could not. "He was unable to cut himself free so he handed back the knife and thanked me," said Miller. The major crawled away.

With the front of the convoy stopped, Chinese troops rushed down from the hill, blowing bugles and whistles. Troops defending the trucks were quickly overrun. "Almost everyone was out of ammo," said Sgt. J. D. Smith, D Company, who was clubbed with a rifle, stomped, and taken prisoner. A soldier on one of the trucks fired a .50-caliber machine gun at the approaching enemy, but the Chinese killed him with a grenade. Capt. Harold Hodge, the A Battery commander, died trying to protect the trucks in the back. Capt. Pop Marr, the Item Company commander, was also killed.

Hungry and freezing Chinese soldiers searched the dead and dying soldiers, taking clothes, equipment, and food and shooting or bayoneting many of those still alive. They siphoned gas from trucks and set them ablaze with wounded men in the rear.

One truck—its driver perhaps panicked or hit by fire—suddenly lurched forward, pushing a three-quarter-ton truck in front of it slowly off the road. As that truck veered right and began to overturn into the ditch, someone shouted a warning to Lt. Jim Campbell, who was in the path. He tried to scramble out of the way, escaping serious injury even though a wheel ran over his foot. The truck "tumbled down the incline and landed upside down, the wounded in it screaming in pain, throwing some of them out," said Campbell. He fired his final rounds at the approaching enemy and got away to the protection of the railroad berm. Campbell teamed up with several soldiers and moved in a crouch toward the reservoir, dragging a wounded soldier with them to the ice.

The truck carrying PFC Williams on the front bumper had sped up, following the other trucks, but upon reaching the roadblock, the driver was killed by a burst of burp gun fire. As Chinese soldiers overran the truck, Williams rolled off the road, crawled into a culvert, and made a simple prayer: "God, I have gone as far as I can go. I am turning it all over to you." Williams immediately passed out.

Following behind the rest of the column, the truck Lee Yong Kak accompanied had been racing down the road but came to a sudden halt, blocked by vehicles in front. Soldiers defending the truck fired at the Chinese on the high ground. "Almost all of us were shot down by the incomparably intensive enemy fire," said Lee. "Patients on the trucks were re-hit by enemy machine guns and hand grenades. Hell couldn't be any worse than this scene. One by one those who stood till the last fell down."

Lee was not hit. His father-in-law and cousin had been executed by the Communists after the North Korean invasion, and he made the instant decision that attempting escape was better than surrender. He crept away as carefully as he could, fearing he would be spotted in the moon's illumination, and made his way out onto the reservoir ice, using the North Star to head south.

With the front of the column in flames, the Chinese closed in on the rear of the convoy. Campbell could see white phosphorus grenades going off in a line of trucks at the rear, one after another.

Lt. Jerry McCabe was unconscious in the back of a truck when he was awakened by the coming slaughter. He heard firing and screams as Chinese troops overran the convoy. "I woke up pretty quickly," McCabe said. He slithered out the back of the truck and crawled into a ravine. He had no feeling in his frozen feet and was weak from his wounds, but he was determined to get away. "I would die before I was taken prisoner," he said. McCabe gathered several other wounded men, and they crawled away.

Seeing the truck he was guarding was about to be overrun, PFC Charles Bennett took blood from a shoulder wound he had suffered that night and smeared it on the back of his neck. He climbed onto a truck tailgate and lay himself sprawled out, his head propped on the body of a dead GI and one leg dangling over the edge. "The Chinese came by, pulled me off the tailgate, dumped me on the ground. They shot into the truck several times, then stuck me twice in the left leg with a bayonet. It took everything I had not to flinch. I knew if I did I was dead."

Sgt. Jim DeLong, K Company, had been guarding a truck of wounded since the breakout began, and now, he was the only one on the truck who still had a rifle and ammunition. He talked the situation over with some of the wounded men as the Chinese closed in. "I knew what they'd do if I opened fire," he said. "They'd massacre us." DeLong smashed his carbine on the bumper and tossed his bullets into the field. Chinese soldiers took him prisoner and made anyone who could walk get off the truck, about 10 or 15 men.

"The rest of the wounded were on the truck," DeLong said. "They got on the truck and started shooting the wounded." DeLong and the other prisoners were marched double time up the road. Then they were stopped, their hands tied behind their backs, and made to kneel in a ditch. DeLong waited for the shot.

Cpl. Anthony Mora, B Battery, was still hanging on to the back of his truck when it was hit by machine gun fire and tipped over. Mora fell clear and crawled away from the road to the railroad berm. He made it to the top and dropped to the other side, landing on his head and injuring his neck. Numb and half-paralyzed from his injuries, Mora got to his feet and ran haltingly through a rice paddy. "The machine gun was shooting at me but it kept missing me because I kept falling down," he said. At one point he looked back and saw many trucks on fire.

Sgt. Jessie Dorsey, driving a truck of wounded for D Battery, 15th AAA, had started the breakout with 15 to 20 wounded but now had 40 to 50 men in the back, many of them already dead. When the truck was overrun, Dorsey and 5 or 6 others were able to escape to the ice. The rest perished.

Lt. Lloyd Mielenz, incapacitated since his mortar injury on the second day, was in the sixth truck from the rear, which had been raked by machine gun fire that killed the driver, Sgt. Robert Cory, a 20-year-old Iowan. Mielenz, lying on the truck bed, could feel bullets hitting the side, and several nearby men fell on top of him as they were shot. Then an incendiary grenade sailed into the back of the truck, landing on top of wounded men. A GI tossed the grenade off the truck before it exploded, but it fell near the tire, below the gas tank. Mielenz could feel the truck bed getting hotter and braced for the gas tank to explode. He could not move, pinned down by the wounded men on top of him. "I thought this probably was the end," Mielenz said. The gas tank did not explode, but there was little time for relief as Chinese soldiers quickly overran the truck.

Mielenz and other wounded from the truck were rounded up and directed up the road, prodded with bayonets. As Mielenz tried to hobble on one leg, he spotted a hole in the snow. He dove in, unnoticed by his captors. It was a culvert, carrying a frozen stream beneath the road. Mielenz crawled underneath, staying quiet as a Chinese guard walked across the bridge every few minutes.

Sgt. Radke was sitting on the right front fender of one of the trucks as it went through a railroad cut approaching Hudong-ni. "The Chinese had machine guns on both sides of that cut, ripping the hell out of us again," he said. Radke rolled to his right, off the fender and into the ditch, and shot his M1 at machine gun flashes on the left, stopping its firing. "Then all of a sudden there's Chinese all over us—everywhere you go—just a mob of Chinese, and not many of them armed, or at least they didn't seem to be." Several tried to grab Radke's rifle, but he pushed them away and managed to wrestle his way to the rear of truck. He hopped on the back just as it took off. "I was holding on with one hand and firing the damn rifle with one hand and we broke through and went like a bat out of hell."

Stamford, moving on foot ahead of the truck, suddenly found himself surrounded and taken prisoner along with several GIs. They were made to lie by the road. Just then, the truck carrying Radke ran through the Chinese blockade. In the ensuing chaos, Stamford and at least one GI managed to escape. The Marine captain ran toward a line of scrub near the shore of the reservoir and began moving south toward Hagaru.

Radke's ride on the back of the truck did not last long. After racing several hundred yards past Chinese troops on the road, the truck came to another blown bridge across the Paegamni-gang, a stream near Sasu-ri, and could go no further. Chinese troops were closing in. "I fired a couple of rounds at the guys chasing us, and I just jumped off the edge of the bridge," he said. "I didn't even look to see how high it was."

Radke followed the stream bed a short distance to Sasu-ri, where he almost immediately ran into a wounded soldier, Sgt. Wayne Ruddick of Item Company, also seeking shelter in the village. The two encountered a North Korean teenage boy with whom Ruddick was able to communicate in broken Japanese. The Chinese were everywhere, the boy reported, and he took them to a nearby house that was heated in the Korean fashion, with a fire beneath the floor,. A wounded Chinese officer lay sleeping, tucked under a blanket on the floor. "It was nice and warm," said Radke. "I went over to the side of the wall and sat down and fell asleep, boom, just like that."

Lt. Gray had taken a position trying to defend the middle of the convoy with about a platoon-sized force. They fired at the approaching enemy, but with their meager numbers and firepower, their stand was woefully inadequate. Gray, his wounded and infected hand grossly swollen, could barely pull the trigger of his rifle. "We were not dropping many of them, and in my case I was simply not hitting my targets at all." They were quickly driven back to the railroad embankment, where they futilely fired at enemy soldiers moving between the trucks.

Chinese troops tossed incendiary grenades into trucks, which burst into flames, and they could hear the screams of wounded men. "Some of them managed to struggle up out of the truck beds in agony, and then fall off the back of the trucks with their clothing on fire," said Gray. "In our helplessness to save our wounded, there was an awful sense of betrayal; a terrible feeling that we had abandoned them."

Gray and the men headed to the ice.

In the back of his truck, Ed Reeves heard the driver call out a warning: "We've got company." The driver reported that the Chinese were burning trucks, and he kept up a running description as the enemy continued in their direction. Those wounded who could walk had already left the truck, but the 22 men remaining, like Reeves, were in too poor a condition to try to escape.

Before long, Chinese soldiers reached Reeves's truck, and he could hear them rattling around the gas tanks, trying to siphon fuel, but there wasn't enough left to start a fire. So 3 soldiers climbed on board and began methodically shooting everyone on board, working in Reeves's direction. The men faced their executioners stoically, none of them pleading. "I got to fight with these men, but soon we'll all be dead, and nobody will know how brave they were," Reeves thought.

When his turn arrived, Reeves said, "Jesus, here I come," he said. Reeves felt the muzzle blast but soon realized he was not dead. The shot had grazed his scalp, and the Chinese moved on to the next truck.

Maj. Miller, moving away from the trucks, encountered two GIs who joined him in crawling south in the roadside ditch. When Miller fell behind, one came back to help. "I told him to go ahead while they had a chance, and they both soon disappeared," said Miller. Eventually, he found a stick he could use as a crutch and hobbled his way across a field toward Sasu-ri. His right hand, white and hard as a rock, was frozen stiff around his crutch, and what remained of his left hand was frozen as well. At the blown-out bridge over the Paegamni-gang, he worked his way down the bank and tried to cross on the ice and rocks. He was almost over when his left foot slipped and plunged through the ice, filling his boot with freezing water. But he made it into town and found an empty house with comforters on the floor. Miller sat down, pulled out his pen knife, opened it with his teeth, cut the left boot laces, and removed his boot. He had extra socks under his shirt and got one on his left foot. By now he felt no pain, just numbness, so he pulled a comforter over himself and fell asleep.

Approaching Hagaru, Maj. Jones and his group, now numbering about 40, saw flashes of machine gun and artillery fire from the perimeter. Although worried about moving into the middle of a firefight between Chinese and Marines, they decided to move forward rather than risk being captured or freezing. Lt. May had the men disperse ten yards apart to keep from losing a large number if they came under fire. Before long, they were startled by a loud and unmistakable American voice ordering them to halt. "Boy, that was the best word I had ever heard in my life," said Hugh Robbins.

While the wounded were taken for medical care and other soldiers taken to a mess tent, Jones and May reported to the 1st Marine Division headquarters, according to a memo May later wrote. "Major Jones reported to the Marine Commander and requested a small armored task force to return for the rescue of our wounded comrades, but this was denied on the basis that all personnel were needed to protect the present Hagaru-ri perimeter," May wrote.

May was bitter. "It is my considered opinion that Army, Corps and Division had written us off and left us on our own to do the best we could with a little air support," he wrote in a 1981 letter. "This feeling was more supported when we tried to set up a rescue team at the Marine base at Hagaru-ri. The Marine general gave an emphatic no to any effort to set up such a rescue attempt."

Maj. Curtis was walking alone on the reservoir with his makeshift crutch. At one point he became completely disoriented and was unable to find his compass, but he found his direction using the North Star. Exhausted and dehydrated, he ate snow constantly but was unable to quench his thirst. Curtis moved toward the artillery fire and arrived at the perimeter around 2:00 a.m. He was taken to a Marine aid station, where a corpsman put a pressure bandage on his wounded leg.

Shortly afterward, Lt. Rolin Skilton, a liaison officer with the 31st RCT rear headquarters, arrived in a jeep. Curtis told Skilton that Faith was mortally wounded and said that he needed to see Hodes. The general was still in Hamhung, but Skilton told Curtis that Hodes was trying to organize an attack up the road at dawn.

"I told him there would be nothing left there by dawn," Curtis said.

Hagaru Northeast Perimeter, Early Saturday Morning

At the 1st Marine Motor Transport Battalion, Lt. Col. Beall had extra men on duty to watch the ice for arriving soldiers. Word was put out to exercise caution before shooting at movement. "About 0200 we heard some sounds from the ice and shot off flares, and a sight I will never forget greeted our eyes," said Tom Elliott, one of the Marines. "It seemed like hundreds of soldiers were approaching. . . . Some were carrying others, some were dragging bodies behind them, others were crawling."

Soldiers kept arriving through the night, many of them straying unknowingly into a minefield protecting the Marine perimeter. Staff Sgt. Scott was with a group that made it all the way through without tripping anything. "The Marines said it was a miracle," said Scott. "They had thought an ant wouldn't be able to get through."

Lt. Edward Smith, an officer with the Marine transport battalion, figured 200 or 300 men walked through the minefield without being blown up. He raised hell about it with the engineers. "Some minefield!" he complained. "They said it was probably the weather."

The arriving men were challenged for Marine passwords, which none of the GIs knew. "We finally convinced the Marines we were Americans by the use of a lot of filthy language such as the Chinese wouldn't have known," said PFC Tom Marker.

Jordan's group safely made it to Marine lines. "We informed them of the plight of the column and requested assistance from them," said Jordan. Every man in the group was suffering from wounds or frostbite, and they were taken to a Marine aid station.

The group led by Capt. Bigger and Lt. Mortrude arrived around 3:30 a.m. Mortrude's appearance—including the white pillow sheet on his helmet, the Chinese great coat he was wearing, and the Chinese potato masher grenades he was carrying—caused some consternation among the Marines. "They wisely insisted on divesting me of my coat and remaining grenades before escorting me to the aid station," said Mortrude.

Out on the ice, Lee Yong Kak caught sight of red machine gun tracer fire far to the south. It was a hopeful sign indicating the direction of the Marine base, but the tracers were a long way away. He was thirsty, hungry, and mostly exhausted, and began hallucinating that he was home in Seoul in a nice warm room. He fell down on the ice and was soon asleep.

Somebody shook his shoulder. "Here, wake up. Wake up!" he heard. Lee opened his eyes and saw three GIs. They helped him to his feet. "Do you know where the Marine base is?" one asked. Lee told them he did. "I was dragged by them until I got my awareness back," he recalled. After hours of walking, they reached the safety of the Marine perimeter. Lee ate two trays of hot chow and fell into a long, deep sleep.

Sgt. DeLong and his fellow captives had been kneeling in the ditch for an hour, waiting to be shot, when a Chinese officer, apparently a political commissar, came down the road holding a piece of paper and ordered that the prisoners be marched up the road north. The same thing had happened with PFC Grant McMillin, who, along with the other POWs in his group, had been spared their expected execution and instead had joined the movement north.

But the horror was by no means over. The GI in front of DeLong was limping and having trouble keeping pace. One of the Chinese guards "puts his rifle up and just blew this kid's head right off," said DeLong. "And I had to step over that kid, and I had dreams of that for years."

McMillin was luckier. With his wounded foot, he had trouble keeping up with the other 9 GIs in his group despite using a stick another prisoner had given him to use as a crutch. But every time McMillin fell behind, the guard would stop the men. "They would wait until I caught up and then keep going," said McMillin.

DeLong and McMillin were just 2 of approximately 150 31st RCT soldiers who had been taken prisoner and were being marched north in long columns.

One truck made it well past the roadblock at Hudong—the one being driven by PFC Barney. Don Faith was in the cab, "blue with cold," and either dead or dying. He had been hit again during the ride, this time with small-arms fire. With the bridge over the Paegamni-gang blown, the truck likely crossed the stream downstream, where it was broad and shallow. The truck came to a stop along the road south of Sasu-ri. Perhaps it had run out of gas or been disabled by fire, or perhaps Barney thought he would be safer out of the truck.

Faith was dead when Barney left on foot, he later reported. The truck was just a mile and a half from Hagaru, closer to reaching it than any other vehicle.

Lt. Gray's group headed west on the white ice toward the opposite shore, hoping they might find the Marines there. The group exchanged fire with pursuing Chinese, with several men killed or wounded, and they became scattered in the process. The windswept and frozen surface was slippery, and between his thigh wound, blood loss, and exhaustion, Gray kept falling, each time almost blacking out from the pain. He lost his helmet and compass.

They made it to the west shore and took cover in the brush. Gray felt too weak to continue and feared he was slowing down the progress of the men. Gray directed Cpl. Helmuth Bertram, M Company's acting reconnaissance sergeant, to lead the men south, following the shoreline. They should leave him in the brush, and he would follow later if he recovered his strength. Bertram was a large fellow who had served in World War II with the German

Wehrmacht, including at Stalingrad, and he had joined the U.S. Army seeking American citizenship.

Bertram drew himself to his full height. "Never will I leave my officer," he declared. Bertram put Gray's arm around his neck, and they began limping toward Hagaru. "I wasn't about to prefer any charges for disobedience," Gray said.

They had just reached the south end of the reservoir when a machine gun opened up on them. The men hit the ground and took cover in a small depression. Unsure whether it was a Chinese or American gun, they decided to wait until daylight before moving. When dawn finally lightened the morning, they could see tents and smoke rising from heating stoves, and then Gray spotted an American flag. "My goodness, I felt like Francis Scott Key did when he wrote the Star-Spangled Banner," Gray recalled. "Our flag was still there."

Chapter 16

THE DAY AFTER

Saturday, December 2

From inside the four-foot-wide culvert where he had hidden through the night, Lt. Lloyd Mielenz heard an American voice shouting, "Come out, they're gone." He looked out in the early morning light and could see wounded men stirring about near the wreckage of the destroyed convoy.

Along the east shore of the Chosin Reservoir, several hundred soldiers were still alive—some hiding in culverts, ditches, or brush; others, moving cautiously out on the ice, along the road, or by the shoreline, singly or in small groups. Some were still trapped in or around the trucks; many had taken shelter in huts, sheds, and barns, often with the help of courageous North Korean civilians. The Chinese had largely pulled back into the hills.

Mielenz crawled out from the culvert. Wounded men were on the frozen ground, calling for water. A ROK assigned to Mielenz's B Battery walked up and started crying when he spotted the lieutenant. The Korean soldier was barefoot, with his feet black and his toes frozen together. The Chinese had captured him and taken his boots, and he had been walking barefoot in thirty degrees below zero temperature. "Yet in his pain, he gathered firewood and water for the wounded," recalled Mielenz. "We built a fire and dragged as many of the wounded as we could near it."

But before long, the activity attracted the attention of Chinese on the hill, and they opened up with a machine gun. The wounded scattered for cover. Mielenz and 3 other wounded men started crawling toward the railroad berm, going through a culvert underneath the tracks and then onto the frozen reservoir. They had made it about three hundred yards out on the ice when Mielenz heard a bullet whizzing overhead. He looked back and saw a Chinese soldier shooting at them from the road. They crawled faster until the firing stopped. In the distance Mielenz could see C-119 cargo planes dropping loads with parachutes. He figured that was the direction to go. The men crawled south.

Ray Radke, sleeping solidly in the house in Sasu-ri where he and Sgt. Ruddick had taken shelter, woke up shortly after dawn when he was poked in the chin with a rifle held by a Chinese soldier. Radke was relieved to find he and Ruddick were being taken prisoner rather than executed. "Now if it'd been me, I would have shot me," Radke later reflected. "They were pretty damn decent, really, when you get down to it."

Radke and Ruddick were taken outside and, along with several other POWs, marched up a hill above Sasu-ri. But when the guards and prisoners were strafed by a U.S. plane, they reversed course, and the captives were taken to a farmhouse near Hudong-ni, where other prisoners were being held. A guard pushed Radke into the building, and he fell to his knees in a corner, where he spotted several cloves of garlic. Radke ate them—his first food in days.

Maj. Crosby Miller awoke at daylight when a North Korean woman and her son came into the home he had found during the night. The woman was frightened, but she dressed his finger stumps with some kind of powder, gave him some powdered milk, and hurriedly left. Before long, Miller heard shots in the village and figured the Chinese were searching houses. He had no place to hide, so he lay where he was. Two Chinese soldiers came in, one carrying a rifle and the other, a Tommy gun. "They each took a cigarette from me, laughed when I pointed out my wounds, and then left," Miller said. "Soon two more Chinese came in. They took all my cigarettes and lighter, ransacked the house and left. A third pair came in, took a can of meat and beans from my pocket, searched the house and left."

A bit later, a young GI crept in the back door. Peering outside, the two could see no more Chinese in the village, and Miller decided they should try to get away. "We got no more than two houses down the street when two Chinese appeared, shoved me in a shed and marched the soldier with me off up the road," Miller recalled. The major assumed he looked too wretched for the Chinese to bother taking him prisoner. "Unshaven, dirty, covered with blood and with frozen fingers now beginning to blister and turn black, I believe I was being left to die," Miller said. He crawled behind a wood pile in the shed and fell asleep.

At the northeast perimeter manned by the 1st Marine Motor Transport Battalion, Lt. Col. Olin Beall had a hunch—a quite accurate one, as it turned out—that there might be survivors on the ice in need of help. Beall, 52, was an old-school Marine who had enlisted in the Marine Corps in 1917, served in France, chased bandits in Haiti, and seen combat at Okinawa. "He was what you'd call an old-timer—he knew all the tricks," said his driver, PFC Ralph Milton.

Beall and Milton chopped a hole in the ice and decided it was thick enough to support a jeep. Along with Navy corpsman Oscar Biebinger, they drove up the center of the reservoir and, before long, spotted a half-dozen wounded men on the ice. When the Marines tried to drive closer, they came under Chinese sniper and automatic weapons fire, so they got out of the jeep and approached the group on foot. They were all seriously wounded men who had managed to crawl from the trucks and get to the ice. "They were out of their minds, because it was a slaughter," said Milton.

They could see many more men were out on the ice and along the shore. Beall sent the first 6 men back on Milton's jeep and ordered more vehicles brought to the perimeter.

Hagaru, 7:00 a.m. Saturday

Soon after daylight, a small Army liaison plane appeared over the Hagaru airstrip, making a spiral descent on its way to landing to avoid small-arms fire from all around the perimeter. Hank Hodes, the assistant 7th Division commander, stepped out of the plane. Two days after Dave Barr had pulled him out of Hagaru to avoid awkward command issues with Smith, Hodes had insisted on returning to see if anything could be done now to help the 31st RCT convoy. But it was soon clear it was too late.

Hodes had hoped to send the 31st Tank Company north at dawn to assist the Task Force Faith column. The 1st Marine Division had approved a limited operation. Lt. Col. Berry Anderson, the do-nothing 31st RCT rear commander, had been given the authority to make preparations but had done nothing.

Now that he was on the scene and after meeting with Smith and his staff, Hodes did not press the matter, recognizing there was no longer a column to save. "On the morning of 2 Dec it was too late to risk sacrifice of another force, if such could have been gotten together," said his operations aide, Maj. Lynch. "The stories by the survivors reported the men left with the trucks were either captured, dead or dying." Aerial reconnaissance reported many bodies scattered around the trucks.

Maj. Curtis and Capt. Bigger saw Hodes early Saturday morning, when they were brought to the airstrip to be evacuated due to their wounds. Bigger went over to speak to the general. "Hodes was sorely distressed and frustrated," recalled Bigger.

After his arrival at Hagaru, Curtis had been given morphine and fallen into a deep slumber, believing that Hodes planned to attack further up the road at daybreak. "When I saw Hodes at the airstrip the next morning, I realized the mistake I had made," Curtis later wrote. "TF Faith was indeed abandoned. No link-up effort was going to be made. I should have stayed with them." Shortly afterward, Curtis and Bigger were loaded onto a C-47 and flown out of Chosin and on to Japan.

Maj. Bob Jones and Lt. Hugh May also spoke to Hodes that morning, according to May. "Major Jones and I appealed to him the decision the Marine Commander had given us of not allowing us a task force for a rescue mission of the remainder of our column," said May. "General Hodes informed us that he had just left the Marine Commander's headquarters and that no rescue mission would be sent out."

It was too late to send tanks to rescue Task Force Faith. But it was not too late to use them to save some of the men. At 10:00 a.m., while Beall's team continued looking for men on the ice, a small force of tanks and infantry was sent up the road along the east side of the reservoir on a limited mission to rescue wounded. The 1st Marine Division headquarters instructed the force to avoid any heavy fighting that could cut the tanks off.

The force included five tanks from Dog Company of the 1st Tank Battalion, 1st Marine Division, and two platoons of infantry. Some tanks from the 31st Tank Company accompanied the patrol and helped recover about 20 wounded, according to a report from Capt. Drake, who did not accompany the mission. Drake was also directed to provide tanks to take position on the reservoir shore in support of stragglers coming over the ice.

PFC George Duncan, a Marine tanker with Dog Company, was stunned at the condition of the GIs they found, both dead and alive. "Some had weapons frozen to their hands," said Duncan. "I will never forget that day as long as I live, the frozen GI bodies, one with a Chinese sword still stuck in him."

Among the GIs they picked up was Cpl. Anthony Mora, who had made it through the night after escaping the convoy. As he and another wounded man struggled south along the road Saturday morning, they were spotted by several North Korean civilians who took them to a hut where other survivors were being collected. A GI who left the hut looking for help soon ran into several Marine tanks coming up the road, and he led them back to the village.

Mora had taken off his boots to warm his toes but could not get them back on because his feet were so swollen. A Marine picked him up and tossed him on a tank. "My feet and my hands got stuck to the tank because it was so cold," Mora recalled. The Chinese fired at the tanks as they returned to Hagaru. "The bullets were bouncing around," said Mora. "But you know, I was in another world or something. I wasn't even scared anymore."

Lt. Mortrude awoke midmorning in a Marine aid tent packed with wounded men. His head wound had been redressed, and he was given a set of crutches that he used to hobble to the mess tent. While there, he saw Maj. Jones, who told him the main body of the task force had been destroyed with heavy losses. "Hungry as I thought myself to be, I actually ate very little," said Mortrude.

A bit later, Jones mustered all the 1st Battalion troops who had made it to Hagaru thus far and were still capable of fighting. They counted about 150 enlisted men and 4 officers: Jones, May, Lt. Cecil Smith, and Capt. John Swenty, a staff officer. Faith was missing and presumed dead, and Maj. Miller, the acting battalion commander, was missing and known to be seriously wounded. Bigger had been evacuated and all the rifle company commanders were dead. Scullion, the Able Company commander, had been killed the first night, and Turner and Seever, the Baker and Charlie Companies commanders, respectively, had been killed in the fighting around Hill 1221.

The picture was similarly devastating for the 3rd Battalion. Storms was presumed dead, and Kitz was the only company commander not wounded or dead. Marr had been killed and Etchemendy and Jordan seriously wounded. Only 5 of the battalion's medics made it back to Marine lines.

The 57th Field Artillery was also decimated. Two young lieutenants who had graduated from West Point five months earlier and been assigned to the firing batteries were dead. Carter Hagler had been killed in the inlet when running a communication wire for A Battery, while Kenneth Takus, a Baker Battery forward observer, was shot in the back of the neck attacking the roadblock at the hairpin curve. Together with George Foster of C Company, burned by the napalm, three members of the West Point class of 1950 were killed at Chosin. In total, A Battery had 1 officer, 13 enlisted men, and 5 ROKs who were not killed or wounded. Only 10 of the 129 men in D Battery, 15th AAA, remained.

First Sgt. Ben Dryden did a headcount of those left from the 31st Heavy Mortar Company. "We went in with 240 men and 100 ROKs," he said. "We came out with no ROKs, one officer and 75 GIs." Capt. George Cody, the commanding officer, had been killed in action.

Hodes walked through the assembly area, where the disheveled and exhausted survivors of Task Force Faith were being counted, supplied, and organized. Tents were being erected, officers and men assembled in their respective companies, troops fed, and equipment checked. "At least each man kept his weapon," Hodes remarked. He spoke with some of the soldiers as he moved about, asking questions, getting updates about men he knew, and taking addresses to pass word to families about who had made it out.

Then Hodes addressed about 100 men and officers and "told it like it was," said Maj. Carl Witte. The Battle of Chosin was not over for them, Hodes said. His message was that "this group had a fight ahead of them and they should get organized, weapons ready and be prepared for what then seemed a rough exodus for both Army and Marines," Lynch recalled.

For some of the GIs who thought they had reached deliverance in Hagaru, the realization that their fight was not over came as a rude shock. Sgt. Clarence White of B Company was part of a group that made it to Marine lines after midnight. They had fallen asleep in a warming tent, snuggled near a stove, feeling they were finally safe. "The next morning . . . they gave us clothes, food and Tootsie Rolls and we were all in heaven!" recalled White. "Then we heard we were still surrounded. It was hard to believe at first."

9th Army Group Headquarters

On Saturday morning, Song Shilun, commander of the 9th Army Group, sent a telegram with the momentous news his superiors had been anxiously awaiting about the Army task force. "The 27th Army has completely annihilated the retreating enemy from Sinhung-ni at the Hudong-ni line, capturing 150 enemy soldiers and most trucks and vehicles," Song reported to Peng Dehuai at the Chinese People's Volunteer Force headquarters in northwest North Korea.

An ecstatic Peng replied immediately. "Congratulations to the 9th Army Group! Congratulations to the 27th Army!"

The news was quickly relayed to Mao Zedong in Beijing. Annihilation was music to his ears, and he sent celebratory telegrams to Peng and Song. "Our 9th Army Group has achieved a great victory after its engagements during the past several days," Mao declared. But he wanted more. "We need to annihilate the surrounded U.S. 1st Marine Division before the end of tomorrow night," Mao instructed Peng and Song.

The "great victory" had come at a great cost to Song's army. In destroying the 31st RCT, two divisions of the 27th Army—the 80th and 81st—had been rendered useless. By fighting to the death over the course of five days, Task Force Faith had kept the two Chinese divisions from continuing south to Hagaru, where they almost certainly would have overrun the beleaguered garrison.

The 80th Division's 239th Regiment, which had begun the battle with 3,800 men, had fewer than 600 troops remaining. The story was similar for the seven other regiments in the two divisions. Between the losses the 80th and 81st Divisions had suffered against the Army and the 79th Division against the Marines at Yudam-ni, the 27th Army had lost more than 20,000 men and was in no condition to continue fighting. The 20th Army to the west and south of Yudam-ni had also suffered serious losses and was in need of relief.

With Peng's approval, Song ordered his reserve force, the 26th Army, to move toward Chosin. But the 26th Army was at least seventy miles north of Hagaru, hardly in a position to quickly relieve the devastated divisions.

West Side Chosin Reservior, Saturday Morning

The 5th Marine Regiment was meeting heavy enemy resistance and taking many casualties Saturday morning in its drive to reach Hagaru from Yudam-ni, and Col. Litzenberg, the regimental commander, radioed division headquarters to report that the situation appeared grave. But early that morning, Lt. Col. Ray Davis and his 1st Battalion, 7th Marines, moved through the punishing cold to link up with the isolated Fox Company at Toktong Pass. The battalion then seized high ground to the east that controlled the road to Hagaru. It was a turning point in the breakout.

Hagaru, Saturday Afternoon

At 2:00 p.m., General Ned Almond departed X Corps headquarters in Hamhung in a small liaison plane, accompanied by his aide, Al Haig. Hodes had already sent word to the headquarters that the 31st RCT "was completely overrun." Landing in Hagaru a short time later, Almond went directly to a meeting with O. P. Smith.

Almond was uncharacteristically reserved, perhaps shaken by the fate of the Army task force he had sent into the Chosin Reservoir with so little preparation and support; he was likely worried whether the outcome would be the same for the 1st Marine Division. "He had very little to say about the tactical situation," Smith noted.

The Marines briefed him on what they had learned about Task Force Faith from Capt. Stamford when he reached the perimeter early that morning. The situation map in the operations center showed blue, rectangular crossed-rifle symbols representing the 1st Battalion, 32nd Infantry, and the 3rd Battalion, 31st Infantry, still positioned at the Pungnyuri inlet where the breakout had begun the morning before. Someone had used a red grease pencil to cross over both of the blue battalion symbols, adding a question mark.

Almond's visit was quick. He apparently did not speak to any of the 31st RCT survivors. Shortly after 3:00 p.m., he and Haig reboarded the plane and returned to Hamhung. Back in his headquarters, Almond sent a cable to MacArthur in Tokyo, reporting that the two Marine regiments on the west side of the Chosin Reservoir were fighting their way to Hagaru and were about seven miles away. "The situation in the Mar Div, while extremely serious, is not critical," Almond assured MacArthur.

As for the Army task force, Almond reported that the 31st RCT "was completely overrun and has lost their tactical integrity."

Beall's rescue mission continued through the day, with many wounded Army survivors on and around the reservoir. "They were scattered over the ice almost as far as I could see," said Marine Sgt. Fred Van Brunt, who joined the rescue team. "It was the most horrible sight I've ever seen. Some of them were practically dismembered." Their hands and sometimes their feet were black from frostbite. It was hard knowing where to pick up some of the men. "Some had so many wounds you could hardly touch them," said Van Brunt.

There was an unspoken arrangement with the Chinese. The Marines would not drive the jeeps too close to the shore, and when they got out, they left their weapons in the vehicles. Beall would direct those wounded who could move on their own to get on the ice and head to the jeeps. Beall and Biedinger would retrieve those who could not move and carry them. The Marines were puzzled by the willingness of the Chinese to let the wounded be collected unmolested. Perhaps it was simply pity for the wretched condition of the Army survivors. Beall saw Chinese soldiers help wounded men get down an embankment so they could get to the ice. Other wounded were given morphine and had their wounds bandaged by the Chinese before being set free. Some Chinese soldiers set GIs free in exchange for cigarettes. Milton's theory was that the Chinese did not want to waste any ammunition on anything that did not pose a threat, and the men on the ice posed no threat. In any event, there was no doubt that the Chinese spared many lives they could have taken.

Beall was also struck by the courage shown by many grievously injured GIs, who insisted that others with worse wounds be saved before them. An Army lieutenant with two terribly wounded legs scooted on the ice past Beall, pulling himself along with his hands. "He wouldn't let me help him," Beall recalled. "The dogface said, 'There's a guy out there with a belly wound who needs help more than I do.'" The lieutenant refused to get in the jeep until two men he had left at the shoreline had been rescued.

Sgt. Joe Medina, an Item Company medic, had stayed through the night, helping care for the wounded on several trucks, despite his own serious leg and arm wounds. He and other soldiers made three trips carrying wounded men from the trucks, but when Beall noticed Medina's wounds, he ordered him into one of the rescue vehicles to get treatment.

"There were many brave men here this day, men shot through the body helping a buddy, men with hands frozen helping a buddy with a broken leg, men with both legs broken dragging themselves along with their hands and elbows," Beall wrote in a report.

Beall, Milton, and the other Marines in the rescue party were among the bravest. Beall crawled within fifty yards of a Chinese machine gun to reach a GI with two broken legs. "Go back, go back they'll kill you," the wounded man yelled. Beall kept crawling and then dragged the soldier to safety, drawing no fire. The rescuers were on the reservoir all day, suffering frostbite from the strong winds blowing across the ice in the afternoon, but they persevered.

Other impromptu rescue operations were underway. Army Lt. Hodges Escue, a liaison officer for the 31st Regiment, had been helping to process the survivors as they arrived at the Marine lines when North Korean civilians handed him notes from wounded soldiers holed up in various huts on the east shore. "To whom it may concern," read one note, written on the USO stationery used by GIs to write letters home. "I'm wounded and I'm here." It included a sketch showing the location near Hudong-ni.

Escue went to work. "I talked with General Hodes and he got me a jeep and a driver," he recalled. Escue and the driver took the road north to Hudong-ni and found the men who had written notes. They drove back with wounded men piled high on the jeep.

Back at Hagaru, Escue told Hodes that he had seen many more wounded in the area who needed rescue. The general got him two Marine two-and-a-half-ton trucks, which Escue led to Sasu-ri. The Chinese displayed the same benevolence toward Escue's rescue operation that they had elsewhere. "I looked around and the Chinese were on the high ground just 150 yards away—just looking," Escue recalled. They continued into the town, going house to house, picking up all the wounded men they could find. "I was astonished that the Chinese let us out," said Escue. "We took out two full truckloads of wounded."

After he saw the condition of the men straggling in, Army Cpl. Bob Harley, a member of an X Corps provisional military police company at Hagaru, took action as well. He found a sled in the village and attached it to a jeep. Harley made many trips out on the ice, collecting all the men he could fit onto the sled and jeep and bringing them back to Hagaru.

In the afternoon an American civilian came out on the ice to join Beall and his crew. "What in the hell are you doing out here?" Beall demanded. It was Buck LeFevre, an International Red Cross field representative for the area, and he stayed out on the ice, helping stragglers coming in until he himself collapsed from cold and fatigue and had to be sent to the aid station.

By the end of the day, the volunteers brought back more than 300 men, all wounded, most of them severely—"quite a remarkable rescue operation," Smith noted.

Though he knew little about exactly what had happened to Task Force Faith, Smith was quick to judge the survivors harshly. "The story of these battalions is a pitiful one and not a credit to many of the personnel of the battalions," he recorded in his daily log. "As far as I can determine, they left their wounded to shift for themselves."

Many more lives were saved thanks to North Korean civilians who gave shelter to survivors, treated their wounds, and delivered dozens of them to Hagaru. A North Korean civilian who was serving as a counterintelligence agent for the 1st Marine Division showed up with 45 wounded and frostbitten men in oxcarts. Some GIs were hidden under rags and junk, but others rode in the open, as the Chinese did not seem to mind. A woman with a small child on her back came in leading an ox dragging a sled with 3 seriously wounded men on it.

North Korean civilian agents were circulating on the east side of the reservoir, looking for stragglers and directing them to go out on the ice of the reservoir, where they could be seen and rescued. In full view of Chinese soldiers, they delivered notes instructing the wounded where to move for rescue. The Chinese did not try to stop the GIs when they left.

Capt. Navarre, the 1st Battalion surgeon, arrived late in the day, riding in a sleigh driven by a Korean woman. Navarre had managed to crawl away when the truck he was riding in was raked by fire at the final roadblock. He had hidden in a nearby foxhole through the night and, at first light, found a pole he could use to slowly hobble away. Navarre had taken shelter in a hut for most of the day before the woman put him and two wounded GIs in the sleigh. Near the perimeter, they encountered a Marine patrol. A Marine aidman splinted Navarre's broken leg with a carbine and placed him in a jeep. After Navarre was flown out and reached a Navy hospital ship, an incredulous sailor who removed the splint asked him, "Do you know that gun was cocked and loaded?"

More survivors continued to make it into the perimeter through the afternoon and into the evening. Lt. Mielenz and his 3 wounded companions had good luck crawling across the ice. They came across four pairs of wool socks and, a bit later, a can of tuna. The supplies had apparently been dropped by a small Army liaison aircraft tracking the survivors. One of the men was having trouble crawling, so the other 3 dragged him along. In the afternoon the plane flew low overhead and dropped a note: "Hang on, help will be coming out." Before long Lt. Robert Hunt, one of Beall's rescuers, approached them on foot and carried the men one by one to his waiting jeep.

Sgt. Ayala arrived with other survivors, pulling a badly wounded soldier in a sleeping bag over the ice. Ayala had been shot in the foot on the way to Hagaru, but he barely felt it because his feet were frozen. "We was filthy dirty," said Ayala. "We had icicles coming down our nose, our eyebrows, and all around." Beall saw the group and said they were "the sorriest bunch he'd ever seen." Mielenz and Ayala were soon on evacuation flights out of Chosin.

All day, wounded soldiers and Marines were flown out from the tiny Hagaru airstrip. A steady parade of C-47s flying out of Yonpo airfield near Hungnam was landing every ten minutes or so. "Our airstrip has been like LaGuardia Airport," said Smith.

The airstrip was only 2,900 feet long, and landing planes would careen down the runway but somehow stop just in time. Most of the arriving aircraft were filled to capacity with ammunition, fuel, and other supplies, which were quickly unloaded, and the cargo space was then filled with wounded troops. The usual load for a C-47 was 27 passengers plus the crew, but the flights out of Hagaru were averaging 34 evacuees, and at least one flight carried more than 40 wounded. The takeoffs were hair-raising, as the twin engines on the C-47s strained to get enough altitude in the high terrain and cold air to clear the ridge to the south, often while taking fire from Chinese in the hills. One C-47 carrying wounded lost power on takeoff and came down hard just outside the perimeter. Troops rushed out to protect the plane and get the wounded back to safety, and miraculously, no one suffered further injury. Lt. John Gray, aboard one of the flights, heard the plane's engines straining as the plane struggled to get over the rapidly approaching hills. Gray wondered if he would have been safer staying in Hagaru. But the plane cleared the ridge with what looked to

Gray to be not more than fifty feet, and soon the engines quieted to a peaceful drone.

Upon landing at Yonpo, the wounded were triaged at an X Corps medical receiving section. Some men were sent by ambulance to nearby field hospitals; others to the Navy hospital ship USS *Consolation*, anchored in Hungnam harbor; and others loaded immediately onto waiting four-engine planes to be flown to military hospitals in Japan.

Most of the planes were C-47s from the Air Force 21st Troop Carrier Squadron, but other aircraft joined the effort, including Marine transports, small Army planes, and at least one Greek cargo plane. Lt. Ted Magill of B Battery, who had made it to the perimeter just before dawn with three other soldiers and a Chinese prisoner, found himself being loaded on a Royal Hellenic Air Force C-47 late that afternoon. As the plane climbed over the hills, it took Chinese machine gun fire, which punched holes in the starboard wing, but the plane made it safely to Yonpo.

Cpl. Mora, rushed to the airstrip after arriving in the perimeter, was loaded onto the first available aircraft—an Army L-5 artillery spotter plane. The plane putt-putted its way over the ridges with its 150-horsepower engine, buffeted by Siberian winds. Before falling asleep, Mora thought he heard bullets peppering against the wood-and-fabric fuselage. He woke up aboard the *Consolation* but thought he might be dreaming. "It was all white and just clean and beautiful," he said. Mora was wearing five sets of fatigues to keep warm, and when the nurses cut them off, pieces of shrapnel fell to the floor—all the clothing had kept them from penetrating his body.

Capt. Bill Etchemendy, the L Company commander, and Lt. Jerry McCabe of the 31st Heavy Mortar Company, both of whom crawled from the trucks at the final conflagration at Hudong-ni and made it to Hagaru, were put on flights and evacuated to Japan. So were Harry Jacobs and Harry Graham from Baker Company, as well as John Williams from Item Company, who woke up in his culvert and made it to Marine lines. Sgt. Via from Able Company was brought to the *Consolation*. Kenzo "Benny" Takatsu, the Japanese houseboy who had been smuggled aboard the troopship by Cpl. Robert Tait to accompany the 57th Field Artillery to Korea, had taken up a carbine and fought beside the artillerymen defending the convoy at Hill 1221. He was wounded in the neck by mortar fire but made it to Hagaru with a group of ROKs and was evacuated to Japan. Tait had been captured.

PFC Lewis Shannon brought in PFC Floyd Scalph, as he had promised he would. Shannon and several other GIs had formed a protective screen for a group of walking wounded who were moving painfully slowly. Scalph, with his frozen hands and the wounds on his back and feet, was soon on an evacuation flight.

Shannon found that few soldiers from I Company had made it to Hagaru unscathed. "There are only about 20 left of a company 280 strong," Shannon wrote to his mother. "They will never make medals worthy of the bravery a lot of men showed."

By the time darkness fell, 919 men had been flown out from Hagaru, the majority of them soldiers from the 31st RCT. But many of them were not alive by the time they landed. "More than a dozen men died in my arms today," Staff Sgt. James Morris, crew chief of an Air Force C-47, said after his final flight Saturday evening.

That evening, Navy Captain Eugene "Bud" Hering, the senior medical officer with the 1st Marine Division, visited O. P. Smith. "Dr. Hering was convinced that a considerable number of Army men, who were not in fact casualties, had gotten aboard outgoing planes by malingering," Smith said. Hering based this on the fact that he had started the day with 450 men in his hospitals, but by nightfall, 260 remained, even though the planes had carried out 919 men.

Though Smith did not witness this, he later speculated that many soldiers had faked injuries. "What these jokers would do, some of them might have frostbitten fingers, something like that, they would go down to the strip and get a blanket and a stretcher and then groan a bit; the corpsmen would come along and put them on a plane," Smith said.

Smith ordered a screening system established with MPs checking to make sure wounded had medical evacuation tickets before they were boarded on planes. He also summoned Lt. Col. Anderson and directed him "to try to get some semblance of control over the Army personnel straggling into the perimeter."

Doubtless, some lightly injured soldiers took advantage of the chaos to get on flights out of Chosin Reservoir. Yet the reasoning Smith and Hering used to suggest that this was a large-scale problem was flawed. Many of the hundreds of wounded men picked up on the ice that day were taken directly to the airstrip and placed on C-47 aircraft, never stopping at Hering's hospitals.

PFC Milton alone made dozens of trips from the ice to the airstrip in his jeep, usually carrying 5 or 6 wounded at a time. "Most of the time I took them right to the plane because I knew they were going to put them right on, no use clobbering the hospital with them, because the hospital had more than they could handle anyhow," Milton said in a 2022 interview. "I'd just take them right to the plane and stick them on, and then right back to the reservoir I'd go."

None of the Task Force Faith survivors he brought to the airstrip were faking injuries, Milton said. "Most of them probably didn't even live to Tokyo," he said.

By nightfall, many wounded survivors remained scattered around the reservoir, holed up in huts, hiding in brush, or working their way cautiously toward Hagaru. PFC Roy Oxenrider and John Parker, a fellow wounded soldier from Able Company who had escaped from their truck when it was overrun near the first blown bridge, had been on the move for almost twenty-four hours. Oxenrider was using a tree branch as a crutch, and Parker had no boots. Oxenrider had given him an extra pair of socks and insoles to provide a bit of protection, but by the time they reached the village of Sasu Saturday evening, Parker could no longer walk on his frozen feet. Oxenrider pushed open the door of a house and spotted the frightened faces of the elderly North Korean couple who lived there. Three other GIs, one badly wounded, were already inside. The soldiers made plans to try to reach friendly lines in the morning. Then they tried to rest for the remainder of the night.

Crosby Miller awoke to find himself being dragged outside by two Chinese soldiers, who had discovered him sleeping in the shed. They took his wallet and tore his ID card in half but gave him back his folder of family pictures. One of the soldiers put a round into the chamber of his rifle and pointed it at him. "After what seemed to be an eternity, [he] turned and walked away," said Miller. "At a temperature of at least 20° below zero, I still wiped sweat from my face."

Miller retrieved the largest piece of his ID card and then crawled to another house off the street. Inside, he found two wounded GIs hiding. Once again, he slept.

When darkness fell, Sergeant J. D. Smith and two dozen other prisoners who had been held all day in a barn hidden in the hills above Hudong-ni were taken back down a trail to the road. They were herded up and prodded north. The route took them over the ground that had been the site of so much desperate fighting—past burned trucks, destroyed weaponry, and blown bridges—to the scene of the napalm horror, then on through the Pungnyuri inlet. "We retraced our steps on the road which was still strewn with our dead, frozen in grotesque shapes, most of them shoeless, plainly visible on the snow-covered ground under bright moonlight," said Smith.

If anything, the scene in the eerie light was even more ghastly now that the fight was over. "There were still Chinese and American dead everywhere you looked—frozen corpses, some of them sitting up with their eyes open," said another captive, PFC Lawrence Bailey of C Company. "It was a terrible sight."

Part IV

The Aftermath

Chapter 17

OUT OF CHOSIN

The first reports of the shocking disaster suffered by the 7th Infantry Division at the Chosin Reservoir hit American newspapers Sunday morning, December 3. "Wounded G.I.'s Burned Alive, Bayoneted by Red Chinese," read the headline in *The Boston Globe*.

United Press reporter Charles Moore interviewed three 31st RCT survivors who had been evacuated to Hungnam. His story, published around the country, described the Chinese destruction of the truck column in horrifying detail. "They poured gasoline over the truckloads of wounded men and set them afire," PFC Jackie Brooks, a 31st Regiment rifleman, told Moore. "There must have been about 40 men in each one. . . . I could hear the men on the trucks screaming 'Help me.' I couldn't do anything." A high-ranking officer told Moore it was "a story the American people ought to know."

Newspaper headlines warned that MacArthur's forces faced a potential Dunkirk. The *New York Herald Tribune* reported the Marines and remaining Army troops would attempt "what looked like a desperate attempt at escape" to the coast. Beijing radio was reported as saying that the remaining U.S. forces at Chosin were surrounded and "complete annihilation" was just a matter of time.

Adding to the alarm in Washington, a dire cable arrived at the Pentagon Sunday from Douglas MacArthur in Tokyo, warning that annihilation was indeed possible for both the 8th Army and X Corps. MacArthur said his forces in Korea were "facing the entire Chinese nation in an undeclared war and unless some positive and immediate action is taken, hope for success cannot be justified and steady attrition leading to final destruction can reasonably be contemplated." He demanded "ground reinforcements of the greatest magnitude," as well as "political decisions and strategic plans" to meet the new realities on the ground—a pointed slap at the White House and Pentagon. "In this, time is of the essence as every hour sees the enemy power increase and ours decline. Signed MacArthur."

The Joint Chiefs of Staff convened Sunday at the Pentagon to consider how to respond to MacArthur's unnerving assessment. While his cable reported that X Corps was being withdrawn into the Hamhung area "as rapidly as possible," the chiefs worried that he was not moving with enough urgency, and they debated ordering him to get his troops to the beachhead at once. But Secretary of Defense Marshall, who believed theater commanders should have wide latitude, balked at giving such specific direction.

With Truman's approval, the Joint Chiefs sent a short message to MacArthur, emphasizing the need to save his troops. "We consider that the preservation of your forces is now the primary consideration," it read. "Consolidation of forces into beachheads is concurred in."

Gen. Matthew Ridgway, who sat in on the meeting as deputy chief of staff for operations, was frustrated at the lack of forceful action. "Why don't the Joint Chiefs send orders to MacArthur and *tell* him what to do?" Ridgway asked General Hoyt Vanderberg, the Air Force chief of staff.

Vanderberg shook his head. "What good would that do? He wouldn't obey the orders."

Given the danger that the fighting with Chinese troops could trigger a war with the Soviet Union, the Joint Chiefs also agreed that U.S. forces worldwide be placed on full alert, and they sent a message to theater commanders around the globe: "The JSC consider that the current situation in Korea has greatly increased the possibility of general war."

East of Chosin, Sunday, December 3

More than twenty-four hours after the breakup of Task Force Faith, survivors were still out on the ice, moving along the shore or hiding in huts. It was still dark when PFC Roy Oxenrider and two other walking wounded GIs took off from the house where they had taken shelter, leaving John Parker and another seriously wounded soldier behind. Before departing, Oxenrider gave Parker his .45, which had one round left, and promised they would send help if they found it. They came under fire on the road but continued unharmed. With his leg wounds, Oxenrider could only move slowly, but the other two soldiers stuck with him.

Around 10:00 a.m., as they approached the Hagaru perimeter, several Marines stood up and zeroed in on the GIs with their rifles. "My God," Oxenrider thought. "We have come this far, and now our own people are going to shoot us." Instead, the Marines came out, slung their rifles over their shoulders, and carried Oxenrider to a nearby three-quarter-ton truck. "We told them about our two other buddies in the Korean village, and they promised to go find them," said Oxenrider. They did. Oxenrider and Parker were soon on the same C-47 out of Chosin.

When he woke up Sunday morning in Sasu-ri, Maj. Crosby Miller figured he needed to get to Hagaru soon or he would be left behind. The two wounded GIs in the house opted to stay, so Miller hobbled alone down the road until he reached the hamlet of Sasu, southwest of Sasu-ri, where several villagers took him into a home, gave him coffee, and handed him a penciled note. It was one of many written by LeFevre, the Red Cross man, and given to villagers to distribute: "UN Soldiers: Every effort is being made to rescue you. If at all possible, start moving west to the center of the reservoir and then start south. Do this immediately."

One of the civilians guided Miller out of the village but disappeared when they spotted Chinese troops on a hill to the south. Miller continued until two Corsairs flew overhead. He dropped into a ditch just as the planes blasted a house behind him with .50-caliber slugs and then dropped a napalm cannister that ignited about thirty yards behind him. "Took some of the chill out of the air," Miller recalled.

He made it to the reservoir and headed south. "I tripped and fell and almost quit because the snow seemed soft and warm," he said. "I felt as though sleep was all I needed." Miller realized he was freezing to death, so he got to his feet and stumbled on. After what seemed like hours, he could see Hagaru in the distance. Then a jeep rolled up. Miller had made it.

Sgt. Charlie Gebhardt, who had made it to Hagaru with a group of soldiers after daylight on Saturday, had heard a Marine officer chastise the arriving soldiers for leaving men behind. "This bothered me," he recalled. "All that day and night." First thing Sunday morning, he approached Beall, the Marine motor battalion commander, and asked if he could use some of his trucks to search for more survivors.

"If you get some men who are nuts enough to go with you, I'll supply the trucks and drivers," Beall told him. Gebhardt went back to the assembly area and quickly recruited some GIs to go with him. "I've got a bunch of nuts that are willing to go with it," Gebhardt told Beall. They got the trucks, drove up toward Hudong-ni, and picked up every survivor they could find.

When they got back, Beall saluted the men with the highest accolade he knew: "You men are Marines." Soon afterward, Gebhardt collapsed, suffering from pneumonia and frostbite, and was evacuated to Japan.

The number of prisoners being marched up a valley, away from Chosin, with PFC Grant McMillin had swollen to about 50 men. The guards had put the captives inside a large home to spend Saturday night, and the men filled almost every square inch of the floor. McMillin slept on a ledge in the corner of the house, the only space he could find.

The prisoners had learned to be wary of aircraft, which were looking to attack Chinese forces moving toward Hagaru, so McMillin was worried when he heard a plane flying over shortly after dawn on Sunday. It dropped a bomb that missed the house by about twenty feet. "I was the closest one to it, and the blast went over me but it took the whole end of the house out and buried the guys inside," McMillin said. He stumbled to his feet and began helping to dig soldiers from the rubble. Most of the men made it out, but five were killed. They took the bodies out of the house, laid them in a ditch, and covered them with branches. Then the Chinese had them back on the march.

Further north, another group of captives was en route to a prison camp. One of the prisoners, a large American officer, was seriously wounded. It was Col. Allan Maclean, commander of the 31st Infantry Regiment. Maclean had been seriously wounded when he'd been captured after rashly running out on the ice on November 29. For several days he and other captives were marched north, but Maclean was having difficulty walking. His fellow prisoners cared for him and helped him on the march as best they could, but his condition worsened. Maclean died of his wounds on the fourth day. The task force commander was buried in a roadside grave by his men. Then they continued north.

Hagaru, Sunday Evening, December 3

The Marines had broken through Chinese lines and were moving steadily toward Hagaru. With heavy support from Marine air and artillery, Lt. Col. Ray Davis's 1st Battalion, 7th Marines, met little resistance. Song Shilun had sent the 81st Division to plug gaps, but the division, weakened by its fight with the 31st RCT, was "late in mending the broken hole of the defense positions," according to an official Chinese history.

At 7:35 p.m., Davis's battalion arrived at the northwest Hagaru perimeter. His men formed into a column as they entered, marching in cadence and singing "The Marines' Hymn." They were weary and haggard; their parkas, stained with blood and gun oil. A long column of walking wounded arrived, with more serious casualties in trucks or on stretchers lashed across the hoods of bullet-riddled jeeps. Some of the men who had been holding Hagaru wept as they watched. "Look at those bastards, those magnificent bastards," a Navy doctor kept whispering.

Elements of the 5th Regiment arrived later that evening, and the rest of the force would come in through the night and into the following day. The two Marine regiments had come out of Yudam-ni intact, and they had come in proud. It was one of the most celebrated moments in Marine Corps history, and deservedly so.

The contrast with the stragglers from Task Force Faith was inescapable. The arrival of the battered GIs into the Hagaru perimeter had created quite an impression on the Marines who witnessed it, and it was not positive. The Marines saw "the psychiatric aftermath of annihilation, consisting of haggard surviving stragglers, many reduced to subhuman status, driven primarily by the instinct for survival," Lt. John Gray later said.

Most of the Marines knew virtually nothing about what had happened to Task Force Faith. They only saw the aftermath. "Upon reaching Hagaru-ri from Yudam-ni, I heard more damn incriminating tales about the 'crappy' 7th Infantry Division," Marine Capt. George W. Howe reflected years later. Had the Marines "known the true circumstances of the ordeal of the Army troops east of Chosin, perhaps they would have been more sympathetic and have expressed empathy for soldiers in trouble."

Monday, December 4

Aviators spotted more men on the ice Monday morning. After getting the report, Beall headed out in the jeep with PFC Milton. This time the Chinese greeted them with heavy machine gun and sniper fire, but Corsairs were called in, and they were able to reach four wounded men. They had been brought to the reservoir by their Chinese captors and shot in their legs when they began walking away. Of the 4 GIs, 3 had two broken legs, and the 4th had one broken leg and one broken arm. Beall sent them back in the jeep and then moved ashore by himself to look around.

With the Corsairs still overhead, Beall felt safe. Near Hudong-ni he spotted a line of Army trucks. It was the forward section of the Task Force Faith convoy, the trucks that had been destroyed at the final roadblock approaching the village. Beall went from truck to truck, looking for anyone alive, but there were no survivors. Beall counted 300 bodies. "I went through that convoy and saw the dead in each vehicle, stretchers piled up with men frozen to death trying to pull themselves out from under another stretcher," Beall later reported. "Yes, I saw this and shall never forget it."

By midafternoon Monday the last Marine elements from Yudam-ni had reached Hagaru, having met "considerably slackened pressure" from the Chinese, according to Col. Alpha Bowser, the division's chief of operations. Smith met Monday night with his commanders, including the senior remaining Army officers, to review plans for breaking out from Hagaru. The first objective would be to reach Koto-ri, eleven miles to the south, which was still held by Puller's 1st Marine Regiment but surrounded by Chinese.

Smith had decided to wait two days, until December 6, to begin moving south. The Marines who had fought their way from Yudam-ni needed to rest, reorganize, and resupply. Hering, the chief medical officer, estimated they would need another full day to evacuate all the casualties, including the 1,500 who had been brought in by the Marines from Yudam-ni.

Waiting "was a considered risk," Smith acknowledged, as it would give the Chinese time to build up their forces. But as Smith noted, "the enemy showed no inclination to launch a strong attack." Bowser was puzzled by this, as the 5th and 7th regiments were still recovering from their ordeal and Hagaru remained vulnerable. But the "CCF appears to have missed its greatest opportunity," Bowser wrote in a subsequent report. "Seemingly they could not be regrouped to take advantage of the situation."

9th Army Group Headquarters, Monday, December 4

The 26th Army, with nearly 49,000 troops in four desperately needed divisions, was late. Song Shilun had expected his reserve force would be in place for an attack on Hagaru Sunday evening, but the divisions were too far away, and the attack had been postponed a day.

"Where is the 26th Army," Song yelled at his staff Monday. When told that most of the troops had not yet arrived at Chosin, Song flung his teacup to the ground.

The 88th Division, lacking current maps, got lost in heavy snow and fog, while the 77th Division spent a day trying to find the right route. The other two divisions were not close either. The main failure was that Song had left the 26th Army with a nearly seventy-mile march through frozen mountainous terrain to reach Chosin, "a crucial miscalculation," historian Xiaobing Li noted.

The 20th Army and the 27th Army, gravely weakened by their fights with the 31st RCT and 1st Marine Division, were in no position to launch a strong attack. Adding to Song's frustration, Mao was "extremely attentive" to Chosin, asking for updates several times on Monday alone. Mao had not yet learned of the Marine breakout and was expecting quick annihilation. He personally wrote a news release for the official state news agency, Xinhua, saying, "[The Chinese volunteer forces] have cut off and surrounded the invader 1st Marine Division and the U.S. 7th Division near Chosin Reservoir. The majority has been annihilated, and the remnant is being pursued and destroyed soon."

Hagaru, Monday Afternoon

Ned Almond made another of his near-daily fly-in visits to Hagaru on Monday, watching the ongoing evacuation operation and then meeting with Smith at his CP, where he promised "every effort within the power of X Corps and the Air Force" to assist the withdrawal from Hagaru.

Before departing, Almond asked Smith to line up with Lt. Col. Murray and Col. Litzenberg, the commanders of the 5th and 7th Regiments, respectively, as well as Beall, who had saved so many Army lives. "He came up and gave us all the Distinguished Service Cross, and he was weeping," Smith later said. "I don't know what he was weeping about, whether from the cold or from emotion or what it was."

Beall and his team were not done rescuing soldiers. He and PFC Milton, checking out a report of men on the ice, spotted people in a small flat-bottomed boat that was frozen in the ice near the reservoir shore. Milton approached cautiously on foot, wary of an ambush, and directed them to stand up with their hands in the air. They had trouble doing that. "As I got closer I could see they were Americans," Milton said. It was Cecil McMorris of B Company and Arcadio Agunod, a 44-year-old World War II veteran with the 57th Field Artillery. McMorris had suffered six bullet wounds during the breakout but crawled to the reservoir, eventually finding the boat. Agunod, also with serious leg wounds and frozen feet, had joined him. They had been hiding in the boat for several days. Milton loaded them into the jeep.

Nearby, the Marines spotted another GI on the ice. It was Ed Reeves. After surviving the executioner's shot the night the convoy was overrun, Reeves had stayed alive in his truck, thanks to the bit of warmth provided by his sleeping bag. He had played dead every time Chinese soldiers poked around the truck, looking for boots or clothing. But on Sunday several soldiers rifling through the truck discovered him alive. They pulled him out of his bag, beat him, and tossed him off the truck. After they left, Reeves crawled on his elbows and knees, crossed the railroad berm, and reached the reservoir. He had survived a night on the ice when Beall and Milton found him.

"You look like Santa Claus to me," Reeves told Beall. Milton drove them straight to the airstrip.

Hudong-ni, Monday Night, December 4

At the farmhouse near Hudong-ni where Ray Radke and Wayne Ruddick were being held, more captives had been brought in, including Lt. Col. Tolly, the acting 57th Field Artillery commander, who had been shot in the arm and captured by a Chinese patrol near the reservoir Saturday evening. Tolly had folded his collar to hide the oak leaves, trying to conceal his rank from the Chinese. The house had been strafed by American planes a couple of times, but the captives had escaped injury.

Chinese troops moving south toward Hagaru were constantly crowding into the house to warm up. Then someone would blow a whistle, and the troops would move out. Nobody paid much mind to the prisoners. Radke and Ruddick decided Monday night to take advantage of the chaos. "We thought maybe when the whistle blows, we'd move out with them, and see what happened," Radke recalled.

The next time the whistle blew, Radke, Ruddick, Tolly, and 5 others headed for the door. "We walked out with them in the dark and cold, joined the ranks, marched with them," said Radke. "I'm sure the Chinese soldiers knew it, but it was too frigging cold to cause a fuss."

After a bit the GIs peeled off from the column, cutting into a culvert running through the railroad embankment, and made it to the reservoir. It was dawn when they reached Marine lines and traipsed through the minefield. Like everyone else, they did not set off any mines. Marines called for them to halt and asked for the password. "I said, 'I don't know your damn password,'" Radke recalled. "Then they gave me a baseball question, and I didn't know shit about baseball." But eventually, the Marines were satisfied, and Radke, Ruddick, and Tolly were soon on an evacuation flight.

With survivors still turning up, Bob Jones held a fleeting hope that Faith might be found alive. Every day, he checked all the Marine aid stations, looking for Faith. "He was never brought in," Jones said.

But a day or so before the column was to pull out of Hagaru, Capt. Sterling Morgan, the 3rd Battalion surgeon, drove up the road toward Sasu-ri, accompanied by Lt. Robert Reynolds of the 32nd Heavy Mortar Company. They came by a lone Army truck and saw bodies inside. Morgan examined them in case anyone was still alive. They were all dead. One of the men, Morgan later told other officers, was Lt. Col. Don Faith.

Hagaru, Tuesday, December 5

Hagaru had become a mass of humanity by Tuesday, with the addition of nearly 8,000 Marines from Yudam-ni and preparations for the attack south in full swing. Survivors from the 31st RCT were still coming in. Almond, flying in for another visit Tuesday morning, spotted a group of 30 people on the reservoir ice with two large objects, likely sleds, making their way to Hagaru.

A wave of news correspondents arrived in the perimeter on Tuesday, having finally wrangled their way onto flights coming into Hagaru. "The correspondents almost missed the boat," Smith noted. Big names arrived, including

Homer Bigart and Marguerite Higgins of the *New York Herald Tribune*, Keyes Beech of the *Chicago Daily News*, and photographer David Douglas Duncan of *Life* magazine. There were reporters from Britain and France. A television crew filmed scenes of the aerial evacuation and interviewed Smith.

With their news stories capturing the drama of a garrison surrounded by a much larger enemy force deep in the frozen mountains of North Korea, Hagaru was becoming a household name across America. The correspondents were stunned at the condition of the gaunt-faced, exhausted, and hollow-eyed troops, their faces swollen and bloodied from the cold wind, some with hands or feet blackened from frostbite. Beech served with the Marines as a combat correspondent at Iwo Jima and Tarawa, "but at neither of these places did I see such mass suffering as I witnessed" at Chosin, he later wrote.

Now the 1st Marine Division and 31st RCT survivors were faced with fighting their way to the sea in subzero temperatures. A British correspondent asked Smith whether the movement was properly referred to as a withdrawal or a retreat. "We are not retreating, we are just attacking in a different direction," Smith replied.

One of the reporters jazzed the quote up a bit, throwing in a little profanity, which Smith was not given to using. "Retreat, hell," Smith was supposed to have barked. "We are just attacking in a different direction."

Smith seemed to have nothing but contempt for the soldiers of Task Force Faith. "I had quite a time with those Army people—they had no spirit," he later said. In his journal he complained that the soldiers did little but sit around. "They apparently considered that as far as they were concerned the war was over," Smith wrote. In fact, many 31st RCT soldiers were helping the Marines man the Hagaru perimeter, including PFC Hode Hensley and the rest of his M16 crew, who were assigned to bolster the defenses of East Hill as soon as they'd arrived. Lt. Hugh May, working to collect airdrops, was hit by mortar fire and evacuated. "Army soldiers fought and died on the Marine perimeter," Rasula noted.

By Smith's account, the 31st RCT soldiers were little more than wards of the state. "They felt it was up to us to take care of them, feed them and put up tents for them," he later said. Smith's own chief of operations, Bowser, told a different story. "By this time the Army had 4 galleys operating in the area," Bowser said in a report he made a month later. The Marines had given harbor to the Army troops as they arrived in the perimeter, he noted. "Now as the 5-7 column began folding to within the area, the Army facilities were directed toward helping the Marines," Bowser reported. The Army galleys operated twenty-four hours a day, each serving 1,000 men at every meal.

The grunts were appreciative. "I met only one authentic hero, an Army mess sergeant," Sgt. David Dowdakin, a squad leader with Davis's 1/7 Battalion, later said. When his squad made it into the perimeter, the Army cook walked up to him. "Have you and your boys had anything to eat?" the cook asked. "Go to that mess tent. We have hot food." Said Dowdakin, "This gentleman is, of course, my all-time hero. We hadn't eaten in three days."

Marine PFC Charles Carmin and his fire team were not happy when one of the 31st RCT survivors was assigned to their foxhole on the perimeter. "But we figured what the hell, a little more body heat won't hurt us, even if he is a soldier," Carmin recalled. They were even happier around midnight, when they heard footsteps crunching in the snow and discovered it was an Army cook delivering hot coffee for everyone.

The next morning, the cooks set up field stoves in the back of a truck placed near the perimeter. "We could smell the coffee and pancakes," said Carmin. "Those Army cooks were OK. After they fed their men, they just kept on cooking. They fed every Marine they could until they ran out of stuff to cook."

Of the approximately 2,800 troops from the 31st RCT who had been trapped by the Chinese east of Chosin, only 385 able-bodied soldiers remained at Hagaru to fight their way out. They joined the 325 soldiers, including Drake's 31st Tank Company, who had been safely withdrawn from Hudong-ni prior to Task Force Faith's attempted breakout.

The survivors were reorganized into a provisional 31st Regiment under Lt. Col. Anderson, the ranking officer remaining. The troops were divided into two mini battalions, each with three small rifle companies.

Maj. Bob Jones took command of the 1st Battalion, which included the remaining men from Faith's 1st Battalion, while the 3rd Battalion, including what was left of the 3rd Battalion, 31st Infantry, was commanded by Maj. Carl Witte, the 31st Regiment intelligence officer. Anderson assigned half of the remaining men in the 57th Field Artillery to the 1st Battalion and half to the 3rd Battalion.

The makeshift Army regiment numbered 490 men, including Army engineers and other soldiers from various Army units at Hagaru. It was attached to Litzenberg's 7th Marine Regiment. Drake's 31st Tank Company was kept separate from the provisional regiment and attached to the 5th Marine Regiment to help defend the rear of the column.

The provisional 31st received its mission Tuesday evening. The 7th Marine Regiment would lead the way out, with its 2nd Battalion at the point. Davis's 1st Battalion would be on the right flank. Litzenberg assigned the provisional 31st to guard the left flank, moving on the high ground to the east of the road.

It was surprising that the Army unit was being given such a critical and difficult task. The provisional 31st was a shell of its former self, having suffered roughly 85 percent casualties, including the bulk of their officers and NCOs. It was much weaker than the Marine battalions—less than half the size, with no organic supporting arms and no forward observers to guide fire. Many of the remaining troops were clerks, artillerymen, or ROKs, jumbled together in makeshift units with men they did not know. Moreover, the left flank was generally on the uphill side of the road, over difficult, steep, frozen terrain.

"After Anderson had a meeting with the Marines and told me what the mission was, I was incredulous," Witte said. "Why did they give the rough terrain to the 31st? Why no supporting fires?" Litzenberg's regiment had suffered many casualties at Yudam-ni and on the way back to Hagaru, but he may not have fully recognized how weak the remaining 31st RCT was.

Lt. Rasula learned he would be commanding one of the rifle companies, mostly made up of survivors from the 57th Field Artillery, including some ROKs. His three infantry platoon commanders were all artillery officers. There was no weapons platoon, except for one .30-caliber machine gun that did not work. They had no mortars. "Other than M-1 rifles and carbines, that was it," said Rasula. When he asked about communications, he learned he had one backpack-mounted SCR-300 radio with a sketchy battery.

Even among the 385 Task Force Faith survivors still able to fight, many had wounds or frostbite. Staff Sgt. Harry Scott, who had been wounded by a grenade and had frozen feet, was tagged for evacuation but got his back up when he overheard another sergeant making a snide remark. "So I decided to stay and fight," he said. "Big mistake on my part."

SFC Bill Donovan, the L Company weapons platoon sergeant, was among the last men to make it back to Hagaru. Donovan had been shot in the stomach while leading an assault up Hill 1221 and suffered a concussion from the friendly air strike. Both his eyes had bled from the concussion, and he could barely see. He had frostbite as well, as he had given his knit cap and gloves to a mortally wounded soldier. "He wanted to die with his hands warm," Donovan recalled. He and two other wounded GIs from L Company had taken shelter in a hut and were hidden from the Chinese by the residents. Donovan wrote a note describing their location, which the civilians then delivered to Hagaru. LeFevre, the Red Cross man, arranged for them to be brought in by ox sled.

Once in the perimeter, Donovan was rushed to the airstrip to catch one of the final planes out. There was only time to give him some pain medication before the C-47 took off. "I remember the guy giving me two shots in the leg and looking at me and shaking his head like, I don't think you're going to make it," Donovan said.

The last flight took off from the Hagaru airstrip around 6:00 p.m. Tuesday. In all, about 3,150 Marines and 1,050 Army soldiers had been evacuated.

9th Army Headquarters, Tuesday, December 5

By Tuesday evening, only two of the four 26th Army divisions had arrived, and Song's long-planned attack was once more postponed until the following day. The 20th and 27th armies would therefore need to remain in contact with U.S. forces, but they could scarcely do so in their weakened condition. The 27th Army could only provide 2,000 men of the 50,000 troops available before their fight with the 31st RCT and 1st Marine Division. Capt. Wang Xuedong had only 18 men left in his 58th Division company near Hagaru and had to combine with two other companies to make one complete unit. The troops had nearly exhausted their ammunition and food.

Wednesday Morning, December 6

The night passed with no attacks on Hagaru, other than by an Air Force B-26 bomber, which mistakenly dropped six five-hundred-pound bombs inside the perimeter, miraculously injuring no one. The breakout from Hagaru kicked off at 5:00 a.m. with the 7th Marine Regiment leading a column of 10,000 men, including more than 9,000 Marines, 818 Army soldiers, and 125 Royal Marines. The provisional 31st was on the left flank.

The attack down the road was met with heavy Chinese fire on the left flank. The movement paused while the Marines hit the Chinese positions with mortars and napalm. When the firing ceased, Witte sent Rasula's I Company around the left flank, and an assault platoon of artillerymen rushed into Chinese fire. "Within moments after the assault began the Chinese began coming out of their foxholes with hands raised in surrender," Rasula said. Four of his men had been wounded.

But resistance soon stiffened. While Rasula's men turned 115 prisoners over to Marine MPs, Maj. Witte sent L Company, under Lt. Robert Boyer, forward to attack a fire block. "Much of the action was on the left flank and it was over high, rough, frozen ground," said Witte. "The left flank was fought over and secured by unsupported Army riflemen." Boyer was killed leading the attack, and Lt. Skilton, commanding one of the platoons, took two slugs to the stomach while checking on a wounded man. "The boys who carried him to the ambulance say he looked pretty bad," Rasula reported.

Toward evening, as Witte and several soldiers passed a farmhouse thought to be occupied by civilians, a flurry of grenades came flying out. Witte and the men knocked down a wooden door and killed a half-dozen Chinese soldiers in a furious firefight. But Witte was wounded by a grenade, and his radio operator was killed. "The cold weather kept me from bleeding to death," said Witte, who struggled forward on foot but was unable to continue command. In just a short time, the already skeletal battalion leadership had been gutted.

The 1st Battalion under Bob Jones took over the 3rd Battalion's position and attacked a roadblock that was holding up the column. Able Company, under Lt. Smith, and Charlie Company, under Lt. Barnes, overran a machine gun nest, suffering more casualties but enabling the column to move forward. By nightfall Litzenberg replaced the weakened provisional 31st on the left flank with his 3rd Battalion.

It had been a mistake to assign such an important assignment to the battered provisional 31st. To make matters worse, many of the Army radios had stopped working in the cold. The single radio in Rasula's company lasted long enough to receive one message before dying by noon. Anderson told Litzenberg's executive officer that "he had lost control of his battalion, that he had no communications with any of the units."

Drake's 31st Tank Company, attached to the Marine 5th Regiment, remained in Hagaru most of Wednesday as part of the rear guard for the column. Marine units moved all day through the tanks' position astride the road leading to Koto-ri, and it was dark before the final convoys cleared the area. "Then, as we anticipated, all hell broke loose," Drake recalled. The 26th Army finally launched its attack on Hagaru Wednesday evening, and though late, it was fierce. Many 5th Regiment Marines considered the attack more ferocious than what they had seen at Yudam-ni. "Never before had they seen the Chinese come on in such numbers or return to the attack with such persistence," the official Marine Corps history reported. So much enemy fire came in that Drake was able to read his map by the light of the tracers. But the Chinese were unable to stop the rear guard from escaping. "Thank God, most of the CCF paused to plunder the booty left behind at Hagaru-ri or the outcome might have been far different!" Drake recalled.

For the Chinese, moving into Hagaru was a disappointment. Wang's men had hoped to find supplies and food, he said, "but they burned everything."

By early Thursday morning, December 7, the lead elements of the column had reached Koto-ri. The 31st RCT was at long last linked up with the 2nd Battalion, 31st Infantry, which had never made it to Chosin. The 2nd Battalion troops could scarcely recognize the 31st RCT survivors, who came in wearing a hodgepodge of outer garments picked out of Marine supply dumps to replace the bloodied and torn uniforms in which they had arrived in Hagaru. "Some seemed to be in shock even though they continued to walk," said PFC Norman Deptula. There was little talk of what had transpired over the past ten days. Reidy, the 2nd Battalion commander, "seemed to avoid conversation," Rasula noted. Most of the men collapsed for some sleep in the 2nd Battalion tents while the rest of the column continued to fight its way during the day into the Koto-ri perimeter. Witte was put on an evacuation flight from the Koto-ri airstrip.

Once the entire force had safely arrived in Koto-ri, there was growing confidence that the Chinese would not be able to stop the withdrawal. By joining up with Puller's regiment and other units at Koto-ri, the force had grown to 14,000 men. "Day-by-day it became more obvious the Chinese did not have the capability of stopping this breakout," said Rasula. "Mass was on our side."

But a major obstacle remained: The Chinese had blown a critical bridge in the Funchilin Pass. This left a twenty-four-foot-wide gap on the precarious stretch where the road ran along a nearly sheer cliff as it crossed four enormous pipes carrying water down from the Chosin Reservoir. Lt. Col. John Partridge, commander of the 1st Marine Division's engineer battalion, was unfazed. After making an aerial reconnaissance, Partridge proposed that the Air Force airdrop Treadway bridge sections that could be used to span the gap. By good fortune, the Army happened to have two Brockway trucks from the 58th Engineer Battalion at Koto-ri that could carry the bridge sections and erect them at the site. The 2,500-pound bridge sections were dropped into the Koto-ri perimeter on Thursday.

Marine Corps Headquarters, Arlington, Virginia, Thursday Afternoon, December 7

Maj. Gen. Merwin H. Silverthorn, assistant commandant of the Marine Corps, was ecstatic Thursday afternoon when the tickertape at headquarters spit out a wire story with a quote attributed to O. P. Smith: "Retreat, hell," he exclaimed. "We are just attacking in a different direction."

As the smallest military service, the Marine Corps had learned that savvy public relations could pay big dividends, particularly with a president in office who was skeptical of a push to have the Marines represented on the Joint Chiefs of Staff. "The Marine Corps is the Navy's police force and as long as I am President that is what it will remain," Truman had told a congressman a few months earlier. "They have a propaganda machine that is almost equal to Stalin's."

Silverthorn immediately gave orders to the Marine public information office to spread Smith's quote far and wide. He dashed off a note to Smith. "I am sure the press of the United States will recognize that as a quotation which will rank high with expressions of commanders of the past," Silverthorn wrote. "It is the best quote to come out of the Korean war to date."

Indeed, "Retreat, hell" was quickly picked up by radio broadcasts and newspapers across the land, with Smith reported to have variously "growled" or "snorted" the expression. It did not matter that Smith had not actually said those words. "It was simply not in character to describe our situation in those terms," Smith later said.

Chosin had the potential to become an iconic moment in Marine Corps history, just as Marines raising the American flag atop Mount Surabachi on Iwo Jima had five years earlier. "The raising of that flag on Suribachi means a Marine Corps for the next 500 years," Secretary of the Navy James Forrestal had said when he witnessed the moment from a landing craft.

The nation was getting a sense that another epic military campaign was underway at Chosin Reservoir—a Marine Corps epic. After the initial stories about the destruction of the Army units east of Chosin, almost all the coverage now focused on the 1st Marine Division's fight to reach the sea. "If you have a father, brother, or son in the 1st Marine Division," columnist Walter Winchell said in his weekly radio broadcast heard around the nation, "pray for him tonight."

La Feria, Texas, Thursday, December 7

It had taken a week for Helen Storms to find the strength to pick up her pen and write to Harvey.

> *My Precious Husband,*
>
> *Somewhere, I feel, you are still living, still breathing, still wanting to be here with us, and still holding tightly to your faith in God's power to keep and protect you for the life that you so desire to live. For days I have failed to write you. I have not failed to think of you, cry for you, and pray for you. But to write you—well, my heart was too sorrowful, too broken and too worried to do that. . . .*

Christmas was approaching, her mother was in the hospital for abdominal surgery, and the baby was due in weeks. None of that seemed to matter compared to the news from Chosin.

> *I have been able to do nothing except listen and dial [the] radio to catch every word that passes over the air about you and your whereabouts. I'll never know it all but oh, I pray that you will live to be with us again.*

Koto-ri, Friday, December 8

The 7th Marine Regiment led the way out of Koto-ri Friday morning in a heavy swirling snowstorm, with the provisional 31st RCT again on the left flank. The weather was worsening. Thick fog and snow covered the town and surrounding peaks, which meant no air support.

As the column continued to move out from Koto-ri, a mass grave was being dug. A Marine bulldozer scraped the frozen ground of an artillery command post to make it large enough to hold the bodies of 117 men, about 100 of them Marines and the rest, Army soldiers and Royal Marines. Their numbers included Lt. Boyer and Lt. Skilton, who had died from his wounds. Trucks brought the frozen bodies over to the hole. A handful of journalists and officers, including Smith, attended a brief service. The Marines were wrapped in ponchos, and some of the British commandos wore berets. "They were laid beside men of the 7th Infantry Division in a kind of final fraternity," Maggie Higgins wrote. "The chaplain spoke the psalm, 'The Lord is my shepherd,' but the tobogganing wind swept away his words." When the service ended, the bulldozer pushed a mound of frozen earth over the bodies. The column continued its slow push out of Koto-ri and into the treacherous Funchilin Pass.

The casualties from combat and frostbite had further shrunk the provisional 31st, which was so small now that the two battalions were relabeled as companies, one under Capt. Rasula and the other under Capt. Kitz. Anderson, perhaps recognizing his limits as a combat commander, spent most of his time bundled up in a jeep. He turned over immediate command of the provisional 31st to Maj. Jones.

The Army soldiers launched an attack in a blinding snowstorm midafternoon on Friday against Chinese positions on the high ground of Hill 1457 overlooking Funchilin Pass. Three artillerymen were hit in the close-in fighting, and one was killed. Together with the Marine battalion on their left flank, the provisional 31st cleared the hill.

Down on the road, Maj. Marty Hoehn, the 3rd Battalion chaplain, came upon a tank that was slowly sliding sideways on the ice toward the edge of the road and a sheer drop of several hundred feet. With no officers around, the crew looking helpless, and the column behind them blocked, Hoehn sprang into action, as was his wont. He instructed men to pour gasoline onto the ice near the tracks and ignite it. The ice melted, the tank inched forward, and the column was soon again underway.

The night of December 8 was likely the coldest of the entire campaign, reaching an "unbelievably low" forty-five degrees below zero, according to the

Chinese military history. Several hundred Chinese soldiers waiting south of Koto-ri froze to death in their thin uniforms.

The provisional 31st stayed in position on the cold high ground all night Friday. The next morning, they moved south to high ground overlooking the blown bridge. The soldiers watched from the side of the mountain as the engineers put the sections of the Treadway bridge in place. Late Saturday afternoon, December 9, the bridge was completed. The first vehicles began to cross at 6:00 p.m.

The provisional 31st remained on the mountain, guarding the flank, as the vehicles below crossed all night. Soldiers would rotate coming down off the mountain to warm up a bit and get food. "I found a seat in [the] front of a jeep," recalled Sgt. Clarence White. "No one liked to ride or drive because of sniper fire. They were the first to get hit. I didn't care if I got hit. I was that tired and cold."

Lt. Col. Robert Taplett, commander of the 3rd Battalion, 5th Marine Regiment, believed some of the Army troops were abandoning their position on the mountain and confronted Anderson about it. Anderson said the men needed a break from the cold. Taplett called him a son of a bitch. "I don't want troops as lousy as yours out there on our flank," Taplett told him. "We'll take care of it."

The Marines were scathing in their criticism of the provisional 31st. "They were pitiful," said Smith. Oddly, the one person Smith thought did a good job was Anderson, whom he described as "a pretty good fellow; he tried to get them under control and get them back."

Capt. William Hopkins, a company commander with the Marine battalion at Chinhung-ni, shared the low opinion of the Army soldiers. But he changed his mind years later, when he learned what had happened to the 31st RCT prior to the march out of Chosin. "It is a tribute to these survivors that they participated in the remainder of the fighting against the Chinese," he said.

Sunday, December 10

At 7:30 a.m. on Sunday, the 7th Marine Regiment started down the pass and across the bridge, with the provisional 31st following directly behind. There was little Chinese resistance en route to the bottom of the pass, where troops from the Army's 3rd Infantry Division had been sent north to relieve the Marine garrison at Chinhung-ni.

Smith had contempt as well for the 3rd Division troops who had come to help. "My goodness, what a bunch of tramps," he later said. "They had one regiment of Puerto Ricans, they had black battalions in each of the other regiments—oh, it was a mess!" Smith was particularly annoyed at suggestions that the 3rd Division had come to the Marines' rescue.

It was Sunday night when the provisional 31st reached the friendly lines at Chinhung-ni. "I'll never forget when I saw the insignia of the 3rd Division soldiers holding open the lines for us to get in," remembered White. "What a happy moment."

The arriving Army troops mounted trucks that were waiting just inside the perimeter. Within an hour, the trucks got rolling and didn't stop until they reached the 7th Division assembly area at Hamhung about midnight. "They really took care of us when we got in—hot chow right off the bat and then a sack in a warm room, WONDERFUL!" Rasula wrote to another officer. "But there was one thing that hit me the next day—that feeling of not being in the same outfit—too many strange faces, which reminded us that we had lost a lot of good friends."

Monday, December 11

The final troops and vehicles crossed the bridge in the Funchilin Pass early Monday morning, and at 2:00 a.m., Marine engineers blew it up. Song Shi-lun and his commanders were dumbfounded at the engineering feat, having expected the column would be held up in the pass long enough for Chinese troops to regroup and attack again. "It provided the only passage to American marines from death hell to living world," the Chinese military history noted.

Yonpo Airfield, Monday, December 11

With the safe arrival of the column into the Hamhung beachhead, MacArthur and his senior staff, including Pinky Wright and Maj. Gen. Doyle Hickey, the acting chief of staff, flew into Yonpo Airfield. X Corps had established a twenty-mile-long, semicircular defensive perimeter encompassing the city of Hamhung and the port of Hungnam. It was manned by the 3rd Infantry, the ROK I Corps, and 7th Division troops from units that had not been at Chosin.

Initial plans for X Corps to remain over the winter at the Hungnam beachhead had been scrapped. In keeping with the preferences of the Joint Chiefs, MacArthur had decided to evacuate Almond's force by sea and join it up with the 8th Army along a united front in South Korea. MacArthur met with Almond and his staff in the pilot briefing room to review plans for evacuating X Corps from Hungnam by ship. Almond basked in MacArthur's praise. "He was most cordial and he praised the 'Brilliant operations of the X Corps,'" Almond reported to Margaret. "He was almost lyrical and it pleased me to have the staff, as well as Hickey and Wright, hear him say so."

MacArthur then met privately with Almond and told him he was recommending him for promotion to lieutenant general. MacArthur asked Almond whether he wanted to return to Tokyo to resume his position as chief of staff or remain in command of X Corps—with the caveat that if he did, Almond would no longer report directly to MacArthur. X Corps would be placed under the command of Johnnie Walker, the 8th Army commander. It was a tacit admission that having X Corps as a separate command had been a disaster. Nonetheless, Almond quickly decided to stay with X Corps. Relinquishing command and leaving Korea would doubtlessly be seen as a rebuke for Chosin.

Upon his return to Tokyo, MacArthur wasted no time declaring victory. "This enemy plan has failed," he said in a statement. "All our units are intact and the losses inflicted on the enemy have been staggering." In his original draft, MacArthur wrote, "The suggestion widely broadcast that the command has suffered a rout or debacle is pure nonsense." But that line was not included in the version approved by the Pentagon. Perhaps the claim was seen as a stretch. It was hard to disguise that MacArthur's venture to the Yalu had ended in disaster. China had entered the war decisively, UN forces were retreating back to the south, and hopes of a unified Korea were shattered.

The Chinese offensive against the 8th Army in the west and X Corps at Chosin had irrevocably broken the spell of MacArthur's omniscience. Secretary of State Dean Acheson would call it "the greatest defeat of American arms since the Second Battle of Bull Run." Though MacArthur would claim that his drive to the Yalu had been a reconnaissance in force meant to discover Chinese intentions and that they had been "forced prematurely" to launch their offensive, his credibility at the White House and Pentagon had sunk. Public support for the war had plummeted. "When MacArthur underestimated the enemy and showed his military fallibility, the world was shocked and angry," wrote Maggie Higgins. "He had broken his legend, and the world could not forgive him for being human after all."

Hamhung, Tuesday, December 12

Musters of the 31st RCT survivors conducted at Hamhung showed that most of the companies had suffered roughly 85 percent casualties. There had been further whittling of the number in the retreat from Hagaru. For the entire 1st Battalion, Jones counted 47 enlisted GIs, 7 ROKs, and 3 officers, including himself, who'd made it to Hamhung.

Jones went to the 7th Division headquarters Tuesday morning to meet with Gen. Barr. "Knowing his close relationship with LTC Faith, I felt that he would want to know everything that had happened during the Chosin operation, and particularly what happened to LTC Faith," Jones recalled.

It was the first substantial report Barr had received about the destruction of Task Force Faith. Jones described Faith's actions during the breakout and the sketchy details he knew about his death. "[Barr] asked me what decoration I thought Col. Faith deserved," Jones said. "There was only one—The Congressional Medal of Honor." Barr told Jones to get the paperwork started for the award. Then the general wrote a letter to Faith's wife, Barbara, in Louisiana. Her husband and his men had faced "insurmountable odds estimated at two divisions," Barr told her.

Barr had been powerless to stop Almond's reckless demand to rush the 31st RCT to Chosin, but he doubtless felt guilt for his ineffective efforts to get any help for the task force. "Dave Barr was practically in tears over this," recalled Col. Herbert Powell, the 17th Regiment commander. "I don't think he ever got over this."

According to Maj. Hoehn, one of the 7th Division chaplains went to the general's office "and called him every kind of a son-of-a-bitch for bringing us into such a mess."

Hungnam, Tuesday Evening, December 12

Ned Almond called together his three division commanders—Smith, Barr, and Maj. Gen. Robert Soule, commander of the 3rd Division—ostensibly for a briefing on the plans for the evacuation from North Korea, but really so they could attend a dinner party celebrating Almond's 58th birthday at his relocated command post in Hungnam. Delicacies, including a cake baked by his wife, Margaret, had been flown in from Tokyo.

Almond's chief of staff, Gen. Ruffner, "gave a short eulogy of General Almond, and stated, in effect, that never in the history of the Army had a

Corps in such a short period of time done so much," Smith recalled. Lieutenant General Lem Shepherd, commander of Fleet Marine Force, Pacific, who attended VMI with Almond, chimed in with his own complimentary remarks.

Almond was delighted with the tributes. "It has been a wonderful day for me," he wrote that evening to Margaret. "We had a fine dinner, nice speeches about me and the X Corps and all topped off by your cake which was one of the best anyone has ever cooked. The candles set it off!"

Almond seemed to have convinced himself that the drive to the Yalu had been a success. He told Margaret that X Corps operations in the past month were "nearly as spectacular as the Inchon Landing, though not so popular a subject just at present."

In letters to friends, Almond admitted things had not worked out quite as he hoped. Still, he had no trouble absolving himself and MacArthur of any responsibility. "It is a great disappointment to me, of course, having reached the Yalu on my left and to be within 50 miles of Vladivostok on the right, to have suddenly to retire," he wrote in one letter. "There is no one to blame, of course, for the turn of events except the dominating Soviet influence." Almond expressed relief to be out of "this cesspool of humanity centered around Chosin Reservoir [and] those cursed mountains." The 1st Marine Division would recover rapidly, he predicted, but added, "Combat Teams of the 7th Division must be rebuilt, practically en toto. In spite of this local difficulty the Corps has performed magnificently and the spirit, courage and resolution of the commanders and their troops are without parallel in my experience."

The original plan for the sea evacuation from Hungnam was to have the 1st Marine Division stay to defend the final beachhead and be the last X Corps division to evacuate. Smith did not like that idea. "We had taken all the casualties of the X Corps," Smith later said. "The 7th Division, outside of the two battalions that got messed up at the reservoir, had had no casualties." It was a strange thing to say, as both divisions had suffered heavily at Chosin. The 31st RCT had lost more than 1,000 killed, missing, or captured and about 1,500 wounded. The Marines had suffered about 750 dead, nearly 200 missing, and 3,000 wounded. Almond agreed the Marines should leave first, and Smith's division began loading onto ships on Monday, December 11, and finished on December 13.

On Wednesday, the same day the Marines finished shipping out, the remnants of the 31st RCT assembled on the Hungnam beach. "The survivors of the Chosin experience had only individual weapons, sleeping bags and the clothes on their back," said Jones.

They waded into the surf and onto landing craft, which took them out to the USS *General George M. Randall*. It was the same troopship that had carried many of them to Inchon three months earlier, which now seemed like a lifetime ago. Just climbing up the rope landing net to board the ship was a struggle for some, weakened as they were from the Chosin ordeal.

"Rumors had it that we were headed for Japan, but no soap," Rasula wrote in a letter. The ship was heading to Pusan, South Korea, where they were to go by rail to assembly areas for reorganization, rest, and training to return to combat.

As the *Randall* set sail, Rasula stood at the rail on the deck and looked at the snow-covered mountains of North Korea in the distance, thinking of the many who were never coming out "and wondering what happened, and why."

On December 15, acting on orders from Peng Dehuai, the 9th Army Group formally ended its offensive in northeast North Korea. Like MacArthur, Peng Dehuai declared victory. "You have fought against enemy forces for over half a month under the extremely difficult conditions of ice, snow and shortage of food and ammunition," he said in a cable to the 9th Army Group command. Peng claimed they had succeeded in "defeating the U.S. 1st Marine Division and 7th Division."

On one score, Peng was certainly correct: "The Korea war situation has been fundamentally reversed," he said. The Chinese offensive had made a mockery of MacArthur's drive to the Yalu and his prediction that the troops would be home by Christmas. Mao cabled his congratulations to Peng and Song Shilun: "Under extremely difficult conditions, the 9th Army Group has accomplished its gigantic strategic task." Even Stalin weighed in with what the Chinese military history termed "very rare warm congratulations" in a telegram to Mao.

But Peng was "extremely heavy in heart" at the casualties reported by the 9th Army Group. It lost more than 48,000 men, nearly one-third of its total force, including more than 19,000 combat casualties and nearly 29,000 to severe frostbite. Song's three armies would effectively be out of the war for months. The 27th Army took more than 20,000 casualties during five days of fighting, from November 27 to December 1, and none of its regiments would be able to fight again for at least six months.

Even the hard-hearted Mao, not known for shedding tears at loss of life, was taken aback at the numbers. "After reading the combat report of the east front, I am deeply saddened," he told Peng and Song. "The casualties exceeded 40,000 men. . . . What a painful lesson! A huge blow to our combat effectiveness."

Mao suggested bringing the 9th back to China to recuperate and reorganize, but Song and Peng successfully argued that trying to move so many wounded through the harsh North Korean terrain and winter would be a nightmare and that they were better off remaining around Hungnam until spring. "The entire 9th Army Group became a giant field hospital for its wounded," recalled Capt. Wang.

HUNGNAM, DECEMBER 24

By Christmas Eve the evacuation of X Corps from North Korea was nearly complete. The spent Chinese forces made no real effort to attack the perimeter. Some 105,000 American and ROK troops, 17,500 vehicles, and 350,000 tons of cargo were carried out on 109 ships, with some making several trips. The success of the evacuation represented a measure of redemption for Almond, not that he thought he needed it.

The ships also sailed with 100,000 North Korean civilian refugees. Almond had approved the recommendations of his staff to evacuate civilians, including those who had worked for the Americans and Christians targeted by the communists. Many other refugees who made it to Hungnam and desperately crowded onto beaches were evacuated as well. One ship, the *Meredith Victory*, carried out 14,000 refugees alone. Sadly, their numbers included few if any of the civilians who helped the Task Force Faith survivors on the east side of Chosin and the Marines at Hagaru-ri. The blowing of the bridge in the Funchilin Pass had left most of them stranded.

After the last ships had been loaded, Almond asked Lt. Haig what had happened to the mosaic bathtub they had built for the general's villa in Hungnam. Haig replied that it had been left untouched. "What the hell is wrong with you, Haig?" Almond thundered. "Go back and blow it up—no damn

Russian is going to use my bathtub." Haig wearily went back to the villa and dropped a thermite grenade into the tub.

At 2:00 p.m. on December 24, as Almond and other senior officers watched from the deck of the USS *Mount McKinley*, engineers triggered spectacular explosions—including from four hundred tons of dynamite and two hundred drums of gasoline left behind—that sent the entire port sky high. An accompanying massive barrage of naval gunfire completed the destruction of the Hungnam port. "Nothing has been left to the enemy," Almond cabled to MacArthur. Then he went to his cabin and fell into a dead sleep.

Truman cabled his personal thanks to MacArthur, Almond, and Admiral Joy, the naval forces commander: "This saving of our men in this isolated beachhead is the best Christmas present I have had."

Across the United States, the families of the more than 1,000 dead or missing soldiers of the 31st RCT received dreadful news.

Barbara Faith was staying with her parents in Alexandria, Louisiana, when she was notified that Don Faith was missing in action. "All those nights I sat up with Barbara at my house in order that she might talk out some of her grief and frustration," a family friend, Susie Moseley, later recalled. "How I did suffer with her and how much I wanted to ease some of her pain!"

Barbara took her 4-year-old daughter Bobbie for a drive and told her that her father was not coming home. Barbara was not sure her daughter would understand what that meant, but Bobbie did. "She just had to pull the car over because I was terribly upset," Bobbie remembered.

Some weeks later, an Army captain and sergeant who had been with Faith at Chosin came to the house to tell Barbara Faith what they knew. "She was told of his heroism, that he saw every man, both whole and wounded, on trucks while he commanded their withdrawal," Moseley recalled. "They were caught in a situation with all odds against them, and there was Paddy, giving what was reported to have been brilliant and fearless leadership." The two soldiers were angry that no column had been sent from Hagaru to help the task force.

At the Storms family farmhouse in La Feria, Texas, Sam Storms was washing dishes and his mother Helen was preparing lunch when they heard a knock at the door. He trailed behind his mother, still pregnant with his youngest brother, as she opened the door to two men in Army uniforms. They handed over a telegram and apologized. Maj. Harvey Storms was reported missing in action.

Helen Storms thanked them, went back into the kitchen, opened the refrigerator door, and stared inside. "Sammy, I don't know what we are going to do, but God is going to take care of us," she told him.

It was close to Christmas at the French home in Childress, Texas, when Myrtle French received a telegram. She was expecting word that Huey French was on his way home, as she had been assured when she had reported to authorities that he was only 15 years old. Instead, the telegram reported that he was missing in action. "It ate at her the rest of her life, and she never got over it," recalled Huey's twin sister, Joan.

In San Juan, Puerto Rico, where Capt. James Conner had served on the staff of the Episcopal Cathedral of St. John the Baptist before becoming an Army chaplain, his wife, Bernice, was notified just before Christmas that her husband was missing in action. She waited until after Christmas to tell their three young children. Chaplain Hoehn wrote her a letter suggesting there was little chance Conner had survived and that "he was fortunate to have probably died," he recalled. Hoehn thought the blunt letter would help her move on. He seemed surprised to learn that it instead "shook her up."

In Smithsburg, Maryland, Roy DeLauter received a telegram reporting that his son, Cpl. Roy DeLauter, D Company, 32nd Infantry, was missing in action. The next day, a second telegram arrived, saying that his 17-year-old son Boyd DeLauter had been wounded elsewhere in Korea. The senior DeLauter, a 43-year-old veteran of World War II, went straight to the Army recruiting office at City Hall. "I'm going back into the Army if they'll take me and avenge what the Reds have done to my two sons," he said. "My job as a carpenter foreman doesn't mean anything now."

PFC Harry Jacobs woke up in a hospital bed in Osaka. The soldier in the bed next to him was covered head to toe with shrapnel wounds. "What outfit you with?" Jacobs asked.

"2nd Division," the soldier answered. It was an 8th Army unit badly mauled by the Chinese in the west.

"My brother's in there, Sergeant James Jacobs," Jacobs said.

"He got killed," the soldier said.

Jacobs asked the nurse for stationery, an envelope, and a stamp. He wrote a letter to his mother and father in Wilkes-Barre, Pennsylvania.

In Kirkwood, Missouri, Mrs. John Moore, the mother of Lt. Henry Moore, terribly burned by the napalm strike and killed by the friendly fire air strike atop Hill 1221, learned only that her son was dead. "To you he was only another man that lost his life defending his country, but to me, his mother, and to his Dad, our first born is gone, our circle at home is forever broken," she wrote to Almond.

She pleaded for any information about how her son was killed and if his body was buried. "I have read in the papers about some of the wounded being burnt alive on trucks," she wrote. "Was Hank one of those? Is that why we have not received his personal belongings?"

Almond could offer little except to say that perhaps future Red Cross negotiations could lead to the recovery of his body. "I pray that your son may be among those found and returned for burial," he wrote.

In Old Saybrook, Connecticut, Barbara Skilton received a letter written on December 5 by her husband, Lt. Roland Skilton, letting her know he was safe in Hagaru. Then she received a telegram reporting he went missing in action on December 6. Skilton's men contacted her to tell him he had been wounded on the way to Koto-ri and that they had carried him and placed him in a Marine ambulance. "He was thought to have been evacuated but there isn't a record of him at any hospital," she wrote in a letter to O. P. Smith, seeking help. Smith wrote back a sympathetic note but suggested her information might be erroneous. "Are you sure of the authenticity of the report that your husband, after being wounded, was placed in a vehicle?" he asked. "The Division had a record of the dead and the wounded who were brought into Koto-ri. Manifestly, if the Division reports that it has no record of your husband, he was not brought into Koto-ri." It would be many months before Barbara learned that her wounded husband was indeed brought into Koto-ri but had died and was buried there in the mass grave.

In Johnston, Rhode Island, Jennie Mazzulla took up a pen and wrote a letter to Gen. Almond. She had not heard anything from her son, Lt. Anthony Mazzulla of B Company, 32nd Infantry, since November 10. "He is a good soldier and fought in World War Two at the age of eighteen," she wrote. "His conduct is beyond reproach. I know he would write to me if he could."

Almond gave the letter to his staff for a response, but they could give him no information. "There are no survivors in B Company of the 32nd Infantry Regiment present for duty able to furnish additional details regarding the disappearance of Lt. Mazzulla," Colonel R. H. Harrison, Almond's personnel chief, reported back. "Nearly the entire Company was either KIA, WIA and evacuated or MIA."

Maj. Crosby Miller, lying in serious condition in an Army hospital in Japan, knew the answer, but no one asked him, perhaps fortunately. Jennie Mazzulla did not learn that her son had been frozen in his own blood in the back of a truck, unable to cut himself free.

CHAPTER 18

THE SHAME AND GLORY

MASAN, KOREA, JANUARY 14, 1951

BARELY A MONTH AFTER CHOSIN, HOLLYWOOD WAS COURTING THE MARINE Corps. "Among my other concerns, I am now getting involved in the movies," O. P. Smith wrote to his wife, Esther, from the 1st Marine Division's new headquarters in South Korea.

Smith had received a message with the news that day from Gen. Cates, the Marine Corps commandant: "Warner Brothers Studio plan production of a feature picture based on Marines' break-out from Changjin Reservoir, tentatively entitled 'Retreat, hell!' Title extracted from your now famous quoted statement, 'Retreat, hell, we're just attacking in a different direction.' Request you forward this headquarters your exact statement on this epic occasion."

Smith was still not exactly sure what he had said or to whom he'd said it. But he told Cates it was a reasonable summary of the situation and his frame of mind at Chosin.

According to press reports, John Wayne was expected to get the lead role. That news upset Hollywood director John Ford, who was in Korea working on a documentary for the U.S. Navy about the war. Ford went to see Smith to protest. "He says John Wayne is under contract to him," Smith wrote Esther. Smith told Ford he knew nothing other than the news clippings he had been sent.

Smith was dubious about the whole movie idea. "There is a dramatic story to be told, but Hollywood is incapable of telling it," he told Esther. But the commandant's office enthusiastically supported the movie, and it was full steam ahead.

"Retreat, hell!" had already entered the pantheon of famous quotes by American commanders, rivaling those from past wars: Oliver Hazard Perry declaring, "We have met the enemy and they are ours," after his victory on Lake Erie during the War of 1812; Admiral David Farragut exclaiming, "Damn the torpedoes, full speed ahead!" at the Battle of Mobile Bay in the Civil War; and "Nuts," General Anthony McAuliffe's one-word reply to a German demand for surrender at the Battle of the Bulge.

The 1st Marine Division's withdrawal from Chosin was being rightly celebrated as a remarkable accomplishment. *Time* magazine (which reported that Smith "snapped" his famous line) called Chosin "a battle unparalleled in U.S. military history. It had some aspects of Bataan, some of Anzio, some of Dunkirk, some of Valley Forge, some of the 'Retreat of the 10,000' (401–400 B.C.) as described in Xenophon's *Anabasis*."

Press reports credited the Marine performance at Chosin with bolstering efforts in Congress to expand the Marine Corps and give the commandant a seat on the Joint Chiefs of Staff. Even Harry Truman, the Marine skeptic, shook his head in admiration. "Those Marines have old Xenophon beat a mile," he said. "There's only one man, no two, that I've ever read about who could do as well and I mean Stonewall Jackson and Robert E. Lee."

Life magazine had published David Douglas Duncan's pictures of the breakout from Chosin—some of the finest and most memorable war photographs ever taken, capturing the harrowing march through the Funchilin Pass, the exhaustion in the men's faces, and the cruel toll of the frozen world. Duncan had trained his lens almost exclusively on Marines rather than the Army troops in the column. That was understandable since the Marines dominated the breakout and Duncan was a former Marine. But it was easy for the public to forget the Army had even been at Chosin.

Family expecting the 31st RCT soldiers would return home after the Chosin ordeal were disappointed. Gen. Matthew Ridgway, the new commander of the 8th Army, was planning a counteroffensive against the Chinese, and the battalions that had fought at Chosin would be needed.

Ridgway had taken command of the 8th Army after Gen. Walker was killed on December 23, when the jeep in which he was riding—being driven far too fast, as Walker always demanded—collided with a South Korean weapons carrier. Ridgway kept Ned Almond in command of X Corps, considering him a fighter, but he made it clear the Corps would be under the 8th Army's control. In keeping with Smith's wishes, the 1st Marine Division was no longer part of X Corps. At Almond's insistence, Dave Barr was replaced as commander of the 7th Division in late January.

In the midst of his work to revive the 8th Army, Ridgway took time to write several letters to Barbara Faith, mourning the loss of his longtime aide during World War II. He reported to her in late January that some task force survivors had said if Faith had lived, he would have led all his men to safety. It was "the ultimate in trust and admiration" that any leader could hope to obtain, he wrote. In another note, Ridgway told her not to save the bottle of Napoleon cognac that he and Faith had hoped to drink together one day, as they had often done in quiet moments during World War II. "I believe I could not swallow for the memories that would flood over me," he wrote.

At the headquarters of the 1st Battalion, 32nd Infantry, in a schoolhouse south of Taegu, Maj. Bob Jones and a skeleton staff were trying to put "a shattered unit" back together. They were starting almost from scratch, procuring jeeps, uniforms, weapons, and rations just so they could function. Sister battalions from the 32nd Regiment began sending officers and men to fill out the decimated 1st Battalion companies. "We gradually got our mail, but there was an awful lot of mail addressed to people that weren't there," said Jones. The tasks kept Jones and the men busy, but there was a hollow feeling. "How do you adjust to seeing 10, 15, 20, 25 and 50 of your friends—personal friends, lost in a war?" he asked.

One loss in particular stung. "I have lost many friends and acquaintances in both wars, but I am sincere when I say that I have never felt a loss so keenly—and that feeling is not felt by me alone, I assure you—he had a battalion that felt the same way," Jones wrote to Barbara Faith.

Gradually, some old familiar faces were released from hospitals and returned to the 1st Battalion. After recovering from head and leg wounds for two months in the hospital, Lt. Jim Mortrude was sent back to the 32nd as an assistant operations officer in February, just as a daughter was born to him back home in Seattle. Capt. Erwin Bigger, who'd suffered multiple wounds and nearly lost his eye, returned to the regiment to command the heavy mortar company. Maj. Wes Curtis came back after six weeks in the hospital. Lt. Hugh May recovered from his mortar wounds and returned to the battalion. Monty

Piercefield, who had marched out of Chosin as part of the provisional 31st, was soon commissioned as an officer. But many others faced long recoveries. Roy Oxenrider was flown to the United States and spent nine months at Percy Jones Army Hospital in Battle Creek, Michigan, where many of the worst frostbite cases were treated.

The 3rd Battalion, 31st Infantry, and the 57th Field Artillery faced their own struggles to rebuild. Lt. Col. Reilly, grievously wounded the first night at the inlet and evacuated by helicopter, had recovered from his injuries but did not return to command the 3rd Battalion; he was assigned instead to a staff job in Tokyo. "He never got over the fact that he had to leave his men, and of course when he saw what happened after he left them, that was really devastating," said Jerry Francois's wife, Dawn. Lt. Col. Ray Embree, also evacuated from the inlet, was still hospitalized in Japan and faced a yearlong recovery. "He was very proud of the way the 57th FA Battalion had performed but quite sad about the very heavy casualties," recalled Lt. Ted Magill, who was also recuperating from his wounds but would soon rejoin the battalion.

Lt. John Gray spent more than two months at the 155th Army Station Hospital in Yokohama, undergoing multiple operations and seventy-two shots of penicillin for his infected thigh wound, nearly losing his leg to gangrene. Painful frostbite on his cheeks, nose, and ears made it difficult to fall asleep, and when he did drop off, the popping of cables in a nearby elevator shaft and thumping of ward doors closing made for fitful dreams of being back at Chosin.

Though Gray's wounds remained tender and pink, he received an expedited discharge from the hospital in late January. Combat arms officers were desperately needed for Ridgway's planned counteroffensive. Gray was sent back to the 31st Regiment, where he was greeted with a bear hug from the M Company commander, Capt. Earle Jordan, who'd also recently returned from hospitalization. Only 7 men out of the 53 in Gray's old mortar platoon remained.

Staff Sgt. Harry Scott, who had volunteered to march out of Chosin with the provisional 31st—even though he had been tagged for evacuation from Hagaru-ri—spent eight weeks recovering from his wounds at a hospital in Japan and then rejoined the 3rd Battalion. Three surviving squad leaders from the destroyed 31st Intelligence and Reconnaissance Platoon—Sam Muncy,

John Q. Adams, and Richard Cooper—recovered from their wounds in Army hospitals and rejoined the platoon.

After four months in a hospital in Japan and almost losing his hands and feet from frostbite, Robert Ayala was sent back to Battery D, 15th AAA, and made a squad leader on an M19. "There was no one from the old outfit," he recalled. "I thought I was the only survivor." After five months in the hospital, Bob Hammond made it back to A Battery of the 57th and found it full of strangers, with no one from his platoon and just a dozen of the original men in the entire battery.

By the time Ridgway's first counteroffensive, dubbed Operation Killer, was launched on February 21 against Chinese and North Korean forces in South Korea, the battalions that had made up the 31st RCT at Chosin had rejoined the fight. Ridgway "has completely changed things in the Eighth Army," Jones wrote to Barbara Faith on March 14. "Two months ago we were all ready to quit, but now confidence has been regained, morale is high, and, in my humble opinion, this war is being fought the way it should be."

The horrors of Chosin had not ended for approximately 150 31st RCT soldiers who had been captured during the battle. Many of them were marched north and west every night for eighteen days. "I carried one guy for 50 miles," said Jim DeLong. "Died on my back, just froze to death." Many more died along the way before they arrived at their first prison camp, near Kanggye. The Chinese turned them over to North Koreans, and their treatment grew worse.

Soon after they arrived, Grant McMillin and Jerry Francois helped several other POWs trying to amputate the frozen and gangrenous legs of PFC Tully Cox, a 17-year-old from Alabama, who had been shot in both legs while defending the convoy. Two GIs tried to saw off his legs with a rusty pair of scissors they found in their hut but gave up, exhausted, after an hour. McMillin picked up the scissors and finished the job, then tore up his shirt to bandage Cox's feet. Cox survived, but many others did not. Men died almost every day from starvation, cold, dysentery, diseases, and untreated wounds. The GIs took to calling the place Death Valley. By spring half of them were gone.

On February 5, the military newspaper *Stars and Stripes* published a commendation issued by Almond saluting the "gallant and heroic actions" of the 31st RCT at Chosin Reservoir. "With an undaunted spirit and the will to win, these men fought ceaselessly in the face of overwhelming forces, sub-zero weather and rugged mountainous terrain," Almond stated. "Although isolated and cut off from normal logistical support, and suffering cruel losses, they regrouped and reorganized successfully on the east side of Chosin Reservoir."

O. P. Smith was incensed when he read Almond's praise in the newspaper, offended by the suggestion that the task force had fought its way back to Hagaru-ri. Smith wrote a confidential letter on February 10 to Gen. Silverthorn, the Marine Corps deputy commandant, accusing Almond of a "lack of integrity" for distorting facts "to cover up poor performance on the part of one of his units. . . . Even the enlisted men who were at Hagaru-ri recognized this story for what it is and their feeling is one of disgust. . . . It may be that initially those battalions of the 31st and 32d Infantry fought gallantly, but we know that after their breakup they straggled into Hagaru-ri over a period of three or four days with no semblance of organization," Smith wrote. "We know also the able-bodied men came in first."

While heaping much disdain on the stragglers, Smith admitted he knew little about the events that led to the destruction of the 31st RCT. "I have never found out exactly what happened," he wrote Marine Commandant Cates on December 17. Nor did he make much of an effort to find out, even though the 31st RCT was under his command when it was destroyed.

Reviewing Smith's comments years later, George Rasula was struck by Smith's lack of curiosity about the destruction of the task force. "It's difficult to understand how a division commander could ignore an attached infantry regiment, and then after the regiment is destroyed by the enemy while part of his command, not ask 'What happened and why?'" Rasula said.

Smith's judgment of the 31st RCT was largely colored by what he'd seen and heard about the survivors who'd made it to Hagaru-ri, and he was strongly influenced by Beall's unsparing criticism of Army officers who had come in ahead of the wounded. The volatile Beall wrote a statement saying that some of the wounded rescued by the Marines said that "they had been left to die" by their officers. "I can honestly state here that that is my opinion too and I will further state that it is the opinion of the undersigned that these so called officers are yellow and unfit to be officers, incompetent and a damn disgrace to our American boys whose lives and safety are placed in their charge," Beall wrote.

By Beall's account, the 31st RCT was "an outfit whose officers cry, 'Each man for himself, get out the best way you can,' or officers who send them down a road straight into Chinese ambush, then flee across the ice of the reservoir and come in crying, "We've been through hell, we are the sole survivors of our units."' Beall's harsh words were probably justified for some officers and men who had left the convoy early and arrived first in Hagaru. But they painted a distorted picture that unfairly tarnished the great majority of officers, many of whom fought to the death trying to get the wounded men out.

Navy Lieutenant Commander Otto Sporrer shared Smith's contempt for the 31st RCT. Sporrer, 38, had served as a Catholic chaplain with the 1st Marine Division at Chosin. Originally from Buffalo, New York, Sporrer had been ordained in Los Angeles and served as a Navy chaplain in World War II. He was highly regarded by the Marines, and he had been awarded the Silver Star for leading a litter party of Korean civilians who brought in wounded Marines while under fire in August. Sporrer had been at Yudam-ni when the Chinese had launched their attack, and he had given last rites to dying Marines.

Sporrer had a reputation for being single-minded and "somewhat of a crusader." He resented that an Army general had sent the Marines so far inland, considering it a misuse of an amphibious force. He chafed at seeing the luxury that had prevailed at Almond's headquarters. After making it back to Hagaru-ri with the Marines from Yudam-ni, Sporrer boiled over with indignation at what he saw and heard about the 31st RCT.

In late January, soon after returning home to California to take up a new assignment as a chaplain at the San Diego Naval Hospital, Sporrer wrote a lengthy letter to an unknown recipient, saying that he wanted "to bring attention to the sad and deplorable deficiencies which exist in the United States Army." The letter was soon shared with *Fortnight*, a biweekly California newsmagazine founded by Oliver Keep, a Marine Corps veteran with aspirations of creating the *Time* of the West coast. On February 19, the magazine published Sporrer's dispatch, attributing it to an anonymous "fighting man."

Sporrer's letter lambasted the Army officer corps in Korea, calling it "riddled with incompetency" and "corrupted with a luxurious love of the comforts of life." The Army units were peopled by malcontents who had not been properly toughened and had no will to fight.

"To indicate this spirit of selfishness and cowardice, let me narrate a little incident that occurred . . . when the 31st Regiment was attacked by the Chinese on Nov. 28, 1950," Sporrer continued. "This unit in the face of that attack, which was not overwhelming by any means, was completely routed. Several of the officers got into jeeps and drove to the rear, leaving their companies to lieutenants and sergeants, telling them to make their way back as best they could." Sporrer further suggested that the Army battalions "never waited for the enemy to get that close."

The article was accompanied by a banner headline on the cover of *Fortnight*: "The Shame and Glory of Korea." The implication was clear: The glory belonged to the 1st Marine Division, and the shame belonged to the Army 31st RCT.

The reaction to the *Fortnight* article was muted initially. The magazine did not circulate much beyond California, and the article was not seen for several weeks in Washington, Tokyo, or the 8th Army headquarters in South Korea. Then in mid-March, Senator William Knowland of California, a member of the Senate Armed Services Committee, forwarded the article to the Pentagon, and Senator Lyndon B. Johnson, the junior senator from Texas and chairman of the Senate Preparedness Subcommittee, asked Secretary of the Army Frank Pace for a detailed report on the *Fortnight* allegations. In response, Maj. Gen. Floyd Parks, the Chief of Army Information, denounced the article as "irresponsible and ill-considered."

Fortnight began banging the drum, calling for Johnson's subcommittee to hold hearings and summon witnesses. Keep, the magazine's publisher and editor, told the Associated Press that the Army was "covering up" scandalous behavior by its officers. There were enough clues in the article that reporters were soon able to identify Sporrer as the possible author of the letter. Sporrer would not confirm this when a reporter asked him on March 17, but he said, "Whoever wrote that article has nothing to be ashamed of. It was a public service."

Several days later, another tiff erupted in the Pentagon, highlighting the festering anger between the Army and the Marine Corps over what had happened at the Chosin Reservoir. A Navy documentary, *The Hungnam Story*, about the Marine withdrawal from Chosin and the evacuation of Hungnam, was completed in March and screened at the Pentagon. The film did not mention the 31st RCT or even the Army until a sardonic comment near the end by the narrator—an actor playing the role of an old Marine sergeant. The *New York Times* described the scene: "The old Marine sergeant—after all the fighting is done and the bitter retreat is over—catches a glimpse of the Army near the beach at Hungnam and says out of the side of his mouth: 'Well, whaddaye know—the Army!'"

It might have been funny except for the 1,000 31st RCT soldiers dead or missing and 1,500 more recovering from wounds. The film "caused a small explosion in the Pentagon" when it was shown, the *Times* reported. Parks demanded the Navy make changes to the film.

Sporrer was outraged when he learned of Parks's complaints about the film, believing the Army was asking for credit it did not deserve. By his account, this spurred him to publicly identify himself as the author of "The Shame and Glory of Korea." Sporrer gave interviews on March 28 to newspapers and a San Diego television station, painting himself as a truth teller who was speaking out at risk of his career. "There are times when a man, and especially a priest, if he is to sleep with himself and his conscience, must put justice and honor before discretion and caution," he told reporters.

Sporrer expanded his attacks on the Army, claiming the 31st RCT had made a "disgraceful showing" at Chosin and calling its troops "cowardly." He claimed that 400 "physically fit" soldiers had faked injuries in order to get evacuated. "I remember with shame and mortification that when we most needed every living body who could fire a gun in the magnificent withdrawal, as we were about the start back from Hagaru-ri, over 400 American soldiers . . . laid down on stretchers beside the air strip, and feigning wounds, had themselves put aboard planes and flown out to safety," Sporrer said. He contrasted them to "those magnificent Marines" who concealed wounds and frostbite to avoid being evacuated.

Sporrer's allegations were now broadcast and printed across the country. "Copies of Fortnight began popping up all over the Pentagon; most of them were being exultantly waved by officers of the U.S. Marine Corps," *Time* magazine reported.

Fortnight basked in the attention, boasting that its article "practically blew the roof off the Pentagon." Keep used the contretemps to call for an expanded Marine Corps, while a letter writer suggested abolishing the Army altogether and building up the Marines in its place.

At Percy Jones Army Hospital in Michigan, SFC Bill Donovan lay in a hospital bed, his intestines riddled with holes from his wounds, leaving him with inflamed organs and life-threatening peritonitis. He had lost all his toes to frostbite and could barely move. He felt sicker still when he heard about Sporrer's accusations. "I hate to say it, but I'd choke him today if I saw him," Donovan said decades later. "That's an awful thing to say, but that's the way I feel about him."

Capt. Bigger was outraged by the accusation that the task force had abandoned its wounded. "It is incomprehensible to me how Chaplain Sporrer came up with such an irrational concept," he later said. "The underlying concept in our breakout plan was to care for the wounded."

The Army tried to mobilize defenses, holding a Pentagon press briefing on March 29 with Army Colonel S. L. A. Marshall, a well-known military historian who had spent months in Korea, observing operations, including considerable time with the 1st Marine Division. Marshall shook with anger in denying Sporrer's allegations of cowardice. The chaplain, said Marshall, "does not know what he is talking about."

The Marines felt otherwise. "The briefing did not go too well as Marshall had to admit he was not at Hagaru during the action," Silverthorn chortled in a report to Smith.

Parks proposed to Marine headquarters that the Army and Marine Corps issue a joint statement denying Sporrer's allegations, but he received no help. "I . . . refused to consent to such a proposition," Silverthorn told Smith. Brig. Gen. Johnny McQueen, the chief Marine spokesman, would only say that the Marine Corps "looks with disfavor on any interservice bickering."

Parks cabled MacArthur's headquarters for support. "It is imperative that General Smith, commanding the 1st Marine Division, make a public statement as to the truth in the matter and clear the good name of the Army personnel involved," Parks wrote.

An X Corps public information officer telephoned Marine Capt. Michael Capraro, Smith's public information officer, asking "to get a statement from me commending the conduct of elements of the 7th Infantry Division in the Chosin Reservoir area," Smith wrote in his log. "I, of course, will furnish no such statement."

He explained further in a letter to Esther. "I do not know how these troops fought because I was not with them, but I am cognizant of the wreckage which came into Hagaru-ri," he wrote. It was a disingenuous excuse. Smith had not been with the Marines at Yudam-ni either, but he had rightfully saluted their heroic performance in fighting back to Hagaru. Parks's cable had not asked Smith to "commend" the 31st RCT; it asked him to tell the truth. Smith was well aware that much of what Sporrer said was wrong. "His allegations were about 60 percent correct," Smith later wrote in his family journal. Accepting his calculation meant that 40 percent of Sporrer's allegations were false. But Smith was unwilling to correct them.

Some of Sporrer's most inflammatory allegations were obviously untrue and could have been easily refuted by Smith. The assertion that several officers "got into jeeps and drove to the rear" was ludicrous. Even if one accepted the false charge that officers took off in jeeps, not a single vehicle from Task Force Faith made it to Hagaru-ri, as Smith knew.

Perhaps even more egregious was Sporrer's absurd claim that the Chinese force that attacked the 31st RCT "was not overwhelming by any means." While Smith did not know the full size of the 9th Army Group's attack, he knew from 1st Marine Division intelligence that at least one—and probably two—Chinese divisions had attacked the Army task force.

Smith did nothing to correct those falsehoods. "I wasn't going to disavow any chaplain," he later said. Smith gave Sporrer greater consideration than the more than 2,000 Army soldiers who had died, were missing, or were wounded, many of them while under his command—or their families. Among the men Sporrer had besmirched was Capt. James Conner, the Episcopalian chaplain for the 3rd Battalion, who died trying to save men from being burned by the Chinese, and Capt. Lawrence Brunnert, the Catholic chaplain for the 1st Battalion, who had volunteered to stay behind with the wounded. Brunnert died a captive on December 20, at the end of the march to Death Valley.

Matt Ridgway, after receiving copies of *Fortnight* in Korea via courier, felt the best way to tamp down the burgeoning controversy would be to stop talking about it. "I . . . decided to do all I could to prevent any public statements being made," he wrote in his diary on April 2. MacArthur had ordered his inspector general to immediately investigate the allegations and have a "determination made as to personal knowledge or hearsay of each accusation."

That morning, Ridgway met alone with Almond at the latter's CP, where the X Corps commander agreed to make no public statements. Ridgway then spoke privately with Smith at an airstrip near the Marine headquarters and again met with no disagreement. "I told him that I did not want to get involved in the controversy, that I had made no statement and that I would not make one," Smith said.

Ridgway expected Almond and Smith to each meet with the inspector general, though Smith bristled at being interviewed. "One would almost think we are on trial," he complained to Esther. When a colonel from the inspector general's office arrived from Tokyo to interview him on April 4, Smith spoke to him off the record and told him he had little to offer. "I pointed out to him that I could . . . not see why I should be used to help prosecute Sporrer; that what he had done was a matter between him and the Navy Department," Smith said. He limited his testimony to answering three questions, none of which addressed the charges of cowardice on the part of the 31st RCT or the size of the attack the soldiers had faced.

Some of the 31st RCT soldiers interviewed by the inspector general had more to say in their testimony:

> Sgt. Stephen Lewis, C Company, 32nd: "I believe if it hadn't been for our officers there wouldn't be a man alive from this unit today. Our officers carried on although some of them were wounded two or three times. I believe they did everything in this world to get everybody out."
>
> SFC Carroll Price, A Battery, 57th: "I was in the Bulge and it was nothing like this at Chosin Reservoir. This was something."
>
> Cpl. Helmuth Bertram, M Company, 31st: "I fought in the German Army in the last war around Stalingrad and Moscow and I never saw anything like this before, for four days against such an outnumbering force. I never saw such bravery."
>
> Lt. Ted Magill, B Battery, 57th: "I heard it said that the Army troops in the area had taken off without firing, which was a lie. There were so many feats of incredible heroism that it almost challenges the imagination. It was commonplace. That is all, sir."

At the 31st Regiment headquarters, a group of "boiling mad" soldiers told Joe Quinn of United Press that they were demanding a retraction and public apology from Sporrer, who they said had "slandered some of the bravest men who ever wore the uniform."

"I am certain there were a hundred acts of bravery for every act of cowardice," said Sgt. Daniel Hart. Sgt. Joe Medina, the Item Company medic who'd helped rescue many men after the convoy was overrun, was particularly bitter about Sporrer's claim that they had abandoned their wounded. "It's a damn lie," Medina said. "Ask two of the four chaplains who were with us. You can ask only two because the others were killed while helping us care for the wounded."

Tokyo, April 11, 1951

MacArthur had requested a report on Sporrer's allegations by the second week of April, but on April 11, the controversy was abruptly overshadowed by a shocking news flash from Washington. Shortly after 3:00 p.m. Tokyo time, an Armed Forces Radio announcer read a statement from President Truman relieving MacArthur of command and designating Ridgway as his successor.

Truman had been quietly mulling the move for over two weeks, believing that MacArthur had been sabotaging all attempts by Washington to negotiate an end to the war or at least to keep it from escalating into a wider conflict. Though he had been warned against publicly airing policy differences with Washington, MacArthur had been giving interviews hinting at just that. Then on April 5, House Minority Leader Joe Martin, a fierce critic of Truman's policies, read a letter from the general on the House floor that implied support for Martin's proposal to have Chiang Kai-shek's Nationalist army invade the Chinese mainland. "There is no substitute for victory," MacArthur wrote, suggesting that negotiations with the communists amounted to appeasement.

Truman called it "rank insubordination" in his diary and was determined to fire MacArthur. Secretary of Defense Marshall and Gen. Bradley were initially reluctant, fearful of the firestorm that was sure to result and hoping a less drastic solution could be found to rein in MacArthur. But by April 8, Marshall and the Joint Chiefs had agreed he should be relieved.

Bradley thought MacArthur was driven by an ego bruised by the humiliating 8th Army and X Corps retreat from North Korea. "The only possible means left to MacArthur to regain his lost pride and military reputation was now to inflict an overwhelming defeat on those Red Chinese generals who had made a fool of him," Bradley later wrote. "In order to do that he was perfectly willing to propel us into an all-out war with Red China and possibly with the Soviet Union, igniting World War III, and a nuclear holocaust."

MacArthur had picked up rumors of what was happening in Washington. Almond, who was in Tokyo on home leave, went to say goodbye to MacArthur on April 9, before his return to Korea. "[MacArthur] looked rather disconsolate and said to me, 'I may not see you anymore, so goodbye, Ned,'" Almond recalled. When Almond expressed puzzlement, MacArthur said, "I have become politically involved and may be relieved by the President." Almond insisted that Truman would not take such drastic action and that MacArthur would soon be back in Korea to visit X Corps. "Well, perhaps so," MacArthur replied.

The delivery of the news to MacArthur was botched. Army Secretary Pace, visiting Korea, was sent a cable instructing him to proceed immediately to Tokyo to inform MacArthur that he was relieved. But fearing the news was leaking, the White House rushed the announcement, releasing Truman's statement at a news conference at 1:00 a.m. Washington time.

Almond, a loyal MacArthur devotee until the end, immediately wrote to the general from Korea to "express my astonishment and indignation. . . . My sincere hope is that this dismissal will meet the contempt of the American people as it richly deserves." Smith did not seem as upset. "It is too bad that Gen. MacArthur did not go home after the Inchon landing," Smith wrote Esther. "He was at his peak then."

When MacArthur, accompanied by Jean and their son Arthur, departed Tokyo on April 16, Almond's wife Margaret was part of the procession that followed the general to the airport. "From the gates of the Embassy to the doors of the plane, all six miles, there was a solid line of guards, Japanese police, soldiers, sailors, airmen and marines," she wrote her husband. "And behind them thousands lined the streets the entire way. I have never seen anything like it."

After a flyover by four B-29s and eighteen jet fighters, the MacArthurs and their entourage boarded the *Bataan*, and an Army band played "Auld Lang Syne." Then MacArthur was off, on his way to set foot on the United States mainland for the first time in fourteen years.

Smith and Almond would depart not too long after MacArthur. In April Smith learned that he would rotate back to the United States in the summer to take command of the Camp Pendleton Marine base in California. On April 14, Ridgway asked Almond if he preferred to stay "indefinitely" as the X Corps commander or leave for another assignment. With MacArthur relieved, Almond decided he would prefer leaving for a combatant command stateside. He had to settle for command of the Army War College in Carlisle, Pennsylvania. Almond would leave Korea in July with a final furious fusillade, with 286 artillery pieces and tank cannons firing a salute at once across the X Corps zone, the thunderous sound carried over open radio channels.

The inspector general's investigation into Chaplain Sporrer's allegations was completed May 31, and the results were sent to General Ridgway. On June 12, the Army publicly released a strongly worded letter from Ridgway to Pace, summarizing the results of the Army's investigation. Sporrer had "slandered the reputation of many brave and honorable soldiers, both dead and alive," Ridgway wrote. Sporrer had been interviewed by both Army and Navy investigators. "[His allegations] are without basis in fact," Ridgway wrote. "These opinions are apparently based on rumors, hearsay, speculations and half-truths."

The 31st RCT "withstood repeated attacks" by more than 20,000 Chinese troops before being overrun, the investigation summary reported. "Evidence clearly show that the 31st Regiment Combat Team was struck by the full fury of more than two CCF divisions," the report added. As for the cowardly officers, the investigation found that 90 percent of the task force officers had been casualties. "The allegations that officers fled to the rear in jeeps is fantastic and impossible," the summary said. "The unit was completely surrounded." Sporrer had not seen 400 physically fit soldiers lie down on stretchers so they could be evacuated. Nobody had seen it, because it did not happen. "The allegation that the army left its wounded because of negligence and cowardice is a gross distortion of the truth," the report concluded.

Smith was not impressed. "It was a whitewash," he later said, though he did not offer specific refutations. The Navy's inquiry into Sporrer's actions was the real whitewash. Ridgway's letter said that action against the chaplain was "imperatively in order." The Navy told reporters that Secretary of the Navy Francis Matthews had written Sporrer "a very strong, critical letter" demanding he explain his actions. But that was not entirely true. The Navy had planned stern action against the chaplain. However, Cardinal Francis Spellman, a powerful figure in the Catholic church who served as the vicar of the United States

Armed Forces, intervened and insisted that Sporrer should not be punished because he had written the letter according to the dictates of "his conscience and his God." Admiral Forrest Sherman, the chief of Naval Operations, "decided the case was too hot for him to handle and turned the matter over to Mr. Matthews," according to Smith. Matthews, who was "one of the leading Catholic laymen" in the country, as Smith noted, apparently had little interest in going against Cardinal Spellman's wishes.

Shortly after Smith returned to California, he paid a social call on Matthews at the St. Francis Hotel in San Francisco, where Matthews was attending a chaplain's convention. "Before leaving I asked him out of curiosity what he had done about the Sporrer case," Smith wrote in his family journal. "He laughed, and said he had given the chaplain a letter of caution (a minor reprimand), and that the letter of caution was not for having written the letter which was published in *Fortnight*, but for participating in a TV program covering the same ground after he had been warned to cease and desist."

Perhaps emboldened by the slap on the wrist he had received, Sporrer continued to speak out against the "pampering" of combat troops, writing a letter urging the American War Dads Association to support measures at its annual convention in Topeka that fall to put the Army on a "Spartan-like" training regimen emphasizing self-denial. "Rigid measures should be taken by communities adjacent to military post to curtail and stifle gyp joints, prostitution and uncontrolled beer joints, gambling houses and burlesque houses," Sporrer wrote.

Though Matthews sent out a directive instructing all naval service personnel to not make "any comment reflecting adversely upon or belittling the role of any other branch of service," the Marines' disparagement of the Army troops continued. Chesty Puller, the commander of the 1st Marine Regiment, told reporters that the soldiers needed more "beer and whisky" and less ice cream and candy.

The Pentagon, June 21, 1950

Four-year-old Bobbie Faith, wearing a pink dress with matching ribbons in her hair, looked tiny in the cavernous Pentagon auditorium, standing on the stage with her mother next to General of the Army Omar Bradley. Bradley and Don Faith's father, retired Brigadier General Don Faith Sr., had served together in the Army when they were junior officers. Now Bradley presented the Medal of Honor posthumously to the younger Faith, handing the medal to Bobbie, who clutched the case with two hands. "Mrs. Faith, I have known Don since he was a little boy, and I'm not surprised at his leadership and courage," Bradley said.

The Army had notified Barbara Faith on April 18 that it had changed his status from MIA to KIA, expected but hard news for the family and the many in the Army who had known him. "In very recent weeks I have seen strong men cry in this country when they first heard that Don Faith was missing in action and later that he had been killed," said Senator Harry Cain of Washington, who had served with Faith on Ridgway's staff in Europe.

There were whispers in Marine circles that Faith had been awarded the Medal of Honor as a sop to the Army to soothe ruffled feelings. "Lieutenant Colonel Faith received it for simply doing his duty, and not very well at that," Capt. Capraro, Smith's public information officer, later said.

Few soldiers who saw Faith at Chosin questioned the medal's legitimacy. Among surviving officers, there was unanimity. "We all agreed he deserved the Medal of Honor," said John Gray. Wes Curtis, the officer on Faith's staff who'd been most critical of his tactical decisions and leadership style, had no doubts. "He was a gallant and determined young commander, and was fully deserving of the Medal of Honor," Curtis later said. Bill McCaffrey, who had considered Faith an "egotistical whiner," would alter his opinion. "In times of desperation heroism wells up in men and must be recognized and applauded," he said.

"It is little enough, but deserved many times over, and I hope will help you to bear your loss a little easier," Bob Jones, who had written the original recommendation, told Barbara Faith.

Certainly, there was no shortage of Marine heroes from Chosin, including 14 who received the Medal of Honor and 70 who were awarded the Navy Cross, among the highest number of honorees from any single battle in American history.

By comparison, there were "pitiful few awards" made to soldiers from the 31st RCT, Jones noted. Soon after they arrived in Taegu, Jones had gathered three dozen Chosin survivors from the 1st Battalion to talk about the submission of awards to members of the unit. "Much to my surprise I found a great reluctance on the part of most of the survivors to provide statements of actions they witnessed or could corroborate," he recalled.

Part of it was trying to choose what actions and what soldiers deserved recognition over others, including their own actions. "Under the circumstances that prevailed, heroic acts were happening continuously, concurrently, endlessly, and were in fact somewhat commonplace," said Jones.

Some men felt uncomfortable being honored for their actions when so many of their comrades had been killed doing equally brave—or even braver—acts. Others felt ashamed that they had not safely brought the convoy into Hagaru-ri and did not think anyone should be honored. Many men simply did not want to relive the horrors of Chosin, as writing up awards would require. "Bigger and I were told by the regimental exec to write each other up for the Silver Star, which we, by mutual agreement, refused to do," Curtis recalled. "It was a bitter experience for those personally involved—the sooner forgotten the better."

So many officers and NCOs were killed or missing that many actions were difficult to substantiate. "Witnesses were hard to find as most had become casualties," said Jones. "As a result there were many, many individuals who were not recognized with awards as they should have been."

Many men who saw Harvey Storms during the breakout thought his actions were worthy of the Medal of Honor. He received a Silver Star. "There were no surviving senior commanders to officially report what happened, nor were there surviving official reports, such as unit journals and after-action reports to reconstruct battle events, for these were destroyed along with those who maintained them," said John Gray.

Some thought Marine Capt. Ed Stamford rated the Medal of Honor for his handling of close air support and the leadership he showed in trying to keep the convoy moving. He was awarded the Silver Star by the Army.

Some did receive high recognition. Sgt. Charles Garrigus, the truck driver killed in the final attempt to break though the Chinese block, received the Distinguished Service Cross (DSC) for his repeated acts of heroism in shepherding trucks to safety. Though he did not seek it, Jones received the DSC for "extraordinary heroism" during the breakout, based on Lt. Hugh May's recommendation. "He surely deserved it," said May, who received a Silver Star.

Col. Maclean, still listed as MIA, received the DSC at Barr's instigation for his "unflinching courage and intrepid actions" at Chosin. Capt. Jordan, Lt. Gray, and Lt. Schmitt of M Company each received the DSC for their actions—in Schmitt's case, posthumously. Sgt. Charlie Gebhardt was awarded the DSC for the rescue mission he led from Hagaru to pick up task force survivors.

Many soldiers singled out the men of Battery D of the 15th AAA as deserving of recognition. "Every damn one of them was worthy of the Medal of Honor," said Ray Radke. "Their gunners were prime targets—one would be knocked off another took his place." Sgt. Harold Haugland, who did not make it back to Hagaru-ri and was listed as MIA, was awarded the DSC, while 15 men in the battery received Silver Stars, including Capt. Jim McClymont, Sgt. Grantford Brown, Sgt. Robert Slater, and, posthumously, Cpl. Celestino Chavez.

But there were many heroes who went unrecognized. "The most deserving were dead or missing," said Curtis.

Camp Pendleton, California

Filming for *Retreat, Hell* began in September 1951. Eager to assist the production, the Marine Corps allowed Warner Brothers to shoot the movie at Camp Pendleton, the sprawling Marine base in southern California where, conveniently enough, Smith had taken command.

A rugged, hilly area of the installation was chosen for the filming. Crews bulldozed a road up a ravine and sprinkled the entire area with gypsum to make it look like snow. "One difficulty was that the actors had to wear parkas in the summery weather of Camp Pendleton, and they sweated instead of freezing," said Smith. A wind machine was brought in to blow the gypsum around and create snowstorms. With John Wayne unavailable, Frank Lovejoy was cast in the lead role as a tough but lovable Marine battalion commander.

Smith was shown a copy of the script and was appalled at the liberties the screenwriter had taken with the story. "They have done violence to history," he wrote to McQueen, the Marine chief public information officer. "I hope the Marine Corps will not be asked to endorse this picture as a historically accurate account of what transpired in Korea, for it is not that." Smith requested that his name not be used in the film and that he be referred to simply as the division commander. "Definitely I would like to remain anonymous in this picture," he said. It would fall to Lovejoy, in the role of the battalion commander, to utter the famous "Retreat, hell" line.

The assistance and location provided by the Marines saved Warner Bros. more than $1 million, close to half the total cost of the film. Smith fretted that "unfriendly sources could make something of this." But he suggested to Silverthorn that the Marine Corps use that cost savings as leverage to demand changes to the film from Warner Brothers if necessary. Silverthorn assured Smith the Marine Corps would preview the film and that "the producer will be required to make any changes determined prior to release of the picture."

They need not have worried. The commandant and his staff were delighted after seeing the preview. "In the opinion of many of us the film is by far the finest war picture produced," McQueen wrote Smith. For his part, Smith allowed that "as wartime movies go, it was not a bad picture."

Retreat, Hell, released in February 1952, received decent reviews and did reasonably well at the box office. The film lionized the Marine Corps but made no mention of the 31st RCT.

A far more consequential slight was in the works for Task Force Faith.

Soon after the Chosin battle, Smith had been confident that either the Army or the Navy would award the entire 1st Marine Division a Distinguished Unit Citation, the highest honor that could be conferred on a military unit, for its performance during the Chosin Reservoir campaign. The Navy had already awarded the citation to the 1st Marine Division for the Inchon landing.

Army policy at the time generally saw the award as more appropriate for smaller units, such as battalions, but it had made exceptions. Certainly, Almond had no problem commending Smith and the 1st Marine Division, awarding Smith the Distinguished Service Cross, the Distinguished Service Medal, and the Air Medal. Almond sent Smith a commendation saluting his "splendid fighting force" in February 1951. "I wish to express my admiration and respect for the valiant actions of the 1st Marine Division," Almond wrote. "My highest praise goes to you, General Smith, and to the members of your command." Smith conceded in a letter to Esther that "Gen. Almond has gone out of his way to commend us."

Nonetheless, as the months went by with no action on the unit citation, Smith suspected a deliberate snub. "There appears to be a studied attempt on the part of the Army to minimize the contributions [of the 1st Marine Division]," Smith wrote Major General Gerald Thomas, his successor as commander of the division. "It seems inconceivable to me that . . . [the] Division could have gone through what they did without receiving from the Army some form of recognition in the way of a DUC."

By the time Smith and Almond departed Korea in the summer of 1951, no recommendation for a Distinguished Unit Citation had been made. "If, as it appears, the Army intends to make no recommendation, I feel that the Navy should step in again," Smith wrote in August to Lt. Gen. Shepherd, commander of Fleet Marine Force, Pacific.

Shepherd responded to Smith's letter harshly. "I personally feel the responsibility for the failure of the 1st Marine Division to be recommended for the Army Distinguished Unit Citations rests to a large measure on your own shoulders," Shepherd replied. "You were in a position, while in command of the Division, to take up and press this matter personally not only with General Almond, but with General Ridgway and General MacArthur as well. . . . Be that as it may, I am afraid the time has now passed and the bitterness that has developed by criticism, much of which was warranted, I'll admit, of the Army as a result of the Chosin Reservoir Campaign, precludes any official recognition of the Division as a unit for an Army Citation."

According to a biography of Smith written by his granddaughter Gail Shisler, Shepherd was jealous of the accolades showered upon Smith after Inchon and Chosin, viewing him as a rival to become the next commandant of the Marine Corps. Shepherd did not want to do anything "that might add to Smith's luster," she wrote.

The Navy also seemed disinclined to make the award, Smith concluded after making inquiries. "The attitude of the Army and the Navy toward awarding of unit citations to Marine Ground Units is hard to understand," Smith complained to Thomas. It appeared the effort was dead.

Smith had been revising his already low assessment of Task Force Faith, dropping it even further. In January 1952, he reviewed a Marine Corps board study evaluating the Marine performance in Korea through the end of the Chosin operation. Smith wrote extensive comments on the study, including its section covering the rescue of wounded survivors from Task Force Faith.

"I believe there is a misconception as to the type of casualties rescued," Smith wrote. "Since the Chinese closed in and threw grenades into the trucks carrying the wounded I doubt if any of the seriously wounded of the convoy escaped. The men our people rescued were those who were able to make their way out on the surface of the reservoir. Our last report from TF Faith was that there were 400 wounded in the truck convoy. Admitting we evacuated 1500

Army personnel it is apparent the bulk of this number could not have come from the convoy. Most of those evacuations were, I believe, frostbite cases."

Smith was claiming that few of the Task Force Faith survivors were seriously wounded. It was an astonishing statement. Smith's assertion that none of the seriously wounded men in the trucks were rescued was contradicted by numerous survivor accounts, and it also ignored the graphic reports from Lt. Col. Beall and other Marines who described the horrific wounds of the men they rescued. Some of those wounded men had died on the evacuation flights, others died at hospitals, and others were left with lifelong disabilities. The Marines would revise the estimate of 1,500 Army troops evacuated, dropping it to 1,050. But Smith's suggestion that the task force only had 400 wounded soldiers because that was the number when the breakout began ignored the hundreds of additional soldiers who were wounded in the desperate fight to get to Hagaru. Saying that most of the 31st RCT soldiers evacuated were simply suffering from frostbite was outrageous.

In March 1952, learning that an effort was underway to award the Distinguished Unit Citation to two Marine battalions for their performance at Chosin, Smith made another push to award the citation to the entire division, arguing it was wrong to only honor a few of its units. "Probably no large unit of the Marine Corps has ever had to face odds comparable to those faced by the 1st Marine Division during the Chosin Reservoir Operation," Smith wrote in a formal recommendation to Shepherd, who was now commandant. "In this operation the division had cut its way through seven Chinese divisions and parts of three others." He did not mention that the small Army task force on the east side of Chosin fought two of those divisions. Nor did Smith include the 31st RCT in his list of units that should receive the award, reflecting his disdain for the destroyed task force.

Smith did include some Army units, including the 31st Tank Company, which he had approved removing from Hudong-ni prior to the breakout to join the Marine defenses at Hagaru; the 2nd Battalion, 31st Infantry, which had arrived too late to join the 31st RCT and had remained at Koto-ri; and the troops of the provisional 31st, the makeshift unit of survivors who had participated in the breakout from Hagaru-ri to Chinhung-ni. Smith also included units that made up Task Force Drysdale; among them are B Company, 31st Infantry Regiment, and the Royal Marines from the British 41st Commando

Battalion. Smith also included various small Army detachments that had been at Hagaru-ri or Koto-ri, including engineers, signals troops, MPs, and headquarters units. All these units had contributed to the breakout, made sacrifices, suffered casualties, and deserved to be included in the citation. But the Army unit that had contributed, sacrificed, and suffered the most—the soldiers of Task Force Faith—had been excluded.

In April Shepherd, perhaps no longer seeing Smith as a rival, endorsed the recommendation and forwarded the proposed citation to Vice Admiral Robert Briscoe, commander of Naval Forces Far East. Briscoe decided it would be appropriate to award the division the Navy Presidential Unit Citation, the service's equivalent to the Army Distinguished Unit Citation. He sent the recommendation to Army General Mark Clark, who had succeeded Ridgway as commander of the Far East Command, asking that he provide a list of Army units "deserving" of inclusion.

Clark sent the request down his Army chain of command for review, and in August 1952, Brigadier General Wayne C. Smith, then the commander of the 7th Division, recommended that all elements of the 31st RCT be included in the citation, noting they were under the operational control of the 1st Marine Division during much of the Chosin battle. The 3rd Division commander added one of his units—the 3rd Battalion, 7th Infantry—which had relieved the Marines at Chinhung-ni and held the line for the troops moving out of the Funchilin Pass. In September Briscoe and Clark each endorsed awarding the Navy Presidential Unit Citation to the 1st Marine Division and attached Army units, including the 31st RCT. But they asked that the Department of Army be further consulted because, as Briscoe put it, there was "some variation" between the Army units now included in the proposed citation and the original recommendation by Smith, who had excluded the 31st RCT.

The recommendation bounced around between offices for some months until February 1953, when the Navy Board of Decorations and Medals sent it to the Army Office of the Chief of Military History, asking that it provide a definitive list of all Army units that participated in the Chosin operation. On March 19, 1953, the Army office sent a list of units they recommended be included, among them the 31st RCT.

The Navy board sent the Army's list to Smith on March 27 for review. Over the next two weeks, Smith composed a recommendation objecting to the inclusion of the 31st RCT and several other Army units. Smith argued that the citation should only include those units "which made a direct contribution to the successful breakout of the 1st Marine Division from the Chosin Reservoir Area."

Smith then listed the five most critical ground operations that allowed the breakout to succeed, the first being the breakout of the 5th and 7th Marine Regiments from Yudam-ni to Hagaru. The second most important, Smith explained, was the defense of Hagaru pending the arrival of the 5th and 7th Marines. Smith was, in essence, saying that the 31st RCT's four-day, five-night fight played no role in protecting Hagaru.

In fairness to Smith, he did not know that Song Shilun had ordered the main effort of the 9th Army Group away from the Marines at Yudam-ni and toward the east side of the reservoir, to annihilate the 31st RCT.

But Smith knew quite a bit by the time he wrote the citation recommendation. The 1951 Marine board study, which Smith had carefully reviewed, had concluded that the "80th and probably 81st" Divisions had attacked the Army units on the east side. Smith knew the 31st RCT had been in intense combat for four days, from the start of the attack on November 27. He and Col. Bowser, knowing that the Marine defenses were in danger of being overrun, had been both puzzled and relieved that the Chinese had not directed more force at Hagaru. It should have been evident to Smith that Task Force Faith's fight on the east side of the reservoir played a big role in preventing the Chinese from mounting a heavier attack on Hagaru.

The two divisions attacking the 31st RCT—the 80th and 81st—had been decimated by the fight and were never able to attack Hagaru. "East of Chosin, the Chinese had succeeded in overrunning and scattering RCT 31, but they were reduced to uselessness in doing so," Patrick Roe, who served as an intelligence officer with the 7th Marine Regiment at Chosin, concluded after examining Chinese military histories. "RCT 31, in fighting to destruction, had kept the Chinese from concentrating two more divisions at Hagaru-ri."

Smith was a scrupulously honest and thoughtful commander. Without his calm and cautious leadership and foresight, all of the X Corps force at Chosin might have been lost. Yet Smith had a glaring blind spot when it came to the 31st RCT.

In his recommendation, Smith said nothing about the size of the Chinese force that had attacked the 31st RCT. All Smith said of the battle fought by the Army task force was that it was cut off from Hagaru-ri and was "overwhelmed by the Chinese." Smith instead emphasized the wretched condition of the survivors who made it to Hagaru: "These men came in small groups without any semblance of organization. Many had discarded their weapons. They brought out no equipment or vehicles. Most of them were suffering from frostbite."

On April 14, Smith sent the recommendation to the Navy Board of Decorations and Medals with the 31st RCT removed, including the 1st Battalion, 32nd Infantry; the 3rd Battalion, 31st Infantry; and the 57th Field Artillery. "I do not consider it justifiable to include the complete units as proposed by the Department of the Army," Smith wrote. The recommendations did not go back to the Army for review, so there was no opportunity to protest. The Navy Presidential Unit Citation as modified by Smith was approved and signed by Secretary of the Navy Robert Anderson on May 19, 1953, in the name of President Dwight D. Eisenhower.

Smith had refused honors to the Army unit that had suffered destruction at Chosin, fighting to its death.

Chapter 19

THE CHOSIN FEW

It was not much of a welcome home for Grant McMillin and other 31st RCT prisoners of war who were released after thirty-three months of captivity following the July 1953 armistice ending hostilities in the Korean War. The POWs were taken from a camp along the Yalu River to the demilitarized zone (DMZ) established along the border by the armistice, then walked across the Freedom Bridge into South Korea. They were flown by helicopter to Inchon and boarded a ship, arriving in San Francisco eighteen days later. McMillin was given several months' back pay and instructed to report to Fort Sheridan, Illinois, in thirty days.

"They did nothing for us," McMillin recalled. "We were just dumped off the ship in San Francisco and told, 'Find your own way home, and be back in a month to get your discharge.'" McMillin travelled by train and Greyhound bus to his parents' home in Lake Geneva, Wisconsin. The lack of services for the returning POWs "kind of smarted," McMillin said. But the real slap, he said, was when he heard about Chaplain Sporrer's accusation that "we all threw our weapons down and ran. There was no place to run. We were surrounded."

Jerry Francois had done his best to make the Chinese rue the day they captured him. Always challenging his captors, he was labeled a reactionary and twice put before a firing squad but not shot. Sometimes at night, he would crawl on his belly to steal extra rations to share with the men. If caught, he would be put in a small wooden box as punishment. Francois weighed seventy pounds upon his release and spent a year recovering at an Army hospital.

Johnny Snock had prayed that his twin brother Joey would be among the returning captives. He was not. Joey had been wounded at the inlet and dragged off by the Chinese while Johnny ran for a medic. The Snock family in Apollo, Pennsylvania, was informed Joey had died in captivity from malnutrition and lack of medical care in late December 1950. Johnny Snock "felt devastated that he came home and his brother didn't," his niece recalled.

Army officials showed up at the home of Cpl. Robert Witt, A Company, 32nd Infantry, in Bellflower, California, and told his parents that their son had died of malnutrition at a prison camp in January 1951. "My dad had brown hair the day before, but the day after, his hair was gray," Robert's sister, Laverne Minnick, said. "Nobody said anything that day. We just hugged each other."

Dodie Maclean learned in March 1954 that her husband had died on the march to the camps. Col. Allan Maclean, the highest-ranking combat leader killed in action in the Korean War, left behind a daughter, Catherine, who was three years old when her father disappeared.

Returning prisoners testified to the "devoted" service Chaplain Lawrence Brunnert gave to other captives before he died.

The families of hundreds of MIAs had held out desperate hope that their loved ones would turn up among the released prisoners. Returning POWs sometimes had answers. It was rarely good news.

PFC James Colasanti of Item Company was still listed as missing in action. Returning POWs reported that Colasanti was seen accompanying the convoy as it approached the last roadblock at Hudong, still moving on foot despite a wound to his thigh. He subsequently died from his wounds. One of the released POWs from I Company, Master Sgt. Kenneth Hemric, had promised to write Colasanti's mother in Syracuse, New York, and tell her what he knew. Hemric had just spent $3,370 of his back pay to buy a fire-engine red Mercury convertible, and he put eight hundred miles on it in three days in September 1953, driving the roads near his home in Yadkin County, North Carolina, with another released POW, enjoying their restored freedom. But the car went off the road rounding a bad curve and smashed into a power pole, killing both. Hemric "never got a chance to tell my mother about James's death," recalled Dan Colasanti, James's younger brother.

Portia Marshburn's son, Lt. Herbert Marshburn—a West Point class of 1949 graduate and much-admired A Company platoon leader—was also missing in action and was not among the returning prisoners. For years Portia wrote to survivors from her home in Alabama, trying to find out what had happened. Wes Curtis received a letter asking when he had last seen her son and if he thought he might still be alive. "It was difficult to write the poor woman," Curtis recalled. "I could offer her no hope."

The answer lay with Lt. Jim Mortrude. Whether Portia Marshburn ever learned it is unclear. When Mortrude was grazed in the head by a sniper's bullet on the road below Hill 1221, his friend Marshburn volunteered to continue forward with Mortrude's men. A short time later, Marshburn was shot in the head and killed, possibly by the same sniper. "I have always felt Marshburn died in my place at the head of our platoon," Mortrude later said.

In 1954 the remains of nearly 3,000 American troops who died in North Korea were turned over to the United States as part of the terms of the armistice. The transfer, called Operation Glory, included remains from the mass grave at Koto-ri, various battle sites and POW camps, and American cemeteries in Hungnam, Pukchong, and other locations that were abandoned when X Corps and the 8th Army withdrew in December 1950.

Some of the remains were from east of Chosin, including those of 15-year-old Huey French, who was returned to his parents for burial in Childress, Texas. Also among them was Capt. Henry Wamble, the 31st Medical Company executive officer who was wounded when the Chinese ambushed the medical company the first night. The remains of Lt. Richard Coke, the Intelligence and Reconnaissance Platoon commander, who had died after eleven months in captivity, were returned to Texas and interred at Fort Sam Houston National Cemetery. Lts. Skilton and Boyer came home from Koto-ri.

But most of the dead from the 31st RCT remained lost—Allan Maclean, Anthony Mazzulla, Charles Garrigus, Ed Scullion, Herb Marshburn, Harold Haugland, Celestino Chavez, Joey Snock, and Donald Hamilton, to name just a few. In Greene County, Indiana, Oval Hamilton kept the porch light on and the backdoor unlocked at his farmhouse in case Donald came home. "Send me just one bone of my son, and I'll accept his death," he told the Army.

In January 1956, the Army declared the remains of Don Faith "non-recoverable" and notified the Faith family. Barbara Faith would not speak with Bobbie about the details of her father's death. "She was very distressed," recalled Bobbie. "She knew what the Marines were saying." Nor would Faith's father and mother, retired Brigadier General Don Faith Sr. and his wife Katherine. "I think it was so painful that they had no words," said Bobbie. She had little more than her memories. "What I recall most about my father was that he was happy," she said. "I still can hear him laughing."

Barbara Faith married another Army officer, Warren Bennett. But she made sure Bobbie never forgot her father. By the time Barbara died of breast cancer in 1960, recalled Bobbie, "She had instilled in me the respect and honor that he was due."

La Feria, Texas

Helen Storms gave birth to her fourth child in February 1951. It was another boy, Robert. Harvey Storms remained missing. "Every morning, she read her Bible and prayed on him, and a lot of mornings I'd get up early and she'd be on her knees in front of that couch, sometimes sobbing, then she would go get her newspaper," recalled her eldest son, Sam Storms. "And they always listed the POWs. And she would always read that list to see if she knew anyone on that list, including my daddy." Harvey Storms was never on that list.

Helen wrote to 31st Regiment officers and their spouses, including Capt. Rasula's wife, Lucy, trying to find out anything she could. George Rasula did not want to tell her about the severe wounds Maj. Storms had received as he kept fighting in his final hours. "Mrs. Storms wrote to Lucy the other day and asked . . . but it sure is hard for me to say anything to the women, so I didn't," George Rasula wrote to another officer in February 1951. "This I believe should be told her—that he displayed gallantry in action which was terrific." The Army changed Storms's status from missing in action to killed in action in 1951, but his body was not among those turned over in 1954.

Helen and the boys stayed in La Feria, with Harvey's parents still living next door. She tried her best to fill in for Harvey's absence, once taking Sam into town to a haberdashery to learn how to tie a tie.

Helen died of cancer in 1960, at age 46, leaving the four boys as orphans, but they never felt that way. She had arranged for relatives, eventually including Harvey's mother, to move into the home and raise the boys. Neighbors would always keep an eye out for them, and if they got into any mischief, the news reached home before they did.

While recovering from his wounds at the Army hospital in Osaka, Ray Radke fell in love with Chiyoko, the woman changing his bedpan. After the war ended, he came back to Japan and married her.

Maj. Crosby Miller spent nine months in the hospital, recovering from leg and hand wounds. The remaining fingers on his left hand were amputated and those on the right, removed to the first joint. He returned to duty at Fort Knox and later taught at the Command and General Staff School at Fort Leavenworth.

Many survivors recovered from horrific wounds and began new lives in the civilian world. Cecil McMorris, rescued from the rowboat on the reservoir by Ralph Milton, lost both his legs beneath his knees to his wounds and frostbite and was fitted with artificial legs. During a visit to a Veterans Administration facility in Lubbock in his home state of Texas, he befriended the owner of a prosthetic limb company and began working for him. Eventually, McMorris bought the business and renamed it Lubbock Artificial Limb. Word spread that any veterans who needed prosthetics should go see Cecil and they would get the best care, whether they could pay for it or not.

The Army doctors treating Ed Reeves in Michigan told his parents in Illinois not to come to the hospital, as the operations he needed to cut out the gangrene would probably kill him. "Stay home and remember your son as he was," they advised. Reeves's parents were at his side the next day, and the surgeries began, removing both his feet and all his fingers. He was released from a VA hospital after more than two years of reconstructive surgery, and he was soon married, raising a family, and earning a college degree.

Many survivors were left with as much mental trauma as physical. After his release from the hospital, Jerry Francois visited his brother in Denver, where he met a young nursing student, Dawn Emery. They married in 1956. She did not know much about what had happened to him in Korea, but it was not long before she realized he had what is now known as posttraumatic stress disorder (PTSD). "At first he wouldn't talk about it at all to me," she recalled. "And then on our honeymoon trip, I don't know why he would pick a hotel close to the airport but he did, and a jet came in and he lit out of the bed, and he knocked a table over, and he tried to get under the bed. And I said, 'Okay this is it, either you tell me what's going on or I'm going home to my mama.' And then he started talking about it and opened up to me about it." They settled in Colorado Springs, where they raised four daughters and ran a commercial towing company. But what happened in North Korea never left him.

Back home in Wilkes-Barre, Harry Jacobs's parents wanted him to explain what had happened to him at Chosin, as well as what he knew about the death of his brother, James, with the 2nd Division. They could get little out of him. "One day my father says, 'Harry, let's go for a beer.' So I said 'OK,' we went, we ordered a beer, he says, 'Harry, I want you to tell me how everything was, you and James in the war.'"

Jacobs tried to reply but felt as if his mouth were frozen. "I couldn't talk," he recalled. "I said, 'Dad, I can't talk. I can't tell you.' It took me I don't know how many years before I could open up."

Many felt survivor's guilt. "So many people did so much more than I," said Jerry McCabe, who'd spent months recuperating from his wounds and frostbitten feet before returning to service. "You come out and say, 'Why the hell did I survive?'"

Roy Oxenrider was always haunted by the memory of men in the truck in which he had been riding calling for help when the Chinese overran it while he lay wounded and hiding in the nearby brush. "I knew there was nothing I could do," he recalled decades later. "Nevertheless, the self-questioning has never stopped."

Wes Curtis tortured himself for his decision to leave the column just before it was overrun, once writing out a series of questions to himself and then answering them:

> Question: What should you have done?
>
> Answer: I should have remained with the truck column—regardless of the consequences.
>
> Question: Has this bothered you—your conscience?
>
> Answer: Yes—for the past 30 years.

Seeing violent death on such a massive scale made it hard for some to form close attachments. "I have no close male friends, as I remember the hurt I felt at the loss of my friends at the Reservoir," said Don Mayville. When Mayville was hospitalized, recovering from his wounds, Army officials interviewed him, trying to verify the names of men he knew had been killed so their next of kin could be informed that they were dead. It took two days.

"Not many nights go by, if any, that I don't dream or wake up living through it again," said Clarence White. He finally began writing down his memories of Chosin when he woke up in the middle of the night, hoping it would help him sleep. "Maybe I'll find some peace and stop getting up at 3 and 4 a.m."

On vacation in Hawaii in 1968, Bob Hammond went with his wife to the National Memorial Cemetery of the Pacific in Honolulu, known as the Punchbowl for its location at a volcanic crater. As they walked through, they came upon courts with walls listing the names of missing service members, including a section with the names carved of 8,210 missing from the Korean War. Since the moment Sgt. Billy Allen had ordered him to get into a truck at the start of the breakout, Hammond had never again seen any member of his squad, either when he'd rejoined A Battery or anywhere else. He scanned the names on the wall. "One by one I found them," he recalled. "My whole squad. All of them. I was looking at the proof of what I had suspected all these years. They never got out." Hammond leaned against the wall and sobbed.

As the years wore on, the survivors grew angry that the sacrifice of so many comrades had been forgotten—or even worse, denigrated. They felt as if the 31st RCT had been written out of history. Chosin had taken its place as one of the most legendary and heroic battles in American history. Yet it was almost exclusively a Marine legend, one regarded by the Corps as being on a par with Belleau Wood and Iwo Jima. "No other operation in the American book of war quite compares with this show by the 1st Marine Division," historian S. L. A. Marshall wrote.

Many accounts of Chosin largely ignored the Army. So little was known about the Army role that Chosin had become almost entirely a Marine story. "When and if mentioned it is in a negative context, otherwise we appear not to have been there," said Rasula.

Histories of Chosin relied heavily on the papers and journals of O. P. Smith, which harshly criticized Task Force Faith and downplayed the Army's contribution. Smith concluded that the 31st RCT had only fought the 80th Division. Moreover, he did not credit the Army with inflicting much damage, telling a historian in 1956 that the 80th Division had attacked the 1st Marine Division south of Hagaru after overrunning the 31st RCT. In fact, both the 80th and 81st Divisions had been so damaged by the fight with the 31st RCT that they were unable to attack Hagaru. Smith wrote that of an estimated

37,500 Chinese casualties during the Chosin Reservoir operation, "22,500 [were] inflicted by Marine ground forces, and 15,000 by air." By that calculation, none of the casualties were inflicted by the Army.

The performance of the 1st Marine Division at Chosin required no embellishment. "The Marines at Chosin lose no part of their well-earned glory by acknowledging the crucial role played by the doomed men of the 7th Division who through the fortunes of war were swept up in the maelstrom east of Chosin," Bill McCaffrey observed.

Task Force Faith was largely forgotten, other than occasionally cited—usually by Marines—as a telling example of Marine Corps superiority over the Army. "The Marines as usual received plaudits and were canonized in the public press—the Army troops were denigrated," historian Roy Appleman observed. "Why could not the Army troops do what the Marines had done at Chosin?"

It must be recognized, as Appleman did, that the 1st Marine Division at Chosin "was one of the most magnificent fighting organizations that ever served in the United States armed forces. It had to be to do what it did." The bulk of this powerful force was at Yudam-ni when the attack began—two infantry regiments and most of the artillery regiment.

To expect the small Army task force—not even an entire regiment, with less than one artillery battalion, cobbled together from different units, poorly equipped for winter fighting, infuriatingly undersupplied with fuel and ammunition, still arriving at Chosin and not fully in place when the Chinese attacked—to perform at the same level as the 1st Marine Division was wholly unrealistic. "The major cause of the disaster came at the very outset: the operation of moving 31st RCT to Chosin was too hastily conceived and too hastily executed," Bob Drake observed.

Smith had the 1st Marine Division under his command at all times and was able to fight as a division. Almond committed the 7th Division piecemeal, leaving Dave Barr with little control of his division and Maclean little control of his regiment. "Battalions were moved by the Corps Commander—and that is *not* the way to do it," said Curtis.

"Sometimes I have bristled at comparisons of the Marines' gallant withdrawal there with the failure of ours," said John Gray. "In actuality, we were the 'few good men' who were too few, and the Marines, in this case, were the many."

The Army survivors were generally grateful to the Marines for the life-saving shelter at Hagaru and their rescue of hundreds of men, often at great risk to themselves. But they deeply resented what had been said and done in the years since. "Glory to the Marines, the hell with the Army guys" was how Harry Graham summed it up.

"I still get hot under the collar when I hear Marines talk as if they alone were in the fighting at Chosin," said Harry Scott. "If they could talk, the . . . Army men who died would dispute that."

What was particularly incendiary was the common Marine accusation that Task Force Faith had abandoned its wounded. The truth was Faith and hundreds of his officers and soldiers fought to their deaths trying to get the wounded out. "The mission was to get that damn column through," said Radke. "And dammit, we tried, but didn't make it."

There were soldiers and officers who precipitously abandoned the column. But they were a minority. "Of course there were cowards among the soldiers of the 7th Division, just as there were among the Marines, but it is the cruelest of falsehoods to categorize entire units in those terms," said McCaffrey. "When the story of the Seventh Division is finally told, it will be a tragic but gallant page in our history."

The men who made it to Hagaru were called stragglers. In reality, most were defeated soldiers who had fought with courage beyond the limits of physical endurance. "I would never call them deserters," said Charlie Gebhardt. "Never, ever. I wouldn't stand for it."

Among the survivors there was a palpable anger at O. P. Smith. Many of them believed, rightly or not, that he could have done more to assist the 31st RCT. Beyond that, they resented that the Marine general never seemed to appreciate that the reason the Army task force was sent to Chosin in the first place was to meet Smith's wise demand of Almond that the 1st Marine Division be relieved of responsibility for the east side of the reservoir before launching its attack from Yudam-ni.

It certainly was not Smith's fault that Almond had rushed the 31st RCT to the east side of the reservoir with none of the methodical preparations that Smith had made for the 1st Marine Division, preparations that were key to escaping Chosin. But had the Army task force not rushed, Smith's 5th and 7th Marine regiments would have been on opposite sides of the reservoir when the

Chinese attacked on the night of November 27—a potentially fatal division of his force. And had the 31st RCT not fought for four days and five nights against an overwhelmingly larger Chinese force, Hagaru likely would have been overrun. It made Smith's claim that the 31st RCT had not contributed to the 1st Marine Division's withdrawal and, therefore, not entitled to the Presidential Unit Citation hard for survivors to stomach.

Smith remained determined to keep the 31st RCT off the list of units included in the PUC. "I trust this list will remain undisturbed," Smith wrote to Marine Corps headquarters in 1954. "There has been a persistent effort on the part of the Army to include units in this citation that had no valid claim to the citation."

Smith was hardly the only target of ire for the Army Chosin veterans. Many blamed Douglas MacArthur for sending them recklessly north and failing to read Chinese intentions. Normally mild-mannered Charlie Gebhardt would become animated at the mention of MacArthur. "He should have been drawn, quartered and hung from a telephone pole like Mussolini, that's my viewpoint," he said.

MacArthur's insistence on splitting command of X Corps from 8th Army, as well as on rushing his forces deep into the extremely cold and rough terrain of North Korea with his Army units at "dangerously low levels" of ammunition, clothing, and food, was "largely responsible" for the heavy casualties, Matt Ridgway later said. MacArthur received a hero's welcome upon his return from Japan in 1951. He was given an enormous ticker tape parade in New York City, and he addressed a joint session of Congress in Washington. "I now close my military career and just fade away—an old soldier who tried to do his duty as God gave him the light to see that duty," MacArthur said. "Goodbye." And he did fade away.

The Chosin veterans directed even more anger at Ned Almond, especially for his fatal refusal to recognize the danger the 31st RCT faced until it was too late. "Our worst enemy at the reservoir was not the cold or the Chinese," said Anthony Biebel. "It was Almond and his so-called X Corps headquarters."

For his part, "[Almond] was never reconciled to our inability to come to their aid," according to Al Haig. Almond retired from the Army in 1953, earlier than he had expected, after not getting a fourth star; he suspected his continued dogged defense of MacArthur had irritated the political hierarchy.

Haig would rise to four stars and serve as White House chief of staff and secretary of state.

Though Dave Barr and Hank Hodes lacked much command and control at Chosin, they came under heavy approbation for not doing more to get the ammunition, supplies, and replacements for wounded officers that might have saved the 31st RCT. "I've never been able to shake the sick feeling in my stomach that had there been a fierce desire to prevail within the senior officers of the 7th Division much of TF Faith could have been extricated," Bill McCaffrey later said.

Barr clearly felt the weight of the failure to save the 31st RCT and his role in the death of an officer whom he'd treated like a son. He retired from the Army in 1952 and stayed close to Barbara Faith for the rest of her short life.

Hodes was frustrated with every level of higher command, including Barr, Almond, Smith, and MacArthur's headquarters. "I am sure that this whole episode troubled him the rest of his life," said Lynch, his operations aide. McCaffrey thought Hodes should have been court-martialed for not taking over the 31st RCT after Maclean disappeared. Others say he had little choice once Barr ordered him out. "He did all he could do without being insubordinate," said Carl Witte. Chosin did not harm Hodes's career, as he had a quick rise to four stars and served as commander of the U.S. Army in Europe.

Don Faith loomed large in the memories of the survivors, his charisma lingering long after his death. "It took years for me to quit dreaming about Col. Faith," Erwin Bigger said in 1980. "In my dreams I had always found him alive." Bigger named one of his sons after Faith and kept a photo of Faith and Maclean on the wall of his den in Knoxville.

"He was more than my commanding officer to me—he was a friend, a confidant, an ideal," Bob Jones once told Barbara Faith. "It may sound as if I am putting him on a pedestal—perhaps—but if so, he was one who did not have feet of clay."

Army historian Russell Gugeler interviewed soldiers from Faith's battalion soon after the battle. "In Korea when I talked to men they became almost reverent when they spoke of Faith," he recalled. "I don't believe I've known of any leader who had the respect and affection these men showed, unless it would be a captain about whom Ernie Pyle wrote during the Italian campaign." It was an allusion to the war correspondent's most famous column, about the death of Capt. Henry Waskow in 1944.

Some soldiers in the other battalions considered Faith a showboat and were resentful that his Medal of Honor overshadowed the heroism of others. But Faith had the undying admiration of the men of the 1st Battalion. "He'd do anything for all the guys who fought under him," said Harry Graham.

Most of the men recognized that Faith made mistakes at Chosin; among them were his push to move the 1st Battalion north before all the task force had arrived, his failure to try to improve communication with higher headquarters, and his lack of planning and organization for the breakout.

Hugh May served with Faith from his first day of command of the battalion through the last of his life at Chosin. "He was a brave, courageous and dedicated soldier in over his head, and not by his choice or design," May said. "He was placed in this untenable position and situation by the bumbling decisions and plans by incompetents at higher headquarters, mostly I think at 10th Corps and at MacArthur's headquarters. 7th Division headquarters also contributed its part in this fiasco."

The men had mixed feelings about Maclean, who some faulted for his lack of caution. "Some people want to make Maclean out to be a superhero and others want to vilify him," said his radioman, Frenchy Mercier, the last man to speak to the colonel before he crossed the ice. "He was a good soldier."

Faith and Maclean "both were confronted with a situation well beyond their control—and with inadequate resources to deal with it," said Wes Curtis. "But given the situation they both made mistakes—we all did."

In the view of the most perceptive officers who survived Chosin—among them Curtis, May, Bob Jones, Ray Lynch, Bob Drake, and Crosby Miller—the fundamental failures came from higher headquarters. "Their inadequacy and shortcomings did surely spell out the doom of the 31st RCT," said May.

"No commander placed in these exact circumstances and under these exact conditions could have performed any better," May added. "As for Col. Faith being in over his head, we were all in over our heads from the word go."

The Chosin Few

In 1983 Frank Kerr, who had served at Chosin as a Marine sergeant, and Jack Hessman, who had been there as a Navy corpsman, decided to organize a reunion of veterans from the battle, inspired by a recently published book, Eric

Hammel's *Chosin: Heroic Ordeal of the Korean War*. The idea soon blossomed into creating a veterans group that they called the Chosin Few. With a nod to Shakespeare, they adopted as their motto "We few, we Chosin Few, we eternal band of brothers."

They soon had hundreds of members, drawn by a bond formed through service together in one of the most harrowing military campaigns in American history. Veterans from all services and nations who served with the UN forces at Chosin were invited to join, including Army, Navy, Air Force, South Korean ROKs, and British Royal Commandos. But the organization was understandably dominated by Marines. In December 1985, the first international reunion was held in San Diego, a four-day gala affair.

A small group of 31st RCT veterans attended, including Jerry Francois, Ed Reeves, Jim DeLong, and George Rasula. "I think there were 21 Army guys and 1,400 Marines," recalled Dawn Francois. Though the organizers had made a point to include them, the Army veterans did not feel particularly welcomed by the rank-and-file members. It was a Marine celebration through and through. "They felt so out of place and so unwelcome," said Dawn. "And that's when they decided that they had to have their own group."

Back home in Colorado Springs, Jerry Francois got to work trying to band together as many Army survivors from the east shore of the Chosin as he could find. In early 1986 he sent out a letter. "There are so few of us that survived and we have such a common bond," he wrote.

So little was known about the Army role that Chosin had become almost entirely a Marine story, Francois believed. The sacrifice of so many soldiers was unknown, even among the Marines who had been at Chosin, and to the extent that it was remembered, the men had been labeled as cowards.

"I have felt for years that the Army history of what happened at the Chosin on the east bank was incomplete and as many of us found out at the reunion is virtually nonexistent," Francois wrote. "The ones who were our leaders did not make it home in many instances. The truth must be recorded. Time is running out."

At Francois's suggestion, they met in June 1986 at Fort Sill, Oklahoma, where some of the Chosin veterans would be attending a reunion of the 31st Regimental Association. "Jerry pulled the guys together and told them to meet at the swimming pool area at the hotel if they wanted to be part of an Army Chapter of the Chosin Few," recalled Dawn Francois.

About 16 of them gathered around the pool. Dawn took the notes. Ed Reeves—who had raised 8 children, including two adopted Korean orphans, with his wife Beverly—was appointed secretary. Oliver "Robbie" Robertson, the 3rd Battalion deputy operations officer and close friend of Harvey Storms, was chosen to be president, and George Rasula became the chapter historian.

It was official: They were now the Army Chapter of the Chosin Few. Its creation "was a declaration by Army veterans of the Chosin Reservoir campaign that they, too, were part of the legend," John Gray later said.

The Army chapter, with full support from the national Chosin Few, was an instant success. Word spread via letters, word of mouth, and notices in veteran publications. Harry Graham, living in Pennsylvania, read about it in the *VFW Magazine*. "I said, 'Hell, I'm one of those guys.'" He joined and was reunited with old B Company friends like Clarence White and Harry Jacobs. He never missed a chapter reunion after that. They soon had dozens and, before too much longer, several hundred members.

In those pre-internet days, there had been little contact between survivors, scattered as they had been after the battle. Veterans showing up at reunions were shocked to find comrades whom they had long assumed had died at Chosin. For decades Robert Ayala thought he was the only survivor from D Battery, 15th AAA, but he was soon reunited with a half-dozen men, including Jim McClymont, Grantford Brown, Hode Hensley, and Robert Slater.

Clarence White had marked off Cecil McMorris on a list as KIA, but he found him alive and well. Ray Radke had spent thirty years in the Army, retiring as a sergeant major, but he had never run into another Chosin veteran until he attended a reunion.

"They would sit and talk and talk," said Dawn Francois. "And the wives would listen to some of this and couldn't believe it because their husbands never talked about anything. And to hear the stories and to hear them open up and discuss things, and when they got home the wives would tell me what a difference it made just getting together, just being together in the fellowship, being able to talk about things that nobody else would understand, other than somebody that had been there. So it was a blessing for a lot of them."

Don McCallister and 4 other soldiers from A Company held a mini reunion in Knoxville. "We could talk to each other about things that happened there that no one else seems to understand," he wrote afterward in a letter. "Like how the hell did we get out of there? How did we keep the 10-to-1 odds from killing us? What happened to our buddies? Did they make it out? Where are they? Why didn't we get help when we needed it?"

"Well, I feel better after seeing some of the men and buddies. I think if it wasn't for The Chosin Few, no one would ever know or understand the circumstances we endured."

At one reunion Graham gave White a copy of an old Baker Company roster. Looking over the names while back home in Columbia, South Carolina, White realized that his friend Ralph Boughman—killed next to him on the day of the breakout—had been from Union, not far from where he lived. His remains had never come home. "I got the operator on the phone and told her what I was trying to do," White wrote. "The Lord had to be guiding this. The very first number she dialed for me knew exactly who he was. I've had telephone conversations with his brother, sister and cousins. It's exciting yet it's hard. Hard for me and I know terribly hard for the family. After all these years, I have come into their lives, trying to find peace for me and I hope and pray peace for them."

Grant McMillin was reunited with Tully Cox, the soldier whose legs he'd amputated at the prison camp. McMillin's son arranged to bring his father to Cox's home near Altoona, Alabama. McMillin was nervous about it, wondering if Cox might hold a grudge about losing his legs. But when they pulled up in the car, Cox came striding out on his prosthetic legs and stuck his hand through the open car window. "I want you to know this is the guy who saved my life," Cox announced to everyone in sight.

Reeves became good friends with Ralph Milton, the Marine who'd picked him up off the reservoir. For years, Reeves would call Milton at his home to thank him every December 5, the anniversary of their jeep ride together.

Some survivors wanted nothing to do with the group, at least initially. "There *are* men out there who do *not* want to talk about Chosin," Rasula wrote in a 1987 letter. "There is a feeling of guilt among many who survived Chosin. Those who have joined us, talked it out (at times showing deep emotions), end up for the better. We realize that PTSD is not limited to the Vietnam veterans. After 37 years the burden continues to be heavy."

Bill Etchemendy, the L Company commander who recovered from his three wounds at Chosin, went on to serve of thirty-two years in the Army, including counterinsurgency operations during the Vietnam War. At first, he refused to respond when Robbie Robertson contacted him about the Army chapter. But when he learned how little was known about the heroism of Harvey Storms as well as his own soldiers, he joined the chapter and tried to correct the record.

Ed Stamford was a regular at reunions, the only Marine member of the Army chapter. Stamford was a great champion for the 31st RCT, always defending the soldiers when they were bad-mouthed by Marines. "There was so much BS coming out of uninformed sources of the Marine Corps that I found myself a single voice defending the Army operation on the Chosin," Stamford recalled. "I shut many, or left many a mouth hanging open, by letting them sound off and then informing them that I had been in Task Force Faith's command party."

Benny Takatsu, the Japanese houseboy smuggled to Korea aboard the troopship, recovered from his wounds and opened a restaurant catering to Americans in Hokkaido, Japan. He attended Chosin Few reunions and met in Maine with the family of his friend Robert Tait, who died in captivity and whose remains had not been returned. "If I had the chance, I would return to North Korea to search for the missing in action," Takatsu said. "I am ready to stow away again on a ship, if necessary."

Mysteries were solved, such as the fate of the 31st Intelligence and Reconnaissance Platoon. Accounts of the battle said the platoon had simply vanished and was never heard from again. Surviving task force officers had heard rumors after the battle that some members of the platoon had made it back, but they were never able to locate any of them. "Exactly what happened to the I&R Platoon would remain a mystery for the next 35 years when a few survivors appeared at reunions to tell their story," said Rasula. Three squad leaders—Sam Muncy, Dick Cooper, and John Q. Adams—were reunited, along with Jim Arie and Roy Shiraga.

Every time they gathered, the Army chapter veterans asked a lot of questions. Why had the 2nd Battalion, 31st Infantry never made it to the inlet? How could X Corps screw up the transportation? Why didn't they get more airdrops of the ammunition they needed so desperately, and how was it possible they never received any ammo for the Twin 40s?

One question was asked with special bitterness: Why had the tanks been withdrawn from Hudong-ni? "If they'd left those tanks there, it would be a much different story," said Radke. Instead, Hudong-ni became the final graveyard for the 31st RCT. Bob Drake would "hesitatingly" agree that removing the tanks was a major mistake. "In retrospect, I hate to think how easy it would have been to have helped TF Faith," he said.

The men began asking another question: Why had the 31st RCT been left off the Presidential Unit Citation? The omission was a stinging rebuke. Some Chosin Few Marines supported asking the Navy to add the 31st RCT to the citation, but others insisted that the Army task force did not deserve the award. At the request of the Army chapter, the national Chosin Few board sent a letter to the Navy in March 1989, asking that the PUC be amended to include the Army units. Months later the Army chapter received an informal reply. "The Navy has stated, through the Marine Corps, that any further action on the PUC is not practical," Rasula reported in the March 1990 chapter newsletter.

There were other slaps. When the Navy announced an Aegis guided missile cruiser would be named USS *Chosin*, Navy Secretary James Webb, who served in combat in Vietnam with the Marine Corps, left little doubt that he thought it was solely a Marine honor. Chosin "was one of the great moments in Marine Corps history," he said in his 1987 announcement. "While other units disintegrated, the Marines fought their way out in bitter cold, never abandoning their equipment, their wounded or even their dead."

In October 1989, when the USS *Chosin* was christened in Pascagoula, Mississippi, veterans of the battle were in attendance, including several Army Chosin Few members. Among them were two comrades from Able Company, Roy Oxenrider and Willis Via. When they looked through the handout given to the guests at the ceremony, they found it spoke only of the 1st Marine Division and made no mention of the 31st RCT or any other Army units. It saluted the more than 700 Marines killed at Chosin but ignored the more than 1,000 dead or missing Army soldiers. The speakers paid tribute to the Marines at Chosin but said nothing about the Army men.

Oxenrider and Via sent letters complaining about the ceremony. The Navy and Ingalls Shipbuilding, which had organized the event, promised to correct the oversight when the ship was ready for commissioning. But the slight rankled.

Chickamauga Battlefield, Summer 1990

In the summer of 1990, John Gray traveled to Chattanooga, Tennessee, to attend the hundredth anniversary reunion of the Legion of Valor, a prestigious veterans' organization open only to recipients of the nation's two highest honors for valor in combat—the Medal of Honor or the individual armed services awards for extraordinary heroism in combat—the Army Distinguished Service Cross, the Navy Cross, and the Air Force Cross. Gray had retired from the Army as a colonel after thirty years of military service, including two tours in Vietnam.

On a tour of the nearby Chickamauga Civil War battlefield, Gray chatted with a distinguished gentleman in a business suit. The two men soon realized they had both served at the Chosin Reservoir. Gray learned he was speaking with retired Gen. Ray Davis, the legendary Marine who was awarded the Medal of Honor for his heroic leadership of the 1st Battalion, 7th Marines, in relieving Fox Company at Toktong Pass.

When Davis asked Gray if he had been part of the Army task force, Gray gave a detailed account of the action on the east side of the reservoir, telling the general that he believed the 31st RCT had bought time for Davis and his Marines to reach Hagaru-ri. Davis was surprised at what he heard, calling it "quite a story, and one of which he was unaware," Gray recalled. Davis said he wanted to learn more about it, and he suggested Gray join the Chosin Few.

Gray joined both the national Chosin Few and the Army chapter, though he was reluctant at first to attend a reunion, fearing it would bring back too many traumatic memories and sad recollections of those lost. But in the spring of 1991, he and his wife went to Fort Sill for the annual Army chapter reunion. Robbie Robertson greeted him as a long-lost brother, recalling how Gray's M Company had given refuge to soldiers from the headquarters company when it was overrun. Jerry Francois had suffered a stroke in 1988 and could no longer speak. But when he spotted Gray, he ran up to embrace him, weeping. Gray, too, had tears in his eyes as he recognized old soldiers. As they reminisced, Gray recalled, "I could sense a pervasive resentment against the Marines because of their subjective, partisan and often negative portrayal of the Army's role at Chosin as inconsequential."

The Army veterans worked at changing Marine attitudes. George Rasula gave a presentation at the 1992 national reunion, presenting a chronology of the attacks on the east shore and detailing the small size of the 31st RCT. "It was a revelation to most of the Marines," recalled Radke. Few had understood how undermanned and poorly equipped the Army unit was. After the presentation, a Marine veteran plopped into a seat next to Radke and looked at his name tag, which identified him as being with the 31st RCT. "He said, 'Damn, I didn't know there were only a couple of battalions over there. I thought the whole 7th Division was there."

But other Marines reacted negatively. "You're trying to rewrite history," some told Rasula.

At the 1994 Army chapter reunion in Rapid City, South Dakota, Gray was elected as chapter president, promising to try to gain proper recognition for the 31st RCT. Gray was the perfect point man for the fight as someone who had been awarded the DSC for heroism at Chosin. Perhaps even more importantly, he'd served in combat with the Marine Corps during World War II. That gave him credibility with many Chosin Marines. "As a World War II Marine and member of the 'once a Marine always a Marine' fraternity, I felt I still spoke the Marine language, and that our Chosin Few Marines would listen if I had a provable case to change their minds," he recalled.

Some strong evidence was emerging in the 1990s. Patrick Roe, who had been an intelligence officer with the 7th Marine Regiment at Chosin, served with Rasula on the national Chosin Few historical committee. As part of his research into the battle, Roe examined newly obtained translations of Chinese documents and studies, including *The Chinese People's Volunteers: A History of the War to Resist U.S. Aggression and Aid Korea*, published by the PLA in 1988. The Chinese history showed that the 31st RCT had fought two full divisions, the 80th and 81st divisions. Moreover, a third division, the 94th, had been held in reserve in case it was needed.

An attack by two divisions aligned with what the 1951 Marine Corps board study believed likely and what the Army Sporrer investigation the same year had concluded. Many 31st RCT survivors had always believed they had been fighting more than one division.

But in the years following the battle, O. P. Smith's more conservative estimate of one division had become the accepted figure. The official Marine

Corps history published in 1957, *The Chosin Reservoir Campaign*, by Lynn Montross and Nicholas Canzona, said only the 80th Division attacked the 31st RCT and that there was "no report of contact" with the 81st Division until after the battle was over.

In 1987, Roy Appleman's authoritative *East of Chosin* concluded that "the CCF 80th Division was the only enemy formation engaged against the 31st RCT." Clay Blair's monumental 1987 Korean War history, *The Forgotten War*, which relied heavily on Appleman in its account of the Army fight at Chosin, likewise said only the 80th Division had attacked the Army task force. Shelby Stanton's excellent 1989 study of X Corps in Korea, *America's Tenth Legion*, said the same. So did the official Army history of that period of the war, Billy Mossman's *Ebb and Flow* in 1990, as well as various academic papers.

By Roe's calculation, the attacking Chinese forces outnumbered the 31st RCT east of Chosin by a ratio of 6:1 the first two nights and 9:1 the last two nights. By comparison, the two Marine regiments at Yudam-ni faced attack ratios ranging from 3.9:1 to 5.5:1, according to Roe's study. At Hagaru-ri the defenders were confronted with ratios ranging from 4.8:1 to 8:1, Roe calculated. "Whatever one can say about RCT 31 the striking thing is that they took, proportionally, the hardest hit of any major force at Chosin," he concluded.

Gray sent a letter in late December 1994 to all Chosin Few board members and chapter presidents, highlighting the information. "With this new perspective of such a large enemy force on the east shore, it can now be readily understood why the 31st RCT was decimated," he wrote.

At the national reunion in Portland, Oregon, in 1996, Roe made a presentation based on the research, while Ted Magill, who had become a well-known trial lawyer in Florida, gave a powerful account of what B Battery, 57th Field Artillery had faced. The presentations changed the long-held views of many Chosin Few Marines about the 31st RCT. A Marine board member came up after the seminar with tears in his eyes, saying, "We didn't know," recalled Rasula.

Gray and the Army chapter had also gained an important ally. Gen. Ray Davis had become convinced by the evidence that the 31st RCT had made a vital contribution to the withdrawal. Davis was the guest speaker for the banquet at the May 1996 Army chapter reunion in Asheville, North Carolina. "First of all, I wish to thank all of you, my Army brothers, for the time you bought at a sacrificial price in fending off the Chinese and keeping them out of Hagaru-ri," Davis told the audience.

It was a watershed moment in the fight to restore honor to the 31st RCT, a tremendous gesture of recognition for the task force veterans, coming from one of the most honored and respected Chosin Marines.

But just as momentum was building for a renewed campaign to correct the PUC, it was nearly derailed by a bitter rift that broke out later in 1996 within the national Chosin Few leadership. Retired Marine Warrant Officer Dick Oly was elected as next president of the Chosin Few, but the result was challenged by some of the board members, including cofounders Kerr and Hessman. Soon the warring factions each had their own board claiming the right to control the assets of the Chosin Few. Though the push for Army recognition had nothing to do with the split, it was in danger of becoming collateral damage.

In June 1998, the dueling factions each held their own reunions: the Oly group in Jacksonville, Florida, and the Kerr group in Indianapolis. Gray, who had been elected to represent the Army chapter on the Oly board, presented the case for the 31st RCT to the directors in Jacksonville, showing them the translated excerpts from the PLA history. The Oly board unanimously agreed that the PUC should not have excluded the 31st RCT, and they voted to retroactively seek to amend the award. The board authorized its awards and decorations committee, chaired by retired Marine Colonel Bob Parrott and including Gray, Rasula, and Marine Chosin veteran Tom Kalus, to prepare a letter to send to the Marine Corps commandant making the case.

Before they could make much progress, the Kerr faction sued the Oly faction in federal court. The federal judge hearing the case approved a consent decree in November 1998 that restored the Chosin Few board to its composition prior to the 1996 split. That meant Oly was out as president. The consent agreement also barred the Chosin Few board from taking any executive or governmental actions without permission from the court.

This raised a dicey question for the awards committee: Who would sign the letter forwarding the case to the commandant? Parrott, who had received the Silver Star for his heroism while commanding an artillery battery at Yudam-ni, decided that as chairman of a standing committee not included in the judge's order, he had the authority to sign the letter on behalf of the Chosin Few.

To bolster Parrott's authority to proceed with the matter, the awards committee asked for support from three retired generals who were senior members of the Chosin Few: Ray Davis; retired Marine Lt. Gen. Alpha Bowser, who had been Smith's operations chief at Chosin; and retired Army Lt. Gen. Bill McCaffrey, the X Corps deputy chief of staff. All three agreed to support and sign the letter.

The letter, drafted by Gray and dated February 23, 1999, described the research that proved the enormous size of the force that had attacked the Army unit. "If this avalanche of Chinese manpower had bypassed the 31st RCT to initially attack East Hill at Hagaru-ri, instead of spending nearly five days laying siege to this strategically inconsequential Army force, then Hagaru-ri might have tragically fallen, and the bulk of the First Marine Division at Yudam-ni would not have had this vital logistic/staging base to which to withdraw," it read.

The letter said that because of a lack of intelligence about the Chinese force, "General Smith could not have known how critical the 31st RCT's defensive role was in protecting his command post and garrison" at Hagaru. It expressed confidence that Smith "would have promptly ordered inclusion of the 31st RCT" in the original citation had he known "the extent of the enemy reservoir east shore threat." It was a dubious claim—but a nice diplomatic touch. They did not want to be seen as criticizing Smith, a revered figure in Marine Corps history.

More than 4,000 members of the Chosin Few—80 percent of them Marines—"have gone on record as wishing to extend Navy PUC recognition to their soldier brothers," the letter added. The three generals signed the letter, each adding handwritten endorsements. "Actions East of Chosin were essential to our efforts," Davis wrote. Bowser, who, soon after the battle, had considered Marine criticism of the Army performance at Chosin "mostly justified," had a change of heart after seeing the evidence of what the 31st RCT had faced. "I am in full accord with the recommendation" to award the PUC, he wrote. McCaffrey called it "both a generous and long overdue gesture by the gallant Marines who fought at the Chosin." Having the endorsement of the three highly respected generals was critical. Davis and Bowser, Marines with impeccable Chosin credentials, had the stature to counter Smith, who died in 1977.

After the Army's Military Awards Branch endorsed the recommendation in June 1999, Parrott brought the letter to the Marine Corps Commandant,

General James L. Jones, who approved the recommendation on July 12. Secretary of the Navy Richard Danzig, "after carefully considering the recommendations," signed a memorandum on September 14, 1999, stating, "[The Army units of the 31st RCT] are hereby authorized to participate in the Presidential Unit Citation previously approved to First Marine Division, Reinforced for the period 27 November 1950 to 11 December 1950." Nearly a half century after the battle, the record had been corrected.

"At first, the Marines had nothing but contempt for the 7th division, for the performance of the 31st RCT," said McCaffrey. "They now understand if it hadn't been for that group of leaderless kids fighting up there for their lives, they probably would have been overrun."

The Presidential Unit Citation did not stop the denigration of Task Force Faith. Even as the award gained approval, a new book about Chosin appeared in 1999: Martin Russ's *Breakout: The Chosin Reservoir Campaign, Korea 1950.* It was a classic of narrative history, considered by some as the finest account of Chosin. Russ, who'd served with the 1st Marine Division in Korea during the final year of the war, saluted the Marine performance at Chosin while savaging the 31st RCT.

Russ portrayed "Faith's tattered mob" as shirkers and cowards of low character who largely had themselves to blame for their fate. At the Pungnyuri inlet, where the 31st RCT fought for days, "the GIs waited passively for the next thing to happen," Russ wrote. Faith did not bother to set up a real perimeter, according to Russ; "it was more like a number of scattered groups warming themselves up around fires." During the breakout, he wrote, "few of the GIs even bothered to raise their rifles, let alone fire them; that would be too provocative, too dangerous." Russ reported as fact that "many survivors of Task Force Faith were feigning wounds or frostbite" in order to be evacuated from Hagaru-ri, repeating the claims of Smith and Sporrer.

Russ conceded that the 31st RCT may have provided the narrow margin that enabled the Marines to hold Hagaru. "But the Army's performance," he wrote, "was in no way commendable; by default, they played the part of sacrificial lamb, and the lamb was slaughtered."

Bob Hammond, Battery A, 57th, read *Breakout* with two highlighters, one color for marking positive comments about the Army and the other for negative. He only had to use one color. "Marines did one hellava job at Chosin under extremely tough conditions, and they have every right to be proud of it. I am proud of them!" Hammond wrote in the Army chapter newsletter. "But I'm also proud of the men I knew in my outfit that fought to their deaths under impossible conditions. Martin Russ has no idea what these men faced, or for that matter, what I faced. And to make them seem as cowards by repeating slanderous rumor which has been proven untrue is to do the greatest disservice to these young men who should be held with the highest respect. And he dishonors them."

Lancaster, Pennsylvania, June 10, 2000

Emotions were high as the old soldiers of the 31st RCT stood at attention for the presentation of the Navy Presidential Unit Citation at the 2000 Army Chapter reunion in Lancaster, nearly a half century after the Battle of Chosin Reservoir. Two color guard contingents from the 31st and 32nd Regiments, then part of the 10th Mountain Division in Fort Drum, New York, presented the colors, each accompanied by their respective battalion commander and command sergeant major. Maj. Gen. Arnold Fields, the Marine Corps Headquarters chief of staff, presented the award on behalf of the Navy and Marine Corps. John Gray read the citation: "For extraordinary heroism and outstanding performance of duty in action against enemy aggressor forces in the Chosin Reservoir and Koto-ri area of Korea from 27 November to 11 December 1950." Battle streamers for the Chosin Reservoir Campaign were affixed to the pikes carrying the colors of the 31st Regiment and the 1st Battalion, 32nd Infantry. An Army band played a stirring rendition of "The Battle Hymn of the Republic" to conclude the ceremony. "Some of these old soldiers had tears in their eyes," said Gray. "This is closure at last, after all these years."

It was a moment of vindication for the veterans at the ceremony—Jerry Francois, Joe Ager, Harry Graham, Max Guernsey, Jerry McCabe, Ray Vallowe, George Rasula, and Grant McMillin among them. But the award, they knew, had been largely earned by the men who were not there, who had fallen in the battle and, in many cases, still lay at Chosin—men such as Harvey Storms, Ernest Fontaine, Henry Moore, Celestino Chavez, and Don Faith, to name just a few. "Task Force Faith owns that page on the east side of that reservoir," said Vallowe. "We paid a high price for it, and we will not yield that page in history to anyone."

McCabe, who had retired as a colonel after thirty years of service in the Army, had always expected the day would come that the 31st RCT would be recognized. "I was there," he said. "I know what happened. The things that were said we knew were said by people who weren't there and didn't know. I don't think there could be a prouder unit. We were fighters."

The honor would not have happened without the support of the Chosin Few Marines. "We, who were on the east shore, will be forever indebted to our Marine brothers for the refuge at Hagaru-ri that saved us, but we also like to think that we helped some in saving Hagaru-ri," Gray said. "Our mutual support for one another at Chosin indeed makes us an eternal band of brothers."

The dynamic between the Army and Marine veterans of Chosin had changed. The national Chosin Few reunion in San Diego in December 2000, marking the 50th anniversary of the battle, drew the largest Army crowd yet. They noticed a big difference in the way that Marines warmly recognized soldiers for their role at Chosin. Army veterans were asked to stand and be recognized at meetings. Retired Marine Lt. Gen. Steve Olmstead, who had been a rifleman at the reservoir and was now president of the Chosin Few, told the crowd at the banquet that the Army troops "saved our bacon." There was a camaraderie that had not existed before.

"All this time the Marines didn't know . . . what happened on the east side," recalled Bob Ayala. "All they heard was hearsay. Now that the facts have come out after 50 years, the Marines know what had happened out there, and now they accept us as people."

A few days later, on December 12, 2000, soldiers from the 31st RCT stood shoulder to shoulder with Marines from the 1st Marine Division at the Navy Memorial in Washington, DC, for a solemn and proud national commemoration marking the 50th anniversary of the battle.

Retired Marine Brig. Gen. Edwin Simmons, who commanded a weapons company at Chosin and subsequently served as director of Marine Corps History and Museums, paid tribute to the Marine and Army troops who served with a string of memories: "We remember the terrible fate of the 31st RCT. . . . We remember the rows of grotesquely frozen corpses. . . . We remember the breakout from Hagaru-ri. . . . We remember the rescue of 100,000 refugees. . . . There's a great deal to remember," Simmons concluded. "It's not the forgotten war, for us."

George Rasula, addressing Navy Secretary Danzig on behalf of the Army Chapter of the Chosin Few, expressed appreciation for the recognition finally given to the soldiers of Task Force Faith, including the hundreds of them still missing in action in North Korea: "The long battle of Chosin is now over."

Epilogue

Chosin Reservoir, Fall 2002

On September 12, 2002, a Russian-made North Korean military helicopter touched down in a base camp at Hill 1221, on the east shore of the Chosin Reservoir. Retired Army Col. Ted Magill and retired Marine Gen. Ray Davis stepped out, the first American veterans of Chosin to return to the scene. A half century after the battle, they had come to witness a joint United States-North Korean search for the fallen soldiers of the 31st RCT.

The delegation, including American Department of Defense officials and two North Korean Army colonels accompanying the veterans, traveled by road in Japanese-made SUVs up to the Pungnyuri inlet, where Task Force Faith had been surrounded.

Magill and Davis stood by the shore of the reservoir, now a placid lake with no ice, and gazed at the quiet surrounding hills. The frozen landscape where they had fought looked very different on a balmy day with no snow and the trees on the hills in full foliage. "It took a while to get oriented because everything was covered with greenery," Magill recalled. Much of the land was being cultivated, including acres of potato fields.

They drove up the Pungnyuri trail to the site where the 31st Intelligence and Reconnaissance Platoon had been overrun on the first night of the battle. There, a U.S. military team from the Defense Prisoner of War/Missing Personnel Office (DPMO) assisted by North Koreans was excavating a site with shovels. It was slow, painstaking work, but it was being done "with great dignity," Magill said. The delegation drove down the road toward Hagaru, following the route that Task Force Faith had taken on its breakout. The drive took them over bridges that had replaced the ones blown during the battle, around the hairpin curve, and along the south side of Hill 1221, which was now being farmed. They passed through Hagaru and continued up the western side of the reservoir to Yudam-ni, where the 1st Marine Division had fought. They saw few vehicles or machinery, mostly villagers traveling on foot or by bicycle. "The roads are much the same as they were 52 years ago and Hagaru is the same miserable place it was when we were there," Magill joked.

The excavations at Chosin had begun a year earlier. The veterans' visit had been arranged by DPMO to allow them to see a recovery operation firsthand, and report back to veterans' organizations and family groups in the United States. Eventually, the DPMO team working on the east side of Chosin would find the remains of 5 soldiers in a mass grave.

For Davis and Magill, it was emotional to watch the search for the remains of fallen soldiers at Chosin. "It's hard to believe, after 50 years, there's a chance for them to be returned to their families," Davis said.

Davis and Magill "are stoic type of men," noted Ashton Ormes, a senior DPMO researcher who led the delegation. "They wouldn't have survived what they went through if they weren't. But some of the things they said made me think they were remembering lost friends."

It had been a long journey to that moment. Representatives from DPMO began meeting with North Korean officials in the DMZ in 1989, trying to negotiate a way to bring home some of the more than 6,000 American servicemembers whose remains were still in North Korea at that time. In 1990 Pyongyang turned over boxes holding the remains of 16 Americans, the first MIAs recovered from North Korea since Operation Glory, thirty-five years earlier. Many more boxes were turned over during the next several years—208 in all. The K-208 boxes, as they were designated, were eventually found to hold the highly comingled remains of more than 700 individuals. Identifying them would take many years.

In 1996, after more negotiations, Pyongyang allowed a U.S. military team to work with the North Korean People's Army (KPA) on a joint recovery operation in North Korea for the first time. Several more joint recovery operations in ensuing years recovered 65 sets of remains. But until September 2001, no U.S. team had been allowed to go to Chosin.

The 12-member team was led by Army Capt. Eric Frensley and accompanied by a civilian archaeologist. As part of the agreement with North Korea, the team hired locals to assist with the operation—the locals were required to be KPA soldiers, and their main job seemed to be keeping an eye on the Americans.

The team was taken to a site where they had been told farmers had discovered human remains in 1979. It was close to the Pungnyuri inlet bridge. From photographs taken during the battle, they could see the present-day road and bridge lay in the same location as they had in 1950. "Nothing had changed since the war," said Johnny Webb, a DPMO official. "It was still exactly the same."

The team did most of the digging with shovels, but once suspected remains were located, they used trowels and brushes to expose the remains. Over the course of the month-long excavation of three different sites at the inlet, the team found 14 sets of remains, including 11 from one shallow grave. "Of course, it didn't take long for morale to get pretty bad in North Korea, but as soon as you found remains of an American, the morale of the team just skyrocketed," Webb recalled. The cold and dry conditions at Chosin were excellent for bone preservation. The team returned to Chosin in late October, this time investigating four sites on Hill 1221 and one at the inlet, recovering the remains of 5 more soldiers. All the remains were flown to the U.S. military's identification laboratory in Hawaii for examination.

They had found clues, including some clothing and three sets of dog tags found at one of the inlet excavation sites: Cpl. Frank Friedenberger of M Company, as well as SFC Carl Brewington and SFC Billy Donahoe of Texas, both of K Company. Friedenberger, it turned out, was alive and well and living in Altoona, Pennsylvania. He had lost his dog tags during the fighting at the inlet and was subsequently wounded, but he had made it across the ice to Hagaru. But Brewington and Donahoe were missing. After the Army obtained a DNA sample from his son, Brewington was identified in 2003 and buried at home in Missouri. When Donahoe had been reported missing in December 1950, his mother sent a letter to the Army. "Don't ever give up. Find my Billy for me," she asked. In 2004, after his remains were identified using dental records, Billy Donahoe was buried in a plot in a Houston cemetery that had been reserved for him next to his mother.

In September 2003, a team began the first excavation at the northern perimeter, where Faith's 1st Battalion had been the first two nights of the battle. The team found a shallow grave with the remains of at least 4 GIs. One of them was Cpl. Charles Williams, who had been part of an Able Company mortar section that was overrun the first night. Williams had been found dead in his foxhole the next morning, with his .45 pistol in his hand and several dead Chinese around him. All the bodies had been left at the northern perimeter when Faith's battalion left to consolidate with the rest of the task force at the inlet.

Williams's younger brother, Thomas, had always hoped Charles would be brought home, but he did not think it was possible. His children convinced him to submit a DNA sample. In March 2004, Thomas Williams got a phone call saying they had a positive match. "Dad was in shock to say the least," said his son, Larry Williams. "He could not believe that after all these years his brother could finally come home."

Further excavations around the A Company position led to the recovery of Ed Scullion, the company commander killed at the start of the attack. He was returned to his daughter in Virginia and buried at Arlington National Cemetery.

As the excavations continued, it was sometimes possible for the teams to get a glimpse of the conditions faced by the troops in 1950. During one visit to examine some proposed sites for future excavation, heavy snow fell, blanketing the mountains in white and making travel hazardous. Webb was driving with his North Korean Army counterpart to reach the team's location, and as the road worsened, the North Korean said they should turn around. But Webb persuaded him to continue, and they reached the site safely. "We were pushing the limits, trying to get in as much time as possible," said Webb.

Another time, a truck hauling potatoes from Chosin fell through a decrepit bridge, blocking the road indefinitely. Webb and the team surveyed the area and found a spot where they thought they could cross with their four-wheel-drive vehicles. After some negotiations with the North Koreans, they were allowed to proceed.

Sometimes, GIs were found exactly where they died. During an excavation at the inlet, Webb accompanied team members up to a ridge where they found the remains of two Americans, still in a fighting position. "They had a bazooka and a round that exploded in the tube and killed both of them," he recalled.

At other times, it was clear the remains had been planted there recently. The Americans believed that the North Koreans were holding the remains of a number of GIs either to use as bargaining chips or to encourage the United States to spend more money on recovery operations.

While not paying for remains, the U.S. government was paying North Korea millions of dollars for its support of the work, a sum eventually reaching more than $22 million. Excavating remains was a lucrative source of much-needed foreign currency for Pyongyang. "The North Koreans, I think, wanted us to be successful and so we were getting close to the end of the mission, and they would come to us and say, 'We talked to a witness, and we think if you go dig right here, there should be some remains there,'" recalled Webb. "And sure enough, we'd dig, and there would be remains there, but more often than not . . . , it was remains that had recently been placed there." It was frustrating because identification would be more difficult since the remains had been moved and often comingled with others. But the most important thing was that they were recovering remains.

On September 11, 2004, a new joint recovery operation began near the inlet. After over a week of excavation without finding any remains, KPA representatives came forward with another witness statement: A local road maintenance worker had found remains at the site ten years earlier and reburied them at a nearby location. The team was allowed to interview the worker, now retired, and learn more about where the remains had been reburied. They were in a cultivated field immediately south of the inlet. Several team members investigated the second site and, on September 22, found human remains in a mass grave less than fifty feet from the road. The entire team came the next day and, over the course of three days, recovered the comingled remains of at least 5 individuals, along with uniform fragments, including insignia worn by Army infantry and field artillery.

After some analysis, DPMO concluded that neither the first nor the second site were the original burial site of the remains. In the months or years after the battle, the remains had likely been collected from various locations on the east shore and reburied at the first site, possibly by a Chinese military burial detail or by North Korean villagers clearing the ground so they could resume farming. Then, at some point in the more recent past, the remains had been moved to the second site.

The remains collected in 2004 took years of painstaking analysis to identify. Between July 2005 and April 2012, 101 bone and tooth samples recovered from the burial site were sent to the Armed Forces DNA Identification Laboratory for mitochondrial DNA testing. The results, as they trickled in, were intriguing. A positive match had come up with DNA samples donated by Bobbie Broyles, or, as she had once been known, Bobbie Faith, the only child of Don Carlos Faith. Eventually, 19 of the samples were associated with Faith. Other information matched up. The remains were consistent with Faith's height. The upper left arm bone showed signs of trauma. The clincher was a lower jawbone fragment that indicated the subject lacked two rear molar teeth on the lower left—the same "dental deficiency" that had kept Faith out of West Point.

The DPMO teams had always hoped they might find Faith, but to actually do so was "just amazing," Webb said. "We knew there was a possibility, but until you get the remains back to the laboratory you can never be sure," he said. "When you know the story of Colonel Faith and how he performed, that is quite the emotional day to know that we've been able to recover one of the heroes of the Korean War."

In late September 2012, Bobbie Broyles received a telephone call at her home in Baton Rouge from Michael Mee, a senior Army official, with the news. A few days later, Mee and two Army casualty assistance officers in dress blues came to her home and sat in her living room for hours with a briefing book hundreds of pages thick, giving a detailed account of how her father had been found and identified.

"I never thought it would happen," she said. "Well, once upon a time I thought it would happen." But as the years went by, given how inaccessible North Korea was and the amount of time that had passed, it seemed unrealistic to think he would ever be found. Yet he had been. "The Army did not give up," she said.

Soon after Bobbie was notified, the Army Chapter of the Chosin Few got word of Faith's recovery. Her telephone answering machine was soon full of messages from the men of Task Force Faith. "They've been calling me for weeks and weeks and talking about my father and telling me they wouldn't have gotten out without him, that he saved their lives," she said.

Frenchy Mercier wished he could come to the funeral from his home in Montreal, but he was too frail to travel. "I'm glad they found him," said Mercier, weeping as he spoke. "He's a real hero to me."

Arlington National Cemetery, April 17, 2013

Don Faith's remains were wrapped in a white shroud and covered in an Army blanket for his funeral service at the Main Post Chapel at Fort Myer, adjacent to Arlington National Cemetery. His folded dress blue uniform lay atop the blanket. At Bobbie's request, the casket was open during the service. That was unusual for a partial remains service, but her father had been gone sixty-two years, and she wanted to see him. "He's here," she said. "I want it clear that he's here."

The Right Reverend James B. Magness, bishop for the Armed Forces for the Episcopal Church, delivered the sermon at the chapel, filled with members of the extended Faith family, active-duty Army officers, and Korean War veterans, including some 31st RCT survivors, among them John Gray, George Rasula, and Ray Vallowe. "Don Faith kept the faith," Magness said. "In the midst of war and challenges of command too numerous to count, Don set an example of what it meant to keep faith with his men and with the country that sent him to war."

An Army band and honor guard led the procession through Arlington National Cemetery. Seven horses drew the black caisson carrying Faith's flag-draped casket. It was a beautiful spring afternoon, and the procession moved along winding roads, beneath blossoming trees, toward the awaiting hilltop grave.

Near the grave site, the procession stopped, and a casket team carried Faith's remains to the waiting grave site. Behind them, a soldier carried a Medal of Honor flag with white stars on a light blue field, the same as the ribbon on the medal Faith had earned. Faith's grave lay next to his parents, Don Faith Sr. and Katherine. Bobbie only learned when the Army briefed her on the funeral preparations that her grandparents had reserved the plot next to them decades ago in the hope that their son would one day be found.

The current commander of the 1st Battalion, 32nd Infantry, Lt. Col. Theo Moore, was at the funeral, as were the last three officers who had commanded the battalion. Each of the former commanders had taken the battalion on combat tours in Afghanistan with the 10th Mountain Division, and each had lost men. Moore would be taking the battalion there in 2014. They all felt compelled to be at the burial. Faith's name carried a mystique for their battalion, which had adopted the name Chosin Battalion with the motto "Against all odds."

Gray was now 88, and his Army dress blues hung loosely on his frame, but his blue eyes still burned bright as an Army rifle team fired a three-volley salute and a lone bugler blew out a mournful "taps."

"Now the soldier is coming home," Gray said. "I wish there was some way he could recognize that all his sacrifice and valor was not for nothing."

Faith's remains were among the last to return from the joint excavations in North Korea. The operations ended in April 2005 amid worsening United States-North Korean relations and growing American concern about the safety of the excavation teams. Over the course of ten years, some 230 remains had been recovered, and the painstaking identifications continued for many years afterward.

Johnny Snock was identified in 2014, thanks to DNA provided by Joey, his twin brother. But it came too late for Joey, who died in 2007. Harold Haugland, the M19 commander whose heroics during the battle earned him the Distinguished Service Cross, was recovered in 2004, in the same excavation as Faith. He was identified in 2016 and returned to his family in Montana for burial.

The remains of Cpl. Eldon Ervin, 57th Field Artillery, recovered in a 2001 excavation, were identified in 2016. His best friend, Ray Vallowe, 85, who was at Ervin's side when he bled to death 66 years earlier after mortar shrapnel gashed his throat, traveled from his home in Illinois to the funeral in Seneca, Missouri. "My regrets that your life was cut short before you had the opportunity to raise a family haunt my thoughts always," Vallowe wrote in a eulogy. "But you did not die alone: I was there with you."

Many Chosin MIAs have been identified in recent years from the remains buried at the National Memorial Cemetery of the Pacific, the Punchbowl, which included 967 unknown service members killed during the Korean War who could not be identified following their return in 1954, during Operation Glory. It was long thought that the chemicals used to preserve the bodies when they were buried had destroyed any chance for DNA identification. But by 2012, based on improved capabilities, DNA testing began on the remains of unknowns at the Punchbowl, and to date, 232 from the Korean War have been identified. Sgt. Charles Scott of C Company was identified in 2013, in time for his 98-year-old mother to attend his funeral in Lynchburg, Virginia.

The Chosin Few continued making differences in the lives of the veterans. At the reunions, the Chosin veterans noticed that an inordinate number of them were suffering from joint deterioration, skin diseases, extreme sensitivity to cold, and impaired blood circulation. The frostbite so many suffered at Chosin had damaged blood vessels and nerves, causing conditions that were worsening with age. "Oh my God, I suffer all the time with it," said Harry Graham. Bob Ayala was plagued all his life with pain in his hands, arms, legs, feet, and joints. "My hands, they lock up on me," he said. "My fingers, I have to pull them out, and they hurt like heck."

When Chosin veterans went to the VA for treatment, they were often asked for documentation that they had been treated for a cold injury while in Korea. The aid stations at Chosin had been far too overwhelmed with life and death wounds for surgeons and medics to record such treatment. In many cases, veterans had no documentation, and the VA would deny their claims.

The Chosin Few created the Cold Injury Committee, led by retired Marine Gunnery Sergeant Ernest Pappenheimer and retired Army Colonel John Zitzelberger, who had been a medic at Chosin. They compiled a mountain of evidence, including a climatological study of the killing cold at Chosin in November and December of 1950. Eventually, the VA agreed to stop denying disability payments to Chosin veterans who lacked supporting medical records for frostbite or cold-weather-injury disabilities. Ayala and many others finally received a 100 percent disability.

It was often the families of those lost at Chosin who received the most comfort from the Army Chapter of the Chosin Few. Michael Couch was 5 years old when his father, Maj. Cliff Couch, the executive officer for Reilly's 3rd Battalion, was mortally wounded in the Chinese attack on the battalion CP. Michael's son, doing research on the grandfather he'd never known, learned of the Chosin Few and contacted the Army chapter. At Rasula's invitation, Michael Couch and his family attended the next reunion and met soldiers who had served with his father. "Those men embraced our family as if we were one of them and brought my Dad to life for me," Michael Couch said.

Gray invited Catherine Maclean, 3 years old when her father, Allan Maclean, was captured on the ice, to attend the 2005 chapter reunion. "I was disarmed, enlightened and tickled at the members' ability to merge the greatest depths of sorrow, fear and loss with humor and transcendence," she said.

Chosin can be seen today as one of the decisive battles of the twentieth century, with repercussions that reverberate three-quarters of a century later. These include a direct connection to two of the world's most dangerous flash points today: the nuclear threat posed by North Korea, as well as a potential Chinese invasion of Taiwan that could lead to a new armed conflict with the United States.

With MacArthur on the verge of reunifying Korea, the Chinese intervention rolled UN forces back to the south and ensured the survival of North Korea to this day. Despite enormous casualties, the 9th Army Group succeeded in driving X Corps out of North Korea, and it did not return. The heroic escape from Chosin and evacuation of Hungnam, for all the "Retreat, hell, we're just attacking in a different direction" talk, was still a retreat.

The 9th Army Group, which was to spearhead Mao's planned invasion of Taiwan in 1950, was instead diverted to Chosin and the invasion postponed, for three-quarters of a century now. Today, Taiwan remains unfinished business for the Chinese government, which still views the island as part of China.

The Korean War is anything but forgotten in China. It was "a formative moment" in the nation's modern history, in the view of historian Xiaobing Li, enabling Mao to consolidate Communist control of the country and placing China on the world stage. By fighting the most powerful nation in the world to a stalemate, China established itself as a rising major power and demonstrated that the United States could be challenged in Asia. The most important result of the Chinese offensive in late 1950 was "the broken myth" of American military invincibility, a PLA history boasted in 2006.

Chosin, or Changjin as it is known in Korea and China, looms especially large in the Chinese consciousness and has been used by Xi Jinping's government in recent years to stoke Chinese nationalism and anti-American sentiment. In a country where children are taught that South Korea began the war as a pretext for a U.S. attack on China, Chosin is portrayed as a heroic victory against American aggression. A blockbuster Chinese film about Chosin, *The Battle at Lake Changjin*, was commissioned by the government as part of the celebration of the hundredth anniversary of the Communist Party of China and was released in China in September 2021. It featured movie star and martial artist Wu Jing as a CCF company commander leading his troops against American invaders bent, according to the film, on crossing the Yalu River into China. At a cost of $200 million, it was the most expensive Chinese film ever made and the highest-grossing Chinese-language film ever. But beyond its propaganda value, Chosin is seen as holding potential lessons for a future conflict between the United States and China. "Chinese military historians and strategists now want to learn more from Chosin instead of merely continuing to glorify it politically," Li noted.

Though remarkably little remembered today by Americans, Chosin and the Chinese intervention had a profound effect on Cold War history. Even before the battle had ended, Congress approved a White House request for an additional $16.8 billion in defense spending, putting the United States on a path for an enormous rearmament that would continue for decades.

"The Cold War was an abstract idea until Chosin Reservoir, but the battle—as brutal as any ever fought—showed that it was very real, and convinced Americans that fears of dominos or red hordes were not exaggerated, and any amount of money spent opposing them was justified," James Carter, a historian of modern China, observed in 2021. "The arms race and the global cold war can be said to have started in the frozen hills around Chosin Reservoir."

WONSAN, NORTH KOREA, JULY 27, 2018

On the sixty-fifth anniversary of the armistice that ended hostilities in the Korean War, a U.S. Air Force C-17 landed at Wonsan, the port city in North Korea where X Corps began landing in late October 1950 on its ill-fated mission to reach the Yalu River. The American cargo plane had arrived to pick up fifty-five boxes containing the remains of missing service members.

The return was a goodwill gesture following a summit in Singapore a month earlier between North Korean Supreme Leader Kim Jong-un and President Donald Trump. Based on intelligence, the United States believed the North Koreans were holding the remains of at least 200 Americans to use as bargaining chips. But when Johnny Webb and the rest of the American delegation met with North Korean officials to arrange details, getting the boxes was a struggle. "The senior colonel who was heading up the negotiation said, 'Well, we don't have any remains, but we might be able to go out and recover some in the next few months,'" Webb recalled. "Well, we were sure that that was not a factual statement. So we continued to press and continued to press. And he finally said, 'We can probably find 50 remains.' Of course, again we had good intel that they had more than that, so we continued to press, and the best that we could get him to agree to return was 55 remains."

At the Wonsan turnover, the North Korean representatives seemed surprised that the American delegation included a Korean-born woman. Dr. Jennie Jin was the lead scientist on the Korean War project team for the Defense POW/MIA Accounting Agency (DPAA), the successor agency to DPMO. Jin's grandparents were among the 100,000 North Korean civilian refugees who escaped aboard ships when X Corps evacuated Hamhung in December 1950. Born in Seoul in 1979, Jin had paid little attention to Korean War history and her own family story until her husband's job took them to Hawaii in 2010. She took a job with the U.S. military lab, even though forensics was not her medical specialty. But Jin became drawn into the work as she studied the bones and realized that many of them were connected to her grandparents' escape. "I looked at the remains, and where did these guys die? In Chosin Reservoir. It gave me chills," she said.

Her grandfather, now in his 90s, had been the same age as many of the soldiers of Task Force Faith—kids 18, 19, or 20 years old—when he escaped North Korea. "So my grandfather is still alive, when these young soldiers didn't make it home. And I can only imagine what that was like for their families," she said. "After that, it became my mission. I can do something for the families who are still waiting."

Each of the fifty-five boxes was wrapped in a United Nations flag—the flag the men had fought under—and carried by an honor guard onto the C-17. After the boxes were secured in the cargo bay, an Army chaplain performed a blessing of sacrifice and remembrance. Once the plane crossed out of North Korean airspace, it was greeted by three F-16 fighter jets and escorted to Osan Air Base in South Korea. Then the boxes were flown to Hickam Air Base in Hawaii and transferred to the DPAA lab, where the work began.

The remains in each box were carefully laid out and tagged on lab tables. Some boxes contained only broken fragments of arm bones, while others had intact femurs, teeth, or pieces of skulls. Bits of equipment and uniforms—combat boots, helmets, buttons, knife sheaths, a canteen, and a mess kit—were also in the boxes.

After some analysis Jin and her team estimated that the K-55 boxes, as they were designated, held remains from about 250 individuals, about 100 of them from Americans and many of the rest from the ROKs who fought beside them. Possibly, the remains also included those of some Chinese soldiers who died next to them. Examination made it clear that many of the bones had been held in storage for a long time by North Korea. "They had been out of the ground for decades," said retired Air Force Gen. Kelly McKeague, the DPAA director.

The K-55 boxes had less intermingling than the K-208 boxes. The latter came from multiple locations, including POW camps, clusters along the DMZ, the east side of Chosin, and other battlefields, often with remains from different locations mixed in the same box. By contrast, the K-55 boxes came from only two locations: The majority of them, thirty-five boxes, came from the eastern shore of Chosin and twenty boxes, from the 8th Army's desperate fight against the Chinese along the Chongchon River Valley in late 1950. Each box held comingled remains, but each individual in the box came from the same location. This made identification easier in some cases. The remains of 80 ROKs were returned to the South Korean government. And by late 2018, remains started to be returned to families in the United States.

In July 2019, Sam Storms, then 79, was driving his pickup truck filled with brush to the dump near his home in Pflugerville, Texas, when he got a phone call. "I've got some good news for you," an Army official told him. "We found your Daddy."

Storms was stunned. He had last seen his father, Harvey Storms, on the train platform in Tokyo in 1950. "I just started bawling and had to pull off the road," he said. He called his three brothers with the news. They had all given DNA samples in the 1990s, but never really thought their father would be found, believing his remains had likely burned in the truck he was riding. "I kept hoping but never figured I'd ever see him," said Sam. The remains of Harvey Storms had been identified in one of the K-55 boxes. It was only two bones, his left femur and his right humerus, but it was their father. In June 2021, Harvey Storms was buried with honors at Arlington National Cemetery with his four sons and dozens of relatives in attendance.

National Chosin Few Reunion, Arlington, Virginia, September 10, 2022

A handful of Army Chosin veterans made it to the 2022 National Chosin Few Reunion at the Hilton Crystal City. Joe Ager and Max Guernsey were there, along with Monty Piercefield, who was now confined to a wheelchair. John Gray, George Rasula, and Ray Vallowe had all passed away in 2019. With the Army chapter closed down in 2021, the national reunion was the best opportunity for those left to catch a few of their old comrades. They also felt the need to stay vigilant for any slights directed at the 31st RCT. That came at a luncheon when a Marine Corps historian gave a talk about the battle and described the the Army task force's actions. "The soldiers are throwing down their arms, they're not even carrying their weapons anymore," he said. "They're just in this pell-mell kind of retreat towards Hagaru-ri."

Ager could feel his blood boiling. As soon as the presentation ended, he popped out of his seat and addressed the speaker. "My name is Joe Ager, and I was east of the Chosin Reservoir, and I'm one of the 387 survivors who walked out of the frozen Chosin," he said. "You made a statement that has been repeated for years about those of us that were east of the Chosin Reservoir." For seventy years, Ager said, he'd been hearing the claims that the soldiers of Task Force Faith had given up and run away. Nothing is ever said "about the bravery, and the gallantry and the sacrifice that we made east of the Chosin."

"So, I wish that the record is set straight about those of us east of the Chosin," he said. "We didn't throw down our guns and not fight. We fought to the very end."

Ager received loud and long applause from the audience. The Marine historian apologized profusely. Afterward, a stream of well-wishers came by Ager's table to thank him for standing up for the 31st RCT. "John Gray'd be proud of me, getting up and saying what he used to say," Ager chuckled.

No further remains have returned from North Korea since 2018, and there has been no response from Pyongyang about returning more of the estimated 5,300 American service members still in the north. But remains from the K-55 boxes and the Punchbowl continue to be identified at a steady clip in recent years.

In January 2022, 93-year-old Evelyn DeLauter Eccard was at a doctor's office in Smithsburg, Maryland, dealing with a lung cancer diagnosis, when she got a phone call that her kid brother, Sgt. Roy "Buddy" DeLauter, D Company, had been identified. "I never thought it would happen in my lifetime," she said. A military honor guard greeted DeLauter's remains when they arrived at Baltimore-Washington International Airport in April, and Maryland State Police escorted the motorcade to Hagerstown, in western Maryland. Firefighters stood on highway overpasses, saluting as the motorcade passed below.

Inside the funeral home, Evelyn broke down and sobbed atop her brother's flag-draped casket.

The funeral was held in nearby Boonsboro on April 22, 2022, on what would have been Buddy's 93rd birthday. His parents, including his father who tried to reenlist in the Army when he learned his son was missing, were long gone. But Evelyn was there, as were Buddy's two younger sisters, whom he had loved to tease, Margaret Carr and Jane Kline, both now in their late 80s. So were Buddy's two daughters, Sharlene DeLauter and Sue Draper, who were ages 3 and 2 when their father disappeared at age 22. They had been waiting their entire lives for his return. "I watched war movies thinking I would see my Dad," Sharlene said.

The Willow Brook Seventh-day Adventist Church was filled with family members, friends, and Korean War veterans. A military attaché from the South Korean embassy spoke of the debt his country owed DeLauter and saluted his casket. McKeague, the DPAA director, described DeLauter's recovery and identification as "nothing short of a miracle" and presented the family with a collage of photographs showing DeLauter in uniform and the recovery of the K-55 boxes. Sharlene spoke on behalf of the family, keeping her emotions in check until she said these final words: "He was a much-loved father, husband, brother, and friend to those he left behind."

Such moments are being experienced in small towns and big cities across the country almost every month. Anthony Mazzulla, the B Company platoon leader frozen to his seat in the back of a truck, was returned to Rhode Island in October 2021 and buried with his family, including his mother, Jennie, who never stopped hoping he would be found. Ralph Boughman, Clarence White's friend, came home to South Carolina in 2021. Charles Garrigus, the truck driver awarded the DSC for his heroism, was identified in 2022. He was escorted by representatives of thirteen police agencies to a cemetery in Greenwood, Indiana, and buried with honors in April 2023. Another 13 soldiers from the 31st RCT were identified in 2024. Celestino Chavez, the M19 loader who refused to leave his post when he was wounded, was identified in April 2025.

But many other Task Force Faith soldiers remain missing, some 400 as of July 2025. Oval Hamilton left the back porch light on for his son Donald at his home in Indiana until he died in 1996. Charlene Cox, Donald's niece, has done so ever since at her home, but the C Company medic who turned back to help wounded has not yet returned. Allan Maclean has never been found. Dale Seever, the C Company commander, remains missing. James Conner, the Episcopalian chaplain whose daughters were presented with a Silver Star that he was posthumously awarded in 2004, remains missing, as does Lawrence Brunnert, the Catholic chaplain who stayed with the wounded on the road at Hill 1221. Henry Moore, the platoon leader who was severely burned by the napalm and then died leading an assault on Hill 1221, remains missing.

Frenchy Mercier said this before he died in 2020: "Real heroes are still there."

Acknowledgments

THIS BOOK BEGAN ON A WINTER DAY IN LATE 2000, WHEN I DROVE DOWN TO Southern Maryland and sat down in the living room of Jerry McCabe and his wife, Peg. I was writing a series of stories for *The Washington Post* marking the fiftieth anniversary of the Korean War, and I wanted to learn about his experience at the Chosin Reservoir in 1950 with the Army's 31st Regimental Combat Team.

Like many Americans interested in military history, I was familiar with Chosin as one of the most dramatic and brutal battles the United States ever fought, but I knew it almost entirely as a legendary Marine Corps story. The 1st Marine Division, surrounded by a much larger Chinese force at the frozen reservoir, successfully fought its way back to the sea—rightfully one of the proudest episodes in the Corps' history. But I knew almost nothing about the Army's role at Chosin and the fate of Task Force Faith. The account Jerry gave me over the next several hours was at once fascinating, horrifying, tragic, and infuriating. But the story of how Army survivors had banded together in recent years to combat allegations of cowardice made after the battle was inspiring.

After writing my article, I knew there was much more I wanted to learn about the Army's experience at Chosin, and I became convinced more people needed to know the story. I stayed in touch with some Chosin veterans and their families and wrote about the recovery of the remains of MIAs from North Korea in subsequent years.

In 2013, when the recovered remains of Don Faith were buried at Arlington National Cemetery, I was there to help cover it for *The Washington Post*, but by then, it was more than a story to me. I took my then-13-year-old son, Donald, out of his seventh-grade class that day and brought him with me, something I had not done before. He had been born in 2000, the same year I'd learned about Task Force Faith, and now he was only a few years younger than many of the young men who died at Chosin. It felt both deeply moving and close to miraculous to watch the flag-draped casket carrying the long-lost Faith pass before me, as well as to see that flag presented to Bobbie Faith Bennett Broyles, who was 4 years old when her father died.

I am grateful to Bobbie and her husband, Stephen, for inviting me to their home in Baton Rouge in 2022, where Bobbie shared with me letters, photos, and other memorabilia related to her parents. Deep thanks also to Sam Storms and his family for sharing with me the moving wartime letters of Harvey and Helen Storms. It was a privilege to meet the Storms brothers at the dedication of the Wall of Remembrance at the Korean War Memorial in July 2022 and to join them on a visit to their father's grave at Arlington National Cemetery.

Special thanks to Charmaine Francois-Griffith, daughter of Jerry and Dawn Francois, who welcomed me to the final reunion of the Army Chapter of the Chosin Few and gave me much guidance on the project. Charmaine and Dawn kept their promise to Jerry to look after "the guys" in the chapter after he passed away. Thanks also to Byron Sims, longtime editor of the Army chapter newsletter and an honorary member of the chapter.

Many family members of fallen soldiers graciously helped me. One in particular is Dan Colasanti, who was 9 years old when his older brother James went missing in action at Chosin. In 2018, frustrated by the lack of available information on many MIAs from the battle, Dan spent long months creating a spreadsheet with the names and known fates of more than 2,000 U.S. soldiers who served with the 31st RCT in Korea. Dan's database was of enormous help during my research. James Colasanti remains MIA.

Ferd Protzman and Ron Jensen, two seasoned journalist friends from my reporting days in Germany, gave the manuscript careful readings, suggesting many improvements. Thanks also to the late Bobbye Pratt, an extraordinary *Post* researcher, who helped me track down veterans and family members. Gene Thorp, another former *Post* colleague, is the superb mapmaker. Thanks also to longtime coworker Phyllis Jordan and her husband, Brian Wilson, for hosting me during my research in California.

The story of the 31st RCT would be almost impossible to tell today without the prodigious research of Army historian Roy Appleman. After retiring from government service, Appleman became consumed by the Army fight at Chosin, and in the 1970s and 1980s, he doggedly tracked down key participants, collecting records and valuable accounts for *East of Chosin*. The research papers and interviews conducted by authors Eric Hammel and Clay Blair were also extremely helpful. The groundbreaking work of Xiaobing Li in *Attack at Chosin*, which examines the battle from the Chinese perspective, was invaluable. Also of great value were Patrick Roe's *The Dragon Strikes*, Shelby Stanton's *America's Tenth Legion*, Ed Simmons's *Frozen Chosin*, John Gray's *Called to Honor*, Randy Mills's *Honoring Those Who Paid The Price*, and Hampton Sides's *On Desperate Ground.* Julie Precious's excellent documentary, *Task Force Faith: The Story of the 31st Regimental Combat Team*, was also a valuable resource.

Thanks to Nick Mueller in New Orleans for introducing me to the preeminent Korean War historian Allan Millett, author of *The War for Korea* volumes, who generously shared with me the translation of a People's Liberation Army history of the war. Historian Mike Neiberg, at the U.S. Army War College, connected me with his colleague, Michael Lynch, the author of the fine recent biography *Edward M. Almond and the US Army*, who graciously provided research insights and connections. I'm also indebted to historian Gina DiNicolo for fueling my early interest in Task Force Faith.

At the U.S. Army Heritage and Education Center, Tom Buffenbarger and Justine Melone cheerfully fielded my countless requests for documents. Thanks also to Jessica Sheets and Andy Hayt with the Marine Corps History Division, Jim Zobel at the Douglas MacArthur Memorial Archives, and Megan Harris with the Veterans History Project. Ashley Wright at the Defense POW/MIA Accounting Agency helpfully set up interviews and provided information about the recovery of the missing.

The Korean War Project, a website (https://www.koreanwar.org/) founded by Hal Barker and maintained with his brother Ted, is a tremendous resource with biographical information and remembrances of many of the men who fell at Chosin. The Korean War Educator (https://thekwe.org/home.htm) is another valuable site featuring memoirs from many Chosin veterans.

Thanks to my mother, Joan Vogel; my webmaster and brother Peter Vogel; and my children, Donald, Charlotte, and Thomas, for their love and support. Any time there were complaints about freezing weather, the kids were conditioned to hear me mutter, "It was a lot colder than this at Chosin."

George Rasula, a Chosin veteran and longtime historian for the Army Chapter of the Chosin Few, jump started my research in 2000 with a parcel of papers about the 31st RCT. In 2001 Norm Strickbine sent me a copy of *Korean Vignettes: Faces of War*, a remarkable collection of firsthand accounts he helped compile from fellow GIs. Warren Wiedhahn, the president of the

Chosin Few since 2018, has helped many times over the years. Special thanks to Ray Radke, Charlie Gebhardt, John Gray, Harry Jacobs, Max Guernsey, Harry Graham, Grant McMillin, Ray Vallowe, and Monty Piercefield. I'm grateful to all the Chosin veterans I interviewed, some of them many years ago and others in more recent years. Most of them are gone now, but their story will not be forgotten.

Note on Sources

References for one or more paragraphs are often grouped in a single note. The order of the citations in each note generally corresponds to the information or quotation referenced. The following abbreviations are used in the endnotes and bibliography:

CFND: The Chosin Few News Digest

CJBC: Clay and Joan Blair Collection, USAHEC

DFP: Don Faith Papers

DMA: Douglas MacArthur Memorial Library and Archives

DPAA: Defense POW/MIA Accounting Agency

EAC: Edward M. Almond Collection, USAHEC

EHPP: Eric Hammel Personal Papers Collection, MCH

FOW: Korean Vignettes: Faces of War

GRP: George A. Rasula Papers, Hoover Institution

HHS: Harvey and Helen Storms letters

KWE: Korean War Educator (https://thekwe.org/home.htm)

KWP: Korean War Project (https://www.koreanwar.org/)

MCH: Marine Corps History, Archives Branch

NAC: Newsletter of the U.S. Army Chapter of the Chosin Few

NARA: National Archives and Records Administration

OPSC: General Oliver P. Smith Collection, MCH

RAC: Roy Appleman Collection, USAHEC

REA: Roy E. Appleman

RG: Record Group

SV int: author interview

TCC: The Chosin Chronology

USAHEC: U.S. Army Heritage and Education Center

VHP: Veterans History Project Collection, Library of Congress

WP: Washington Post

Notes

Prologue

Except as otherwise noted, the prologue is based on the author's notes and interviews during the Army Chapter of the Chosin Few reunion in Springfield, Missouri, August 29–31, 2021.

xii Chosin was the moment: Carter, "The Real Battle at Lake Changjin."

xiv A magazine article: "The Shame and Glory of Korea," *Fortnight*, February 19, 1951; "O. P. Smith to Navy Board of Decorations and Medals," 14 April 1953, Box 40, OPSC.

xvi One pressing issue: *NAC*, May–June 2004, 5.

Chapter 1: An End to the Peace

2 Army Lieutenant Alexander Haig: Haig and McCarry, *Inner Circles*, 19–20.

2 "Ned Almond could precipitate": Blair Interview with John Chiles, Combat Leadership in Korea, Box 2, CJBC, n.d.; Haig and McCarry, *Inner Circles*, 42.

3 Almond was in: Almond Testimony to Senate Internal Security Subcommittee, November 23, 1954, Almond folder, Box 29, RAC (hereafter Almond Testimony, SISS).

3 "It couldn't be, I told myself": MacArthur, *Reminiscences*, 327.

3 Whatever orders came: Wesley Curtis to REA, August 21, 1983, Curtis file, Box 8, RAC.

3 News of the North: Hoehn, "Chosin, Korea," Account for Eric Hammel, February 1979, Hoehn folder, Box 6, EHPP.

4 At Camp Haugen: Mills, *Honoring Those Who Paid the Price*, 39–40.

4 President Harry Truman: Truman, *Memoirs by Harry S. Truman*, 332.

4 It was quite: Blair, *The Forgotten War*, 54; Halberstam, *The Coldest Winter*, 63.

5 Back in Washington: David McCullough, *Truman* (Simon & Schuster, 1992), 777; Truman, *Memoirs by Harry S. Truman*, 334; Appleman, *South to the Naktong*, 38.

5 MacArthur later admitted: Jim G. Lucas, "Gen. MacArthur: An Historical Memorandum," *Washington Daily News*, April 8, 1964.

6 Contingency plans: Almond Testimony, SISS.

6 Accompanied by Almond: Manchester, *American Caesar*, 658; Weintraub, *MacArthur's War*, 50–51, 53; Halberstam, *The Coldest Winter*, 143.

6 The visit lasted: Blair, *The Forgotten War*, 77, 83–85; Halberstam, *The Coldest Winter*, 101.

7 The 7th Infantry: Blair, *The Forgotten War*, 50, 120; Almond Testimony, SISS.

7 The 24th Division: Blair, *The Forgotten War*, 88–89; Haig and McCarry, *Inner Circles*, 128; Mills, *Honoring Those Who Paid the Price*, 40.

8 On July 1: SV int, Brad Smith, June 2000; SV int, Carl Bernard, June 2000; Steve Vogel, "Unprepared to Fight," *WP*, June 19, 2000.

8 In six years: Weintraub, *MacArthur's War*, 12; Manchester, *American Caesar*, 660; James and Sharp Wells, *Refighting the Last War*, 39.

8 MacArthur was the Army's: Weintraub, *MacArthur's War*, 1; William McCaffrey, Draft Book Review of Korea: The Untold Story of the War, July 15, 1983, McCaffrey folder, Box 29, RAC.

8 MacArthur had been: Halberstam, *The Coldest Winter*, 128; Ricks, *The Generals*, 126.

9 The general rarely: Weintraub, *MacArthur's War*, 11, 13; James, *The Years of MacArthur*, 371.

10 GHQ in Tokyo: Halberstam, *The Coldest Winter*, 105.

10 Only one outsider: Halberstam, *The Coldest Winter*, 163; Appleman, *Escaping the Trap*, 45; Lynch, *Edward M. Almond and the US Army*, 1; Stanton, *America's Tenth Legion*, 4; "Sic 'Em Ned," *Time*, October 23, 1950.

10 Almond was commissioned: Biographical Sketch, Edward Almond Oral History, Box 1, EAC, USAHEC (hereafter Almond Oral History), 4–6; Almond VMI profile, n.d., Almond folder, Box 29, RAC; Lynch, *Edward M. Almond and the US Army*, xii.

11 In the months: Stanton, *America's Tenth Legion*, 9–10; Blair, *The Forgotten War*, 149.

11 Almond disgracefully blamed: Rick Atkinson, *The Day of Battle: The War in Sicily and Italy, 1943–1944* (Henry Holt, 2007), 383; Ricks, *The Generals*, 153.

11 After a reorganization: Appleman to Ridgway, March 19, 1978, Ridgway Correspondence folder, Box 20, RAC; Stanton, *America's Tenth Legion*, 11, 15; Almond to Emma Hoskins, June 8, 1951, Personal Correspondence June 1951 folder, Box 77, EAC.

11 Reflecting the Army's: Halberstam, *The Coldest Winter*, 160; Haig and McCarry, *Inner Circles*, 43.

12 With his career: Conversations Between Lieutenant General Edward M. Almond and Captain Thomas G. Fergusson, Senior Officers Debriefing Program, U.S. Army Military History Institute, Section 3, 47, Box 1, Almond Oral History; Stanton, *America's Tenth Legion*, 16.

12 MacArthur, skeptical: Lynch, *Edward M. Almond and the US Army*, 300; Haig and McCarry, *Inner Circles*, 43; Blair, *The Forgotten War*, 32–33; Almond Oral History, Section 3, 59–60, 73.

12 MacArthur liked to play: McCaffrey to REA, July 11, 1979, McCaffrey folder, Box 29, RAC; James, *The Years of MacArthur*, 380–81; Bill Paddock to Blair, November 15, 1984, 7th Division folder, Box 71, CJBC; Gurfein to Hammel, April 2, 1979, Folder 6, Box 5.

12 Some grumbled: Halberstam, *The Coldest Winter*, 163; Lynch, *Edward M. Almond and the US Army*, 186; McCaffrey to REA, July 19, 1983, McCaffrey folder, Box 29, RAC; McCaffrey interview by Blair, McCaffrey folder, Box 80, CJBC.

13 MacArthur, for his: Haig and McCarry, *Inner Circles*, 143; Wright interview, 20, Box 7, RG 6, DMA.

13 After the demise: Lynch, *Edward M. Almond and the US Army*, 180; Almond, "How Inchon Korea Was Chosen for the X Corps Amphibious Landing There on 15 September

1950," Almond folder, Box 29, RAC (hereafter "How Inchon Was Chosen"); Simmons, *Over the Seawall*, 3, 8.

14 MacArthur left the 7th: Barr, "Address Given by Major General Barr," February 21, 1951, USAHEC, 2.

14 The 7th Division was now: Appleman, *South to the Naktong*, 491; Almond to Claude Ferenbaugh, May 1, 1951, Personal Correspondence June 1951 folder, Box 77, EAC; Almond Oral History, Section 4, 22; Hugh May to REA, July 24, 1981, Hugh May folder, Box 9, RAC.

14 Originally activated: Carroll, E. D. *Bayonet: A History of the 7th Infantry Division* (n.p., 1953); Appleman, *South to the Naktong*, 5; "History of the Bayonet Division," n.d., 7th Division folder, Box 71, CJBC; Paddock to Blair, November 15, 1984, 7th Division folder, Box 71, CJBC.

15 One of the division's: John E. Gray, *Called to Honor: Memoirs of a Three-War Veteran* (R. Brent, 2006), 76–77; Blair, *The Forgotten War*, 276; SV int, Charlie Gebhardt, May 10, 2016.

15 That was part of its appeal: SV int, Ray Radke, August 29, 2021; Hoehn, "Chosin, Korea."

15 Cpl. Ray Vallowe: "Official Obituary of Cpl. William Eldon Ervin," Paul Thomas Funeral Home, posted March 26, 2016, https://www.paulthomasfuneralhomes.com/obituaries/Cpl-William-Eldon-Ervin?obId=832059.

16 Many of the regiment's: SV int, Jerry McCabe, December 2000; SV int, Sam Storms, July 26, 2022; Helen Storm to friends, July 14, 1949, HHS.

16 Now that it was clear: SV int, Ray Radke, November 19, 2021; Blair, *The Forgotten War*, 291; Carl Witte to Blair, June 16, 1986, 31st Regiment folder, Box 71, CJBC; Hoehn, "Chosin, Korea."

17 Not surprisingly: Jerry Francois interview with Blair, February 15, 1986, 31st Regiment folder, Box 71, CJBC; Blair, *The Forgotten War*, 276; *TCC*, 18; Berquist, "Organizational Leadership in Crisis," 10.

17 Most considered: Charles Davis interview with Blair, n.d., David Barr folder, Box 76, CJBC; Bob Jones to REA, March 2, 1981, Bob Jones folder, Box 8, RAC; Blair, *The Forgotten War*, 292.

18 Faith launched: "Col. Robert Ellis Jones Interview," Korean War Educator (hereafter Jones Memoir, KWE).

18 In spring 1950: Beauchamp to Barbara Faith, February 3, 1951, DFP.

18 Faith was big: *East of Chosin*, 20; Wes Curtis interview with REA, May 6, 1979, Curtis folder, Box 8, RAC; Don Carlos Faith Certificate of Service, 1947, DFP.

18 Faith was from: "Don Carlos Faith," DFP; "In Memoriam Edward C. Faith," DFP; Ridgway to Blair, June 29, 1984, 32nd Regiment folder, Box 71, CJBC.

18 Given his name: SV int, Bobbie Broyles, April 11, 2013; Martin Mumaw III, "Remembering a Hero," 1998, DFP; Wes Curtis to REA, February 20, 1978, Curtis folder, Box 8, RAC.

19 Brig. Gen. Matthew: Clay Blair, *Ridgway's Paratroopers: The American Airborne in World War II* (Dial Press, 1985), 20, 195; Ridgway to Barbara Faith, February 27, 1951, DFP; Ridgway to Jerome Cox, November 5, 1976, Ridgway folder, Box 20, RAC.

19 After the war: Jones to REA, March 2, 1981, Jones folder, Box 8, RAC; Jones Memoir, KWE, 16; Wes Curtis to REA, February 20, 1978, Curtis folder, Box 8, RAC; Kirkland, "Soldiers and Marines at Chosin," 258.

20 In Tokyo: Almond, "How Inchon Was Chosen," Almond folder, Box 29, RAC; Almond Oral History, Section 4, 29.

21 Almond wasn't the only: Weintraub, *MacArthur's War*, 111; Halberstam, *The Coldest Winter*, 158; Lynch, *Edward M. Almond and the US Army*, 172–73, 188.

22 For MacArthur, what: Stanton, *America's Tenth Legion*, 43; Lynch, *Edward M. Almond and the US Army*, 185; McCaffrey to REA, July 11, 1979, McCaffrey folder, Box 29, RAC.

22 Mao Zedong's alarm: Goncharov, Lewis, and Litai, *Uncertain Partners*, 146; Halberstam, *The Coldest Winter*, 50–51; Li, *Attack at Chosin*, 16, 25.

22 The speed: Goncharov, Lewis, and Litai, *Uncertain Partners*, 158; Li, *Attack at Chosin*, 25–27.

23 In early August: The 7th Bill Paddock, "Pre Korean Notes on the 7th Div," August 1950, 7th Division folder, Box 71, CJBP (hereafter Paddock journal); "U.S. Marines Combined Arms Training Center, Camp Fuji," U.S. Marines, n.d., https://www.fuji.marines.mil/About/; Jones Memoir, KWE, 17; Herbert Powell interview by Clay Blair, Powell folder, Combat Leadership in Korea Box 6, CJBC; SV int, Jerry McCabe, December 2000; SV int, Bobbie Broyles, April 11, 2013.

23 Harvey and Helen Storms: Harvey to Helen Storms, August 21, 1950, and October 11, 1950, HHS; SV int, Sam Storms, July 26, 2022.

Chapter 2: We Shall Land at Inchon

25 The race to rebuild: Paddock journal, Box 71, CJBP.

25 MacArthur ordered: "Equipping of the Seventh Infantry Division," August 4, 1950, folder 2, Box 2, RG 6, DMA; Almond, "How Inchon Was Chosen," Almond folder, Box 29, RAC.

25 Across the United States: SV int, Lloyd Mielenz, June 16, 2023; Lloyd Mielenz interview, AFC/2001/001/41636, VHP; Mielenz, "Lloyd Mielenz Remembers Chosin," 4; Widener, "Young Teenage GIs Take On Communists," 36–37; SV int, Grant McMillin, August 29, 2021.

26 Some of the new: Gray, *Called to Honor*, prologue, 72, 76.

27 Two highly experienced: Appleman, *East of Chosin*, 21–23; Curtis to REA, February 20, 1979, Curtis folder, Box 8, RAC; Miller to REA, July 29, 1980, Miller file, Box 9, RAC.

27 But Curtis was concerned: Curtis to REA, February 20, 1979, Curtis folder, Box 8, RAC; Berquist, "Organizational Leadership in Crisis," 15; Appleman, *East of Chosin*, 349.

27 In all, some 390: Almond, "How Inchon Was Chosen," Almond folder, Box 29, RAC; Appleman, *South to The Naktong* , 492; Haig and McCarry, *Inner Circles*, 42.

28 Faced with this: Lynch, *Edward M. Almond and the US Army*, 190; Appleman, *South to The Naktong*, 386; SV int, Ray Radke, August 29, 2021; "Comments by Major General David G. Barr," n.d., 7th Division folder, Box 71, CJBC.

28 Lt. John Gray: Gray, *Called to Honor*, 78; Paddock journal, Box 71, CJBP; Address Given by Major General Barr Before the Army War College, 2, USAHEC.

29 Like many MacArthur: "Fremont 'Monty' Piercefield memoir," KWE; Lester Olson to Clay Blair, June 27, 1986, 31st Regiment folder, Box 71, CJBC; Gray, *Called to Honor*, 79.

29 It fell to the squad: Curtis to REA, January 1, 1977, Curtis folder, Box 8, RAC; Bigger, "Reflections and Comments"; Harvey to Helen Storms, September 15, 1950, HHS.

29 The Americans and Koreans: John Zitzelberger to Eric Hammel, June 18, 1984, 31st Regiment folder, Box 71, CJBC; Oxenrider, "A Week of Eternity," 5; Paddock journal, Box 71, CJBP.

42 MacArthur pushed ahead: Appleman, *South to The Naktong*, 498; Halberstam, *The Coldest Winter*, 295–97; Blair, *The Forgotten War*, 230.

30 Maj. Gen. Oliver: Russ, *Breakout*, 186; Family Album and Journal of Oliver Prince Smith, OPSC, 331 (hereafter Smith Family Journal); General Oliver P. Smith oral history interview by Benis M. Frank, 1973, MCH (hereafter Smith Oral History), 199–200; Haig and McCarry, *Inner Circles*, 44.

31 The tensions: Lynch, *Edward M. Almond and the US Army*, 190–92; Simmons, *Over the Seawall*, 16; John Chiles interview by Clay Blair, Combat Leadership in Korea Box 2, CJBC.

31 On August 23: Interview with Lieutenant General Edward M. Almond, January 20, 1967, RG 32 Oral Histories, DMA; James, *The Years of MacArthur*, 470–71; MacArthur, *Reminiscences*, 351.

31 The same day: Goncharov, Lewis, and Litai, *Uncertain Partners*, 171; Halberstam, *The Coldest Winter*, 305, 372.

32 On August 26: Stanton, *America's Tenth Legion*, 38; Gray, *Called to Honor*, 80.

32 It wasn't clear: Appleman, *East of Chosin*, 26; Mortrude to Merrill Needham, November 14, 1985, Mortrude folder, Box 8, RAC.

32 Almond inspected: Lt. Gen. Edward M. Almond Diary Korea: August 1950–July 1951, Almond Diary file, July 31, 1950, Box 29, RAC (hereafter Almond Diary); Almond interview notes by REA, April 8, 1977, Almond folder, Box 29, RAC.

33 The Marines, for their: Smith to Lynn Montross, June 28, 1955, Monograph correspondence 1953 folder, Box 21, OPSC; Haig and McCarry, *Inner Circles*, 42; McCaffrey notes for REA received March 2, 1981, McCaffrey correspondence folder, Box 20, RAC.

33 In the first days: Harvey to Helen Storms, September 15, 1950, HSS; Appleman, *South to The Naktong*, 501; Gray, *Called to Honor*, 80; Reeves, *Beautiful Feet and Real Peace*, 5.

34 Aboard the *Randall*: SV int, Ray Radke, August 29, 2021; Takatsu, "Deception and Decency"; "Fremont 'Monty' Piercefield Memoir," KWE, 2.

34 After four days: "Order of Battle US Seventh Infantry Division 1 September 1950–31 December 1950," 7th Infantry Division Chosin folder, Box 7, RAC; Harvey to Helen Storms, September 15, 1950, HSS; "Sunday, September 10, 1950, Earthquake," Earthquakes.Zone, last updated 2025, https://earthquakes.zone/1950/09/10/03:21:22-000; Appleman, *South to The Naktong*, 502; Blair, *The Forgotten War*, 267.

34 Given the narrow window: Harvey to Helen, September 15, 1950, HHS; James Dill diary, September 12, 1950 to December 31, 1951, Dill Diary folder, Box 78, CJBC (hereafter Dill Diary); SV int, Harry Graham, August 29, 2021; Charles Beauchamp, interviewed by Clay Blair, Beauchamp folder, Box 76, CJBC; White, "Korean War Memories"; Haig and McCarry, *Inner Circles*, 39; Almond Oral History, Section 4, 45; Dill to Harry Summers, November 26, 1984, Dill Diary folder, Box 78, CJBC.

35 Adm. Doyle: Smith, "Aide-Memoire Korea," 127; James, *The Years of MacArthur*, 474; Gray, *Called to Honor*, 80; "Fremont 'Monty' Piercefield Memoir," KWE, 2.

35 The North Koreans: Halberstam, *The Coldest Winter*, 305; Blair, *The Forgotten War*, 269–70; James, *The Years of MacArthur*, 476; Smith, "Aide-Memoire Korea," 149.

36 Almond was anxious: Stanton, *America's Tenth Legion*, 83; Interview with Captain Edward P. Stamford, 16 March 1951, 44, MCH (hereafter Stamford Interview); "Fremont 'Monty' Piercefield Memoir," KWE, 2; Heinl, *Victory at High Tide*, 157.

36 Moving forward on September 20: Stanton, *America's Tenth Legion*, 88; Stamford Interview, 47.

36 Capt. Bob Jones: Jones, *FOW*, 41; Miller to REA, September 29, 1979, Miller folder, Box 9, RAC; Jones Memoir, KWE; "It Takes More than That to Stop Captain Jones," *Citizen* (Poynor, TX), November 24, 1950.

37 By the end: Col. Alpha Bowser, Comments on Marine Corps Board Study, December 29, 1951, COP's comments folder, Box 67, OPSC; Lynn Montross and Nicholas A. Canzona, *The Inchon-Seoul Operation—U.S. Marine Operations in Korea*, vol. II (Headquarters U.S. Marine Corps, 1955), 221.

37 The 31st Regiment Polar Bears: Appleman, *South to The Naktong*, 522; Gray, *Called to Honor*, 81; Harvey to Helen Storms, September 22–September 23, 1950, HHS.

37 Two big fights: Stanton, *America's Tenth Legion*, 62; James, *The Years of MacArthur*, 480; Appleman, *South to The Naktong*, 513, 527; Almond Oral History, Section 4, 50, 53; Smith, "Aide-Memoire Korea," 264.

38 Almond was infuriated: Blair, *The Forgotten War*, 289; Almond Oral History, Section 4, 53–54; Almond to Margaret, September 24, 1950, Correspondence with Wife folder, Box 77, EAC.

39 A heavy ground: Blair, *The Forgotten War*, 292; Heinl, *Victory at High Tide*, 220–21; Appleman, *South to The Naktong*, 528–30; Beauchamp interview notes by Clay Blair, 32nd Regiment folder, Box 71, CJBC; Mortrude to Needham, November 14, 1985, and March 23, 1986, Mortrude folder, Box 8, RAC.

39 Almond soon decided: "Excerpt from Personal Notes of Lt. Gen. E. M. Almond," September 1950–July 1951; Almond folder, Box 29, RAC; McCaffrey to REA, December 5, 1975, McCaffrey folder, Box 29, RAC.

39 After speaking: Lynch, *Edward M. Almond and the US Army*, 205; Almond Oral History, Section 4, 55; Smith Family Journal, OPSC, 356.

40 As he had been: Heinl, *Victory at High Tide*, 239; Blair, *The Forgotten War*, 293.

40 The next morning: Stamford Interview, MCH, 62; Beauchamp interview notes, 32nd Regiment folder, Box 71, CJBC; Jones Memoir, KWE, 21; Mortrude to Needham, November 14, 1985, Mortrude folder, Box 8, RAC; Mortrude DSC, folder 1, Box 9, RG 6, DMA.

40 Lt. Col. McCaffrey: McCaffrey interview with Clay Blair, McCaffrey folder, Box 80, CJBC; Barr to Henry Hodes, September 26, 1950, William R. Lynch folder, Box 8, RAC.

40 Among the C Company: Widener, "Young Teenage GIs Take On Communists," 37; Mills, *Honoring Those Who Paid the Price*, 22, 58, 98.

41 As MacArthur predicted: Appleman, *South to The Naktong*, 572–73; Harvey to Helen Storms, September 25, 1950, HHS; Blair, *The Forgotten War*, 315–16; Gray, *Called to Honor*, 81.

Chapter 3: An Unkind and Inexorable Fate

42 Ned Almond had: Smith, "Aide-Memoire Korea," 313; James, *The Years of MacArthur*, 483; Stanton, *America's Tenth Legion*, 112; Halberstam, *The Coldest Winter*, 312; Haig and McCarry, *Inner Circles*, 47; Blair, *The Forgotten War*, 319.

42 Inchon had succeeded: Smith, "Aide-Memoire Korea," 325–26; James, *The Years of MacArthur*, 488; "Record of the Actions Taken by the Joint Chiefs of Staff . . . from 25 June 1950 to 11 April 1951" for the Senate Armed Forces and Foreign Relations Committees, April 30, 1951, Record of Actions folder, Box 64, CJBC (hereafter Record of the Actions JCS); Marshall to MacArthur, September 30, 1950, folder 4, Box 9, RG 6, DMA.

43 On September 28: Almond Testimony, SISS; Appleman, *South to The Naktong*, 610; Stanton, *America's Tenth Legion*, 125–26.

43 But MacArthur's grand: Weintraub, *MacArthur's War*, 165, 168; Lynch, *Edward M. Almond and the US Army*, 207–8; Halberstam, *The Coldest Winter*, 313–15; Stanton, *America's Tenth Legion*, 121; James, *The Years of MacArthur*, 492; "Comments by Major General David G. Barr," n.d., 7th Division folder, Box 71, CJBC; Beauchamp interview notes, 32nd Regiment folder, Box 71, CJBC; McCaffrey interview with Blair, McCaffrey folder, Box 80, CJBC.

44 Even MacArthur's nominal: J. Lawton Collins, *War in Peacetime: The History and Lessons of Korea* (Houghton Mifflin, 1969), 141–42.

44 Shortly after midnight: Roe, *The Dragon Strikes*, 103; Millett, *The War for Korea*, 293, 298–99; Li, *Attack at Chosin*, 28, 219.

45 That same day: Appleman, *South to The Naktong*, 632; Lynch, *Edward M. Almond and the US Army*, 211–12.

45 Accidents were the: "James DeLong's Experience," *NAC*, March 1990, 11; Harvey to Helen Storms, October 7 and October 11, 1950, HHS; Blair, *The Forgotten War*, 345; Paddock to Blair, November 15, 1984, 7th Division folder, Box 71, CJBC.

46 Adding to the uncertainty: Blair, *The Forgotten War*, 294; Ovenshine to Blair, October 19, 1984, 31st Regiment folder, Box 71, CJBC.

46 Mao notified Kim: Li, *Attack at Chosin*, 30–31; Appleman, *East of Chosin*, 52–53; "The Unforgotten Korean War," 178; Roe, *The Dragon Strikes*, 73; Zhou, "Mao's Telegrams," 4.

47 Douglas MacArthur did not: Truman, *Memoirs by Harry S. Truman*, 364–65; MacArthur, *Reminiscences*, 361; James, *The Years of MacArthur*, 505;

47 MacArthur briefly reviewed: "Substance of Statements Made at Wake Island Conference on 15 October 1950," Foreign Relations of the United States, 1950, Office of the Historian, Department of State, https://history.state.gov/historicaldocuments/frus1950v07/d680.

47 MacArthur was not alone: Blair, *The Forgotten War*, 338; James, *The Years of MacArthur*, 516–17.

48 The soldiers of the 7th: Mills, *Honoring Those Who Paid the Price*, 115; SV int, Harry Graham, August 29, 2021; SV int, Grant McMillin, August. 29, 2021; "Comments by Major General David G. Barr," n.d., 7th Division folder, Box 71, CJBC.

48 As they waited: Stamford to REA, October 28, 1980, Stamford folder, Box 9, RAC; Charles Beauchamp, "Allan Duard MacLean," Assembly, West Point, January 1955, 52; Herbert Powell interview, Powell folder, Combat Leadership in Korea Box 6, CJBC; Beauchamp interview, Beauchamp folder, Box 76, CJBC.

49 Maclean made a quick: Hoehn, "Chosin, Korea"; George Rasula to Lucy Rasula, November 2, 1950, *Changjin Journal*, November 1, 2002; Francois, Recollections transcripts.

49 Most of Maclean's staff: SV int, Ray Radke, November 19, 2021; Rasula to Hammel, March 16, 1979, Rasula folder, Box 5, EHP; McCaffrey to REA, March 11, 1978, McCaffrey correspondence folder, Box 20, RAC.

49 On October 19: James, *The Years of MacArthur*, 496; Headquarters X Corp Special Report on Chosin Reservoir, X Corps Command Report folder, Box 13, RAC, (hereafter X Corps Special Report); Blair, *The Forgotten War*, 346, 363–64; Halberstam, *The Coldest Winter*, 369.

50 Ned Almond was beside: Stanton, *America's Tenth Legion*, 153; Blair, *The Forgotten War*, 343; Haig and McCarry, *Inner Circles*, 53–54; "Sic 'Em Ned," *Time*, October 23, 1950; Almond to Leo Clarke, November 3, 1950, Correspondence CG X Corps folder, Box 55, EAP.

51 The main body: Stanton, *America's Tenth Legion*, 153–54; McCaffrey interview, McCaffrey folder, Box 80, CJBC; X Corps Special Report, Box 13, RAC.

52 Halloween was approaching: Harvey to Helen Storms, October 15, October 23, and October 29, 1950, HHS; Dill Diary, October 18, 1950, Box 78, CJBC; Storms to Ruth, Kay and Jo, October 30, 1950, HHS.

Chapter 4: Into North Korea

53 The 7th Division: *Philadelphia Inquirer*, October 30, 1950, 2,; GHQ press releases Aboard USS *Eldorado*, October 29 and October 30, 1950, Folder 9: Miscellaneous Press Releases, August 1950–11 April 1951, Box 1, RG 7, DMA; SV int, William McCaffrey, December 2000; McCaffrey to REA, April 14, 1981; Mortrude to Needham, March 23, 1986, Mortrude folder, Box 8, RAC.

53 Barr, from Nanafalia: David Goodwin Barr biography, Department of Army, Barr folder, Box 76, CJBC; Blair, *The Forgotten War*, 274–75; "Secret Testimony in 1949 Forecast Victory of Mao," United Press International, in *Rocky Mountain News*, December 13, 1976; Almond Oral History, Section 4, 33, EAC.

54 Barr and Almond: Stanton, *America's Tenth Legion*, 54; Almond interview notes by REA, April 8, 1977, Almond folder, Box 29, RAC; Blair, *The Forgotten War*, 275; Chiles to Blair, April 8, 1986, and Boniface Campbell to Blair, April 5, 1986, Barr folder, Box 76, CJBC; Paddock to Blair, December 3, 1984, 7th Division folder, Box 71, CJBC.

54 The same day the 7th: Li, *Attack at Chosin*, 33; Zhou, "Mao's Telegrams," 4.

55 Warnings were flashing: Appleman, *East of Chosin*, 4; Millett, *The War for Korea*, 301; Record of the Actions JCS, Record of Actions folder, Box 64, CJBC.

55 Almond, at least: Almond Oral History, Section 4, 68, and Section 5, 23–24, EAC; Stanton, *America's Tenth Legion*, 162–63; Almond Diary, 30 October 1950, Box 29, RAC; McCaffrey to REA, March 30, 1978, McCaffrey correspondence folder, Box 20, RAC.

56 Charles Willoughby: Halberstam, *The Coldest Winter*, 376; Blair, *The Forgotten War*, 377; Smith to Davis Merwin, August 29, 1962, Monograph correspondence folder, Box 21, OPSC; Roe, *The Dragon Strikes*, 167.

56 Regardless of Willoughby's: Appleman, *South to The Naktong*, 678; Richard Stewart, *The Chinese Intervention: 3 November 1950–24 January 1951* (Center of Military History, U.S. Army, ca. 2000), 3; Smith Family Journal, OPSC, 370.

57 The 31st Regiment Polar: Donovan, "Photographs of Korea," 60; Dill Diary, November 1, 1950, Box 78, CJBC; SV int, Grant McMillin, August 29, 2021; November War Diary Summaries, Headquarters X Corps, 1 November to 30 November 1950, X Corps War Diary folder, Box 13, RAC.

57 Beauchamp's 32nd Regiment: Curtis, "Operations of the First Battalion," 1; Bigger, "Reflections and Comments."

58 The Chinese attack: CINCUNC to JCS 7 November 1950, JCS outgoing folder, Box 45, RG 9, DMA; Marshall to MacArthur, November 7, 1950, folder 11, Box 1, RG 6, DMA; Blair, *The Forgotten War*, 395, 403.

59 Reflecting MacArthur's concern: Smith to Major General Stephens, November 15, 1957, Monograph correspondence folder, Box 21, OPSC; Almond to Hoke Smith, November 17, 1950, Box 85, EAC.

59 There were hints: Rasula to Lucy, November 7 and November 15, 1950, *Changjin Journal*, November 1, 2002; Storms to Helen, November 20, 1950, HHS; Appleman, *South to The Naktong*, 733; Rasula to Hammel, September 16, 1980, Rasula folder, Box 5, EHPP; Gray, *Called to Honor*, 86; Bryant, "Four Days and Five Nights."

61 However, Maclean's report: Blair, *The Forgotten War*, 390; Beauchamp interview, Beauchamp folder, Box 76, CJBC; Beauchamp to Blair, March 25, 1986, 32nd Regiment folder, Box 71, CJBC.

61 Then, as quickly: Appleman, *Escaping the Trap*, 10–11; Li, *Attack at Chosin*, 46; "The Unforgotten Korean War," 178.

61 Peng's plan: Roe, *The Dragon Strikes*, 233; Zhou, "Mao's Telegrams," 4; Li, *Attack at Chosin*, 32–34, 42, 46.

62 The Joint Chiefs: JCS to CINCFE, November 9, 1950, JCS 30 June 1950–5 April 1951 folder, Box 45, RG 9, DMA; Roe, *The Dragon Strikes*, 194, 201; Schnabel, *Policy and Direction*, 259.

63 In his reply: CINCFE to DA, November 9, 1950, folder 6, Box 9, RG 6, DMA; Halberstam, *The Coldest Winter*, 44.

63 As went MacArthur: Smith, "Aide-Memoire Korea," 581; Appleman, *South to The Naktong*, 734; Lynch, *Edward M. Almond and the US Army*, 221; Blair, *The Forgotten War*, 417; Powell interview, Powell folder, Combat Leadership in Korea Box 6, CJBC.

63 The dangers of the: Smith, "Aide-Memoire Korea," 577; Rasula to Lucy Rasula, November 14, 1950, *Changjin Journal*, November 1, 2002; Appleman, *Escaping the Trap*, xi.

64 The Marines were relatively: Marker, "A Soldier Remembers," 4; John Zitzelberger to Hammel, June 18, 1984, 31st Regiment folder, Box 71, CJBC; G-4 to CG, "Mountain Sleeping Bags for ROK Personnel," 1950, and "Evaluation Cold Injury 7th Division," November 22, 1950, Information Bulletins, X Corps folder, Box 62, EAC; Haig and McCarry, *Inner Circles*, 59; Harvey Storms to Helen, November 15, 1950, HHS.

64 The situation was only: Beauchamp to Blair, March 25, 1986, 32nd Infantry Regiment folder, Box 71, CJBC; SV int, Charlie Gebhardt, May 10, 2016; Ryder, "The Coldest Battle"; "What Well-Dressed GIs Wore with Temps in the Freezer," *NAC*, January–February 2012, 12; Jerry Francois interview with Blair, February 15, 1986, Box 71, CJBC; Oxenrider, "A Week of Eternity," 1; Curtis, "Operations of the First Battalion," 1; Stamford Interview, MCH, 69; CG X Corps to CG 8th Army, November 17, 1950, X Corps in November 1950 folder, Box 89, RG 9, DMA.

64 By November 15: Curtis, "Operations of the First Battalion," 3; Stamford, February 1951 Statement, 1; SV int, Charlie Gebhardt, May 10, 2016; Stamford account, October 1, 1979, Stamford folder, Box 9, RAC.

65 The 7th Marine Regiment: Halberstam, *The Coldest Winter*, 432–34; Bowser, "The Real Story," *CFND*, 1985, 3; Smith Oral History, MCH, 217–18; Almond comments on Schnabel, *Policy and Direction*, February 20, 1969, Almond folder, Box 29, RAC.

65 After the meeting: Smith to Cates, November 15, 1950, in Smith, "Aide-Memoire Korea," 604–10; Gurfein to Hammel, March 14, 1979, Gurfein folder, Box 5, EHPP.

66 The single road: Smith to Esther Smith, November 14, 1950, Correspondence 2 November to 31 December 1950 folder, Box 27, OPSC.

66 Though there would be: CG X Corps to CG 1st Mar Div, November 17, 1950, 1st Mar Div Historical Diary November 1950 Appendixes 3, 4, and 5 folder, Box 61, OPSC; Almond to MG Ed Hume, Chief of Medical Section FEC, February 19, 1951; Smith, "Aide-Memoire

Korea," 586, 607. See, for example, Joseph C. Goulden, *Korea: The Untold Story of the War* (Times Books, 1982; repr., Dover Books, 2020), 304.

67 Almond was not thinking: McCaffrey to REA, July 2, 1983, McCaffrey folder, Box 29, RAC; Almond to REA, October 29, 1975, Almond folder, Box 29, RAC; Haig and McCarry, *Inner Circles*, 58.

67 Almond had eleven: William C. Barnard, "Luray Man's Tenth Corps Stopped Great Chinese Spring Offensive," Associated Press, in *Richmond Times-Dispatch*, June 24, 1951; Almond to Doyle Hickey, November 15, 1950, Korean War Correspondence of CG X Corps, Box 85, EAC; Kenneth E. Lay, "Korea's Blue Goose," Box 55, EAC; Lynch, *Edward M. Almond and the US Army*, 249.

67 Almond's aggressive push: Roe, *The Dragon Strikes*, 243, 248; Appleman, *South to The Naktong*, 745–46, Lynch, *Edward M. Almond and the US Army*, 221; X Corps Special Report, Box 13, RAC, 9; Stanton, *America's Tenth Legion*, 192.

68 But MacArthur sided: Appleman, *East of Chosin*, 7; Roe, *The Dragon Strikes*, 250; Schnable, *Policy and Direction*, 286; Blair, *The Forgotten War*, 417–18; Toland, *In Mortal Combat*, 274.

68 Almond's plan did call: X Corps Special Report, Box 13, RAC, 9; Roe, *The Dragon Strikes*, 260.

68 Through his stubborn: Paddock to Blair, November 15, 1984, and April 6, 1986, 7th Division folder, Box 71, CJBC; Blair, *The Forgotten War*, 389, 418.

69 Almond was feeling: Almond to Margaret, November 18, 1950, and December 14, 1950, Correspondence with wife folder, Box 77, EAC; Smith to Esther, November 2, 1950, Correspondence 2 November to 31 December 1950 folder, Box 27, OPSC; Blair, *The Forgotten War*, 288; Weintraub, *MacArthur's War*, 216; Haig and McCarry, *Inner Circles*, 60.

70 Helen Storms was tired: Helen to Storms, November 19, 1950; Storms to Helen, November 20, 1950, HHS.

70 George Patton had: Haig and McCarry, *Inner Circles*, 57; Address Given by Major General Barr Before the Army War College, 9, USAHEC; Appleman, *South to The Naktong*, 736–37; Paddock to Blair, April 6, 1986, 7th Division folder, Box 71, CJBC; CG X Corps to Barr, November 21, 1950, X Corps in November 1950 file, Box 89, RG 9, DMA.

71 The first of the three: Li, *Attack at Chosin*, 47, 50, 53; Peters and Li, *Voices from the Korean War*, 24, 119; Millett, *The War for Korea*, 300, 319.

72 To the west: Millett, *The War for Korea*, 336; Blair, *The Forgotten War*, 435; Li, *Attack at Chosin*, 37, 54; "The Unforgotten Korean War," 180.

73 Almond issued instructions: CG X Corps to CG 1st Mar Div, November 21, 1950, 1st Mar Div Historical Diary November 1950 Appendixes 3, 4, and 5 folder, Box 61, OPSC; Captain Jones to Signal Officer, X Corps, November 22, 1950, Service messages folder, Box 62, EAC; Almond Diary, 23 November 1950, Box 29, RAC; Smith, "Aide-Memoire Korea," 630–31; "Thursday, 23 November 1950," Korean War Log 23–27 November folder; Box 65, OPSC.

73 At the 31st Regiment: SV int, Ray Radke, August 29, 2021.

74 Thanksgiving came: Curtis, "Operations of the First Battalion," 3; Blair, *The Forgotten War*, 418; Stamford Interview, MCH, 67, 70, 75; Beauchamp interview, Beauchamp folder, Box 76, CJBC; SV int, Harry Jacobs, January 15, 2022; White, "Korean War Memories"; Mortrude to Needham, November 14, 1985, Mortrude folder, Box 8, RAC; Oxenrider, "A Week of Eternity," 1.

Chapter 5: To Chosin

75 A tremendous barrage: Blair, *The Forgotten War*, 436; Record of the Actions JCS, Record of Actions folder, Box 64, CJBC; Weintraub, *MacArthur's War*, 233; MacArthur, *Reminiscences*, 373; Sides, *On Desperate Ground*, 137; Powell interview, Powell folder, Combat Leadership in Korea Box 6, CJBC.

76 Back in Tokyo: CG X Corps to all commands, November 24, 1950, relaying MacArthur communique, X Corps in 16–30 November 1950 folder, Box 89, RG 9, DMA; Roe, *The Dragon Strikes*, 263–64; Blair, *The Forgotten War*, 435.

76 Almond had done nothing: Smith to Cates, December 17, 1950, Correspondence with HQMC folder, Box 21, OPSC; Roe, *The Dragon Strikes*, 260; Ruffner to Hammel, February 12, 1979, folder 5, Box 5, EHPP; McCaffrey to REA, December 11, 1976, McCaffrey correspondence folder, Box 20, RAC.

76 The 1st Marine Division: Roe, *The Dragon Strikes*, 261; Blair, *The Forgotten War*, 420; Smith, "Aide-Memoire Korea," 727; November War Diary Summaries, Headquarters X Corps, 1 November to 30 November 1950, X Corps War Diary folder, Box 13, RAC; Address Given by Major General Barr Before the Army War College, 10, USAHEC; Smith Oral History, MCH, 218.

78 Before dawn, Faith's 1st Battalion: Appleman, *East of Chosin*, 19, 21; Miller to REA, July 29, 1980, Miller folder, Box 9, RAC.

78 Around 9:00 a.m.: Curtis, "Operations of the First Battalion," 4–5; Miller, "Chosin Reservoir," 1; Blair, *The Forgotten War*, 958.

79 With one infantry: Paddock to Blair, November 15, 1984, 7th Division folder, Box 71, CJBC; Blair, *The Forgotten War*, 457; Appleman, *East of Chosin*, 337; Coombs, "Changjin (Chosin) Reservoir, Korea, 1950," 68.

80 At the 7th Division CP: Robbins, "Breakout," 1; Curtis to Blair, March 17, 1984, 32nd Regiment folder, Box 71, CJBC; Paddock to Blair, April 6, 1986, 7th Division folder, Box 71, CJBC.

80 When Helen Storms: Helen to Storms, November 24, 1950, HHS.

80 After eighteen hours on the road: Miller, "Chosin Reservoir," 1–2; Curtis, "Operations of the First Battalion," 5; Appleman, *East of Chosin*, 24; Smith, "Aide-Memoire Korea," 503–5; SV int, Charlie Gebhardt, May 10, 2016.

81 Even wearing all: Gugeler, *Combat Actions in Korea*, 54; Mortrude, "Autobiographic Chronology of Chosin"; SV int, Harry Jacobs, January 15, 2022.

82 The reservoir lay: Sides, *On Desperate Ground*, 82–83, 119; Vallowe, *What History Failed to Record*, 70; "The Unforgotten Korean War," 2; White, "Korean War Memories"; Miller, "Chosin Reservoir," 3.

82 They were heading: Raymond Murray oral history, MCH, 17; Smith to Geer, July 28, 1951, Box 24, OPSC; Curtis to Blair, March 17, 1984, 32nd Regiment folder, Box 71, CJBC; Curtis, "Operations of the First Battalion," 6; Robert Drake to REA, January 20, 1980, Drake folder, Box 7, RAC; Appleman, *East of Chosin*, 306.

83 It was 3:00 p.m.: Stamford Interview, MCH, 71; Mortrude, "Autobiographic Chronology of Chosin"; Roe, *The Dragon Strikes*, 260; Bowser interview, January 2, 1951, MCH, 5.

83 The 1st Battalion now: Appleman, *South to The Naktong*, 24, 28; Mortrude "Autobiographic Chronology of Chosin"; Mortrude to Needham, March 23, 1986, Mortrude folder, Box 8, RAC; Curtis to REA, November 27, 1980, Curtis folder, Box 8, RAC.

84 As soon as the 1st: Stamford Interview, MCH, 71; Appleman, *East of Chosin*, 26; Curtis, "Operations of the First Battalion," 6.

84 The 8th Army offensive: Blair, *The Forgotten War*, 440.

85 Two infantry battalions: Robbins, "Breakout," 1; SV int, Ray Radke, August 29, 2021; *TCC*, 174.

85 Intelligence was all: Marine Corps Board Study: An Evaluation of the Influence of Marine Corps Forces on the Course of the Korean War (4 August 50–5 December 50), II-C-54, Box 67, OPSC (hereafter Marine Corps Board Study); X Corps Special Report, Box 13, RAC, 29; Bowser interview, January 2, 1951, MCH, 3; Roe, *The Dragon Strikes*, 256; Ruffner to Hammel, February 12, 1979, Ruffner folder, Box 5, EHA; Matthew Ridgway oral history, April 18, 1984, Ridgway interview folder, Box 82, CJBC; Appleman, *South to The Naktong*, 757.

85 But there were some: Special Action Report (SAR), 5th Marines, 1st Marine Division, Period: 8 October–15 December 50, Box 58, OPSC; Marine Corps Board Study, II-C-50, Box 67, OPSC; Smith, "Aide-Memoire Korea," 745; Smith to Esther, November 27, 1950, Box 27, OPSC; Stamford, February 1951 Statement, 1; Stamford Interview, MCH, 71–72.

86 On November 26: Marine Corps Board Study, II-C-50, Box 67, OPSC; Roe, *The Dragon Strikes*, 267; Russ, *Breakout*, 79–80; Appleman, *East of Chosin*, 51.

86 The weather was: Curtis, "Operations of the First Battalion," 7; Curtis to REA, February 20, 1978, Curtis folder, Box 8, RAC; Address Given by Major General Barr Before the Army War College, 11, USAHEC; Blair, *The Forgotten War*, 276; Lynch interview with REA, June 12, 1978, Lynch folder, Box 8, RAC; Davis interview with Blair, June 9, 1986, Barr folder, Box 76, CJBC; Lynch to REA, January 21, 1977.

86 Hodes told Faith: Curtis, "Operations of the First Battalion," 7; SV int, Charlie Gebhardt, May 10, 2016.

87 At X Corps headquarters: Appleman, *East of Chosin*, 52; Rasula to REA, October 12, 1984, Rasula folder, Box 9, RAC.

87 At 6:00 p.m., a messenger: 5th Marine Regiment SAR, Box 58, OPSC; Smith, "Aide-Memoire Korea," 890; Curtis, "Operations of the First Battalion," 8.

88 Maclean arrived: Curtis, "Operations of the First Battalion," 8; Jones to REA, March 2, 1981, Jones folder, Box 8, RAC; Bigger to REA, March 29, 1981, Bigger folder, Box 9, RAC; Curtis to REA, February 20, 1978, Curtis folder, Box 8, RAC.

88 Maclean reported that: Miller, "Chosin Reservoir," 3; Curtis, "Operations of the First Battalion," 8.

88 It was a fateful: Curtis to REA, February 20, 1978, Curtis folder, Box 8, RAC; Berquist, "Organizational Leadership in Crisis," 80.

88 Maclean established his: Robbins, "Breakout," 1; Curtis, "Operations of the First Battalion," 8; *Changjin Journal*, July 10, 2003; Appleman, *East of Chosin*, 160.

89 The 5th Marines began: 5th Marine Regiment SAR, Box 58; OPSC, 20; Appleman, *East of Chosin*, 44; Curtis to REA, January 30, 1977, Curtis folder, Box 8, RAC.

89 Maclean was equally: Robbins, "Breakout," 1; Appleman, *East of Chosin*, 35; Embree to REA, March 18, 1979, RAC.

90 Faith's 1st Battalion began: Stamford Interview, MCH, 71; Curtis, "Operations of the First Battalion," 9; "Truck Platoon at Chosin," *NAC*, August/September 2004, 12; SV int, Joe Ager, September 10, 2022.

90 The Marines left: Miller, "Chosin Reservoir," 3–4; Appleman, *East of Chosin*, 47–49; Simmons, *Frozen Chosin*, 52.

91 Song Shilun was: "The Unforgotten Korean War," 180; Li, *Attack at Chosin*, 58, 60; Appleman, *East of Chosin*, 87.

91 But there were surprises: Roe, *The Dragon Strikes*, 295–96; Li, *Attack at Chosin*, 58; "The Unforgotten Korean War," 181, 184.

92 The Marine attack west: Appleman, *East of Chosin*, 56; Weintraub, *MacArthur's War*, 240; Blair, *The Forgotten War*, 450; Smith Family Journal, 380; Address Given by Major General Barr Before the Army War College, 13, USAHEC.

92 More elements of Task: SV int, Warren Wiedhahn, September 20, 2021; Gray, *Called to Honor*, 87; Francois, Recollections transcripts.

93 Reilly was well liked: Francois, Recollections transcripts; McCaffrey interview, McCaffrey folder, Box 80, CJBC; Willard P. Donovan interview, AFC/2001/001/41595, VHP; Celeste Reilly to REA, March 13, 1977, Reilly folder, Box 8, RAC; "William R. Reilly," RCM Collection, https://www.rcmcollection.com/reilly.

93 The Polar Bears: Rasula, "Thinking About the Chosin Reservoir," 1981, Rasula folder, Box 5, EHPP.

93 Maclean had the 3rd: Appleman, *East of Chosin*, 36, 154; Curtis to REA, February 20, 1978, Curtis folder, Box 8, RAC; SV int, Charlie Gebhardt, May 10, 2016.

94 Lead elements: Ray Embree to Hammel, September 6, 1979, Embree folder, Box 6, EHPP; Vallowe, *What History Failed to Record*, 104; Blair, *The Forgotten War*, 421; Appleman, *East of Chosin*, 36–37; Embree to REA, March 18, 1979, and August 15, 1980, Embree folder, Box 8, RAC; SV int, Grant McMillin, August 29, 2021.

94 Key additional firepower: Appleman, *East of Chosin*, 37, 89; "D Battery," *NAC*, July 2000, 11.

95 Back at the regimental: Roe, *The Dragon Strikes*, 298; Appleman, *East of Chosin*, 36; Mortrude to REA, November 3, 1980, Mortrude folder, Box 8, RAC.

95 When the 31st Regiment Intelligence: Roy Shiraga, *FOW*, 119; *TCC*, 42; "Once Were Lost," *NAC*, June–July 2002, 10; "My Favorite Officer," *The Graybeards*, May–June 2005, 23; Embree to Hammel, September 6, 1979, Embree folder, Box 6, EHPP.

95 Convoys carrying Reilly's: Vallowe, *What History Failed to Record*, 104; Gray, *Called to Honor*, 86; Robbins, "Breakout," 1; William McNally transcript, McNally folder, Box 5, EHPP; Oliver Robertson to Blair, July 5, 1986, 31st Regiment folder, Box 71, CJBC; Coombs, "Changjin (Chosin) Reservoir, Korea, 1950," 30.

96 Captain William Etchemendy's: Etchemendy to REA, November 24, 1989, Etchemendy folder, Box 9, RAC; "William E. (Bill) Etchemendy," *NAC*, May–June 2015, 4; Gray, *Called to Honor*, 87, 89, 91; Willard P. Donovan interview, AFC/2001/001/41595, VHP; Appleman, *East of Chosin*, 79.

96 In midafternoon: Drake to REA, November 17, 1977, and January 10, 1977, Drake folder, Box 7, RAC.

97 At the 1st Battalion's: Miller, "Chosin Reservoir," 4–5; Curtis, "Operations of the First Battalion," 10; Oxenrider, "A Week of Eternity," 2.

97 Late in the afternoon: SV int, Charlie Gebhardt, May 10, 2016; Appleman, *East of Chosin*, 61; Stamford Interview, MCH, 1–2; Bigger interview by REA, March 11, 1981, Bigger folder, Box 9, RAC.

97 Shortly before dark: SV int, Monty Piercefield, September 30, 2021; "Fremont 'Monty' Piercefield Memoir," KWE, 3; Curtis interview by REA, June 1981, Curtis folder, Box 8, RAC.

98 By early evening: Address Given by Major General Barr Before the Army War College, 11, USAHEC; Lynch to REA, December 19, 1976; Appleman, *East of Chosin*, 88; Robbins, "Breakout," 1.

98 When Maclean arrived: Appleman, *East of Chosin*, 79; "I&R Platoon," *NAC*, March 1990, 7; 1st Battalion 32nd Infantry 27–29 November 1950, excerpt from 7th Division diary, copy in Rasula folder, Box 5, EHPP; *TCC*, 42; Robbins, "Breakout," 1.

98 After receiving a copy: Jones to Robert Coombs, January 15, 1975, Jones folder, Box 8, RAC; Appleman, *East of Chosin*, 57; Curtis, "Operations of the First Battalion," 1; Curtis interview with REA, June 1981, Curtis folder, Box 8, RAC.

99 A bitter, ceaseless: Miller, "Chosin Reservoir," 3–4; Appleman, *Escaping the Trap*, 62; SV int, John Edward Gray, April 17, 2013; Roe, *The Dragon Strikes*, 133; Li, *Attack at Chosin*, 62; White, "Korean War Memories"; Mortrude, "Autobiographic Chronology of Chosin."

99 Across the reservoir: *Changjin Journal*, March 31, 2000, and November 27, 2005; Smith Oral History, MCH, 280–81; Jones Memoir, KWE, 23.

99 All Mortrude could do: Mortrude, "Autobiographic Chronology of Chosin"; Willis Via, *FOW*, 107; Miller, "Chosin Reservoir," 4.

100 Four miles south: Gray, *Called to Honor*, 92; Francois, Recollections transcripts; Smith, "Aide-Memoire Korea," 891; Smith Oral History, MCH, 219.

100 Task Force Maclean: Appleman, *East of Chosin*, 42; Berquist, "Organizational Leadership in Crisis," 74; Francois, Recollections transcripts.

Chapter 6: The First Night

102 With darkness approaching: "Once Were Lost," *NAC*, June–July 2002,10; "I&R Platoon," *NAC*, March 1990, 7; Roy Shiraga, *FOW*, 119; James E. Arie interview, AFC/2001/001/41535, VHP.

105 A 31st Medical Company: Hoehn, "Chosin, Korea"; Clifton Hancock narrative, 1979, and Hancock to Hammel, July 20, 1979, Hancock folder, Box 5, EHPP; *TCC*, 102.

105 In their hillslope: Oxenrider, "A Week of Eternity," 2; White, "Korean War Memories"; Curtis, "Operations of the First Battalion," 11.

106 It quieted down: Miller, "Chosin Reservoir," 5; Gugeler, *Combat Actions in Korea*, 59.

106 The firing could be: 7th Division Command Report, Chosin Reservoir, 7th Infantry Division folder, Box 7, RAC; SV int, Charlie Gebhardt, May 10, 2016; Bigger interview with REA, May 8, 1980, Bigger folder, Box 9, RAC; Mortrude, "Autobiographic Chronology of Chosin."

106 The wait to attack: Li, *Attack at Chosin*, 86–88, 220; Appleman, *East of Chosin*, 53.

107 The 240th Regiment: Li, *Attack at Chosin*, 87; Combat Intelligence Bulletin No. 1, Enemy Tactics and Equipment, 1951; Information Bulletins, X Corps folder, Box 62, EAC; Russ, *Breakout*, 61; Simmons, *Frozen Chosin*, 48.

108 Around 12:30 a.m.: Oxenrider, "A Week of Eternity," 2

108 At the A Company: Curtis, "Operations of the First Battalion," 10–11; Bigger, "Reflections and Comments"; Stamford, February 1951 Statement, 2–3; McCalister to REA, October 3, 1985, Mortrude folder, Box 8, RAC; John McGuire, *FOW*, 153.

109 Reports started coming: James A. Smith to REA, July 6, 1990, 1990 correspondence folder, Box 21, RAC; Appleman, *East of Chosin*, 136–37.

109 A garbled message: Bigger, "Reflections and Comments"; Bigger interview with REA, May 8, 1980, Bigger folder, Box 9, RAC; Appleman, *East of Chosin*, 71, 88; Miller, "Chosin Reservoir," 6; SFC Jeremiah Casey Service Member Profile, DPAA.

110 No artillery fire: Stamford, February 1951 Statement, 4, 16; Marker, "A Soldier Remembers," 4; Marker to Rasula, January 25, 2005, folder 9, Box 15, GRP; Bigger to REA, March 29, 1981, Box 9, RAC; Appleman, *East of Chosin*, 75.

111 Capt. Clifton Hancock: Hancock narrative, 1979, Hancock folder, Box 5, EHPP; Galloway to Hammel, May 22, 1979, Box 6, EHPP.

112 But even as the message: *TCC*, 102, 108; "Hill 1221—The Beginning and the End," *NAC*, March 1989, 4; Lynch to REA, July 30, 1980, Lynch folder, Box 8, RAC.

112 The radios the task: Jones to Coombs, January 15, 1975, Jones folder, Box 8, RAC; Operations Summary by Lt. Col. Berry Anderson, 31st Infantry, December 1950, DFP; Curtis to REA, January 1, 1977, Curtis folder, Box 8, RAC; Stanton, *America's Tenth Legion*, 248.

112 A frustrated Hodes: Lynch to REA, July 30, 1980, Lynch folder, Box 8, RAC; Appleman, *East of Chosin*, 87–88, 306.

112 Hodes decided to: "Hill 1221—The Beginning and the End," *NAC*, March 1989, 4; Witte to Hammel, January 24, 1980, Witte folder, Box 5, EHPP; Lynch to REA, December 19, 1976, Lynch folder, Box 8, RAC.

113 The night had begun: Robert Kitz report, Box 3172, RG 407, NARA; Appleman, *East of Chosin*, 79; Farley to Hammel, February 14, 1979, Farley folder, Box 6, EHPP; Report from Sgt. Bill G. Rowland, Box 3172, RG 407, NARA; Reeves, *Beautiful Feet and Real Peace*, 6; Rasula to Martin Russ, September 21, 1984, Rasula folder, Box 9, RAC; Reeves to Rasula, April 23, 1988, 1988 correspondence folder, Box 21, RAC.

114 The collapse of K: Gray, *Called to Honor*, 94; Etchemendy to REA, Etchemendy folder, Box 9, RAC; Lewis Shannon and William Mahon statements, IG investigation folder, Box 7, RAC; Appleman, *East of Chosin*, 81; Shannon, "A Letter Home"; "7th Division Units at Chosin Reservoir," 7th Division Diary, Rasula folder, Box 5, EHPP; Sgt. John Gibbs and Sgt. John Sweatman statements, IG investigation, Box 7, RAC.

114 Hundreds of Chinese: Gray, *Called to Honor*, 93; Harry Scott, *FOW*, 151; Francois, Recollections transcripts; Li, *Attack at Chosin*, 89.

115 The soldiers of the 9th: Li, *Attack at Chosin*, 61, 67, 95; Simmons, *Frozen Chosin*, 48; O. P. Smith to Eric Goldman, April 10, 1956, Monograph correspondence folder, Box 21, OPSC; Stanton, *America's Tenth Legion*, 199; 1st Marine Division SAR, 8 October–15 December 1950, Box 67, OPSC; Combat Intelligence Bulletin No. 1, Enemy Tactics and Equipment, 1951; Information Bulletins, X Corps folder, Box 62, EAC.

116 Troops from the CCF 2nd: Earle Jordan to REA, January 5, 1979, Jordan folder, Box 8, RAC; Appleman, *Escaping the Trap*, 96; Celeste Reilly to REA, March 13, 1977, Reilly folder, Box 8, RAC; Li, *Attack at Chosin*, 90.

116 More Chinese troops who: Gray, *Called to Honor*, 92; Jordan to REA, January 5, 1979, Jordan folder, Box 8, RAC; Reeves, *Beautiful Feet and Real Peace*, 6.

117 The 105 mm howitzers: Sickafoose statement, IG investigation folder, Box 7, RAC; Lloyd Mielenz interview, AFC/2001/001/41636, VHP; Kitz report, Box 3172, RG 407, NARA; Robert Hammond, *FOW*, 117; Hammond, "Memories of War," 6; Mielenz, "Lloyd Mielenz Remembers Chosin," 4; Robert Ayala, *FOW*, 117; Edward Magill to Hammel, July 7, 1979, Magill folder, Box 6, EHPP.

118 Cpl. Anthony Mora: Edward Magill to Hammel, July 7, 1979, Magill folder, Box 6, EHPP; Anthony T. Mora interview, AFC/2001/001/55589, VHP; Distinguished Service Cross citation for Corners, DSC folder, Box 31, RAC; Magill statement, IG investigation folder, Box 7, RAC.

119 Four miles to: Stamford, February 1951 Statement, 3; Appleman, *East of Chosin*, 68, 71, 73; Willis Via, *FOW*, 197; Bigger, "Reflections and Comments"; Distinguished Service Cross citation for Godfrey, DSC folder, Box 31, RAC.

120 Along the battalion's right: Curtis, "Operations of the First Battalion," 11; Appleman, *East of Chosin*, 76; SV int, Harry Jacobs, January 15, 2022.

120 Dr. Lee Yong Kak: Lee, "Dr. Yong Kak Lee," 58; Miller, "Chosin Reservoir," 6; Cowdrey, *The Medics' War*, 120.

121 Dawn was approaching: "D Battery," *NAC*, July 2000, 11; SV int, Grant McMillin, September 27, 2021; "Army Chapter of the Chosin Few Grant McMillin interview," posted May 28, 2017, by TheRbrooks502, YouTube, https://www.youtube.com/watch?v=AODJzZTF7M8 (hereafter McMillin Army Chapter interview).

121 Heavy mortar fire: Vallowe, *What History Failed to Record*, 298; McClymont, "Narrative of Chosin," 4–6; Magill to Hammel, July 7, 1979, Magill folder, Box 6, EHPP; Appleman, *East of Chosin*, 97–98.

123 The arrival of dawn: Celeste Reilly to REA, March 13, 1977, and Bill Reilly to his parents, December 17, 1950, Reilly folder, Box 8, RAC; Jordan to REA, February 28, 1980, Jordan folder, Box 8, RAC.

123 Just to the north: Lt. Thomas J. Patton and Shannon statements, IG investigation folder, Box 7, RAC; Li, *Attack at Chosin*, 90–92; Lloyd Mielenz interview, AFC/2001/001/41636, VHP; Appleman, *East of Chosin*, 120.

Chapter 7: The First Day

125 With the morning light: Gray, *Called to Honor*, 95–96; Li, *Attack at Chosin*, 91–93.

126 The Chinese offensive: Li, *Attack at Chosin*, 62; "The Unforgotten Korean War," 8–9; Roe, *The Dragon Strikes*, 299–301; Russ, *Breakout*, 114; Zhou, "CCF Order of Battle," 8.

126 The Chinese attack at Yudam-ni: Marine Corps Board Study, II-C-55, Box 67, OSPC; Russ, *Breakout*, 121; Curtis, "Operations of the First Battalion," 10.

126 But the Chinese success: Li, *Attack at Chosin*, 58–59, 61–63, 92.

127 With the Chinese withdrawal: Curtis interview with REA, June 1981, Curtis folder, Box 8, RAC; Oxenrider, "A Week of Eternity," 2; Appleman, *East of Chosin*, 76; Gugeler, *Combat Actions in Korea*, 59; Curtis, "Operations of the First Battalion," 10; Miller, "Chosin Reservoir," 7; Stamford, February 1951 Statement, 18; May, "Report from Capt. Hugh," 1; Jones Memoir, KWE, 20; SV int, Monty Piercefield, September 30, 2021; "Fremont 'Monty' Piercefield Memoir," KWE, 3.

128 At first light: Robbins, "Breakout," 1–2; Stamford, February 1951 Statement, 18; Oxenrider, "A Week of Eternity," 2. Maclean may have also visited the inlet perimeter that morning, as two soldiers say they saw the colonel speak with Reilly, the 3rd Battalion commander, but further evidence has not been found. See Francois, Recollections transcripts, and Rasula to Miller, March 11, 1988, Crosby Miller folder, Box 14, GRP.

128 PFC James "Doc": Blohm, *FOW*, 125; Magill to Hammel, July 7, 1979, Magill folder, Box 6, EHPP; Reilly to parents, December 17, 1950, Reilly folder, Box 8, RAC; Bryant, "Four Days and Five Nights."

129 Litter parties: Blohm, *FOW*, 125; *TCC*, 125; Francois, Recollections transcripts; Galloway to Hammel, May 22, 1979, Galloway folder, Box 6, EHPP; Gray, *Called to Honor*, 96.

130 Reilly remained in command: Jordan to REA, February 29, 1980; Farley to Hammel, February 14, 1979, Farley folder; Box 6, EHPP; Kitz report, Box 3172, RG 407, NARA; Etchemendy to REA, November 24, 1989, Etchemendy folder, Box 9, RAC.

130 But SFC Bill: Donovan, "Photographs of Korea," 121; Willard P. Donovan interview, AFC/2001/001/41595, VHP; Donovan interview, in Precious, *Task Force Faith.*

130 Further south, Sergeant: DeLong, "Inside King Company," 11; DeLong interview, in Precious, *Task Force Faith.*

131 At the 31st Regiment: Drake to REA, March 22 and June 21, 1978, Drake folder, Box 7, RAC; Appleman, *East of Chosin*, 109; *TCC*, 109; James Burton, *FOW*, 157.

131 Hodes rode with Drake: Drake to REA, January 10, February 1, and February 12, 1977, Drake folder, Box 7, RAC; Appleman, *East of Chosin*, 112. Beryl Williams interview, AFC/2001/001/41742, VHP; Li, *Attack at Chosin*, 93; Robert E. Drake, "The Infantry Regiment's Tank Company," *Armor*, September–October 1951; Lynch to REA, July 30, 1980, Lynch folder, Box 8, RAC; Witte interview with Blair, 31st Regiment folder, Box 71, CJBC; Hancock narrative, 1979, Hancock folder, Box 5, EHPP.

133 Maj. Marty Hoehn: Hammel, *Chosin*, 141; McCaffrey to REA, March 6, 1981, McCaffrey correspondence folder, Box 20, RAC; Drake to REA, February 22, 1978, and May 6, 1980, Drake folder, Box 7, RAC; "Frontline Chaplain," *Pacific Stars and Stripes*, December 20, 1950; Drake to REA, May 1, 1987, Drake folder, 1987 folder, Box 21, RAC.

133 Ned Almond was not: Roe, *The Dragon Strikes*, 310–12; Almond Oral History, Section 5, EAC, 11; X Corps Special Report, Box 13, RAC, 14–15; Smith, "Aide-Memoir Korea," 951; Coombs, "Changjin (Chosin) Reservoir, Korea, 1950," 40; Shisler, *For Country and Corps*, 198.

134 Almond wanted to visit: Almond to REA, February 24, 1977, and May 22, 1978, Almond folder, Box 29, RAC; Russ, *Breakout*, 195; "Korea: The Forgotten War Remembered," *Northwest Quarterly*, Summer–Fall 2015.

134 Standing outside: Almond to Dora Maclean, December 14, 1950, Correspondence CG X Corps folder, Box 85, EAC; McNally transcript, McNally folder, Box 5, EHPP; Hammel, *Chosin*, 137; May to REA, July 24, 1981, May folder, Box 9, RAC.

135 That Almond would make: Roe, *The Dragon Strikes*, 313; SV int, Ray Radke, August 29, 2021; Lynch, *Edward M. Almond and the US Army*, 232; Blair, *The Forgotten War*, 463; SV int, Charlie Gebhardt, May 10, 2016.

135 Almond did not use: May to REA, July 24, 1981, May folder, Box 9, RAC; Almond to Maclean, November 14, 1950, Box 85, EAC.

135 To Faith and the men: Curtis to Rasula, March 2, 1988, 1988 correspondence folder, Box 21, RAC; SV int, Ray Radke, August 29, 2021; McNally transcript, McNally folder, Box 5, EHPP; Gugeler, *Combat Actions in Korea*, 62; SV int, Charlie Gebhardt, May 10, 2016; Jones to REA, March 2, 1981, Jones folder, Box 8, RAC; Excerpt from Martin Blumenson report on 1st Battalion, 32nd Infantry, 1984 correspondence, Box 21, RAC; Curtis to REA, January 30, 1977, Curtis folder, Box 8, RAC.

136 Then Almond addressed: Gugeler, *Combat Actions in Korea*, 61; SV int, William McCaffrey, December 2000; Roe, *The Dragon Strikes*, 313.

136 Pulling Faith aside: Almond to REA, February 24, 1977, Almond folder, Box 29, RAC; May to REA, July 24, 1981, May folder, Box 9, RAC.

137 Hammering Hank: Lynch to REA, January 21, 1977, and July 30, 1980, Lynch folder, Box 8, RAC; Berquist, "Organizational Leadership in Crisis," 45.

137 Maclean and Faith knew nothing: Appleman, *East of Chosin*, 155, 306; Roe, *The Dragon Strikes*, 312; Kirkland, "Soldiers and Marines at Chosin," 268; Almond to REA, March 8, 1977, Almond folder, Box 29, RAC.

137 Hodes's view darkened: Lynch to REA, January 21, 1977, and May 18, 1981, Lynch folder, Box 8, RAC; Parker and Batha, *A History of Marine Observation Squadron Six*, 21.

138 To make matters: Lynch to REA, July 30, 1980, Lynch folder, Box 8, RAC; *TCC*, 104; Appleman, *East of Chosin*, 165–67, 178, 306; Curtis to REA, May 9, 1976, Curtis folder, Box 8, RAC; Stanton, *America's Tenth Legion*, 250.

139 Almond had squandered: Almond to REA, May 22, 1978, Almond folder, Box 29, RAC; Lynch to REA, December 19, 1976, Lynch folder, Box 8, RAC.

139 After extricating: 31st Tank Company Operations Summary, November 25–December 11, 1950, December 12, 1950, Box 3172, RG 407, NARA; Hancock narrative, 1979, Hancock folder, Box 5, EHPP; Hoehn, "Chosin, Korea."

139 Back at Hudong: Burton, *FOW*, 157; Drake to REA, June 28, 1978, and November 17, 1977, and Jimmy Howle to Drake, February 18, 1986, Drake folder, Box 7, RAC; Appleman, *East of Chosin*, 115.

140 All afternoon: Jordan to REA, February 28, 1980, and January 5, 1979, Jordan folder, Box 8, RAC; Lynch to REA, July 30, 1980, Lynch folder, Box 8, RAC; Gray, *Called to Honor*, 96–97; "D Battery," *NAC*, July 2000, 11; Magill, "57th Field Artillery," 112.

140 Reilly ordered: Farley to Hammel, February 14, 1979, Farley folder, Box 6, EHPP; Francois, Recollections transcripts; McClymont, "Narrative of Chosin,", 5; Simmons, *Frozen Chosin*, 48; 1st Marine Division SAR, 8 October–15 December 1950, Box 67, OSPC, 30.

141 Late in the afternoon: Appleman, *East of Chosin*, 122; Francois, Recollections transcripts; Reeves, "Chaplain's Corner," *NAC*, October 2002; Hill, "An Unknown Chaplain," 12.

142 What comfort: Miller, "Chosin Reservoir," 7; Farley to Hammel, February 14, 1979, Farley folder, Box 6, EHPP.

142 The 1st Battalion fight: Swenty statement, IG investigation folder, Box 7, RAC; Mortrude, "Autobiographic Chronology"; Curtis, "Operations of the First Battalion," 13.

142 Maclean tried to get: Vallowe, *What History Failed to Record*, 351; Sims and Shaw, "Those Are My Boys," 1.

143 With the air support: Mortrude, "Autobiographic Chronology of Chosin"; Miller, "Chosin Reservoir," 7; Appleman, *East of Chosin*, 102, 106; Gugeler, *Combat Actions in Korea*, 61; Bigger to REA, March 29, 1981, Bigger folder, Box 9, RAC.

143 Just before sundown: Stamford, February 1951 Statement, 6; Miller, "Chosin Reservoir," 7.

143 With the Chinese: Robbins, "Breakout," 2; Curtis, "Operations of the First Battalion," 12; SV int, Ray Radke, August 29, 2021.

144 At the battalion aid: Lee, "Dr. Yong Kak Lee," 58; SV int, Joe Ager, September 10, 2022.

144 All day small: "Once Were Lost," *NAC*, June–July 2002, 9; "I&R Platoon," *NAC*, March 1990, 7; Shiraga, *FOW*, 119.

145 As the afternoon progressed: Smith Oral History, MCH, 222; Roe, *The Dragon Strikes*, 314; Appleman, *East of Chosin*, 165; *TCC*, 43; Russ, *Breakout*, 200.

145 "Hagaru had to be held": Smith, "Aide-Memoire Korea," 855; AP, "General Belittles China Red Tactics," *New York Times*, December 26, 1950; "The Unforgotten Korean War," 183–84; Far East Command intelligence digest, January 1953, North Korean and CCF folder, Box 32, RAC, 16–31.

146 Though he had not received: Smith, Korean War log, 23–27 November 1950, Box 65, OPSC, 91; Smith, "Aide-Memoire Korea," 776.

146 Maclean and Faith: Berquist, "Organizational Leadership in Crisis," 50; Appleman, *East of Chosin*, 165; *Changjin Journal*, July 10, 2003.

146 Upon his return: X Corps Command Report, Chosin, Box 13, RAC, 15; Sides, *On Desperate Ground*, 191; Stanton, *America's Tenth Legion*, 231.

146 At the Dai Ichi: CINCFE to JCS, November 28, 1950, Folder 6, Box 2, RG 6, DMA; Weintraub, *MacArthur's War*, 243; Blair, *The Forgotten War*, 465–66; Roe, *The Dragon Strikes*, 321–22.

147 Mao Zedong was: Zhou, "Mao's Telegrams," 5.

147 Billy had a fever: Helen to Storms, November 28, 1950, HHS.

Chapter 8: The Second Night

149 Another attack was: Robbins, "Breakout," 2; Bigger, "Reflections and Comments"; James Campbell transcript, November 29–30, 1980, Campbell folder, Box 8, RAC.

150 The harsh weather: Russ, *Breakout*, 224; Vogel, "Veterans Still Feel Their Hidden Wounds"; Stanton, *America's Tenth Legion*, 317; Willis Via, *FOW*, 107; Oxenrider, "A Week of Eternity," 2.

150 Four miles to: DeLong, "Inside King Company"; James DeLong interview, AFC/2001/001/41567, VHP, 7; DeLong interview, in *Precious, Task Force Faith*.

151 The 80th CCF: 7th Division Command Report, Chosin Reservoir, 7th Infantry Division folder, Box 7, RAC, 4; RCT 31 Command Report, 11 December 1950, Box 3179, RG 407, NARA; Li, *Attack at Chosin*, 94–95; Patton statement, IG investigation folder, Box 7, RAC; DeLong, "Inside King Company"; Kitz report, Box 3172, RG 407, NARA; Sickafoose statement, IG investigation folder, Box 7, RAC; Appleman, *East of Chosin*, 123; Farley to Hammel, February 14, 1979, Farley folder, Box 6, EHPP.

151 Lt. John Gray's: Gray, *Called to Honor*, 98–101.

152 As with the previous: Li, *Attack at Chosin*, 95; Bryant, "Four Days and Five Nights."

152 From there, infiltrators: Bryant, "Four Days and Five Nights"; McClay to Rasula, May 31, 1979, McClay folder, Box 6, EHPP; Celeste Reilly to REA, February 22, 1977, Reilly folder, Box 8, RAC.

153 A Chinese attack: Gray, *Called to Honor*, 101; Li, *Attack at Chosin*, 95.

153 The plane carrying: Almond Oral History, Section 5, EAC, 11; X Corps Command Report, Chosin, Box 13; RAC, 15; Weintraub, *MacArthur's War*, 245; Blair, *The Forgotten War*, 469.

153 MacArthur asked first: Schnabel, *Policy and Direction*, 279; Roe, *The Dragon Strikes*, 327–28; Courtney Whitney, *MacArthur: His Rendezvous with Destiny* (Knopf, 1956), 423.

154 When MacArthur asked about: McCaffrey to REA, January 17, 1977, McCaffrey folder, Box 29, RAC; Appleman, *East of Chosin*, 170; Almond to REA, December 21, 1976, Almond folder, Box 29, RAC; Roe, *The Dragon Strikes*, 333.

154 The evening had remained: Willis Via, *FOW*, 107; Li, *Attack at Chosin*, 95; Mortrude to REA, November 3, 1980, Mortrude folder, Box 8, RAC.

154 At the headquarters: Robbins, "Breakout," 2; Miller, "Chosin Reservoir," 7; Curtis, "Operations of the First Battalion," 13; Curtis to REA, January 1, 1977, Curtis folder, Box 8, RAC.

156 Faith did not take: Jones, "Report to Major Lynch," 1; Gugeler, *Combat Actions in Korea*, 63; Appleman, *East of Chosin*, 128, 132; Curtis, "Operations of the First Battalion," 13; Robbins, "Breakout," 2; Lee, "Dr. Yong Kak Lee," 58.

156 Sgt. Grantford Brown: "Robert Ayala Memoir," KWE; Robert Ayala interview, August 12, 2011, AFC/2001/001/82143, VHP; "D Battery," *NAC*, July 2000, 11; McClymont, "Narrative of Chosin," 6–7; Magill to Hammel, August 9, 1979, Magill folder, Box 6, EHPP.

157 The 57th Field Artillery guns: Magill, "57th Field Artillery," 112–13; Eichorn statement, IG investigation folder, Box 7, RAC; Magill to Hammel, July 7 and August 9, 1979, Magill folder, Box 6, EHPP; Magill to Rasula, October 28, 1987, folder 5, Box 15, GRP.

158 The K Company line: DeLong, "Inside King Company"; DeLong interview, in Precious, *Task Force Faith*; James DeLong interview, AFC/2001/001/41567, VHP.

159 Bullets were flying: Lee, "Dr. Yong Kak Lee," 58; Robbins, "Breakout," 3; SV int, Ray Radke, November 19, 2021; Curtis, "Operations of the First Battalion," 13; Appleman, *East of Chosin*, 131; May, "Report from Capt. Hugh R. May," 3; Miller, "Chosin Reservoir," 8.

159 Drivers began trying: Robbins, "Breakout," 3; May, "Report from Capt. Hugh R. May," 2–3; SV int, Joe Ager, September 10, 2022.

160 Trucks, ambulances: Robbins, "Breakout," 2–3; Jones, "Report to Major Lynch," 1; Curtis to REA, January 1, 1977, Curtis folder, Box 8, RAC; Gugeler, *Combat Actions in Korea*, 63; Mortrude, "Autobiographic Chronology of Chosin"; Campbell transcript, November 29–30, 1980, Campbell folder, Box 8, RAC; Appleman, *East of Chosin*, 135.

160 B Company held: Appleman, *East of Chosin*, 135; SV int, Harry Graham, August 29, 2021; "Army Chosin Few Reunion 2017 Harry G. Graham Jr. Interview," posted July 4, 2019, by TheRbrooks502, YouTube, 17 min., 37 sec.

161 A Company, still: Miller, "Chosin Reservoir," 9; Appleman, *East of Chosin*, 137; Robbins, "Breakout," 3; Oxenrider, "A Week of Eternity," 2; Li, *Attack at Chosin*, 78, 96.

161 About halfway to: Jones to REA, January 5, 1979, Jones folder, Bob 8, RAC; Jones, "Report to Major Lynch," 1.

163 While the column: Bigger, "Reflections and Comments"; Stanford Statement, 6; Gray, *Called to Honor*, 104; Curtis to REA, January 1, 1977, Curtis folder, Box 8, RAC.

163 The command party: Appleman, *East of Chosin*, 138, 145; Jones, "Report to Major Lynch," 1; Curtis to REA, February 16, 1981, Curtis folder, Box 8, RAC; Mortrude "Autobiographic Chronology"; Mortrude to REA, November 3, 1980, Mortrude folder, Box 8, RAC.

164 Faith, Maclean, and the: Bigger interview with REA, March 11, 1981, Bigger folder, Box 9, RAC; Bigger, "Reflections and Comments"; Address Given by Major General Barr Before the Army War College, 11, USAHEC; Jones to REA, January 5, 1977, Box 8, Jones folder, RAC; Stamford, February 1951 Statement, 8; Curtis to REA, January 1, 1977, Curtis folder, Box 8, RAC.

164 Maclean grew alarmed: Bigger, "Reflections and Comments"; Bigger to REA, May 11, 1981, Bigger folder, Box 9, RAC; Jones to REA, January 19, 1981, Jones folder, Box 8, RAC; Bigger interview with REA, March 11, 1981, Bigger folder, Box 9, RAC.

165 With that, Maclean: SV int, Arthur Mercier, April 11, 2013; Sims and Shaw, "Those Are My Boys," 2; Bigger, "Reflections and Comments."

165 From different vantage: Jones to REA, January 19, 1981, Jones folder, Box 8, RAC; Curtis to REA, January 1, 1977, Curtis folder, Box 8, RAC; Gugeler, *Combat Actions in Korea*, 64; RCT 31 command report, 11 December 1950, Rasula folder, Box 5, EHPP; Magill, "57th Field Artillery," 113; McCaffrey to REA, March 6, 1981, McCaffrey folder, Box 20, RAC; Bigger, "Reflections and Comments."

Chapter 9: The Second Day

166 Shocked as he was: Appleman, *East of Chosin*, 140; Lieutenant Colonel Don C. Faith Medal of Honor citation, Box 31, RAC; Curtis, "Operations of the First Battalion," 14; Jones to REA, March 14, 1981, Box 8, Jones folder, RAC; John Swenty statement, IG investigation folder, Box 7, RAC.

166 Across the ice: Bryant, "Four Days and Five Nights"; Kitz report, Box 3172, RG 407, NARA; Francois, Recollections transcripts; Gray, *Called to Honor*, 184.

167 Faith joined B Company: Miller, "Chosin Reservoir," 10; Appleman, *East of Chosin*, 140; Robbins, "Breakout," 3; Mortrude, "Autobiographic Chronology of Chosin"; Bigger to REA, March 11, 1981, Bigger folder, Box 9, RAC; Curtis to REA, January 1, 1977, Curtis folder, Box 8, FAC; Jones to REA, June 5, 1979, Jones folder, Box 8, RAC.

167 The convoy carrying: Robbins, "Breakout," 3; Jones, "Report to Major Lynch," 1; Jones to REA, March 2, 1981, Jones folder, Box 8, RAC; Miller, "Chosin Reservoir," 10-11.

168 Just about every vehicle: Mills and Mills, "His Valorous Conduct," 347–49; Charles Garrigus Distinguished Service Cross citation, DSC folder, Box 31, RAC; Gugeler, *Combat Actions in Korea*, 69.

168 Most of the GIs: Stamford, February 1951 Statement, 7; Oxenrider, "A Week of Eternity", 3; Marker, "A Solder Remembers," 4.

168 With the American: Li, *Attack at Chosin*, 95–98; "One Reservoir, Two Battles," *CFND*, July-September 2021, 15; "The Unforgotten Korean War," 187; Roe, *The Dragon Strikes*, 329.

169 Once all the wounded: Bigger, "Reflections and Comments," 6; Lieutenant Don C. Faith Medal of Honor citation, Box 31, RAC; Willis Via, *FOW*, 108; Oxenrider, "A Week of Eternity," 3; Robbins, "Breakout," 3; Lee, "Dr. Yong Kak Lee," 58; Gray, *Called to Honor*, 184; Stamford, February 1951 Statement, 19.

170 Robbins made: Robbins, "Breakout," 3; Francois, Recollections transcripts.

171 Faith came in: Gray, *Called to Honor*, 104; Stamford, February 1951 Statement, 16; Robbins, "Breakout," 3–4; Miller, "Chosin Reservoir," 10; Jones, "Report to Major Lynch," 1; Miller to REA, July 29, 1980, Miller folder, Box 9, RAC; Curtis to REA, October 4, 1980, Curtis folder, Box 8, RAC; Bigger, "Reflections and Comments," 6; Oxenrider, "A Week of Eternity," 3.

171 At 8:00 a.m., Capt.: Appleman, *East of Chosin*, 158; 31st Tank Company Operations Summary, Box 3172, RG 407, NARA; Burton, *FOW*, 157; Witte to REA, May 26, 1980, Witte folder, Box 8, RAC; Li, *Attack at Chosin*, 97; Drake to REA, March 22, 1978, Drake folder, Box 7, RAC.

172 As the day wore: SV int, Harry Graham, August 29, 2021; White, "Korean War Memories"; Knox, *The Korean War*, vol. 1, 552; Francois, Recollections transcripts; Lewis Zink, *FOW*, 159.

173 The Chinese had three: Stamford, February 1951 Statement, 9; Gray, *Called to Honor*, 106; Appleman, *East of Chosin*, 153; Jones, "Report to Major Lynch," 2; Miller, "Chosin Reservoir," 10; Curtis, "Operations of the First Battalion," 14; Curtis to REA, January 1, 1977, Curtis folder, Box 8, RAC.

174 Mortrude's C Company: Mortrude, "Autobiographic Chronology of Chosin"; Willis Via, *FOW*, 108; Bryant, "Four Days and Five Nights"; SV int, Harry Jacobs, January 15, 2022.

175 With ammunition: Robbins, "Breakout," 4; Stamford, February 1951 Statement, 18; Francois, Recollections transcripts; Reeves, *Beautiful Feet and Real Peace*, 6; Patton statement, IG Investigation folder, Box 7, RAC; Bigger, "Reflections and Comments," 8.

175 Capt. Navarre set: Gugeler, *Combat Actions in Korea*, 69; Lee, "Dr. Yong Kak Lee," 61; Miller, "Chosin Reservoir," 11–12.

176 McClymont's men had: McClymont, "Narrative of Chosin," 7; SV int, Ray Radke, November 19, 2021.

176 Around 3:30 p.m.: Miller, "Chosin Reservoir," 10; Gray, *Called to Honor*, 109; Robert Hammond, *FOW*, 115; Robbins, "Breakout," 4; SV int, Ray Radke, August 29, 2021; McClymont, "Narrative of Chosin," 7; 7th Division Command Report, Chosin Reservoir, 7th Infantry Division folder, Box 7, RAC, 4; Stamford, February 1951 Statement, 8; Drake to REA, January 10, 1977, Drake folder, Box 7, RAC.

177 At his headquarters: Li, *Attack at Chosin*, 85–86, 98; "The Unforgotten Korean War," 188–89; "One Reservoir, Two Battles," *CFND*, July-September 2021

15.

178 In the tiny crossroads: RCT 31 command report, 11 December 1950, Box 3179, RG 407, NARA; Stanton, *America's Tenth Legion*, 255; Appleman, *East of Chosin*, 160.

179 Late in the day: Lynch to REA, January 21, 1977, Lynch folder, Box 8, RAC; Reilly to parents, December 17, 1950, Reilly folder, Box 8, RAC; SV int, Grant McMillin, September 27, 2021; Magill interview, folder 5, Box 15, GRP; Miller, "Chosin Reservoir," 10; Galloway to Hammel, May 22, 1979, Galloway folder, Box 6, EAC; Sterling Morgan to Galloway, December 1, 1951, Galloway folder, Box 6, EAC; Bryant, "Four Days and Five Nights."

180 It's puzzling why: Parker and Batha, *A History of Marine Observation Squadron Six*, 14; Berquist, "Organizational Leadership in Crisis," 58, 78; Appleman, *East of Chosin*, 155–56.

213 Some task force officers: Garrett, "Task Force Faith," *Infantry Magazine*, 29; Bigger, "Reflections and Comments," 8; Appleman, *East of Chosin*, 314; McCaffrey to REA, June 5, 1981, McCaffrey correspondence folder, Box 20, RAC; Celeste Reilly to REA, February 22, 1977, Reilly folder, Box 8, RAC.

181 There were many steps: Appleman, *East of Chosin*, 308; Mortrude to REA, November 3, 1981, Mortrude folder, Box 8, RAC; Bigger interview with REA, March 11, 1981, Bigger folder, Box 9, RAC.

181 Darkness was falling: Almond to Margaret, November 30, 1950, Correspondence with wife folder, Box 77, EAC; Stanton, *America's Tenth Legion*, 237; Almond to REA, March 22, 1976, Box 29, Almond folder, RAC.

181 Inside the X Corps: Almond Oral History, Section 5, EAC, 12; Almond diary, 29 November 1950, Box 29, RAC; Roe, *The Dragon Strikes*, 334.

182 The Marine base: Smith, "Aide-Memoire Korea," 820–21; 1st Marine Division historical diary, November 1950, Box 61, OPSC; Roe, *The Dragon Strikes*, 317; Simmons, *Frozen Chosin*, 62; Russ, *Breakout*, 218.

182 Koto-ri, held: Blair, *The Forgotten War*, 505, 509; Lynch to REA, July 30, 1980, Lynch folder, Box 8, RAC; Appleman, *East of Chosin*, 164.

183 By 9:00 p.m.: Almond diary, 29 November 1950, Box 29, RAC; X Corps Special Report, Box 13, RAC, 13; X Corps War Diary, Box 13, RAC, 8; Appleman, *East of Chosin*, 164, 294; Almond to REA, March 8, 1977, Almond folder, Box 29, RAC; Roe, "Destruction of the 31st Infantry," Part 5, 4; Smith to Cates, December 17, 1950, Correspondence with HQMC folder, Box 21, OPSC.

184 The news from Korea: "Communists in Intensified Attacks Continue Driving Back U.N. Forces in Korea," *New York Times*, November 29, 1950, 2; Helen to Storms, November 29, 1950, HHS.

Chapter 10: The Third Night

185 The calm: Curtis, "Operations of the First Battalion," 15; Miller, "Chosin Reservoir," 10; McClymont, "Narrative of Chosin," 9; White, "Korean War Memories."

185 Late that night: James Campbell transcript, November 29–30, 1980, Campbell folder, Box 8, RAC; Appleman, *East of Chosin*, 174; Oxenrider, "A Week of Eternity," 3; Gray, *Called to Honor*, 109; McCaffrey to REA, July 3, 1979, McCaffrey correspondence folder, Box 20, RAC; Knox, *The Korean War*, vol. 1, 552; Willis Via, *FOW*, 107; Mortrude, "Autobiographic Chronology of Chosin."

186 In the surrounding hills: Li, *Attack at Chosin*, 97; "The Unforgotten Korean War," 193.

186 Around midnight, the moon: Gray, *Called to Honor*, 110; *TCC*, 57; "D Battery," *NAC*, July 2000, 11; McClymont, "Narrative of Chosin," 9; Robbins, "Breakout," 4.

187 The Chinese had plotted: Bryant, "Four Days and Five Nights," 3; McClymont, "Narrative of Chosin," 9; Haugland DSC citation, DSC folder, Box 31, RAC; Robert Ayala interview, August 12, 2011, AFC/2001/001/82143, VHP; "Celestino Chavez Jr. Remembrance," KWP; "Celestino Chavez Silver Star Citation," Hall of Valor, Military Times, posted 2024, https://valor.militarytimes.com/hero/25032; Ayala, *FOW*, 117; "Robert Ayala Memoir," KWE.

188 The heaviest attack: Curtis, "Operations of the First Battalion," 15; May, "Report from Capt. Hugh R. May," 4; Appleman, *East of Chosin*, 172; White, "Korean War Memories."

188 The attacks had been: Magill, "57th Field Artillery," 113; Appleman, *East of Chosin*, 175; Ayala, *FOW*, 117.

Chapter 11: The Third Day

190 Dawn once again: Gray, *Called to Honor*, 111; Stamford, February 1951 Statement, 9; SV int, Ray Radke, November 19, 2021; Gugeler, *Combat Actions in Korea*, 67; Mortrude, "Autobiographic Chronology of Chosin"; Mortrude to REA, November 3, 1980, Mortrude folder, Box 8, RAC; Farley to Hammel, March 5, 1979, Farley folder, Box 6, EHPP.

190 The soldiers also used: Stamford interview with REA, October 28, 1980, Stamford folder, Box 9, RAC; Gray, *Called to Honor*, 104; Blohm, *FOW*, 125; SV int, Charlie Gebhardt, May 10, 2016; Robert Hammond, *FOW*, 115; Hammond, "Memories of War," 9.

190 Around the inlet: Patton statement, IG investigation folder, Box 7, RAC; Robbins, "Breakout," 4; Willis Via, *FOW*, 108.

191 After waiting almost: Joseph Gurfein to Hammel, February 16, 1979; Command Report, 2nd Battalion, 31st Infantry, 29 November to 12 December 1950, Box 7, RAC; McCaf-

frey to REA, March 28, 1978, McCaffrey correspondence folder, Box 20, RAC; *Changjin Journal*, July 10, 2003.

191 The bleak situation: McCaffrey to REA, June 5, 1981, and March 6, 1981, McCaffrey correspondence folder, Box 20, RAC; Appleman, *East of Chosin*, 176.

192 As of 8:20 a.m.: RCT 31 command report, 11 December 1950, Rasula folder, Box 5, EHPP; Smith, "Aide-Memoire Korea," 896; Smith diary, 30 November 1950, Box 72, OPSC; Russ, *Breakout*, 228–29; Bowser interview, January 2, 1951, MCH, 11.

192 Smith told Hodes: Smith, "Aide-Memoire Korea," 959; Smith to Cates, December 17, 1950, Correspondence with HQMC, December 1950, Box 21, OPSC; Smith comments on Marine Corps Board Study, January 1952, COP's comments folder, Box 67, OPSC; *TCC*, 81.

193 Bad as the situation: Smith, "Aide-Memoire Korea," 960; McCaffrey to REA, June 5, 1981, McCaffrey correspondence folder, Box 20, RAC; Drake to Needham, n.d., 1988 correspondence folder, Box 21, RAC; Lynch to REA, July 30, 1980, Lynch folder, Box 8, RAC.

193 At 8:00 a.m., Ned Almond: Almond Oral History, Section 4, 17; Montross and Canzona, *The Chosin Reservoir Campaign*, 239; Appleman, *East of Chosin*, 180; Almond diary, 30 November 1950, Box 29, RAC; Almond to Dora Maclean, December 14, 1950, Correspondence CG X Corps folder, Box 85, EAC.

194 Almond and Barr considered: McCaffrey to REA, June 5, 1981, McCaffrey correspondence folder, Box 20, RAC; Almond diary, 30 November 1950, Box 29, RAC; Smith, "Aide-Memoire Korea," 897.

194 With 18 remaining: Appleman, *East of Chosin*, 183–84; Drake to REA, January 10, 1977, Drake folder, Box 7, RAC; Hoehn, "Chosin, Korea."

194 With Hodes in Hagaru: Rasula to Russ, September 21, 1984, Rasula folder, Box 9, RAC; Rasula to Lucy, October 8, October 17, and October 30, 1950, *Changjin Journal*; January 31, 2002, *Changjin Journal*; Drake to REA, January 12 and December 23, 1977, Drake folder, Box 7, RAC; Hoehn, "Chosin, Korea"; Drake to Needham, n.d., 1988 correspondence folder, Box 21, RAC.

195 The schoolhouse: Hoehn, "Chosin, Korea"; *TCC*, 59.

195 At 11:00 a.m., Anderson: RCT 31 command report, 11 December 1950, Rasula folder, Box 5, EHPP; Lynch to REA, July 30, 1980; 7th Division command report, Chosin Reservoir, 7th Infantry Division folder, Box 7, RAC, 7; Smith, "Aide-Memoir," 899; Appleman, *East of Chosin*, 185; Drake to REA, September 27, 1980, February 22, 1978, and January 10, 1977, Drake folder, Box 7, RAC; Drake to REA, May 1, 1987, 1987 folder, Box 21, RAC.

195 Lt. Mortrude had: Mortrude, "Autobiographic Chronology."

196 Several officers escorted: Magill, "57th Field Artillery," 114; Address Given by Major General Barr Before the Army War College, 11–12, USAHEC; Barr to Barbara Faith, December 12, 1950, DFP; McNally transcript, McNally folder, Box 5, EHPP.,

196 Barr described the futile: Miller, "Chosin Reservoir," 11; Robbins, "Breakout," 4; Barr address, Address Given by Major General Barr Before the Army War College, 12, USAHEC.

196 Barr's visit was likely: Jones to REA, March 2, 1981, Jones folder, Box 8, RAC; Appleman, *East of Chosin*, 176; Simmons, *Frozen Chosin*, 72; Robbins, "Breakout," 4; Gray, *Called to Honor*, 112; Magill, "57th Field Artillery," 114.

197 After landing back: Smith Oral History, 236; Smith to Heinl, October 24, 1966, Monograph correspondence folder, Box 21, OPSC; Smith, "Aide-Memoire Korea," 898; Smith to Cates, December 17, 1950, Correspondence with HQMC, December 1950, Box 21, OPSC; Bowser interview, January 2, 1951, MCH, 1.

198 Shortly after 2:00 p.m.: X Corps Special Report, Box 13, RAC, 2; Lynch interview by REA, June 12, 1978, Lynch file, Box 8, RAC; Appleman, *East of Chosin*, 181; Smith to Cates, December 17, 1950, Correspondence with HQMC, December 1950, Box 21, OPSC; Shisler, *For Country and Corps*, 207; Smith, "Aide-Memoire Korea," 898.

198 The discussion turned: Smith Korean War log, 23–27 November 1950, Box 65, OPSC, 91; Smith diary, 30 November 1950, Box 72, OPSC; Appleman, *East of Chosin*, 315; Almond to REA, March 22, 1976; Almond Oral History, Section 5, 13; Roe, *The Dragon Strikes*, 338.

199 Once Almond departed: Smith Oral history, 230; Garrett, "Task Force Faith," *Infantry Magazine*, 29; Stamford to REA, April 7, 1981, and October 1, 1979, Stamford folder, Box 9, RAC; *Changjin Journal*, June 15, 2000, and June 30, 2008; Berquist, "Organizational Leadership in Crisis," 70.

200 Despite the task force's: Robbins, "Breakout," 4; Parker and Batha, *A History of Marine Observation Squadron Six*, 22; McClymont, "Narrative of Chosin," 7.

201 In the mountains: Zhou, "Mao's Telegrams," 5; Zhou, "CCF Order of Battle," 8; "The Unforgotten Korean War," 189; Li, *Attack at Chosin*, 85, 98, 220; Roe, *The Dragon Strikes*, 348.

202 Don Faith had: May to REA, September 5, 1981, and August 5, 1981, May folder, Box 9, RAC.

202 The role of exhaustion: Smith to Esther, December 21, 1950, OPS to Esther 2 November to 31 December 1950 folder, Box 27, OPSC; Stanton, *America's Tenth Legion*, 250; May to REA, September 5, 1981, May folder, Box 9, RAC.

203 Curtis was the most: Curtis to REA, February 20, 1978, Curtis folder, Box 8, RAC; Miller to REA, July 29, 1980, Miller folder, Box 9, RAC; May to REA, October 31, 1981, May folder, Box 9, RAC.

203 As evening approached: McCalister to REA, October 3, 1985, Mortrude folder, Box 8, RAC; Willis Via, *FOW*, 108; May, "Report from Capt. Hugh R. May," 5; Curtis, "Operations of the First Battalion," 15.

204 Some rifle companies: Gray, *Called to Honor*, 104, 113–15; Lee, "Dr. Yong Kak Lee," 62.

204 Airdrops brought: Appleman, *East of Chosin*, 175, 205; Willis Via, *FOW*, 108.

204 Word had spread: McClymont, "Narrative of Chosin"; Magill, "57th Field Artillery," 113; Curtis, "Operations of the First Battalion," 16.

205 By late afternoon: Rasula to REA, October 12, 1984, Rasula folder, Box 9, RAC; Drake to REA, January 10, 1977; 31st Tank Company operations summary and RCT 31 command report, 11 December 1950, Box 3172, RG 407, NARA; "I&R Platoon," *NAC*, March 1990, 7.

205 The Chinese wasted: Rasula to Russ, September 21, 1984, Rasula folder, Box 9, RAC; Hoehn, "Chosin, Korea"; 31st Tank Company operations summary, Box 3172, RG 407, NARA; Drake to REA, September 27, 1980, Drake folder, Box 7, RAC.

205 Hodes, who had: Lynch to REA, July 30, 1980, and June 3, 1981, Lynch folder, Box 8, RAC; Drake to Needham, September 1985, 1988 folder, Box 21, RAC; Appleman, *East of Chosin*, 323.

206 Ned Almond, seemingly: Haig and McCarry, *Inner Circles*, 63; Roe, *The Dragon Strikes*, 340; Almond to MacArthur, 30 November 1950, X 13481, X Corps in November 1950 folder, Box 89, RG 9, DMA; Bowser interview, January 2, 1951, MCH, 13; CG X Corps to CINCFE, 30 November 1950, X 13483, X Corps in November 1950 folder, Box 89, RG 9, DMA; Parker and Batha, *A History of Marine Observation Squadron Six*, 21; Service message,

29 November 1950, dispatched 2130 30 November, Service Messages X Corps folder, Box 62, EAC.

207 The plight: "1st Marine Division Trapped; 2 Infantry Regiments Also Cut Off," November 30, 1950, *Boston Globe*, 1; Geer, *The New Breed*, 308; Rasula to Hammel, March 5, 1979, Rasula folder, Box 5, EHPP; JCS to MacArthur, November 30, 1950, and CINCUNC to DEPTAR for JCS, November 30, 1950, November 50 to April 51 folder, Box 2, RG 6, DMA; James, *The Years of MacArthur*, 376; Omar N. Bradley and Clay Blair, *A General's Life* (Simon & Schuster, 1983), 600; Blair, *The Forgotten War*, 522–23; Weintraub, *MacArthur's War*, 257–59.

208 Helen Storms's: Helen to Storms, November 30, 1950, HHS.

Chapter 12: The Fourth Night

209 Once darkness arrived: "The Unforgotten Korean War," 189; Roe, *The Dragon Strikes*, 342; Curtis, "Operations of the First Battalion," 16; SV int, Harry Jacobs, January 15, 2022; Mortrude "Autobiographic Chronology"; Lee, "Dr. Yong Kak Lee," 62.

210 Soon after dark, Zhan: Li, *Attack at Chosin*, 98, "The Unforgotten Korean War," 189.

210 The attack began: "The Unforgotten Korean War," 189; "One Reservoir, Two Battles," *CFND*, July-September 2021, 16; Li, *Attack at Chosin*, 98; Robbins, "Breakout," 4; Bryant, "Four Days and Five Nights"; Curtis, "Operations of the First Battalion," 16.

211 But after midnight: Curtis, "Operations of the First Battalion," 16–17; Gugeler, *Combat Actions in Korea*, 67; Magill, "57th Field Artillery," 114; McMillin Army Chapter interview; SV int, Grant McMillin, September 27, 2021.

212 Around 3:00 a.m.: Curtis, "Operations of the First Battalion," 17; Cowdrey, *The Medic's War*, 121; Lee, "Dr. Yong Kak Lee," 62; Miller, "Chosin Reservoir," 12; Robbins, "Breakout," 4; Lloyd Mielenz interview, AFC/2001/001/41636, VHP, 5.

212 Captain Cody's: SV int, Jerry McCabe, December 1, 2000; Vogel, "50 Years Later"; Ben Dryden, *FOW*, 149; Fulton, "Korean War Veteran, Missing for 65 Years."

213 Pitched battles: Bryant, "Four Days and Five Nights"; May, "Report from Capt. Hugh R. May," 5; McGuire, *FOW*, 153.

213 For a while: Gray, *Called to Honor*, 115; Stamford, February 1951 Statement, 9; May, "Report from Capt. Hugh R. May," 5; Miller, "Chosin Reservoir," 12; SV int, Charlie Gebhardt, May 10, 2016; McClymont, "Narrative of Chosin," 9; Hensley, *FOW*, 195.

214 As dawn approached: Mortrude, "Autobiographic Chronology of Chosin"; Mortrude interview, in Precious, *Task Force Faith*.

214 The Chinese still held: Gugeler, *Combat Actions in Korea*, 67–68; James Campbell transcript, November 29–30, 1980, Campbell folder, Box 8, RAC; Appleman, *East of Chosin*, 193.

215 At the combined: Li, *Attack at Chosin*, 99; Curtis, "Operations of the First Battalion," 17; Gray, *Called to Honor*, 116; Kitz report, Box 3172, RG 407, NARA, 4; Jones, "Report to Major Lynch," 2.

215 At daylight: Magill, "57th Field Artillery," 114; Willis Via, *FOW*, 108.

216 The 1st Battalion aid: Lee, "Dr. Yong Kak Lee," 62.

Chapter 13: Breakout Morning

218 By dawn: Curtis, "Operations of the First Battalion," 17; Oxenrider, "A Week of Eternity," 3; Gray, *Called to Honor*, 116–17; Curtis to REA, May 6, 1979, Curtis folder, Box 8, RAC; Francois interview with Blair, February 15, 1986, 31st Regiment folder, Box 71, CJBC.

218 It was clear: Curtis, "Operations of the First Battalion," 18; Address Given by Major General Barr Before the Army War College, 12, USAHEC; Jones, "Report to Major Lynch," 2; Stamford, February 1951 Statement, 9; Miller, "Chosin Reservoir," 12.

219 Stamford tried for: John Swenty statement, IG investigation folder, Box 7, RAC; Curtis, "Operations of the First Battalion," 15, 18–19; Appleman, *East of Chosin*, 195–96.

219 Faith huddled: Curtis, "Operations of the First Battalion," 19; Curtis to REA, September 10, 1978, and March 1, 1981, Curtis folder, Box 8, RAC; Appleman, *East of Chosin*, 310–11; Garrett, "Task Force Faith," *Infantry Magazine*, 29.

220 At 10:00 a.m., Faith: Appleman, *East of Chosin*, 196; Miller, "Chosin Reservoir," 13–14; Jones to REA, March 2, 1981, Jones folder, Box 8, RAC; McClymont, "Narrative of Chosin," 9; Curtis, "Operations of the First Battalion," 19.

221 The two-and-a-half-ton trucks: May, "Report from Capt. Hugh R. May,"6; Appleman, *East of Chosin*, 196–97; Miller, "Chosin Reservoir," 13–14; Gugeler, *Combat Actions in Korea*, 70; Curtis, "Operations of the First Battalion," 19; Jones to Coombs, January 15, 1975, and Jones to REA, January 19, 1981, Jones folder, Box 8, RAC; Curtis to REA, September 10, 1978, Curtis folder, Box 8, RAC.

221 When the meeting ended: Robbins, "Breakout," 4; McNally transcript, McNally folder, Box 5, EHPP.

222 About the same time: May, "Report from Capt. Hugh R. May," 6; Campbell transcript, November 29–30, 1980, Campbell folder, Box 8, RAC; Bigger, "Reflections and Comments"; Bigger to REA, March 29, 1981, Bigger folder, Box 9, RAC; Miller, "Chosin Reservoir," 12; Jones Memoir, KWE, 23.

222 At the 1st Battalion CP, Miller: Miller, "Chosin Reservoir," 14; Curtis, "Operations of the First Battalion," 19; Bryant, "Four Days and Five Nights."

222 At the 57th Field: Price statement, IG investigation folder, Box 7, RAC; Curtis to REA, February 15, 1981, Curtis folder, Box 8, RAC; Charles Bennett, *FOW*, 127.

223 Faith, waving: Magill, "57th Field Artillery," 115; Magill to Rasula, October 28, 1987, and April 19, 1991, folder 5, Box 15, GRP; Anthony T. Mora interview, AFC/2001/001/55589 VHP.

223 The troop preparations: Gugeler, *Combat Actions in Korea*, 68; Campbell to REA, April 9, 1981, Campbell folder, Box 8, RAC.

224 At 11:00 a.m.: Appleman, *East of Chosin*, 206; Shisler, *For Country and Corps*, 209; *TCC*, 61.

224 Hagaru had been: Smith, "Aide-Memoire Korea," 963; Drake to REA, January 10, 1977; Lynch to REA, December 19, 1976, Lynch folder, Box 8, RAC; Bowser, Comments on Marine Corps Board Study, December 29, 1951, COP's comments folder, Box 67, OPSC.

224 In the morning: Lynch interview with REA, July 26, 1980, Lynch folder, Box 8, RAC; REA to Drake, March 17, 1978, Drake folder, Box 7, RAC; McCaffrey interview with Blair, McCaffrey folder, Box 80, CJBC.

225 Unlike the Army: Smith, "Aide-Memoire Korea," 752; 30 November 1950, 1st Marine Division Historical Diary for November 1950, Box 61, OPSC; Simmons, *Frozen Chosin*, 80, 84; Russ, *Breakout*, 284; Smith Family Journal, 387–88.

225 As the breakout: Curtis, "Operations of the First Battalion," 18; Robbins, "Breakout," 4–5; Bryant, "Four Days and Five Nights."

226 At Able Company: Roy Oxenrider, *FOW*, 147; Thomas Patton and Helmuth Bertram statements, IG investigation folder, Box 7, RAC; "A Soldier's War," Fall 1983, *CFND*, 4; Appleman, *East of Chosin*, 198; Gray, *Called to Honor*, 116; Hill, "An Unknown Chaplain," 12.

227 Trucks were lining: Appleman, *East of Chosin*, 200–2; "D Battery," *NAC*, July 2000, 11; Robert Ayala interview, August 12, 2011, AFC/2001/001/82143, VHP, 9; McClymont, "Narrative of Chosin," 10; SV int, Jerry McCabe, December 1, 2000; Robert Hammond, *FOW*, 115; Hammond, "Memories of War," 4.

227 The soldiers anxiously: SV int, Joe Ager, September 10, 2022; Bryant, "Four Days and Five Nights"; Magill, "57th Field Artillery," 115; Magill to Hammel, August 9, 1979, Magill folder, Box 6, EHPP.

228 Bigger—still in: Bigger to REA, March 29, 1981, Bigger folder, Box 9, RAC; Kunkle and Vogel, "Korean War Hero Comes Home at Last," *WP*, April 17, 2013; Knox, *The Korean War*, vol. 1, 552; Roy Oxenrider, *FOW*, 147; Mortrude, "Autobiographic Chronology of Chosin."

Chapter 14: Breakout Afternoon

229 The attack began: Mortrude, "Autobiographic Chronology of Chosin"; Appleman, *East of Chosin*, 207–8, 313; Bigger to REA, July 6, 1980, Bigger folder, Box 9, RAC; Lt. Col. Anderson report, 31st Infantry command report, 1, Box 3172, RG 407, NARA.

229 Faith rode: Campbell to REA, December 13, 1980, Campbell folder, Box 8, RAC; Robbins, "Breakout," 5; Knox, *The Korean War*, vol. 1, 552; McClymont, "Narrative of Chosin," 9; Magill, "57th Field Artillery," 115; SV int, Ray Radke, November 19, 2021; Kitz report, Box 3172, RG 407, NARA; "Fremont 'Monty' Piercefield Memoir," KWE, 4; SV int, Monty Piercefield, September 30, 2021.

230 A short way outside: Magill, "57th Field Artillery," 115; "The Unforgotten Korean War," 189; Curtis interview with REA, May 6, 1979, Curtis folder, Box 8, RAC; Appleman, *East of Chosin*, 208; Mortrude, "Autobiographic Chronology of Chosin"; Robbins, "Breakout," 5; Faith Medal of Honor citation, Box 31, RAC; Miller, "Chosin Reservoir," 15.

230 Mortrude watched hopefully: Mortrude, "Autobiographic Chronology of Chosin"; Magill, "57th Field Artillery," 115; Robert Ayala memoir, KWE; Gray, *Called to Honor*, 121; Cowdrey, *The Medics' War*, 121.

230 Maj. Robbins, lying: Robbins, "Breakout," 5; SV int, Ray Radke, August 29, 2021; Edwin Anderson interview with REA, November 3, 1980, Anderson folder, Box 8, RAC; May to REA, August 20, 1981, May folder, Box 9, RAC; Jones to REA, April 5, 1983, Jones folder, Box 8, RAC; Lee, "Dr. Yong Kak Lee," 5; McMillin interview, in Precious, *Task Force Faith*; Stamford to REA, October 3, 1979, Stamford folder, Box 9, RAC.

232 PFC Roy Oxenrider: Roy Oxenrider, *FOW*, 147; SV int, Joe Ager, September 10, 2022; Bigger, "Reflections and Comments," 6; SV int, Charlie Gebhardt, May 10, 2016.

232 Faith's response: Stamford, February 1951 Statement, 18; Appleman, *East of Chosin*, 214; Stamford to REA, March 30, 1980, Stamford folder, Box 9, RAC; Bigger, "Reflections and Comments," 6.

233 Deadly as the napalm: Stamford to REA, October 3, 1979, Stamford folder, Box 9, RAC; Miller, "Chosin Reservoir," 15; Stamford, February 1951 Statement, 10.

233 The 3rd Battalion: Jordan to REA, October 30, 1978, Jordan folder, Box 8, RAC; Gray, *Called to Honor*, 121; McClymont, "Narrative of Chosin," 10; Appleman, *East of Chosin*, 200;

Robert Ayala interview, August 12, 2011, AFC/2001/001/82143, VHP, 9; "D Battery," *NAC*, July 2000, 11.

234 Without the Twin 40: Kitz report, Box 3172, RG 407, NARA, 5; Hensley biography, *NAC*, July 2000, 2; Hode Hensley, *FOW*, 195; Harry Scott, *FOW*, 151; John Williams, *FOW*, 203; Rasula to Olson, February 4, 1951, Long folder, Box 9, RAC; "D Battery," *NAC*, July 2000, 11.

235 With the task force cleared: "The Unforgotten Korean War," 190; Li, *Attack at Chosin*, 99.

235 The column surged: Magill, "57th Field Artillery," 116; Robert Ayala interview, August 12, 2011, AFC/2001/001/82143, VHP, 10; Miller, "Chosin Reservoir," 15; White, "Korean War Memories."

236 Roy Oxenrider's Able: Roy Oxenrider, *FOW*, 147; May, "Report from Capt. Hugh R. May," 6.

236 Sgt. Via, who: Willis Via, *FOW*, 108; Anthony T. Mora interview, AFC/2001/001/55589, VHP, 23–25.

237 The 3rd Battalion, bringing: Bryant, "Four Days and Five Nights"; Etchemendy to REA, November 24, 1989, Etchemendy folder, Box 9, RAC; Kitz report, Box 3172, RG 407, NARA; Appleman, *East of Chosin*, 222; Francois, Recollections transcripts; Donovan, "Photographs of Korea," 139.

238 Up front, the troops: Curtis, "Operations of the First Battalion," 20; Miller, "Chosin Reservoir," 16; Stamford, February 1951 Statement, 101; Jones to Coombs, January 15, 1975, Jones folder, Box 8, RAC; Magill statement, IG investigation folder, Box 7, RAC; Appleman, *East of Chosin*, 230.

238 The truck carrying Hugh: Robbins, "Breakout," 5; Mortrude to REA, October 23, 1980, Mortrude folder, Box 8, RAC; Miller, "Chosin Reservoir," 16; Appleman, *East of Chosin*, 225, 312; Curtis, "Operations of the First Battalion," 20.

239 A few trucks made: Garrigus Distinguished Service Cross citation, DSC folder, Box 31, RAC; Miller, "Chosin Reservoir," 16; May, "Report from Capt. Hugh R. May," 6; Gray, *Called to Honor*, 214; Robert Ayala interview, August 12, 2011, AFC/2001/001/82143, VHP, 10; McClymont, "Narrative of Chosin," 11.

240 Faith surveyed: May to REA, October 31, 1981, May folder, Box 9, RAC; May, "Report from Capt. Hugh R. May," 7; Bigger, "Reflections and Comments," 2; Jones to REA, March 14, 1981, Jones folder, Box 8, RAC; Appleman, *East of Chosin*, 233; Li, *Attack at Chosin*, 100; Stamford interview with REA, October 28, 1980, Stamford folder, Box 9, RAC.

240 As trucks gradually: Robbins, "Breakout," 5; Curtis, "Operations of the First Battalion," 20–21; Lee, "Dr. Yong Kak Lee," 62; Charles Bennett, *FOW*, 127.

240 The roadblock clearly: Bigger, "Reflections and Comments," 2; Appleman, *East of Chosin*, 233–34; Magill, "57th Field Artillery," 116; Mielenz, "Lloyd Mielenz Remembers Chosin"; Stamford, February 1951 Statement, 11.

240 Another threat: Curtis, "Operations of the First Battalion," 20; Appleman, *East of Chosin*, 229–30, 236; Miller to REA, March 26, 1981, Miller folder, Box 9, RAC; May, "Report from Capt. Hugh R. May," 7; Stamford, February 1951 Statement, 11; Miller, "Chosin Reservoir," 17.

241 As the crossing continued: Miller to REA, July 29, 1980, Miller folder, Box 9, RAC; Miller, "Chosin Reservoir," 17–18.

241 Curtis was standing: Curtis, "Operations of the First Battalion," 20; Curtis to REA, February 20, 1978, Curtis folder, Box 8, RAC; Hill, "An Unknown Chaplain," 12; Curtis interview with REA, June 1981, Curtis folder, Box 8, RAC; Appleman, *East of Chosin*, 232.

242 Some men had reached: SV int, Ray Radke, November 19, 2021; Appleman, *East of Chosin*, 278; Jones to Coombs, January 15, 1975, Jones folder, Box 8, RAC; Bryant, "Four Days and Five Nights"; Jones Memoir, KWE, 18.

243 Not every truck made: May to REA, August 20, 1981, May folder, Box 9, RAC; Mortrude to REA, November 3, 1980, Mortrude folder, Box 8, RAC; Roy Oxenrider, *FOW*, 148.

243 The last two trucks: May to REA, August 20, 1981, May folder, Box 9, RAC; Appleman, *East of Chosin*, 226, 313–14; Cpl. George Auger Silver Star citation, Drake folder, Box 7, RAC; Robert Ayala interview, August 12, 2011, AFC/2001/001/82143, VHP, 10–11; Stamford interview with REA, October 28, 1980, Stamford folder, Box 9, RAC.

243 Harvey Storms waited: Bryant, "Four Days and Five Nights"; Appleman, *East of Chosin*, 236; SV int, Sam Storms, July 26, 2022; Trautz, "Man Finds Closure After His Father's Remains"; McClay to Rasula, May 31, 1979, folder 3, Box 16, GRP; "On the East Side of Chosin," Ned Forney, August 6, 2018, https://nedforney.com/index.php/2018/08/06/chosin-reservoir-major-harvey-storms/; Jordan to REA, January 5, 1979, Jordan folder, Box 8, RAC; "Remembering Harvey Storms," *NAC*, March 1990.

244 Faith strode up: Campbell interview with REA, Campbell folder, Box 8, RAC; Gugeler, *Combat Actions in Korea*, 73; SV int, Joe Ager, September 10, 2022; Stamford, February 1951 Statement, 12; Bigger, "Reflections and Comments," 8; Appleman, *East of Chosin*, 379.

245 Bigger volunteered: Bigger, "Reflections and Comments," 2; Robbins, "Breakout," 5–6; White, "Korean War Memories'"; Appleman, *East of Chosin*, 243; Mortrude, "Autobiographic Chronology of Chosin"; Willis Via, *FOW*, 109.

246 Other assaults of Hill: Gray, *Called to Honor*, 125–27; 130–31; "Schmitt Distinguished Service Cross Citation, Robert Gerard Schmitt Remembrance," KWP; Jordan to REA, January 5, 1979, Jordan folder, Box 8, RAC.

247 Down on the road: SV int, Harry Jacobs, January 15, 2022; Magill statement, IG investigation folder, Box 7, RAC.

247 The Bigger attack: Robbins, "Breakout," 5–6; White, "Korean War Memories"; Mortrude, "Autobiographic Chronology of Chosin."

247 Lt. Patton: Patton statement, IG investigation folder, Box 7, RAC; Gugeler, *Combat Actions in Korea*, 74, 77; Appleman, *East of Chosin*, 242.

248 Capt. John MacDonald: SV int, John MacDonald, April 4, 2022; Smith, "Aide-Memoire Korea," 964; MacDonald, "Which Way?"; Patton statement, IG investigation folder, Box 7, RAC.

249 Around 4:00 p.m.: 1st Motor Transport Battalion annex to 1st Marine Division Special Action Report for 8 October to 15 December 1950, Box 58, OPSC, 11; Beall, "Statement, Regarding Dealings with the Army in Korea," 4; Beall, "Statement, in Regards to Rescue of Army Personnel," 1; Appleman, *East of Chosin*, 279, 287; Bowser interview, January 2, 1951, MCH, 12; Patton statement, IG investigation folder, Box 7, RAC.

250 By late afternoon: Robbins, "Breakout," 6; "Survivor reports on Chosin escape," *Dallas Morning News*, December 12, 1950, in *CFND*, July–September 2022; Etchemendy to REA, November 24, 1989, Etchemendy folder, Box 9, RAC.

250 PFC Lewis Shannon: "Shannon and Scalph," The Army at Chosin; Reeves, *Beautiful Feet and Real Peace*, 7; Ben Dryden, *FOW*, 149.

251 Capt. James Conner and Cpl.: SV int, Ray Radke, August 29, 2021; Sgt. Carl Truett statement, IG investigation folder, Box 7, RAC; Hill, "An Unknown Chaplain," 12; Tom Marker, "In Memoriam," Chester Bair folder, Box 74, CJBC; Mills, *Honoring Those Who Paid the Price*, 136; Tim Evans, "Forgotten No More," *IndyStar*, August 26, 2019.

252 PFC Doc Blohm: Blohm, *FOW*, 125.

252 Two trucks carrying: SV int, Grant McMillin, September 27, 2021; McMillin Army Chapter interview.

253 By dusk the air: Appleman, *East of Chosin*, 214, 239; *TCC*, 82, 118; Stamford, February 1951 Statement, 12; Stamford Interview, MCH, 94; Samuel B. Folsom interview, AFC/2001/001/79380, VHP; Folsom to James Dill, March 14, 1983, Dill Diary folder, Box 78, CJBC; Stamford interview with REA, October 28, 1980, Stamford folder, Box 9, RAC; Far East Situation, 3 December 50, Telecons 1–8 December folder, Box 123, RG 9, DMA.

254 A ray of hope: Miller, "Chosin Reservoir," 18; Mortrude, "Autobiographic Chronology of Chosin"; Bigger interview with REA, May 8, 1980, Box 9, RAC; Bigger, "Reflections and Comments," 2; Willis Via, *FOW*, 109; Magill, "57th Field Artillery," 116; Harry Scott, *FOW*, 151.

255 The victims included: May to REA, July 24 and August 20, 1981, May folder, Box 9, RAC; Curtis, "Operations of the First Battalion," 18; Bigger, "Reflections and Comments," 7.

Chapter 15: Breakout Night

256 Don Faith was not: Appleman, *East of Chosin*, 249–52; Jones to Coombs, January 15, 1975, Jones folder, Box 8, RAC; Jones Memoir, KWE, 26; Gray, *Called to Honor*, 132; Jones to REA, January 19, 1981, Jones folder, Box 8, RAC.

257 The friendly fire air strikes: Gray, *Called to Honor*, 132; Jordan to REA, January 5 and February 4, 1979, Jordan folder, Box 8, RAC.

257 A few minutes later: Stamford to REA, September 30, 1979, Stamford folder, Box 9, RAC; Jordan to REA, January 5, 1979, Jordan folder, Box 8, RAC; Jones, "Report to Major Lynch," 3; Campbell to REA, December 13, 1980, Campbell folder, Box 8, RAC; SV int, Charlie Gebhardt, May 10, 2016; SV int, Joe Ager, September 10, 2022; "Lt. Col Don Carlos Faith, Jr.," JPAC, DFP, 4; SV int, Arthur Mercier, April 11, 2013; Anthony Biebel, *FOW*, 169.

258 With Faith being tended: Jordan to REA, January 5, 1979, Jordan folder, Box 8, RAC; Gray, *Called to Honor*, 133; SV int, Joe Ager, September 10, 2022.

259 Maj. Jones was already: Jones to Coombs, January 15, 1975, Jones folder, Box 8, RAC; Gray, *Called to Honor*, 133; Jones Memoir, KWE, 25; "CPT Lawrence Francis Brunnert Remembrance," KWP; May to REA, August 20, 1981, May folder, Box 9, RAC; John Williams, *FOW*, 203; Radke, "Radke Remembers," *NAC*, May–June 2004, 9.

259 At the rear of the: Stamford, February 1951 Statement, 13–14; *Changjin Journal*, February 27, 2000; Appleman, *East of Chosin*, 260; Cowdrey, *The Medics' War*, 121.

259 In the darkness: Jones Memoir, KWE, 25; Jones to Coombs, January 15, 1975, Jones folder, Box 8, RAC; May, "Report from Capt. Hugh R. May," 8; Appleman, *East of Chosin*, 256; May to REA, August 20, 1981, May folder, Box 9, RAC; Gray, *Called to Honor*, 134; John Williams, *FOW*, 203.

260 Jones reconsidered: Jones, "Report to Major Lynch," 3; Jones to Coombs, January 15, 1975, Jones folder, Box 8, RAC; Capt Lawrence Frank Brunnert Service Member Profile, DPAA; SV int, Ray Radke, November 19, 2021; Gray, *Called to Honor*, 137.

260 It was here that: Jones to REA, January 5, 1979, Jones folder, Box 8, RAC; Gugeler, *Combat Actions in Korea*, 75; Jones, "Report to Major Lynch," 3; Jones interview, in Precious, *Task Force Faith*; May, "Report from Capt. Hugh R. May," 8–9; SV int, Monty Piercefield, September 30, 2021; "Fremont 'Monty' Piercefield Memoir," KWE, 4; Robbins, "Breakout," 6.

261 Other groups of soldiers: Jordan to REA, October 30, 1978, and January 5, 1979, Jordan folder, Box 8, RAC; Mortrude, "Autobiographic Chronology of Chosin"; Appleman, *East of Chosin*, 242, 248; Kitz report, Box 3172, RG 407, NARA; SV int, Harry Jacobs, January 15, 2022.

262 At X Corps Headquarters: Lynch to REA, May 18, 1981, and December 19, 1976, Lynch folder, Box 8, RAC; Appleman, *East of Chosin*, 295–96.

263 The troops remaining: Miller, "Chosin Reservoir," 19; Gray, *Called to Honor*, 138–40.

263 Bob Jones and his: May, "Report from Capt. Hugh R. May," 10–11; Jones, "Report to Major Lynch," 3; SV int, Monty Piercefield, September 30, 2021; "Fremont 'Monty' Piercefield Memoir," KWE.

264 Capt. Stamford arrived: Stamford to REA, February 22, 1979, Stamford folder, Box 9, RAC; Stamford, February 1951 Statement, 15.

264 It was another endless: Curtis, "Operations of the First Battalion," 21; Miller, "Chosin Reservoir," 18–19; SV int, Ray Radke, November 19, 2021; Radke, "Radke Remembers," *NAC*, May–June 2004, 9; John Williams, *FOW*, 203; Lee, "Dr. Yong Kak Lee," 63.

265 The trucks that: Curtis to REA, June 5, 1980, January 30, 1977, February 16, 1981, and February 20, 1978, Curtis folder, Box 8, RAC; Ivan Long, *FOW*, 123.

265 By around midnight: Lee, "Dr. Yong Kak Lee," 63; Gray, *Called to Honor*, 140; Curtis, "Operations of the First Battalion," 21; Etchemendy to Crosby Miller, ca. 1954, Etchemendy folder, Box 9, RAC; "Remembering Harvey Storms," *NAC*, March 1990, 6.

266 As one of the last: Gray, *Called to Honor*, 140–41; SV int, John Edward Gray, April 17, 2013; SV int, Charlie Gebhardt, May 10, 2016; SV int, Ray Radke, November 19, 2021.

266 The moon was burning: Vallowe, *What History Failed to Record*, 9; Miller, "Chosin Reservoir," 19–20; Appleman, *East of Chosin*, 270, 274; Gugeler, *Combat Actions in Korea*, 75; Etchemendy to Miller, ca. 1954, Etchemendy folder, Box 9, RAC.

267 Miller rolled off: Miller, "Chosin Reservoir," 20–21; Appleman, *East of Chosin*, 272.

268 With the front: Gray, *Called to Honor*, 141; Smith, *FOW*, 129; Moore, "Wounded GIs Burned Alive"; Appleman, *East of Chosin*, 270–72; Corporal Ambrose Feist statement, IG investigation folder, Box 7, RAC; Campbell to REA, December 13, 1980, Campbell folder, Box 8, RAC; Gugeler, *Combat Actions in Korea*, 76.

269 The truck carrying: John Williams, *FOW*, 203; Lee, "Dr. Yong Kak Lee," 63–64; Campbell to REA, December 13, 1980, Campbell folder, Box 8, RAC; SV int, Jerry McCabe, December 1, 2000; Vogel, "50 Years Later"; Charles Bennett, *FOW*, 127.

270 Sgt. Jim DeLong: DeLong, "Inside K Company"; Anthony T. Mora interview, AFC/2001/001/55589, VHP, 25–26; Dorsey statement, IG investigation folder, Box 7, RAC; Appleman, *East of Chosin*, 259.

270 Lt. Lloyd Mielenz: Mielenz, "Lloyd Mielenz Remembers Chosin," *NAC*, October 2000, 4–5; Mielenz interview, AFC/2001/001/41636, VHP, 7–8.

271 Sgt. Radke: SV int, Ray Radke, November 19, 2021; Stamford, February 1951 Statement, 15–16; Stamford to REA, July 9, 1990, 1990 folder, Box 21, RAC; Appleman, *East of Chosin*, 265–66; Radke, "Radke Remembers," *NAC*, May–June 2004, 10.

272 Lt. Gray had: Gray, *Called to Honor*, 141–42; Reeves, *Beautiful Feet and Real Peace*, 7; Sides, *On Desperate Ground*, 274; Reeves interview, in Precious, *Task Force Faith*.

273 Maj. Miller, moving: Miller, "Chosin Reservoir," 21–22; Robbins, "Breakout," 6; May, "Report from Capt. Hugh R. May," 12–13; May to REA, September 5, 1981, May folder, Box 9, RAC.

274 Maj. Curtis was: Curtis to REA, February 20, 1978, and May 9, 1976, Curtis folder, Box 8, RAC.

274 At the 1st Marine Motor: Tom Elliott, "Ice Marines," *CFND*, 1985, 3; Harry Scott, *FOW*, 151; Russ, *Breakout*, 330; Marker, "A Soldier Remembers"; Jordan to REA, May 30, 1978, and January 5, 1979, Jordan folder, Box 8, RAC; Mortrude, "Autobiographic Chronology of Chosin."

275 Out on the ice: Lee, "Dr. Yong Kak Lee," 64; DeLong interview, in Precious, *Task Force Faith*; SV int, Grant McMillin, August 29, 2021; McMillin Army Chapter interview; Li, *Attack at Chosin*, 101; *TCC*, 63.

276 One truck made it: Appleman, *East of Chosin*, 275–77; Major Edwin Anderson interview with REA, Anderson folder, Box 8, RAC; Notes on Anderson memo to Barr, January 9, 1951, 7th Division at Chosin folder, Box 7, RAC; "Lt. Col Don Carlos Faith, Jr.," JPAC, DFP, 6.

276 Lt. Gray's group: Bertram statement, IG investigation report, Box 7, RAC; Gray, *Called to Honor*, 142–43; SV int, Joe Ager, September 10, 2022; Gray interview, in Precious, *Task Force Faith*.

Chapter 16: The Day After

278 From inside: Mielenz, "Lloyd Mielenz Remembers Chosin," *NAC*, October 2000, 5; Feist statement, IG investigation folder, Box 7, RAC; Mielenz interview, AFC/2001/001/41636, VHP, 9–10.

279 Ray Radke, sleeping: SV int, Ray Radke, November 19, 2021; "Radke Remembers," *NAC*, May–June 2004, 10; Miller, "Chosin Reservoir," 22–23.

280 At the northeast perimeter: Beall, "Statement, in Regards to Rescue of Army Personnel," 1; Appleman, *East of Chosin*, 288; Simmons, *Frozen Chosin*, 16; SV int, Ralph Milton, January 9, 2022; Beall, "Statement, Regarding Dealings with the Army in Korea," 4.

280 Soon after daylight: Captain Joseph McCallister, USAF, transcript, McCallister folder, Box 6, EHPP; Appleman, *East of Chosin*, 294, 298; REA to Drake, June 21, 1978, Drake folder, Box 7, RAC; Bowser interview, January 2, 1951, MCH, 11; Lynch to REA, July 30, 1980, Lynch folder, Box 8, RAC; Stanton, *America's Tenth Legion*, 243.

281 Maj. Curtis and Capt. Bigger: Curtis to REA, June 5, 1980, March 1, 1981, and May 9, 1976, Curtis folder, Box 8, RAC; Bigger to REA, March 29, 1981, Bigger folder, Box 9, RAC; May, "Report from Capt. Hugh," 13.

281 It was too late: O. P. Smith Korean War Log, December 2, Box 65, OPSC; Marine Corps Board Study, Annex C, Box 67, OPSC, 73; Smith, "Aide-Memoire Korea," 900–1; 31st Tank Company Operations Summary, 25 November to 11 December 1950, Box 3172, RG 407, NARA; Drake to REA, January 10, 1977, Drake folder, Box 7, RAC; George C. Duncan, *FOW*, 227; Anthony T. Mora interview, AFC/2001/001/55589, VHP, 25–30.

Though Appleman wrote in *East of Chosin* (chapter 20) that no tanks were sent out on December 2, ample evidence and witness accounts show otherwise.

282 Lt. Mortrude awoke: Mortrude, "Autobiographic Chronology of Chosin"; May, "Report from Capt. Hugh R. May," 13; Swenty statement, IG investigation folder, Box 7, RAC; Curtis to REA, February 16, 1981, Curtis folder, Box 8, RAC; Sterling Morgan to Harvey Gal-

loway, December 1, 1951, Galloway folder, Box 6, EHPP; Mielenz, "Lloyd Mielenz Remembers Chosin," *NAC*, October 2000; "D Battery," July 2000, *NAC*, 12; Hode Hensley, *FOW*, 195; Ben Dryden, *FOW*, 149; SV int, Jerry McCabe, December 2000.

283 Hodes walked through: Lynch to REA, May 8, 1981, and July 30, 1980, Lynch folder, Box 8, RAC; Witte to Hammel, January 24, 1980, Witte folder, Box 5, EHPP; Witte to REA, November 5, 1978, Witte folder, Box 8, RAC; White, "Korean War Memories."

284 On Saturday morning, Song: Li, *Attack at Chosin*, 101, 111; Zhou, "Mao's Telegrams," 5; "The Unforgotten Korean War," 191; Roe, *The Dragon Strikes*, 342, 352; Smith, "Aide-Memoire Korea," 753.

285 At 2:00 p.m., General Ned: X Corps Special Report, Box 13, RAC, 16; Stanton, *America's Tenth Legion*, 243; Smith, "Aide-Memoire Korea," 996–67; Gray, *Called to Honor*, 145; Almond to MacArthur, December 2, 1950, X Corps in December 50 to April 51 folder, Box 89, RG 9, DMA.

286 Beall's rescue mission: "Marines Tell Suffering of Nearly Frozen GIs," *Los Angeles Times*, December 4, 1950; Beall, "Statement, in Regards to Rescue of Army Personnel," 3; Gugeler, *Combat Actions in Korea*, 77; Higgins, "The Bloody Trail Back," 118; Watson, "Army Checks on Behavior"; Beall, "Statement, Regarding Dealings with the Army in Korea," 5; SV int, Ralph Milton, January 9, 2022.

287 Other impromptu rescue: Hodges Escue interview with Rasula, October 17, 1981, Escue folder, Box 12, GRP; *Changjin Journal*, June 30, 2008; "A Cool Customer in Icy Rescue," August–September 2004, *NAC*, 6; Beall, "Statement, Regarding Dealings with the Army in Korea," 5; Geer, *The New Breed*, 345; Smith Family Journal, 390; Smith, Korean War Log, December 2, 1950, Box 65, OPSC.

288 Many more lives: Smith, Korean War Log, December 2, 1950, Box 65, OPSC; S. L. A. Marshall, "CCF Tactics in the Envelopment of a Column," OPSC, 11; Beall, "Statement, in Regards to Rescue of Army Personnel," 3; Hoehn, "Chosin, Korea," 24; Navarre to Stamford, November 30, 1951, Stamford folder, Box 9, RAC; Cowdrey, *The Medics' War*, 122; Mielenz interview, AFC/2001/001/41636, VHP, 11; Robert Ayala interview, August 12, 2011, AFC/2001/001/82143, VHP, 12.

289 All day, wounded: Smith, Korean War Log, December 2, 1950, Box 65, OPSC; Smith, "Aide-Memoire Korea," 992, 999; McCallister transcript, McCallister folder, Box 6, EHPP; Gray, *Called to Honor*, 144–47; "Little Lift Operation," December 9, 1950, GHQ Public Information Office, Folder 9, Box 1, RG 7, DMA.

290 Cpl. Mora, rushed: "Separate Experiences, Now a Brotherhood," November–December 2004, *NAC*, 5; "Hummingbirds and Hornets," *NAC*, May–June 2004, 6; Anthony T. Mora interview, AFC/2001/001/55589, VHP, 29–30; Etchemendy to REA, November 24, 1989, Etchemendy folder, Box 9, RAC; SV int, Jerry McCabe, December 1, 2000; John Williams, *FOW*, 109; Takatsu, "Deception and Decency," 26–27; SV int, Ray Radke, August 29, 2021; Shannon statement, IG investigation folder, Box 7, RAC; "Shannon and Scalph," The Army at Chosin; Shannon, "A Letter Home"; Smith to Cates, December 17, 1950, Correspondence with HQMC, December 1950, Box 21, OPSC; "1000 Wounded Saved in Mass Mercy Flight," United Press, in *Boston Globe*, December 3, 1950.

291 That evening, Navy Captain: Smith, "Aide-Memoire Korea," 903–4; Smith Oral History, MCH, 227; Smith, Korean War Log, December 2, Box 65, OPSC; SV int, Ralph Milton, January 9, 2022.

292 By nightfall many wounded: Roy Oxenrider, *FOW*, 148; Miller, "Chosin Reservoir," 23; Smith, *FOW*, 149; Knox, *The Korean War*, vol. 2, 328.

Chapter 17: Out of Chosin

297 The first reports: Moore, "Wounded GIs Burned Alive, Bayoneted by Red Chinese," *Boston Globe*, December 3, 1950; "Reds Shell Pyongyang; G.I. Dunkirk Threatens," United Press, in *Boston Globe*, December 3, 1950; Christopher Rand, "G.I.s Join Marines for Escape to East Coast Port 40 Miles Off," *New York Herald Tribune*, December 3, 1950.

297 Adding to the alarm: CINCFE to DEPTAR for JCS, 3 December 1950, Folder 6, Box 9, RG 6, DMA; Blair, *The Forgotten War*, 528–30; DEPTAR (JCS) to CINCFE, JCS 97917, 4 December 1950, Folder 6, Box 9, RG 6, DMA.

298 More than twenty-four: Roy Oxenrider, *FOW*, 148; Oxenrider, "A Week of Eternity," 6; Miller, "Chosin Reservoir," 24–25; Red Cross note, Miller folder, Box 9, RAC.

299 Sgt. Charlie Gebhardt: SV int, Charlie Gebhardt, May 10, 2016; Ryder, "The Coldest Battle"; SV int, Grant McMillin, September 27, 2021; McMillin Army Chapter interview; Appleman, *East of Chosin*, 147–48.

301 The Marines had broken: Simmons, *Frozen Chosin*, 87; Lynn Montross, "Breakout from the Reservoir," *Marine Corps Gazette*, November 1951, 35; Bowser interview, January 2, 1951, MCH, 15; "The Unforgotten Korean War," 193; Smith, "Aide-Memoire Korea," 758; Sides, *On Desperate Ground*, 264; Geer, *The New Breed*, 341; Shisler, *For Country and Corps*, 215.

301 The contrast with: Roe, *The Dragon Strikes*, 347; Gray, "One Reservoir, Two Battles," *CFND*, July–September 2021, 14; David Dowadkin to Blair, March 25, 1988, Box 85, CJBC; Howe to REA, July 25, 1987, 1987 folder, Box 21, REA.

302 Aviators spotted more: 1st Motor Transport Battalion annex to 1st Marine Division Special Action Report for 8 October to 15 December 1950, Box 58, OPSC, 11–12; Geer, *The New Breed*, 345; Beall, "Statement, Regarding Dealings with the Army in Korea," 7; Smith, "Aide-Memoire Korea," 904–5.

302 By midafternoon Monday: Bowser interview, January 2, 1951, MCH, 15; Witte to Hammel, January 24, 1980, Witte folder, Box 5, EHPP; Smith, "Aide-Memoire Korea," 756, 972, 994, 1025.

303 The 26th Army: Li, *Attack at Chosin*, 112, 116–18; "The Unforgotten Korean War," 193; Zhou, "Mao's Telegrams," 5.

303 Ned Almond made another: Almond diary, 4 December 1950, Box 29, RAC; Smith Oral History, 231.

304 Beall and his team: SV int, Ralph Milton, January 9, 2022; "Chosin Survivor Turns 99," *NAC*, October–November 2006, 1; "Veterans of Korean War Are Reunited," *NAC*, April 2000, 13; Reeves, *Beautiful Feet and Real Peace*, 8, 10; "Snapshot from Hell," *NAC*, June–July 2007, 1; Sides, *On Desperate Ground*, 286.

304 At the farmhouse: Vallowe, *What History Failed to Record*, 190; SV int, Ray Radke, August 29, 2021; Radke, "Radke Remembers," *NAC*, May–June 2004, 10; 1st Motor Transport Battalion Annex to 1st Marine Division Special Action Report for 8 October to 15 December 1950, Box 58, OPSC, 11.

305 With survivors still: Jones to Barbara Faith, March 14, 1951, DFP; Hugh May sworn statement, January 23, 1951, Headquarters, 1st Battalion, 32nd Infantry, DFP.

305 Hagaru had become: Rasula, *FOW*, 235; Almond diary, 5 December 1950, Box 29, RAC; Smith, "Aide-Memoire Korea," 978; Simmons, *Frozen Chosin*, 90; Higgins, "The Bloody Trail Back," 30, 118; Keyes Beech, *Tokyo and Points East* (Doubleday, 1954), 201; Smith to Robert Leckie, April 3, 1960, Monograph correspondence folder, Box 21, OPSC.

306 Smith seemed to have: Smith Oral History, 228; Smith, "Aide-Memoire Korea," 904; May to REA, August 20, 1981, May folder, Box 9, RAC; Bowser interview, January 2, 1951, MCH, 15; Rasula to Olson, February 4, 1951, Long folder, Box 9, RAC; Dowadkin to Blair, March 25, 1988, Box 85, CJBC; Charles Carmin, *FOW*, 225.

307 Of the approximately: Smith, "Aide-Memoire Korea," 905; Lynch to REA, December 19, 1976, Lynch folder, Box 8, RAC; Statement of Major Robert Jones, Hagaru-ri to Hamhung, HQ RCT 32, December 29, 1950, Jones folder, Box 8, RAC (hereafter Jones Statement, Hagaru-ri to Hamhung); Simmons, *Frozen Chosin*, 92; Lt. Col. Anderson report, 31st Infantry command report, Box 3172, RG 407, NARA, 1.

308 The provisional 31st received: Rasula to Olson, February 4, 1951, Long folder, Box 9, RAC; Witte to Hammel, January 24, 1980, April 6, 1980, and March 7, 1981, Witte folder, Box 5, EHPP; Geer, *The New Breed*, 349; Rasula to REA, February 13, 1989, 1989 folder, Box 21, RAC; Rasula, *FOW*, 235; Harry Scott, *FOW*, 151.

309 SFC Bill Donovan: Willard P. Donovan interview, AFC/2001/001/41595, VHP, 5–7; Smith, "Aide-Memoire Korea," 906, 1000.

309 By Tuesday evening: Li, *Attack at Chosin*, 120, 124; Peters and Li, *Voices from the Korean War*, 124.

309 The night passed: Simmons, *Frozen Chosin*, 90; Smith, "Aide-Memoire Korea," 760, 1027; Rasula to Olson, February 4, 1951, Long folder, Box 9, RAC; *Changjin Journal*, February 28, 2003; Witte to Hammel, April 6, 1980, Witte folder, Box 5, EHPP; Barbara Skilton to O. P. Smith, May 25, 1981, Misc. documents folder, Box 66, OPSC.

310 Toward evening, as Witte: SV int, Carl Witte, December 2000; Witte to Hammel, January 24, 1980, Witte folder, Box 5, EHPP; Jones statement, Hagaru-ri to Hamhung, Jones folder, Box 8, RAC; Simmons, *Frozen Chosin*, 94; Smith, Oral History, 229; Rasula, *FOW*, 235; *TCC*, 70; Knox, *The Korean War*, vol. 1, 571.

311 Drake's 31st Tank: Drake to REA, January 10, 1977, Drake folder, Box 7, RAC; Li, *Attack at Chosin*, 112; Montross and Canzona, *The Chosin Reservoir Campaign*, 291; Drake to CFND, November 17, 1977, Drake folder, Box 7, RAC; Peters and Li, *Voices from the Korean War*, 123.

311 By early Thursday: *Changjin Journal*, February 28, 2003, May 1, 2003, and October 30, 2003; Higgins, *War in Korea*, 192; Simmons, *Frozen Chosin*, 98.

312 Maj. Gen. Merwin: Silverthorn to Smith, December 7, 1950, Corr OFF CMC & AMC folder, Box 21, OPSC; "Truman to Gordon McDonough, August 29, 1950," The Official Website of Marines, https://www.usmcu.edu/Research/Marine-Corps-History-Division/Frequently-Requested-Topics/Historical-Documents-Orders-and-Speeches/The-Marine-Corps-as-the-Navys-Police-Force/; Virginia Smith to O. P. Smith, December 8, 1950, Personal correspondence folder, Box 29, OPSC; Smith to Heinl, August 19, 1960; Paul Stillwell, "Creation of an Icon," *Naval History*, December 2000; Shisler, *For Country and Corps*, 228.

313 It had taken: Helen to Harvy Storms, December 7, 1950, HHS.

313 The 7th Marine Regiment: Smith Family Journal, 405; Simmons, *Frozen Chosin*, 103–4; Rasula to Olson, February 4, 1951, Long folder, Box 9, RAC; Smith, "Aide-Memoire Korea," 1014; Higgins, "The Bloody Trail Back," 119.

314 The casualties from combat: Jones statement, Hagaru-ri to Hamhung, Jones folder, Box 8, RAC; Simmons, *Frozen Chosin*, 97; Anderson report, 31st Infantry command report, Box 3172, RG 407, NARA, 1; Hoehn, "Chosin, Korea," 19.

314 The night of December 8: "The Unforgotten Korean War," 193; Jones statement, Hagaru-ri to Hamhung, Jones folder, Box 8, RAC; Simmons, *Frozen Chosin*, 107; White, "Korean War Memories"; Russ, *Breakout*, 421–22; Smith Oral History, 228–29; Hopkins, *One Bugle No Drums*, 139.

315 At 7:30 a.m. on Sunday: Jones statement, Hagaru-ri to Hamhung, Jones folder, Box 8, RAC; Smith Oral History, 293; Smith to Esther, December 26, 1950, Smith to Esther 2 November to 31 December 1950 folder, Box 27, OPSC; White, "Korean War Memories"; Rasula to Olson, February 4, 1951, Long folder, Box 9, RAC.

316 The final troops: Russ, *Breakout*, 420; Li, *Attack at Chosin*, 123; "The Unforgotten Korean War," 193.

316 With the safe arrival: Almond diary, 11 December 1950, Box 29, RAC; Almond Oral History, Section 5, 21; Simmons, *Frozen Chosin*, 112; Almond to Margaret, December 12 and December 14, 1950, Correspondence with wife folder, Box 77, EAC.

317 Upon his return: MacArthur to Department of Army, December 8, 1950, Folder 6, Box 2, RG 6, DMA; Halberstam, *The Coldest Winter*, 475; Russ, *Breakout*, 433; Higgins, *War in Korea*, 177.

318 Musters of the 31st: *TCC*, 63–4; Jones statement, Hagaru-ri to Hamhung, Jones folder, Box 8, RAC; Jones to REA, March 2, 1981, Jones folder, Box 8, RAC; Jones to Barbara Faith, March 14, 1951, DFP; Barr to Barbara Faith, December 12, 1950, DFP; Powell interview, Powell folder, Combat Leadership in Korea Box 6, CJBC, 94; Hoehn, "Chosin, Korea," 4.

318 Ned Almond called: Weintraub, *MacArthur's War*, 286; Smith Family Journal, 410; Almond to Margaret, December 12 and December 14, 1950, Correspondence with wife folder, Box 77, EAC; Almond to Lt. Gen. Clarence Huebner (Ret.), December 13, 1950, Correspondence CG X Corps folder, Box 85, EAC.

319 The original plan: Smith Oral History, 257; Smith, "Aide-Memoire Korea," 905; Appleman, *East of Chosin*, 302; Sides, *On Desperate Ground*, 327; Almond Oral History, Section 5, 21, EAC; Simmons, *Frozen Chosin*, 112; Jones to REA, March 2, 1981, Jones folder, Box 8, RAC; Rasula to Olson, February 4, 1951, Long folder, Box 9, RAC; "Editor's Page," *NAC*, March 1990, 5.

320 On December 15: "The Unforgotten Korean War," 194–95, 201; Li, *Attack at Chosin*, 128, 131–33, 101; Zhou, "Mao's Telegrams," 5; Peters and Li, *Voices from the Korean War*, 124.

321 By Christmas Eve: CG X Corps to CINCFE, 24 December 50, December 1950 to April 1951 folder, Box 54, RG 9, DMA; Millett, *The War for Korea*, 354; SV int, Alexander Haig, December 2000; Steve Vogel, "U.S. Remembers Heroic Evacuation from Besieged North Korean Port," *WP*, December 28, 2000; Bill Gilbert, *Ship of Miracles* (Triumph Books, 2000); "Who Will Tell the Story of the Refugees at the Chosin Reservoir?" *CFND*, October–December 2022, 22.

321 After the last ships: Haig and McCarry, *Inner Circles*, 65; Simmons, *Frozen Chosin*, 124; Blair, *The Forgotten War*, 545; Almond Oral History, Section 5, 1; Truman to MacArthur, December 27, 1950, Box 58, OPSC.

322 Across the United: SV int, Bobbie Broyles, April 11, 2013; Susie Moseley to Annie Wilbur, n.d., Faith folder, Box 8, RAC; REA to Curtis, April 27, 1980, Curtis folder, Box 8,

RAC; Alison Bath, "Korean War Hero Finally Comes Home," *USA Today*, April 15, 2013; SV int, Sam Storms, July 26, 2022.

323 It was close to Christmas: Widener, "Young Teenage GIs Take On Communists," 37; Hill, "An Unknown Chaplain," 12; Hoehn, "Chosin, Korea," 2; "Smithsburg Father Seeks to Enlist After Second Son Wounded in Korea," newspaper clipping, n.d., courtesy of Sharlene DeLauter.

323 PFC Harry Jacobs: SV int, Harry Jacobs, January 15, 2022; Mrs. John Moore to Almond, March 22, 1951, and Almond to Mrs. Moore, April 14, 1950, Personal correspondence March 1951 folder, Box 77, EAC.

324 In Old Saybrook: Barbara Skilton to Smith, May 25, 1951, and Smith to Skilton, June 12, 1951, Misc documents folder, Box 66, OPSC; Mrs. Mazzulla to Almond, December 28, 1950, and Col. R. H. Harrison to Almond, January 19, 1951, Personal correspondence folder, Box 77, EAC.

Chapter 18: The Shame and Glory

326 Barely a month: Smith to Esther, January 14 and January 19, OPS to Esther January 2 to February 14, 1951 folder, Box 28, OPSC, 195; Smith Family Journal, 424; Smith to Ralph West, March 14, 1951, Box 24, OPSC.

327 "Retreat, hell!" had: "War: Retreat of the 20,000," *Time*, December 18, 1950; Shisler, *For Country and Corps*, 231–32, 238; Hanson W. Baldwin, "Tribute to the Marines," *New York Times*, June 29, 1951; "There Was a Christmas," *Life*, December 25, 1950; Blair, *The Forgotten War*, 541.

327 Family expecting: Mildred Adkins, *CFND*, Fall 1983, 9; Halberstam, *The Coldest Winter*, 493, 498; Lynch, *Edward M. Almond and the US Army*, 242; Shisler, *For Country and Corps*, 232; Smith Oral History, 231; Blair, *The Forgotten War*, 581; Paddock to Blair, December 3, 1984, 7th Division folder, Box 71, CJBC; Ridgway to Barbara Faith, January 26, 1951, 7th Infantry Division Chosin folder, Box 7, RAC; Ridgway to Barbara Faith, February 27, 1951, DFP.

328 At the headquarters of the 1st Battalion: Jones to REA, March 2, 1981, Jones folder, Box 8, RAC; SV int, Monty Piercefield, August 30, 2021; "Mortrude Gets Silver Star," n.d., news clipping, Mortrude folder, Box 8, RAC; Oxenrider, "A Week of Eternity," 9; Jones to Barbara Faith, March 14, 1951, DFP.

329 The 3rd Battalion: Lt. Col. Jay Dasche to Barr, March 16, 1951, DFP; SV int, Dawn Francois, November 17, 2022; Magill to Hammel, August 9, 1979, Magill folder, Box 6, EHPP; Gray, *Called to Honor*, 148–54; SV int, John Edward Gray, April 17, 2013; Harry Scott, *FOW*, 151; Robert Ayala interview, August 12, 2011, AFC/2001/001/82143, VHP; Hammond, "Memories of War," 17; Appleman, *East of Chosin*, 334; Mossman, *Ebb and Flow*, 304; Jones to Barbara Faith, March 14, 1951, DFP.

330 The horrors of Chosin: DeLong, "Inside King Company"; SV int, Grant McMillin, August 29, 2021; "No Knife? No Need," *NAC*, August–September 2011, 1, 3; "Battle of Korea: The Boys Come Home," *Time*, May 11, 1953; SV int, Dawn Francois, November 17, 2022; Knox, *The Korean War*, vol. 2, 328–29; Charles Peckham to Rasula, November 23, 1979, Peckham folder, Box 6, EHPP.

330 On February 5: *CFND*, Spring 1984; Smith to Silverthorn, February 10, 1951, Correspondence with HQMC, February 1951 folder, Box 21, OPSC; Smith to Cates, December 17,

1950, Correspondence with HQMC, December 1950 folder, Box 21, OSPC; *Changjin Journal*, November 1, 2001.

331 Smith's judgment: Beall, "Statement, Regarding Dealings with the Army in Korea," 5, 7.

332 Navy Lieutenant Commander: "Navy Chaplain Honored for Korea Action," *Los Angeles Times*, January 16, 1951; First Marine Division Special Action Report Wonsan-Hamhung-Chosin 8 October–15 December 1950, Annex G, Chaplains, Box 67, OPSC, 3; "Padre Otto Helped the Downtrodden," *Orange County Register*, October 13, 1993; Smith Family Journal, 444; Russ, *Breakout*, 83.

332 In late January, soon: "The Shame and Glory of Korea," *Fortnight*, 16–17; Alan Hensher, "Fortnight: The First Newsmagazine of California," *Southern California Quarterly*, Winter 1972, 353.

333 The reaction to: "Army Accused of Concealing Incompetence," *Baltimore Sun*, March 18, 1951; "Another Voice Heard From," *Fortnight*, April 16, 1951, 12; O. D. Keep, "Senator Lyndon Johnson's Subcommittee Should Call Witnesses," *Fortnight*, April 2, 1951; Senator Lyndon B. Johnson, letter to the editor, *Fortnight*, April 16, 1951; "Chaplains Charge Draws Army's Fire," *Los Angeles Times*, March 18, 1951.

333 Several days later: Baldwin, "Frictions at Pentagon"; Transcript of Sporrer interview with Harold Keen, Sporrer Inquiry folder, Box 19, GRP; Major Carl Witte to Col. T. P. Woodburn, 4th Army HQ, "Facts Relevant to 31st Infantry Regiment," March 30, 1951, Sporrer Inquiry folder, Box 19, GRP; "Chaplain Admits He Wrote Article," *Los Angeles Times*, March 29, 1951; "The Shame & Glory," *Time*, April 2, 1951; *Fortnight*, April 2, 1951, 11; *Fortnight*, March 19, 1951, 4.

335 At Percy Jones: Willard P. Donovan interview, AFC/2001/001/41595, VHP, 8; Donovan interview, in Precious, *Task Force Faith*; Bigger, "Reflections and Comments," 7; Watson, "Army Checks on Behavior"; Silverthorn to Smith, March 30, 1951, Correspondence with HQMC, March 1951 folder, Box 21, OPSC.

335 Parks cabled MacArthur's: Parks to CINCFE Tokyo, DA 87267, April 1, 1951, War DA Class 1–5 April 51 folder, Box 116, RG 9, DMA; Smith Korean War Log, March 30, 1951, Box 65, OPSC; Smith to Esther, April 5, 1951, OPS to Esther April 1951 folder, Box 28, OPSC; Smith Family Journal, 444.

336 Smith did nothing: Smith Oral History, 267; "CPT Lawrence Francis Brunnert Remembrance," KWP.

336 Matt Ridgway, after: CINCFE PA to PIO Presidio, March 30, 1951, March 1951 folder, Box 54, RG 9, DMA; Memorandum for Diary: 2 April 1951, CINC Far East Special File, Box 72, Series 3, Matthew B. Ridgway Papers; E. A, Zundel, IG, CINCFE to 6th Army, March 31, 1951, War Misc Out, Box 48, RG 9 DMA; Smith Korean War Log, April 2, 1951, Box 65, OPSC; Smith to Silverthorn, April 14, 1951, Correspondence with HQMC April–July 1951, Box 21, OPSC.

337 Some of the 31st: Lewis, Price, Bertram, and Magill statements, IG investigation folder, Box 7, RAC; Joe Quinn, "GIs Rap Chaplain's Attack on Officers," United Press, in *Arizona Republic*, April 4, 1951.

338 MacArthur had requested: JCS to MacArthur, JCS 88181, 11 April 1951, Correspondence January–April 51 folder, Box 1, RG 6, DMA; Weintraub, *MacArthur's War*, 317; Millett, *The War for Korea*, 420; Blair, *The Forgotten War*, 783–87; Halberstam, *The Coldest Winter*, 593; Bradley and Blair, *A General's Life*, 616.

339 MacArthur had picked: Weintraub, *MacArthur's War*, 337–39; Almond Oral History, Section 5, 43; Almond to MacArthur, April 12, 1951, Box 77, EAC; Smith to Esther, April 11, 1951, OPS to Esther April 51 folder, Box 28, OPSC; Margaret to Almond, April 16, 1951, Correspondence with wife folder, Box 77, EAC; Weintraub, *MacArthur's War*, 1, 354.

339 Smith and Almond would: Silverthorn to Smith, April 18, 1951, Correspondence with HQMC April–June 1951 folder, Box 21, OPSC; Almond to Ridgway, April 15, 1951, Box 77, EAC; Almond diary, July 15, 1951, Box 29, RAC; Lynch, *Edward M. Almond and the US Army*, 272.

340 The inspector general's: Lt. Col. George Boram, IG, Special Inquiry into Allegations Made by Chaplain (Lt Commander) Otto Sporrer, May 31, 1950, Inquiry folder, Box 19, GRP; "Pace Fires Back at Navy Chaplain," *Baltimore Sun*, June 13, 1951; "Chaplain's Charges All False, Says Army," *WP*, June 14, 1951; "Ridgway Defends 31st Regt in 3-Day Battle," *Stars and Stripes*, June 16, 1951.

340 Smith was not impressed: Smith Oral History, 268; "Navy Demands Chaplain Explain Charges," *Pacific Stars and Stripes*, June 1, 1951; Baldwin, "Frictions at Pentagon"; Smith Family Journal, 445–46; Russ, *Breakout*, 429–30; "Troops 'Pampered,' Navy Chaplain Says," *Stars and Stripes*, October 5, 1951.

341 Four-year-old Bobbie: "Bradley Gives Medal of Honor to Relatives of 11 Army Heroes," *Washington Evening Star*, June 21, 1950; "Lt Col Don Carlos Faith, Jr.," JPAC, 6; Needham to Mortrude, September 23, 1985, Mortrude folder, Box 8, RAC; Russ, *Breakout*, 334; SV int, John Edward Gray, April 17, 2013; Curtis to REA, November 27, 1980, Curtis folder, Box 8, RAC; McCaffrey to REA, February 16, 1981, McCaffrey correspondence folder, Box 20, RAC; Jones to Barbara Faith, March 14, 1951, DFP.

342 Certainly, there was no: Chosin Few fact sheet, 1986, Korean War Associations folder, Box 76, CJBC; Simmons, *Frozen Chosin*, 114–17.

342 By comparison, there were: Jones to REA, March 2, 1981, Jones folder, Box 8, RAC; Curtis to REA, January 30, 1977, Curtis folder, Box 8, RAC; Jones Memoir, KWE, 26.

343 Many men who saw Harvey: Rasula memo for Curtis, Jones, Jordan, and Miller, April 8, 1988, 1988 correspondence, Box 21, RAC; Gray, *Called to Honor*, 149; Rasula to REA, August 12, 1981, Rasula folder, Box 9, RAC; Maj. Gen. Field Harris, USMC, to Hodes, January 23, 1951, Stamford folder, Box 9, RAC; Hodes to Harris, Jan 26, 1951, 1988 folder, Box 21, RAC; May to REA, July 24, and August 20, 1981, May folder, Box 9, RAC; Garrigus, Gray, Jordan, and Maclean Distinguished Service Cross citations, DSC folder, Box 31, RAC; Dasche to Barr, March 16, 1951, DFP; SV int, Charlie Gebhardt, May 10, 2016; Ryder, "The Coldest Battle"; SV int, Ray Radke, August 29, 2021; List of Silver Star recipients, D Battery, 15th AAA, McClymont folder, Box 8, RAC; Curtis to REA, June 5, 1980, Curtis folder, Box 8, RAC.

344 Filming for *Retreat*: Smith Family Journal, 459–60; Smith Oral History, 304; Smith to Brig. Gen. Johnny McQueen, August 23, 1951, Correspondence August 1951 folder, Box 24, OPSC; Smith to Silverthorn, January 29, 1952, Silverthorn to Smith, November 16, 1951, Correspondence with HQMC folders, Box 21, OPSC.

345 They need not have: McQueen to Smith, January 29, 1952, HQMC correspondence, Box 24, OPSC; Smith Family Journal, 460; Jeff Shaara, *The Frozen Hours: A Novel of the Korean War* (Ballantine, 2017), 507; Jay Carmody, "'Retreat, Hell', at the Warner Echoes Marines' Great Fight," *Washington Evening Star*, February 22, 1952.

345 Soon after the Chosin: Smith to Esther, January 5, 1951, OPS to Esther January 2 to February 14 51 folder, Box 28, OPSC; Smith to Shepherd, August 20, 1951, Commendations:

Unit citations folder, Box 40; Smith to Esther, March 1 and March 8, 1951, OPS to Esther 15 February to 30 March 51 folder, Box 28, OPSC; Almond commendation to Smith, 23 February 1951, OPS to Esther 15 February to 30 March 51 folder, Box 28, OPSC.

345 Nonetheless, as the: Smith to Thomas, August 24, 1951, Smith to Shepherd, August 20, 1951, and Shepherd to Smith, August 27, 1951, Commendations: Unit citations folder, Box 40, OPSC; Shisler, *For Country and Corps*, 147–48, 236; Smith to Craig, December 1, 1952, Box 24, OPSC.

346 Smith had been revising: Smith comments on Marine Corps Board Study, January 1952, COP's comments folder, Box 67, OPSC, 40.

347 In March 1952: Smith to Shepherd, Recommendation for award of Distinguished Unit Citation to 1st MarDiv, March 3, 1952, Commandant of the Marine Corps to Commander Naval Forces Far East, First Endorsement, April 4, 1952, and Commander Naval Forces, Far East to Commander in Chief, Far East Command, June 9, 1952, Commendations: Unit citations folder, Box 40, OPSC.

348 Clark sent the request: Brig. Gen. Wayne Smith to CG 8th Army, Recommendation for Presidential Unit Citation, August 19, 1952, Briscoe to Secretary of the Navy, Second Endorsement, September 30, 1952, Commendations: Unit citations folder, Box 40, OPSC; Navy Department Board to Chief, Military History, Eight Endorsement, February 2, 1953, Commendations: Unit citations folder, Box 40, OPSC; Department of the Army, Office of the Chief of Military History, to Navy Department Board of Decorations and Medals, March 19, 1953, Commendations: Unit citations folder, Box 40, OPSC.

348 The Navy board sent: Navy Department Board of Decorations and Medals to Smith, Tenth Endorsement, March 27, 1953, and Smith to Navy Department Board of Decorations and Medals, Eleventh Endorsement, April 14, 1953, Commendations: Unit citations folder, Box 40, OPSC, 1.

The next three ground operations listed by Smith in order of importance were the attack from Hagaru-ri to Koto-ri, the defense of Koto-ri, and the attack from Koto-ri to Chinhung-ni.

349 But Smith knew quite: Marine Corps Board Study, II-C-118, Box 67, OPSC; Smith comments on Marine Corps Board Study, January 1952, COP's comments folder, Box 67, OPSC, 40; X Corps Special Report, "Movement of CCF into X Corps Zone," X Corps War Diary 1–30 November folder, Box 13, RAC, 24.

349 The two divisions: "One Reservoir, Two Battles," *CFND*, July-September 2021, 15; Roe, *The Dragon Strikes*, 352.

349 In his recommendation: Smith to Navy Department Board of Decorations and Medals, Eleventh Endorsement, April 14, 1953, Commendations: Unit citations folder, Box 40, OPSC, 3; *Changjin Journal*, November 1, 2001; J. F. Blakely to Smith, Presidential Unit Citation, August 24, 1953, Commendations: Unit citations folder, Box 40, OPSC.

Chapter 19: The Chosin Few

351 It was not much: SV int, Grant McMillin, September 27, 2021; McMillin Army Chapter interview; SV int, Dawn Francois, November 17, 2022; "Gerard A. 'Jerry' Francois," *NAC*, January–February 2012, 5; "Taps," *NAC*, May–June 2015, 4; Fulton, "Korean War Veteran, Missing for 65 Years"; Tony Perry, "Remains of Southern California Soldier Missing Since Korean War Come Home," *Los Angeles Times*, October 28, 2015.

352 Dodie Maclean learned: Appleman, *East of Chosin*, 147; Charles Beauchamp, "Allan Duard MacLean," Assembly, West Point, January 1955; Roe, *The Dragon Strikes*, 316; Roger R. Venzke, *Confidence in Battle, Inspiration in Peace: The United States Army Chaplaincy 1945–1975* (Department of the Army Office of the Chief of Chaplains, 1977), 85.

352 PFC James Colasanti: Department of Army Report of Death Memorandum, Colasanti, James A., 17 February 1954, courtesy of Dan Colasanti; "The Last Mile," *Time*, September 28, 1953; SV int, Dan Colasanti, January 7, 2022; Curtis to REA, February 15, 1981, Curtis folder, Box 8, RAC; Mortrude, "Autobiographic Chronology of Chosin."

353 In 1954 the remains: "Operation Glory," DPAA fact sheet, n.d.; "Lt Col Don Carlos Faith, Jr.," JPAC, 7; Widener, "Young Teenage GIs Take On Communists," 37; Joan French Blackburn, "Remembering CPL Huey P French, Huey P. French Remembrance," KWP; *NAC*, October–November 2013, 10; "Once Were Lost," *NAC*, June–July 2002, 11; Letter from Brunner R. Coke, *CFND*, Summer 1983, 5; Ray E. Boomhower, "A Family's Heartache," *Traces of Indiana and Midwestern History*, Fall 2002.

354 In January 1956: "Lt Col Don Carlos Faith, Jr.," JPAC, 7; Annie Randolph Wilbur to REA, March 30, 1980; SV int, Bobbie Broyles, May 6, 2022; Vergun, "After 62 Years."

354 Helen Storms gave birth: SV int, Sam Storms, July 26, 2022; Rasula to Olson, February 4, 1951, Long folder, Box 9, RAC; Trautz, "Man Finds Closure After His Father's Remains."

354 While recovering from: SV int, Ray Radke, August 29, 2021; Miller, "Chosin Reservoir," 25; "Cecil McMorris," *NAC*, January 2001, 10; "Taps," *NAC*, September–October 2009, 4; Reeves, *Beautiful Feet and Real Peace*, 8; SV int, Dawn Francois, Novembeer 17, 2022; SV int, Harry Jacobs, January 15, 2022.

356 Many felt survivor's: SV int, Jerry McCabe, December 1, 2000; Vogel, "50 Years Later"; Roy Oxenrider, *FOW*, 148; Curtis to REA, March 1, 1981, Curtis folder, Box 8, RAC; Letter from Don Mayville, *CFND*, Spring 1984; White, "Korean War Memories"; Hammond, "Memories of War," 10–11.

357 As the years wore: Hopkins, *One Bugle No Drums*, ix; Rasula to Ray Lynch, July 24, 1981, Lynch folder, Box 8, RAC.

357 Histories of Chosin: Smith to Eric Goldman, April 10, 1956, Monograph correspondence folder, Box 21, OPSC; Smith Family Journal, 411; McCaffrey comments to REA, March 12, 1981, McCaffrey correspondence, McCaffrey folder, Box 20. See, for example, the description of Army soldiers in Goulden, *Korea: The Untold Story of the War*, 369: "They had thrown away their weapons. Their conduct at Hagaru was disgraceful."

358 Task Force Faith: Appleman, *East of Chosin*, 336, 340; Drake to REA, May 1, 1987, 1989 correspondence folder, Box 21, RAC; Curtis to REA, June 5, 1980, Curtis folder, Box 8, RAC; Gray, *Called to Honor*, 148, 326; SV int, Harry Graham, August 29, 2021; Harry Scott, *FOW*, 151; SV int, Ray Radke, November 19, 2021; McCaffrey to REA, July 19, 1983, McCaffrey folder, Box 29, RAC; Curtis, "Operations of the First Battalion," 2; SV int, Charlie Gebhardt, May 10, 2016.

359 Among the survivors: SV int, Charlie Gebhardt, May 10, 2016; Smith to Lt. Gen. Randolph Pate, October 4, 1954, Commendations: Unit citations folder, Box 40, OPSC.

360 Smith was hardly: SV int, Charlie Gebhardt, May 10, 2016; SV int, Grant McMillin, August 29, 2021; Ridgway to REA, March 6, 1978, Ridgway correspondence folder, Box 20, RAC; Weintraub, *MacArthur's War*, 6–7.

360 The Chosin veterans: Anthony Biebel, *FOW*, 169; Haig and McCarry, *Inner Circles*, 63; McCaffrey to REA, July 20, 1979, McCaffrey folder, Box 29, RAC; Almond Oral History,

Section 5, 63; Bigger to REA, May 11, 1981, Bigger folder, Box 9, RAC; McCaffrey to REA, March 31, 1978, McCaffrey correspondence folder, Box 20, RAC; SV int, Bobbie Broyles, April 11, 2013; Lynch to REA, January 21, 1977, Lynch folder, Box 8, RAC; McCaffrey to REA, September 19, 1990, McCaffrey folder, Box 29, RAC; Witte to Hammel, March 7, 1981, Witte folder, Box 5, EHPP; "Gen. Henry I. Hodes Dies at 62," *New York Times*, February 15, 1962.

361 Don Faith loomed: Bigger, "Reflections and Comments," 6; Jones to Barbara Faith, March 14, 1951, DFP; Gugeler to Needham, December 10, 1984, Faith folder, Box 8, RAC; SV int, Dawn Francois, November 17, 2022; SV int, Harry Graham, August 29, 2021; Mortrude to Needham, November 14, 1985, Mortrude folder, Box 8, RAC; May to REA, September 5, 1981, and October 31, 1981, May folder, Box 9, RAC.

362 The men had mixed: Sims and Shaw, "Those Are My Boys," 2, 8; Curtis to Needham, November 9, 1985, Curtis folder, Box 8, RAC; Miller to REA, September 29, 1979, Miller folder, Box 9, RAC; May to REA, October 31, 1981, May folder, Box 9, RAC.

363 In 1983 Frank: "Chosin Few Band as Brothers," *CFND*, Fall 1983, 1; "Meet the CF Co-Founders," *CFND*, Summer 1983, 12; "1,000 Marines Relive Battle of Korean War," United Press International, December 8, 1985; SV int, Dawn Francois, August 30, 2021; *TCC*, 13.

363 Back home in Colorado: Francois to To Whom It May Concern, February 1986, 31st Regiment folder, Box 71, CJBC; SV int, Dawn Francois, November 17, 2022; "Who Were the AC's Founding Fathers?," *NAC*, November–December 2011, 5; Gray, *Called to Honor*, 326; SV int, Harry Graham, August 29, 2021.

364 In those pre-internet: "Ayala Memoir," KWE; White, "Korean War Memories"; SV int, Dawn Francois, November 17, 2022; SV int, Ray Radke, August 29, 2021; Letter from McCallister, *CFND*, Winter 1984–1985.

365 Grant McMillin was reunited: SV int, Grant McMillin, August 29, 2021; SV int, Ralph Milton, January 9, 2022; "Chaplain Says: It's A Wonderful Life!" *NAC*, January–February 2003, 4; Rasula to REA, November 17, 1987, 1987 folder, Box 21, RAC.

366 Ed Stamford was: Stamford to REA, October 1, 1979, Stamford folder, Box 9, RAC; SV int, Ray Radke, August 29, 2021; "The Saga of Kenzo Takatsu," *The Graybeards*, November–December 2005, 9; Takatsu, "Deception and Decency," 36; "31st I&R Platoon, Where Ya Been?" *NAC*, September–October 2010; *TCC*, 46; Mortrude, "Autobiographic Chronology of Chosin"; Drake to REA, May 1, 1987, 1987 folder, Box 21, RAC.

367 The men began asking: SV int, Grant McMillin, September 27, 2021; *Changjin Journal*, May 6, 2000; *TCC*, 13; "The PUC," *NAC*, March 1990, 2, 4; "U.S. Navy Announces Cruiser to Be Named Chosin," *CFND*, October 1987, 1.

368 In the summer of 1990: Gray, *Called to Honor*, 324–26; SV int, Dawn Francois, November 17, 2022; SV int, Ray Radke, August 29, 2021; *TCC*, 14.

369 At the 1994 Army: Gray, *Called to Honor*, 328, 372–75; SV int, John Edward Gray, April 17, 2013; *TCC*, 14, 94.

370 But in the years: Montross and Canzona, *The Chosin Reservoir Campaign*, 398; Appleman, *East of Chosin*, 301; Blair, *The Forgotten War*, 459; Stanton, *America's Tenth Legion*, 223; Mossman, *Ebb and Flow*, 92, 98; Berquist, "Organizational Leadership in Crisis," 1; Kirkland, "Soldiers and Marines at Chosin," 257.

370 By Roe's calculation: Roe, "Destruction of the 31st Infantry," Part 5, 6; *TCC*, 14; Gray, *Called to Honor*, 329–30, 371.

371 But just as momentum: Gray, *Called to Honor*, 329–30, 340–42, 401–2.

372 To bolster Parrott's: President, The Chosin Few, to Commandant, United States Marine Corps, Subj: Navy Presidential Unit Citation, January 29, 1999, copy in Gray, *Called to Honor*, Appendix B, 381; Bowser, Comments on Marine Corps Board Study, December 29, 1951, COP's comments folder, Box 67, OPSC; SV int, William McCaffrey, December 2000.

373 The Presidential Unit Citation did: Russ, *Breakout*, 280, 258, 276, 336–37; "Book Review by Bob Hammond," *NAC*, July 2000, 10.

374 Emotions were high: "From the President," *NAC*, July 2000, 3, 8; SV int, John Edward Gray, April 17, 2013; SV int, Grant McMillin, September 27, 2021; Vallowe, *What History Failed to Record*, 6; SV int, Jerry McCabe, December 1, 2000; Vogel, "50 Years Later"; Gray, *Called to Honor*, 371.

375 The dynamic between the: Gray, "From the President," *NAC*, January 2001, 3; Robert Ayala Interview, August 12, 2011, AFC/2001/001/82143, VHP, 14; Steve Vogel, "Military Matters," *WP*, January 10, 2001; *TCC*, 17.

Epilogue

377 On September 12: Vogel, "Chosin Reservoir Veterans Make a Pilgrimage"; "Hill 1221 Revisited," *NAC*, January–February 2003, 15; Magill to Rasula, December 15, 2002, folder 5, Box 15, GRP; "Taps," *NAC*, October–November 2006, 3; Jimmie L. Dorser identification announcement, February 16, 2007, DPAA; "52 Years Later, Little Change," *NAC*, October 2002, 9.

378 It had been: Ashley M. Wright, "Agency Accounts for 700th Missing Korean War Hero," September 13, 2024, DPAA; "A Span of History," *NAC*, October 2002, 6–7; SV int, Johnny Webb, April 11, 2022; SV int, Jennie Jin, March 15, 2023; "Bringing Them Home," *Changjin Journal*, November 27, 2001; "Home, at Long Last," *NAC*, August–September 2004, 8; Anne Marie Kilday, "Soldier Lost in Korea Is Laid to Rest," *Houston Chronicle*, December 29, 2004.

The lab was known as the U.S. Army Central Identification Laboratory in Hawaii (CILHI) until 2003, when it became the Joint POW/MIA Accounting Command (JPAC) Central Laboratory.

379 In September 2003: Larry A. Williams, "The Long Way Home," *NAC*, August–September 2004, 9; Martin Weil, "Remains of Virginia Soldiers Killed in Battle Are Found," *WP*, April 6, 2008.

380 As the excavations: SV int, Johnny Webb, April 11, 2022; Dan Lamothe and Paul Sonne, "For the U.S., a Frustrating History of Recovering Human Remains in North Korea," *WP*, July 4, 2018.

381 On September 11, 2004: "Lt Col Don Carlos Faith, Jr.," JPAC, 8–9; Identification of CIL 2004-142-I-01, in "Lt Col Don Carlos Faith, Jr.," JPAC; SV int, Johnny Webb, April 11, 2022.

382 In late September 2012: SV int, Bobbie Faith Bennett Broyles, April 11, 2013; Vergun, "After 62 Years"; "After Six Decades, LTC Don Faith Returns Home," *NAC*, October–November 2012, 1; Bath, "Korean War Hero Finally Comes Home," *USA Today*, April 15, 2013; SV int, Arthur Mercier, April 11, 2013.

383 Don Faith's remains: Mike Wereschagin, "Ending the Era of Lost Defenders," *Pittsburgh Tribune-Review*, May 27, 2013; "Funeral for LtCol Don Carlos Faith, US Army," April 17, 2013, DFP; "At Long Last, Soldier, Welcome Home," *NAC*, April–May 2013; Greg Jaffe,

"At Arlington, Keeping Faith with a Hero of a Long-Ago War," *WP*, April 22, 2013; Kunkle and Vogel, "Korean War Hero Comes Home at last"; SV int, John Edward Gray, April 17, 2013.

384 Faith's remains were among: SV int, Johnny Webb, April 11, 2022; "Is N Korea Using Remains of GIs to Induce Recovery Work Again?" *NAC*, November–December 2014; Fulton, "Korean War Veteran, Missing for 65 Years"; "Soldier Missing from the Korean War Accounted For (Haugland)," June 9, 2017, DPAA; "Soldier Killed in Korean War Accounted For (Ervin)," March 21, 2016, DPAA; "Official Obituary of Cpl. William Eldon Ervin," Paul Thomas Funeral Home, March 26, 2016.

384 Many Chosin MIAs: "Lt Col Don Carlos Faith, Jr.," JPAC, 7; Wright, "Agency Accounts for 700th Missing Korean War Hero," September 13, 2024, DPAA; Claudia Rupcich, "Remains of Lynchburg Soldier Identified 63 Years Later," *WSET*, August 18, 2013.

385 The Chosin Few continued: SV int, Harry Graham, August 29, 2021; Robert Ayala interview, August 12, 2011, AFC/2001/001/82143, VHP, 14; Gray, *Called to Honor*, 364–65; Jones Memoir, KWE, 28; Vogel, "Veterans Still Feel Their Hidden Wounds."

385 It was often the families: Michael Couch, "The Man Who Never Came Home," *NAC*, October–December 2020, 16; "Catherine Maclean's Note of Gratitude to Board Chairman Ray Phares," *NAC*, April–May 2005, 1.

386 Chosin can be seen: Millett, *The War for Korea*, 335; Li, *Attack at Chosin*, 10, 128; Halberstam, *The Coldest Winter*, 471.

386 The Korean War is anything: Li, *Attack at Chosin*, 11, 13; Blair, *The Forgotten War*, vii; Halberstam, *The Coldest Winter*, 632–33; "The Unforgotten Korean War," 200; John Y. Lee letter, *CFND*, October–December 2021, 13; Carter, "The Real Battle at Lake Changjin."

387 Though remarkably little: Blair, *The Forgotten War*, 468; Millett, *The War for Korea*, 368; Carter, "The Real Battle at Lake Changjin."

387 On the sixty-fifth: SV int, Johnny Webb, April 11, 2022; SV int, Jennie Jin, March 15, 2023; "North Korea Hands Over Remains of Korean War Soldiers to U.S.," *CBS News*, July 27, 2018, https://www.cbsnews.com/news/korean-war-soldiers-remains-returned-north-korea-today-2018-07-27/; "DPRK Returns Possible Remains from Korean War," Defense Visual Information Distribution Service, July 27, 2018; Dan Lamothe, "The Korean War Veterans Who Never Came Home," *WP*, July 26, 2018; Tara Copp, "Corn in the Bones," *Military Times*, September 18, 2018; SV int, Kelly McKeague, April 22, 2022.

389 In July 2019: SV int, Sam Storms, July 26, 2022; Trautz, "Man Finds Closure After His Father's Remains."

389 A handful of Army Chosin: "Battle of the Chosin Reservoir Q&A," National Chosin Few reunion luncheon, September 10, 2022; SV int, Joe Ager, September 10, 2022.

390 No further remains: SV int, Johnny Webb, April 11, 2022; SV int, Evelyn DeLauter Eccard, April 22, 2022; Mary Grace Keller, "Home Again: Korean War Vet's Remains Delivered to Hagerstown," *Frederick News-Post*, April 19, 2022; SV int, Sharlene DeLauter, April 22, 2022.

391 Such moments are: Mark Reynolds, "Remains of Rhode Islander Lost in Frozen Chaos of Korean War Battle Arrive Home," *Providence Journal*, October 13, 2021; "Soldier Accounted For from Korean War (Boughman, R.)," March 1, 2021, DPAA; "Funeral and Burial of Sgt. Charles Garrigus in Indiana," Eyewitness News (WEHT/WTVW), posted March 10, 2023.

391 But many others: Boomhower, "A Family's Heartache," *Traces of Indiana and Midwestern History*, Fall 2002; Evans, "Forgotten No More," *IndyStar*, August 26, 2019; SV int, Arthur Mercier, April 11, 2013.

Selected Bibliography

The list includes books and articles cited multiple times in the text. All others are listed in the notes. *NAS* refers to *Newsletter of the U.S. Army Chapter of the Chosin Few*. *CFND* refers to *The Chosin Few News Digest*.

Books

Appleman, Roy E. *East of Chosin: Entrapment and Breakout in Korea, 1950.* Texas A&M University Press, 1987.

———. *Escaping the Trap: The US Army X Corps in Northeast Korea, 1950.* Texas A&M University Press, 1990.

———. *South to The Naktong, North to the Yalu: United States Army in the Korean War*. United States Army Center of Military History, 1961.

Blair, Clay. *The Forgotten War: America in Korea 1950–1953.* Times Books, 1987.

Colasanti, Daniel R., Sr. *RCT-31: The Sacrificial Lambs of the Chosin Reservoir Campaign, Korea 1950.* Self-published, 2019.

Cowdrey, Albert E. *The Medics' War: United States Army in the Korean War*. United States Army Center of Military History, 1987.

Geer, Andrew. *The New Breed: The Story of the U.S. Marines in Korea*. Harper & Brothers, 1952.

Goncharov, Sergei N., John W. Lewis, and Xue Litai. *Uncertain Partners: Stalin, Mao and the Korean War*. Stanford University Press, 1993.

Gugeler, Russell A. *Combat Actions in Korea: Army Historical Series*. Office of the Chief of Military History, 1954. Reprint, United States Army Center of Military History, 1987.

Haig, Alexander, and Charles McCarry. *Inner Circles: How America Changed the World. A Memoir*. Warner Books, 1992.

Halberstam, David. *The Coldest Winter: America and the Korean War*. Hyperion, 2007.

Hammel, Eric. *Chosin: Heroic Ordeal of the Korean War*. Vanguard, 1981. Reprint, Zenith, 2007.

Heinl, Robert Debs, Jr. *Victory at High Tide: The Inchon-Seoul Campaign*. J. B. Lippincott, 1968. Reprint, Nautical and Aviation Publishing Company of America, 1979.

Higgins, Marguerite. *War in Korea: The Report of a Woman Combat Correspondent*. Doubleday, 1951.

Hopkins, William. *One Bugle No Drums: The Marines at Chosin Reservoir*. Algonquin Books, 1986.

James, D. Clayton. *The Years of MacArthur: Volume III Triumph and Disaster 1945–1964*. Houghton Mifflin, 1985.

———, and Anne Sharp Wells. *Refighting the Last War: Command and Crisis in Korea, 1950–1953*. Free Press, 1993.

Knox, Donald. *The Korean War: An Oral History*. Vol. 1. Harcourt Brace Jovanovich, 1985.

———. *The Korean War: An Oral History*. Vol. 2. Harcourt Brace Jovanovich, 1988.

Li, Xiaobing. *Attack at Chosin: The Chinese Second Offensive in Korea*. University of Oklahoma Press, 2020.

Lynch, Michael. *Edward M. Almond and the US Army: From the 92nd Infantry Division to the X Corps*. University Press of Kentucky, 2019.

MacArthur, Douglas. *Reminiscences*. McGraw-Hill, 1964.

Manchester, William. *American Caesar: Douglas MacArthur 1880–1964*. Little, Brown, 1978. Reprint, Dell, 1979.

Millett, Allan R. *The War for Korea, 1950–1951: They Came from the North*. University Press of Kansas, 2010.

Mills, Randy K. *Honoring Those Who Paid the Price: Forgotten Voices from the Korean War*. Indiana Historical Society Press, 2002.

Montross, Lynn, and Nicholas A. Canzona. *The Chosin Reservoir Campaign: U.S. Marine Operations in Korea 1950–1953*. Vol. 3. Historical Branch Headquarters, U.S. Marine Corps, 1957.

Mossman, Billy. *Ebb and Flow: November 1950–July 1951. United States Army in the Korean War*. United States Army Center of Military History, 1990.

Parker, Gary W., and Frank M. Batha, Jr. *A History of Marine Observation Squadron Six*. History and Museums Division, Headquarters, U.S. Marine Corps, 1982.

Peters, Richard, and Xiaobing Li. *Voices from the Korean War: Personal Stories of American, Korean and Chinese Soldiers*. University Press of Kentucky, 2019.

Rasula, George. *The Chosin Chronology: Battle of The Changjin Reservoir, 1950*. Self-published, 2006.

Reeves, Ed. *Beautiful Feet and Real Peace*. Melcher, 1997.

Ricks, Thomas E. *The Generals: American Military Command from World War II to Today*. Penguin Books, 2012.

Roe, Patrick C. *The Dragon Strikes: China and the Korean War: June–December 1950*. Presidio, 2000.

Russ, Martin. *Breakout: The Chosin Reservoir Campaign, Korea 1950*. Penguin, 1999.

Schnabel, James F. *Policy and Direction: The First Year. United States Army in the Korean War*. United States Army Center of Military History, 1992.

Shisler, Gail B. *For Country and Corps: The Life of General Oliver P. Smith*. Naval Institute Press, 2009.

Sides, Hampton. *On Desperate Ground: The Epic Story of Chosin Reservoir—the Greatest Battle of the Korean War*. Doubleday, 2018.

Simmons, Edwin H. *Frozen Chosin: U.S. Marines at the Changjin Reservoir*. Marines in the Korean War Commemorative Series. U.S. Marine Corps Historical Center, 2002.

———. *Over the Seawall: U.S. Marines at Inchon*. Marines in the Korean War Commemorative Series. U.S. Marine Corps Historical Center, 2000.

Stanton, Shelby L. *America's Tenth Legion: X Corps in Korea, 1950*. Presidio, 1989.

Toland, John. *In Mortal Combat: Korea 1950–1953*. William Morrow, 1991.

Truman, Harry S. *Memoirs by Harry S. Truman: Volume Two: Years of Trial and Hope*. Doubleday, 1955.

Vallowe, Ray C. *What History Failed to Record: A Phantom Force Lost to History*. Self-published e-book, 2015.

Weintraub, Stanley. *MacArthur's War: Korea and the Undoing of an American Hero*. Free Press, 2000.

Wilson, Arthur W., and Norman L. Strickbine, eds. *Korean Vignettes: Faces of War*. Artwork Publications, 1996.

Articles

Baldwin, Hanson W. "Frictions at Pentagon." *New York Times*, August 6, 1951.

Bryant, Herbert L. "Four Days and Five Nights." *Changjin Journal*, October 30, 2000.

Carter, James. "The Real Battle at Lake Changjin." *The China Project*, December 1, 2021. https://thechinaproject.com/2021/12/01/the-real-battle-at-lake-changjin/.

"D Battery—15th AAA at the Chosin Reservoir." *NAC*, July 2000.

DeLong, James. "Inside King Company, 3/31: James DeLong's Experience." *NAC*, March 1990.

Fulton, Sarah. "Korean War Veteran, Missing for 65 years, Laid to Rest." Scripps Howard Foundation Wire, July 7, 2015.

Garrett, Anthony R. "Task Force Faith: At the Chosin Reservoir." *Infantry Magazine*, September–December 1999.

Higgins, Marguerite. "The Bloody Trail Back." *The Saturday Evening Post*, January 27, 1951.

Hill, Donald. "An Unknown Chaplain." *NAC*, November–December 2004.

Kirkland, Faris B. "Soldiers and Marines at Chosin Reservoir: Criteria for Assignment to Combat Command." *Armed Forces & Society*, Winter 1995/96.

Kunkle, Fredrick, and Steve Vogel. "Korean War Hero Comes Home at Last." *WP*, April 17, 2013.

MacDonald, John. "Which Way?" *Friends Journal*, Summer 2010.

Marker, Thomas F. "A Soldier Remembers," *CFND*, Summer 1983.

Mielenz, Lloyd. "Lloyd Mielenz Remembers Chosin." *NAC*, October 2000.

Mills, Randy. "'It's Hard to Write with Mittens On': Hoosier Letters from the Korean War." *Traces of Indiana and Midwestern History*, Fall 2002.

———, and Roxanne Mills. "His Valorous Conduct: The Story of a Hoosier Hero in the Korean War." *Indiana Magazine of History*, December 2000.

Moore, Charles. "Wounded GIs Burned Alive, Bayoneted by Red Chinese." United Press in *Boston Globe*, December 3, 1950.

"Once Were Lost But Now They're Found." *NAC*, June–July 2002.

"One Reservoir, Two Battles." A translated excerpt from *The Chinese People's Volunteers: A History of the War to Resist U.S. Aggression and Aid Korea*. PLA Military Science Publishing House, 1998. *CFND*, July-September 2021.

Radke, Ray. "Radke Remembers." *NAC*, May–June 2004.

Rasula, George, ed. *The Changjin Journal*. Series of 76 essays published on the New York Military Affairs Symposium website from 2000 to 2012. Accessed 2025. https://archive.nymas.org/text_resources /The+Changjin+Journal/changjinjournalTOC.html.

Ryder, Robert Randall. "The Coldest Battle." *The American Legion Magazine*, October 2020.

"The Shame and Glory of Korea." *Fortnight*, February 19, 1951.

"Sic 'Em Ned." *Time*, October 23, 1950.

Sims, Byron, and Chuck Shaw. "Those Are My Boys!" *NAC*, June–July 2012.

Trautz, Deana. "Man Finds Closure After His Father's Remains Are Recovered in Korea." *Austin American-Statesman*, October 28, 2019.

Vergun, David. "After 62 Years, Korean War Medal of Honor Recipient Rests in American Soil," *Army News Service*, April 17, 2013.

Vogel, Steve. "Chosin Reservoir Veterans Make a Pilgrimage to a Land of Loss." *WP*, October 6, 2002.

———. "50 Years Later, An Army Force Gets Its Due." *WP*, December 11, 2000.

———. "Veterans Still Feel Their Hidden Wounds," *WP*, June 21, 2000.

Watson, Mark. "Army Checks on Behavior." *Baltimore Sun*, March 30, 1951.

Widener, Robert. "Young Teenage GIs Take On Communists in Korea," *VFW Magazine*, June/July 2013.

Yong-kak, Lee. "Dr. Yong Kak Lee at the Chosin Reservoir." *The Graybeards*, May/June 2004.

Zhou, Jing. "CCF Order of Battle Near Chosin." *CFND*, July–September 2021.

———. "Mao's Telegrams for the Deployment of the IX Army Group," *CFND*, October–December 2021.

Academic Papers

Berquist, Paul. "Organizational Leadership in Crisis: The 31st Regimental Combat Team at Chosin Reservoir, Korea, 24 November–2 December 1950." U.S. Army Command and General Staff College, Fort Leavenworth, KS, 2007.

Coombs, Robert. "Changjin (Chosin) Reservoir, Korea, 1950: A Case Study of United States Army Tactics and Doctrine for Encircled Forces." U.S. Army Command and General Staff College, Fort Leavenworth, KS, 1975.

Roe, Patrick C. "Destruction of the 31st Infantry: A Tragedy of the Chosin Campaign." Monograph, c. 2000.

"The Unforgotten Korean War." Academy of Military Science, People's Liberation Army, 2005–06.

Personal Papers, Reports, and Reminiscences

Almond, Edward M. "Lt. Gen. Edward M. Diary Korea: August 1950 – July 1951." Almond Diary file, Box 29, RAC.

Almond Testimony to Senate Internal Security Subcommittee. November 23, 1954. Almond folder, Box 29, RAC.

Barr, David. "Address Given by Major General Barr Before the Army War College." Fort Leavenworth, Kansas, February 21, 1951, Lectures AY 1950-1951, Folder 10, Box 1950/1951-1, Army War College Archives, USAHEC.

Beall, Olin L. "Statement of Lieutenant Colonel Olin L. Beall, 01937, U.S. Marine Corps, in Regards to Rescue of Army Personnel." MCH, n.d.

———. "Statement of Liuetenant Colonel Olin L. Beall, 01937, U.S. Marine Corps, Regarding Dealings with the Army in Korea." MCH, n.d.

Bigger, Erwin. "Reflections and Comments." Bigger letter to REA, July 6, 1980, Bigger folder, Box 9, RAC.

Curtis, Wesley J. "Operations of the First Battalion, 32nd Infantry Regiment, Seventh Infantry Division, in the Chosin Reservoir Area of Korea During the Period 24 November–2

December 1950. Personal Experience of the Battalion Operations Officer." Paper written at West Point, 1951–53, draft copy in Curtis folder, Box 8, RAC.
Donovan, Willard P. "Photographs of Korea: Pictures Taken with L Company, 31st Infantry Regiment, August to December 1950." Courtesy of Byron Sims.
Francois, Gerard "Jerry." Recollections transcripts. Courtesy of Charmaine Francois-Griffith.
Hammond, Robert. "Memories of War." AFC/2001/001/41597, VHP.
Hoehn, Martin. "Chosin, Korea." Account for Eric Hammel, February 1979. Hoehn folder, Box 6, EHPP.
Jones, Robert. "Report to Major Lynch. December 4, 1950." Major Jones folder, Box 8, RAC.
"Lt Col Don Carlos Faith, Jr." Joint POW/MIA Accounting Command (JPAC), 2012. DFP.
Magill, Edward. "57th Field Artillery Battalion." *TCC*, 112–17.
May, Hugh. "Report from Capt. Hugh R. May." October 28, 1957. Hugh May folder, Box 9, RAC.
McClymont, James. "Narrative of Chosin, 1980." McClymont folder, Box 8, RAC.
Miller, Crosby. "Chosin Reservoir." October 1953. Miller folder, Box 9, RAC.
Mortrude, James O. "Autobiographic Chronology of Chosin Reservoir Operation." 1980. Mortrude folder, Box 8, RAC.
Oxenrider, Roy. "A Week of Eternity." Author's collection.
Robbins, Hugh. "Breakout." Written in Army hospital 1950–51. Robbins folder, Box 8, RAC.
"Shannon and Scalph." The Army at Chosin. https://31rct.tripod.com/shannonscalph.html.
Shannon, Lewis. "A Letter Home After the Battle of Chosin." The Army at Chosin. https://31rct.tripod.com/shannon.html.
Smith, Oliver P. "Aide-Memoire Korea." Box 68, OPSC.
———. "The Family Album and Journal of Oliver Prince Smith." Written after his retirement in 1955. OPSC.
Stamford, Edward. Statement written in February 1951 at Marine Corps Base Quantico. Stamford folder, Box 9, RAC.
Storms, Harvey, and Helen Storms. Letters from 1950. Courtesy of the Storms Family.
White, Clarence. "Korean War Memories." Self-published, circa 2009. Courtesy of Harry Graham.
Takatsu, "Benny" Kenzo. "Deception and Decency: Unforgettable Incidents." Self-published, circa 2003. Courtesy of Ray Radke.

Archives

Don Carlos Faith Papers, Baton Rouge, LA. Courtesy of Bobbie Faith Bennett Broyles.
Douglas MacArthur Memorial Library and Archives, Norfolk, VA. RG 6 (Records of General Headquarters Far East Command), RG 7 (United Nations Command), RG 9 (Radiograms).
Hoover Institution Library and Archives, Stanford University, Stanford, CA. George A. Rasula Papers.
Library of Congress, Washington, DC. Veterans History Project Collection, American Folklife Center.
Marine Corps History Division, Archives Branch, Quantico, VA. General Oliver. P. Smith Collection, Eric Hammel Personal Papers Collection.
National Archives, Modern Military Records, College Park, MD. RG 407 (Records of the Adjutant General's Office).

U.S. Army Heritage and Education Center. Roy E. Appleman Collection, Edward M. Almond Collection, Clay and Joan Blair Collection, Matthew B. Ridgway Papers.

Documentaries

MacLowry, Randall, dir. *American Experience*. "The Battle of Chosin." Produced by Randall MacLowry. Film Posse Production, WGBH, Boston, 2016.

Precious, Julie, dir. *Task Force Faith: The Story of the 31st Regimental Combat Team*. Produced by Julie Precious and Vincent Gaines. Julie Precious Studios, 2013.

Author Interviews

Joe Ager, September 10, 2022
Carl Bernard, June 2000
Bobbie Faith Bennett Broyles, April 11, 2013, and May 6, 2022
Dan Colasanti, January 7, 2022
Ray Davis, October 2002
Sharlene DeLauter, April 22, 2022
Evelyn DeLauter Eccard, April 22, 2022
Dawn Francois, August 30, 2021, and November 17, 2022
Charlie Gebhardt, May 10, 2016
Harry Graham, August 29, 2021
John Edward Gray, April 17, 2013
Alexander Haig, December 2000
Harry Jacobs, January 15, 2022
Jennie Jin, March 15, 2023
John MacDonald, April 4, 2022
Jerry McCabe, December 1, 2000
William McCaffrey, December 2000
Kelly McKeague, April 22, 2022
Grant McMillin, August 29, 2021, and September 27, 2021
Arthur Mercier, April 11, 2013
Lloyd Mielenz, June 16, 2023
Monty Piercefield, August 30, 2021, and September 30, 2021
Ray Radke, August 29, 2021, and November 19, 2021
Brad Smith, June 2000
Sam Storms, July 26, 2022
Johnny Webb, April 11, 2022
Warren Wiedhahn, September 20, 2021
Carl Witte, December 2000

Index

Note: Photo insert images indicated by *p1, p2, p3,* etc.